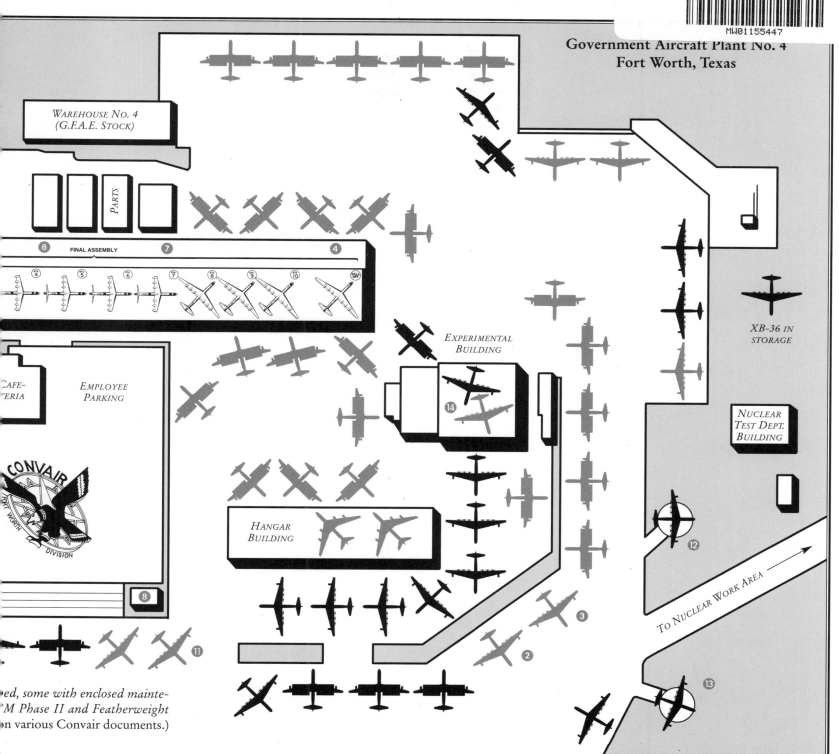

WAREHOUSE NO. 4
(G.F.A.E. STOCK)

PARTS

FINAL ASSEMBLY

CAFE-
TERIA

EMPLOYEE
PARKING

CONVAIR
FORT WORTH
DIVISION

HANGAR
BUILDING

EXPERIMENTAL
BUILDING

XB-36 IN
STORAGE

NUCLEAR
TEST DEPT.
BUILDING

TO NUCLEAR WORK AREA

*...ed, some with enclosed mainte-
...M Phase II and Featherweight
...n various Convair documents.)*

MAGNESIUM OVERCAST

The Story of the Convair B-36

Dennis R. Jenkins

ISBN 1-58007-042-6

specialtypress
PUBLISHERS AND WHOLESALERS

39966 Grand Avenue
North Branch, MN 55056 USA
(651) 277-1400 or (800) 895-4585
www.specialtypress.com

Printed in China

Distributed in the Uk and Europe by:

Midland Publishing
4 Watling Drive
Hinckley LE10 3EY, England
Tel: 01455 233 747 Fax: 01455 233 737
www.midlandcountiessuperstore.com

Library of Congress Cataloging-in-Publication Data

Jenkins, Dennis R.
    Magnesium overcast : the story of the convair B-36 / by Dennis R. Jenkins.
    p. cm.
    ISBN 1-58007-042-6
    1. B-36 bomber--History. 2. Strategic bombers--United States. I. Title.

UG1242.B6 J4626 2001
623.7'463'0973--dc21   2001049195

On the front cover: *Near the end. A Featherweight III B-36H-40-CF (51-5737) arrives at Davis-Monthan AFB in Arizona during January 1958 to be scrapped. These were the final markings worn by most B-36s after the white "high altitude camouflage" paint was added to the lower surfaces.* (Frank Kleinwechter via Don Pyeatt)

On the front dust jacket flap: *This aircraft (44-92080) sits on the ramp at San Diego as a newly-converted B-36D-45-CF – it had arrived in San Diego as a B-36B-20-CF. Very shortly after being redelivered to the Air Force, on 29 January 1952, the aircraft would be lost in a crash at Fairchild AFB. Fortunately all of the crew survived.* (Convair)

On the front page: *The last B-36A (44-92025) comes down the assembly line in Building 4 at Government Aircraft Plant No. 4 in Fort Worth, Texas. Note the overhead monorail extending the length of the almost mile-long building.* (Lockheed Martin)

On the title page: *Like all of the reconnaissance models, as originally delivered this RB-36D-10-CF (49-2688) carried the three large ferret electronic countermeasures (FECM) radomes under what should have been bomb bay No. 4. These would be moved under the aft pressurized compartment when it was decided to activate the bomb bay to carry nuclear weapons and switch the aircraft's primary mission to strategic deterrent instead of strategic reconnaissance.* (Lockheed Martin)

For the Dedication: *The B-36 was an imposing aircraft, especially when more than one of them passed overhead at low level. In addition to their sheer size, the sound made by the six Pratt & Whitney R-4360 piston engines and 19-foot diameter pusher propellers is the first thing recalled by most people that have ever seen the bomber. The aircraft to the right in this photo (B-36H-10-CF, 51-5701) only has bullet sealing pads installed under the two inboard fuel tanks (between the inboard nacelle and the fuselage). The other three aircraft have the pads installed under all of the fuel tanks.* (Lockheed Martin)

On the back dust jacket flap: *At top, a mixture of A- and B-models shows how effective the red arctic paint was at making the aircraft more visible.* (National archives via Stan Piet)

On the back cover: *This B-36B-1-CF (44-92033) shows off the red arctic markings that were used by the Project GEM-modified aircraft. Note that the undersides of the horizontal stabilizer are not completely red – this is different than most of the aircraft where the entire stabilizer and elevator were painted.* (Lockheed Martin)

First Printing:	October 2001
Second Printing:	September 2002 (with corrections, added index and addendum)

TABLE OF CONTENTS

AN UNUSUAL STORY

The story of the B-36 is unique in American aviation history. The aircraft was an interesting blend of concepts proven during World War II combined with budding 1950s high-tech systems. The program survived near-cancellation on six separate occasions during an extremely protracted development process. It was also the symbol of a bitter interservice rivalry between the newly formed Air Force and the well-established Navy over which organization would control the delivery of atomic weapons during the early years of the Cold War. The atomic mission brought with it the lion's share of the funding and prestige, things both services wanted to keep largely for themselves. As a result of the bickering, the aircraft was the subject of numerous Congressional investigations as well as countless newspaper and magazine articles, all with no firm conclusions.

The B-36 was on the books for only 10 years, but was a potentially effective aircraft for only 3–4 of those. The first 5 years were spent working the bugs out, followed by a few useful years of operational service. By 1955 it was clear that the big aircraft could no longer penetrate serious defenses, although delays in the B-52 program would keep a small number of B-36s in service a while longer.

In reality, there had always been questions as to whether the B-36 could accomplish its assigned mission. Nobody denied the aircraft was slow, although sometimes it was hard to ascertain just how slow it really was in comparison to other aircraft of the era – politics, security, and an aversion to allowing one's weaknesses to be seen contributed to the confusion. However, the B-36 flew so high that it probably did not really matter – at least initially. Few fighters of its era could climb as high, and operational surface-to-air missiles were still in the future. The aircraft also had very long legs, a necessary attribute for the first truly intercontinental bomber. It is difficult to imagine a modern aircraft remaining airborne for 2 days without refueling, but it was not particularly unusual for the B-36 to do so. It took a long time to fly 10,000 miles at 250 mph.

The B-36, despite its seemingly conventional appearance, pushed 1950s' state-of-the-art further than any other aircraft of its era. Its sheer size brought structural challenges, while its high-altitude capabilities brought engine cooling and other problems. Sophisticated gun and bombing systems presented development, maintenance, and operational headaches. A lack of training for the ground crews, and severe spare parts shortages exacerbated the problems. All were eventually overcome, and the B-36 served well as the first "Big Stick" of the Cold War.

There have not been many books on the B-36. A few short monographs, including one of my own, made up the early works. The only attempt at a serious history was by Meyers K. Jacobsen, who assembled six other authors to create *Convair B-36 – A Comprehensive History of America's "Big Stick"* published by Schiffer Military History, 1998. The oversized-book's 400 pages allowed the authors to go into more detail on several subjects than is possible here. However, they also seemed to miss some subjects entirely, and perpetuated various misconceptions about others. Nevertheless, someone truly interested in the B-36 should look at a copy of Meyers' book.

The intent of this work is to cover the development and production of the aircraft itself, and therefore its operational use is mentioned only when it brings to light information relevant to its design and construction. This is not meant to minimize the efforts of those who served, but is simply a limitation based on the size of the book and my own interests. Hopefully, some future historian will write a book detailing the operational use of the B-36.

AND THE THANKS GO TO ...

No book can be produced in a vacuum and, more so than most, this one is the product of tremendous cooperation from a great many people. As always, my good friends Peter M. Bowers, Walter J. Boyne, Frederick A. Johnsen, Tony Landis, Jay Miller, Terry Panopalis, and Mick Roth supplied information and photographs. Many B-36 enthusiasts also contributed from their personal collections. Don Pyeatt was first and foremost, going to great lengths to secure photos for me for my B-36 monograph in the *WarBirdTech* series. Don went on to publish an excellent CD-ROM book on the restoration of the last B-36, but he continued to collect data and photos for me. He also put me in contact with many others: Max Campbell, Ed Calvert, Richard Freeman, Frank Kleinwechter, Richard Marmo, Wendell Montague, Bill Plumlee, George Savage, Joe Trnka, Bert Woods, and John W. "Zimmy" Zimmerman. All contributed greatly.

Photos and other material from the Jay Miller Collection in Little Rock are used courtesy of the Aerospace Education Center and the Central Arkansas Library System. The assistance of Rob Seibert and others at the collection is greatly appreciated. This constantly growing Collection is becoming a truly world-class resource for aviation history researchers.

DEDICATION

To the crews and families who served during the uncertain
1950s. Long hours away from home and friends, and
frequent danger; their sacrifices are remembered.

However, the unique content of this book is largely attributable to Mike Moore, Karen Hagar, and Diana Vargas at Lockheed Martin Aeronautics Company in Fort Worth (the former Convair). Mike spent many hours looking through the archives and uncovered things that everybody assumed were lost forever, if anybody knew the items existed in the first place. Many of the photos presented here have never been seen outside Convair. The efforts of Mike and his mentor, C. Roger Cripliver, are also responsible for much of the data that shed long-overdue light on many subjects covered herein.

Others who graciously contributed include: James Baldwin, Bob Bradley (formerly of Convair, San Diego), Mark Cleary (45th SW/HO), Doug Davidge, Dwayne A. Day, Scott Deaver, Robert F. Dorr, James Foss (P&W), Wesley Henry (Air Force Museum), T. A. Heppenheimer, Teresa Vanden-Heuvel (AMARC Public Affairs), Ellen LeMond-Holman (Boeing St. Louis), Marty Isham, Colonel Doug Kirkpatrick (USAF, Ret.), Mike Lombardi (Boeing Historical Archives), MSgt. Gary T. McNeece (Fairchild Heritage Museum), David Menard, Claude S. Morse (AEDC/ACS), Major Bill Norton, Stan Piet, Greg W. Roberts (P&W), Frederick N. Stoliker, Sheila Stupcenski (P&W), Warren F. Thompson, and Ben Whitaker.

Ray Wagner and A.J. Lutz at the San Diego Aerospace Museum graciously allowed me access to their extensive photo archive – easily one of the best in the world when researching Convair subjects. My sincerest thanks go to Ed Lieser, also at the San Diego Aerospace Museum, who was largely responsible for getting me interested in aviation history in the first place.

On the personal side, my deepest admiration and appreciation goes to my mother, Mary E. Jenkins, for always encouraging me to do my best, and to my friends Sandy Gettings and Patti Gibbons who managed to distract me from this work and help me remain sane.

Chapter 1

Above: *The XB-36 (42-13570) on an early test flight. Note the lack of doors over the main landing gear and the absence of armament or radar installations.* (Consolidated-Vultee Aircraft Corporation)

Right: *A later test flight, given that the main landing gear doors have been installed, but the buzz numbers have yet to be painted on the forward fuselage. Note the lack of the forward upper blisters and the relatively small glazed area for the bombardier.* (Lockheed Martin)

DESPERATION – AND REPRIEVE

The first known description of strategic air power was written by H.G. Wells in his 1908 *War from the Air*. However, the concept of aerial bombardment had been discussed by British officers from the Royal Engineers as early as the Chicago Exposition of 1893. During World War I, all sides conducted some form of strategic bombing – the Germans with Zepplins and Gothas, the British with DH-4s, and the French with a variety of aircraft types. None were terribly effective.[1]

The strategic bombardment doctrine employed by the Army Air Corps may be traced to the writings of Colonel (later Brigadier General) William "Billy" Mitchell and General Giulio Douhet of Italy. Both were proponents of creating independent air arms for their nation's military and the effective use of the resulting air power. However, the two men could not have used more diverse tactics. Mitchell was the outspoken rebel, something that eventually earned him a court-martial for insubordination; Douhet published theory sanctioned by the Italian War Ministry. Mitchell thought that air power should be directed against military and industrial targets almost exclusively; Douhet believed that breaking the will of the enemy should be the primary objective, and advocated mass bombing of cities as well as military targets. By the mid-1920s, however, the overarching philosophy of the two men had largely converged – air power would allow a nation to command the skies, and strategic bombing would allow that nation to destroy its enemy.[2]

In 1926 the Air Corps Tactical School* (ACTS) published a book – *Employment of Combined Air Force* – that emphasized the potential of aerial bombardment. The text agreed with Douhet that the true objective in war was to crush the will of the enemy to resist, but followed Mitchell in emphasizing precision attacks against specific military targets rather than more generalized attacks on industrial or population centers. By the early 1930s, strategic bombing had become the dominant doctrine at the ACTS, but it continued to advocate the concept of attacking military and industrial targets in an attempt to minimize collateral damage to civilians.[3]

At the same time, the ACTS began to accept the premise first put forth by Douhet that a defensive bomber formation could provide sufficient self defense to overcome attacks by enemy pursuit formations without the aid of escorting fighter aircraft. The view adopted at the school was that "a well planned and well conducted bombardment attack, once launched, cannot be stopped." This doctrine led to the development of a generation of heavy bombers, such as the Boeing B-17 Flying Fortress and Consolidated B-24 Liberator, that included extensive (or so the planners believed) defensive armament. The development of long-range fighters was afforded a lower priority. It would prove to be a mistake.[4]

The first occasion to use this strategic bombing doctrine came at the beginning of World War II. When the Army Air Forces (the AAF had superseded the Army Air Corps on 20 June 1941) entered combat in Europe in 1942, they did not fully appreciate the lessons that had been learned by the British during the previous 2 years. During 1939 and 1940, the Royal Air Force had attempted daylight precision bombing, but heavy losses to German antiaircraft fire and fighters soon convinced the RAF that unescorted daylight attacks were too costly. In March 1941 the RAF switched from precision daylight bombing† to area bombing at night.[5]

The Convair plant in San Diego, California, shown during 1950. This is where B-36 development began, but it was quickly transferred to the larger facility in Fort Worth where the aircraft would be built. (Jack Kerr via Frank Kleinwechter, scan and digital processing by Don Pyeatt)

---

* Originally the Air Service Field Officers School, later renamed the Air Service Tactical School, and still later the Air Corps Tactical School. The school was established at Langley Field, Virginia, and moved to its present home (as the Air University) at Maxwell Field (AFB), Alabama, in 1931.
† The difference in tactics is important. In precision bombing – which during 1940 almost demanded daylight – bombs are aimed at specific targets (a factory, bridge, etc.) and every attempt is made to limit damage to other areas. In area bombing (also called carpet bombing), bombs are spread over a wide area that encompasses the intended target, eliminating the need for great precision, but extending the damage over a far greater area and requiring many more bombs.

The initial American raids early in the war were against lightly-defended targets in occupied France and the Low Countries close to the English Channel. Since the targets were within range of its escort aircraft, the RAF provided fighter coverage to keep the Luftwaffe at bay, although the Americans were convinced it was not really necessary. A combination of factors resulted in the American losses being light, and the bombing was sufficiently accurate that the raids were considered successful. Despite knowing that the experience was not representative of operations over Germany, General Henry H. "Hap" Arnold was quick to point out the superiority of the new B-17 and noted that: "Either I'm an optimist or just plain dumb, but I think the British still have much to learn about bombing."[6]

It was the AAF that had much to learn. During four unescorted raids deep into Germany in October 1943, the Eighth Air Force lost 148 heavy bombers to enemy fighters – over 12 percent of the strike force. Damage to the targets was minimal because the bombers were too busy dodging fighters and antiaircraft fire to effectively use the Norden bombsights (which required, more or less, straight and level flying during the target run). This finally caused the AAF to acknowledge that the concept of using unescorted bomber formations to conduct daytime precision strikes was flawed. Nevertheless, the AAF was not ready to abandon daylight raids, electing instead to wait until P-51 escort fighters were available in sufficient quantity to accompany the bombers all the way to Berlin. During the final 16 months of the war, the AAF attacked Germany almost every day, eventually resorting to area bombing of entire cities. It still took ground troops capturing Berlin to bring the final surrender. Strategic bombing had undoubtedly played a role, but did it win the war?[7]

After the war a study entitled *United States Strategic Bombing Survey* (USSBS) was conducted. The study found that the most decisive results of strategic bombing in Europe had been against the German oil production industry, but these in themselves did not halt the production of fuels. Attacks against the German aircraft industry had been somewhat effective, but the Germans simply moved production out of large plants into smaller facilities spread around the country and continued to manufacture aircraft, albeit at a much slower pace. Attacks against ball bearing plants were found to have been the least effective.[8]

Others criticized the accuracy of strategic bombing, both in daylight using the much-heralded Norden bombsight and in bad weather or at night using the H2X radar bombing system. The USSBS report commented that, "In many cases bombs dropped by instruments in 'precision' raids directed against specific targets fell over a wide area comparable to that covered normally in an 'area' raid."[9]

The air war in the Pacific did not fare much better, although the problems were somewhat different. In April 1944 the first missions against Japan were undertaken by the XX Bomber Command from bases near Chengtu, China. The new long-range Boeing B-29 Superfortress had a combat radius of about 1,800 miles, but this allowed only targets in western Honshu, Kyushu, and Manchuria to be attacked. Even then, bomb loads were generally limited to less than 4,000 pounds, and only 2,880 tons of bombs were dropped between June and October 1944. It is questionable whether the costs of this effort were outweighed by the results, and the logistics were insane. Only 14 percent of the combat capabilities of XX Bomber Command were brought to bear against the Japanese – the remainder was used to ferry fuel and supplies from India to support the few operational missions. They were desperate times.[10]

By November 1944, bases constructed on the Mariana Islands allowed B-29s to strike at the Japanese Home Islands less than 1,300 miles away. However, these bases had come at a terrible price in casualties – both Allied and Japanese. For the next 5 months the XXI Bomber Command attacked Japan using the same high-altitude daylight precision bombing techniques that had been tried in Europe, with the same lack of results. According to the USSBS survey after the war: "Weather constituted the most serious obstacle … clouds often obscured a clear view of the aiming point [for the Norden bombsight] … necessitating a radar drop on the secondary target. Bombing accuracy, as a result … was not satisfactory. Urban areas, readily identifiable on the radar scope were usually designated as secondary targets since accuracy limitations of the APQ-13 radar prevented successful radar bombing of pinpoint industrial targets from high altitudes."[11]

The lack of success of these early operations caused Major General Curtis E. LeMay, commander of XXI Bomber Command, to rethink his tactics. During March 1945 he ordered the operational units to remove the defensive armament from the B-29s to allow more fuel and bombs to be carried. Long-range P-51 escort fighters would accompany the bombers, using airstrips on islands closer to Japan that had recently been captured. Tactics were changed from high-altitude precision attacks on strategic targets using high-explosive bombs, to low-level incendiary strikes against Japanese cities. These proved much more successful. Although originally aimed at destroying Japan's war production, these raids were soon seen as a method of eliminating Japan's will to fight, returning to Douhet's original premise.

For the remainder of the war, area fire bombing of Japanese cities constituted the primary effort, although a few medium-altitude precision strikes were mounted against specific hardened industrial targets. This represented a decided change of tactics for the Army Air Forces, but publicly LeMay and others still maintained that daylight precision (strategic) bombing was the most effective way to fight a war.[12]

The ultimate statement of strategic bombing took place on 6 August 1945 when a B-29 flying at high altitude dropped a Mk I "Little Boy" atomic bomb on Hiroshima – more than 4 square miles of the city were destroyed, killing 66,000 people and injuring another 69,000. Three days later, another B-29 dropped a Mk III "Fat Man" atomic bomb on Nagasaki, destroying 1.5 square miles of the city, killing 39,000 people and injuring 25,000 more. Interestingly, as devastating as these attacks were, the total amount of damage and casualties paled in comparison to the fire bombing that had been conducted against Tokyo, Nagoya, Osaka, and Kobe. For instance, during one ten-day period during the summer of 1945, XXI Bomber Command burned over 32 square miles of urban-industrial centers in those cities, and by early August, the incendiary bombs had destroyed over 50 percent of the urban areas in Japan and killed over a million people. Yet, it is the atomic bombs that will forever be remembered.

AN INTERCONTINENTAL BOMBER

The idea for a true intercontinental bomber had its roots during the early days of 1941. At that time it appeared England might fall to a German invasion, leaving the United States without any bases outside the Western Hemisphere. It had taken Hitler just 20 days to crush the Polish Army in September 1939, and but a few weeks for the Blitzkrieg to speed across the Low Countries and France in 1940. Hitler's rapid successes against Russia would serve to underscore the concern.

Consequently, the Army Air Corps felt it needed an aircraft that could attack targets in Europe from bases in North America. To accomplish this, the Army Air Corps drafted requirements for a bomber with a 450-mph top speed, a 275-mph cruising speed, a service ceiling of 45,000 feet, and a maximum range of 12,000 miles[*] at 25,000 feet. The aircraft should be able to carry 10,000 pounds of bombs over a radius of 5,000 miles, or a maximum load of 72,000 pounds over a much shorter distance. It was an ambitious concept.[13]

During the early 1940s, the concept of aerial refueling was not considered practical for an operational aircraft, although experiments with it had been conducted as early as 1928. This meant that any aircraft with the range required of the new bomber would of necessity be very large, if for no other reason than to accommodate all of the fuel required for the trip. However, experience constructing very large aircraft was largely limited to the Boeing XB-15[†] and the Douglas XB-19[‡] flying laboratories, both of which were considerably smaller and slower than the aircraft envisioned by the Army.

The new requirements were a significant leap over existing aircraft – the contemporary Boeing B-17E and Consolidated B-24D paled in comparison. The B-17E had a top speed of 317 mph, with a cruising speed of 195 mph and a service ceiling of 36,600 feet. Combat radius was 1,000 miles with 4,000 pounds of bombs, or 3,300 miles with no bomb load. The B-24D had a top speed of 303 mph and could cruise at 200 mph. Its service ceiling was only 32,000 feet, but it could fly 1,150 miles with 5,000 pounds of bombs, or 3,500 miles with no bombs. Even compared with the B-29 – which did not fly until 21 September 1942 and had a troubled development period – the new aircraft was a major step forward. The production B-29 was capable of 361 mph, with a cruising speed of 230 mph and a service ceiling of 32,000 feet. It had a combat radius of 1,900 miles with 16,000 pounds of bombs, or a ferry range of 5,500 miles.[14]

Requests for preliminary design studies were released to Boeing and Consolidated on 11 April 1941. The design competition had a fixed cost of $435,623 with the winner being awarded $135,445 and the remainder going to the loser.[§] Consolidated had been working on the Model 35 concept since September 1940 using company funds, and used this design as the basis for its submission. This high-wing aircraft had a circular fuselage that was 128 feet long and used twin vertical stabilizers like the contemporary B-24. The wing spanned 164 feet and provided 2,700 square feet of area. Power was provided by four engines arranged in two nacelles (one on each wing), each with one tractor and one pusher propeller. This design was slightly larger than the B-29, but as impressive as it was, did not meet the requirements laid out by the Army.

On 27 May 1941 Jack Northrop was asked to provide further information on his "flying wing" design, although the aircraft only had an estimated combat radius of 3,000 miles with 10,000 pounds of bombs. Later, the Glenn L. Martin Company was also solicited, but declined because of a shortage of engineering personnel due to work on the XB-33 design and a Navy production contract. Separately, in possible support of the very long-range aircraft program, on 19 April 1941 Douglas was awarded a contract to determine if the Allison V-3420 liquid-cooled engine could be used in a bomber. It appears that North American Aviation also toyed with designs that could potentially meet these requirements, but never officially submitted them for consideration. On 3 May 1941 Boeing, Consolidated, and Douglas submitted preliminary design data for the very long-range bomber.

The results were not encouraging. All of the manufacturers were having trouble defining an aircraft that met the requirements. A conference, attended by Robert A. Lovett, Assistant Secretary of War for

Although pursuing the concept of a true intercontinental bomber, the Army Air Forces nevertheless began experimenting with the concept of in-flight refueling. Here a B-24D tanker (40-2352) is refueling a B-17E (41-2539) over Eglin Field during 1943. The experiments worked, but in-flight refueling was not pressed into operational service for another 15 years. (U.S. Air Force via the Frederick A. Johnsen Collection)

---

[*] It should be noted that until the early 1950s, the range and speed of aircraft were usually shown in statute miles. Afterwards, the Air Force began to measure speed in knots and range in nautical miles.

[†] The Boeing XB-15 had first flown on 15 October 1937, and was the largest aircraft built in the United States at the time. The experimental bomber looked much like the early B-17s, but had a wing span almost half again as long (149 feet) and was 20 feet longer (87.5 feet). It had a maximum weight of just over 70,000 pounds.

[‡] The Douglas XB-19 dwarfed all previous U.S. aircraft, with a wing span of 212 feet and an overall length of over 132 feet. Maximum weight was 162,000 pounds – about 20,000 pounds more than a fully-loaded B-29. The aircraft made its first flight on 27 June 1941.

[§] This was not unusual at the time. The rationale was that the winner received a large development and production contract and would eventually recoup expenses and make a tidy profit. The loser was essentially reimbursed for expenses plus a small fee.

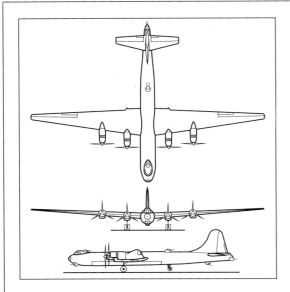
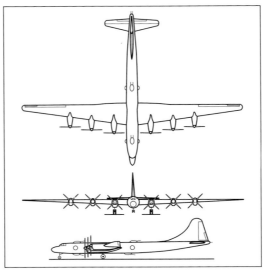
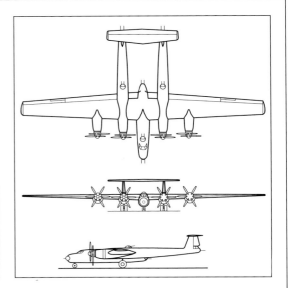

The two Boeing proposals (Model 384 on the left; Model 385 in the center) were considered to be half-hearted attempts by the Army Air Forces. Neither design could meet the specifications laid down by the military, although the Model 385 came relatively close. Each design featured four fuselage turrets plus a tail turret for self defense. Note the relatively narrow chord wing on both designs, something that would probably have been a handicap at the extreme altitudes where the B-36 eventually operating. (Boeing Historical Archives)

Very little information could be found about this North American Aviation NA-116 proposal except that it was designed around the same time as the B-36 competition. The aircraft featured bomb bays in both booms as well as the main fuselage. (Boeing Historical Archives)

Air, Major General George H. Brett, Chief of the Air Corps, and ranking officers of the Air Staff was held on 19 August in an attempt to accelerate the bomber project, mainly by relaxing the specification. This was a relative concept, and the revised requirements were still a tall order – a range* of 10,000 miles, and an effective combat radius of 4,000 miles with a 10,000-pound bomb load. The requirements also specified that the bomber should have a cruising speed between 240 and 300 mph and a 40,000-foot service ceiling. This was still four times the combat radius of the B-17 while carrying over twice the bomb load. Each of the three contractors revised their preliminary data to accommodate the new requirements, and submitted updated proposals in early September 1941.[15]

After a review of the data from Boeing, Consolidated, and Douglas, Brigadier General George C. Kenney,[†] commander of the Experimental Division and Engineering School at Wright Field, Ohio, issued a recommendation to pursue the Consolidated concepts. Major General Henry H. "Hap" Arnold[‡] concurred with the recommendation, and Consolidated entered into contract negotiations.

Consolidated had been the most aggressive of the contractors, but their preliminary data covered two different designs. A revised Model 35 was an evolution of the design proposed in May 1941. The second[§] design, the Model 36, was unusual for an American design in that it featured six engines buried in a thick wing driving pusher propellers instead of the more traditional tractor arrangement. This was somewhat ironic since engineers at Wright Field had been working on a six-engine pusher design independently. Great minds, apparently, think alike.

On the other hand, Douglas stated that it did not desire to undertake an "out-and-out 10,000-mile airplane project" and proposed the development of the 6,000-mile range Model 423, which was rejected. The Boeing designs (Models 384 and 385) were "overly conservative" and the Army Air Forces believed that Boeing had not yet "really tackled the [long-range] airplane design with the necessary degree of enthusiasm." Given that Boeing was heavily involved in the B-29 project (as well as the continuing B-17 evolution) at the time, this was probably understandable. In early October, Consolidated was requested to submit detailed cost estimates for both of its concepts.

Consolidated's detailed proposal was submitted on 6 October 1941 and requested $15 million plus a fixed-fee of $800,000 for the development, mockup, tooling, and production of two experimental very long-range bombers. Consolidated also stipulated that the project could not be "entangled with red tape" and have constantly changing requirements. Prophecy it was not – the resulting airplane probably got tangled up in more red tape than any other defense project of the era.

---

* The word "range" is often qualified with good reason. In this context it indicates how far an aircraft can fly under given operating conditions, from takeoff until fuel exhaustion. This differs from "combat radius" which is the distance an aircraft can fly, then turn around and return to its point of departure, with a given payload at a given speed and altitude. The combat radius is usually a great deal less than half of the maximum range of the aircraft for a variety of reasons.

† Kenney went on to become the first commander of the postwar Strategic Air Command.

‡ Arnold became Commanding General of the Army Air Forces in March 1942 and was promoted to a four-star General in 1943.

§ There seems to be some confusion over whether this was always called the Model 36 – some early sketches of the six-engine design say Model 35, and the earliest surviving report carries a "35" number (usually indicating the model number), but has hand corrections that read Model 36. Regardless, by the time the first engineering drawings were produced, the aircraft was known as Model 36.

On 15 November 1941 a contract (W535-ac-22352) was issued for two XB-36 experimental aircraft to be built at the Consolidated facility in San Diego, with the first being delivered in May 1944 and the second 6 months later. On 22 November engineers at Wright Field concluded that the six-engine Model 36 design offered the most promise and should be selected instead of the four-engine Model 35 concept. Consolidated immediately began constructing a full-scale wooden mockup in San Diego that would be used extensively to check the proposed equipment and armament installation. Consolidated knew it would be faced with design problems that had not been previously encountered, mostly stemming from the aircraft's sheer size and operating altitude.[16]

The Model 36 had a wing that spanned 230 feet with an area of 4,772 square feet and was powered by six new 28-cylinder Pratt &

Whitney "X-Wasp" air-cooled radial engines, each driving a 19-foot diameter, three-bladed Curtiss-Wright propeller in a pusher configuration. The engines were to be accessible for maintenance in flight through the wing, which was 7.5 feet thick at the root. Gross weight was estimated at 265,000 pounds, and the top speed was expected to be 369 mph at 40,000 feet.

Six fuel tanks with a capacity of 21,116 gallons were incorporated into the wing. The 163-foot-long fuselage had four separate bomb bays with a maximum capacity of 72,000 pounds. Forward and aft crew compartments were pressurized and a 25-inch diameter, 80-foot-long pressurized tube ran through the bomb bays to connect the two. Crewmen could use a wheeled trolley to slide back and forth. Four rest bunks, a small galley, and a toilet were provided in the aft compartment. Defensive armament was to consist of five 37-mm cannon

The Model 35 used an unconventional engine arrangement with both pusher and tractor propellers. This design had three bomb bays and the characteristic Consolidated twin vertical stabilizers. The 164.4-foot wing only provided 2,700 square feet of area – just over half that of the final B-36 design. (San Diego Aerospace Museum Collection)

This is likely the first drawing to use the Model 36 designation – notice that it has been overwritten on top of "35," but the report number still begins with "ZD-35," usually indicating the model number. The 230-foot wing provided 4,800 square feet of area, very close to the final design. (San Diego Aerospace Museum Collection)

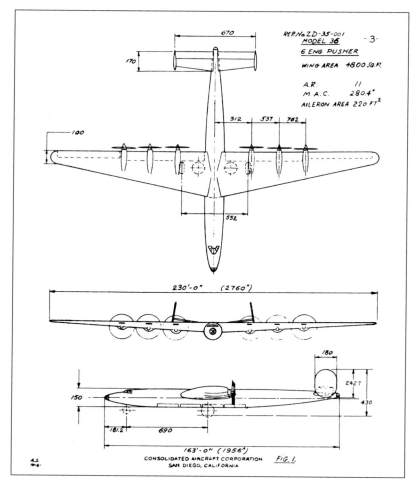

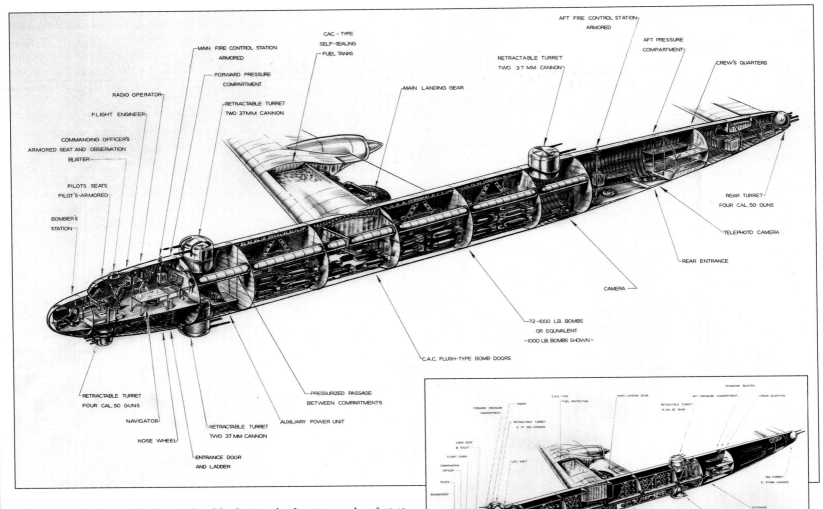

The XB-36 design evolved considerably during the first 3 months of 1942. In January (above) the nose came to a sharper point, there were only three retractable turrets, and most of the aft fuselage was pressurized. By 27 March (right) the nose had taken on the shape that would be built, the aft fuselage compartment was considerably smaller, and the crew transfer tube had moved from a position high in the fuselage to one near the waterline. (San Diego Aerospace Museum Collection)

and ten 0.50-caliber machine guns distributed between four retractable turrets (two on top of the fuselage, two on the bottom) and a radar-directed tail turret, although the actual configuration remained in a state of flux for several years.

The 10,000-mile range was a challenge, dictating that the aircraft would spend almost 2 days in the air. Every effort would have to be made to minimize the base drag of the aircraft, meaning particular attention would need to be paid to the aerodynamic smoothness of the skin and skin joints. To emphasize the problem at hand, Consolidated constantly reminded engineers that for every pound of extra weight, it took 2 pounds of fuel to complete the 10,000 mile mission.

To help reduce drag, during early 1942 Consolidated began developing a metal adhesive strong enough to support primary aircraft loads. In addition to lowering drag, the use of adhesives was expected to speed manufacturing by eliminating the need for thousands of pop-rivets. Dr. Glenn Havens, a noted research scientist, was hired by Consolidated to head the research. Consolidated eventually invested almost $3 million in the program that eventually yielded a high-strength glue in both liquid and tape forms. After it was perfected, Consolidated licensed the product to Narmco, Inc. (which called it Metlbond) and Pacific Laminates (Silabond). Other companies, notably Chrysler, also manufactured similar products. Consolidated pioneered the use of the products in the aviation industry, and by early 1950, approximately 30 percent of the exterior skin of the B-36 was assembled using the technique.[17]

Fatigue tests showed that parts joined by metal bonding had a superior fatigue life compared to mechanical fasteners. For instance, a spot-welded joint could withstand 12,000,000 fatigue cycles, while a riveted joint withstood 18,000,000. The same parts using metal bonding techniques withstood 240,000,000 cycles. The technique proved to be extremely useful on the magnesium skin used on the B-36, but its future applications were not nearly as great as Consolidated once thought.[18]

Based primarily on a desire to reduce weight, the hydraulic and electrical systems were selected for significant advances. Additional rationale included a belief that the 1,500-psi hydraulic systems that were standard at the time were inadequate to effectively move the large landing gear and flaps required for the new aircraft. With assistance from Wright Field, Convair began developing a new 3,000-psi hydraulic system – pumps, valves, and actuators all had to be designed from scratch. Interestingly, 3,000-psi systems would remain a standard for the aircraft industry until the Bell V-22 Osprey pioneered (with great difficulty) a 5,000-psi system in the late 1990s. Wright Field had also been developing a new 400-cycle, 208-volt, 3-phase alternating current (ac) electrical system to replace the direct current (dc) systems used by other aircraft. This permitted the use of lighter-weight motors – for instance a 16-hp ac motor weighed only 23 pounds, compared to 100 pounds for an equivalent dc motor. There was also less chance of the ac motors arcing at high altitudes, and they were considered generally more reliable.[19]

A methyl-bromide fire extinguishing system was developed to replace the usual carbon-dioxide systems provided in engine nacelles.

Methyl-bromide had a lower boiling point than carbon-dioxide, allowing it to be stored at lower pressures in lighter-weight cylinders. As it ended up, the new system was not available in time for inclusion in the XB-36 or XC-99, but was installed on the second bomber and subsequent aircraft. The XC-99 had the new system retrofitted at a later date, but the XB-36 did not.

The Consolidated proposal effort had been managed by I.M.* "Mac" Laddon, an executive vice president who had been chief engineer on the Catalina flying boat. Laddon would remain connected in some manner with the B-36 for many years. Harry A. Sutton, manager of the Engineering Department, and Ted P. Hall, manager of the Preliminary Design group, led the actual development of the prototype design. Ralph L. Bayless, Ken Ward, and Robert H. Widmer worked on getting the exterior shape right and setting up the wind tunnel program.

The first wind tunnel model was a 1/26-scale model designed to be run in the tunnels at the Massachusetts Institute of Technology and at GALCIT (the Guggenheim Aeronautical Laboratory of the California Institute of Technology). Originally Consolidated had chosen a NACA 65 airfoil for the laminar flow wing, but this design exhibited greater than expected drag when first tested in July 1942. A new model was constructed using a NACA 63 airfoil, but the urgencies of war had preempted the B-36 program and it would be over a year before the B-36 entered a wind tunnel again. Further analysis indicated that the trailing edge should be swept forward at 3 degrees to provide a bit more balance and better center-of-gravity tolerance for the design.

---

* Until the 1960s it was normal practice for business correspondence to only use first and middle initials, not first names. Nevertheless, where possible, first names have been provided.

The engine installation also underwent considerable change during the first 3 months of 1942. The January concept is at left; 27 March at right. Note that neither lower nacelle extends all the way to the leading edge of the wing as in the production models. (San Diego Aerospace Museum Collection)

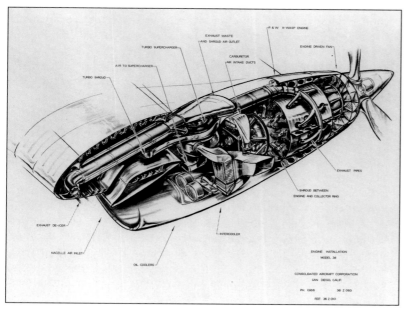

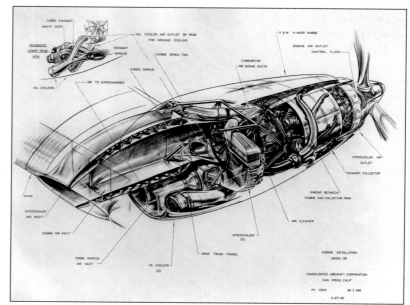

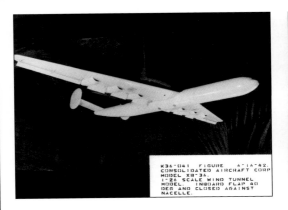
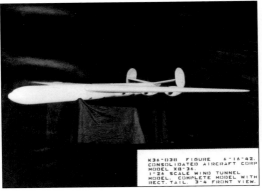

The original 1/26th-scale wind tunnel test model shows the nacelle configuration in mid-1942. Note that the bottom of the nacelle still does not extend all the way to the leading edge of the wing. The amount of dihedral on the horizontal stabilizer is also of interest. (Convair via C. Roger Cripliver)

This display model sent to Wright Field, Ohio, in November 1941 had four-bladed propellers. (San Diego Aerospace Museum Collection)

For six months Consolidated refined the design, exerting every effort to control weight, reduce drag, and eliminate the various developmental challenges typically encountered. In the meantime, Consolidated constructed a full-scale wooden mockup in a large building adjacent to the engineering department at the San Diego plant. The mockup included a complete fuselage, one entire wing, and the twin vertical stabilizers. Particular attention was paid to the defensive armament and landing gear installations.

The B-36 mockup was finally inspected on 20 July 1942, and weight estimates were much higher than expected, resulting in a failure to meet the 10,000 mile requirement. In response, some members of the Mockup Committee wanted to reduce the defensive armament and crew, but other members argued that such changes would render the aircraft tactically useless and relegate it to much the same role as the XB-19 "flying laboratory." If a compromise could not be reached, many members believed that the entire program should be cancelled. The Mockup Committee eventually agreed to delete only "less necessary" equipment such as some crew comfort and survival items. This provided a minor weight reduction, and allowed the program to continue, although the projected range was still considerably less than desired. The Air Force finally approved the mockup inspection in September 1942.

A month after the B-36 mockup inspection, Consolidated suggested shifting the XB-36 program from San Diego to the new

Seemingly, this is the only photo that remains of the XB-36 mockup in San Diego. This was July 1942. (San Diego Aerospace Museum Collection)

Government Aircraft Plant No. 4 in Fort Worth, Texas, some 1,205 miles to the east. The government agreed that this was a prudent move, freeing up space in the San Diego facility and concentrating the engineering staff at the plant that would eventually undertake production of the bomber. The relocation also added a small measure of security to the project – early in the war there had been concern that Japan might mount strikes against the coastal cities of California. Work on the Fort Worth facility had begun in January 1941 as a location to build subassemblies for B-24s being manufactured by Ford at Willow Run. As B-24 production ramped up, additional space was added at Fort Worth, and the plant's first Liberator was completed in April 1941. The plant would go on to build the B-32, B-36, B-58, F-111, and F-16.

The mockup was broken down and packed onto rail cars and, along with 200 engineers, began the trek to Texas. The mockup was reconstructed in the Experimental Building at Fort Worth, but it soon became obvious that the building was too small in which to construct the two prototypes. A new Hangar Building* was constructed nearby for this purpose, finally being completed in early 1944. The move to Texas was completed in September 1942, less than 30 days after being approved, but development was set back several months as the team adjusted to its new surroundings. After the move, R.C. "Sparky" Sebold and Herbert W. Hinckley assumed the leadership of the program in Fort Worth. Progress on the B-36 was also slowed because of the higher priority of the B-24, and later the B-32.[20]

Even before construction of the prototypes had begun, Consolidated wanted the government to place a production order for the B-36, claiming that two years could be saved if preliminary work on production aircraft could be accomplished in parallel with the experimental models. Consolidated also pointed out that it was difficult to get suppliers to expend resources on a program that was only committed to building two airplanes. However, the war in the Pacific was not going well, and the Army Air Forces felt that it should devote

---

* Also called the Development Building.

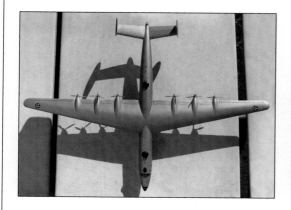  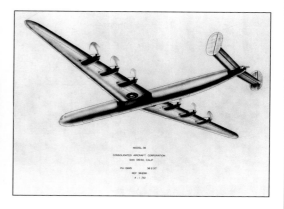

Another early display model shows the overall configuration. Although readily identifiable as a B-36, it differs in almost every detail from what was eventually developed and produced. Note that the engine nacelles extend farther forward than originally. (Convair via C. Roger Cripliver)

The overall configuration on 1 April 1941. Note the exposed main landing gear. (San Diego Aerospace Museum Collection)

its full effort to aircraft which could contribute to the war effort sooner, so the request was denied. The B-24, B-29, and B-32 were all afforded higher priority than the B-36.

Another Consolidated request in the summer of 1942 fared somewhat better. The Army Air Forces agreed to the development of a cargo version of the XB-36, provided that one of the two experimental bombers was produced at least 3 months ahead of the cargo aircraft. Initially, Consolidated had wanted the aircraft to test the engines, landing gear, and flight characteristics of the forthcoming XB-36s, and believed that the cargo variant could be ready to fly much sooner than either of the XB-36s because armament and other military equipment was not required. Nevertheless, Consolidated accepted the government's conditions and a $4.6 million contract was approved by year's end. See Chapter 2 for a discussion of the XC-99.

On 17 March 1943, the Consolidated Aircraft Corporation* merged with Vultee Aircraft, Inc., becoming the Consolidated Vultee Aircraft Corporation.† This name is often truncated to "Convair," although this did not become official until 29 April 1954, when Consolidated Vultee Aircraft Corporation became the Convair Division of the General Dynamics Corporation after the two companies merged. In between Convair referred to itself alternately as CVAC, or CONVAIR (all caps). This book will use "Convair" since it has become the accepted nomenclature, somewhat after-the-fact.[21]

While Convair wrestled with weight increases and various developmental troubles, world events suddenly boosted the importance of the B-36. By the spring of 1943, China appeared near collapse and nei-

ther the B-17 nor B-24 had sufficient range to operate over the vast distances of the Pacific. The B-29 was in the early stage of production, but was proving to be troublesome in initial service. The parallel development of the B-32, generally considered by the Army Air Forces as "insurance" in case the B-29 failed, was also not progressing as well as expected, largely because of a low priority rating in the national production scheme. Neither of these types could reach Japan from the continental United States, and extremely bloody battles would need to be won before the Mariana Islands could become bases for B-29 or B-32 operations. Speeding up B-36 development might provide a way for attacking the Japanese homeland directly.

Unsurprisingly, the war in the Pacific dominated the discussion at the "Trident Conference" between President Roosevelt and Prime

This mid-1942 exploded view of the XB-36 shows a chin turret, one of many configurations studied in an attempt to provide full-hemispheric coverage for the defensive armament. This became more important as the war progressed. (San Diego Aerospace Museum Collection)

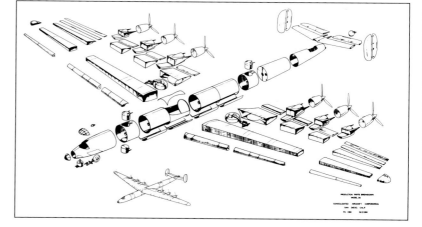

---

* Consolidated had been formed by Major Reuben H. Fleet in East Greenwich, Rhode Island, on 29 May 1923 when certain aviation assets of the Dayton Wright Airplane Company and the Gallaudet Engineering Company were combined into a new company. It moved to Buffalo, New York, in 1925, and then to San Diego in 1935. At the time it had 900 employees. By 1939 the company employed 6,000, and by the middle of 1940 had grown to over 40,000 employees to help with the war effort.

† It is often reported that Consolidated was "owned" by the Atlas Corporation. As far as can be determined, Atlas Corporation was the single largest shareholder of Consolidated stock (about 430,000 of 2,400,000 shares) but otherwise did not control the company. Atlas sold 400,000 of its shares to General Dynamics in April 1953, making GD the largest single shareholder. GD went on to purchase a majority of the stock, becoming the defacto owner of Consolidated.

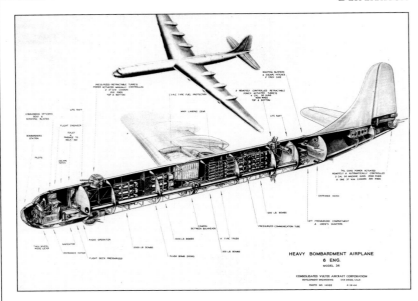

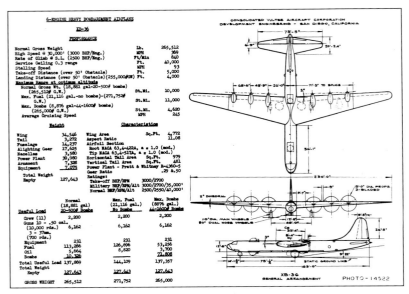

This 19 April 1944 drawing shows the switch to the single vertical stabilizer. Note the arrangement of the defensive turrets in relation to the bomb bays – compare them to the drawing at right. By this time the aircraft was looking much like the XB-36. (San Diego Aerospace Museum Collection)

An undated drawing probably done in very late 1943 or early 1944. Note that the aft turrets are located between bomb bays No. 3 and No. 4, a configuration that would be unique to the XB-36 – the YB-36 would move the turrets aft of bomb bay No. 4. (San Diego Aerospace Museum Collection)

Government Aircraft Plant No. 4 in Fort Worth had been built to manufacture parts for the B-24, and a great deal of work was required to allow it to produce the world's largest bomber. Here a new runway is being constructed to the east of the plant, between the Convair ramp and the existing main Carswell runway. Carswell AFB is the triangular-shaped facility in the upper left corner. Directly north of the plant is Lake Worth, the site of the first B-36 accident. (Convair via C. Roger Cripliver)

Minister Churchill in May 1943. After various consultations, Secretary of War Henry L. Stimson waived the customary procurement procedures and authorized the Army Air Forces to order the B-36 into production without waiting for the completion of the two experimental aircraft. A letter of intent[*] for 100 B-36s was signed on 23 July. The estimated cost of each aircraft was $1,750,000 – just slightly more than 2 days' cost of the war effort. Subsequently, the priority assigned to the B-36 program was raised, although still not to a level equal to the B-29, or even the B-32.

When the Model 36 mockup had been approved in September 1942, it used vertical stabilizers mounted on the ends of each horizontal stabilizer, much like the B-24. There were initial concerns that the vertical stabilizers could shear off during a hard landing or under severe flight conditions – continued evaluation led to the twin tail being deleted in favor of a single 47-foot high vertical stabilizer. This change would decrease structural weight by 3,850 pounds, provide additional directional stability, and lower base drag. It was also in keeping with the general trend in the aircraft industry at the time. Some of the initial designs for the B-29 had twin tails, but Boeing had selected a taller single unit for production. Consolidated had begun with twin verticals on the B-24 and B-32, but both types ultimately used single vertical surfaces (although the B-24 only adapted it very late in its production program). The XB-36 modification was approved on 10 October 1943 as Change Order 7 to the basic contract, along

---

[*] A Letter of Intent was not, technically, a legally-binding document and committed no funds. It was essentially a gentleman's handshake. A Letter Contract, on the other hand, was legally binding, committed funds, and made the U.S. Government liable for default.

  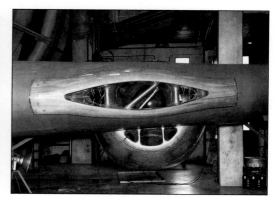

A full-scale power test was conducted on a nacelle in the Air Materiel Command 20-foot wind tunnel at Wright Field, Ohio, during early-to-mid-1944. A great deal of work was done to determine the optimum nacelle configuration; the one shown here is fairly early, with a lower intake that does not extend all the way to the wing leading edge. Note the measuring tubes placed in the air ducts to determine airflow pattern in the photo at right. The same photo gives a good opporunity to describe each duct (top, left to right): intercooler air; engine cooling fan; intercooler air; (bottom, left to right): turbosupercharger air; oil cooler; turbosupercharger air. (U.S. Air Force via C. Roger Cripliver)

A great deal of time was also spent in the N.A.C.A. 40x80-foot full-scale wind tunnel at the Ames Research Laboratory in Palo Alto, California. By October 1945, when these photos were taken, the configuration of the nacelle intakes were nearly finalized. (N.A.C.A. via C. Roger Cripliver)

Functional tests were conducted on essentially hand-made landing gear specimens. (San Diego Aerospace Museum Collection)

Main landing gear mockup. Note that the remarkably detailed "airplane" is made from plywood. (Convair via C. Roger Cripliver)

The XB-36 main landing gear on 13 May 1946. Note the huge brake (right) needed to stop the new bomber. (Convair)

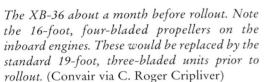

The XB-36 about a month before rollout. Note the 16-foot, four-bladed propellers on the inboard engines. These would be replaced by the standard 19-foot, three-bladed units prior to rollout. (Convair via C. Roger Cripliver)

By August 1945 the XB-36 was listed as 82.5 percent complete, and was briefly rolled out of the Experimental Building so that it could be turned around. Although not of ideal quality, these photos give a good look at the wing structure before the aerodynamic structure and skin were installed. Note the two open turret doors on top of the fuselage – the aft turrets would have been much further forward than on production airplanes. (San Diego Aerospace Museum Collection)

with a 120-day delay in delivery. At best the Army Air Forces would not get the first XB-36 until September 1944. Subsequently, a letter contract (W33-038-ac-7) for the production aircraft was signed on 23 August 1943, replacing the letter of intent issued a month earlier.[22]

In spite of its elevated status, the B-36 program was slow to make progress. Essential wind tunnel tests were postponed until the spring of 1944 because other projects had higher priorities and no alternate test facilities were available. Convair was also concerned over growing weight estimates for the X-Wasp engine. In Convair's opinion,

tying the XB-36 to a single-engine design was a mistake, especially since the new P&W engine was slow to materialize, for many of the same reasons as the B-36 itself. Yet, further study of the liquid-cooled Lycoming BX engine (noted for lower fuel consumption) had been discontinued on the belief that it would require manpower, materiel, and facilities that could not be spared. The Army Air Forces also insisted that development of an alternate engine would only delay "expeditious prosecution" of the B-36 design.[23]

By mid-1944, the military situation in the Pacific had significantly

The hatch directly behind the technician is the access to the fuselage. Crewmembers could use the same hatch to access the wing during flight. (San Diego Aerospace Museum Collection)

The XB-36 on 19 February 1946. The black bars at aft end of rudder hinge slots are loads test equipment. Note the corrugated leading edge spar on the horizontal stabilizer and the open engine cowling. (Convair)

Because it was a slender aircraft, the size of the XB-36 could be deceiving unless you had a basis for comparison. Here a Boeing B-29 poses with the XB-36, showing just how large the new bomber was compared to contemporary aircraft. The fuselage and vertical stabilizers were largely similar in appearance, but the wings and engine configuration differed completely. (Convair via the Marty Isham Collection)

improved. The Marianas campaign was near its end, and preparation was being made to deploy B-29s from these bases to attack the Japanese Home Islands. The B-29's initial difficulties had been mostly resolved, and the Army Air Forces believed that a very-long-range bomber was no longer urgently needed. Nevertheless, the Army Air Forces were still interested in procuring the B-32. On 7 July 1944, General B.E. Meyers from the Air Materiel Command issued a letter that directed "positive and vigorous action to place the B-32 on a Number One priority from an engineering, tooling, and production standpoint, without reference to the effect this action may have on the XB-36 and B-36 programs."

On 19 August 1944, the formal $160 million contract (including a $6 million fixed fee) was finally signed to cover the production of 100 B-36s along with the associated engineering and spare parts. Only now the contract did not carry any priority rating at all, essentially ensuring that no parts or materials could be procured as long as the war lasted. Delivery schedules, however, were unchanged, and the first production B-36 was to be delivered in August 1945 with the last arriving in October 1946.[24]

Following the surrender of Germany and the end of the war in Europe, materiel contracts were drastically cut back. Overall aircraft production was cut by 30 percent on 25 May 1945, a reduction of 17,000 aircraft over an 18-month period. However, the contract for the B-36 was untouched – the enormous losses suffered in seizing island bases in the Pacific confirmed that there was a definite need for a very-long-range bomber. The atomic bomb, unlikely to remain an American monopoly, was another strategic justification. Inasmuch as U.S. retaliation would have to be quick, there would be no time for conquering faraway bases, and realistically, a very-long-range bomber could be the best deterrent for the immediate future. From the economic standpoint, the B-36 also looked good since it out-performed the B-29 and was cheaper by half to operate in terms of cost per ton per mile.[25]

While the fate of the B-36 program vacillated with changing wartime priorities, the aircraft's development remained painfully slow. By 1945 Convair still worried over the weight of the P&W R-4360-25 Wasp Major engine, as the X-Wasp had been designated. Adding nose guns, a new requirement based on wartime experience,

required an extensive rearrangement of the forward crew compartment – the new configuration would become standard beginning with the second XB-36 (subsequently redesignated YB-36). New radio and radar equipment would add at least 3,500 pounds, and the base drag would increase substantially if the antenna of the Western Electric AN/APQ-7 Eagle bombing radar could not be installed in the leading edge of the wing as planned. Coupled with a 2,304-pound increase for the engines, this was a serious problem.

Due to the sheer size of the aircraft, the landing gear presented its own set of concerns. In order to fit the main gear into the wing when it was retracted, Convair decided to use a single 110-inch diameter tire per side. Another reason for this choice was the inability of the industry to provide adequate brakes for a multi-wheel design.

A few B-24s and B-29s used the Western Electric AN/APQ-7 Eagle radar bombing system during World War II. The antenna looked like an auxiliary "wing" under the fuselage between the bomb bays. This installation created a lot of drag, but was easy to retrofit onto the Superfortress. Initial plans for the B-36 were to bury the antenna in the leading edges of the wing. As it ended up, the APQ-7 was replaced by the APQ-23 before any of the Convair bombers were built. (Peter M. Bowers Collection)

Unfortunately, this concentrated most of the aircraft's weight onto two relatively small contact patches, one on each side of the aircraft. Only three runways (at least 22-inches thick) in the world were capable of withstanding the huge stress that a fully-loaded aircraft would impart: Fort Worth, Eglin Field in Florida, and Fairfield-Suisun* Field in California. In addition to the runway restrictions, the landing-weight distribution onto two small contact patches put the entire aircraft at risk if a single tire failed at a critical time.

The 110-inch tires, each weighing 1,475 pounds, were the largest aircraft tires ever manufactured by the Goodyear Tire & Rubber Company. Each tire had a 225-pound inner tube pressurized to 100 psi, and at least 10 were manufactured. The 110-inch diameter wheels were 46 inches wide and weighed 850 pounds each, and the dual mul-

---

* Renamed Travis AFB in honor of Brigadier General Robert F. Travis in November 1950. Interestingly, Fairfield-Suisun had been the terminus for Convairways, an airline run by Convair during World War II.

The XB-36 following its rollout from the Experimental Building in September 1945. The streamlined "airliner" type canopy and nose area are evident in this photo. (San Diego Aerospace Museum Collection)

Except for the 110-inch main gear, from this angle the XB-36 looked much like all early B-36s. All of the control surfaces were covered by doped fabric. Note the absence of landing gear doors. (Peter M. Bowers Collection)

As originally flown, the only significant markings on the XB-36 were old-style national insignia and serial numbers. The buzz numbers would come later. (Convair via Don Pyeatt)

tiple-disk brakes on each wheel added 735 pounds. Complete with the struts and ancillary equipment, each main gear weighed 8,550 pounds. Interestingly, for at least the first few flights of the XB-36 the main landing gear doors were not fitted.

In mid-1945 the Major General Edward M. Powers, Assistant Chief of Air Staff for Materiel, Maintenance, and Distribution, recommended that a new landing gear be developed to distribute the aircraft weight more evenly, thus reducing the need for specially-built runways. As noted, one of the major problems encountered with designing a multi-wheel landing gear for the B-36 had been acquiring adequate brakes. These were finally developed and the production four-wheel bogie-type undercarriage using 56-inch tires allowed the B-36 to use any airfield suitable for the B-29. The new landing gear configuration required "bumps" on top of the wing and on the landing gear doors to provide additional clearance when the landing gear was stowed. Fortunately, the small increase in drag was compensated for by the 2,600 pounds the new landing gear saved.

As a result of the many changes to the original design, the estimated gross weight had increased from 265,000 to 278,000 pounds, and revised projections of the XB-36 performances were proving discouraging. Top speed had gone from an estimated 369 to 323 mph, while the service ceiling had dropped from 40,000 to 38,200 feet. Although it was estimated that the B-36 might not be any faster than later model B-29s, it was still vastly superior in terms of range and payload. A single B-36 would cost three times as much as a B-29, but could carry 72,000 pounds of bombs an estimated 5,800 miles, while the B-29 could only carry 20,000 pounds of bombs a little over 2,900 miles. In terms of airframe weight, the B-36 was 1.85 times as heavy as the B-29, but it could carry over 10 times the bomb load to 5,500 miles.

Meanwhile, faulty workmanship and substandard materials were being discovered in the XB-36. In fairness to Convair, substituting

materials was a generally accepted practice during the war years, especially for experimental aircraft. In addition, labor troubles at the Aluminum Corporation of America frequently held up shipment of materials to Convair. Because of these problems, it was expected that the resultant structural limitations would render the XB-36 useless,

The size of the vertical stabilizer becomes very evident when people are around it. Note the tail bumper under the rear fuselage, something the B-36A and B-36B models would continue. (Peter M. Bowers Collection)

A good comparison of the external changes to the XB-36 over the first few years of its test program. The photo at left shows the original 110-inch main gear and no buzz number on the forward fuselage. The photo at right shows the production four-wheel bogie main gear and the buzz numbers that would adorn most early B-36s. Note the "tail bumper" under the aft fuselage in the photo at right. (Convair)

The national insignia on the side of the XB-36 fuselage was located ahead of the sighting blister rather than behind it as on production models. Note the overall painted finish instead of natural metal. (Convair)

With three of the bomb bays open, this photos shows just how far aft bomb bay No. 4 was located on the XB-36 – the aft gun bays were between bomb bays No. 3 and No. 4 instead of behind No. 4. (Peter M. Bowers Collection)

other than as a test vehicle for the initial flights. Given the changes in configuration expected for production aircraft, this was probably to have been expected in any case.[26]

On 8 September 1945, almost six years after the original contract had been signed, the XB-36 (42-13570) was rolled out in Fort Worth. Given the normal reaction of most people when they first saw the prototype, many had taken to calling it the "Jesus Christ* airplane." In May 1946, Secretary of War Robert P. Patterson told a House subcommittee that the aircraft was "due to fly next month," a prediction that would be repeated several times during the summer. The aircraft finally made its maiden flight on 8 August 1946 piloted by Beryl A. Erickson and G.S. "Gus" Green, along with J.D. McEachern, William "Bill" P. Easley, A.W. Gecmen, Joe M. Hefley, R.E. Hewes, and W.H. Vobbe. At the time, it was the largest and heaviest aircraft ever flown, and the 37-minute flight was generally considered successful.

Early test flights confirmed that the aircraft's top speed was only about 230 mph, and two major problems soon surfaced – a lack of proper engine cooling and a propeller vibration, although both of these had been extensively investigated during wind tunnel testing and using a ground-based test rig. Eventually a two-speed cooling fan was developed that largely eliminated the cooling problem, but nothing could be done to ease the vibration other than strengthening the affected structures (primarily the flaps), which added yet more weight.[27]

After being grounded briefly in late 1946 for modifications, the XB-36 was flown for 160 hours by Air Force pilots. The aircraft was then returned to Convair where company pilots made 53 additional test flights, logging a total of 117 hours. These included a flight to 38,000 feet on 14 August 1947, an impressive achievement at the time.

---

* The first words out of many people's mouths when viewing the aircraft for the first time were "Jesus Christ, its big," or something similar. Other aircraft, particularly the Hughes HK-1 "Spruce Goose" also used the moniker.

One flight in particular made the news. On 26 March 1947, the XB-36 departed Fort Worth on a test flight piloted by Beryl Erickson and Gus Green. Also on board were flight engineer J.D. McEachern, six Convair flight test engineers, three Army Air Forces observers (including Major Stephen P. Dillon), and two technicians from Curtiss-Wright. At about 700 feet Gus Green went to raise the landing gear, "and the plane just went insane." As the hydraulic system attempted to raise the right main gear strut, the actuator exploded, allowing the gear to fall back to the extended position, and smashing the No. 4 engine nacelle and rupturing several fuel and hydraulic lines. The right gear swung from side-to-side in the slip stream. For the next 6 hours the aircraft circled Fort Worth while it burned off fuel. Erickson and Green decided they would attempt to land the aircraft, but ordered the other 12 men to bail out. Erickson flew in a large circle at 5,000 feet around the desired drop zone, and two men jumped at a time, one from each lower aft blister. Unfortunately, the surface winds at the drop zone were around 30 knots, and 9 of the 12 men were injured while landing, although none critically. Dillon hurried back to Fort Worth to guide the aircraft in from a radio in a Jeep. The two pilots managed to set the aircraft down just a little left of the centerline, but had no flaps, no brakes, and no nose wheel steering because of the blown hydraulic system. Fortunately, the right landing gear held, and the aircraft drifted lazily off the left side of the runway into the dirt.[28]

The aircraft was quickly repaired and back in the air. Eventually, the airframe was turned over to the Air Force in mid-1948, but as predicted, the XB-36 had limited operational value and was used primarily for ground training and to evaluate various proposed changes to the interior configuration.

The XB-36 did participate in one further flight test series. In early 1950 an experimental track-type landing gear was installed, similar to ones also tested on a B-50 and C-82 around the same time. The specially-designed Goodyear system of V-belts applied only 57 psi to the runway, compared to 156 psi for the production four-wheel bogie-type undercarriage. This would, in theory, allow very large aircraft to use unprepared landing strips instead of specially-built runways. Each of the two belts on the main landing gear was 16 inches wide, 276 inches in circumference, and had a thickness of 1 inch except for an additional 1 inch in a "V" in the center that fit into a slot on the bogie wheel to keep the track centered. Each belt was made of rubber reinforced with brass-plated steel cables and had a pull-strength of 150,000 pounds. The bogie wheels were made from a magnesium

The XB-36 had largely been retired when it was decided to test a track landing gear system on the aircraft. There was no specific intention to ever equip production B-36s with the odd-looking landing gear, but the XB-36 was a very heavy airplane that was available for tests. Similar tests had been conducted on a C-47, C-82, and B-50. The tests went surprisingly well, considering that tracks are normally associated with slow moving bulldozers and tanks, not aircraft that have to reach high speeds in order to take off. (lower right: Robert F. Dorr Collection; others: Lockheed Martin)

The cockpit of the XB-36 (shown here towards the end of its career) differed considerably from the production cockpit in overall layout and instrumentation. Note the simplicity of the instrumentation. (Convair)

The flight engineer's station of the XB-36 also differed considerably from the production model. This view shows most of the engine instrumentation, throttles, and mixture controls. (Convair)

alloy that contained zirconium. Friction was reduced through the use of 185 tapered roller bearings weighing approximately 500 pounds. The track-style gear added approximately 5,000 pounds to the normal 16,000-pound landing gear. Nevertheless, this was only two-thirds of the expected increase when the project began.[29]

A series of low- and medium-speed taxi tests were conducted during early March 1950 using the runways at Fort Worth. The first flight using the new landing gear came on 29 March 1950, and the resulting "screeching" sound was unnerving to those aboard the aircraft, including Beryl Erickson and Doc Witchell. There was never any intention of using the track-type gear on production B-36s, and the XB-36 was used as a testbed simply because it was a very heavy aircraft that was readily available. This did not stop several organi-

zations (including the Air University) from proposing equipping production B-36s with track-style landing gear, but nothing came of the suggestions.[30]

The Air Force eventually decided it would be too expensive to bring the XB-36 up to production standards, and the aircraft was officially retired on 30 January 1952, although it had last moved under its own power in October 1951. The aircraft was assigned to the nuclear aircraft development program where it was used as a mockup for some aspects of the NB-36H and X-6. Over time the engines and all serviceable equipment were removed, and the aircraft fell into disrepair on a corner of the Fort Worth field. In May 1957 the airframe was turned over to the Carswell AFB fire department to be used as a firefighting aid and was eventually destroyed.[31]

The XB-36 languished for some years after it was retired, shuffled off to a corner of the Convair reservation. After the track landing gear tests, the production-type landing gear was reinstalled, and the engines and other serviceable equipment removed. On 24 May 1957 it posed (left) with the XB-58 for a family portrait. The middle photo shows the XB-36 on the north end of the reservation near the nuclear facility on 20 January 1954. At right, the aircraft sits on Carswell AFB where it was used as an aircraft fire trainer. (right: Frank Kleinwechter via Don Pyeatt; others: Lockheed Martin)

For the 1940s, the XB-35 (left) was a radical-looking aircraft. Counter-rotating propellers were an early attempt to eliminate propeller torque, but it was soon decided that turbojet engines offered a better solution. The YB-49 (center) was the first attempt at replacing the original R-3350 piston engines with jets – eight 3,750-lbf Allison J35-A-15s buried in the wing. The last wing, the YRB-49A, used six 5,000-lbf J35-A-19s; four in the wing and two below it. Notice the open bomb bays on the YB-49, and the bomb falling away from the YRB-49A. (left: Tony Landis Collection; others: Jay Miller Collection)

A FLYING WING

One of the most innovative of the early aviation designers was John K. "Jack" Northrop, who believed that an aircraft should be reduced to its most essential configuration – a flying wing. Early trials by Northrop of a "mostly" flying wing had begun as early as 1929. By July 1940 Northrop had flown the N-1M wing, demonstrating that it was possible for an aircraft to dispense with the normal fuselage and empennage. In theory this would allow a significant savings in weight and drag, and hopefully provide increased performance for any given amount of power.

The piston-powered XB-35 originated from the same competition that spawned the B-36. Based on preliminary data that Northrop supplied in response to the 27 May 1941 Army request, it had been determined that the flying wing would not be able to meet the very-long-range requirements, but the Army Air Forces nevertheless thought the design held promise. On 22 November 1941 Northrop was awarded a contract for 2 prototype XB-35s to be followed by 13 service-test YB-35s. Four 30-percent-scale N-9M models were constructed to test the configuration, and the first XB-35 eventually flew on 25 June 1946 with the second following on 26 June 1947.

Flight test results of the two XB-35s were mixed, with moderate to severe controllability issues encountered under some circumstances. At least a portion of these difficulties were believed to be the result of the propeller torque and, in June 1945, the Army Air Forces directed Northrop to finish subsequent aircraft as YB-49s with eight jet engines in an effort to overcome this. The first YB-49 made its maiden flight on 21 October 1947. Unfortunately the second YB-49 crashed on 5 June 1948, killing Captain Glen W. Edwards – the Muroc test location was renamed Edwards Air Force Base in his honor.

Nevertheless, the Air Force seriously considered producing the bomber – usually at the expense of the B-36 program. At the same time, the Air Force had concerns regarding Northrop's ability to manage such a large production program. Originally, the Air Force proposed a merger between Convair and Northrop, but Jack Northrop seriously objected to this. Eventually, a fee arrangement was worked out that allowed Convair to perform the actual production work. This satisfied a few issues – it allowed a company with a demonstrated ability to produce large bombers to perform the construction, kept a large government facility (Fort Worth) in operation (which it would not be if the B-36 was cancelled), and avoided the need to lay off several thousand workers when the B-36 was cancelled.[32]

On 1 October 1948 Northrop was awarded a production contract for 30 jet-powered B-49A flying wings. The Air Force-brokered agreement between Convair and Northrop was consummated on 13 October 1948 when Convair signed a letter of intent with Northrop to produce 29 of the B-49As under contract. The first aircraft would be manufactured by Northrop in Hawthorne, California, where the prototype XB-35 and YB-49s were built. The agreement called for Northrop to be responsible for all engineering on the B-49A, including the drawing of production tooling. Convair would manufacture the required tooling and actually produce the aircraft. The flying wing assembly line would initially be set up in the 120-foot bay of Building No. 4 alongside the 200-foot bay that was producing the 100-aircraft run of B-36s.[33]

Unfortunately for Northrop, the flying wing continued to demonstrate serious stability and control problems, largely due to its unique configuration and the limitations of the stability-augmentation systems of the era. The continued problems forced the Air Force to defer production, although 30 Convair engineers had already moved to California to assist Northrop in tool design and production planning. Because of the apparent stability problems, the inability of the Northrop aircraft to carry the current generation of atomic weapons, and a growing faith in the B-36, only one more flying wing bomber would fly – the six-engine YRB-49A reconnaissance prototype. In 1951 the Air Force officially terminated the flying wing program and ordered all of the remaining airframes destroyed. Proposals for large commercial airliners and cargo aircraft based on the flying wing concept quietly faded from the scene following the Air Force decision to cancel the bomber program.[34]

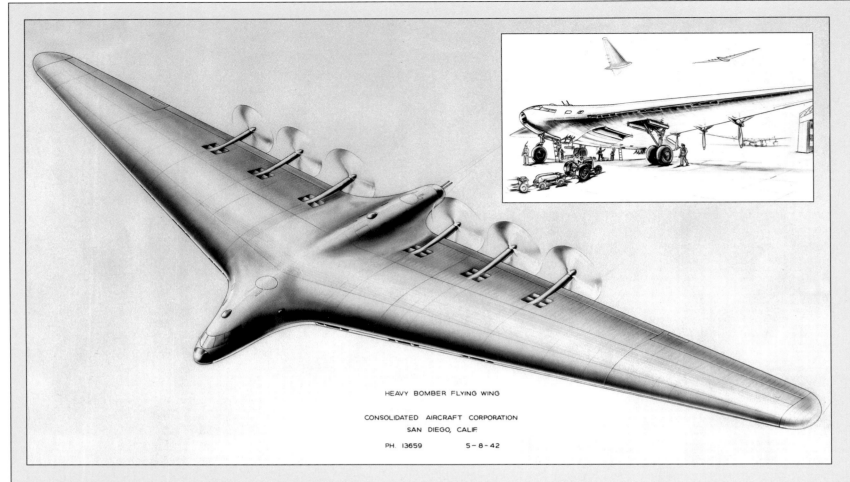

HEAVY BOMBER FLYING WING

CONSOLIDATED AIRCRAFT CORPORATION

SAN DIEGO, CALIF

PH. 13659   5-8-42

This is the flying wing design that Convair investigated as a comparison to the Model 36 under development in 1942. Note the retracted turret on top of the forward "fuselage." It was noted in the final report that the propeller shafts were unrealistically narrow, and there were concerns about engine cooling. The inset shows additional exterior details such as the location of the bomb bays and landing gear. (San Diego Aerospace Museum Collection)

But the initial promise of the flying wing concept had not been lost on Convair. During early 1942 Convair had initiated an in-house study of a very heavy bomber flying wing based around the same requirements being used for the B-36. The goal was to see if the flying wing offered sufficient promise to drive possible changes to the B-36 configuration.

The basic requirements sounded familiar – carry 10,000 pounds of bombs over a range of 10,000 miles. The design used a "special low drag airfoil" with six 19-foot diameter pusher propellers driven by turbosupercharged X-Wasp engines. A tricycle landing gear was envisioned using dual 80-inch diameter main wheels and a single 65-inch diameter nose wheel. The fully-retractable landing gear did not protrude beyond the normal contour of the wing (unlike the later 4-wheel B-36 design). Two pressurized cabins housed a crew of 12 and maintained an 8,000-foot pressure altitude to an actual altitude of 35,000 feet. The front and rear compartments were connected by a 27-inch diameter pressurized tunnel.[35]

The aircraft was designed to carry all of the bomb types then in service with the Army Air Corps, with a maximum bomb load of:

QTY.	TYPE OF BOMB	TOTAL LOAD
12	4,000-pound bombs	48,000 pounds, or
28	2,000-pound bombs	56,000 pounds, or
72	1,000-pound bombs	72,000 pounds, or
134	500-pound bombs	67,000 pounds.

Defensive armament was lavish for the era, consisting of six 37-mm cannon with 300 rounds of ammunition per gun, and eight 0.50-caliber machine guns with 1,000 rounds per gun. The weapons offered "entire sphere" coverage.

A summary letter was written by Harry Sutton to Mac Laddon on 9 May 1942 to accompany the study results. Based on the theoretical figures (no wind tunnel tests had been run), Sutton concluded the flying wing design looked very promising. Compared to the projected B-36A figures, the top speed was 16 mph higher, but a lower wing loading reduced the average cruising speed by 60 mph. The take-off distance was decreased by 400 feet, but the landing distance was 1,000 feet longer. Sutton did not believe the increase in landing distance should be objectionable since it was "still considerably less than the B-36 takeoff distance." The reduction in cruising speed, however, was bothersome.[36]

Sutton cautioned that the largest unsolved problem for a flying wing was how to provide adequate control. In an attempt to solve this, Sutton wrote that Convair was constructing a wind-tunnel model to be tested at the California Institute of Technology. Unfortunately, no results of these tests could be found, if in fact they ever took place. The letter continued that "there seems to be no seri-ous reason why we should not secure satisfactory lateral and directional control by the use of split ailerons. Satisfactory aerodynamic effect can undoubtedly be secured, and there seems to be no reason why such controls could not be adapted to the present system of pilot controls with satisfactory results; that is, the pilot would never know from operating the airplane whether it had normal type of tail surfaces and ailerons or not. The question of longitudinal control may be much more difficult to solve." In the end, Jack Northrop dis-covered the same thing.

Convair continued to investigate flying wing or "tailless" designs for a variety of purposes through at least the middle of 1944, but none were again proposed to replace the B-36. Instead, most concentrated on smaller two- and four-engine bombers and patrol aircraft.[37]

The internal arrangement of the flying wing was similar to Northrop's in concept. Two pressurized compartments, connected by a tunnel, housed the crew – although the rear compartment only contained living and sleeping quarters. The bomb bays were located on either side of the "fuselage" with most of the fuel located in the outer wing panels. The engines were buried at mid-chord, not in the trailing edge like on the Model 36. The main land-ing gear retracted between the two engines on each side. The defensive armament took up most of the rest of the fuselage area, with four completely retractable turrets and a nonretractable tail turret. (San Diego Aerospace Museum Collection)

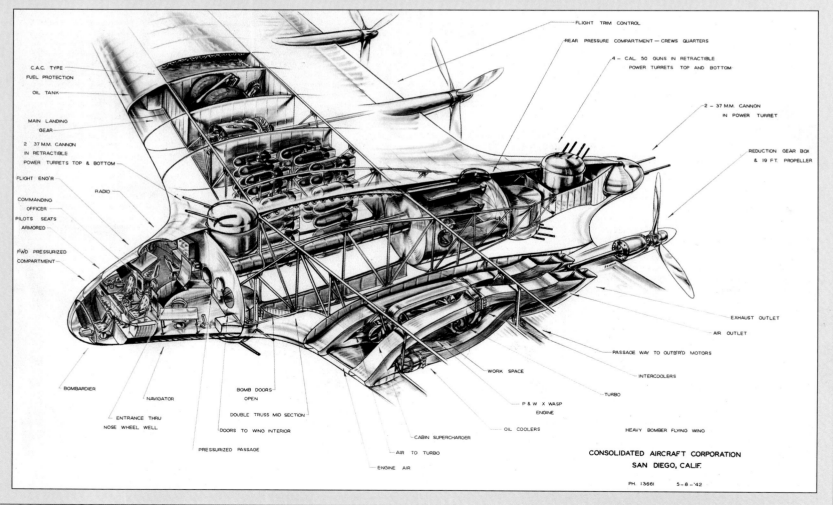

Chapter 2

Above: *The XC-99 in its early operational markings. Note the San Antonio Air Depot logo on the tail.* (Convair via Richard Freeman)

Right: *Early artwork showing a tank driving onto the rear loading ramps of the proposed transport.* (San Diego Aerospace Museum Collection)

WIDE BODY

As early as May 1942 Consolidated had investigated a cargo variant of the XB-36 that used the wing, engines, empennage, and landing gear of the bomber attached to a new fuselage. This aircraft was called the Model 36 Transport, and included the use of the trademark Consolidated twin vertical stabilizers. The Transport was slightly smaller than the XC-99 that would eventually emerge, with an elliptical fuselage that measured 13.5 feet wide, 19.3 feet high, and 173 feet long. The vertical stabilizers stood 40 feet high, while the wing had the same 230-foot span as the B-36. The pressurized fuselage provided seats for 144 passengers in a day arrangement, converting to 68 sleeper berths at night. Up to 12,000 pounds of baggage and mail could also be carried. This was a significant increase over the 40-odd passengers who could be accommodated in the DC-4s of the era. A flight crew of five was provided, with provisions for a five-man relief crew. Seven cabin attendants were aided by a nurse. Unfortunately, the demands of war prevented any immediate commercial prospects.[1]

However, Consolidated believed that construction of a prototype cargo aircraft would be an expeditious way to test many portions of the bomber design, particularly engine cooling, before the XB-36 flew. The cargo variant could be designed and built quicker since it did not require the extensive military equipment specified for the B-36. Of course, having the government pay to develop a prototype would also put Consolidated in a favorable position to sell commercial versions after the war. The project engineer for Consolidated was Roberts R. Hoover. When the B-36 program moved to Fort Worth in September 1942, Hoover and the 17 engineers assigned to the cargo variant moved with it. The two programs were located together in the Experimental Building at Fort Worth, and portions of a fuselage mockup were constructed alongside the XB-36 mockup.[2]

The Army Air Forces finally ordered a single example (43-52436) on 31 December 1942 under a $4.5 million (plus $180,000 fee) contract (W535-ac-34454) that specified the newly-designated XC-99 program was not to interfere with the construction or delivery of the XB-36. Interestingly, the fact that an entire new fuselage needed to be designed was not considered to be high risk, and delivery was set for 21 months later. Fort Worth seemed to be a logical location to build the XC-99 since San Diego was busy with the production of B-24s and developing the B-32. However, as more and more production shifted to the new plant in Fort Worth, it became clear that it might

be advantageous to move the XC-99 program back to San Diego. In early 1944 the Army Air Forces approved the move westward, and Hoover returned with seven engineers in May 1944.

By this time the design had matured considerably, resulting in a new Model 37 designation. The graceful elliptical fuselage cross-section was replaced by an unpressurized ogive shape 20.6 feet high, 14 feet wide, and 182.5 feet long. The twin vertical stabilizers were replaced by a single unit 57.5 feet high. The original Model 36 Transport mockup was not relocated, and partial mockups of the new fuselage were constructed at San Diego to optimize the cargo loading and unloading concepts. A structural test fuselage section was also constructed since this was the first time a large double-load fuselage had ever been built and Consolidated wanted to perform stress testing on it.

The XC-99 was designed to carry over 100,000 pounds of cargo, 400 fully-equipped troops, or 300 litter patients within a total cargo volume of 16,000 cubic feet split between two decks. The aircraft's range was estimated to be 1,720 miles with a 100,000-pound load, or

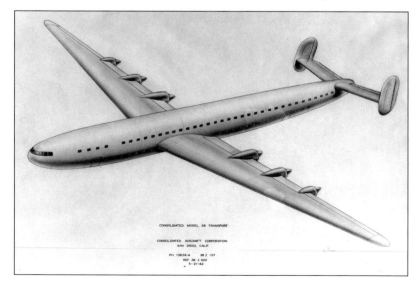

The Model 36 Transport as it looked on 21 May 1942. The wing and empennage were common to the proposed XB-36, mated with a new double-deck fuselage. (Convair)

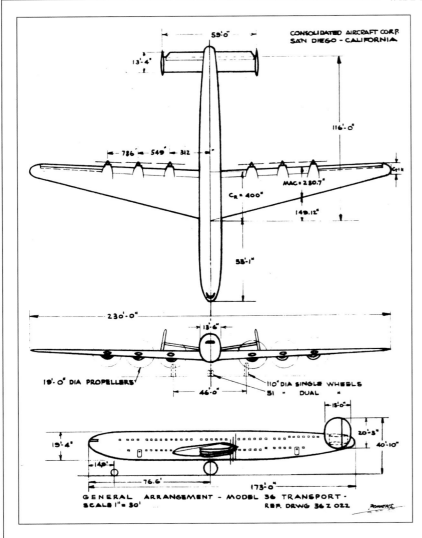

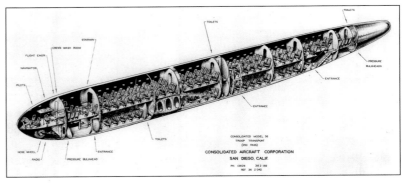

The May 1942 design (left) for the Model 36 Transport included variants that could carry 250 troops (above), each in an individual seat, and also an all-cargo model (below). (Convair)

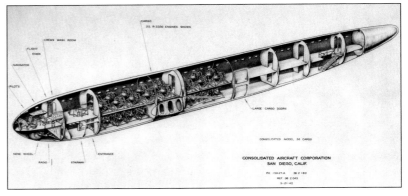

8,100 miles with 10,000 pounds. Cruising speed was 292 mph, with a top speed of 335 mph at 30,000 feet. Eight crewmembers were required to operate the aircraft – pilot, copilot, two flight engineers, navigator, radio operator, and two scanners. The scanners were stationed on the lower deck in the aft fuselage near windows to observe the operation of the engines and landing gear; they also doubled as cargo masters while the aircraft was on the ground. The flight deck was carpeted and soundproofed, and black fluorescent lighting was provided at all crew stations for night flying.[3]

The aircraft had a gross weight of 265,000 pounds, but the operating manual allowed an "over-condition" weight of 295,000 pounds with "favorable atmospheric conditions when operating from known runways." This allowed 117,000 pounds of cargo to be carried, and still permitted a normal 500-feet per minute rate of climb at sea level.[4]

During late 1946 and 1947 the single XC-99 was assembled at the Consolidated plant in San Diego, although the wings and other common B-36 parts were manufactured in Fort Worth and shipped via rail to San Diego for installation. The XC-99 would prove to be the largest piston-engine cargo aircraft ever developed, and made its maiden flight on 24 November 1947 with Russell R. Rogers and Beryl A. Erickson at the controls. Mel Clause and B.B. Gray were the flight engineers, L.J. Bordelon and Larry Brandvig were the scanners, John T. Ready and G.W. Hofeller were the flight test engineers, and William C. Geopfarth was the radio operator for the first flight. Erickson and Geopfarth came from Fort Worth, while the other crew members were from San Diego.

The uneventful hour-long flight was made from Lindbergh Field in front of several thousand spectators. The aircraft was equipped with over 12,000 pounds of flight test instrumentation that provided detailed information on control movements and forces, engine and duct temperatures, duct velocities, and valve movements in the various systems. This information proved very useful on both the B-36 and C-99 programs, just as Convair had intended.[5]

The basic airframe weighed 135,232 pounds, broken down as: fuselage 25,164 pounds, wings 37,100, empennage 4,659, landing gear 18,738, engines and nacelles 42,345, and miscellaneous equipment 7,226. Aluminum alloy accounted for 75,000 pounds, steel for 18,000, and glass for 2,000. The remainder was made up of rubber, plastic, fabric, and other metal alloys. Unlike the B-36, very little magnesium was used, mainly for the tail cone, some of the wing skins, and parts of the cargo doors. There were a variety of reasons for the difference. The use

Unlike the original Model 36 Transport, this 11 August 1942 design study used a fuselage that was more closely related to the XB-36. Unfortunately, the comparatively small diameter fuselage would have limited the utility of the cargo aircraft considerably. (Convair)

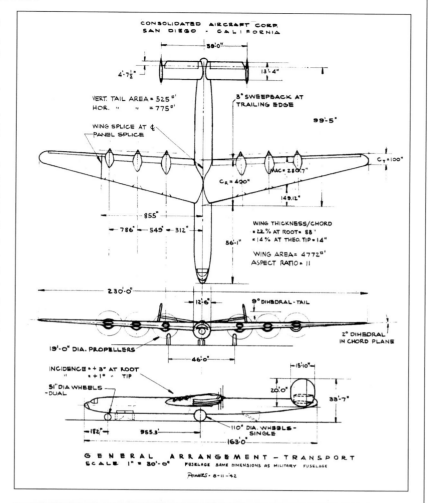

of aluminum simplified manufacturing the one-off aircraft, and any production models were expected to be pressurized – magnesium did not lend itself for use in areas* that underwent pressure cycles.[6]

To provide additional safety for crewmembers and passengers, Convair located the inboard wing fuel tanks some 10 feet from the fuselage. A supplemental bulkhead between the inboard fuel tank and the fuselage served as a secondary dam in the event of fuel leakage and prevented fuel from entering the fuselage. This design eliminated the fire hazard inherent when fuel tanks are located in the fuselage area. Unfortunately, this also reduced the fuel capacity of the aircraft slightly from that of the B-36. If the aircraft had entered production, it is likely that additional tanks would have been installed in the outer wing panels, much like was done on the B-36J. Like the XB-36, the XC-99 was originally fitted with a carbon dioxide fire extinguishing system, but this was replaced during the 1950 modification period by one using methyl-bromide. This allowed the 72 high-pressure tanks originally installed to be reduced to only four low-pressure tanks, saving over 2,000 pounds.[7]

Like the B-36s, the XC-99 used unpowered flight controls. The control surfaces had an area almost equal to the entire wing area of a B-24, and were operated by a series of spring tabs† that looked much like normal trim tabs, only larger. These were directly operated by moving the control stick in the cockpit and caused the larger control surface to move via aerodynamic forces. The use of spring tabs was not original to the B-36/XC-99, but it was the largest aircraft ever equipped with the devices. Also like the early B-36s, the XC-99 used doped fabric to cover the ailerons, elevators, and rudder.[8]

The XC-99 was equipped with two electrically-operated sliding cargo doors on the bottom of the fuselage, one just forward of the wing and one in the aft fuselage. The doors were supported by rollers that moved in tracks, and the fuselage skin had slots to accommodate the door brackets while they moved. The slots were covered flush by spring-loaded strips when the doors were closed. Two pairs of clamshell doors were installed immediately aft of the rear sliding cargo door although the rear sliding door had to be opened before them. Structural limitation prohibited the clamshell doors from being opened in flight, although either sliding door could be opened in order to drop cargo.

Cargo could be loaded, unloaded, or shifted within the cargo compartments by means of four electric hoists. The two hoists in the lower compartment could be used to shift or drop cargo while the aircraft was in flight, but the two hoists in the upper compartment were normally restricted to ground operations. The hoists were set on tracks

---

* This was also true on the B-36 – all pressurized areas used aluminum skin. When the pressurized photographic compartment was added to bomb bay No. 1 on the RB-36 models, the skin was changed from magnesium to aluminum.

† This control system was identical to that used on the B-36. The nomenclature reflected differences between San Diego and Fort Worth – San Diego called them "spring tabs" while Fort Worth used "servo tabs."

The XC-99 landing at Lindberg Field in San Diego. At this point the aircraft sill used the 110-inch main landing gear. (Convair)

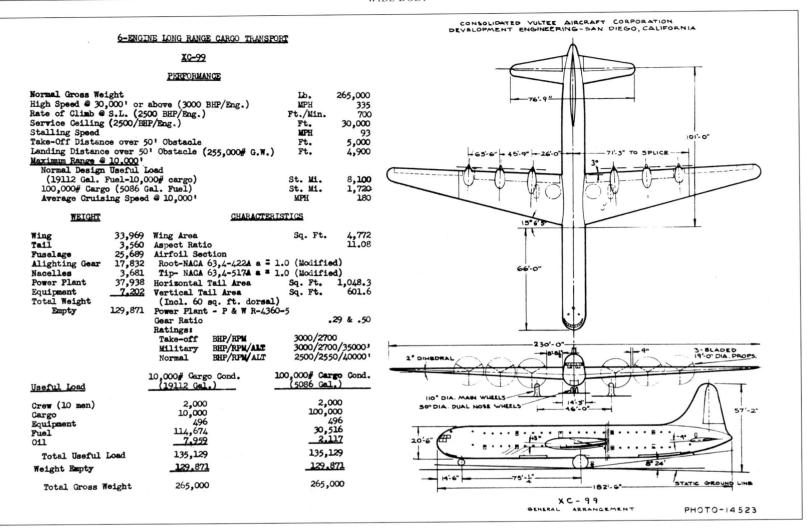

6-ENGINE LONG RANGE CARGO TRANSPORT

XC-99

PERFORMANCE

Normal Gross Weight	Lb.	265,000
High Speed @ 30,000' or above (3000 BHP/Eng.)	MPH	335
Rate of Climb @ S.L. (2500 BHP/Eng.)	Ft./Min.	700
Service Ceiling (2500/BHP/Eng.)	Ft.	30,000
Stalling Speed	MPH	93
Take-Off Distance over 50' Obstacle	Ft.	5,000
Landing Distance over 50' Obstacle (255,000# G.W.)	Ft.	4,900

Maximum Range @ 10,000'

Normal Design Useful Load (19112 Gal. Fuel-10,000# cargo)	St. Mi.	8,100
100,000# Cargo (5086 Gal. Fuel)	St. Mi.	1,720
Average Cruising Speed @ 10,000'	MPH	180

WEIGHT

Wing	33,969
Tail	3,560
Fuselage	25,689
Alighting Gear	17,832
Nacelles	3,681
Power Plant	37,938
Equipment	7,202
Total Weight Empty	129,871

CHARACTERISTICS

Wing Area	Sq. Ft.	4,772
Aspect Ratio		11.08

Airfoil Section
Root-NACA 63,4-422A a = 1.0 (Modified)
Tip- NACA 63,4-517A a = 1.0 (Modified)

Horizontal Tail Area	Sq. Ft.	1,048.3
Vertical Tail Area	Sq. Ft.	601.6

(Incl. 60 sq. ft. dorsal)
Power Plant - P & W R-4360-5
Gear Ratio .29 & .50

Ratings:

	BHP/RPM	
Take-off	BHP/RPM	3000/2700
Military	BHP/RPM/ALT	3000/2700/35000'
Normal	BHP/RPM/ALT	2500/2550/40000'

Useful Load

	10,000# Cargo Cond. (19112 Gal.)	100,000# Cargo Cond. (5086 Gal.)
Crew (10 men)	2,000	2,000
Cargo	10,000	100,000
Equipment	496	496
Fuel	114,674	30,516
Oil	7,959	2,117
Total Useful Load	135,129	135,129
Weight Empty	129,871	129,871
Total Gross Weight	265,000	265,000

The final characteristics of the XC-99 when it was approved for manufacture. Very little would change during production. (Convair)

Three views of the XC-99 early in its flight test program when it was still equipped with the original 110-inch main landing gear. At left the aircraft is seen departing San Diego. At right, workers trying to hand turn the propeller on one of the big R-4360s – it could not have been an easy task. As originally flown the aircraft had a "Convair XC-99" logo on the forward fuselage. (Peter M. Bowers Collection)

The wing and engine installation on the XC-99 was nearly identical to the XB-36 and YB-36 since all three wings had been built at the same time. Initially the XC-99 used –25 engines, but these were upgraded to –41 engines during its time in service. The upgrade was not as straight forward as it should have been, necessitating some changes to the wing structure to accommodate the newer power plants. (San Diego Aerospace Museum Collection)

to accommodate the newer engines. Other changes included installing the methyl-bromide fire extinguishers and a warning system that alerted the pilot when the oil supply for any engine dropped below 25 gallons (each engine normally carried 190 gallons). The 12,000 pounds of flight test instrumentation was also removed.

Unfortunately, while undergoing ground tests on 20 March 1950 an explosion ruptured the left inboard fuel tank. The cause was subsequently traced to static electricity in some servicing equipment that was improperly grounded. Repairs took about 90 days, and were completed on 25 June. The aircraft returned to the air on 3 July 1950 with a 2.5 hour flight around San Antonio piloted by Colonel Fred Bell, then Director of Maintenance at Kelly, and Captain M.W. Neyland. The only problem was slight damage to a nose wheel door that was improperly rigged.[15]

The Air Force decided a long-duration flight was required to verify that all of the modifications were satisfactory. As it happened, there were a quantity of R-4360 engines and Curtiss-Wright propellers in San Diego that needed returned to the San Antonio depot for overhaul in support of the ongoing B-36B conversion work. Operation ELEPHANT was born, and the XC-99 was flown to San Diego on 12 July 1950. After some difficulty loading the material in San Diego, the

XC-99 departed for the 1,150-mile trip back to Kelly AFB on 14 July. The cargo included 10 engines and 16 propellers for a total payload of 101,266 pounds and a ramp weight of 303,334 pounds. On this flight the XC-99 unofficially broke 23 world records for cargo carrying – greatest distance, fastest speed, highest altitude, etc. The crew included Colonel Bell as the aircraft commander, Colonel Theodore W. Tucker as the pilot, and Captain M.W. Neyland as the copilot. During the flight, the No. 6 engine began backfiring and was feathered – the remainder of the flight was made on five engines![16]

After Operation ELEPHANT was completed, the aircraft was turned over to a crew from Carswell AFB and flown to Fort Worth for an uncertain future. Two weeks later, in September 1950, Headquarters Air Force reassigned the aircraft back to Kelly AFB for the purpose of conducting an operational evaluation. Colonel Tucker, the pilot on the Operation ELEPHANT flight, was named the project officer. The goal of the operational evaluation was not specifically to evaluate the XC-99 (although that naturally occurred), but rather to compare a very large cargo aircraft versus the use of many smaller cargo aircraft. The result would determine if the Air Force would seek to purchase more of its existing aircraft, or design and procure larger aircraft for the future.

OPERATIONAL EVALUATION

The first circuit (a combination of individual flights) of the operational evaluation was scheduled to begin on 5 October 1950 – a flight from Kelly AFB to McClellan AFB, California, and return. However, the urgent need for 42 R-2000 aircraft engines to support C-54 operations on the Korean airlift caused a last minute change of plans and the first circuit was rerouted to McChord AFB, Washington. Twenty-seven of the engines were loaded onto the lower deck, and the remaining 15 on the upper deck. During the flight, problems were encountered with high cylinder head temperature indications that were later traced to an error in the thermocouple system. With this exception, and excessive fuel consumption caused by additional drag generated by engine air plugs that were stuck in the open position, the aircraft functioned satisfactorily for the first five hours of the flight. However, serious trouble became apparent when the left scanner reported that the No. 2 propeller was wobbling about its axis. This movement became progressively worse, and about 20 minutes later the propeller was feathered.[17]

The lower deck of the XC-99 showing the two scanner positions. Like the rear gunners on the B-36, these crewmembers checked the engines and landing gear during operations to ensure they were functioning correctly. Note the ladder in the background leading to the upper deck. (Convair)

There was insufficient fuel remaining to continue to McChord on five engines, so the XC-99 landed at Kirtland AFB, New Mexico, where it was determined that the propeller shaft had developed an 18-inch long crack. The engine was changed at Kirtland and the flight continued to Spokane, Washington, after weather conditions at McChord were found to be too poor to land. After a short hop to McChord when the weather improved, the entire manifest of 42 engines was off-loaded in 2.5 hours. The next morning a new cargo destined for McClellan was loaded aboard the aircraft, delivered later that morning, then the XC-99 continued back to Kelly with only minor problems encountered enroute.

The second circuit encompassed a flight from Kelly to Hill AFB, Utah, to McClellan and back to San Antonio. The flight had been scheduled well in advance, and a week prior to the XC-99's arrival the local newspapers and radio in Ogden began announcing the forthcoming visit by the world's largest cargo aircraft. On the request of local authorities, the XC-99 circled the city several times with cameramen photographing the aircraft from a B-25. When the XC-99 landed at Hill AFB, it was greeted by at least 3,000 people, including newspaper and television reporters.

The problems inherent in the ground handling of a very large aircraft became apparent while at Hill. There was not a taxiway that led to the take-off position at the end of the runway, and it was necessary for the XC-99 to taxi down the runway and turn around at the far end. However, it was virtually impossible to turn the XC-99 around

A trio of shots of the XC-99 loading cargo. The hoist configuration was fairly versatile, allowing a variety of loads to be hauled up through the two cargo openings. Note the ladder in the opening at left. (Lockheed Martin)

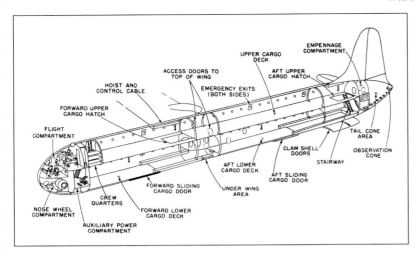

The as-built general arrangement for the XC-99. (Convair)

in less than 250 feet under its own power when fully loaded, and unfortunately the runway at Hill was only 100 feet wide. The heavier the load, the larger the radius because of the scraping action on the tires and gear on the inboard side of the turn.

Cleatracs were hitched to the main gear, and the nose gear was turned by the combined efforts of crew members pushing on a pipe inserted through the nose axle and the pilot using nose wheel steering. After four attempts the aircraft was finally pointed in the right direction. However, several hundred yards of runway lay behind the aircraft, which needed all available length because of the high field elevation. Guided by the crew chief's hand signals, waving, and shouting, the pilot applied power to the propellers in reverse pitch and the XC-99 gracefully backed towards the end of the runway. Later this became a routine operation, but on this first occasion the crew was quite excited and pleased over the ease in which the aircraft backed down the runway. The aircraft took off for McClellan and finally returned to Kelly.[18]

During the third circuit the XC-99 flew to Tinker AFB near Oklahoma City, then on to McClellan. On 31 October 1950 the XC-99 made its first very-long-range flight – 2,300 miles from McClellan to Turner AFB, Georgia. The 86,000-pound cargo consisted of virtually the complete stock of spare parts and equipment necessary to maintain and operate a fighter wing. The gross takeoff weight was 311,864 pounds. McClellan had a field elevation of 74 feet and the runway was 7,000 feet long with a row of 60-foot high power lines only 1,700 feet from the end of the runway. The wind was east-south-east at 4 mph and the temperature was 47 degF. The high performance take-off was well executed and the scanners reported that the main gear cleared the power lines by 30 feet.

The first six hours of flight were conducted at 20,000 feet, and a newly-revamped oxygen system functioned well. A gradual descent to 10,000 feet was begun over Kansas with about five hours of flight remaining. The XC-99 touched down at Turner AFB after a 16-hour nonstop flight of 2,332 miles with a landing weight of 253,184 pounds.

The aircraft had consumed 9,780 gallons of fuel – an average of less than 890 gallons per hour – which was a marked improvement over previous flights. The balance of this circuit continued from Turner to Mobile, Alabama, where an engine check was accomplished, and then from Mobile back to Kelly.

The fourth circuit encompassed flights from Kelly AFB, to Austin, to the Naval Air Station at North Island, California, to the Convair facility at Lindberg Field in San Diego, and back to Kelly. The fifth circuit was Kelly to Macon, Georgia, and return to Kelly. Both circuits were uneventful.

The sixth and last circuit of the XC-99 operational evaluation was made from Barksdale AFB, Louisiana, to Ramey AFB, Puerto Rico, and return. An R-4360 failure on the outbound leg forced the aircraft to land at Tampa, Florida, for an engine change. The remaining flight to Ramey was uneventful. Unfortunately, the pivot shaft forging in one main landing gear broke while the XC-99 was landing at Barksdale on the return. It was determined that it was unwise to move the aircraft very far, so the XC-99 was towed just off the edge of the runway and secured to the ramp. This effectively ended the operational evaluation and curtailed flights for the remainder of 1950. The aircraft was eventually repaired at Barksdale and flown back to Kelly.[19]

During the operational evaluation the aircraft had flown 129 hours and 45 minutes, covering 21,702 miles. A total of 1,306,653 pounds of cargo was carried, not including the original Operation ELEPHANT flight. These tests consumed 120,532 gallons of fuel and 2,917 gallons of engine oil. Four engines were changed and 29 different modifications were incorporated into the aircraft during the evaluation. Convair liked to point out that the XC-99 held numerous unofficial world records for air cargo operations, and continued to break its own records on a fairly routine basis.[20]

Based on the results of the evaluations, Convair determined that the XC-99 was capable of carrying a ton of cargo one airline mile for less than four cents of fuel expended. At the time, the XC-99 was the only aircraft in the Air Force that had demonstrated the ability to carry 100,000 pounds of cargo 2,000 miles nonstop.

MORE USE

Upon its return to Kelly at the end of 1950, the XC-99 underwent numerous modifications during the first six months of 1951. The most significant work was that the fuel tanks were completely resealed by 4 Convair supervisors and 30 Convair technicians from Fort Worth. Other changes included reupholstering the flight deck and adding sound-deadening material to the cockpit. Additional crew-comfort items, based largely on B-36 parts, were also added, including 11 bunks, 2 hot plates, an electric oven, a small refrigerator, a dining table, and a "roomette" where the aircraft commander could relax. A new elevator was installed inside the fuselage to speed loading and unloading cargo. Late-model square-tip propellers replaced the original units, reducing the buffeting suffered by the flat-sided fuselage by approximately 50 percent. The landing gear was strengthened, allowing gross weights of up to 320,000 pounds, up from 312,000 pounds.[21]

The first flight after the modifications occurred on 6 July 1951, and subsequently the aircraft was used extensively by the San Antonio depot. A regular schedule was established where the XC-99 flew to the west coast twice per week – normally to the depot at McClellan, but often to other bases in California as well. On 9 September, for example, the XC-99 traveled between Kelly AFB and Travis AFB with an 80,000-pound payload; the aircraft returned the next day with a 90,000-pound load.

The average usage of the XC-99 was fairly consistent during 1951–52. For instance, during September 1951, the aircraft made 16 flights for 114 hours and 55 minutes while covering 20,760 miles with 964,147 pounds of cargo. During January 1952 the aircraft flew 15 flights totaling 117.25 hours carrying 1,123,000 pounds of cargo. The totals for a 9-month period around the same time were impressive – 7,000,000 pounds of cargo during 115 flights, 65 of which flew over 1,500 miles. It took an average of 54 minutes to load each 10,000 pounds of cargo with a ten-man loading crew. Offloading averaged just over half as long.

The XC-99 cockpit was unusual in that the flight engineer sat between and behind the pilots, and the majority of his instrumentation and controls were on the center console. The engineer also had additional controls on the right side of the cockpit. Jump seats for observers were located behind the flight engineer. This seldom-seen inflight shot was taken on 28 June 1952. (Lockheed Martin)

This is not to say it could not be accomplished quicker, however. During a trip on 3 July 1952, workers at McClellan AFB removed 74,149 pounds of cargo and replaced it with 83,549 pounds in only 3 hours and 45 minutes. This was largely the result of using preloaded

A good photo (dated 19 June 1952) of the nose before the weather radar was added. (Lockheed Martin)

One of the few exterior changes to the XC-99 was the addition of a nose-mounted weather radar in June 1953. (above: Convair; below: A. Kreiger via the Norm Taylor Collection via Richard Freeman)

cargo bins, much like the containers used today by commercial airlines. The bins, each capable of carrying 4,000 pounds of cargo, had been designed and built at Kelly and were introduced in April 1952. On this same flight the XC-99 passed the 1,000 flight hour mark while on its way from Kelly to McClellan.[22]

The only significant external change to the aircraft was made in June 1953 when the XC-99 received a weather radar behind a radome installed on the extreme nose. The 250-pound unit had a range of over 200 miles under ideal conditions, and could detect mountains and other obstacles in addition to thunderstorms. Given the overall size and capacity of the XC-99, the extra weight detracted little from the aircraft performance, although it did change the overall look more significantly than one would think. According to Convair, around 8 August 1953 the Air Force redesignated* the XC-99 as the C-99 (no "X"), although independent confirmation of this could not be obtained.[23]

On 12 August 1953 the XC-99 made its first intercontinental flight, carrying a crew of 23 and 61,000 pounds of cargo from Kelly AFB to Rhein Main AB in Germany. The 4,800 mile flight included overnight stops at Kindley AFB, Bermuda, and Lajes AFB in the Azores. A week later it returned with 62,000 pounds of cargo, stopping at Lajes and Westover AFB, Massachusetts. In all, the mission covered more than 12,000 miles in about 63 flight hours. The flight crew consisted of Captain James M. Pittard, Jr. (who had over 1,900 hours in the XC-99), copilot Major C.W. Potter, and navigator Major James Sanders.[24]

The XC-99 continued to provide useful service to the San Antonio depot, and reportedly flew more flight hours than any other Air Force experimental aircraft. It could carry cargo for $0.16 per pound per mile, compared to over $0.25 per pound for the C-124. However, these rates assumed the XC-99 had a full load, something it rarely did. By June 1957 it was obvious that the aircraft was suffering from structural fatigue, and the Air Force did not want to spend the estimated 145,000 man-hours and $1,000,000 to fix it. The XC-99 was permanently grounded in August 1957. The aircraft had logged 7,430 hours of flight time, and carried over 60,000,000 pounds of cargo.[25]

On 6 November 1957, title for the aircraft was transferred to the Disabled American Veterans, which put the aircraft on public display in a field next to Kelly AFB for the next 30 years. Regrettably, the aircraft fell into disrepair, and in 1993 the Kelly Field Heritage Foundation purchased it for $65,000 and the aircraft was towed back to the west side of the Kelly ramp near the Texas Air National Guard flight line. Plans to establish a museum at Kelly to house the aircraft proved fruitless, and the aircraft was subsequently donated to the Air Force Museum. Officials have stated that the aircraft will be preserved, but its exact future remains uncertain.

MODEL 37 PRODUCTION PLANS

By November 1949 Convair had developed the definitive production version of the C-99 and proposed the aircraft to the Air Force. The redesign had been accomplished by a team led by J.W. Larson, the

---

* Interestingly, a few months later Convair returned to calling the aircraft the XC-99.

Chief Engineer at Fort Worth. The most visible change was a raised "bubble" cockpit common with the production B-36, including the same basic flight-deck arrangement used on the B-36B. The nose landing gear was relocated into a bulge located under the forward fuselage, looking much like the radome under the B-36. The new arrangement did not protrude into the cargo area, and its slightly longer stroke allowed a level floor during ground operations (the XC-99 had a slight forward slope).[26]

A revised fuselage featured a rearranged cargo area with a pressurized upper deck that could accommodate 183 troops. The lower compartment remained unpressurized, but now featured large clamshell doors in the nose and tail that allowed vehicles to drive-on and drive-off at the same time. The doors provided an entrance measuring 12 by 13 feet and could accommodate the Army's 240-mm howitzer and M46 heavy tank. The C-99 was designed to allow vehicles or tanks to be transported with their operating and maintenance crews directly to

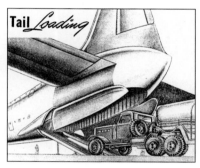

The production C-99 would have looked considerably different – in fact, in many respects it resembled a larger version of the Douglas C-124. Clamshell doors on each end allowed vehicles to drive-on and drive-off simultaneously, and a production-style B-36 cockpit and canopy would have been used. (Convair)

a combat area without the need for a staging area. Ambulances could drive inside the aircraft to unload up to 343 litter patients plus 33 attendants. Equipment that was not self-propelled could be pulled up into the airplane by means of built-in electric hoists.

The C-99 would have had 21,715 cubic feet of available cargo space, compared to 16,000 available on the XC-99. The Fort Worth-based design team believed that 100,000 pounds could be transported 3,800 miles nonstop, with an overload capability of 116,000 pounds over a somewhat shorter distance. If necessary the aircraft could carry 401 fully-equipped troops (unpressurized), allowing an entire airborne division of 17,500 men to be carried on only 44 flights. The aircraft shared the 230-foot wingspan of the standard B-36, but was 182 feet long and 57 feet high at the vertical stabilizer. The maximum gross takeoff weight was 357,000 pounds, the same as mid-life B-36s.

The basic design used the same 3,800-hp R-4360-53 engines scheduled for use in late-model B-36s, but alternate models were prepared using the VDT engines proposed for the B-36C. Other designs used the track-style landing gear tested on the XB-36 to allow rough field operations. The basic C-99 was priced at $1.5 million, competitive with the C-97 and C-124 cargo aircraft being procured by the Air Force. However, by the time funds were available for any possible C-99 purchase, the Air Force was firmly committed to the other aircraft, and in the end, no C-99s were built.

One other entity expressed some interest in the C-99 – the United States Post Office. During the early 1950s, the railroads were trying to force the Post Office into paying higher rates for transporting mail. In response, the Post Office began evaluating moving a larger percentage of mail to air transport. In the case of the C-99, the aircraft would have been equipped not just for moving mail, but also for sorting it while in flight. The economics looked workable, and the Post Office reportedly considered asking the Air Force to loan the XC-99 for trials. For whatever reason this never happened, and the Post Office C-99 never materialized.[27]

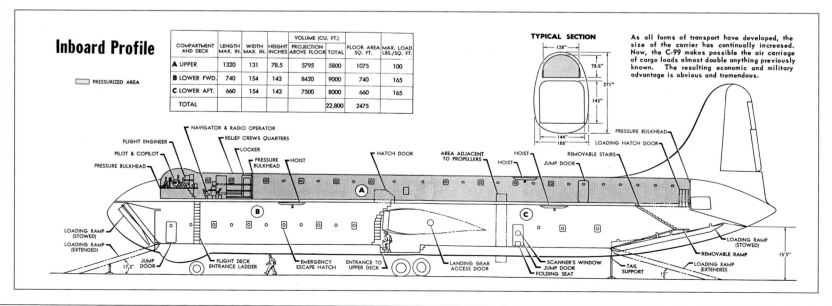

COMMERCIAL DERIVATIVES

Even during the war Consolidated pitched a commercial version of the aircraft to several airlines. For instance, Ralph Bayless, Chief Engineer at San Diego, and Roberts Hoover had extensive discussions with Pan American World Airways during January 1945. Pan Am wanted an aircraft that would allow $90 one-way tickets between San Francisco and Hawaii, and Consolidated was confident that the Model 37 Airliner could achieve this.

Pan Am ordered 15 of the "Super Clippers" in February 1945 with production to begin in San Diego as soon as the war ended. Three of the airliners would be used on the Hawaii routes, but the other dozen would fly up to 443,000 passengers a year between New York and Europe, a trip expected to take only 9 hours instead of the 5 days required by the transatlantic ocean liners. Each of the airliners could carry 204 passengers and 15,300 pounds of baggage and mail. Initial variants used the same R-4360 engines and 19-foot propellers as the B-36 and XC-99, but later concepts used 4,300-hp VDT engines or six unspecified* 5,000-hp turboprop engines. Reportedly, versions with swept wings and jet engines (much like the YB-60) were also investigated.[28]

The interior arrangement featured a mixture of dayplane seats and sleeper berths, with spacious lounges located on each of the two decks, and large circular staircases located on each end of the aircraft. A full galley would offer gourmet meals, and the toilet facilities resembled a fine hotel more than a modern airliner. Noted interior designer Henry Dreyfuss from New York City was commissioned to design the interior furnishings, and some mockups were even built in San Diego.

But it was not to be. The postwar economy was not as robust as expected, and Pan Am soon cancelled the Super Clippers. The "wide body" era would have to wait another 20 years until the Boeing 747 was introduced – by Pan Am.

---

* Probably Curtiss-Wright XT35-W-1 gas turbines since they were showing up on other Convair designs around the same time.

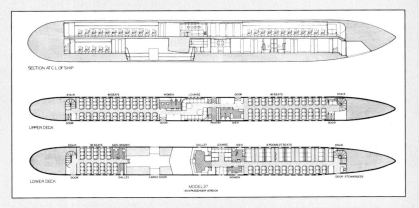

General arrangement for the Model 37 Commercial variant as proposed to Pan Am. (Convair via the San Diego Aerospace Museum Collection)

The Pan Am Super Clippers would have featured luxurious bathrooms and lounges. (Convair via the San Diego Aerospace Museum Collection)

A Flying Boat

Pan Am also asked Convair to investigate a flying boat derivative of the Model 37. The basic design of the aircraft was similar, except the six 5,000-hp turboprop engines drove counter-rotating, three-bladed, 16-foot-diameter tractor propellers instead of the larger pushers. The fuselage incorporated a traditional hull design similar to other Consolidated flying boats. The elimination of the landing gear and its supporting structure allowed a weight savings of 6,500 pounds, even after the modified hull and floats were added.[29]

The additional drag generated by the hull and floats meant the flying boat would need to carry 3,000 pounds more fuel to achieve the same nominal range. Nevertheless, the flying boat could, in theory, carry 3,000 pounds more cargo. The design had a range of 4,200 miles at 25,000 feet and 332 mph – 10 mph slower than the conventional aircraft. Its maximum service ceiling was reduced from 30,000 feet to 29,100, and its takeoff distance from 4,760 feet (for the land plane) to 5,680 feet. It would take 48 seconds for the flying boat to clear the water after it started its takeoff run.[30]

There appeared to be no reason a water-borne version of the Model 37 could not be developed. Yet the age of the flying boat was over, and after the war Pan Am decided to concentrate on more conventional aircraft such as the Lockheed Constellation and Douglas DC-6/7. The water-based version of the Model 37 faded from sight.

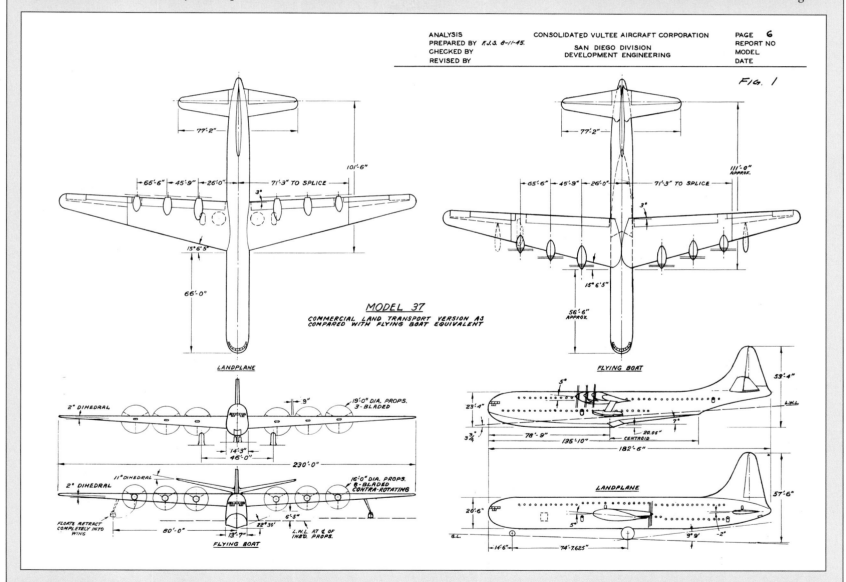

Although Convair engineers at the time considered the big flying boat a derivative of the land plane, in reality it was an almost completely new design. This drawing was supplied with the initial report to illustrate the general configuration. (Convair via the San Diego Aerospace Museum Collection)

Chapter 3

Above: *A B-36B-1-CF (44-92033) shows its clean lines and original markings. The extensive use of magnesium skin shows up well here – the shiny sections are aluminum, the rest is magnesium.* (Lockheed Martin)

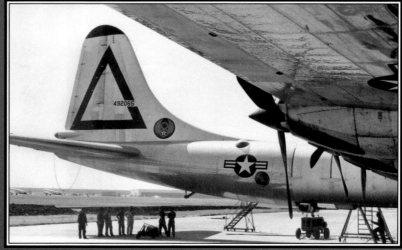

Right: *Geometric unit markings began to appear on the fleet, such as this B-36B-15-CF (44-92065). These markings would undergo several iterations before disappearing during the mid-1950s.* (Peter M. Bowers)

INITIAL PRODUCTION

As the first XB-36 was being built, it became obvious that various changes would be necessary based on new requirements and wartime experience. A decision was made on 27 April 1945 to finish the second XB-36 (42-13571) closer to the expected production standard with a raised flight deck and canopy, redesigned forward crew compartment, bomb bays Nos. 3 and 4 moved together instead of being separated by the aft turret bays, and provisions for a nose turret. The aircraft was redesignated YB-36.

The entire issue of defensive armament for the new bomber had been undergoing many changes. When the XB-36 mockup had been inspected in July 1942, the self-protection suite had included upper and lower forward turrets, each equipped with two 37-mm cannon. Each of these turrets would be controlled by a gunner in the turret, explaining why the XB-36 did not have forward sighting blisters. In the aft fuselage, an upper turret housed two 0.50-caliber machine guns, while a lower turret had four 0.50-caliber guns. These turrets were controlled by two upper and two lower sighting blisters, forcing the fire control system to deal with issues of alternate control and double parallax computations – it was a complicated scheme. A pair of 37-mm tail guns were controlled from a remote position in the aft crew compartment.[1]

By April 1944, the defensive armament had changed considerably. General Electric proposed installing eight retractable turrets – four upper and four lower – plus a tail turret. All would be equipped with two 20-mm cannon and permanently controlled by a single sighting station, eliminating much of the complexity of sharing turrets between gunners. Once this concept was approved, GE believed it could deliver the first two working systems in October 1944 and April 1945 since the new system was based heavily on the computers and sighting stations originally developed for the B-29 and Northrop P-61 Black Widow night fighter. The majority of changes centered around adapting the new units to the ac electrical system (instead of dc) and modifying the computers to permit successive recomputations and corrections.

In January 1945 the nose turret was added, and on 15 July 1945 the AN/APG-3 tail radar being developed for the B-29 was included in the B-36 configuration. Soon afterwards a decision was made to delete the two lower forward turrets to make room for the new radar that would replace the original APG-7 Eagle. At the same time it was decided that the radio operator in the forward cabin would have control of the new radar-directed tail turret.[2]

General Electric ran into unexpected trouble scaling the system up from the B-29 installation. When the defensive system finally came together in early 1946, it was discovered that the fire control electronics interfered with virtually every other item of radiating or receiving equipment on the aircraft. It was soon evident that the device that converted the ac error signals to dc for the turret motors would require some sort of noise suppression. In April 1946 GE indicated that a solution would be in hand in time for the 14th B-36A, but this turned out to be overly optimistic. Six months later GE proposed noise-reduction modifications that would cost $100,000 per aircraft, although it was not completely obvious that this would solve the problems. The Air Force decided not to pursue this pending further investigations. Eventually a combination of less-costly changes was approved that allowed production systems to be delivered, but they did not work very well.

General Electric delivered a single 2CFR87A-1 (commonly called the A-1) fire control system for installation in the YB-36 during the latter half of 1947. An improved system, called the B-1, was scheduled for installation in the B-36A, with an even more advanced system – the C-1 – scheduled for the B-36B. It did not quite turn out that way.[3]

The YB-36 (42-13571) under construction in late 1946. This was the first airplane to move down what would become the production line in Building 4 at Government Aircraft Plant No. 4 in Fort Worth. (Convair)

YB-36

The YB-36 flew for the first time on 4 December 1947. However, as rolled-out, the YB-36 still had the original single-wheel undercarriage, and lacked armament and most production equipment. Convair was expected to retain the YB-36 for 6–12 months for test and evaluation and also to use the aircraft to identify future production line changes.[4]

During its third flight, on 19 December 1947, the YB-36 reached an altitude of more than 40,000 feet, an outstanding achievement for the time. After 89 hours of flight testing, the YB-36 was grounded for modifications on 27 May 1948. The single-wheel landing gear was replaced by the production four-wheel bogie-type undercarriage and 3,500-hp R-4360-41 engines were fitted in place of the original –25s. Although no direct confirmation could be found, this undoubtedly required the same wing modifications made to the XC-99 since the first three wings[*] had been built to the same engineering. The aircraft first flew in this configuration in June 1948, and Convair made 36 test flights that accumulated 97.5 hours of flight time.

In February 1949 the first Farrand hemisphere nose sight and its associated turret were installed in the YB-36 for testing. Around the same time an AN/APG-3 tail radar and its associated turret were also installed for testing. Reports indicate that at least two of the aft sighting stations were installed, but without turrets, and were used simply to evaluate the sighting equipment.[5]

The YB-36 was turned over to the Air Force on 31 May 1949 where it was subsequently used essentially as another B-36A. Subsequently, the YB-36 was returned to Fort Worth in October 1950 to be remanufactured into an RB-36E in lieu of the first B-36A (YB-36A) that had been tested to destruction at Wright Field.

Interestingly, for no particular reason, this aircraft was frequently the first B-36 to go through most of the modifications programs, such as SAM-SAC Cycle One and Cycle Two. The Air Force would add 1,952.5 flight hours to the airframe before it was retired in early 1957. The aircraft was turned over to the Air Force Museum at Wright-Patterson AFB, but it was declared surplus and scrapped when the new museum facility was built. Parts of the aircraft were acquired by Ralph Huffman for $760, or roughly 3/4 of a cent per pound. Huffman subsequently sold the remains to Walter Soplata, and these still exist on his farm in Newbury, Ohio.[6]

B-36A

The B-36A was essentially similar to the YB-36, including the use of 3,000 hp R-4360-25 Wasp Major engines. The four bomb bays could accommodate 72,000 pounds of conventional bombs, but no provisions existed for carrying atomic weapons. The maximum takeoff weight was 310,380 pounds, due mainly to structural limitations of the landing gear. With 24,121 gallons of fuel and a 10,000-pound bomb load the B-36A had a radius of action of 3,880 miles. The reduction in fuel required to carry the maximum 72,000 pounds of bombs resulted in a radius of only 2,100 miles. With full fuel and no weapons the aircraft could be ferried 9,136 miles. Performance was listed as 345 mph at 31,600 feet with 10,000 pounds of bombs, and a service ceiling of 29,100 feet.[7]

Fuel was carried in up to eight tanks. Six of these were permanently installed in the wings and were labeled No. 1 on the outboard left to No. 6 on the outboard right. These tanks were formed by

---

[*] The three wings were used on the XB-36, YB-36, and XC-99.

The YB-36 (42-13571) showing its original configuration with the 110-inch main landing gear. Note that both nose and tail turrets have been installed when this photo was taken. (San Diego Aerospace Museum Collection)

Convair hired Henry Dreyfuss Designs in New York City to design the new raised cockpit of the B-36 – the same company had done much of the interior design work on the proposed commercial XC-99. The B-36 flight deck mockup is depicted as it appeared on 24 August 1945. (Convair)

The first B-36A-1-CF (44-92004) only made two flights – a short flight around Fort Worth (above), then a single ferry flight to Wright Field. Apparently, somewhat after the fact the aircraft was redesignated YB-36A. At Wright Field, the aircraft was slowly tested to destruction to determine its ultimate structural strength. At one point, the airframe had to be turned upside down (sequence at left) so that loads could be applied to the bottom of the wings. Note the four open bomb bays in the last photo of the sequence. The fuselage skin (below center) buckled at 70 percent of the design loads during simulated wind gusts, but the primary structure was not damaged. The photo below right shows the wing supporting 80 percent of the design vertical load with the aircraft (upside down) in a level flight condition. Note the B-45 airframe in the foreground of this photo. (above: Lockheed Martin; left and below: via Ed Calvert via Don Pyeatt)

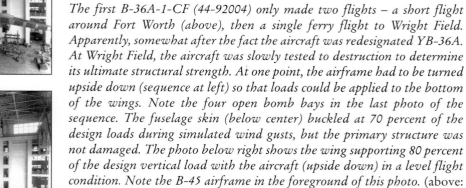

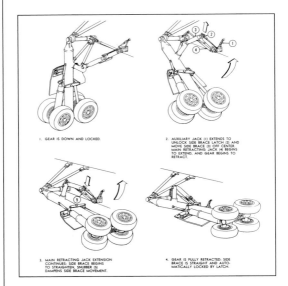

1. GEAR IS DOWN AND LOCKED.

2. AUXILIARY JACK (1) EXTENDS TO UNLOCK SIDE BRACE LATCH (2) AND MOVE SIDE BRACE (3) OFF CENTER. MAIN RETRACTING JACK (4) BEGINS TO EXTEND, AND GEAR BEGINS TO RETRACT.

3. MAIN RETRACTING JACK EXTENSION CONTINUES, SIDE BRACE BEGINS TO STRAIGHTEN, SNUBBER (5) DAMPENS SIDE BRACE MOVEMENT.

4. GEAR IS FULLY RETRACTED; SIDE BRACE IS STRAIGHT AND AUTO-MATICALLY LOCKED BY LATCH.

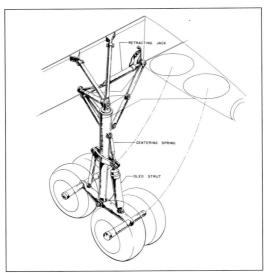

RETRACTING JACK

CENTERING SPRING

OLEO STRUT

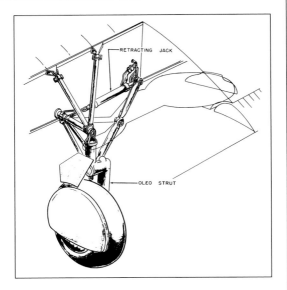

RETRACTING JACK

OLEO STRUT

One of the most noticeable changes in the production B-36s was the main landing gear. Nobody had been completely happy with the 110-inch main gear originally used on the XB-36, YB-36, and XC-99, so a new four-wheel design was developed that used 56-inch wheels. This distributed the weight of the B-36 more evenly and allowed the aircraft to use any runway that had supported B-29 operations. It also minimized the possibility of a single tire failing on takeoff destroying the aircraft. The list of fields available to the B-36 with the new landing gear is at right. (above : San Diego Aerospace Museum Collection; right: Frederick A. Johnsen Collection; below: Jay Miller Collection)

The original 110-inch main gear (right) and the production 4-wheel gear (center). Only the XB-36, YB-36, and XC-99 used the original. (Convair)

9th ABG - 9 MAY 52 - B-36 REPAIRS - TAFB

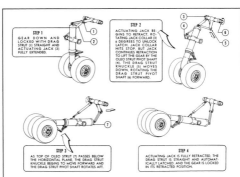

STEP 1
GEAR DOWN AND LOCKED WITH DRAG STRUT (1) STRAIGHT AND ACTUATING JACK (2) FULLY EXTENDED.

STEP 2
ACTUATING JACK BE-GINS TO RETRACT. RO-TATING JACK COLLAR (3) 6 DEGREES TO UNLOCK LATCH. JACK COLLAR HITS STOP, BUT JACK CONTINUES RETRACTION TO LIFT THE GEAR BY THE OLEO STRUT PIVOT SHAFT (4). THE DRAG STRUT KNUCKLE (5) MOVES DOWN, ROTATING THE DRAG STRUT PIVOT SHAFT (6) FORWARD.

STEP 3
AS TOP OF OLEO STRUT (7) PASSES BELOW THE HORIZONTAL PLANE, THE DRAG STRUT KNUCKLE BEGINS TO MOVE FORWARD AND THE DRAG STRUT PIVOT SHAFT ROTATES AFT.

STEP 4
ACTUATING JACK IS FULLY RETRACTED, THE DRAG STRUT IS STRAIGHT AND AUTOMAT-ICALLY LATCHED, AND THE GEAR IS LOCKED IN ITS RETRACTED POSITION.

Several nose gear configurations were investigated for the XB-36 before the definitive arrangement was selected. Very little changed during production and all B-36s used slight variations of the two-wheel nose landing gear. (San Diego Aerospace Museum Collection)

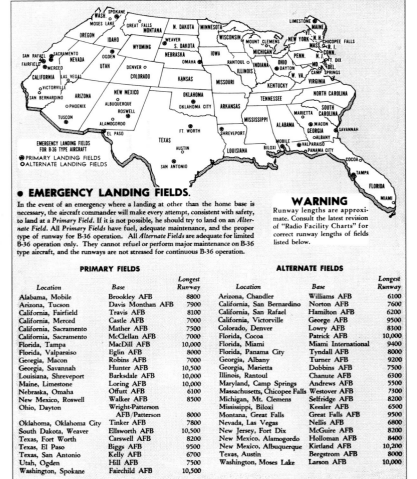

EMERGENCY LANDING FIELDS FOR B-36 TYPE AIRCRAFT
● PRIMARY LANDING FIELDS
○ ALTERNATE LANDING FIELDS

● EMERGENCY LANDING FIELDS.

In the event of an emergency where a landing at other than the home base is necessary, the aircraft commander will make every attempt, consistent with safety, to land at a *Primary Field*. If it is not possible, he should try to land on an *Alternate Field*. All *Primary Fields* have fuel, adequate maintenance, and the proper type of runway for B-36 operation. All *Alternate Fields* are adequate for limited B-36 operation only. They cannot refuel or perform major maintenance on B-36 type aircraft, and the runways are not stressed for continuous B-36 operation.

WARNING
Runway lengths are approximate. Consult the latest revision of "Radio Facility Charts" for correct runway lengths of fields listed below.

PRIMARY FIELDS			ALTERNATE FIELDS		
Location	Base	Longest Runway	Location	Base	Longest Runway
Alabama, Mobile	Brookley AFB	8800	Arizona, Chandler	Williams AFB	6100
Arizona, Tucson	Davis Monthan AFB	7900	California, San Bernardino	Norton AFB	7600
California, Fairfield	Travis AFB	8100	California, San Rafael	Hamilton AFB	6200
California, Merced	Castle AFB	7000	California, Victorville	George AFB	9500
California, Sacramento	Mather AFB	7500	Colorado, Denver	Lowry AFB	8300
California, Sacramento	McClellan AFB	7000	Florida, Cocoa	Patrick AFB	10,000
Florida, Tampa	MacDill AFB	10,000	Florida, Miami	Miami International	9400
Florida, Valparaiso	Eglin AFB	8000	Florida, Panama City	Tyndall AFB	8000
Georgia, Macon	Robins AFB	7000	Georgia, Albany	Turner AFB	9200
Georgia, Savannah	Hunter AFB	10,500	Georgia, Marietta	Dobbins AFB	7500
Louisiana, Shreveport	Barksdale AFB	10,000	Illinois, Rantoul	Chanute AFB	6300
Maine, Limestone	Loring AFB	10,000	Maryland, Camp Springs	Andrews AFB	5500
Nebraska, Omaha	Offutt AFB	6100	Massachusetts, Chicopee Falls	Westover AFB	7300
New Mexico, Roswell	Walker AFB	8500	Michigan, Mt. Clemens	Selfridge AFB	8200
Ohio, Dayton	Wright-Patterson AFB/Patterson	8000	Mississippi, Biloxi	Keesler AFB	6500
Oklahoma, Oklahoma City	Tinker AFB	7800	Montana, Great Falls	Great Falls AFB	9500
South Dakota, Weaver	Ellsworth AFB	10,500	Nevada, Las Vegas	Nellis AFB	6800
Texas, Fort Worth	Carswell AFB	8200	New Jersey, Fort Dix	McGuire AFB	8200
Texas, El Paso	Biggs AFB	9500	New Mexico, Alamogordo	Holloman AFB	8400
Texas, San Antonio	Kelly AFB	6700	New Mexico, Albuquerque	Kirtland AFB	10,200
Utah, Ogden	Hill AFB	7500	Texas, Austin	Bergstrom AFB	8000
Washington, Spokane	Fairchild AFB	10,500	Washington, Moses Lake	Larson AFB	10,000

GLOBAL FLIGHT

On 6 January 1947, the results of a planning exercise for a global flight by a B-36 were published by Convair. The aircraft would be extensively modified – all armor and armament would be removed; all antennas and radomes would be removed and faired over; the sighting blisters would be faired over, the bombardier, radar operator; and all gunners seats, instrument panels, and other equipment would be removed; and the bunks and galley would be replaced by lighter weight versions. Even the forward compartment carpeting would be deleted. In all, the equipment removal would save over 5,000 pounds. Six new flexible fuel cells would be installed in the wings, and four bomb bay fuel tanks would be installed. Bomb bay No. 4 would also include provisions for four Aerojet 4,000-lbf jet-assisted takeoff (JATO)* bottles to be used during takeoff.[8]

The modified aircraft would have a range of 15,075 miles at an average cruising speed of 210 mph. The proposed route used Idlewild Airport, New York, as the departure point, following a great circle route over Scotland, Berlin, the Black Sea, Southern Russia, Tokyo, the Aleutian Islands, Vancouver Island, and landing at Fort Worth. If favorable winds were encountered, a landing back at Idlewild would be attempted. The fact that part of the flight was over Russia – by an American strategic bomber! – did not seem to deter the planners. As far as is known, the flight never took place, but no reason could be ascertained past the fact that no production B-36s actually existed in early 1947.

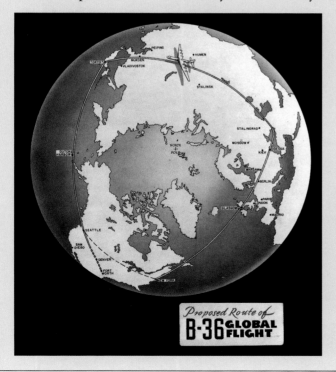

Proposed Route of
B-36 GLOBAL FLIGHT

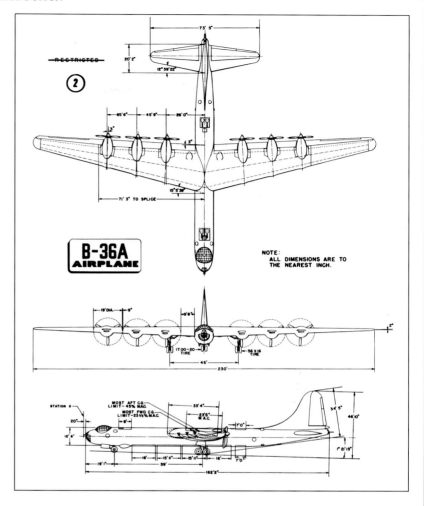

The general arrangement for the B-36A shows the defensive armament that was never installed. The B-36B was virtually identical. (Convair)

sealed compartments between the front and rear wing spars inboard of each engine nacelle. The tanks could be accessed through hatches in the front spar behind hinged leading edge panels. Tanks Nos. 1 and 6 had a capacity of 2,330 gallons, but only 2,248 gallons were usable. Tanks Nos. 2 and 5 could hold 4,206 gallons with 4,073 usable, while the inboard tanks had a capacity of 4,338 gallons with 4,205.5 usable.[†] Total useable internal fuel was therefore 21,053 gallons. In addition, bomb bays No. 2 and 3 could each carry a 3,000-gallon (2,996 usable) fuel cell, expanding capacity to 27,045 gallons. Since aerial refueling had not yet been perfected, the B-36 was not equipped for it.[9]

The first aircraft (44-92004) made its maiden flight on 28 August 1947, actually beating the YB-36 into the air by almost four months.

---

* These were actually rockets, but were often referred to as "jets" at the time.
† Although the size and configuration of the tanks did not change, various issues of the flight and maintenance manuals showed slightly different capacities for them – usually differing by 10–30 gallons per tank. This was probably attributable more to differing test conditions (temperature, aircraft leveling, etc.) when the tanks were measured than to actual variances in the tanks themselves.

This aircraft was designated YB-36A, and was only fitted with enough equipment for a ferry flight to Wright Field* where it was used as a structural loads airframe and tested to destruction. The aircraft was flown to Wright Field (unusual for a static test article) simply because nobody could figure out another method of getting it there. The aircraft accumulated a total of 7 hours and 36 minutes of flight time in its two flights (it had flown once at Fort Worth just to prove it was airworthy), and was formally delivered to the Air Force on 30 August 1947, only two days after its first flight.[10]

The decision to have a structural test airframe had been made in mid-1946, after a convincing argument by General Nathan F. Twining: "Experience has shown that we would have been unable to use our bombers efficiently had we not had this policy in effect in the past. The B-17, originally designed for a gross weight of 37,000 pounds, fought the war flying universally at 64,000 pounds. This could never have been done without accurate knowledge of the strength of the component parts." This policy continued on most aircraft until the 1980s, when sufficient faith in computer modeling was finally gained.[11]

The physical size of the control surfaces – ailerons, elevators, and rudders – on the B-36 essentially prohibited manual control of them, but the final design did not use powered surfaces. Instead, when the pilot moved a control servo, tabs in the floating main surfaces moved up or down in a direction opposite of what the pilot commanded. An up movement of the servo tab produced a down movement of the main surface as a result of the air load on the displaced tab. Likewise, a down tab movement caused the main surface to move up. Control column or rudder pedal movement was only transferred to the flying servo tabs; however, the actuating mechanism was interconnected to the main surfaces through a double-acting spring to provide control feedback to the pilot. In gusty conditions the flying servo tabs actually produced a small damping effect on the main surfaces, creating a crude stability augmentation system.[12]

Each of the four bomb bays was covered with sliding doors reminiscent of the B-24. The structurally-rigid doors were mounted on rollers and moved in tracks around the fuselage contour. All of the doors were operated by electric motors through a cable arrangement.

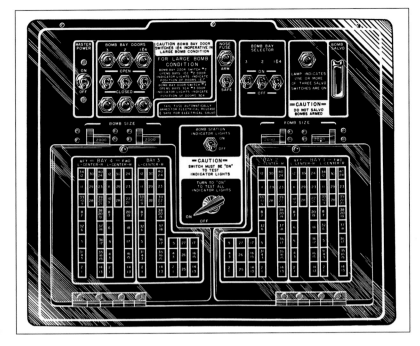

This was the bombing control panel from the B-36A and B-36B. Note that bay doors for No. 1 and No. 4 had to operate as a pair. (U.S. Air Force)

The doors on bomb bays No. 1 and No. 4 were single-piece units that slid up the left side of the fuselage. The two middle bomb bays had doors split down the centerline that slid up both sides of the fuselage – the location of the wing prevented using a single-piece design. The doors were slow to operate, tended to stick in the extremely cold temperatures at 40,000 feet, and significantly increased drag when open. A better solution would need to be found, but all A- and B-models would use these doors.[13]

* Wright Field became Wright-Patterson AFB on 13 January 1948.

A B-36A-15-CF (44-92023) participated in the Air Power Demonstration at Eglin AFB in 1948. (Air Force Historical Research Agency)

1949 saw a B-36A-5-CF (44-92007) at Eglin for the Air Power Demo, shown on a low-level bomb run. (Air Force Historical Research Agency)

The fifth B-36A (44-92008) shows the empty tail turret, although otherwise it looks much like an operational aircraft. (Jay Miller Collection)

Thirty-six removable bomb racks of 15 different types were furnished with each aircraft. The racks and associated equipment were designed to accommodate conventional bombs weighing 500, 1,000, 1,600, 2,000, 4,000, 12,000, 22,000, or 43,000 pounds. In addition, bombs weighing 100, 115, 125, 250, 325, or 350-pounds could be carried at the 500-pound stations. When the three largest bomb sizes were carried, it was necessary to combine two adjacent bomb bays. The lower portion of the bomb bay No. 1 aft bulkhead and the bomb bay No. 2 forward bulkhead (called bulkhead 6.0), incorporated a portion of the bomb bay door tracks and could be swung to the side of the fuselage when the 12,000, 22,000, or 43,000-pound bombs were being loaded and released. The same was true for the bulkhead (8.0) between bomb bays Nos. 3 and 4, although due to the 72,000-pound load limitation, only a single 43,000-pound T-12 bomb could be carried by the A-model.

The bulkheads were moved by electric motors and a push-pull rod arrangement – the motors were actuated by the movement of the bomb bay doors. The bombardier had two circuits to open the bomb bay doors – one was used for small bombs (up to 4,000-pounds each); the other for the larger bombs. The latter circuit included the automatic operation of the swinging bulkheads.[14]

Interestingly, the controls allowed the bomb bay doors on No. 2 and No. 3 to be opened independently, but bomb bays No. 1 and No. 4 were slaved to each other and operated as a pair. When the operator selected a bomb size greater than 4,000 pounds the switch to operate 1/4 became inoperative, and the switches normally used to open/close Nos. 2 and 3 operated the combined large bay doors and bulkheads.[15]

The planned AN/APG-7 Eagle bombing/navigation system had been superseded by the AN/APQ-23 with a radome located beneath the forward fuselage where the lower gun turrets were originally going to be located. Delays in developing the General Electric defensive armament meant that the B-36As were delivered with incomplete fire control systems (only some components were installed on some aircraft), and without turrets or armament of any type. An incomplete B-1 system was installed on the fifth B-36A (44-92008) in September 1948 for tests at Convair. Initially, problems with reliability prevented meaningful testing, but the aircraft was used extensively for continued testing. Finally, in November one of the turrets managed to fire a 20-round belt of ammunition without incident. Still, for a time the Air Force debated scrapping the complex remote-control system and returning to manned turrets equipped with 0.50-caliber machine guns.[16]

The crew complement of the B-36A was listed as 15, but this included eight gunners who had no guns and functioned mainly as spotters when they flew. The other seven crewmembers were a pilot, copilot, radar-bombardier, navigator, flight engineer, and two radiomen.

A B-36A-5-CF (44-92010) was at Andrews AFB during February 1949 along with a YB-49 and XB-47 in order to give members of Congress a first-hand look at the newest Air Force aircraft. (Tony Landis Collection)

The B-36A suffered from many of the types of problems normally encountered when a complex new aircraft enters service. The fuel tanks leaked, the new alternating-current electrical system was troublesome, and engine cooling was still not as good as it should have been. None of the problems were insurmountable, and Convair engineers continued to work on solutions. Nevertheless, a great deal of negative press was generated, largely attributable to the U.S. Navy and its supporters in Congress and elsewhere.

During March 1948 it was announced that the 7th Bombardment Wing (Heavy)* at Carswell AFB – on the other side of the runway from the Convair plant – would become the first operational unit for the B-36. The Strategic Air Command notified the 436th Bomb Squadron that it would transfer six of its B-29s to the 93rd Bombardment Group at Castle AFB, California, to make room for the new aircraft. The 7th BW responded by sending four flight engineers and five crew chiefs to Convair for training. Training equipment for the B-36 began arriving at Carswell by early April.[17]

Finally, in April 1948 the tide began to turn and the B-36 was able to demonstrate its future potential. On 8–9 April a B-36A (44-92013) made a 33 hour and 10 minute flight covering 6,922 miles, shuttling between Fort Worth and San Diego. Beryl Erickson and Arthur S. "Doc" Witchell, Jr. had remaining fuel for another 206 miles if it had been necessary. The aircraft was flown with sufficient ballast to compensate for the lack of defensive armament, and also carried 10,000 pounds of dummy 500-pound bombs that were dropped from 25,000 feet over the Air Force Bombing Range at Wilcox, Arizona, 15 hours into the flight. Unfortunately, problems with two engines limited the average cruising speed to only 214 mph, a disappointment to Convair and the Air Force.

A month later, on 13–14 May 1948, the same B-36A (44-92013) again piloted by Erickson and Witchell, conducted a second long-range simulated tactical mission. Captain Wesley D. Morris and First

---

* The 7th Bombardment Group (Very Heavy) was activated on 1 October 1946, consisting of the 9th, 436th, and 492nd Bombardment Squadrons. On 17 November 1947 the 7th Bombardment Wing (Very Heavy) was established as an overarching organization encompassing the 7th BG plus various support and maintenance groups. On 1 December 1948 the 11th Bomb Group (Heavy) was organized under the 7th Bomb Wing. The 11th was elevated to Wing status on 16 February 1951. This left the 7th BG with no real task since both the 7th BW and 11th BW acted as independent entities. However, it was not until 16 June 1952 that the 7th Bomb Group was officially inactivated. Also during this time period, the term "Bombardment" was replaced with "Bomb" and "Very Heavy" become "Heavy." To ease possible confusion – even though it is technically incorrect – this text will simply refer to the 7th BW and 11th BW regardless of their Group relationships.

Lieutenant Richard Munday from the 7th BW were also on the flight. The aircraft had a gross weight of 299,619 pounds, including 10,000 pounds of dummy bombs, 5,796 pounds of simulated 20-mm ammunition, and ballast to compensate for the lack of turrets and other equipment not fitted to the B-36As. The flight duration was 36 hours and 8 minutes during which 8,062 miles were flown at an average 223 mph. The aircraft landed with 986 gallons of fuel remaining, which would have extended the mission by 508 miles. This was a typical high-altitude mission, with the first 369 miles flown at 5,000 feet, followed by a power climb to 10,000 feet. This altitude was maintained until 30 minutes before the target when the aircraft climbed to 25,000 feet and commenced a maximum speed bomb run including 17 minutes of evasive maneuvers. The flight home was made at 25,000 feet. The B-36 had just demonstrated that it was a true intercontinental bomber.[18]

Four days later another flight dropped 25 2,000-pound bombs from 31,000 feet on the Naval Range at Corpus Christi, Texas. This was followed on 30 June 1948 when a B-36A dropped 72,000 pounds of bombs during a test flight, the heaviest bomb load yet carried by any aircraft.

A few weeks later, on 18–19 July 1948, another B-36A (44-92013, again) completed a 5,983-mile flight at an average speed of more than 301 mph, making it the first airplane to fly that distance at that speed. Gross take off weight was 310,292 pounds, including full wing tanks plus a 3,555-gallon bomb bay tank (144,819 pounds total fuel). Immediately after take off, the pilot set normal rated power (2,550 rpm) and climbed to 26,000 feet. The climb took 1 hour and 23 minutes – this was actually 1 minute less than predicted. The flight continued 620 miles at 26,000 feet, then climbed to 30,000 feet. This altitude was

achieved at a range of 2,120 miles, approximately 7.5 hours after take-off. Fifteen minutes prior to reaching the target the aircraft accelerated to "maximum continuous speed" (about 320 mph) for 30 minutes. Midway through this "bombing run," 15,500 pounds of bombs (31 dummy 500-pounders) were dropped. Twenty of these (10,000 pounds) represented the design bomb load, while the other 5,500 pounds simulated ammunition that would have been expended by the cannon, if they had been fitted. (Non-droppable ballast was included in one bomb bay to simulate the turrets, cannon, etc.). The target had been located and the bombs dropped using the radar bomb/nav system. The bombs were dropped 9 hours and 49 minutes (2,811 miles) after takeoff. Five minutes of evasive action were taken immediately after the bomb drop, and then a climb to 32,700 feet was initiated. This altitude was maintained for about an hour, then the aircraft climbed to 34,200 feet, which was maintained for the rest of the flight home. The aircraft landed with the required 5% fuel reserve. The only difficulties noted on the flight were low oil pressure indications at some altitudes and a non-functional turbo selector for the No. 5 engine.[19]

Defying superstition, on 13 August – a Friday – the 13th B-36A (44-92016) made a successful shake-down flight. The first long-range flight by an all-Air-Force crew was on 22 August when the 492nd Bomb Squadron took a B-36A (44-92007) on a 15,500-mile, 26-hour flight that used 14,000 gallons of fuel. The crew found the B-36 was much more comfortable than the B-29s it was replacing.[20]

On 12 September a dozen B-36s took part in Air Force Day celebrations around the country, all departing and returning to Fort Worth. Ten aircraft flown by Air Force crews logged a total of 152 hours and 45 minutes on long-distance flights; the other two aircraft were flown by Convair crews around the Fort Worth area. In early October 1948 Major Stephen P. Dillon, chief Air Force pilot for the B-36, commanded a mission from Fort Worth to Muroc AFB carrying four 12,000-pound bombs, although one bomb would not release and had to be carried back to Fort Worth. The mission was flown at 37,000 feet averaging 330 mph. Things were getting better.[21]

The Air Force accepted its first B-36A in May 1948 and on 18 June 1948 the aircraft was delivered to the Air Proving Ground Command at Eglin AFB for climatic testing, which lasted most of the following year. The Air Force had previously accepted the YB-36A in August 1947. Twenty B-36As were delivered during 1948 – one in May, five in June, five in July, four in August, and five in September. The 22nd

The third "long-range simulated tactical mission" was conducted by a new B-36A-10-CF (44-92013) on 18–19 July 1948. This 5,983-mile flight included dropping 31 dummy 500-pound bombs midway through the mission. The simulated mission gave the Air Force the data necessary to defend the B-36 before Congress and also allowed planners to begin developing tactics necessary to take the B-36 to war if the occasion was to arise. (Jay Miller Collection)

PRESS INTRODUCTION

During mid-October 1948, the Air Force lifted a bit of the secrecy surrounding the B-36 and invited the national press to spend a day with the airplane. In the days before the widespread use of TV, "press" generally meant newspapers. It was a simpler time, and newspaper articles were, as often as not, meant to enthrall the public into supporting government policy for what was perceived as the common good. Here is a sampling of what was written that day.[22]

Associated Press (wired to more than 4,000 newspapers and radio stations): "The B-36 can put the world in its bomb sights. … From the crew's aft compartment, a look out the observation blisters turns your mouth dry. The nose of the plane is a couple of Pullman car lengths in front of you. Twenty feet behind you is the 47-foot tail, high as a four-story building. And the horizontal control surface is almost as long as the entire wing span of the old Convair B-24.…"

United Press (wired to more than 3,000 newspapers and radio stations): "War is hell … but if a war has to be, the Eighth Air Force's B-36 groups are going to the scene in comfort … (with) … plush leather seats, built-in ash trays, food lockers, gadgets for heating foods, wash basins, beds, and above all, leg room. … One well-planned attack by B-36's carrying atomic bombs could virtually bring down the curtain on any nation's hope for victory."

San Diego Union (local newspaper): "You can see this global bomber and ride in it and still not be able to believe that man has harnessed 21,000 horsepower into one machine that will lift its own weight plus a bomb load of more than 80,000 pounds; and then hurl this mass through space at a speed of better than 350 miles per hour."

American Aviation Daily (trade publication): "… the B-36 is extremely sensitive to control movements and is much easier to handle than World War II bombers. … Flight engineers state that an allowance for 10 minutes of target-area power of about 365 miles per hour (true air speed) at 40,000 feet is figured in maximum range estimates. On a normal mission, the B-36 would fly … at true air speeds ranging from 250 to 350 miles per hour depending upon air density …"

New York Daily News (local newspaper): "Uncle Sam's newest, biggest bomber – the B-36 – is a long, slim Texas gal with a wiggle to her rear. She's a little on the skinny side, but she's beautiful. … Pilots of the bombers which carried newspapermen were unanimous in their admiration for the plane.…"

New York Sun (local newspaper): "This is the mammoth battleship of the air on which the United States would largely depend in carrying the war – and the atom bomb – to Moscow in case its dictators, avid for world domination, start the world's third great conflict in the next few years."

and last B-36A was accepted in February 1949. The first B-36A (44-92015) was turned over to SAC as the *City of Fort Worth* on 26 June 1948, and 19 more B-36As were subsequently delivered to the 7th BW based at Carswell* AFB. Since the aircraft carried no defensive armament and were considered somewhat underpowered, they were used primarily for training and further flight testing. In reality, they were down for maintenance as often as not as Convair and the Air Force worked through various problems. Fortunately, the service life of the B-36A was extremely short, the last one (44-92017) being remanufactured into an RB-36E by July 1951.[23]

B-36B

The B-36B was the first truly operational version, and used uprated 3,500-hp R-4360-41 Wasp Major engines with water injection. These engines had 500 more horsepower than the –25 engine, which allowed a slightly shorter takeoff distance and yielded marginally higher cruising speeds and a higher top speed. The first B-36B made its maiden flight on 8 July 1948 with Beryl Erickson at the controls, and subsequent testing showed that its performance was generally better than expected. The top speed was up to 381 mph, and the service ceiling increased to 42,500 feet. An average cruising speed of 300 mph could be maintained at 40,000 feet.

The bomb bay arrangement was similar to the B-36A, but the B-36B could carry up to 86,000 pounds of bombs, a rather significant 14,000-pound increase. This allowed the B-36B to carry two 43,000-pound T-12 bombs, as well as various more conventional munitions. The same sliding-type bomb bay doors used on the B-36As were retained. The last 54 aircraft (44-92045/92098)[†] were to be equipped from the factory to carry the Mk III/4 atomic bomb in bomb bay No. 1, although only 47 were actually modified (the seven aircraft completed as RB-36Ds were not). Eighteen of the aircraft (44-92045/92062) were also equipped with guidance equipment for two 13,000-pound VB-13 Tarzon-guided bombs. This was an early precision-guided munition that was controlled via radio link by an operator in the B-36 viewing a television picture from the nose of the bomb. It appears that at least the first few B-36Bs were also equipped with the mounting brackets to carry the F-85 parasite fighter, although it is unlikely any equipment was actually installed.[24]

Intentions were to equip the B-36B with the new Farrand Y-1 retractable periscopic bomb sight, but development problems resulted in the tried-and-true M-9 Norden being used instead. Nevertheless, the B-36B used the newly-developed AN/APQ-24 bombing/navigation system with an improved search radar and faster computer. Finally, in November 1949 the first prototype K-1 system was installed in a B-36B-15-CF (44-92072) for testing.[25]

---

* On 1 December 1947 the Fort Worth Army Air Field became the Fort Worth Air Field under the newly-established U.S. Air Force. On 13 January 1948 the field was renamed as Griffiss AFB in honor of Lieutenant Colonel Townsend Griffiss, the first airman to die in the line of duty in Europe during World War II. The change lasted 17 days until 30 January 1948 when the base was renamed in honor of Major Horace S. Carswell, Jr., a Medal of Honor recipient in World War II.

† In the end, the bombers (B-36B and B-36D) beginning with 44-92045 were so equipped, but the B-models (44-92088/92094) that were completed as RB-36Ds were not.

GAS TURBINE-POWERED B-36A

Almost from the beginning, the critics had latched onto the relatively slow speed of the B-36. Hedging its bets, on 14 February 1947 Convair proposed to modify one B-36A with four 5,000-shp Curtiss-Wright XT35-W-1 gas turbine engines driving two tractor propellers on each wing. The installation was expected to cost less than $1.5 million and to be completed by August 1948. The engines were to be installed in the same locations normally used by the inboard and center Wasp Majors, and the outer engine nacelle on each wing would be deleted. Each of the four nacelles would be arranged with the engine mounted aft of the rear spar and an extension shaft extending forward through the rear and front spar to a reduction gear box and a 19-foot diameter propeller. Convair believed the modification "not only will improve the performance of the airplane to a degree that it will compare favorably with new design requirements for very heavy bombers, but also offers to AMC [Air Materiel Command] a means for securing airplanes with such improved performance at a minimum cost either by modifying delivered B-36 airplanes or manufacturing additional airplanes incorporating turbines."[26]

The modifications were actually fairly extensive, but involved very little primary structure. The existing fixed leading edge air intake sections around the inboard and center nacelle would be completely redesigned, and the steel tube diamond truss assembly on the front spar would be replaced with a web-stiffened combination panel with cutouts for the air ducts and extension shafts. The R-4360 engine mount extensions would be redesigned for the smaller-diameter nacelle and revised engine centerline location. The rear spar, rear spar fittings, and wing bulkheads would be unchanged. The wing trailing edge upper and lower surface skin

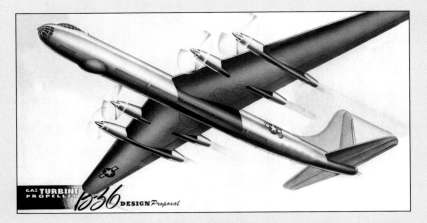

panels would be modified, and the main landing gear strut doors would be redesigned. The upper and lower fixed nacelle sections would be replaced with units that were smaller in diameter. A 25-inch access door would be installed on the lower nacelle surface just forward of the front spar; access to the rear fixed sections of the nacelle would be through removable nacelle panels.[27]

The outboard nacelle was to be completely removed from the aircraft. The fixed leading edge air intake section would be replaced with a smooth contour leading edge, and the front spar steel tube assemblies would be replaced with a web-stiffened combination panel. Fuel cells would be installed between wing bulkheads 22 and 25, taking the place of the outboard nacelle. The trailing edge assembly would be reworked to a continuous skin surface and be configured as an "island" between the outboard flap and the aileron.

Other work included modifying the flaps to fit the smaller diameter nacelles by adding small trailing-edge islands, and all of the controls and instrumentation on the flight deck would be replaced with appropriate items for the gas turbine engines. For the prototype it was expected that the anti-ice and cabin pressurization systems would be inoperative, although this would be corrected for any production aircraft.

Convair actually studied using both the XT35-W-1 and more powerful T35-W-3 engines. Performance estimates with the –1 engine showed a 100-mph increase in cruising speed over the B-36A; the –3 engine increased this speed by 150 mph.

Convair wanted to begin wind tunnel testing no later than 1 May 1947 in order to design and manufacture the appropriate parts by 30 April 1948. The dates were based on B-36A No. 46 (44-92049) entering final production in April 1948. Between April and August the aircraft would be modified off-line at the Fort Worth plant. The engines were expected to be delivered in August 1948, by which time the modifications would be completed and the aircraft ready to accept the powerplants and begin ground and flight tests.

The proposal was declined by the Air Force – the T35 engine was too far in the future for the B-36, and the Air Force believed that the Curtiss-Wright delivery estimates were overly optimistic. Ultimately, the Air Force was correct – the T35 never materialized.

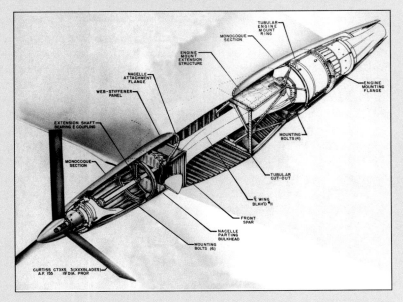

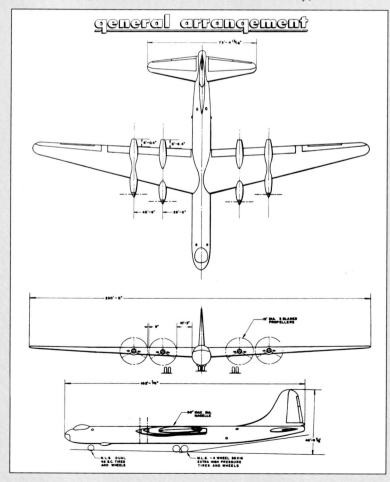

			B-36 WITH (4) T-35-1 GAS TURBINES		B-36 WITH (6) P&W R-4360-25 ENGINES	
			DESIGN GROSS WEIGHT	MAXIMUM ALTERNATE GROSS WEIGHT	DESIGN GROSS WEIGHT	MAXIMUM ALTERNATE GROSS WEIGHT
TAKE-OFF GROSS WEIGHT		LBS.	278,000	328,000	278,000	328,000
Including Fuel at 6 Lbs./Gal.		LBS.	136,190	184,046	119,724	166,683
Including Bombs		LBS.	10,000	10,000	10,000	10,000
COMBAT GROSS WEIGHT						
(D.G.W. Less 1/2 Fuel)		LBS.	209,905	235,977	218,138	244,658
HIGH SPEED AT 30,000 FT. ALTITUDE		MPH	359	349	342	333
SERVICE CEILING (R/C = 100 FT./MIN.)						
Full Engines		FT.	38,250	35,800	39,050	36,000
Half Engines		FT.	17,600	13,500	6,900	
RATE OF CLIMB						
Take-off G.W. at Sea Level		FPM	1,450	1,100	690	430
RANGE AT OPTIMUM ALTITUDES						
With Take-off G.W.						
Minimum R/C Available = 350 fpm		MI.	7,714	9,300	*8,520	*10,310
Minimum R/C Available = 100 fpm		MI.	8,460	10,353		
AVERAGE SPEED FOR ABOVE RANGE						
Minimum R/C Available = 350 fpm		MPH	347	344	222	222
Minimum R/C Available = 100 fpm		MPH	313	311		
TAKE-OFF OVER 50' OBSTACLE						
At Take-off G.W.		FT.	5,260	8,030	**5,300	**9,500
LANDING OVER 50' OBSTACLE						
At Take-off G.W. Less Bombs		FT.	4,180	4,860	4,180	4,860

NOTES:
Performance Estimates Are For Combat G.W. Except As Noted. Range Includes Fuel Consumed And Distance Covered In Climb, But Not In Descent. All Bombs Are Dropped At 1/2 Range.
*The Maximum Range Is Obtained With Reduced Powers On The Reciprocating Engine, And Both Minimum Allowable Rates Of Climb Shown Are Always Exceeded With Rated Power On All Points Of The Optimum Altitude Flight Path.
**Based On 2850 Propeller Shaft Horsepower Per Engine.

(all illustrations Convair via Bob Bradley)

In addition, the defensive armament was installed, making these the first true combat versions of the B-36. The 2CFR87B-2 system had superseded the proposed B-1 system before any units had been delivered. The major changes were all internal, and included the substitution of an improved AN/APG-32 tail radar for the APG-3 in the B-1 system. Unfortunately, the APG-32 was delayed and most B-36Bs were delivered with the APG-3 instead. There were six retractable remotely-operated turrets each equipped with a pair of 20-mm M-24A1 cannon, plus two more 20-mm cannon each in nose and tail turrets. There were two retractable turrets in the upper forward fuselage, two in the upper aft fuselage, and two in the lower aft fuselage. This was the most formidable defensive armament yet fitted to any warplane and was based largely on World War II experience. The guns were aimed using computing gunsights situated at two blisters on the forward fuselage and four blisters on the aft fuselage. The tail turret was directed by a gun-laying radar while the nose turret was aimed using a gunsight located in the glazed nose compartment. Bolt-in armor panels were provided to protect all but the inboard fuel tanks (they would be empty and purged by the time the aircraft was under threat) and all of the engine oil tanks.[28]

Like the B-36A, the crew of the B-36B was normally fifteen: a pilot, copilot, radar-bombardier, navigator, flight engineer, two radiomen, three forward gunners, and five rear gunners. In this case the gunners actually had something to do, although continuing problems with the gun system did not allow them to do it well.

A technician in Fort Worth checks the alignment of a turret and gunsight prior to installation in a B-36B. (Convair)

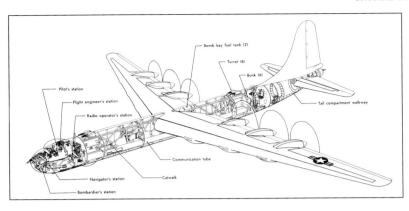

The B-36B general arrangement diagram from the flight manual. (U.S. Air Force)

In November 1948, a B-36B flying out of Fort Worth took aim at a "target ship" off the coast of Florida in the Gulf of Mexico. The aircraft was flown by Convair's Doc Witchell and Captain E. J. Crahan, an officer from the test wing at Eglin AFB, Florida. Captain Wesley D. Morris from the 7th BW was the bombardier. The 2,000-mile mission included a low-level bombing run before a group of high-ranking Air Force officers on hand for an air show at Eglin. The B-36B dropped two salvos of dummy bombs into the water as demonstrations, then scored a direct hit from 10,000 feet on a simulated target ship (actually, a platform sitting on pilings off the coast). By all accounts, the platform was heavily damaged by the dummy bomb load. Also on board for the flight were F. Hanley and C. J. Driskell as engineers, J. C. Shirley and W. R. Camp as observers, photographer Fred Carlisle, armament engineers W. N. Stevenson and A. D. Tuttle, flight test engineer R. P. Scott, and navigator Lieutenant Harkness.[29]

After the demonstration, the Air Force accepted its first B-36B (44-920026) on 25 November 1948 and assigned it to the 7th BW at

Despite being designed as a high-altitude bomber, many early B-36 flights included a very low-level bomb run. This undated photo depicts a B-36B-1-CF (44-92032), probably at Eglin AFB. (via Don Pyeatt)

Carswell AFB, which already operated the B-36As in a training role. The 11th BW would also be activated at Carswell with the B-36B, receiving its first aircraft (44-92050) on 18 March 1949. Plans were made for additional B-36 groups to be based at Rapid City, South Dakota, and Fairfield-Suisun, California. In 1947 construction had also begun on a new SAC base at Limestone, Maine, and the installation was being built to accommodate 60 B-36s. However, the sheer size of the B-36 presented problems to the crews constructing facilities at the bases, and progress lagged behind schedule.

On 15 January 1949 a five-ship formation of B-36s from the 7th BW was flown in an air review over Washington D.C., commemorating the inauguration of President Harry S. Truman. Several low-level runs were flown over the U.S. Capitol, resulting in a series of photographs that have been reproduced extensively, usually in conjunction* with accounts of the "Revolt of the Admirals."[30]

The B-36 presented some unique challenges to maintenance workers, and specialized equipment such as dollies, jacks, and work stands proved to be in short supply. The aircraft was too large to fit in any existing hangar, and the cost of new hangars was prohibitive given the budget constraints at the time. Even ground refueling, normally a routine process, proved cumbersome. Because of the height of the wing fuel tanks, the ground-based fuel pumps had to work harder than expected, causing them to fail frequently. New, higher-capacity, pumps had to be designed and procured.[31]

Given the location of many B-36 operating locations, including Fort Worth, maintenance work was frequently halted during periods of bad weather. Both extreme cold and extreme heat were problems, along with winds, rain, snow, etc. In late 1949 Convair came up with a solution in the form of a "maintenance dock" that covered most of the wing and three engines. A pair of these docks were installed in such a way that all six engines and both main landing gear, along with other systems mounted in the wing, could be worked on in relative comfort.[32]

The docks included a "floor" at a convenient level to work on the wing leading and trailing edge, along with a metal "front" and "roof" to protect against the elements. On early docks a canvas "back" covered the propellers and provided weather protection, but this was changed to removable aluminum panels that provided better protection against the wind on later docks. Canvas continued to be used around the ends where the wing protruded through. Mobile heating units provided some warmth during the winter months, but the docks were not air conditioned in the summer – at least their roofs kept workers out of direct sunlight. The docks were equipped with compressed air piping and electrical outlets that could be connected to base support systems, and floodlights were also built in. Each set of docks consisted of four sections, each 36 feet in depth and 30 feet long. When in place the docks enclosed 60 feet of wing on each side of the aircraft. By the end of 1950 all of the docks had been equipped with carbon dioxide fire-extinguishing systems.[33]

---

* The Revolt of the Admirals and the controversy surrounding the National Security Act of 1947 and subsequent development of the Strategic Air Command are outside the scope of this book. Several good studies have been done on these events. See Jeffery G. Barlow, *Revolt of the Admirals: The Fight for Naval Aviation, 1945-1950*, (Washington D.C.: Naval Historical Center, 1994) for instance.

The B-36 assembly line in full swing during December 1948 building B-models. Note that the fuselage skin extends through the area that will be covered by the wing after the aircraft is completely assembled. (Lockheed Martin)

Two types of docks were eventually designed and built. The first was a permanent installation that was provided at the factory, Kelly AFB, and a few of the B-36 bases. It required only 15 minutes for an aircraft to be towed into the dock and set up for maintenance. The second type was a mobile dock that could be moved from aircraft to aircraft. It required about 30 minutes to move a dock and install it around the aircraft to be serviced. These mobile docks were constructed such that they could be disassembled and transported to remote operating locations as needed, but it is unclear if this ever happened. In addition, a nose dock was developed that covered the extreme forward fuselage and canopy area. Interestingly, in photographs of the damage caused by the 1952 tornado at Carswell AFB, it appears as if a great deal of it was the result of the maintenance docks impacting the aircraft.[34]

Eventually, money was found to build some hangars. For instance, at Rapid City AFB the Air Force constructed a hangar 314 feet long, 369 feet wide, and 95 feet tall. The structure covered 3.5 acres, and 18 miles of radiant heating pipes were buried in the floor to help combat

Naming the B-36

Officially, the B-36 never had a name, but it was not for lack of trying on Convair's part. In the 8 December 1948 issue of the employee newspaper *Convairiety*, a contest was announced for all Convair employees to name the new bomber. "Needed is a name appropriate to their size and purpose – a name which will be in keeping with the fine, historic traditions of Convair's fighting ships in days gone by, the Liberators, Catalinas, Coronados, and Vengeance dive bombers." As first announced, there were few restrictions: "the name should be one word and should not be a 'made-up' combination. Duplication or possible confusion with other Army or Navy aircraft names should be avoided. Preference will be given to names which relate to the size, weight, power, range, purpose, and mission of the B-36."[35]

As 1948 came to a close, Convair established 28 February 1949 as the deadline for submitting names for the B-36. A more complete set of rules was published, the most significant being that each employee could only submit a single name between 5 January and 28 February 1949. The judging committee was also named – Major General Roger M. Ramey, commander of the Eighth Air Force; Amon Carter, publisher of the *Fort Worth Star-Telegram*; and LaMotte T. Cohu, president and general manager of Convair. The winner would receive a special certificate, a $50 cash prize, and would "… also feature prominently in publicity attending the naming of the aircraft." In addition, the employees from Fort Worth who submitted the top five names would be eligible for a ride in a B-36 (employees from other locations were not included due to the logistics involved).

The rules also explained that the selected name would not become official until approved by the Air Force Munitions Board Aircraft Committee, which could at its sole discretion, chose any other name if desired. In an effort to be as fair as possible, Convair stated, "If some name submitted by a Convair employee other than the winner of the contest is subsequently selected by the … Munitions Board … the employee who submitted the name so chosen will also be awarded a $50 prize."[36]

Of the 624 submissions from Fort Worth, 49 of them were for the name "Peacemaker," followed by "Peacebinder," Peace Eagle," "Peacekeeper," and "Peacemaster." At San Diego, 11 of the 173 submissions were for "Peacemaker."[37]

In their search for a suitable name, some employees attempted to add a bit of humor. R.G. Cranfill of Fort Worth suggested "Bloodhound" because, "It [the B-36] can smell with radar, and has loud, barking guns." Sadie I. Peteet, also of Fort Worth, liked "Eureka" because, "At last, the king of airplanes has been found."

Other humorous submissions included "Unbelievable" ("every one says it is unbelievable") and "King Kong Bomber."[38]

Interestingly, ancient birds were popular entries, among them "Sacorhampus Gryphus," "Garuda," and "Diatryma." Not surprisingly, many Fort Worth entries had a Texas theme – "Longhorn," "Texas," and "Texan" being the most popular. SARG, an acronym for "size, altitude, range, and guardian" was entered by J. R. Mathis of Fort Worth. Employees at San Diego favored "Condor" and "Crusader" after Peacemaker. One entry that would live long, even after it was not selected, was "The Big Stick," described as "fitting the shape of the B-36 and standing for Teddy Roosevelt's words: 'Talk softly and carry a Big Stick, you'll get far!'"[39]

It had been hoped that the winner would be named by the end of March, but the 30 March 1949 edition of *Convairiety* contained the note: "Judges in the B-36 naming contest apparently were having troubles this week, for there was no official word forthcoming as to the winners. They hoped, however, that some decision will have been reached and the names cleared for copyright before the next issue …."[40]

Finally, on 13 April 1949, *Convairiety* announced that "Peacemaker" had been chosen by the judges and would be forwarded to the Air Force Munitions Board Aircraft Committee for approval.

Peacemaker name certificate. (via Ed Calvert via Don Pyeatt)

According to Evatts Haley, of Canyon, Texas, historian and authority on early Texas, the word Peacemaker was most frequently applied to a Colt 0.45-caliber revolver often used to settle disputes in the old west. Entrants in the Convair contest explained that in 1949 the B-36 occupied much the same position as the famous gun, and could become the world's greatest peace maker.[41]

A drawing was held on 14 April between the 60 submissions to establish who would receive the $50 prize. Ray O. Ryan, division manager, drew the name of J. G. Bohn, a Fort Worth tool and die maker. Four other names were also drawn – J. L. McDaniel, L. R. Harris, G. E. McKenzie, and C. W. Cannon – to accompany Bohn on a one-hour flight in a B-36B on 15 July 1949. All 60 entrants who submitted "Peacemaker" received certificates signed by Ramey, Carter, and Cohu. The certificates read, "Since the ultimate purpose of the B-36 aircraft is to secure and maintain peace throughout the world, we, the undersigned judges of the contest, have unanimously selected 'Peacemaker' from more than 600 suggestions, and have respectfully recommended that the U.S. Air Force adopt the name as official for the B-36."[42]

Unfortunately, objections to the name were raised by various religious groups, and the Air Force deferred making any official decision. In the end, the B-36 came and went without ever being assigned an official moniker, although "Peacemaker" is most often attributed to the aircraft.

the minus 30 degF winters in South Dakota. Even as the last B-36 was being produced, the Air Force was completing a larger hangar (building 1050) at Carswell AFB to house them. At a price of $2,750,000 the four-story-high hangar could accommodate four B-36s at a time. In all, supporting the B-36 was not a simple process.[43]

On 5 December 1948, a B-36B from the 7th BW flew a 4,275-mile mission at 40,000 feet and, except for climb and descent, an average cruising speed of 303 mph was maintained during the entire 14-hour flight. This was bettered a week later when another B-36B averaged 319 mph during a similar mission.

In a maximum range demonstration, a B-36B from the 7th BW/436th BS flew a 35-hour round-trip simulated bombing mission from Carswell to Hawaii on 7–8 December 1948 piloted by Major John D. Bartlett and Lieutenant William H. Grabowski. A 10,000-pound load of dummy bombs was dropped in the ocean a short distance from Hawaii. The flight covered over 8,100 miles, although the average cruising speed was only 236 mph. Nevertheless, this proved the B-36 was a true intercontinental bomber, and given the right circumstance, the aircraft could attack almost any target in the world. Interestingly, the B-36 penetrated Hawaiian airspace without being detected by the defensive forces on the islands, an embarrassment they did not appreciate coming 7 years to the day after Pearl Harbor. A B-50A from the 43rd BG flew a similar mission from Davis-Monthan AFB at the same time.[44]

The Cold War dictated that bases closer to the Soviet Union be found in order to shorten the response time and allow deeper penetration. The bases chosen were all located in the far north, with flight paths that took them near (or over) the North Pole – a route that caused new problems. The magnetic compasses that were still being used as the primary navigation tool at the time did not function well at the North Pole. As a result, Project GEM (global electronics modification) was initiated to provide equipment for worldwide navigation and various cold-weather modifications to the SAC bomber force (B-29s and B-50s also received air-to-air refueling capabilities as part of GEM). Interestingly, the APQ-24 and later K-systems were incapable of obtaining accurate wind or drift values when flown over either water or snow. The Air Force investigated adding an AN/APN-81 Doppler radar to the K-system, but this was not completed before the decision was made to remove the B-36 from service (although it found use on the B-52).[45]

On 17 January 1949 Convair and the Air Force took a B-36 to Ladd AFB, Alaska, for cold-weather testing. The aircraft had departed a balmy Eglin AFB, Florida, and 18 hours and 15 minutes later arrived at Ladd where the temperature was –38 degF. The aircraft remained in Alaska for 2 months, and included a public "B-36 Day" at Ladd on 29 January. The aircraft and crew returned to Fort Worth in early April, accompanied by a pair of Alaskan Huskies that were adopted while at Ladd.[46]

More demonstrations followed. On 29 January 1949, a B-36B established a record bomb lift by taking a pair of dummy 43,000-pound bombs aloft at Muroc AFB (now Edwards AFB). The first was released at an altitude of 35,000 feet, the second from 41,000 feet, both

A B-36B, B-50, B-17, B-26 (A-26), and F-51 pass at low level during an Air Power Demonstration at Eglin AFB. (Air Force Historical Research Agency)

at a speed of 350 mph. The entire flight averaged over 250 mph and covered 2,900 miles. The bombs were 26.85 feet long and 4.5 feet in diameter and had to be released in a specific sequence – the forward one was dropped first, and the sudden release of weight jolted the nose upward. If the rear one had been released first, the resultant nose-down moment might have been too severe to recover from. The aircraft was piloted by Major Stephen P. Dillon and Doc Witchell.[47]

During late March 1949 the B-36 was used for a somewhat unusual purpose, given the secrecy that usually surrounded SAC bombers. England's top-ranking test pilot, Arthur John Pegg, was allowed to fly a B-36B at Fort Worth in order to evaluate the handling of a very large aircraft prior to embarking on the first flight of the eight-engine Bristol Brabazon transport in England. Pegg related, "Before flying the Brabazon, I wanted to find out from your people who fly B-36s if there is anything particularly difficult, anything peculiar to flying such a large craft. I found out. So far as the B-36 is concerned, there isn't." Pegg became the first foreign pilot to fly the B-36 and commented, "The B-36 flies beautifully, and I was very impressed both with its performance and its handling. Everything about it seems to be completely normal, which is why I say that it is surprisingly unsurprising." Accompanying Pegg on his flight was Captain Robert Walling and a 7th BW crew. A few months later, in October 1949, Beryl Erickson inspected the Brabazon at the Bristol plant in England as a guest of Pegg.[48]

A red-tail B-36B-1-CF (44-92027) being prepared for a mission. Note the 43,000-pound T-12 bomb and three cargo carriers around the aircraft. On many early missions, the cargo carriers were used to carry zinc bars to simulate ammunition and other items. (Lockheed Martin)

On 12 March 1949, a B-36B from the 7th BW/492nd BS was used to establish a distance record of 9,600 miles flown in 43 hours 37 minutes, with enough fuel remaining for 2 more hours of flying – the B-36 could remain aloft for 2 days, totally self sufficient. In this case the B-36 had been carrying a simulated load of 10,000 pounds that were dropped at the 5,000-mile point in the flight. The flight departed Carswell, then flew over Minneapolis, Great Falls, Key West, the Gulf of Mexico (where the bombs were dropped), Houston, Fort Worth, Denver, Great Falls, Spokane, and back to Fort Worth. Severe headwinds were encountered over the Rocky Mountains, leaving little doubt that a 10,000-mile mission was possible under ideal conditions. The crew for the flight included Captain Roy R. Showalter as pilot; Lieutenant Clarence F. Horton, copilot; Captain Earl N. Yaden; Major Joseph A. Brown; MSgt. John L. Corley; MSgt. Carl W. Arey; TSgt. J. P. Fleming; SSgt. Clarence E. Pawkett; SSgt. P.C. Cothran, Jr.; and SSgt. Albert L. Claggett. Two men who had participated in the 7 December 1948 mission over Hawaii, mission commander Major John D. Bartlett and Lieutenant William H. Grabowski, were also aboard.[49]

Although confidence building, these missions were not truly representative of the state of the B-36 fleet. During 1949, SAC rarely had more than 40 B-36s on hand, and only 5–8 of these were considered operationally capable. The 7th BW was, in essence, a service test unit. Because of maintenance problems and continued modifications, there was little opportunity to train crews extensively and their proficiency with the aircraft and its systems was questionable. Presumably the wing could have launched a few sorties in the event of war, but as late as June 1950 the B-36 force could hardly be considered a major asset.[50]

In October 1949 the Strategic Air Command held its second* bombing competition, something that would become an annual event for the next couple of decades. The rules set demanding standards that involved the flight crews, ground crews, and most support personnel from the competing units. Equipment failures were not a valid excuse for poor performance. Although the competitions boosted morale, in reality they were used by LeMay to assess the capabilities of the units under his command. Thirteen bomb groups participated in the com-

petition that year – three B-36, eight B-29, and two B-50. Each participating crew conducted three visual bomb runs and three radar bomb runs, each at 25,000 feet.[51]

In this competition, a B-36 crew from Rapid City won the overall event with an average visual bombing error of 441 feet and an average error in radar bombing of 1,053 feet. Although impressive, these scores (highly classified at the time) still cast doubts on the ability of a strategic bomber to conduct "precision strikes" with conventional bombs. They were a long way from "hitting a pickle barrel" as General LeMay liked to claim his crews could do. The 7th BW placed 4th overall, while the 11th BW came in 13th and last.[52]

Still, everything was not working as well as it could be. The APQ-24 was neither as reliable nor as accurate in service as it had been during testing. The problem was eventually traced to faulty vacuum tubes and inadequate training. The complex General Electric remotely-controlled turrets were prone to frequent failures. A lack of 20-mm ammunition had delayed the start of operational testing until mid-1949, and the eventual results were disappointing. The entire system was unreliable, and when it did work, it was not terribly accurate. Although conceptually similar to the defensive armament installed on the B-29, the system was much more complex, a necessity to ensure it was capable of handling the ever-increasing speeds of the fighters it was designed to shoot down. The extreme cold at 40,000 feet created problems as did the vibration of the six large engines. The APG-3 gun-laying radar for the tail turret also proved to be remarkably troublesome. As late as February 1950, the commander of the 8th Air Force was complaining that there was little point in driving a B-36 around carrying a lot of guns that didn't work.

Many of the B-36B's initial problems resembled those of any other new and complex aircraft. Parts shortages were acute, and it was often necessary to cannibalize some B-36Bs to keep others flying. The problems seemed larger than normal, but the B-36 was a larger than

---

* The first bombing competition had been held 20–27 June 1948 at Castle AFB, California. No B-36 groups were operational to participate in the event, which was essentially limited to B-29s.

normal aircraft. Equipment such as empennage stands, dollies, and jacks were in short supply. Because there was no funding for new equipment, maintenance crews utilized some of the tools and equipment left over from the old B-29s. The aircraft were constantly being reconfigured or awaiting modification, and in reality, an operational capability was not achieved until 1952. Personnel turnover in the postwar environment further hampered progress. Nevertheless, by early 1951, many B-36s were available and, if called upon, were capable of giving the Soviets, at a minimum, a reason to pause.

Additional tests were performed at Ladd AFB in Alaska between 14 December 1949 and 8 April 1950. During this evaluation, the "lows" were around –53 degF while the "highs" were –39 degF. Following the GEM modifications, the 7th BW routinely deployed B-36Bs to airfields near Goose Bay, Labrador, and Fairbanks, Alaska, on a rotational basis. These aircraft had their tails and wingtips painted bright red in case they were forced down in the rough terrain (day-glo paint had not been perfected yet).

The move North continued. Eighth Air Force Operations Order 19-49 ordered the 7th BW to establish a forward operational area at Eielson AFB, Alaska, for training and pre-strike staging. In response, Operation DRIZZLE was initiated to provide arctic experience for crews from the 7th BW. One of the more interesting stories concerning these exercises, which continued through 1952 on a less intense basis, was Operation WATERMELON. Crews from Carswell AFB wanted to find a way to repay some of the hospitality shown by members of Eielson. When it was discovered that watermelons were a prized delicacy, the Carswell crews arranged to transport 4,000 pounds of the fruit during the next routine flight.[53]

In his book, Meyers Jacobsen mentions one of the more ironic problems encountered by the B-36 units at Carswell. When a part was needed that was manufactured by Convair, which was located a mile across the runway, the 7th BW had to request the part from the

Air Materiel Command depot at San Antonio, which in turn requested it from the manufacturer. Convair then shipped the part to San Antonio, which turned around and shipped it to Carswell. Finally, somebody in the Air Force realized the irony of the situation, and allowed Convair simply to drive the parts across the runway and deliver them to the B-36 units.

While the B-36Bs were being built, Convair was attempting to develop the reengined B-36C as a means of increasing the performance of the aircraft. When this did not pan out, the Air Force approved a more modest upgrade that added General Electric J47-GE-11 jet engines to the basic B-36B configuration, creating the B-36D. This change was approved while the B-36Bs were being manufactured. Convair was contracted[*] to build 73 B-36Bs, but the Air Force directed 11 of them to be modified with jet engines on the production line. Four of the 11 appeared on Air Force rolls as B-36Ds, and seven as RB-36Ds. Therefore, Air Force records indicate that only 62 B-36Bs were accepted – 31 in FY49, 30 in FY50, and the last one in September 1950 (FY51).[†] This disparate accounting has led to some confusion over the years.

The B-36B phase-out from service was almost as quick as that of the B-36A. Twenty-five B-36Bs were already undergoing conversion into D-models during the first half of 1951, and the last of the 60 converted B-36Bs were redelivered by February 1952. Two of the bombers had crashed before they could be converted. Nevertheless, at least one aircraft (44-92073) managed to accumulate over 1,000 flight hours during 22 months of operation before being delivered to San Diego for conversion.[54]

Interestingly, only the first four conversions (44-92026, 034, 053, and 054) took place at Fort Worth – the rest were performed in San Diego. This was an attempt to relieve the workload at Fort Worth, but the decision was made after an additional 91,000 square yards of concrete pads had been poured at Fort Worth to support the conversion effort (which would have occurred outdoors). The area did not go to waste since it was later used for the various SAM-SAC, ON TOP, and ECM upgrade programs. On the other hand, San Diego now found

---

[*] The original 100 aircraft contract did not specify models, but resulted in 22 B-36As and 73 B-36Bs – 5 aircraft were cancelled to cover the costs of the stillborn B-36C project.

[†] The government fiscal year ended in June at this time.

At left is another assembly line shot, this time showing the "communications tubes" used by crewmembers to travel between the two pressurized compartments. The other two photos show a B-36B-5-CF (44-92043) being rolled out of the north end of Building 4. Note that the red arctic markings were painted on the assembly line, and the angle of the nose to ensure the tail cleared the door as the aircraft left the building. (Lockheed Martin)

Night operations on the ramp at Convair Fort Worth on 23 July 1953. The factory worked around the clock at times in order to produce B-36s on schedule, and also to fix all the latent defects discovered in the aircraft – especially fuel tank sealing problems. (Lockheed Martin)

itself needing more ramp space – or more specifically, *stronger* ramp space. The original ramp had been built to support B-24s, and could not safely accommodate the B-36. Concrete and black-top was ripped out, and almost 10,000 square yards of 7-inch-thick concrete was poured in its place. Building 3 at the plant was also extensively modified by removing various support columns to allow the large aircraft to be parked partially indoors (the empennage was still outside).[55]

When it was decided to move the B-36B conversion work to San Diego, nine all-weather maintenance docks were constructed there to facilitate the effort. Five additional docks were added later. In addition, a variety of other items were built, including horizontal stabilizer stands and two rudder stands. These were transferred to Fort Worth beginning in July 1952 after the last of the D-model conversions and SAN-SAN maintenance were completed in San Diego. Fort Worth needed the docks to outfit additional work areas in preparation for SAM-SAC and other modernization work. The docks were partially disassembled and shipped via rail.[56]

B-36C

Although the B-36's performance since mid-1948 kept exceeding early expectations, the aircraft's relatively slow speed continued to cause concern. Much of the concern resulted from the immediate postwar enthusiasm for speed – becoming more intense after Chuck Yeager broke the sound barrier in 1947 – more than any real operational requirement. However, tests had shown that altitude was also very important in protecting a bomber, and the B-36 excelled at flying high. General LeMay recognized this and it was one of the primary drivers for his unwavering support of the B-36. Nevertheless, a burst of speed over a target or while under attack significantly increased a bomber's chances of survival.

In March 1947, Convair proposed that 34 aircraft out of the original 100 be completed as B-36Cs powered by 4,300 hp Variable Discharge* Turbine (VDT) R-4360-51 Wasp Majors. In the VDT, exhaust gases from the engine would pass through a General Electric CHM-2 turbosupercharger with a clamshell nozzle that created jet thrust by varying the size of the turbine exit. Unfortunately, the use of the VDT engines on the B-36 would dictate a change from a pusher to a tractor configuration – requiring a significant redesign of some structure. Although the engine would remain in the normal position behind the main wing spar, its orientation would be changed to face forward, and each engine would drive a tractor propeller through 10-foot shafts that extended through the entire wing chord. Air intakes would be located on the wing leading edge on either side of a very streamlined nacelle that held the propeller extension shaft. The installation was very reminiscent of the T35 turboprop proposal.

Convair estimated that the VDT engine (also proposed for the B-50C) would give the B-36 a top speed of 410 mph, a 45,000-foot service ceiling, and a 10,000-mile range with a 10,000-pound bomb load. To offset the cost of adapting the VDT engine to the B-36, Convair suggested financing the airframe modification for one prototype by slashing three B-36s from the original procurement contract. This was approved by the Air Materiel Command in July 1947. Convair hoped additional VDT-equipped B-36Cs would be ordered if the prototype proved successful, and a proposal was submitted for additional aircraft on 5 May 1947. A decision on this matter was deferred.

The possible B-36C contract and general concerns over how to keep the plant in Fort Worth busy were interrelated. At the beginning of August 1947, Convair approached Generals Carl A. Spaatz (Army Air Forces Chief of Staff), Hoyt S. Vandenberg (Vice-Chief), and LeMay (Commander of Research and Development) with the dilemma concerning future operations of the plant, and reiterated their 5 May proposal for additional B-36Cs. However, as part of forming the newly-independent Air Force, all of the general officers deferred the matter to the just-created Aircraft and Weapons Board.[57]

The new Aircraft and Weapons Board first met on 19 August and strategic bombing was the subject to be reviewed. Some board mem-

---

* There seems to be some confusion over whether this was 'discharge' or 'displacement' with contemporary literature using both terms. Most P&W documentation, however, uses 'discharge' so that is what will be used in this book.

bers considered the B-36 obsolete and favored buying fast jet bombers, an obvious gamble since early models would have very limited range and not be available for several years. Others wanted to increase the speed of the B-36 with the new VDT engines and use it as a general-purpose bomber. Still others preferred the B-50 because it was faster than the B-36, although otherwise less capable.

After prolonged discussion, a consensus emerged to retain the B-36 as an atomic bomber that would eventually be replaced by the B-52, and to produce the B-50 as a general-purpose bomber to be replaced by the B-47. Given this, there was no particular reason for installing the VDT engine in a prototype B-36, and no additional B-36 procurement would be needed past the 100 aircraft already on order. General Spaatz, who had been appointed by President Truman as the first Air Force Chief of Staff, promptly approved the board's recommendations, and the B-36C prototype was cancelled on 22 August 1947.[58]

The cancellation of the prototype did not stop Convair from proposing on 4 September 1947 that the last 34 B-36s in the original contract be completed as B-36Cs. A service-test YB-36C could be delivered in November 1948, with production aircraft available in August 1949. Production would ramp up to four aircraft per month by November 1949. Convair estimated that the extra cost of the B-36Cs could be met by reducing the overall order to only 95 B-36s, and that the B-36Cs could be produced without delaying the program by more than six months. It was even suggested that the remaining B-36A and B-36B aircraft could be retrofitted to B-36C standards, although no details were forthcoming on how to accomplish this.[59]

The Convair proposal was forwarded to Major General Lawrence C. Craigie, Chief of the Research and Engineering Division at Wright Field. Craigie expressed a concern that the engine availability schedule was overly optimistic, noting that VDT engine production would have to be shared with the B-50C (later redesignated B-54) and Republic F-12 (XR-12) Rainbow programs. Lieutenant General Nathan F. Twining, the Commander of AMC, also indicated that although the cost of the airframes might be absorbed by cutting five aircraft off the production run, other expenses and government-furnished equipment might run as high as $15 million – money the Air Force did not have.[60]

General Vandenberg sent Convair an interim answer that effectively said the matter was being deferred until the next meeting of the Aircraft and Weapons Board. The rationale was that since the Board had previously cancelled the B-36C prototype, Vandenberg believed that each member of the Board should have the opportunity to vote on the new proposal. General Joseph T. McNarney, the new commander of the Air Materiel Command recommended approval of the B-36C on the grounds that the performance figures, production costs, and delivery schedule all appeared feasible. Nevertheless, General Kenney from SAC still opposed continued production of any B-36 variants, although he conceded that they might be useful for reconnaissance and as tankers. The Strategic Air Command did not believe that 34 B-36Cs represented a viable force and cast the lone dissenting vote at the Board meeting in November 1947. Despite Kenney's misgivings, the Board accepted the Convair proposal for the 34 new-build B-36Cs on 5 December 1947, although no decision was made on

Other applications for the VDT engine included the XR-12 (left) and B-54 (right). (left: Tony Landis Collection; right: Peter M. Bowers Collection)

retrofitting the 61 existing B-36s. By this time, SAC's future hopes were firmly pinned on the B-52, but exactly what it would look like and when it would be available were cause for some concern.[61]

Unfortunately, the B-36C project quickly ran into technical difficulties. Ground testing revealed problems with engine cooling generated by the aircraft's high-operating altitude, subsequently degrading engine power and making the Convair performance estimates unachievable. Instead of the original 410-mph top speed, revised estimates showed only 385. Monthly conferences between the Air Force, Convair, and Pratt & Whitney showed that there was nothing wrong with the R-4360 engine, and the General Electric turbine also seemed to be operating satisfactory. The problem was the B-36 installation.

On 12 April 1948 an engineering conference took place at Fort Worth that included representatives from Convair, P&W, General Electric, and Curtiss-Wright (propellers). Further revised cooling requirements were presented at the conference that showed a substantial reduction in power output. The two culprits were the location of the engine and turbine at the rear of the B-36 wing, and the extremely high altitudes at which the B-36 operated. The additional horsepower required to operate a much larger than expected cooling fan resulted in the loss of 49 mph. The drag from the openings in the wing leading edge to feed the cooling system resulted in a further loss of 9 mph, and the additional weight of the installation cost another few miles per hour. The revised cruising speed over a range of 7,250 miles was only 262 mph – 23 mph *slower* than a standard B-36B over the same range.[62]

By the spring of 1948, it had become apparent that the VDT-equipped B-36C was not going to materialize, and the Air Force once again considered cancelling the entire B-36 program. By this time, some officers in SAC had lost confidence in the B-36 as a long-range strategic bomber and believed the relatively slow aircraft would be useful only for such tasks as sea-search or reconnaissance. The B-50 was usually proposed as a replacement.

Much of this was based on emotion and misinformation. In August 1949, Major General Frederic H. Smith, Jr. testified before the House Armed Services Committee that a series of evaluations in late 1948 had showed that the standard B-36B surpassed the B-50 in cruising speed at very long range, had a higher service and cruise ceiling, a larger payload capacity, and a much greater combat radius than the B-50 (assuming no refueling). The speed tests had been conducted to the B-50's maximum range – if the tests had been conducted to the B-36's maximum range, then the results would have favored the B-36 even more since the B-50 would have had to slow down to refuel. An evaluation at the same time showed that the B-36B was superior to the proposed B-54 in all regards except speed over the target, and the addition of the jet pods on the B-36D would cure this deficiency.[63]

Although the B-36 was slow, it flew at altitudes that contemporary fighters could not easily or routinely achieve. When a fighter did manage to get to 40,000 feet, it was usually as slow or slower than the bomber, and often unable to maneuver except on essentially ballistic trajectories. The B-36's large wing area allowed it to be fairly maneuverable at high altitudes, and the standard defense against a fighter attack was to make a sharp turn, something the fighter could not follow. The Navy disagreed with the conclusions from these evaluations but presented little evidence* at the time to support its claims. It now seemed that the B-36 might be a better aircraft than anyone had expected, and that any hasty reduction in the program might be a mistake.

The Air Force was still faced with several decisions. Limited B-36 procurement was one solution, but finding some use for the government-owned Fort Worth plant, soon to be idle, was another problem. Nobody in the government wanted to see the Fort Worth plant mothballed, fearing it would not be feasible to reactivate the plant if the need arose to increase production as had been the case during World War II. The Air Force also could not stand by as Convair's dejected B-36 work force sought and probably secured more stable employment before completion of the B-36 program. There were further complications. Funds had been appropriated during the war for the 100 B-36s, but any amount unspent by the end of June 1948 would have to be reappropriated by Congress. Given a general budget-trimming trend, this was considered unlikely. Production speedup was one solution. If Convair turned out 6 aircraft every month, the 100th B-36 would be delivered in January 1949. This would only leave 7 months of production (July 1948–January 1949) for which new funds would have to be provided.[64]

Chiefly because of shortages of government-furnished equipment, accelerating production proved impossible. This was just as well since it would have hastened the end of the Fort Worth activities. On 1 May 1947 Convair and representatives of the Air Materiel Command met at Wright Field and agreed on a monthly production rate of four B-36s. However, this carried another pitfall – postponing delivery of the last B-36 to November 1949. This would extend the production time for which Convair would have to plan by 17 months with no assurance that money would ever be available to complete the program. Frank A. Learman, the sales manager at Convair Fort Worth wrote a letter to the Air Materiel Command on 4 May 1947 pointing out that careful scheduling of airframe production – especially if the B-36C variant was approved – would be required to ensure smooth operations of the plant. Any prolonged gap in production could result in unplanned costs of up to $1 million per month to keep the plant idle.[65]

---

* In reality, both Navy and British – and possibly Soviet – fighters would have stood a better chance than Air Force fighters at high altitudes. The U.S. Air Force had adopted a doctrine that emphasized a fighter's speed over most other attributes, resulting in a generally higher wing loading than aircraft from other countries (or the Navy). This greatly diminished the USAF fighters' high-altitude maneuverability.

Also in December 1947, Frank Watson, the contracts manager at Convair, wrote to General Joseph T. McNarney, Commander of Air Materiel Command, bluntly expressing the dilemma that Convair faced over the funding issue:[66]

There seems to be a general awareness of the difficulties involved in attempting a five year aircraft program on two year appropriations. All such general discussion is no doubt meritorious and should in due time result in necessary action. However, this contractor is faced with the problem immediately and seriously and is at a loss as to where to turn for some form of assurance on how to proceed.

Deliveries are presently scheduled through 1949. The funds expire on June 30, 1948. Contractor has been advised very properly by Air Materiel Command that if present funds are not extended by Congress or new funds not made available prior to June 30, 1948, it will be necessary for Contractor to go to the Court of Claims for recovery of any amounts due and payable to subcontractors and vendors after such June 30th date.

It would seem a simple matter for Contractor to wait patiently until a few days before June 30th and then if new funds have not been appropriated, to bring the program to a close. This, however, ignores the lead times necessary in an airplane program as complicated as the B-36 program. Contractor cannot wait until just before midnight on June 30th to adjust the flow of materials from subcontractors and vendors. ...

Contractors alternatives: to decide, not after Congress has had a full period of time to consider new appropriations, but by January or February of this coming year [1948] whether: (a) to cut back the program at great loss to the government and with fair certainty that such action means the end of the B-36 program and the end of [the Convair] Fort Worth [plant] as an effective unit in the national defense, or (b) to gamble that the funds will be available for continuing the contract after June 30, 1948. ... it is a gamble of going out of business to a substantial degree.

Aware of the contractor's predicament, in late December 1947 Brigadier General H. A. Shepard, Chief of the Procurement Division at Wright Field, promised to request a reappropriation of B-36 funds when Congress reconvened in January 1948.[67]

When it became obvious that the VDT-powered B-36C was not going to materialize, the Air Force once more thought of cancelling the entire B-36 program. Yet, various factors had to be considered. Twenty-two of the basic and relatively slow B-36As were nearly completed, and a great deal of money had already been spent on the controversial program. The Air Force, therefore, decided to postpone any decisions. It instructed the Air Materiel Command to waive the modification of several shop-completed B-36s that had been awaiting adjustments, and to expedite their ("as-is") delivery. This would allow Convair to speed up the aircraft's flight-test program, as consistently recommended by the Air Force. In addition, new metrics were established to compare the basic B-36's performance with that of other bombers under similar conditions. The new metrics measured the four most important and interdependent characteristics of any given bomber – speed, range, altitude, and payload. The B-36 came out on top of all existing types.[68]

As a result, General McNarney listed four possible courses of action for the B-36 program.[69]

- Continue original program – 22 B-36As and 78 B-36Bs. This would cost an additional $1.5 million to compensate for the VDT development work.
- Terminate the contract after 61 aircraft – 22 B-36As and 39 B-36Bs. This would allow the recovery of approximately $92 million.
- Terminate the contract after 41 aircraft – 22 B-36As and 19 B-36Bs. This number was chosen because there were already 18 B-36Bs slated to go through Project GEM, plus one B-model test aircraft. This would allow the recovery of approximately $113 million.
- Terminate the contract after 22 aircraft – all B-36As. This would allow the recovery of $167 million.

McNarney made no specific recommendation other than to point out that the second option was the most economical since it gave the Air Force the most aircraft for the dollars spent.

Lieutenant General Lauris Norstad, Deputy Chief of Staff for Operations, commented that the most desirable course would be to terminate production after 66 aircraft since that would allow the formation of a single Very Heavy Bombardment Group with 22 B-36Bs and 22 war-reserve spares. The 21 B-36As could then be converted into tankers for the medium bomber force using either the existing British-developed probe and drogue method, or the flying-boom system being developed by Boeing.

General Kenney at SAC still recommended cancelling the entire program, firmly believing that the B-50 was the better airplane. This was understandable since no B-36s had been delivered to SAC yet, and the performance of the aircraft during early testing had been generally unimpressive. The exception to this was the flight to Hawaii on 13–14 May – in fact, this single flight is largely regarded as causing Secretary of the Air Force Stuart W. Symington to decide on 24 May 1948 to continue with the production of at least 61 B-36s.

Despite just spending a relative fortune to produce the B-36, Symington had yet to actually see one in flight. This would be cured 4 days after the decision when Symington visited Dallas. Beryl Erickson and William "Bill" P. Easley were in a lightly-loaded B-36A (44-92007) that had just departed from the same airport as the Secretary. As soon as Symington's C-54 became airborne, Erickson formed up on the C-54 and flew alongside for a while, then sped up and made a complete circle at close range. The experience impressed Symington, who subsequently got a ride in a B-36 on 18 November 1949 at Carswell.

However, it was probably the Soviets who were actually responsible for saving the B-36 program. On 18 June 1948 the blockade of Berlin began. On 25 June 1948, Secretary Symington decided to continue the B-36 program in its entirety since it was the only truly intercontinental bomber then available. General Kenney endorsed this decision, although only a month earlier he had recommended cancelling the B-36 program. Kenny explained his change of heart was due partly to new performance data that showed the B-36 was better than expected, and also as a reaction to the crisis in Berlin. The

VDT-equipped B-36Cs that had been ordered would revert to standard B-36B configuration. Five aircraft (44-92099 through 44-92103) still had to be cut from the original order for 100 aircraft to compensate for inflation and to pay for the cost of the ill-fated B-36C project.[70]

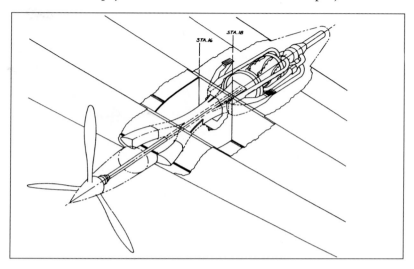

The proposed B-36C used six tractor-style P&W VDT engines, but ran into severe development problems. (above: Convair; below: redrawn by the author from Convair documents supplied by Bob Bradley)

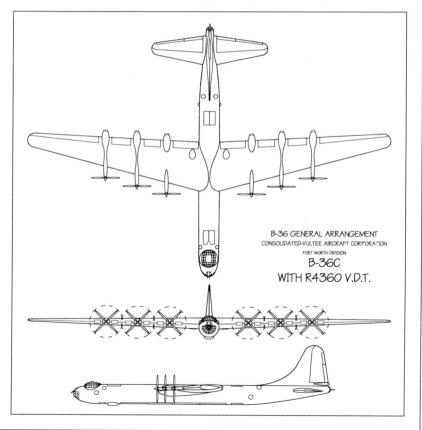

Chapter 4

Above: *The last B-36J (52-2827) is ready to come off the production line on 1 July 1954. The white "camouflage" was not painted on the production line even this late in production. Note that the censor has scratched out the Convair production number in both of these photos. (Lockheed Martin)*

Right: *A line-up of new H-models at Convair in November 1952. The portion of a wing in the foreground shows damage that resulted from the September 1952 tornado that has not yet been repaired. The two closest aircraft are B-36Hs, followed by two recce aircraft. (Lockheed Martin)*

VERY HEAVY BOMBERS

Fortunately, the VDT-powered B-36C was not the only way Convair had devised to increase the speed of the B-36. On 5 October 1948 Convair proposed installing a pair of turbojet engines underneath each outer wing panel. These engines could be used during takeoff and for short bursts of speed at critical times, and would have only a minimal effect on range, more as a result of the additional drag than the relatively small amount of fuel used by the jet engines.

Unlike the extensive changes needed to install the VDT engines, only minor modifications would be required to mount the jet nacelles. In fact, Convair was confident that a prototype B-36 with jet engines would be ready to fly less than 4 months after Air Force approval. The Air Force did not question the obvious merits of the Convair proposal – approval was delayed because of the budgetary restrictions looming in December 1948 and the decision a month before to convert the B-36As into RB-36E reconnaissance aircraft. It should be noted that as originally planned, the RB-36Es did not include jet engines – they were simply remanufactured B-36As with photo and radio-intercept reconnaissance capabilities.

B-36D

The most obvious change for the B-36D was two pairs of 5,200-lbf General Electric J47-GE-11 (later –19s) turbojets in pods underneath the outer wing panels. In order to save money and simplify production, the pods were essentially the same as those developed for the inboard engines on the Boeing B-47 Stratojet. The outrigger landing gear and some of the supporting structure was deleted, although the aerodynamic fairing and taxi light on the bottom of the pods were retained. Initially, the struts and pods were even manufactured by Bell Aircraft Company* on the same Buffalo, New York, production line used to make B-47 pods. Beginning in May 1951, the pods were manufactured in a new Bell facility located 12 miles from the Convair Fort Worth plant. Special collapsible aerodynamic covers were installed over the engine inlets to minimize drag when the engines were not operating. About 5 percent of the normal airflow was allowed to pass through when the covers were closed, mainly to keep the compressor

turning to prevent it from freezing. Hot air from the anti-icing system could also be ducted to the turbojets to prevent freezing when operating at extreme altitude.[1]

Like the R-4360s, the General Electric jet engines were government-furnished equipment. Once the engines and struts/pods arrived at Fort Worth, they were completely assembled in an area separate from normal B-36 production. The complete units were then taken to the final assembly line where they were hung on the wing. The engines themselves were modified to burn standard aviation gas instead of jet fuel so that the B-36 could feed them from the existing fuel supply. This resulted in the engines producing slightly less power than normal, but the trade-off was considered worthwhile. Surprisingly, very little structural modification was required to support the new engine pods, a tribute to how strong the basic B-36 wing was. Controls for the jet engines were mounted on a separate panel above the pilots' heads, while instrumentation was spread across two subpanels added below the main instrument panel. Interestingly, the flight engineer station received essentially no changes due to the jet

The new jet pods introduced on the B-36D would finally make the B-36 a viable weapons system – at least for a while. The last aircraft visible on the line is a reconnaissance version. (Lockheed Martin)

---

* Bell also manufactured the pods for the B-47. The B-36 pods were under direct subcontract to Convair, while the B-47 pods were under subcontract to Boeing.

Proof of concept demonstrations were conducted using a B-36B-10-CF (44-92057). The jet pods used for the demonstration differed from production units – no lower sculpting and no sway braces. The aircraft was otherwise a stock B-model, with none of the other changes intended for the B-36D. Note that the nose turret has guns installed. (Lockheed Martin)

installation. Additional 20-gallon oil tanks were installed in the outer wing panels to hold 13 gallons* of the special oil the jet engines required. Engine operating time was limited by the amount of oil available, but this seldom presented any operational problems.

The reciprocating engines remained the same 3,500-hp R-4360-41 Wasp Majors that had powered the B-36B, although they would be updated to –41A models with the same horsepower sometime during the service life of the aircraft. The maximum gross weight was increased to 357,500 pounds, a figure that would remain constant across all models until the advent of the B-36J. Another major improvement was that most of the flying surfaces were now covered with magnesium skin instead of doped fabric. The retractable tail "bumper" that had been installed on the A/B-models was deleted on new-builds, but it appears that the bumper was retained on at least the B-36Bs that were completed as D-models.

The B-36D was supposed to use an improved K-3 bombing and navigation system. However, development problems prevented the K-3 from being delivered in time to equip the first B-36Ds, which used a K-1 unit that was little more than a refined version of the APQ-24 used in the B-36B. The Farrand Y-1 retractable periscopic bomb sight had run into apparently insurmountable development problems. In its place, Farrand developed a nonretractable version called the Y-3, and this was installed in most B-36Ds. (It is unclear if the B-36Bs completed as B-36Ds carried the Y-3 or the Norden initially.) The substitution of the Y-3 for the Y-1 in the K-system resulted in a new K-3A designation.[†] All B-36Ds were eventually retrofitted with the K-3A. Since the Y-3 bomb sight used a small periscope protruding from the right side of the forward fuselage bottom, the flat glazed panel in the nose was often covered over with aluminum. Of course, on aircraft still equipped with the Norden bomb sight (and all RB-36s), this panel was still glass, complete with its own windshield wiper.[2]

An AN/APG-32A gun-laying radar replaced the APG-3 to direct the tail turret. However, it appears that at least the B-36Bs that were completed on the production line as D-models were equipped with the APG-3 initially, and subsequently modified with the newer unit (the two systems were externally identical).

The B-36D was fitted with "snap-action" bomb bay doors (called "clam shell" by Convair at the time) as opposed to the sliding type fitted to the preceding B-36A/Bs. These doors could open and close in only 2 seconds, minimizing the drag penalty usually associated with getting ready to drop bombs over the target. The doors were hydraulically actuated and proved to be more reliable than the earlier cable-operated sliding doors. Only two sets of doors were provided, one set covering the forward bomb bays (Nos. 1 and 2) and the other covering the aft bays (Nos. 3 and 4). All B-36Ds were delivered with the ability to carry a Mk III/4 atomic bomb in bomb bay No. 1 (this was chosen primarily because the bombs still had to be armed in flight, and the forward bomb bay was the most accessible). Conventional bomb capacity was generally similar to the B-model.

Two additional 4,800-gallon (4,788.5 usable) "auxiliary" fuel tanks were added into the inboard section of the wings, bringing the total to eight tanks carrying 36,622 gallons. Each of these new tanks consisted of four interconnected bladder-type fuel cells made of rubber impregnated nylon fabric and were not self-sealing or armored. Removable bullet sealing pads could be installed on the undersurface of the wing between the engine nacelles to protect the main fuel tanks. The flight manual contained a warning that the "auxiliary" fuel tanks differed in size from aircraft to aircraft, often by as much as 100 gallons. On most aircraft the plumbing was deleted from bomb bay No. 2, and only a

---

* The remaining 7 gallons of volume were reserved for oil foaming.
† The K-3A installed in the B-36D and the K-4A installed in the B-47 differed primarily in the periscopic bomb sights used – otherwise they were nearly identical.

Puerto Rico played host to many B-36s, including the B-36D-35-CF (49-2654) from the 7th BW landing at Ramey AFB shown at left. In the center, a B-36D-10-CF (44-92026) from the 7th BW was photographed at Detroit MAP on 19 August 1951. At this point the buzz number on the forward fuselage had been shortened to just the last three or four digits of the serial number – without the original "BM" prefix. The B-36D-45-CF (44-92065) at right was assigned to the 92nd BW/326th BS at Fairchild AFB in May 1955 – note that this aircraft has a small piece of nose art (it was not readable on the original print, either). (all W. Balogn via the Norm Taylor Collection via Richard Freeman)

single 3,000-gallon (2,996 usable) tank could be carried in bomb bay No. 3. However, the documentation is confusing because various issues of the flight manuals for B-36s show bomb bay fuel tanks in one, two, or all four bomb bays. It is likely that the plumbing was changed during various ON TOP or other modification programs.

The nomenclature for the B-36D's 15 crewmembers changed slightly: aircraft commander, two pilots, two engineers, navigator, bombardier, two radio operators, and forward observer; and five gunners aft. In reality, one of the radiomen operated the ECM equipment, the other operated the nose turret, while one of the pilots and the observer operated the forward upper gun turrets. Although the aft cabin of all

B-36s had always contained six bunks for crewmembers, it was found that in service the crew in the front cabin seldom traveled aft and slept in their seats instead. Convair devised a way to mount two fold-down bunks in the forward cabin, and this change was made during the D-model production run. Kits were provided that allowed the operational units to add the bunks to aircraft already delivered. One bunk was hung from the top of the radio operator's compartment and was high enough to not interfere with the work of other crewmembers. The second bunk folded up flat against the top of the navigator's compartment when not in use. Convair had investigated using hammocks that could be strung up, but rejected the concept as less than ideal.[3]

The B-36 also played movie star on occasion – this B-36D-5-CF (49-2652) was painted up in unique "Hollywood" markings for a film that was never released. The tail code, buzz number, and unit insignia are all fictitious. Note the large ground air conditioning unit in the photo at right that provided heating/cooling for the crew compartment while the aircraft was on the ground. (Peter M. Bowers)

RESTRICTED
AN 01-5EUC-2

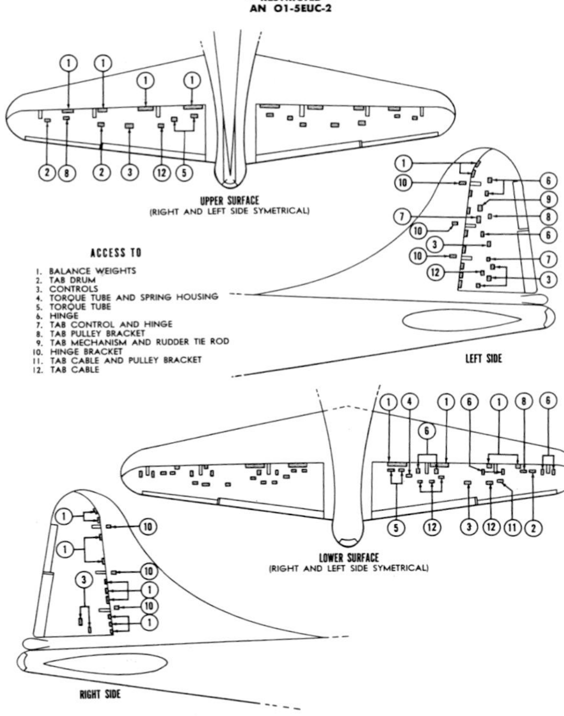

UPPER SURFACE
(RIGHT AND LEFT SIDE SYMETRICAL)

ACCESS TO
1. BALANCE WEIGHTS
2. TAB DRUM
3. CONTROLS
4. TORQUE TUBE AND SPRING HOUSING
5. TORQUE TUBE
6. HINGE
7. TAB CONTROL AND HINGE
8. TAB PULLEY BRACKET
9. TAB MECHANISM AND RUDDER TIE ROD
10. HINGE BRACKET
11. TAB CABLE AND PULLEY BRACKET
12. TAB CABLE

LEFT SIDE

LOWER SURFACE
(RIGHT AND LEFT SIDE SYMETRICAL)

RIGHT SIDE

Figure 3-3. Empennage Access Doors and Inspection Plates
RESTRICTED

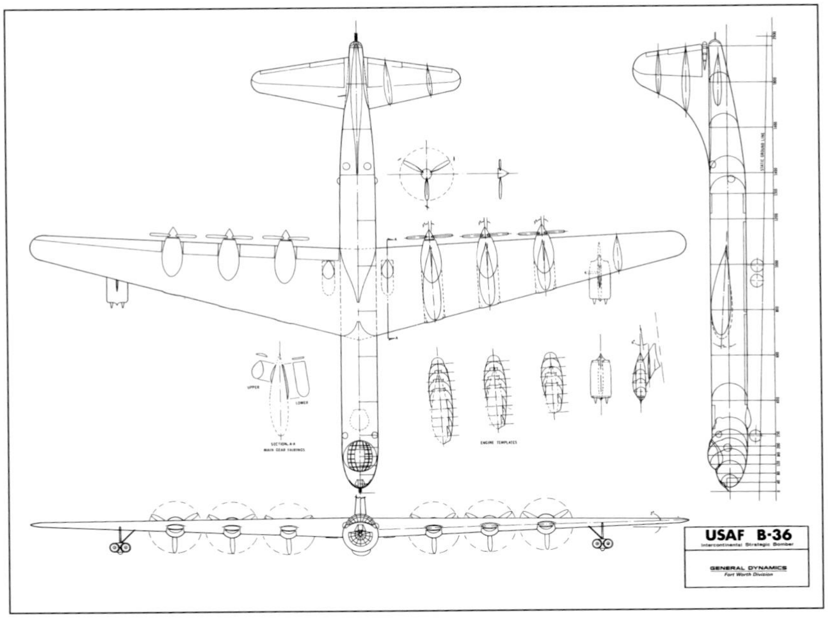

USAF B-36
Intercontinental Strategic Bomber

GENERAL DYNAMICS
Fort Worth Division

RESTRICTED
AN 01-5EUC-2

DOORS
OPENINGS
PANELS

RESTRICTED
AN 01-5EUC-2

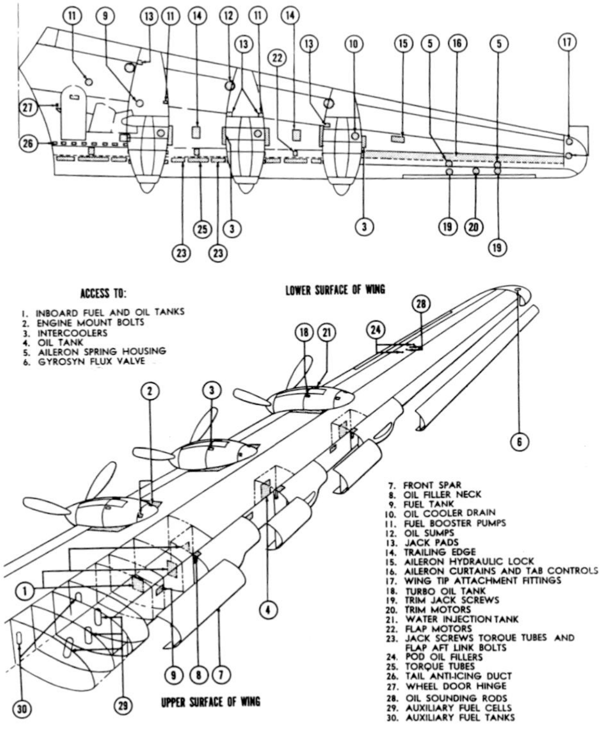

ACCESS TO:
1. INBOARD FUEL AND OIL TANKS
2. ENGINE MOUNT BOLTS
3. INTERCOOLERS
4. OIL TANK
5. AILERON SPRING HOUSING
6. GYROSYN FLUX VALVE

LOWER SURFACE OF WING

7. FRONT SPAR
8. OIL FILLER NECK
9. FUEL TANK
10. OIL COOLER DRAIN
11. FUEL BOOSTER PUMPS
12. OIL SUMPS
13. JACK PADS
14. TRAILING EDGE
15. AILERON HYDRAULIC LOCK
16. AILERON CURTAINS AND TAB CONTROLS
17. WING TIP ATTACHMENT FITTINGS
18. TURBO OIL TANK
19. TRIM JACK SCREWS
20. TRIM MOTORS
21. WATER INJECTION TANK
22. FLAP MOTORS
23. JACK SCREWS TORQUE TUBES AND
    FLAP AFT LINK BOLTS
24. POD OIL FILLERS
25. TORQUE TUBES
26. TAIL ANTI-ICING DUCT
27. WHEEL DOOR HINGE
28. OIL SOUNDING RODS
29. AUXILIARY FUEL CELLS
30. AUXILIARY FUEL TANKS

UPPER SURFACE OF WING

Figure 3-1. Wing Access Doors and Inspection Plates
RESTRICTED

ACCESS TO:
1. NOSE TURRET
2. LOOP ANTENNA
3. CONTROLS
4. INTERPHONE CIRCUIT FILTER
5. FORWARD CABIN
6. CATWALK
7. COMMUNICATION TUBE
8. NOSE WHEEL
9. GUN TURRETS
10. EXTERNAL POWER RECEPTACLE
11. HYDRAULIC LINES
12. OXYGEN FILLER VALVE
13. WING CRAWLWAY
14. AFT CABIN
15. TAIL SECTION
16. FIN
17. STABILIZER
18. ELEVATOR
19. TAIL TURRET
20. STABILIZING JACK PAD
21. RADOME AND EQUIPMENT
22. HYDRAULIC BRAKE HAND PUMP
23. BOMB BAYS

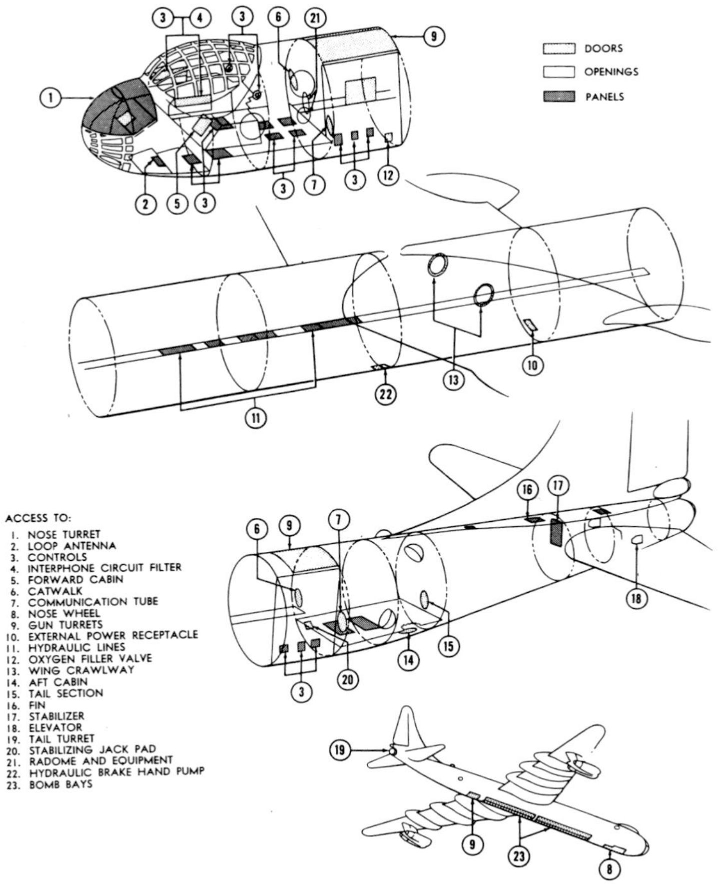

Figure 3-2. Fuselage Access Doors and Inspection Plates
RESTRICTED

Opposite page: *Access diagrams from the B-36 erection manual, plus the three-view drawing that General Dynamics handed out to the public during the 1970s. The two sides of the aircraft were largely mirror images of each other, especially the wings.* (U.S. Air Force and General Dynamics)

The modification of a B-36B (44-92057) to include the jet engines was authorized on 4 January 1949, and the aircraft made its first flight on 26 March 1949. Due to the unavailability of J47 engines, it had four Allison J35-A-19 engines in the pods under the outer wing panels. The pods on this aircraft differed somewhat from production models by not having the sculpted lower surface that housed the outrigger landing gear and landing light on the B-47. The production pods delivered by Boeing were externally identical to their B-47 counterparts, although they deleted some internal structure and the landing gear doors were fixed in the closed position. The prototype installation also did not include the sway-brace between the pylon and lower wing surface that was used on production examples to correct a small vibration problem. A second B-36B (44-92046) was also equipped with J47-GE-11 engines for additional high-altitude testing. Neither of these aircraft were equipped with the other changes specified for the B-36D (bomb bay doors, etc.), and both were among the last B-models converted to the full B-36D configuration. The first aircraft was also used to evaluate the potential use of 16-foot, four-bladed propellers in place of the normal three-bladed units. This was intended to mitigate a vibration problem that had long plagued the B-36. The tests were reportedly inconclusive but led, at least indirectly, to the development of a revised square-tip, three-bladed propeller that would be introduced on the B-36H.

As usual for a B-36 first flight, Beryl Erickson and Doc Witchell were at the controls of 44-92057 when it made its first flight with the jet pods. Also on board were William "Bill" P. Easley, J.D. McEachern, MSgt. G.S. Fish, R.O. Garlington, and Robert Moller. Although the first flight took place at 17:50 hours on a Saturday, several thousand Convair employees turned out to watch it. The flight lasted 3 hours and 15 minutes.[4]

The last 11 B-36Bs were equipped with the jet engines on the assembly line, with seven becoming[*] RB-36Ds and four being completed as B-36Ds prior to delivery. All of these aircraft were completed to the full D-model standard on the line. On 19 January 1949 the Air Force issued a new contract (AF33-038-2182) to Convair to cover the production of 39 additional[†] B-36s beyond the 95 on the original contract. By October 1949 the contract had increased to 75 new aircraft, and would ultimately be extended to cover 205 aircraft up through most of the B-36H models.

The original order for 100 (later reduced to 95) B-36s was based on a unit cost of $4,692,392 per aircraft, of which nearly 50 percent was government-furnished equipment (GFE). The breakdown was: airframe, $2,530,112; engines (installed), $589,899; propellers, $184,218;

B-36s undergoing modification and maintenance in San Diego. When the ramps immediately around the Convair facility were full, aircraft were shuffled off to auxiliary areas by the bay. Note the three maintenance docks facing the road. (San Diego Aerospace Museum Collection)

---

[*] This has led to a lot of confusion over the years. The Air Force considered these aircraft new-build B/RB-36Ds and carried them as such on official paperwork. Since they had been ordered as B-36Bs, Convair continued to count them as B-models that were modified into D-models.
[†] This covered all of the new-build B-36D and RB-36D aircraft.

Project SAN-SAN performed major maintenance and modifications on the B-36 fleet. Here a B-36D-15-CF (49-2657) is shown at San Diego – the program was also active at the San Antonio depot in Texas. As with most B-36 activities at San Diego, work continued well into the night in order to maintain a credible strike force. (San Diego Aerospace Museum)

electronics, $55,974; ordnance, $30,241; armament, $747,681. Modification of these aircraft to RB-36E and B/RB-36D standard added $1,556,294 per aircraft, for a total of $6,248,686. The second increment of 75 B-36s only cost $4,732,939 per aircraft, including a new bomb/nav system and upgraded engines. Part of this reduction was based on the write-off of the production tooling costs after the initial production run. The breakdown of these later aircraft was about 58.2 percent GFE and 41.8 percent Convair. Including the $435,623 cost to design the bomber and $39,475,234 for the two experimental models (XB-36 and YB-36), the first 95 B-36s cost the government $988,506,574 in FY49 dollars.[5]

The third B-36D (44-92090) was used for an accelerated service test program, and flew more than 500 hours during the first 73 days. During this period, the aircraft underwent a thorough inspection that required a 7-day down period every 120 hours. Each flight was a simulated tactical mission that was accomplished as close as practical to how a normal Air Force unit would fly the airplane. The missions attacked "targets" that ranged from the Dakotas to Florida, and from the Pacific to the Atlantic. Most of the simulated bombing runs were conducted at 40,000 feet. Flights averaged approximately 25 hours each, although one lasted over 39 hours.

The program was intended to evaluate how various components behaved under extended operation at high altitudes and long ranges. The flights also served two other purposes, although they were decidedly secondary in nature. First, they allowed many Air Force personnel an opportunity to train on long-range flights with Convair engineers offering advice. The flights also allowed engi-

A B-36D-25-CF (49-2658) at RAF Lakenheath on 20 January 1951 during Operation UNITED KINGDOM. A couple of months later, on 27 April 1951, this aircraft crashed 25 miles northeast of Oklahoma City after a midair collision with a North American F-51 Mustang. Twelve crewmen in the B-36 were killed in the accident. (U.S. Air Force via the Robert F. Dorr Collection)

neering and design personnel the chance to better familiarize themselves with the problems that occurred during long-duration missions. The last flight of the test program was in mid-November 1950, completing 1,008 flight hours.[6]

The first new-build B-36D (originally ordered as a B-model) flew on 11 July 1949, and the Air Force accepted its first B-36D (49-2653) on 22 August 1950. Although officially assigned to the 11th BW at Carswell, the aircraft was immediately sent to Eglin AFB for testing. The 26 new-build B-36Ds were delivered five in August 1950, five in September, one in October, two in November, one in December, three in January 1951, six in March, two in April, and the last one in August 1951 (FY52). This last aircraft carried an early serial number (49-2655), but a very late block number (35) and was delivered substantially after its production line mates. This aircraft had been used by Convair as the prototype for various "crew comfort" items that would be introduced on later models, explaining its late delivery.[7]

A decision was made to retrofit the jet engines to all existing B-36Bs (becoming B-36Ds)* as well as the B-36As being remanufactured into RB-36Es. The Air Force authorized the conversions as an extension of contract AF33-038-2182, the current production contract. The Fort Worth plant was already consumed building new B-36s and remanufacturing the B-36As, so after the first four B-36Bs (44-92026, 034, 053, and 054) were converted, the modification effort was transferred to San Diego. At either location, each aircraft was completely overhauled and new control surfaces, jet engines, and the snap-action bomb bay doors were added. The effort was extensive – all of the control surfaces were removed, the outer wing panels were taken off to be strengthened to accommodate the jet pods, the engines and all accessories were removed and sent to Kelly AFB, the existing fuel tanks were resealed, and the new auxiliary fuel tanks were added into the inner wings. In addition, the electronics were brought up-to-date. Still, it was much less effort than required to remanufacture a B-36A into an RB-36E. Most of the disassembly occurred outdoors in the new work docks, but reassembly was accomplished with four aircraft at a time mostly enclosed in Building 3 – only the empennage could not be accommodated by the building. The aircraft were reassigned later block numbers, although some overlapped block numbers applied to the new-build D-models.

The first B-36B (44-92043) arrived at San Diego on 6 April 1950, and made its initial flight as a B-36D on 5 December 1950. The aircraft made two additional test flights, on 10 and 16 December, before being redelivered to the Air Force the following day. The last modified aircraft (44-92081) was redelivered to the Air Force on 14 February 1952. Before beginning test flights at San Diego, modified aircraft had their engines run up, navigation equipment checked, and the guns were fired into a special gun butt built across the runways from the Convair plant. Each gun fired approximately 50 rounds of nonexplosive ammunition, and the first test was conducted on 21 November 1950. Similar tests were conducted on each B-36 at Fort Worth prior

The B-36s ventured far and wide, usually without stopping or refueling. Here is Mt. Fuji in Japan as seen from a B-36. (Dave Fleming via the Frederick A. Johnsen Collection)

to delivery. In fact, by the end of 1950, B-36 tests had fired 50 tons (200,000 rounds) of 20-mm ammunition in the gun butt at the north end of the Fort Worth facility.[8]

The performance benefit from the jet engines was significant. Although originally the Air Force claimed the jet engines boosted the top speed to 439 mph at 32,120 feet and the service ceiling to 45,020 feet, this was later revised to 406 mph at 36,200 feet and a service ceiling of 43,800 feet. Whether this discrepancy was due to miscalculation, some overzealous public relations (the Congressional hearings were underway at the time), or changes in the aircraft themselves is not certain. The use of the jet engines reduced the takeoff run by almost 2,000 feet and effectively doubled the normal rate of climb to 900 feet per minute. The B-36 flew well on four or even three piston engines, so it was common practice to shut down some of the engines during cruise. The turbojets were normally used only over the target area or for takeoff and climbout.

Although still a great deal lower than the performance expected from the B-52, the B-36 was no longer considered a "sitting duck" and could outrun most contemporary fighters at high altitude. (The speed quoted for an aircraft is usually at its best operating altitude; for contemporary fighters this was about 20,000 feet. The fighters generally lost several hundred miles per hour by the time they got to 40,000 feet, if they could get there at all.) The Air Force was satisfied to rely on the B-36 until the development of the new Boeing B-52 was completed.

On 16 January 1951, six B-36Ds were flown from Carswell to the United Kingdom, landing at RAF Lakenheath after having staged through Limestone AFB, Maine. The flight, dubbed Operation UNITED KINGDOM, was led by Colonel Thomas P. Gerrity, commander of the 11th BW. The flight returned to Carswell on 20 January, marking the first time that B-36s had deployed outside the United States.

---

* All of the B-36Bs that were converted after production became B-36Ds; none were converted into RB-36Ds.

The long missions usually flown by the B-36 caused a great deal of fatigue for the crew. In an effort to improve the environment inside the aircraft, during mid-1951 Convair began installing sound deadening panels inside each pressurized compartment. Different-sized panels made of wool and fiberglass were designed that snapped onto bulkheads inside the aircraft and were installed as the aircraft rotated through San Diego or Fort Worth for upgrades. There were 97 panels in the forward compartment and 59 in the aft cabin. Although each panel began by being cut from a template, each was tailored to the particular aircraft into which it was installed. In addition, 30 pieces of vinyl carpeting were installed on the floor. These modifications also provided a certain amount of thermal protection inside the aircraft, further increasing crew comfort. Unfortunately, these would be among the items removed during the Featherweight program.[9]

By this time the Air Force and Convair were also installing additional crew comfort items, including expanded galleys, better bunks complete with mattresses, blankets, and pillows, and a variety of storage areas for personal items. The new galley, equipped with two electric burners, was located in the aft compartment and included skillets, pots, pans, and lids for cooking, along with knives, forks, spoons, and ladles. Two plug-in hot cups were provided for heating soups, coffee, and other liquids, and an electric oven allowed baking bread or other foods. A small refrigerator was provided to store perishable foods.[10]

Two folding tables were installed along the sides of the aft compartment where the lower bunks could be used as chairs. This allowed up to four men to eat in relative comfort. A special container was provided that allowed hot meals to be transferred to the forward cabin using the normal dolly. Strung between the bunks were small racks for storing personal items, and new storage compartments near the top of the cabin were provided for kit bags and other items that were previously stored on the floor. The aft cabin lavatory facilities were upgraded with a sink, mirror, commode, and privacy curtains. A smaller, but similar, lavatory was added to the forward compartment.

A flight to French Morocco was made on 6 December 1951 when six B-36s of the 11th BW landed at Sidi Slimane AB, having flown 5,000 miles nonstop from Carswell. During the 20-hour flight the crews made good use of the new bunks and galleys that had been installed, and reportedly ate steaks, bacon, and eggs during the flight. For the next five years, it would become relatively routine for B-36s to deploy to Sidi Slimane and nearby Nouasseur AB.[11]

Despite 2 years of engineering test flights and high-priority modifications, many of the problems remained unsolved, although progress was being made through gradual modifications and carefully devised fixes. Changes in the electrical system had largely eliminated fire hazards during ground refueling operations. Better sealant introduced during 1952–53 reduced fuel tank leakage, but sealing the fuel tanks required a lot of work. Each B-36 had approximately 26,000 rivet heads that protruded into the fuel tanks. In order to seal the rivets, a worker first had to clean and dry the area around each rivet. A brush was then used to apply a light coat of a putty-like compound called Proseal, which was then allowed to dry. Each rivet head was then covered by a small "dimple" of Proseal that was applied and formed by hand. Then the entire area around all rivets was covered by a light coat of Proseal and allowed to dry for 24 hours. An average worker could apply 350 dimples during an 8-hour shift. The landing gear struts and some bulkheads had been prone to developing stress cracks due to the sheer size and weight of the aircraft, but better casting and machining techniques resulted in these failures being almost totally eliminated in new aircraft. Earlier aircraft were repaired as necessary. Nevertheless, problems persisted.[12]

At the end of 1951 the B-36's defensive armament system still remained operationally unsuitable. In fact, SAC viewed the "gunnery and defensive armament as the weakest link in the present B-36 capability." This was despite the fact that beginning in May 1950 a series of 6 major and 74 minor changes had been made to the B-2 system that finally reduced the dispersion condition to acceptable limits.[13]

In April 1952 SAC ordered a series of gunnery missions known as FIRE AWAY to be completed by July. These showed that the marginal performance of the B-36's defensive armament system was due to roughly equal parts of design deficiencies, poor maintenance, and inadequate gunnery crew training. This prompted TEST FIRE, a 3-month exercise that began in September 1952 using RB-36Ds from the 28th SRW.

Actually, this was not the first time the B-36 had conducted an indepth gunnery evaluation. In October 1949 a single B-36B (44-92042) from the 11th BW/26th BS was modified with a 35-mm Vitarama camera in lieu of the right 20-mm gun in the tail turret. The first mission was flown at 25,000 feet on 25 October over the range at Eglin AFB, Florida. Additional tests were conducted at Eglin against F-80s during November, then continued at Carswell against F-82 Twin Mustangs based at Bergstrom AFB, Texas. Additional tests were conducted with a B-36D (49-2653) from the 11th BW during September 1950.[14]

B-to-D conversion work at night in San Diego. Note how much of the aircraft has been disassembled and the protective coating over the glazed panels. (San Diego Aerospace Museum Collection)

As anticipated, TEST FIRE confirmed the overall conclusion of FIRE AWAY that the performance of the B-36's defensive armament was unsatisfactory. In light of this, HIT MORE was launched in early 1953 to pool the efforts of the Air Force, Convair, and General Electric to finally devise an effective defensive system. The first step was the modification of six B-36Ds to assess the actual airborne accuracy of the fire-control system after several new or updated components had been incorporated. The HIT MORE results proved encouraging, and by midyear no critical problems had been uncovered. The B-36's defensive armament could be made to work, after numerous minor modifications. More effective training of the gunners and maintenance personnel was the final link in obtaining a truly operational system. In many ways, however, it was a moot victory. Although the B-36 had the most impressive defensive armament ever fitted to a production aircraft, its capabilities were largely overcome by events. The second generation of jet fighters would prove to be too fast to engage accurately, and the development of air-to-air and surface-to-air missiles would render the guns worthless.

One of the aircraft (44-92054) modified for HIT MORE would continue in the role of an armament test aircraft for the rest of its career. It was finally retired in September 1957 after making 244 flights that covered 400,000 miles in 1,600 flight hours. This was the last B-36 based at Fort Worth except for the NB-36H atomic research aircraft. During its time as a B-36 armament testbed the aircraft fired more than 250,000 rounds of 20-mm ammunition. In 1955 the aircraft had a radome grafted onto its nose to test various nose-defense radar systems, and at various times sported other protuberances (such as two RB-style ECM radomes) from the nose. The aircraft spent its last 2 years testing various B-58 systems. The aircraft was also the prototype for the R-4360-53 engine installation. Doc Witchell took the aircraft on its first flight on 18 February 1949, but the aircraft "belonged" to G.I. Davis who was the pilot on 158 of its 244 flights.[15]

In August and September 1953, several B-36s from the 92nd BW completed the first flight to the Far East, visiting bases in Japan, Okinawa, and Guam. Operation BIG STICK was a 3-day exercise that came shortly after the end of hostilities in Korea and demonstrated U.S. determination to keep peace in the region. On 15–16 October 1953, the 92nd BW left Fairchild AFB, Washington, for a 90-day deployment to Guam, marking the first time an entire B-36 wing had been deployed overseas.

B-36F

On 13 April 1949, the Air Force ordered 36 additional B-36s from Convair under the same contract (AF33-038-2182) that had initiated B-36D production. This initial order consisted of 17 B-36Fs and 19 RB-36Fs, although an additional 19 bombers and 5 RB-36Fs would be ordered the following year. The B-36F differed from the B-36D primarily in having improved R-4360-53 engines rated at 3,500 hp (dry) or 3,800 with water/alcohol injection. The –53 installation had already been tested on a modified B-36D (44-92054), but would still prove troublesome in initial service. Among 25 major improvements in the

No, its not an RB-36 – this is the armament test ship (B-36D-10-CF, 44-92054) with its flight crew after its last flight on 30 August 1957. Note the two RB-36-style radomes under the nose and the object over the glazed panel. The aircraft had been used to test various B-36 and B-58 systems, and had sported a variety of bumps and bulges during that time. Interestingly, the nose gun sight has been removed. (Lockheed Martin)

new engine was the use of direct fuel injection and a new ignition system that greatly increased reliability during high-altitude operations. The engines boosted the top speed to 417 mph, and the service ceiling rose to 44,000 feet. Late production aircraft (beginning with 50-1064) also had two A-7 dispensers capable of dropping 1,400 pounds of chaff to confuse enemy radar, although some aircraft used one A-6 and one A-7 dispenser instead. All aircraft were delivered with the K-3A bomb/nav system and the offensive capabilities were unchanged. There were very few other changes, mainly just a minor rearrangement of some cabin equipment.[16]

There were major changes in the defensive systems, however. Initially, the B-36F featured a new 2CFR87C-1 fire-control system. This replaced the mechanical computing mechanism with a new electrical unit capable of continuous high-speed output. It also contained improved gyroscope measuring circuits, improved attack factors, and was designed to be easier to maintain. Beginning with 50-1064 an improved C-2 system was installed. The C-2 further improved the electronics, and also featured new Rhodes-Lewis gun chargers in an effort to reduce gunfire dispersion.[17]

The first B-36F was inspected by an 18-man "689* Board" during March 1951, including a demonstration by an 8-man Convair mainte-

---

* At the time, inspection committees recorded their results on a "Form 689," hence the name.

nance team of how to remove and replace one of the new –53 engines. The Convair team detached the propeller and air plug, then removed the engine and placed it on a stand where it was configured like a replacement engine would have been from the depot. The team then installed the engine and reattached the propeller and air plug. Discounting the need to reconfigure the engine, the elapsed time for the engine swap was 4 hours and 42 minutes, a new record.[18]

The first B-36F made its maiden flight on 18 November 1950 and began "accelerated service tests" by a combined Convair and Air Force test team. The aircraft were flown by Air Force personnel, but maintained jointly by Convair and Air Force personnel. The purpose of the tests was to provide information for the development of systems and assemblies, and to provide operational and maintenance data on the airplane and the new –53 engine. By operating the aircraft at Convair's facilities, the service life of parts or assemblies could be carefully evaluated and at the same time, the factory maintenance facilities and methods could be used as examples to improve Air Force procedures. Under these conditions, the Air Force pilots, engineers, and crewmen were exposed to "the optimum in training by 'living with' the developments and operational problems evolved on the B-36F and RB-36F airplanes almost from the time of their operational inception."[19]

Six B-36Fs (49-2703, 49-2704, 49-2705, 49-2670, 49-2671, and 49-2672) were used during the accelerated service tests, and Convair conducted detailed inspections of the aircraft every 100 flight hours. The flying phase of the test series ended on 11 July 1951, followed by some paperwork before the first F-model (49-2671) was delivered to the 7th BW/9th BS on 18 August 1951. All 34 B-36Fs were delivered to the 7th BW at Carswell.[20]

At first, the R-4360-53 engines were not entirely satisfactory because of excessive torque pressure as well as ground air cooling and combustion problems. However, these problems were resolved fairly quickly, and the new engines proved to be quite reliable in service. The fuel injection, in particular, eased much of the maintenance and operational constraints from the engine.[21]

On 6 March 1952, a new B-36F (50-1067) burned on the ramp at Carswell after its left main landing gear failed while the aircraft was parked. Fortunately, only minor injuries were sustained by the crew and ground personnel. This prompted concerns over the integrity of the landing gear on the F-model, and beginning on 20 March all B-36Fs were cycled through inspections and repairs. A special team from the San Antonio depot arrived at Carswell to perform the work. It was subsequently decided that all B-36s required landing gear modifications,

In the foreground is a B-36F-5-CF (49-2683), but of more interest is the "Boston Camera" airplane (ERB-36D-1-CF, 44-92088) in the background. Note the large opening on the side of the fuselage so that the Boston Camera could be used, and that the aircraft retained her guns even as a test ship. An early AFFTC marking may be seen on the side of the B-36 nearest the camera. The photo was taken at Edwards in 1955. (AFFTC via the Tony Landis Collection)

The Convair delivery line in November 1952. The nearest aircraft (only part of the tail visible) is a B-36H-35-CF (51-5730). Next in line is B-36H-25-CF (51-5723). Interestingly, both aircraft appear to have fabric rudders. (Lockheed Martin)

and aircraft were cycled through a modification center at San Diego as well as being modified in San Antonio and Fort Worth. The bad luck surrounding the F-model's introduction to service continued on 5 August 1952 – gasoline overflowed from the No. 3 tank vent on a B-36F (49-2679) and was ignited by the exhaust from a B-10 power unit on the ramp. Three crew members sustained minor injuries, and the aircraft from the 7th BW/436th BS was a complete loss.[22]

By the time the B-36F was being delivered, a revolution was beginning, although few realized it at the time. Previously, on the B-36 and all other aircraft programs, complex mathematical equations had been solved by engineers using slide rules, or by "computers" – usually young women trained in specific areas of calculus or other higher math. During early 1951 Convair purchased an "electronic brain" called REAC (Reeves Electronic Analog Computer) that used 625 vacuum tubes. The $77,000 computer was an "all-electronic differential analyzer for speed dynamic solution of simultaneous differ-

ential equations." Convair estimated that one sample problem would have taken 2,950 man-days – almost 11 years – to accomplish using the best hand methods. REAC solved the problem in only 108 man-days. The cost saving was significant. The hand method would have cost $73,750 in salary and benefits, while REAC totaled only $3,240 for the effort. REAC had been manufactured by the Reeves Instrument Company in New York and weighed 5,800 pounds. A similar analog computer had been purchased by the San Diego division in 1947 to assist in the Atlas ballistic missile program.[23]

B-36G

The B-36G was the designation initially applied to a swept-wing, jet-powered version of the B-36F. Two B-36Fs (49-2676 and 49-2684) were ordered converted to B-36Gs, but the designation was changed to YB-60 before they were built. See Chapter 10 for more details.

A typical mid-life B-36 arrives in San Diego on 6 December 1950. A close examination will reveal that the periscopic bomb sight has been installed, although the glazed panel remains. Unusually, there are no production numbers on the nose or aft fuselage, making identification impossible. (Convair)

B-36H

First announced on 5 November 1950, the B-36H was the major production version of the B-36, with a total of 83 being built. The initial contract (an extension of AF33-038-2182) for 15 B-36H and 8 RB-36H aircraft was announced on 5 September 1951. However, the contract had been signed over a year earlier resulting in the aircraft having FY50 serial numbers. An additional 44 bombers and 39 reconnaissance variants would be ordered in FY51, with 24 more B-36Hs and 26 RB-36Hs ordered in FY52.

The B-36H was substantially similar to the B-36F that preceded it, but relocated the K-system electronic components into the pressurized compartment to facilitate in-flight maintenance, and featured a rearranged flight deck with a second flight engineer station.[*] In addition to the second flight engineer station, the revised flight deck featured a new instrument panel for the pilot and copilot, and improved night lighting at all four crew stations. The mockup of the new flight deck arrangement had been inspected during August 1950, at essentially the same time as the first B-36D was delivered. Despite the attention to detail paid during the development of the new flight deck, Air Force evaluators found a few items to criticize once the aircraft entered service. For instance, the pilot's gyro horizon was considered too small and was unreliable – interestingly, the copilot's was found to be adequate in all regards. The space available on the flight deck was considered "highly unsatisfactory" and it was recommended that the flight engineer's panel should be moved aft about 12 inches and the pilot's pedestal shortened by 6 inches to "enhance the emergency escape of the co-pilot and assistant flight engineer."[24]

The B/RB-36H-1 models (12 aircraft) were equipped with the same C-2 defensive system as the later B-36Fs. However, beginning with Block 5 aircraft, a new C-3 system was introduced that incorporated dynamic gun mounts designed to further eliminate the fire dispersion problem that had plagued the B-36 since the beginning. This consisted of a spring cushion arrangement that allowed the cannon to move back and forth on tracks along the line of fire, allowing some of the shock to be absorbed by the springs instead of being transferred to the turret.[25]

A new AN/APG-41 gun-laying tail radar was introduced on 51-5742. This improved unit used twin tail radomes, and was essentially two APG-32s that were coupled together, allowing one radar to track an immediate threat while the second continued to scan for other threats. The left-hand (facing the tail) unit could scan from 60 degrees right to 80 degrees left; the right-hand unit could scan 80 degrees right to 60 degrees left.[26]

The engines were six R-4630-53s and four J47-GE-19s, the same as on the B-36F. Slightly improved ECM equipment was included, as were two A-6 or A-7 dispensers that carried 1,400 pounds of chaff to confuse enemy radars (something introduced on late B-36Fs).[27]

The B-36H made its first flight on 5 April 1952, although deliveries to operational units did not begin until December 1952. One of the reasons deliveries were held up was that an RB-36F had suffered a pressure bulkhead failure while flying at 33,000 feet. The accident was traced to a defective bulkhead, and all B-36s were restricted to altitudes below 25,000 feet until the entire fleet could be inspected and defective

---

[*] There had always been a second flight engineer as part of the crew, but the B-36H was the first model to provide a second station for him.

bulkheads replaced. While the accident investigation was ongoing, the Air Force declined to accept any new aircraft from Convair.

The B-36's original propeller blades had structural limitations that resulted in flight restrictions which hampered performance. There had also been constant concerns over propeller-induced vibrations and buffeting against the fuselage sides and the horizontal stabilizer. This had been recognized even before the first flight of the XB-36, leading to investigations of using 16-foot, four-bladed propellers instead of the normal 19-foot, three-bladed units. Similar propellers had been test-fitted on the XB-36 prior to its roll-out, and had been flight test-ed on a B-36B (44-92057) during 1950. Since the B-36 was capable of cruising with some of the engines shut down, many pilots opted to shut down the inboard engines and feather the propellers, easing the vibration on the fuselage and buffeting on the stabilizer. The evaluations of the four-bladed propeller were apparently inconclusive, and the decision was made to develop a new three-bladed unit instead.

A revised blade, made by a special flash-welding process, had a slightly broader chord and less pitch to minimize buffeting. The new propeller could be used freely except for landing and takeoff. The new unit was called a "high-altitude propeller" by Convair. The obvious external difference was the use of square blade tips instead of the orig-inal rounded tips. This blade weighed an extra 20 pounds (1,170 pounds each), but its greater efficiency promised to compensate for the small loss in aircraft range. A batch of 1,175 of the new blades were ordered for installation on B-36Hs on the production line. Additional blades were subsequently ordered and retrofitted to most earlier aircraft, including the XC-99.[28]

The Air Force accepted 32 B-36Hs in FY52 – seven in December 1951, five in January 1952, three in February, five in March, and four in each of the next 3 months. It received 43 B-36Hs in FY53 – four in July 1952, four in August, seven in September, three in October, four in November, two in December, four in January 1953, and three dur-ing each of the next 5 months. Eight B-36Hs were accepted in FY54 – three in July 1953, three in August, and two in September.[29]

The B-36H cost $11,321 more than the B-36F. Airframe costs were lower, but the price of the engines showed an increase, as did arma-ment, electronics, and propellers. The new costs were: airframe, $2,077,785; engines (installed), $874,526; propellers, $214,186; elec-tronics, $80,272; ordnance, $30,241; and armament, $872,436.

A B-36 deployment on 2–21 February 1953 turned out to be par-ticularly tragic. As part of a simulated tactical mission (Operation STYLESHOW) to RAF Fairford in the United Kingdom, 18 B-36s from the 7th BW flew from Carswell to the staging base at Goose Bay, Labrador on 2 and 3 February. One B-36 developed mechanical prob-lems and returned to Carswell. On 6 February, the remaining 17 air-craft departed Goose Bay headed for Fairford, encountering severe weather enroute. Although 16 aircraft managed to land safely, one B-36H (51-5719) ran out of fuel after holding for an excessive amount of time and executing two missed GCA (ground controlled approach) approaches. The GCA center at Fairford was understaffed and manned by inexperienced controllers, and this undoubtedly played a role in the crash. The aircraft was abandoned in flight, and there were

no injuries in the 7 February crash. For the next week, the B-36s flew training missions out of Fairford. Fourteen of the B-36s departed for Goose Bay on 13 February; two B-36Hs remained in the UK for "special weapons training." Unfortunately, on 13 February the GCA controllers at Goose Bay misdirected one B-36H (51-5729) which flew into a hill while attempting to land. Two of the 17 crew members aboard were killed and the aircraft destroyed. The 13 remaining air-craft eventually returned to Carswell, with the last arriving on 21 February. The two aircraft that had stayed at Fairford returned to Carswell on 23 February.[31]

Although unusual, the B-36 could be safely landed with very few engines running. On 27 March 1954, Captain Berry H. Young from the 7th BW/9th BS successfully landed his B-36H at Carswell with all three R4360s on the right wing and all four jets inoperative. To further complicate matters, a hydraulic failure meant that the landing gear had to be lowered manually, and the flaps were inoperative. The landing proved somewhat uneventful, and the crew and aircraft were intact. Around Carswell this became known as the "miracle landing." The crew was presented the Carswell "Crew of the Month" award, and also received a personal commendation from General LeMay.[32]

TANBO XIV

One B-36H (51-5706) was converted into a prototype in-flight refu-eling tanker. The "XIV" referred to the Mark XIV refueling reel that was eventually installed. Searching for a tanker that could refuel jet air-craft at higher altitudes and speeds, in late 1951 SAC became interested in a readily convertible B-36 tanker-bomber (Tanbo). On 15 January 1952 the Air Force authorized Convair to equip one B-36 with a probe-and-drogue refueling system for tests. The modification contract was approved in February 1952 and the work was completed in May. A large reel for the refueling hose was bolted into bomb bay No. 4 and bladder fuel tanks to hold jet fuel were permanently installed in the other three bomb bays. The removable portion of the design consisted of a framework mounted in bomb bay No. 4 that supported a Mark XIV reel, fuel transfer pumps, and an extendable hydraulically-operated boom. Removing the reel would allow atomic weapons to be carried in bomb bay No. 4, but the other bomb bays were unavailable

This is, apparently, the only remaining exterior photo of Tanbo (above). To the right of it, a poor shot of the retractable refueling boom that deployed the hose from a reel in bomb bay No. 4 – Tanbo used the British probe-and-drogue technique instead of the later U.S. "flying boom" design. At right is the refueler's control panel inside the B-36. The program ran into unexpected problems and little real progress was made before the Air Force elected to proceed with the KC-135 instead. (Lockheed Martin)

since the jet fuel tanks were permanently installed. A windmill-type power source was mounted on the boom to feed the fuel pumps and to provide a means of extending the refueling hose away from the airplane. The boom could be retracted entirely within the airplane, and when extended the bomb bay doors formed a tight seal around the boom. There were almost 16,000 gallons of fuel available for transfer at a rate of 600 gallons per minute. This was equivalent to a B-47's internal and external fuel, but more probably could "top off" two or three B-47s on the way to their target. The converted B-36H tanker had a crew of nine and could be returned to a bomber configuration in 12 hours.[33]

Testing began in March 1953 using an F-84 as a receiver. However, due to difficulties with the British-made reel mechanism, the non-availability of adequate hose, and problems with governing the propeller transferring power to the fuel pumps, the tests were suspended on 27 May. The problems were not addressed before the advent of the Boeing KC-135 eliminated the need for the Tanbo concept. The Tanbo B-36H was released to the Rascal production program on 6 July 1954, and on 21 July the Air Force officially cancelled the Tanbo XIV project.

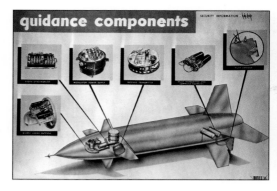

The Rascal was a sophisticated missile for the 1950s, with both internal and radio-relay guidance capabilities. The three-view drawing shows the dimensions. (Jay Miller Collection)

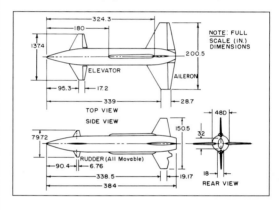

The photos in the center and right of the page (above) show the launch platform and recess fairing installed in bomb bay Nos. 3 and 4 to accommodate the Rascal. The drawing below shows the same items. The modifications were not permanent and could be removed as necessary if conventional bombing missions were required. In addition, a removable electronics package was installed in bomb bay No. 1 (see next page). (Lockheed Martin)

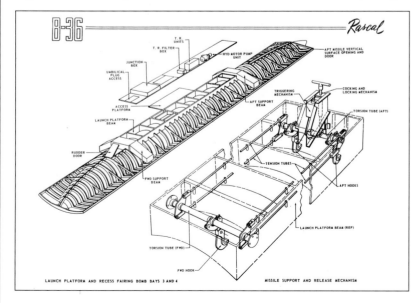

DB-36H

On 7 July 1952 the Air Materiel Command issued contract AF33(600)-21997 to Convair to integrate the B-36 with the Bell B-63 (later GAM-63) "Parasite Pilotless Bomber," more commonly called Rascal. The name "Rascal" was actually an acronym which stood for RAdar SCAnning Link, named for the guidance system that was used during the missile's dive on the target. The guidance system, developed jointly by Bell Avionics, Radio Corporation of America (RCA), and Texas Instruments, was installed aboard the controlling aircraft. The GAM-63 was powered by a Bell-designed 4,000-lbf liquid-fueled rocket engine made up of three vertical in-line thrust chambers. The missile was 31 feet long with a body diameter of 4 feet and could carry a 3,000-pound nuclear warhead up to 110 miles at a maximum speed of Mach 2.95. A retractable radio antenna was installed in the aft fuselage of the DB-36H to provide a data link to the missile. The missile itself was carried semi-submerged in the combined bomb bay Nos. 3 and 4,

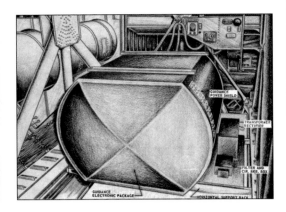

The left and center photos show a live Rascal being loaded into the YDB-36H (51-5710) at Kirtland AFB, New Mexico. All Rascal tests – except for some inert fit-checks – took place at Kirtland. A pressurized electronics package (right) was loaded into bomb bay No. 1 to provide the unique equipment necessary to launch and guide the Rascal. The two photos below are of Rascals at Kirtland, not necessarily for the B-36 program. (Jay Miller Collection)

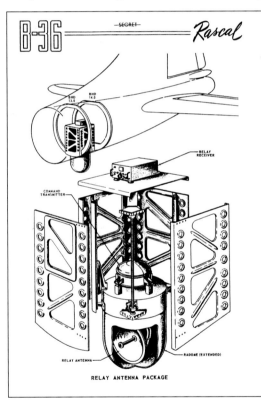

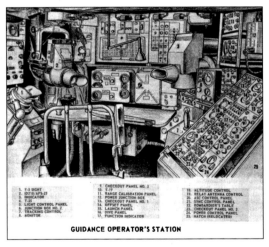

The only permanent modifications to the DB-36s were the addition of a retractable director antenna (above left and center) and some minor changes to the bombardier's station to allow him to check out, launch, and guide the missile. It was believed that these minor changes would not adversely impact the normal bomber mission if strikes were flown without the Rascal. In the end, the program was cancelled and only 3 of the original 11 aircraft were ever modified. (Lockheed Martin)

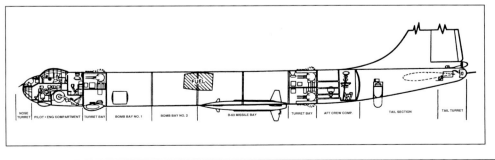

The only known series of photographs showing a Rascal being launched from a B-36 (51-5710, in this case). Note the deployed director antenna in both the shot above and the photo on the ground. (Jay Miller Collection)

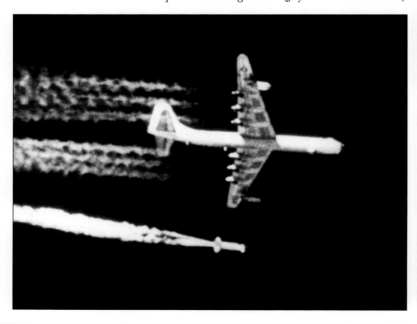

Photographic evidence that the early J-models were indeed equipped with turrets, contrary to some reports. The second aircraft in line, a B-36J-1-CF (52-2218), has its upper aft turrets deployed. (Convair)

hanging down about 18 inches while being carried. The "dished out" area of the bomb bay was equipped with a fiberglass cover that protected the inside of the bomb bay after the missile was released. An electronic guidance package was installed in bomb bay No. 1.[34]

Otherwise, the Rascal carriers were expected to be identical to the standard Featherweight II* B-36H configuration, including the use of R-4360-53 engines and J47-GE-19 turbojets. The standard crew of 15 was expected to be carried, except that the bombardier would have the added responsibility of launching and guiding the missile. Aircraft performance was expected to be unchanged from the standard B-36H.[35]

The contract included 30 hours of wind tunnel tests of the missile and B-36 in the mated configuration and during missile separation. Also included was a mock-up of the forward cabin with the new missile controls and a separate mock-up of the aft bomb bays (Nos. 3 and 4). A single B-36H (51-5710)† was ordered converted into a YDB-36H prototype, and the contract included provisions to modify a total of 12 B-36Hs into the "director-bomber" configuration. The production option was exercised on 26 May 1953 and the original schedule was to deliver all 11 DB-36Hs to the Air Force by the end of 1954. However, delays in the development of the Rascal and its guidance system quickly delayed the program by approximately 1 year. The final schedule called for two deliveries in late 1955 and eight more before 15 November 1956.[36]

The idea behind the Rascal was to improve the kill probability of the B-36 by significantly increasing the "target zone performance" using the Mach 2 Rascal. This also improved the chances of the B-36 surviving the mission since it no longer had to directly overfly the target and could remain well outside the enemy defense perimeter. The Rascal

equipment was designed to be easily removable from the B-36, allowing the aircraft to return to its basic bomber configuration in less than 12 hours. However, certain parts of the DB-36 modification were permanent, although they did not seriously detract from the normal bomber mission. For instance, the modifications to the bombardier's position included specialized guidance equipment that would remain with the aircraft, as would the retractable missile guidance antenna in the aft fuselage. Convair demonstrated that a fully-configured DB-36H could be converted back to its basic bomber configuration in 3 hours and 12 minutes – well short of the 12-hour requirement.[37]

The Rascal was loaded into the aft bomb bays and a guidance electronics package was loaded into bomb bay No. 1. In theory bomb bay No. 2 was available for small bomb loads, or perhaps to carry Buck Duck decoys, but this was never explicitly stated. The missile was dropped from the bomber approximately 100 miles from the target, and the rocket motors were ignited by a lanyard pull after the missile was free of the carrier aircraft. If the lanyard or its associated switch malfunctioned, a timer started the rockets a set time after release. The initial leg of Rascal flight was controlled by a self-contained inertial system that obtained reference information from the B-36 K-3A bomb/nav system prior to launch. This required some modifications to the K-3A, but none of these detracted from the primary functionality of the system. As the missile approached the target area, the bombardier in the B-36 took over guidance of the missile through the data link. The bombardier's station was equipped with a launch panel, terminal guidance equipment, relay antenna controls, and miscellaneous system controls. The guidance package installed in bomb bay No. 1 contained all of the Rascal interface equipment that did not require in-flight access.[38]

A typical mission profile involved loading the missile, taking off, cruising at an optimum altitude (probably around 25,000 feet), climbing to the 42,500-foot launch altitude, launching the missile, guiding the missile to the target, then returning to base. After takeoff, the missile control operator was responsible for keeping current wind and navigation data loaded into the K-3A system for downloading to the Rascal. Before the mission reached the point-of-no-return, the missile operator verified that the missile and its guidance system were functional. This included tuning the video relay receiver, altitude phasing, adjusting the terminal guidance tracking indicator, and verifying that the missile control surfaces were functional. As the mission approached the launch point, the terminal guidance system would be checked again.

The missile was partially preprogrammed for a given flight path, and it was necessary for the carrier to approach an "aim point" along a heading that connected the aim point and the target. A computer in the guidance package tracked the aircraft heading and azimuth to the target and automatically dropped the missile when the proper position was reached. Immediately after launch, the carrier aircraft initiated a rapid turn to return home while the missile operator (bom-

---

* A Standard Aircraft Characteristics was issued for a Featherweight III version, but close examination shows that the data is for a Featherweight II (as were the drawings, etc.) – it appears that the cover is misidentified. It could not be ascertained if there was ever an intent to use Featherweight III aircraft as B-63 carriers.

† The AFFTC test report and some other Air Force documentation lists this as a YDB-36H, but the aircraft history card does not confirm this. Still, it will be used here since it seems appropriate.

bardier) established a video link with the missile. Although the missile was flying based on its own inertial guidance, the B-36 operator could make minor adjustments via the data link. The missile typically would reach 50,000 feet altitude and a speed of approximately Mach 2.5 during its flight. The terminal guidance portion of the missile's flight was controlled by the operator in the B-36 via the video data link. For airburst detonations, the missile would still be traveling at approximately Mach 1.29 at the time the warhead exploded.[39]

The fuselage and cabin mock-ups were inspected by the Air Force on 18 November 1952, and the YDB-36H made its first flight on 3 July 1953. The Air Force conducted six flight tests to determine drag changes introduced by carrying the B-63 on the B-36. A total of 20 hours and 5 minutes were accumulated during the tests that ran from 31 July to 16 August 1953. The basic weight of the DB-36H was 175,917 pounds, with the B-63 adding another 18,200 pounds. During the tests, 500 gallons of fuel were purposefully left in each inboard wing tank to ensure that center-of-gravity limits were maintained while carrying the missile. Interestingly, the test series revealed no discernible difference in drag characteristics with or without the missile attached, or with the aft radome deployed. In fact, the test report noted that "… if the pilot did not know he was flying a YDB-36 he would not be able to detect any change in the handling characteristics as compared to a normal B-36F or B-36H under the same weight and c.g. conditions."[40]

The test group did, however, find a few minor items that needed to be corrected. The primary item centered around the retractable lower stabilizer on the missile. When the missile was installed on the ground, the stabilizer was folded 90 degrees from normal (i.e., it was parallel to the ground instead of perpendicular). Once the aircraft was airborne, the navigator or scanner used a hydraulic hand pump to lower the stabilizer to its flight position. If the B-36 needed to land, the procedure was reversed and the stabilizer folded since attempting to land otherwise would damage both the missile and the DB-36. The test group believed that an electrically-driven hydraulic pump operated from the navigator's station should be provided. The retractable aft radome also proved unsatisfactory, with the retraction mechanism generally refusing to work at high altitudes.[41]

The first Rascal air-launch test occurred on 30 September 1952 from a modified Boeing DB-50D. The first unpowered Rascal drop test from the YDB-36H was on 25 August 1953, and all went well. The aircraft was then grounded while the Bell-designed guidance system was installed. This was completed on 26 February 1954 and the aircraft redelivered to the Air Force on 22 July. On 6 July 1954 the Air Force released the B-36H (51-5706) that had been used in the Tanbo XIV experiments to the Rascal program. A week later this became the first aircraft to enter the Rascal production program, and was redelivered to the Air Force on 21 December. The next day it flew to Holloman AFB to participate in the Rascal test program.[42]

A total of 14 "F-series" Rascals were available for test launches from the DB-36s, and at least two live firings occurred in the first 6 months of 1955. In addition, six "D-series" missiles were launched from DB-50s during the same time period. Only two of these launches were considered successful – five of the failures were caused by various

power plant malfunctions, and one failure was caused by a bad roll rate gyro. It could not be determined how many of the remaining missiles were launched before the DB-36/GAM-63 program was cancelled.[43]

In the meantime, during 1953, the Air Force decided to modify a B-47B (51-2186) as a Rascal carrier under the designation YDB-47B. A single Rascal was suspended from the starboard side of the fuselage below the wing – the Rascal was a large missile for the medium bomber and could not be carried semisubmerged as it was on the B-36. In addition, two B-47Es (51-5219/5220) were earmarked for conversion to YDB-47E Rascal carriers.

SAC felt that equipping the B-47 fleet with the large and bulky externally mounted Rascal would degrade the aircraft's performance to such extent as to make the whole concept of dubious value. SAC also feared that the guidance system would never work very well, and was reluctant to add even more complex electronic equipment to an already electronically packed B-47. Modification costs (about a million dollars per aircraft) were high, and personnel training demands were considerable. Nevertheless, the Air Force decided in June 1955 that the B-47 and not the B-36 would carry the GAM-63. By this time, all 12 of the DB-36H modification kits had been manufactured, although they had only been installed on two aircraft.[44]

As part of the new program, 30 B-47Bs would be converted to DB-47 configuration as Rascal carriers. Despite a successful Rascal launch from a DB-47E in July 1955, the entire project seemed to falter. In May 1957, it was announced that only one rather than two DB-47/GAM-63 squadrons would be fielded. That still did not satisfy SAC which felt that the Rascal program would be outmoded by the time it achieved operational status. Nevertheless, by the end of 1957, crews of the 321st Bomb Wing were involved in Rascal training. The Rascal turned out to be a fairly accurate and effective weapon, but the concept rapidly became obsolete in the face of new developments in the field of air-launched missiles. The Rascal program itself was cancelled on 9 September 1958. On 18 November, AMC was directed to dispose of the 78 experimental and the 58 production Rascal missiles that had been accepted. By this time the three DB-36s had already been scrapped.[45]

An unidentified B-36 in San Diego on 11 November 1950. (San Diego Aerospace Museum)

B-36J

The B-36J was the final production version of the B-36. It had an additional fuel tank in each outer wing panel that increased the fuel load by 2,770 gallons, bringing total fuel capacity (with bomb bay fuel tanks) to 36,396 gallons. The aircraft had a stronger landing gear that permitted a gross takeoff weight of 410,000 pounds, resulting in a slightly degraded top speed of only 411 mph. A new AN/ARC-21 high-frequency command radio was also installed. The only external change was a single elongated radome to cover the twin antennas of the APG-41A gun-laying radar in the tail, something introduced somewhere during B/RB-36H production.[46]

The first B-36J made its maiden flight in July 1953. Flight testing soon discovered an unsatisfactory aileron control characteristic that resulted in the rerigging of the control cables. The Air Force accepted 28 B-36Js in FY54: two in September 1953 and two in October, three each month from November 1953 through March 1954, none in April, four in May, and five in June. Five more B-36Js were accepted in FY55: four in July 1954 and one in August. The final 14 of the 33 B-36Js were completed as Featherweight III aircraft. These were the only Featherweight aircraft to be completed as such on the production line (others were modified after production).[47]

The last B-36J (52-2827) was rolled out on 10 August 1954 and was delivered to the Air Force on 14 August. "This last B-36 will join others to become an integral part of the nation's insurance that we are in business to keep the peace, but prepared to bring defeat to those who might be so stupid as to break it." Those were the closing words of Major General Francis H. Griswold, vice commander of SAC, just before the last B-36 roared into the skies on the way to its home at Fairchild AFB, Washington. Over 11,000 people were on hand to watch the end of an era at Fort Worth. The aircraft was piloted by Major Laurence Nickerson, but also on board were three men who had been on the first flight of the XB-36 eight years earlier: Gus Green, J. D. McEachern, and Joe Hefley.[48]

The B-36J cost half a million dollars less than the preceding B-36H: airframe, $1,969,271; engines (installed), $639,651; propellers, $214,186; electronics, $77,691; ordnance, $32,036; and armament, $707,379. Featherweights cost approximately $100,000 less, mainly because they did not carry the 20-mm cannon or turrets. By the time the B-36 production program was completed, the Air Force had spent over $1,000 million on the aircraft.[49]

FEATHERWEIGHTS

Even given the great range of the B-36, there were compromises between the weapons that could be carried and the distance to the targets that could be attacked. In the early 1950s it was not yet evident that high-yield thermonuclear weapons ("H-bombs") would eventually become fairly small and lightweight. Devising a means to extend the range of the bombers was paramount. Interestingly, although in-

flight refueling would become standard on almost all Air Force aircraft – including some ancient B-29s and most B-50s – it never seems to have been seriously considered for the B-36 fleet.

As an alternative, on 28 January 1954 the Air Force approved the first phase of Project Featherweight* to increase the operational altitude and range of the B-36. The major objectives of the Featherweight program was to eliminate the need to pre-strike stage.[50]

The classic takeoff photo of the last B-36 (52-2827), departing from the Fort Worth plant. The final 14 J-models had been completed as Featherweight III aircraft on the assembly line. (Lockheed Martin)

The delivery ceremony for the last B-36J (52-2827) on 14 August 1954 at Fort Worth – over 11,000 people attended. The white paint had been added in the time between roll-out and the ceremony. Note the lack of national insignia on the fuselage in both of these photos, although there is one on the upper wing. (San Diego Aerospace Museum Collection)

---

* At the time this was always written in all caps – FEATHERWEIGHT.

Prior to the Featherweight program, standard B-36 aircraft – except the 42nd BW based at Limestone AFB, Maine – were forced to pre-strike stage in order to have sufficient range to attack "significant targets" in the Soviet Union regardless of the route chosen. Such pre-strike staging was vulnerable, time consuming, costly in terms of propositioned materiel and airlift, and subject to adverse weather conditions. In addition, strike missions mounted from some of the more remote pre-strike bases required a sacrifice of bombing altitude. It was also possible that the pre-strike bases – most of which were located outside the United States – might be rendered unusable by political or hostile action.[51]

It became evident to the Air Staff and SAC planners that a requirement existed for an aircraft that could: (1) strike through the arctic without pre-strike staging, or (2) attack from more remote pre-strike bases without a corresponding sacrifice in altitude, or (3) attack significant targets with pre-strike and post-strike staging through North American bases. The only aircraft available in early 1954 that could possibly meet these requirements was a modified B-36. The basic idea was to remove sufficient weight from each aircraft so that maximum fuel could be carried on all missions – previously, most missions had been flown with less than maximum fuel due to gross takeoff weight restrictions based on landing gear limitations. Interestingly, the concept of refueling the B-36s in flight at the edge of American airspace does not appear to have been considered.[52]

Three configurations were initially considered for the Featherweight program. Configuration I involved the tactical unit (i.e., Bomb Wing) removing all of the retractable turrets, auxiliary bomb racks (i.e., for conventional bombs), and crew comfort items immediately before a retaliatory strike. This tactic was rejected because of the potential delay (possibly several days) in the unit being able to undertake missions. Eventually, however, all aircraft went through a general "housekeeping" in the field with many unused or unneeded brackets, spare parts, etc. being removed during normal maintenance at the squadron level.

Configuration II ("Tactically Stripped Featherweight") involved removing all the extraneous equipment from each aircraft, except the guns, ECM equipment, auxiliary bomb racks, and crew comfort items. The turrets were slightly reconfigured to allow their rapid removal when required. In addition, as many external protuberances as possible were removed from the aircraft to decrease drag. Periscopic sextants and high-altitude operating equipment were added and flush covers for all six sighting blisters were procured but not normally installed. These modifications were accomplished at the depot level (either Convair or San Antonio) and resulted in an actual weight reduction of 4,800 pounds. If needed, the tactical unit could quickly (less than a day) remove the turrets and install the flush blister covers to eliminate several thousand additional pounds. Surprisingly these seemingly small modifications resulted in an increase in range of between 25 percent with guns and 39 percent without guns. This program was applied across all types of B/RB-36s, and the aircraft had a "-II" appended to their designation (sometimes written as "(II)" – B-36D-II or B-36D(II) – being equivalent).[53]

MODEL	DESIGN G.W. (LBS)	PRESSURIZED CREW COMPARTMENTS	CREW	ENGINEER'S STATION	RECIP ENGINES	WING FUEL TANKS	GUN TURRETS	BOMB BAYS	BOMBING SYSTEM
B-36D	357,500	2	15	SINGLE	R4360-41	8	8	4	K( ) & UNIVERSAL
B-36D-II	357,500	2	15	SINGLE	R4360-41	8	8	4	K( ) & UNIVERSAL
B-36D-III	357,500	2	13	SINGLE	R4360-41	8	1	4	K( ) & UNIVERSAL
B-36F	357,500	2	15	SINGLE	R4360-53	8	8	4	K( ) & UNIVERSAL
B-36F-II	357,500	2	15	SINGLE	R4360-53	8	8	4	K( ) & UNIVERSAL
B-36F-III	357,500	2	13	SINGLE	R4360-53	8	1	4	K( ) & UNIVERSAL
B-36H	357,500	2	15	DUAL	R4360-53	8	8	4	K( ) & UNIVERSAL
B-36H-II	357,500	2	15	DUAL	R4360-53	8	8	4	K( ) & UNIVERSAL
B-36H-III	357,500	2	13	DUAL	R4360-53	8	1	4	K( ) & UNIVERSAL
B-36J-III	410,000	2	13	DUAL	R4360-53	10	1	4	K( ) & UNIVERSAL
RB-36D & E	357,500	3	22	SINGLE	R4360-41	8	8	2	CONV. & UNIVERSAL
RB-36D & E-II	357,500	3	22	SINGLE	R4360-41	8	8	2 or 3	CONV. & UNIVERSAL
RB-36D & E-III	357,500	3	19	SINGLE	R4360-41	8	1	2 or 3	CONV. & UNIVERSAL
RB-36F	357,500	3	22	SINGLE	R4360-53	8	8	2	CONV. & UNIVERSAL
RB-36F-II	357,500	3	22	SINGLE	R4360-53	8	8	2 or 3	CONV. & UNIVERSAL
RB-36F-III	357,500	3	19	SINGLE	R4360-53	8	1	3	CONV. & UNIVERSAL
RB-36H	357,500	3	22	DUAL	R4360-53	8	8	2	CONV. & UNIVERSAL
RB-36H-II	357,500	3	22	DUAL	R4360-53	8	8	2 or 3	CONV. & UNIVERSAL
RB-36H-III	357,500	3	19	DUAL	R4360-53	8	1	3	CONV. & UNIVERSAL
GRB-36D-III	357,500	3	19	SINGLE	R4360-41	8	1	2	NOT UTILIZED

The "main differences" table from a B-36 flight manual shows the major changes between each model. By the time this chart had been issued, all J-models had been converted to Featherweight IIIs – earlier charts had listed straight J-models. (U.S. Air Force)

The ultimate Featherweight was Configuration III, also conducted at the depot level. Under this program all defensive armament except the tail turret and its radar was permanently deleted, as were the forward and upper aft sighting blisters. The lower aft blisters were retained on most aircraft since they provided a convenient location for crewmembers to observe the engines for oil leaks, etc. On some aircraft these blisters were replaced by flat Plexiglas, providing another small decrease in drag. The chaff dispensers and ECM equipment were retained, and in some cases brought up to a later standard. Most of the remaining crew comfort equipment (bunks, galley, sound deadening, carpet, etc.) was also deleted, along with the astrodome on top of the cockpit. On bombers (not RBs) equipped with the –53 engines – since they could attain higher altitudes due to the use of fuel injection instead of carburetors – five additional oxygen bottles were installed in the area previously occupied by the upper forward turrets.[54]

Without guns, the crew could be reduced, usually by two of the aft gunners (the forward gunners generally had other duties, such as navigating). Since most of the insulation had been removed from the pressurized compartments, the temperature at high altitude would be unbearable so provisions for heated flying suits were installed. The new flying suits contained integral communications equipment, so the fixed intercom system and speakers were removed. These modifications resulted in an actual weight reduction of 15,000 pounds, and resulted in a range increase of between 25 and 40 percent (depending on the B-36 model) over the Featherweight II configuration.[55]

The weight and drag reduction increased the top speed of the modified B-36Ds to 418 mph and modified B-36Hs increased to 423 mph. Perhaps more importantly, the reduction in weight allowed a significant increase in operating altitude – up to 47,000 feet officially, and well over 50,000 feet according to many former crew members. These aircraft had a "-III" appended to their designations.[56]

In addition, both configurations of Featherweight aircraft had their main landing gear pivot shafts beefed up, the "large bomb fitting" on the rear wing spar modified to withstand additional gust load factors, and bulkhead 12.0 in the aft fuselage strengthened by adding a layer of fiberglass cloth to its aft face. Various navigation and radio equipment was also updated (for instance, the AN/ARC-27 command set was replaced with an AN/ARC-33 unit). The B-36 had been built with removable armor panels surrounding the integral fuel tanks in the wings – Featherweight removed these. Surprisingly, the anti-ice and fuel tank purging systems were also deleted.[57]

The entire operational B-36 and RB-36 fleet underwent Featherweight modifications. Where feasible the Air Force accomplished other modifications at the same time the aircraft were being converted to Featherweights – including improved thermonuclear capabilities, SAM-SAC, ON TOP Phases 8–10, and the K-system recycling effort. From the beginning the plan was to bring some aircraft up to the full Featherweight III configuration, while leaving others in Configuration II to conduct missions where defensive armament might be necessary. For instance, of the 104 B/RB-36s assigned to the Fifteenth Air Force, only 32 were scheduled for the full Configuration III modifications, and this included the 10 aircraft being modified into GRB-36D FICON carriers. All B-36 modifica-

tions were to be completed by December 1954, with all RB-36s following by March 1955. The last 14 B-36Js were manufactured to the Featherweight configuration III.[58]

Concurrently with the Featherweight modifications, in conjunction with ON TOP Phase 10, all RB-36s were returned to a primary bombardment mission. The aircraft retained a "dormant" reconnaissance capability that could be used in the "exploitation phase of conflict or peacetime operations." This is when the ferret ECM equipment and associated radomes were relocated from between bulkheads 8.0 and 9.0 (bomb bay No. 4) to between bulkheads 10.0 and 12.0 in the aft fuselage. Also as part of ON TOP Phase 10, at least some aircraft (B and RB) received a 10-inch scope for the APS-24 at the bombardier's station instead of the original 5-inch scope. On bomber aircraft the 5-inch scope was relocated to the navigator's station.[59]

There was some disagreement between SAC and the Air Force Systems Command over the removal of the second photographer from the standard crew list. AFSC suggested retaining the second crewmember and removing the split vertical and forward oblique camera installations to achieve an equivalent weight reduction. SAC argued that since the aircraft no longer had a primary reconnaissance role, the second photographer was not needed (although why all the camera equipment was retained was not stated). In the end, the cameras were retained and the second photographer was not manifested for strike missions. SAC also began postponing reconnaissance training and instead concentrated on sending RB-36 crews through the normal bombardment training.[60]

The only major challenge experienced during the Featherweight conversions was a shortage of altimeters. Originally a new C-19 altimeter (also called an N-1) had been specified that measured between zero and 60,000 feet. Unfortunately, the vendor could only supply 35 units per month, while up to 86 B-36s were being modified in some months. Ultimately, the Air Force decided that some aircraft (usually the Configuration II bombers) could be equipped with modified C-12 (J-1) units capable of measuring between zero and 55,000 feet. The first Featherweight Configuration II aircraft began its modification in February 1954 and was redelivered in August 1954. The last modified bomber was redelivered in November 1954, with the last reconnaissance version following 6 months later.

Beginning in late 1954, most (maybe all) aircraft (B and RB) received "high altitude camouflage paint" (under ECP-2309B). In reality, this involved painting the bottom of the fuselage and most of the lower wing surface with "anti-flash white" paint. The painting was accomplished concurrently with the aircraft undergoing ON TOP Phase 10, Featherweight, or SAM-SAC Cycle 2 modifications. The first few aircraft were painted in the Experimental Building, but most later aircraft were painted out-of-doors on a secluded part of the ramp. A few aircraft also had the top of the forward crew compartment painted white, although no record of an ECP that authorized this could be found. At the same time, any aircraft that still had fabric-covered ailerons was modified (ECP-2315) with metal-covered surfaces. Bomber aircraft also had their "bomb-spotting camera" relocated from just behind bulkhead 9.0 to just behind bulkhead 10.0 for undetermined reasons.[61]

Snow covers several B-36s as they sit at Fort Worth. Note that the airplane in the foreground has had its propellers removed. (Lockheed Martin)

MODIFICATION PROGRAMS

The B-36 probably spent more time in various maintenance and modification programs than any other operational aircraft of the era. Much of this had to do with the pace of technical change during the early 1950s – new weapons and electronics were constantly being added to the aircraft. Fixing latent defects in the aircraft – sometimes caused by the Air Force's desire to take delivery of the aircraft early before Convair had finished fixing it – caused other problems. The sheer amount of maintenance, coupled with a lack of personnel in the Air Force, forced the Air Force to subcontract with Convair for many organizational and depot functions. The first 95 airplanes spent a majority of their early careers being modified – Appendix B shows a timeline for each aircraft.

A few of the modification programs – such as Featherweight and FICON – have been discussed in the text. Others – such as the ON TOP and UBS atomic weapons modifications – have been mentioned where appropriate. There were a multitude of others that, although important for keeping the B-36 fleet operational, did not materially effect the configuration of capability of the aircraft at a level of concern to this book.

Between 1953 and 1957 Convair and the Air Force jointly ran a program called SAN-SAN (for San Diego and San Antonio, the two locations it was performed) under contract AF33-038-30498. This was a general maintenance effort where the B-36 fleet was cycled through for inspection, repair, and modernization as required. Project CREW COMFORT installed refrigerators, bunks, improved lavatories, and other items beginning in 1950, although all of this equipment was subsequently removed during the Featherweight program. Project RELIABLE processed already-delivered 39 aircraft between 1 February 1952 and the end of the year, as well as 28 aircraft that were diverted from the production line prior to delivery. RELIABLE relocated

The first B-36J (52-2210) after it was converted to the Featherweight III configuration and received the white paint. (John "Zimmy" Zimmerman)

most of the K-system components into the pressurized area of the forward fuselage. This kept the components at a more constant temperature and allowed in-flight access for monitoring and repair.[62]

Project WORTHMORE processed 53 airplanes between 2 June 1952 and 6 August 1953. This was a general maintenance effort that included IRAN (inspect and repair as necessary) work and the incorporation of various modifications. Project FIXIT ran in parallel with WORTHMORE and was responsible for fixing damage caused by the 1952 tornado that hit Carswell AFB (see Chapter 8 for more details). The decontamination program processed six B-36s and four RB-36s that had been used to monitor atomic testing. Various phases of

Typical clothing during a summer crew briefing at Fairchild AFB. Note the "fuzzy" demarcation on the white paint. (Fairchild Heritage Museum)

A winter crew briefing, with a great deal more survival and personal equipment lined up on the ramp. (Fairchild Heritage Museum)

Project ON TOP and the ECM Follow-On program kept the nuclear weapons and ECM capabilities of the fleet up-to-date. The FECM-DECM program processed 64 RB-36s between 20 July 1954 and 13 July 1956 under contract AF41(608)-6977 to increase the effectiveness of their electronic systems.[63]

Not surprisingly, some of the various B-36 modifications programs came in over budget, while others came in under the estimate. What follows is a partial list of modifications, their final cost (in 1955 dollars), and their original budget.[64]

Description	Actual	Budget	Delta
SAM-SAC Cycle I (Seq. 1–204)	44,951,063	47,888,178	2,937,115
FICON 9,417,515	7,539,334	(1,878,181)	
SAM-SAC Cycle I (Seq. 205–348)	23,231,063	24,065,733	834,670
SAM-SAC Cycle II	28,588,025	25,731,622	(2,856,403)
ECM Phase II Prototype	1,712,830	1,815,854	103,024
ECM Follow-On	7,460,116	7,158,930	(301,186)
ON TOP Phase X	592,291	615,658	23,367
Fire Protection Mods	1,560,517	1,758,906	198,389
Featherweight	9,446,851	9,578,054	131,203
Decontamination	1,415,241	1,417,516	2,275
WORTHMORE, RELIABLE, FIXIT	27,278,897	27,905,511	626,614
Total	*155,654,409*	*155,475,296*	*(179,113)*

Rear view of half of an all-weather service dock built by Convair. The complete dock consisted of four sections, each 36 feet in depth that enclosed 60 feet of each wing, including all of the R-4360 engines. Two different types of docks were built – one set up permanently on the ramp, and the other mobile that could be moved as necessary. Similar docks were built at the San Antonio depot, the Convair San Diego plant, and most of the permanent B-36 bases. (San Diego Aerospace Museum Collection)

SAM-SAC

In June 1953 Convair announced that it would be initiating "an unprecedented program of prime importance to the entire aircraft industry." The hyperbole referred to Project SAM-SAC (Specialized Aircraft Maintenance-Strategic Air Command), "a continuing maintenance and modernization program which eventually will encompass all B-36 aircraft." The goal of SAM-SAC was to standardize the B-36 fleet around a set number of standard configurations, allowing parts to be interchanged more easily and for maintenance procedures to be standardized. The program meant that roughly 25 B-36s would be undergoing heavy maintenance at Fort Worth constantly through 1957.[65]

August C. Esenwein, vice president and Fort Worth division manager, announced that "SAM-SAC is the first contract to be awarded in keeping with the Air Force's new maintenance concept of returning a product to the manufacturer for maintenance and modernization. … That concept is based on the theory that it is more economical for the manufacturer to overhaul the airplane …"

SAM-SAC was an outgrowth of Project WORTHMORE. At Convair, K. A. Day was the modernization manager in charge of both WORTHMORE and SAM-SAC. He explained, "SAM-SAC will be the accomplishment of cyclic maintenance and modernization work to be completed in three cycles." Bringing the aircraft through three times was meant as a way of providing maintenance in a timely manner without keeping the aircraft out of service for a long period of time. The first (un-named) cycle was essentially the same as the normal depot-level overhaul accomplished on most aircraft by the San Antonio Air Materiel Area (SAAMA).

Cycle One included a DIR (depot inspection and repair) of the control surfaces, leading and trailing edges of the wings, outer wing panels, empennage, and engine nacelles. To accomplish this, all of the control surfaces and the engines were removed from the aircraft during the receiving inspection. The control surfaces were thoroughly washed, repainted, and balanced prior to being reinstalled. All of the turrets and fire-control system were also removed and shipped to General Electric for modifications and refurbishment. The 20-mm cannon were refurbished locally by Convair. The refurbished turrets were mounted in test stands for functional tests, then reinstalled, boresighted, and harmonized.[66]

The rest of the airframe received a major inspection, and outstanding TCTOs (time compliance technical orders – modifications) were incorporated. In addition, the nacelles were reworked to allow engines to be installed in any position and to be interchanged between aircraft and positions without excessive rework. This was in support of the Quick Engine Change (QEC) program that involved the build-up of an engine and accessories into a power package that could be installed quickly in the field. Applied to other aircraft as well, the QEC program for B-36s ran from 1953 until 27 August 1957. At any given time, between 50 and 100 QEC engines were available for use by SAC.[67]

Cycle Two included a DIR of the center wing section, fuel tanks, and bomb bays, plus a major inspection of the rest of the aircraft and again having any outstanding TCTOs incorporated. The landing gear was also overhauled, including installing new lynch pins that raised the maximum allowable gross weight of all aircraft (except the J-models) to 370,000 pounds. The aircraft were also repainted as necessary. Convair created 23 work areas at the outset of the program, expanding it to 29 after all of the maintenance docks arrived from San Diego. At the peak of SAM-SAC, Convair had 5,800 employees dedicated to SAM-SAC.[68]

The first aircraft to enter the SAM-SAC program was an RB-36E (42-13571) during early June 1953. Ironically, this presented something of a dilemma for the workers at Fort Worth. It was standard practice when a B-36 was at Convair to paint its assembly line number on the nose and aft fuselage to help workers more readily identify it (most documentation used the assembly number, not the serial number). However, this aircraft had begun life as the YB-36, and did not have an assembly number since it was not part of the production program. The answer was to paint "YB" on the nose and fuselage where the assembly number normally went. The work on the YB was completed by the end of July and the aircraft was redelivered to the Air Force on 4 August 1953. By September 1954, 215 B-36s had been processed through Cycle One. The YB was also the first to arrive for Cycle Two of SAM-SAC, being redelivered to the Air Force (for the fourth time) on 14 July 1955.[69]

Part of SAM-SAC included resealing the wing fuel tanks, something that had always been somewhat of a problem on the B-36, although revised sealants and techniques had greatly reduced problems in later years. Previously, the job of removing the old sealant in preparation to reseal the tanks had been largely a manual job. During the early 1950s it had not been unusual for an aircraft to be down for 2–3 months while its fuel tanks were being resealed.

For SAM-SAC, Convair devised a new technique. First, the leading edges of the wings were removed to allow access to the fuel tanks. Then the nose of the aircraft was raised about 3 feet. A chemical stripper was then sprayed through 1,140 nozzles inserted into the fuel tanks. These fan-shaped nozzles sprayed 2,280 gallons per minute of the stripper that was maintained at a constant temperature via a refrigeration unit and heat exchanger. The dissolved material was strained and stored in a waste-water tank at the site for later disposal. After all of the old sealant was removed, the tanks were thoroughly cleaned and new sealant applied by hand. Interestingly, as each aircraft was delivered to Convair, the amount of fuel in the tanks was carefully measured before it was removed. When the aircraft was returned to the Air Force, the same amount of fuel was filled into the tanks.[70]

Surprisingly, given the nature and duration of B-36 flight operations at Convair, there were only two fatalities. Both occurred during a SAM-SAC test flight on 6 February 1956 when a flash fire erupted in the aft compartment of a B-36 on a test flight. The two scanners in the compartment, J. E. Cunningham and Fred J. Verrips, elected to bail out of the compartment after the smoke became too thick. Unfortunately, neither man had time to pull the rip cord on his parachute before hitting the ground. These were the first fatalities during flight operations at Convair since November 1943 when a B-24 had crashed.[71]

The last aircraft (52-2216) to go through SAM-SAC was redelivered to the Air Force on 29 April 1957. A total of 494 aircraft had been

The first B-36D (44-92095) in the foreground and the first RB-36D (44-92088) in the background pose with the XB-52 at Edwards AFB. Note that the bomber has square-tip propellers, indicating that this was a fairly late photo. (AFFTC via the Tony Landis Collection)

processed through SAM-SAC – 204 through the first Cycle One contract (AF41(608)-6464), 144 through a follow-on Cycle One contract (AF41(608)-7125), and 146 through Cycle Two (AF41(608)-7272). SAM-SAC had used 137 acres at the Fort Worth plant with 38 maintenance docks to process an average of 13 aircraft per month. The average turn-around time for an aircraft was 59 days.[72]

An unidentified Featherweight III B-36 at Edwards. Note the B-50, B-52, F-86s, and F-100s in the background. (Tony Landis Collection)

REMOVE BULLET SEALING PADS

EFFECTIVITY: CONFIG. II & III
REF. ACA'S 2310 A,B,C, OR D-12

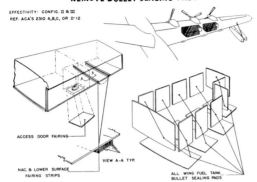

ACCESS DOOR FAIRING

NAC. & LOWER SURFACE
FAIRING STRIPS

VIEW A-A TYP.

ALL WING FUEL TANK
BULLET SEALING PADS

PARTIAL CREW COMFORT REMOVAL (FWD CABIN)

EFFECTIVITY CONFIG. II & III
REFERENCE ACA'S 2310 A,B,C, OR D-4

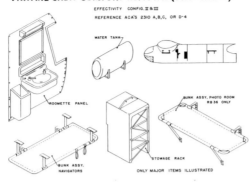

WATER TANK

ROOMETTE PANEL

BUNK ASSY, PHOTO ROOM
RB-36 ONLY

STOWAGE RACK

BUNK ASSY.
NAVIGATORS

ONLY MAJOR ITEMS ILLUSTRATED

PARTIAL CREW COMFORT REMOVAL (AFT CABIN)

EFFECTIVITY: CONFIG. II & III AIRCRAFT   REFERENCE ACA'S 2310 A,B,C, OR D-4

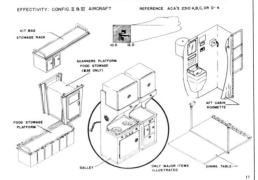

KIT BAG
STOWAGE RACK

SCANNERS PLATFORM
FOOD STOWAGE
(B-36 ONLY)

FOOD STOWAGE
PLATFORM

AFT CABIN
ROOMETTE

GALLEY

ONLY MAJOR ITEMS
ILLUSTRATED

DINING TABLE

17

MISC. REMOVALS AND REWORK

EFFECTIVITY: CONFIG. II & III   REF. ACA'S 2310 A,B,C, OR D-6,-8 (EXCEPT AS NOTED)

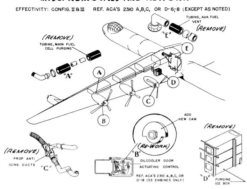

TUBING, AUX. FUEL
VENT   (REMOVE)

(REMOVE)
TUBING, MAIN FUEL
CELL PURGING

"A"

ADD
NEW CAM

(REMOVE)

(REMOVE)
PROP ANTI
ICING DUCTS   "C"

(RE-WORK)
"B"   OILCOOLER DOOR
ACTUATING CONTROL

REF. ACA'S 2310 A,B,C, OR
D-18 (53 ENGINES ONLY)

PURGING
ICE BOX   "D"

ASTRODOME REMOVAL AND PERISCOPIC SEXTANT INSTL.

EFFECTIVE ON ALL CONFIGURATION II & III AIRCRAFT
REF. ACA 2310 A,B,C, & D -3-1 & 3-2

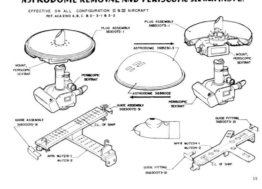

PLUG ASSEMBLY
36830072-1

PLUG ASSEMBLY
36830073-1

MOUNT,
PERISCOPIC
SEXTANT

ASTRODOME 36B5230-3

MOUNT,
PERISCOPIC
SEXTANT

PERISCOPIC
SEXTANT

ASTRODOME 36B6002

PERISCOPIC
SEXTANT

GUIDE ASSEMBLY
36830072-31

GUIDE ASSEMBLY
36830072-31   C.L. OF SHIP

GUIDE FITTING
36830073-21

APPX WJ723-1
WJ723-2

GUIDE FITTING
36830073-21   C.L. OF SHIP

15

INSTALL PROVISIONS FOR HEATED FLYING SUITS

EFFECTIVITY: CONFIG. III AIRCRAFT ONLY
REFERENCES: ACA'S 2310 A & C-10

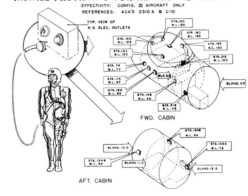

TYP. VIEW OF
H.S. ELEC. OUTLETS

FWD. CABIN

AFT. CABIN

UPPER FWD TURRETS REMOVAL AND ADDITIONAL OXYGEN INSTL.

EFFECTIVITY & REFERENCES AS NOTED:

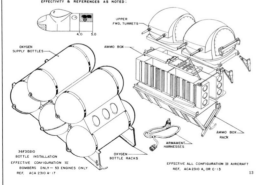

UPPER
FWD. TURRETS

OXYGEN
SUPPLY BOTTLES

AMMO BOX

AMMO BOX
RACK

36F3021O
BOTTLE INSTALLATION
EFFECTIVE CONFIGURATION III
BOMBERS ONLY - 53 ENGINES ONLY
REF. ACA 2310 A-17

OXYGEN
BOTTLE RACKS

ARMAMENT
HARNESSES

EFFECTIVE ALL CONFIGURATION III AIRCRAFT
REF. ACA 2310 A, OR C-13

13

LOWER AFT TURRETS AND EQUIPMENT REMOVAL

EFFECTIVITY- CONFIG. III AIRCRAFT   REF.- A.C.A. 2310A, OR C-13

NOTE: LOWER AFT TURRET DOOR WILL BE LOCKED IN A
CLOSED POSITION ON CONFIG. III BOMBER
AIRCRAFT ONLY

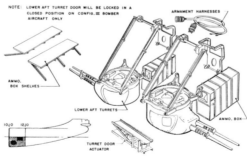

ARMAMENT HARNESSES

AMMO.
BOX SHELVES

LOWER AFT TURRETS

AMMO. BOX

TURRET DOOR
ACTUATOR

REMOVE SIGHTING BLISTERS-PLUG OPENINGS WITH HATCH DOORS

EFFECTIVITY CONFIG. III AIRCRAFT ONLY   REF. ACA'S 2310 A, OR C-3

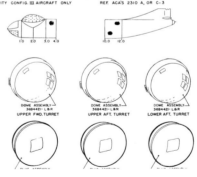

DOME ASSEMBLY
36B4421- L & R
UPPER FWD. TURRET

DOME ASSEMBLY
36B4421- L & R
UPPER AFT. TURRET

DOME ASSEMBLY
36B4421- L & R
LOWER AFT. TURRET

UPPER AFT TURRETS AND EQUIPMENT REMOVAL

EFFECTIVE CONFIGURATION III AIRCRAFT ONLY   REF. ACA 2310A, OR C-13

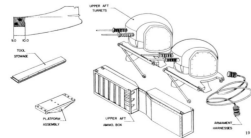

UPPER AFT
TURRETS

TOOL
STOWAGE

PLATFORM
ASSEMBLY

UPPER AFT
AMMO. BOX

ARMAMENT
HARNESSES

19

How to "featherweight" a 357,000 pound airplane. These charts are from the "Featherweight Project Manufacturing Plan" prepared by Convair in preparation for converting the B-36 fleet to Featherweight Configuration II and III airplanes. A lot of equipment was removed during the process. (Convair)

REMOVAL OF NOSE TURRET AND INSTALLATION OF FAIRING

EFFECTIVITY: CONFIG. III AIRCRAFT ONLY
REFERENCE: ACA'S 2310 A, OR C-13

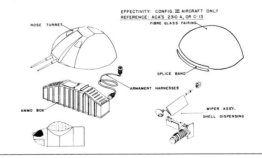

NOSE TURRET

FIBRE GLASS FAIRING

SPLICE BAND

ARMAMENT HARNESSES

AMMO BOX

WIPER ASSY.

SHELL DISPENSING

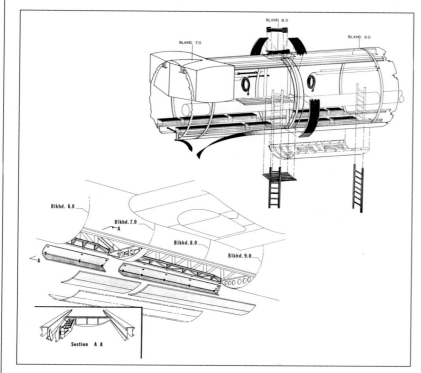

Section 1

DESCRIPTION, DIMENSIONS, AND LEADING PARTICULARS

Bomb bay No. 4 on the RB-36 fleet was activated by Project ON TOP Phase X. To accomplish this, the ferret ECM package located between bulkheads 8 and 9 was moved aft, the bulkheads reinforced, and the bomb bay doors were reconfigured to more closely resemble the bombers. (Convair)

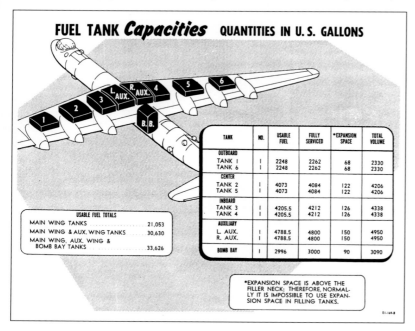

FUEL TANK *Capacities* QUANTITIES IN U. S. GALLONS

TANK	NO.	USABLE FUEL	FULLY SERVICED	*EXPANSION SPACE	TOTAL VOLUME
OUTBOARD					
TANK 1	1	2248	2262	68	2330
TANK 6	1	2248	2262	68	2330
CENTER					
TANK 2	1	4073	4084	122	4206
TANK 5	1	4073	4084	122	4206
INBOARD					
TANK 3	1	4205.5	4212	126	4338
TANK 4	1	4205.5	4212	126	4338
AUXILIARY					
L. AUX.	1	4788.5	4800	150	4950
R. AUX.	1	4788.5	4800	150	4950
BOMB BAY	1	2996	3000	90	3090

USABLE FUEL TOTALS	
MAIN WING TANKS	21,053
MAIN WING & AUX. WING TANKS	30,630
MAIN WING, AUX. WING & BOMB BAY TANKS	33,626

*EXPANSION SPACE IS ABOVE THE FILLER NECK; THEREFORE, NORMALLY IT IS IMPOSSIBLE TO USE EXPANSION SPACE IN FILLING TANKS.

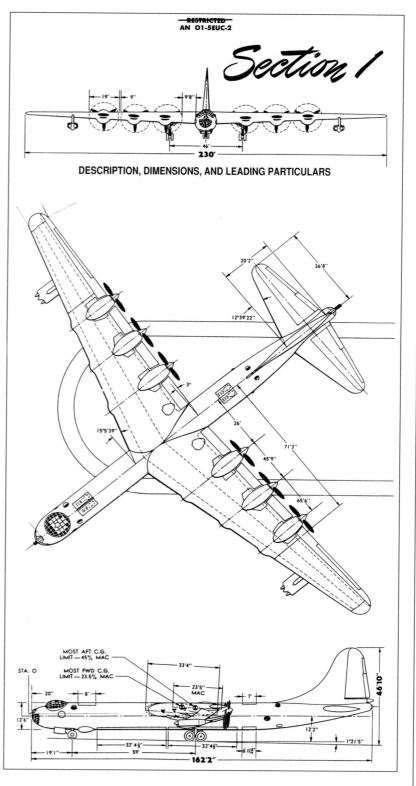

Although from the B-36H flight manual, this chart is generally applicable to all models except the B-36J. (U.S. Air Force)

Dimensional data for a B-36D that is generally applicable for all models of the airplane. (U.S. Air Force)

Chapter 5

Above: *A trio of RB-36Ds from the 5th SRW. The closest (49-2695) and furthest (49-2694) aircraft from the camera would both be converted to GRB-36Ds. (5th BW archives via the Frederick A. Johnsen Collection)*

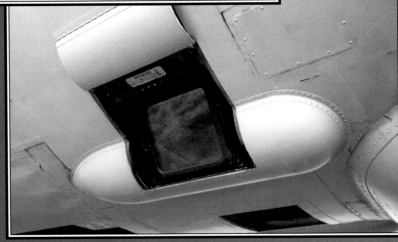

Right: *The forward oblique camera port with the protective door open. This is the RB-36H (51-13730) on display at Castle AFB, California. (Dennis R. Jenkins)*

STRATEGIC RECONNAISSANCE

General LeMay strongly influenced the decision to produce a reconnaissance version of the B-36. He had commanded B-29 strikes against Japan in World War II and was disturbed by the lack of a reconnaissance capability that could photograph the same targets the bombers could attack. One of his first actions upon taking command of SAC was to insist on an up-to-date supply of strategic reconnaissance aircraft. The B-36 was chosen as a reconnaissance aircraft for much the same reasons as it was for a strategic bomber – altitude and range. In fact, all of the original SAC bombers – B-29, B-36, B-45, B-47, and B-50 – had reconnaissance variants at General LeMay's urging. Initially, there was even a reconnaissance variant of the B-52 specified, although very few were produced before SAC decided it would rather have more bombers and rely on the Lockheed U-2 and other assets for intelligence gathering. The remanufacturing of the B-36As into RB-36Es ahead of the production of RB-36Ds attested to the urgency of the SAC Commander's request.

In the case of the B-36, just over one-third (142) of the production aircraft were configured for reconnaissance. The aircraft were assigned to the 5th Strategic Reconnaissance Wing (SRW) at Travis AFB, 28th SRW at Rapid City (later Ellsworth) AFB, the 72nd SRW at Ramey AFB, Puerto Rico, and the 99th SRW at Fairfield-Suisun (later Travis) AFB, California. Although new RB-36 deliveries con-

tinued until late 1953, by 1954 all of them were being reconfigured for a primary nuclear strike capability, with reconnaissance left to the much faster, but shorter-ranged, RB-47s.

The B-36 reconnaissance program was proposed and approved during early 1948, and a mock-up of the camera installation was completed on 17 March 1949. This mock-up was subsequently reviewed and approved by the Air Force. The RB-36D and RB-36E programs progressed almost simultaneously, with the largest difference being the fact that all the RB-36Ds would be new-builds while the 22 RB-36Es were remanufactured from the YB-36 and 21 of the B-36As. In actuality, there was little difference between the aircraft other than their production heritage. The two types proceeded down the production line interspersed. The official explanation of the RB-36 missions was "… to carry cameras and electronic equipment which, in event of war, would gather information about the enemy."

The reconnaissance variant was inspected by the 689 Board beginning on 21 November 1949. This was a group of Air Force officers and civilian specialists who inspected all new Air Force models before they entered series production. This board was headed by Brigadier General George W. Munday from the Air Materiel Command, and consisted of 75 members from Air Force Headquarters, AMC, SAC, the Continental Air Command, and the

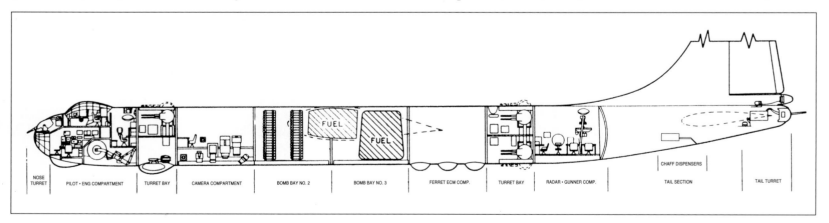

This was the original internal arrangement for all of the RB-36 models (except D-models and early B-36Fs did not have chaff). Later the Ferret ECM equipment and radomes would be moved into the aft fuselage and bomb bay No. 4 reactivated to carry nuclear weapons. (U.S. Air Force)

Air Proving Ground. The Convair project engineer, Norm B. Robbins, headed the group of Convair engineers who answered the board's questions during the 5-day inspection.[1]

There were more differences than met the eye between the reconnaissance variant and the normal bomber version. The RB-36 was outwardly similar, but carried a crew of 22, the additional crew members were needed to operate and maintain the photographic and electronic reconnaissance equipment. The area that normally contained bomb bay No. 1 was converted into a 16-foot long pressurized compartment that contained 14 K-17C, K-22A, K-38, and K-40 cameras, as well as a rudimentary darkroom that allowed the film cartridges to be reloaded in flight. Adding the compartment involved changing the forward and aft bulkheads into pressure domes, reconfiguring the bomb bay doors, and changing the exterior skin around this area to aluminum since magnesium could not tolerate the pressure cycles. This provides easy identification of the reconnaissance aircraft. Several camera windows were installed on each side and the bottom of the compartment, each covered by a sliding door.

The standard photo-reconnaissance configuration included seven camera positions inside the pressurized compartment that could accommodate up to 14 cameras. Five of the stations – the trimetrogon, vertical, split vertical, multi, and forward oblique – were remotely controlled from the photographer's station in the photo compartment, or the photo-navigator's station in the nose of the aircraft. The left- and right-side oblique cameras were controlled by switches at their respective stations by the photographer. The vertical camera could be used for night photography when the target was illuminated by photo-flash bombs. A photocell trip unit was installed that caused the camera shutter to be tripped when the photo-flash bomb went off after being dropped from bomb bay No. 2. Through a combination of airspeed, altitude, and intervalometer settings, the desired photographic overlap could be obtained with the remotely-controlled cameras. A vacuum system, defrosting system, and electrically-operated camera doors formed an integral part of each camera system. In addition to the cameras in the photo compartment, a pair of C-1 radar scope cameras were carried as was a single A-6 motion picture camera – both could be used by the photo-navigator in the forward fuselage.[2]

The K-40 camera – with a 48-inch focal-length lens – had been an early requirement for the RB-36, but quickly ran into development problems. Development of the K-40 had been initiated in late 1948, and the first experimental model was delivered in June 1950. But as late as March 1951 the camera was still undergoing service testing and

A very confusing airplane. This is the first B-36B-1-CF (44-92026) that was subsequently converted to a B-36D-10-CF. However this photo shows the aircraft with a full complement of RB-36 radomes under the nose and bomb bay No. 4 and no guns installed in the nose turret. The position of the ECM antennas under the buzz number would have prohibited the sliding bomb bay doors from opening, and there appears to be part of the forward oblique camera door immediately behind the APS-23 radome. The fuselage skin around bomb bay No. 1 is still the dull magnesium, indicating that the area has not been converted into a pressurized compartment. The official lists indicate this aircraft was used for "propeller vibration tests" between the time it was completed and the time it was the first aircraft converted to a D-model at Fort Worth – it does not appear to have been delivered to the Air Force as a B-model. It was also, apparently, used to test at least the aerodynamic portions of the reconnaissance variant. (San Diego Aerospace Museum Collection)

had not made it to the operational fleet. Nevertheless, the camera continued to be listed as a B-36 asset until the last RB-36 was retired.[3]

The "communication tube" that allowed crew members to travel between the forward and aft pressurized compartments in the bomber models was substantially modified in the RB-36s. Instead of a single tube extending all the way from the aft of the forward compartment through both turret bays and all four bomb bays to the front of the aft compartment, the RB-36 featured two tubes. The first tube extended from the forward pressurized compartment through the forward turret bay into the new photo compartment. Since this tube was comparatively short, it did not include a movable cart. The second tube ran from the back of the photo compartment through the three bomb bays (or two bomb bays and electronics compartment) and the aft turret bay to the pressurized compartment in the rear of the aircraft. This tube still used the cart.

As initially configured, the RB-36 was not equipped to carry bombs. Bomb bay No. 2 was modified to carry eighty 100-pound T86 (or M46) flash bombs, and bomb bay No. 3 generally contained an auxiliary fuel tank but could carry flash bombs instead. As originally delivered a single set of 33.66-foot doors covered the two middle bomb bays (a substantial difference from the bomber versions). Since the aircraft were not equipped as bombers, the K-system (K-1 or K-3A, as appropriate for the model) was not installed, although the aircraft continued to carry the APQ-24 search radar. The reconnaissance models were not equipped with either Norden or periscopic bomb sights.

As built, the last bomb bay (No. 4) was deleted from the reconnaissance variants, and this area instead contained a special pallet that held ferret ECM (FECM) equipment. Three large radomes were mounted on the bottom of the fuselage where the aft bomb bay doors were normally located. Using the ferret equipment, operators onboard the RB-36 could record and analyze radar and communications signals while the aircraft flew close to* Soviet territory. In deleting the last bomb bay, Convair took the opportunity to lighten the aircraft slightly by using different bulkheads on each end of the area that did not contain the reinforcements necessary to mount bomb racks. In addition, certain parts of the aft wing spar and some fuselage frames were also lightened. A single set of 33.66-foot long doors covered the remaining two bomb bays (Nos. 2 and 3). All of this would mean significant rework was required when it was later decided to use the RB-36s as bomb carriers. The normal defensive armament of sixteen 20-mm cannon was retained on all production RB-36s.

The concept of operations for the reconnaissance version did not differ significantly from the bomber version. Instead of the normal bombardier, a photo-navigator sat in the glass nose where he had nearly unrestricted views in front and to the side of the aircraft. As the aircraft approached the photo target, the pilot turned the steering controls over to the photo-navigator, just as was done for a bombardier when a B-36 was starting a bomb run. The photo-navigator steered the aircraft into the proper position, then operated the cameras remotely. The photographer in the photo compartment actually did

This photo was taken of RB-36H-25-CF (51-13720) after the successful completion of flight tests with Ford-built R-4360 engines. It provides a good look at the shiny aluminum skin used around the pressurized photo compartment in the area that was bomb bay No. 1 on the bombers. Both the side-oblique and forward-oblique camera doors may be seen in their closed positions. (Lockheed Martin)

little operating of the cameras. Most of his time was spent loading film magazines and ensuring the proper operation of the cameras, pressurization, and heating/dehumidifying systems.[4]

On 16 June 1954, SAC's four RB-36-equipped heavy strategic reconnaissance wings were assigned a primary mission of strategic bombing with reconnaissance becoming a secondary capability. By this time the Air Force had shifted most strategic reconnaissance to the RB-47, and the RB-36s were more useful as nuclear deterrents, although they retained a fairly comprehensive latent reconnaissance capability. On 1 October 1955, the RB-36 reconnaissance wings were redesignated heavy-bombardment wings, although little changed but the name. The RB-36 aircraft themselves underwent two or three concurrent modification programs to provide a nuclear delivery capability, although the primary changes were performed as part of ON TOP Phase 10 beginning in late 1954.

As built, all reconnaissance models carried various types of FECM equipment in the area that was bomb bay No. 4 on the bomber models (e.g., between bulkheads 8.0 and 9.0). (Most of the defensive ECM – DECM – equipment continued to be carried in the forward fuselage, just like the bombers.) As part of activating the bomb bay to carry atomic weapons, this equipment was moved into the aft fuselage between bulkheads 10.0 and 12.0 – the three large radomes were relocated at the same time. In order to save weight,

---

* Or perhaps over, although no records could be found to indicate that the RB-36s ever conducted overflights.

Above: *An often-used photo of RB-36D-10-CF (49-2688) shows the original location of the ferret ECM radomes under the fuselage. All reconnaissance variants were manufactured with the radomes in this location. The contrast between the magnesium skin and the aluminum skin also shows up well here.* Below: *When bomb bay No. 4 was converted to carry nuclear weapons, the FECM radomes (and equipment) were moved under the rear fuselage below the forward edge of the tail. At the same time the bomb bay doors were reconfigured.* (both: Lockheed Martin)

bulkheads* 7.0, 8.0, and 9.0 in the reconnaissance aircraft had been redesigned and were not capable of supporting bomb racks. These were replaced or modified during the conversion, although it was not a simple matter and required a fair amount of disassembly. The bomb bay doors were also changed to more closely match the bomber models – Nos. 3 and 4 were covered by a single set of new 32.375-foot long doors, while bomb bay No. 2 was covered by a set of 16-foot doors that were modified from the original set of doors.[5]

Most RB-36s also received the "weather reconnaissance" modification that allowed them to collect rudimentary meteorological data during flight. A weather observer's station was added in the lower part of the extreme nose compartment. The station included a humidity indicator, clock, altimeter, and the instrumentation for a new radio altimeter. The antennas for the radio altimeter were flush mounted on the underside of the horizontal stabilizer, and the electronics were added to the unpressurized area of the aft compartment. A barometric pressure, temperature, and humidity probe was added to the right

---

* Bulkhead 5.0 was the front of bomb bay No. 1; bulkhead 6.0 was the front of bomb bay No. 2; bulkhead 7.0 was the front of bomb bay No. 3; bulkhead 8.0 was the front of bomb bay No. 4; and bulkhead No. 9.0 was the pressure dome between bomb bay No. 4 and the aft pressurized compartment.

The weather reconnaissance modification added an instrument boom on the right forward fuselage (left) and a new weather observer's position inside the nose compartment (right). (Lockheed Martin)

side of the extreme nose just behind the glazed panels. A radiosonde equipment rack was added at the intermediate frequency ECM operator's station at bulkhead 10.0 in the aft compartment. The dispenser itself was installed in the floor on the centerline of the rear pressurized compartment where the strike camera was carried in the bombers. Controls for the dispenser were installed at the high-frequency ECM station on the right side of the aft compartment, and also at the right lower gunner's blister. Interestingly, the Featherweight program initially removed this equipment, only to have it reinstalled (by ECP 2310J) a few months later.[6]

RB-36D

The first RB-36D (44-92088) made its maiden flight on 14 December 1949, only 6 months after the jet demonstrator had flown and less than a month after the 689 Board had approved the aircraft for production. This flight lasted 7 hours and 1 minute, and was piloted by George Davis and Francis Keen. Other members of the crew included

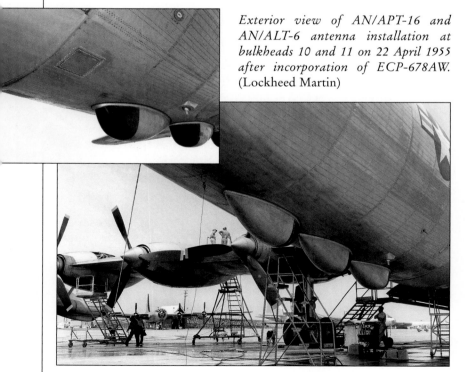

Exterior view of AN/APT-16 and AN/ALT-6 antenna installation at bulkheads 10 and 11 on 22 April 1955 after incorporation of ECP-678AW. (Lockheed Martin)

J.D. McEachern, William "Bill" P. Easley, S.A. Mayfield, Bert L. Woods, and C.J. Driskell. Observers included the RB-36 project engineer Norm B. Robbins, Gil A. Hofeller, Captain R.G. Newbern, Captain R.E. March, Captain, L. LeCouvre, Lieutenant H.F. Smith, Lieutenant D.B. Ingram, Lieutenant P.W. O'Dwyer, and Sgt. P.R. McNamara. Numerous reports have suggested that the first flight of the RB-36D was conducted without the jet pods, but most likely researchers are confusing this with photos of the single B-36B (44-92026) that had been used to evaluate the aeroduynamic effect of the RB-36 radomes – all indications are that the jet pods were installed on the first RB-36D when it made its maiden flight.[7]

The RB-36D actually preceded the B-36D into service with SAC by a couple of months, and the first seven RB-36Ds came off the production line before any bomber-versions of the jet-augmented design. All of the 24 RB-36Ds were "new-builds," although the first 7 had originally been ordered as B-36Bs and were completed on the production line and delivered as RB-36Ds. None of the B-36Bs that had been delivered without jet pods were converted into RB-36Ds because of the extensive rework required.

All RB-36Ds were delivered to the 28th Strategic Reconnaissance Wing at Rapid City AFB, North Dakota (now Ellsworth AFB). Three RB-36Ds were delivered in June 1950 and the remaining 21 were delivered between July 1950 and May 1951. Due to various materiel shortages, the RB-36Ds did not become operationally ready until June 1951, although several operational "peripheral" reconnaissance missions had apparently been flown as early as July 1950.

Convair established a photo test target at the south end of the Fort Worth plant to demonstrate the camera equipment aboard the RB-36s during flight tests. This target consisted of a series of white lines of varying size against a black background. The target took up part of the south parking lot near the Grant's Lane entrance, and employees were reminded not to park in the area.[8]

An RB-36D on the assembly line shows the original bomb bay doors that covered both center bomb bays. (Lockheed Martin)

The Boston Camera initially tested on the first RB-36D is now on display at the Air Force Museum. (Terry Panopalis)

Testing the RB-36D had its interesting moments. One was on 22 April 1950 when Beryl Erickson and Francis Keen were 15 hours into a test flight somewhere over North Dakota. At the last minute the Air Force requested that a jet-powered RB-36 participate in the Eglin air show later that day for President Truman – there were no jet-powered bomber models available. In fact, the aircraft Erickson was flying was the only aircraft that might be able to make it. Erickson turned the aircraft around and headed for Eglin. "Eglin shows are always machine-like precision affairs," Erickson explained. "We were given 15 seconds leeway in our timing to put the [R]B-36 through its paces in front of the president's reviewing stand." Smoke was thick over the field as the RB-36 swooped in at low level with full power on. Erickson pulled the aircraft up and into a steep climbing bank at the end of the field. Immediately behind, two Air Force B-36Bs dropped full loads of live 500-pound bombs. After the dramatic flyby, the RB-36 landed and was put on static display for the president. The aircraft flew back to Fort Worth the following day, having logged 47.75 flight hours.[9]

The performance of the RB-36D was similar to its bomber counterparts with a few subtle differences. Since the reconnaissance version generally took off with fewer bombs but more fuel, it tended to be a little faster and fly a little higher early in the mission. But because it did not drop its major payload (the reconnaissance gear), it was a little heavier on the return flight than the bombers, so it was a little slower.[10]

The longest known B-36 flight was made by a Convair test crew flying an RB-36D (44-92090). The flight took off at 09:05 on 14 January 1951, and landed at 12:35 on 16 January – exactly 51.5 hours in the air. Although this flight was unusual, most B-36 flights lasted more than 10 hours, and it was not unusual for missions to last 30 hours. The average training mission was scheduled for 24 hours. At least one aircraft from the 717th SRS at Rapid City managed to log 200 hours in a single month – January 1951. During March 1951 the 28th SRW managed to fly over 1,000 hours with their RB-36s, a milestone recognized during a ceremony at Rapid City AFB on 15 May.[11]

The first RB-36D (44-92088) spent its entire career as a reconnais-sance testbed and was reportedly redesignated ERB-36D. At one point the aircraft was modified to carry a "Boston Camera" with a 240-inch focal-length lens. Even the B-36 could not actually carry a camera over 20-feet long, so the lens used a set of mirrors to achieve the 240-inch effective length. A large opening was cut in the left side of the camera compartment, and the camera was meant to shoot sideways from a long standoff distance. A much smaller opening was cut further back on the fuselage to allow a small aiming-telescope the same basic field-of-view as the Boston Camera. Each piece* of film measured 18 by 36 inches, and the camera was reportedly able to photograph a golf ball from 45,000 feet. The modifications began on 7 December 1953, and the aircraft was delivered to the Air Force on 2 March 1954. The camera was tested for about a year before being removed from the RB-36D in 1955 and installed in a C-97. The camera was never used operationally and was donated to the Air Force Museum in 1964. After the Boston Camera was removed, the Air Force determined it would cost $200,000 to bring the aircraft back to production standards. Since it was the oldest RB-36D in the fleet, the Air Force decided to retire the aircraft instead. The engines and other equipment were removed and returned into the spares inventory and the aircraft was scrapped at Kelly AFB in late 1955.[12]

RB-36E

In an effort to quickly gain an intercontinental reconnaissance capability, General LeMay ordered the B-36A fleet converted into RB-36Es. The Air Force authorized the conversions as an extension of contract AF33-038-2182, the current production contract. Since the YB-36A (the first B-36A) had been destroyed during structural testing, the original YB-36 (42-13571) was also modified to RB-36E standard to give the Air Force 22 aircraft. As originally envisioned,

---

* Actually, the film was stored on two 18-inch wide rolls – each "frame" consisted of an 18-inch square piece from each roll that formed a single 18 by 36-inch image.

On 5 April 1950, at least eight partially-stripped B-36A airframes were sitting on the Fort Worth flight line waiting to be disassembled during the A-to-E remanufacturing process. At this point the outer wing panels, engines, and empennage control surfaces had been removed, along with most internal systems. Each aircraft would soon be disassembled into its major assembly parts. These would be inspected and repaired as necessary to bring them up to the same standard as new-build RB-36D assemblies. The aircraft would then proceed down the main assembly line interspersed with B/RB-36Ds. (Lockheed Martin)

The photos above and below show a B-36A (44-92016) with its forward fuselage on a special trailer being demated from the rest of the aircraft on 18 July 1950. Note the radome on the ground in front of the wing. (Lockheed Martin)

One of the B-36As in the process of being stripped of all serviceable parts. Bracing is being built up around the fuselage in preparation for the airframe being disassembled. Photo dated 15 July 1950. (Lockheed Martin)

The forward fuselage did not stay on the trailer for long. As soon as it was clear of the wing, the fuselage section was picked up by a crane and placed on a special stand to wait for its turn in manufacturing. (Lockheed Martin)

Three B-36A forward fuselages (44-92021, 023, and 027) sit and wait on 17 July 1950. Note the gun turret bay detail. The "island" at the forward end in the middle of the turret bay was unique to the A- and B-models, and would remain even after the conversion to E- and D-models. New-build Ds and all subsequent aircraft did not have the island. (Lockheed Martin)

B-36A aft fuselages, main wing boxes, and vertical stabilizer assemblies stored between the Hangar Building (left) and Building 4 (right) on 15 September 1950. Apparently, for unexplained reasons, one RB-36E went through major mating and final assembly in this area of the yard. (Lockheed Martin)

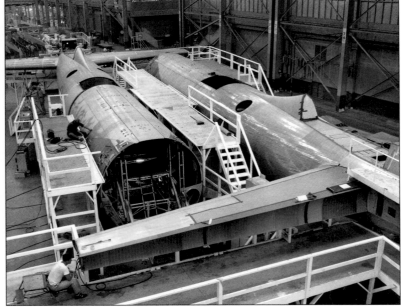

One of the A-models (44-92011) coming back together as an RB-36E on the main assembly line. At this point the fuselage and wings have been mated and the aircraft will enter final assembly. (Lockheed Martin)

B-36A aft fuselages after being demated and moved inside the main assembly building for refurbishment. Note that the main structure for the horizontal stabilizer was not removed. (Lockheed Martin)

these were really "RB-36Bs" in that the 22 aircraft would be brought up to B-36B standard and be equipped for reconnaissance. The decision to install jet engines on the last few B-36B production aircraft (and call them B-36Ds) resulted in the same changes being extended to the RB-36E configuration.

Although generally described as a "modification," in reality the RB-36Es were remanufactured, not converted. The process began with the aircraft arriving in Fort Worth where what little operational equipment that had been installed was removed. The aircraft were stripped of all other equipment, engines, etc., and then most of them sat on an isolated portion of the Convair ramp for several months. Eventually the aircraft were disassembled into their major manufacturing components (forward fuselage, center fuselage, aft fuselage, wing center box, etc.). These components were refurbished, brought up to the B/RB-36D standard, and reintroduced onto the production line interspersed with D-models. On the production line the RB-36Es were treated just like any other new-build B-36, and at the end of the line the RB-36Es were rolled out for a second time. For unexplained reasons, there was a single exception to this – one aircraft (44-92008) went through the remanufacturing process in the open air on the ramp next to Building 4. (The aircraft was neither the first nor the last to be remanufactured, so there appears to be no rationale.)

As completed, the R-4360-25 engines were replaced by R-4360-41s, and the aircraft were also equipped with the four J47-GE-19 jet engines. The same reconnaissance cameras and electronic systems scheduled for the RB-36D were used, although in common with the RB-36D the planned 48-inch K-40 camera was not available until late 1951. The aircraft were also fitted with the 20-mm defensive armament that had not been ready when they were initially built, and they also received the new "snap action" bomb bay doors used on the RB-36Ds. The first remanufactured aircraft made its maiden flight on 7 July 1950. The first RB-36E was delivered to the 28th SRW at Rapid City AFB on 28 July 1950, and the last conversion was completed on 27 April 1951.[13]

RB-36F

The 13 April 1949 order for 36 additional B-36s from Convair under the same contract (AF33-038-2182) that initiated B-36D production included 19 RB-36Fs, and 5 additional aircraft were ordered the following year. The RB-36F made its maiden flight on 30 April 1951. The first four RB-36Fs were accepted in May 1951, with the last being delivered in December 1951. The reconnaissance equipment in the aircraft was generally similar to the RB-36D while the other aircraft systems were the same as the B-36F.[14]

During early 1952 an RB-36F suffered a pressure bulkhead failure while flying at 33,000 feet. The accident was traced to a defective bulkhead, and all B-36s were restricted to altitudes below 25,000 feet until the entire fleet could be inspected and defective bulkheads replaced. While the accident investigation was ongoing, the Air Force declined to accept any new aircraft from Convair. Eventually Convair traced the problem to a comparatively minor manufacturing flaw and instituted a fix for all affected aircraft.

The last A-model (44-92017) to be remanufactured into an RB-36E nears the end of the final assembly line in Building 4 on 26 April 1951. Note that the Convair manufacturing number has been covered with paper for security reasons and that the nose turret is not installed. (Lockheed Martin)

A newly-completed RB-36E (44-92024) on the ramp at Convair on 25 July 1950 prior to its redelivery to the Air Force. (Lockheed Martin)

Operation Pinocchio

On 22 August 1951 two RB-36Es were involved in a ground accident at Travis AFB, California. One aircraft (44-92022) had taken off early in the morning on a 15-hour training flight with 22 crewmembers on board. After completing its mission, the aircraft returned to Travis 90 minutes earlier than planned, landing in the dark. The aircraft commander was directed to taxi to the squadron parking area. During the taxi the aircraft steered and braked normally, and the aircraft was parked on the south end of the ramp.

During the postflight checklist, the flight engineer advanced the throttles to 1,000 rpm for a static magneto check. As soon as the throttles were set at 1,000 rpm, the aircraft began to move forward. This initial movement was not noticed by other members of the crew, including the aircraft commander, who were busy "policing" the aircraft after the long flight. In addition, a gusting crosswind had been bucking the aircraft since landing, making the crew less sensitive to movement. The parking area was under construction and had no area lights, leading to darkness around the aircraft.

After the aircraft had moved 200–300 feet towards another RB-36E (44-92019), the aircraft commander finally realized what was happening and immediately applied the brakes. Nothing happened. The pilot also applied brakes with the same lack of result. Another crew member began to hand pump the emergency brake, but to no avail. The aircraft commander pulled the emergency ignition switch to OFF and ordered the crew to abandon the aircraft. There was only one minor injury. Nobody was aboard the other aircraft at the time.

The left wing of 022 impacted the right jet pod on the parked 019. The aircraft continued to come together until the jet pod on 022 struck the fuselage of 019 just under the right wing root. When the wing of 022 reached the fuselage of 019, it caused the fuselage to twist and break in two at the forward turret bay. The moving aircraft then swerved sharply to the left and came to rest with its wing covering the mangled nose section of 019.

Despite the magnitude of the damage, the Air Force elected to have Convair repair 019 (022 required only minor repairs, mostly accomplished locally by the 5th SRW). Since it was obvious that 019 could not be returned to Fort Worth, Convair dispatched a team to Travis to survey the damage. Subsequently, another Convair team arrived to remove all of the damaged parts from 019 and place the aircraft into storage while new parts were fabricated by Convair. Operation PINOCCHIO was born.

A new forward fuselage was fabricated in Fort Worth and shipped via two rail cars and a barge (to cross San Francisco Bay) to Travis in late March 1952. The new nose was grafted on at Travis, then Doc Witchell flew the aircraft back to Fort Worth for final repairs.

Above and below: The mangled forward fuselage of 44-92019 after being hit by 44-92022 during a bizarre ground accident. The aircraft broke apart around the forward turret bay, but the entire fuselage forward of the wing was a write-off. (U.S. Air Force)

A crew from Convair traveled to Travis in order to strip all of the damaged parts off of the aircraft and prepare 019 for storage while new parts were being fabricated in Fort Worth. While the aircraft was out of service, the engines and other components were also overhauled. (U.S. Air Force)

The nose gear was attached to the aft lower turret compartment for the aircraft to rest on while in storage. (U.S. Air Force)

Presenting a bit of an odd sight, 44-92019 sits in storage awaiting a new nose. (U.S. Air Force)

A different Operation PINOCCHIO motif adorned each side of the forward fuselage, with the one on the left being the one usually published. Note that no guns are installed in the nose turret. (U.S. Air Force)

Above: *An entirely new photo compartment was manufactured, making the second time this area had been replaced (once during A-to-E conversion).* Below: *the photo compartment packaged on its rail car for shipment.* (Convair)

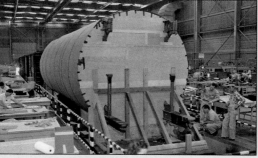

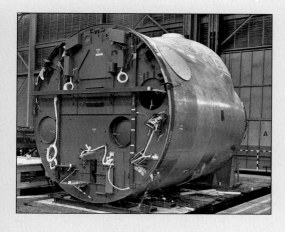

A good look at the forward turret bay area. Above is the aft face of bulkhead 4.0 – the pressure bulkhead at the back of the forward crew compartment. The circular hatch on the left of the photo will lead to the communications tube. The other hatch leads to the turret bay. The photo below is the front end of the forward fuselage. The turret bay is nearest the camera, followed by the pressure bulkhead that forms the forward part of the camera compartment. Note the six oxygen cylinders over where the APS-23 radar antenna motor will be located, and the wiring for the upper turrets. (Convair)

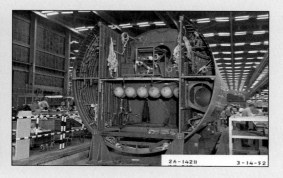

After the new nose was grafted on, the RB-36E (44-92019) looked like any of its contemporaries. The aircraft was subsequently modified into a Configuration II Featherweight. (U.S. Air Force)

RB-36H

The Air Force bought 73 reconnaissance versions of the B-36H. The initial contract (an extension of AF33-038-2182) for 15 B-36H and 8 RB-36H aircraft was announced on 5 September 1951, although it had been signed over a year earlier meaning that the aircraft carried FY50 serial numbers. An additional 39 reconnaissance variants would be ordered in FY51 and 26 more in FY52. Twenty-three RB-36Hs were accepted during the first 6 months of 1952; 42 others were delivered between July 1952 and June 1953, and the last eight were accepted during FY54 (three in July 1953, three in August, and two in September). The camera and ECM/ferret equipment were generally similar to the earlier RB-36s, while all other systems were identical to the B-36H.[15]

MISSIONS

Surprisingly little is known about the missions flown by RB-36s. It is fairly certain that the aircraft never performed overflights of the Soviet Union, at least not from the European side. What it did on the Pacific and Arctic sides is much less clear – still, direct overflights of interior targets are unlikely. It is, however, entirely possible that RB-36s flew peripheral signal gathering missions along the Pacific and Arctic coasts of the Soviet Union.[16]

One deployment that is known involved two RB-36s from the 5th Strategic Reconnaissance Wing from Travis AFB during March 1954. For 2 weeks the aircraft flew missions out of Thule, Greenland, to determine if "clandestine Soviet communications activities existed in an area of interest along the northeastern coast of Greenland, between latitudes 080-00N and 070-00N.[17]

The RB-36s, from the 23rd and 72nd Strategic Reconnaissance Squadrons, each flew two missions in support of Project 54AFR-11. During the first mission, the area of interest was monitored for 24 continuous hours – 12 hours by each aircraft – to detect Soviet transmissions. The mission was considered "highly successful" but the actual results could not be ascertained. On the second mission, each aircraft continued to monitor Soviet transmissions but also conducted experimental flash photography over the highly reflective surfaces to the north of Greenland. This latter mission "was accomplished only to a limited degree."

An RB-36 being prepared for roll-out gives a good look at the original bomb bay door configuration with a single set of doors covering bomb bays Nos. 2 and 3. All aircraft were delivered in this configuration. See the top of the following page for the later configuration. (Lockheed Martin)

The later RB-36 bomb bay door configuration was a single set of short doors covering bomb bay No. 2, and a set of doors identical to the bomber versions covering bomb bay No. 3 and the newly activated bomb bay No. 4. Note the various ECM antennas protruding from the fuselage and the radome for the APS-23 search radar. This photo was taken on 16 May 1955 after all the major modifications had been incorporated. (Lockheed Martin)

An RB-36H-25-CF (51-13720) takes off from Fort Worth for its delivery flight on 10 July 1952. The next couple of years would see the RB-36 fleet modified into nuclear bombers. (Lockheed Martin)

An RB-36H-55-CF (52-1384) undergoing maintenance at Fort Worth. Note the nose dock covering the forward fuselage and the fact that the tail radome has been removed to service the APG-41. (Lockheed Martin)

Two 5th SRW aircraft: an RB-36E-10-CF (44-92020) on the left, and another RB-36E-10-CF (44-92023) on the right. (Frederick A. Johnsen Collection; Warren Bodie via Richard Freeman)

This RB-36F-1-CF (49-2703) from Fairchild AFB lost its rudder while enroute to the inauguration ceremonies for the temporary Air Force Academy at Lowery AFB, Colorado, on 11 July 1955. The aircraft commander, Major William J. Deyerle, maintained control of the aircraft and successfully landed at Ellsworth AFB. (Fairchild Heritage Museum)

An RB-36H-30-CF (51-13730) with the upper turrets deployed and all of the ECM antennas installed. (Frederick A. Johnsen Collection)

The side oblique (upper left) and forward oblique camera ports with the doors open on the RB-36H on display at Castle AFB. (Dennis R. Jenkins)

The side oblique camera port with the door open. (Dennis R. Jenkins)

Looking straight up into the main camera port under the fuselage. (Dennis R. Jenkins)

The main vertical camera port under the fuselage with the door open. (Dennis R. Jenkins)

STATION	CAMERA	FOCAL LENGTH-INCHES	QUAN-TITY	USE
Trime-trogon	K-17C	6	3	Charting and Mapping
Vertical	K-17C, K-37, K-22A, or T-11	6, 12, or 24	1	Mapping, Intelligence, and Night Photography
Split Vertical	K-38	24	2	Mapping, Reconnaissance, and Intelligence
Multi	K-38 or K-40	36 48	5	Reconnaissance and Intelligence
Forward Oblique	K-22A	12	1	Reconnaissance and Intelligence
Left Oblique	K-22A	12 or 24	1	Reconnaissance and Opportunity
Right Oblique	K-22A	12 or 24	1	Reconnaissance and Opportunity
Photo-Navigator and Radar Observer	C-1		2	Radar Scope Photography
Photo-Navigator	A-6		1	Motion Picture Reconnaissance and Intelligence

The camera summary chart from the RB-36H flight manual shows the types of cameras that could be installed at each station and its primary use. The focal lengths available for each camera are also listed. (U.S. Air Force)

COLOR & INTERIOR PHOTOGRAPHY

The XB-36 during early tests. Note that the main landing gear doors have not been fitted in the photo below—this shot was likely taken prior to the first flight. The photo at above shows that the main landing gear doors have been fitted, so it was taken a while after first flight. The streamlined "airliner style" nose on the XB-36 was much sleeker than the production unit. Amazingly little ground support equipment was used 50 years ago. (Lockheed Martin)

Late 1940s view of Carswell AFB showing 29 pre-jet B-36s including 10 with red arctic colors. The partially disassembled B-36As are in front of the Convair plant (top of photo) awaiting conversion to RB-36Es. Lake Worth is to the right at the end of the runways. (Jack Kerr via the Frank Kleinwechter Collection via Don Pyeatt)

The first B-36B (44-92026) at an open house after it had been converted to a D-model. The small radome just in front of the landing gear covers a direction finder antenna for the navigation system. The attachment point for the liaison radio's wire antenna may be seen just below and aft of the sighting blister. (E.W. Quandt via Dave Menard)

Above and Below: The XB-36 with its track landing gear on display at Carswell during an open house on 20 May 1950. (Jack Kerr via the Frank Kleinwechter Collection via Don Pyeatt)

It was not unusual to cruise with the inboard propellers feathered. (Frank Kleinwechter via Warren F. Thompson)

Another view from inside, this time from the 72nd BW during a sunset in 1957. (C. Martin via Marty Isham)

Right: One of the few surviving color photos of the McDonnell XF-85 Goblin that had been intended to be carried by the B-36, shown here on its special ground handling dolly. (Tony Landis Collection)

The 15th Air Force insignia on this RB-36F-1-CF (49-2704) is located further from the leading edge than was normal practice for the other numbered Air Forces. (National Archives via Stan Piet)

The YB-36A (44-92004) in the static test rig at Wright Field, Ohio, shortly after arriving. The airframe would be tested to destruction in a variety of positions. (National Archives via Stan Piet)

This B-36B-5-CF (44-92038) has the small UNITED STATES AIR FORCE written across the forward fuselage, no buzz number, and no numbered Air Force insignia on the tail. The area around the serial number on the tail and the USAF on the wing panel were silver, not red. (San Diego Aerospace Museum Collection)

A good overhead view of a B-36B-1-CF (44-92031) on 13 April 1949 while flying over the Guadaloupe Mountains in west Texas. The location of the national insignia and USAF on the wings shows up well here – compare these to later jet-assisted aircraft where the markings were moved well outboard. (Frank Kleinwechter via Don Pyeatt)

A red tail B-36B-1-CF (44-92028) being prepared for flight. Note the blue exhaust smoke at the extreme right. By this time the numbered Air Force insignia had been added to the tail, along with the unit badge on the nose. (National Archives via Stan Piet)

Another B-36B (44-92036) seen on 13 April 1949. Note the absence of USAF on the right wing panel compared to the photo on the previous page. (Frank Kleinwechter via Don Pyeatt)

The tail turrets on the red-tail B-36Bs (this is 44-92033 at Carswell) were painted silver, with the radomes left in their natural gray. (Frank Kleinwechter via Don Pyeatt)

The numbered Air Force insignia on the tail of a B-36B-5-CF (44-92041) at Biggs AFB near El Paso, Texas, on 5 May 1949. (Frank Kleinwechter via Don Pyeatt)

Frank F. Kleinwechter, Jr.'s first flight as a B-36 crewmember was in this B-36A-10-CF (44-92014), shown here on 5 December 1948 during an open house at El Paso. (Frank Kleinwechter via Don Pyeatt)

An unidentified B-36B displays its upper aft gun turrets at the Albuquerque, New Mexico, air show on 6 August 1949. Note the yellow propeller spinners and the early-style round-tip propellers (Frank Kleinwechter via Don Pyeatt)

This B-36A-1-CF (44-92006) appears to be undergoing fuel tank sealing since the wing leading edges have been removed and the tank access panels are open. (National Archives via Stan Piet)

The City of Ft. Worth (52-2827) was the last B-36 manufactured and was placed on display in Fort Worth after its retirement. It was one of the few airplanes with the white upper fuselage over the forward crew compartment. (Jack Kerr via the Frank Kleinwechter Collection via Don Pyeatt)

Interestingly, this B-36B does not have any cannon installed in its nose turret, although the nose gun sight can clearly be seen projecting from the glazed area beneath the empty turret. The photo was taken on 14 May 1950 at Fairfield-Suisun, California. Note the early faired-type ECM antennas on the forward fuselage. (Frank Kleinwechter via Don Pyeatt)

A good shot of the upper fuselage detail on an early B-36 at Carswell on 26 May 1950. Note the open engine cowling at right. (Frank Kleinwechter via Don Pyeatt)

The Tom-Tom test aircraft (JRB-36F-1-CF, 49-2707) had orange and blue trim applied to the nose and wingtip pods. Note the test boom protruding from the nose. (Lockheed Martin)

This photo of maintenance operations at Carswell on 26 May 1950 shows the amount of variation in markings. The nearest airplane (B-36B-15-CF, 44-92073) shows the small forward fuselage markings, and the full complement of tail markings. The second airplane (B-36B-20-CF, 44-92084) shows the abbreviated "buzz" numbers (no "BM" prefix), and only the numbered Air Force insignia on the tail. (Frank Kleinwechter via Don Pyeatt)

The XC-99 (43-52436) is shown (above) at San Diego in its original natural metal finish with the 110-inch main landing gear. A few years later (below) at Washington National it had been painted in overall silver lacquer. (above: Convair; below: via Dave Menard)

This was the paint scheme the XC-99 wore in September 1954 – overall silver with a white top above the flight deck. The SAAMA insignia on the tail changed several times over the years. (via Dave Menard)

The size of the XC-99 and B-36 made working on the vertical stabilizer an adventure. Here is the tail stand designed to wrap around the vertical, but workers are still using ropes as well. (National Archives via Stan Piet)

The data block on the side of the fuselage reads EB-36H-30-CF (51-5726) from the 4925th Test Group (Atomic) at Kirtland AFB. There were actually two EB-36s based at Kirtland – the one shown plus an EB-36H-55-CF (52-1358). Both aircraft participated in a variety of military-related and scientific tests. (National Archives via Stan Piet)

Far left: *Captain Wayne Tidbury from the Canadian Department of National Defense Squadron 417, CFB Cold Lake, Alberta, stands in the wreckage aft of the bomb bay of B-36B-15-CF (44-92075) in British Columbia. One of the 20-mm cannon units is visible over his right shoulder in this 11 August 1997 photo.* (Doug Davidge)

Below: *The "leatherette" cover of an early B-36 flight test report.* (Jay Miller Collection)

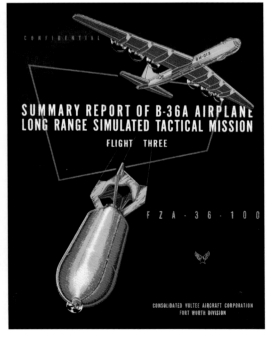

The crew compartments of an RB-36H-5-CF (50-1110) from the 5th SRW. Above: clockwise from lower left: 1LT James Shively is the navigator, Captain William Merrill is the photo-navigator, A1C Albert Brown is the nose gunner and weather observer, and Captain Franklin O'Donald is the radar observer. Right: SSGT John McCarl in the radio operator's position in the RB-36. (National Archives via Stan Piet)

This B-36D-50-CF (44-92033) was photographed flying along with an F-94B (51-5450) from the Oregon Air National Guard. Note the stripe around the tail of the B-36. This B-36 would never be converted to the Featherweight III configuration, and would carry a full set of cannon for its entire career. The white anti-flash paint on the aft fuselage shows up well here. The photo was taken from another F-94, with its tip tank visible at the bottom. (Lt.Col. C. Toynbee via Dave Menard)

A B-36F-1-CF (49-2677) was used to carry the B-58 static test article from Fort Worth to Wright-Patterson AFB on 12 March 1957. The inboard propellers were removed and the landing gear was left extended for the entire flight since the B-58's wing would have interfered with retracting the gear. This limited the B-36's top speed considerably, but it was still better than disassembling the B-58 and figuring out how to transport it overland Note the location of the red stripe on the vertical stabilizer compared to the photo above. (Peter M. Bowers Collection)

Looking rather the worse for wear, the Air Force Museum's B-36J-1-CF (52-2220) displays the markings it was retired in. Apparently only a few airplanes received the white anti-flash paint around the top of the forward crew compartment – no documentation could be found that authorized the change, but both the Air Force Museum's and the Fort Worth aircraft were so equipped. (Peter M. Bowers)

Miss Featherweight, *a B-36H-1-CF (50-1086), at Eglin AFB, Florida, on 10 October 1955. Note the rail system used to transport the bombs, and the bomb lift temporarily installed on top of the airplane. A portable crane (at right) lifts the bombs from the flatbed truck onto the rail system. A pair of 22,000-pound T-14 Grand Slam bombs are shown below, while a 43,000-pound T-12 is at lower right (shown at a Carswell open house in May 1950). (lower right: Jack Kerr; others Frank Kleinwechter via Don Pyeatt)*

The NB-36H was probably the most elegantly marked B-36, with a graceful blue and red trim line extending the length of the fuselage and red nacelle trim. Originally the side of the aircraft had "Convair Crusader" written in the blue cheat line, but the "Crusader" was subsequently painted over for unexplained reasons.(above left: Lockheed Martin; above right: Convair; below: San Diego Aerospace Museum Collection)

One of the early signs (above left) marking the entrance to Carswell AFB, Texas. At right is Frank F. Kleinwechter, Jr. at Goose Bay on 23 January 1952 with a B-36F-5-CF (49-2680) in the background. The snow plows were in constant operation at Goose Bay in an often futile attempt to keep the ramps and runway clear. (Frank Kleinwechter via Don Pyeatt)

Not the best photo, but unusual in that it shows a DB-36H (51-5710) carrying a Rascal missile at Kirtland AFB. Note the DB-47 with a Rascal in the background. All of the test Rascals were painted day-glo orange with white and black photo-reference markings around the nose. The DB-36 markings were standard except for the red nacelle trim. (Lockheed Martin)

Another marginal photo of an unusual Kirtland aircraft. This EB-36H (51-5726) was painted this way to assist in calibrating various optical sensors on the Atlantic Missile Range and elsewhere. Another EB-36H (52-1358) was similarly painted. (Courtesy of the Air Force Research Laboratory, Phillips Research Site History Office)

The YB-60 was flown in the same natural metal finish as contemporary B-36Fs, but had a bright red cheat line and red nacelle trim. Note the tail wheel in the shot at left and how it is pivoted opposite of the nose wheels to assist in ground handling. (upper left: Frank Kleinwechter Collection via Don Pyeatt; lower left: Lockheed Martin; upper right: Tony Landis Collection; lower right: Terry Panopalis Collection)

With a crew of between 15 and 22, depending on the version, there was a lot inside the B-36. The next dozen pages will show most of the crew stations inside the airplane. While most interior photos are grouped here, there are also a few crew station photos spread throughout the rest of the book: the XB-36 cockpit in Chapter 1, the XC-99 cockpit is shown in Chapter 2, the Tanbo in Chapter 4, FICON in Chapter 9, and the NB-36H is detailed in Chapter 11. Even given the great size of the B-36, it was still not a particularly wonderful place to spend 2 days cooped-up with a dozen other men. Still, it was – at least during its mid-life – much more comfortable than the World War II bombers. When the Featherweight program began stripping out the crew comfort items and forced the crew into heated flight suits, the 2 days became much less pleasant. Fortunately, there were only a couple of years of useful service left.

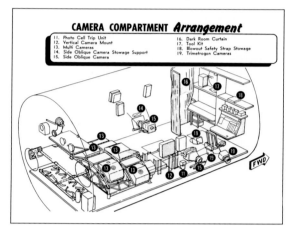

CAMERA COMPARTMENT Arrangement

11. Photo Cell Trip Unit
12. Vertical Camera Mount
13. Multi Cameras
14. Side Oblique Camera Stowage Support
15. Side Oblique Camera
16. Dark Room Curtain
17. Tool Kit
18. Blowout Safety Strap Stowage
19. Trimetrogon Cameras

The forward crew compartment of a B-36D (right) was representative of the D, E, and F-models before the majority of the K-system components were moved inside. The photo compartment (above) of the RB-36D was also representative of the early models. (U.S. Air Force)

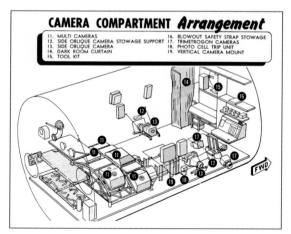

CAMERA COMPARTMENT Arrangement

11. MULTI CAMERAS
12. SIDE OBLIQUE CAMERA STOWAGE SUPPORT
13. SIDE OBLIQUE CAMERA
14. DARK ROOM CURTAIN
15. TOOL KIT
16. BLOWOUT SAFETY STRAP STOWAGE
17. TRIMETROGON CAMERAS
18. PHOTO CELL TRIP UNIT
19. VERTICAL CAMERA MOUNT

The B-36H (right) shows the rearranged flight deck used on the H and J-models. Much of the lower-deck arrangement would later be duplicated in earlier aircraft, the new flight deck remained unique to the last two models. The RB-36H camera compartment (above) was not significantly different from earlier models. (U.S. Air Force)

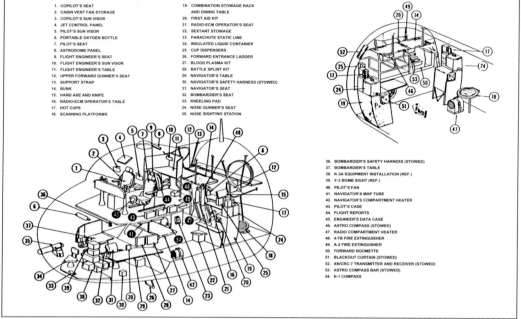

1. COPILOT'S SEAT
2. CABIN VENT FAN STORAGE
3. COPILOT'S SUN VISOR
4. JET CONTROL PANEL
5. PILOT'S SUN VISOR
6. PORTABLE OXYGEN BOTTLE
7. PILOT'S SEAT
8. ASTRODOME PANEL
9. FLIGHT ENGINEER'S SEAT
10. FLIGHT ENGINEER'S SUN VISOR
11. FLIGHT ENGINEER'S TABLE
12. UPPER FORWARD GUNNER'S SEAT
13. SUPPORT STRAP
14. BUNK
15. HAND AXE AND KNIFE
16. RADIO-ECM OPERATOR'S TABLE
17. HOT CUPS
18. SCANNING PLATFORMS
19. COMBINATION STOWAGE RACK AND DINING TABLE
20. FIRST AID KIT
21. RADIO-ECM OPERATOR'S SEAT
22. SEXTANT STOWAGE
23. PARACHUTE STATIC LINE
24. INSULATED LIQUID CONTAINER
25. CUP DISPENSERS
26. FORWARD ENTRANCE LADDER
27. BLOOD PLASMA KIT
28. BATTLE SPLINT KIT
29. NAVIGATOR'S TABLE
30. NAVIGATOR'S SAFETY HARNESS (STOWED)
31. NAVIGATOR'S SEAT
32. BOMBARDIER'S SEAT
33. KNEELING PAD
34. NOSE GUNNER'S SEAT
35. NOSE SIGHTING STATION
36. BOMBARDIER'S SAFETY HARNESS (STOWED)
37. BOMBARDIER'S TABLE
38. K-3A EQUIPMENT INSTALLATION (REF.)
39. Y-3 BOMB SIGHT (REF.)
40. PILOT'S FAN
41. NAVIGATOR'S MAP TUBE
42. NAVIGATOR'S COMPARTMENT HEATER
43. PILOT'S CASE
44. FLIGHT REPORTS
45. ENGINEER'S DATA CASE
46. ASTRO COMPASS (STOWED)
47. RADIO COMPARTMENT HEATER
48. 4-TB FIRE EXTINGUISHER
49. A-2 FIRE EXTINGUISHER
50. FORWARD ROOMETTE
51. BLACKOUT CURTAIN (STOWED)
52. AN/CRC-7 TRANSMITTER AND RECEIVER (STOWED)
53. ASTRO COMPASS BAR (STOWED)
54. N-1 COMPASS

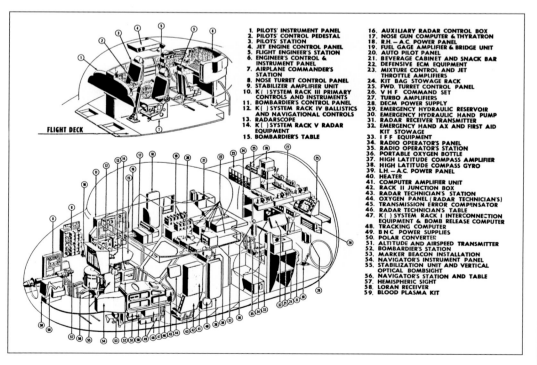

FLIGHT DECK

1. PILOTS' INSTRUMENT PANEL
2. PILOTS' CONTROL PEDESTAL
3. PILOTS' STATION
4. JET ENGINE CONTROL PANEL
5. FLIGHT ENGINEER'S STATION
6. ENGINEER'S CONTROL & INSTRUMENT PANEL
7. AIRPLANE COMMANDER'S STATION
8. NOSE TURRET CONTROL PANEL
9. STABILIZER AMPLIFIER UNIT
10. K( ) SYSTEM RACK III PRIMARY CONTROLS AND INSTRUMENTS
11. BOMBARDIER'S CONTROL PANEL
12. K( ) SYSTEM RACK IV BALLISTICS AND NAVIGATIONAL CONTROLS
13. RADARSCOPE
14. K( ) SYSTEM RACK V RADAR EQUIPMENT
15. BOMBARDIER'S TABLE
16. AUXILIARY RADAR CONTROL BOX
17. NOSE GUN COMPUTER & THYRATRON
18. R.H. – A.C. POWER PANEL
19. FUEL GAGE AMPLIFIER & BRIDGE UNIT
20. AUTO PILOT PANEL
21. BEVERAGE CABINET AND SNACK BAR
22. DEFENSIVE ECM EQUIPMENT
23. MIXTURE CONTROL AND JET THROTTLE AMPLIFIERS
24. KIT BAG STOWAGE RACK
25. FWD. TURRET CONTROL PANEL
26. V H F COMMAND SET
27. TURBO AMPLIFIERS
28. DECM POWER SUPPLY
29. EMERGENCY HYDRAULIC RESERVOIR
30. EMERGENCY HYDRAULIC HAND PUMP
31. RADAR RECEIVER TRANSMITTER
32. EMERGENCY HAND AX AND FIRST AID KIT STOWAGE
33. I F F EQUIPMENT
34. RADIO OPERATOR'S PANEL
35. RADIO OPERATOR'S STATION
36. PORTABLE OXYGEN BOTTLE
37. HIGH LATITUDE COMPASS AMPLIFIER
38. HIGH LATITUDE COMPASS GYRO
39. L.H. – A.C. POWER PANEL
40. HEATER
41. COMPUTER AMPLIFIER UNIT
42. RACK II JUNCTION BOX
43. RADAR TECHNICIAN'S STATION
44. OXYGEN PANEL (RADAR TECHNICIAN'S)
45. TRANSMISSION ERROR COMPENSATOR
46. RADAR TECHNICIAN'S TABLE
47. K( ) SYSTEM RACK I INTERCONNECTION EQUIPMENT & BOMB RELEASE COMPUTER
48. TRACKING COMPUTER
49. B N C POWER SUPPLIES
50. POLAR CONVERTER
51. ALTITUDE AND AIRSPEED TRANSMITTER
52. BOMBARDIER'S STATION
53. MARKER BEACON INSTALLATION
54. NAVIGATOR'S INSTRUMENT PANEL
55. STABILIZATION UNIT AND VERTICAL OPTICAL BOMBSIGHT
56. NAVIGATOR'S STATION AND TABLE
57. HEMISPHERIC SIGHT
58. LORAN RECEIVER
59. BLOOD PLASMA KIT

This was pretty much how all B-36 main instrument panels looked until the advent of the H-model. The main panel (above) is from a B-36D (44-92096), while the overhead panel (left) is from an RB-36E (44-920019). The jet engine instrumentation was split between two subpanels next to the center pedestal, with the controls, switches, and circuit breakers located on the overhead panel. Non-jet-equipped aircraft were generally similar, but naturally lacked the jet instrumentation and controls. Note the fans provided in front of each seat to help cool the pilots. Six red warning lights are located at the top center of the main panel – these indicated an uncommanded propeller reversal. Normally, each control wheel had a lacquered "horn button" in the center with the Consolidated Vultee logo on it (right); both seem to be missing when this photo was taken. (right: via Don Pyeatt; others Convair)

The B-36H (52-1352 shown here) featured a completely rearranged flight deck and a new instrument panel, something carried through to the J-model. The jet instrumentation was integrated onto the main panel, although the throttles and other controls were still located on a redesigned overhead panel (right). The two panels on top of the anti-glare shield are T-18 control boxes for the nuclear weapons in bomb bays Nos. 1 and 4 – on aircraft equipped to carry nuclear weapons in all four bomb bays, two identical control panels were installed at the lower edge of the jet control panel. Additional controls were at the bombardier's (or photo-navigator's) position. The round knob on the center console is the rudder trim control; the two larger wheels on the sides of the center console control the elevator trim. Interestingly, although this aircraft was equipped with a relatively modern (for the era) APS-54 radar warning system, indicators were not provided directly to the pilots. (Lockheed Martin)

The flight engineer's station on the B-36H received major revisions from previous models. The most obvious was that there were seats for two engineers. Although B-36s had almost always carried two flight engineers, seating was only provided for one on earlier models. Interestingly, the jet engines were still not included on the flight engineer's panels except for a fuel flow gauge for each jet at the very top of the main instrument panel. The jet throttles remained on the pilot's overhead panel, and all of the jet engine instruments were now located in the center of the pilot's main panel. Nevertheless, the new panels were better organized and easier to understand. (photos: Lockheed Martin; drawings: U.S. Air Force)

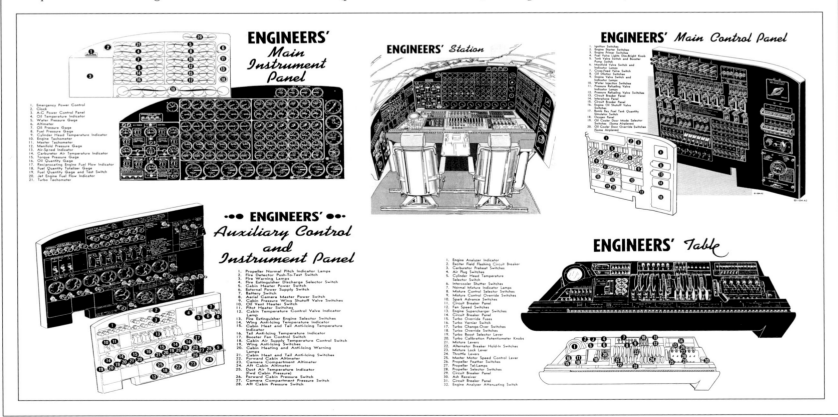

ENGINEERS' *Main Instrument Panel*

1. Emergency Power Control
2. Clock
3. A-C Power Control Panel
4. Oil Temperature Indicator
5. Water Pressure Gage
6. Altimeter
7. Oil Pressure Gage
8. Fuel Pressure Gage
9. Cylinder Head Temperature Indicator
10. Engine Tachometer
11. Master Tachometer
12. Manifold Pressure Gage
13. Air-Speed Indicator
14. Carburetor Air Temperature Indicator
15. Torque Pressure Gage
16. Oil Quantity Gage
17. Reciprocating Engine Fuel Flow Indicator
18. Fuel Quantity Totalizer Gage
19. Fuel Quantity Gage and Test Switch
20. Jet Engine Fuel Flow Indicator
21. Turbo Tachometer

ENGINEERS' *Station*

ENGINEERS' *Main Control Panel*

1. Ignition Switches
2. Engine Starter Switches
3. Engine Primer Switches
4. Fuel Valve Lights Dim-Bright Knob
5. Tank Valve Switch and Booster Pump Switch
6. Manifold Valve Switch and Indicator Lamps
7. Cross-Feed Valve Switch
8. Oil Dilution Switches
9. Engine Valve Switch and Indicator Lamps
10. Water Injection Switches
11. Pressure Refueling Valve Indicator Lamps
12. Pressure Refueling Valve Switches
13. Circuit Breaker Panel
14. Interphone Panel
15. Circuit Breaker Panel
16. Engine Oil Shutoff Valve Switches
17. Bomb Bay Fuel Tank Quantity Simulator Switch
18. Oxygen Panel
19. Oil Cooler Door Mode Selector Switches (Some Airplanes)
20. Oil Cooler Door Override Switches (Some Airplanes)

••• ENGINEERS' ••• *Auxiliary Control and Instrument Panel*

1. Propeller Normal Pitch Indicator Lamps
2. Fire Detector Push-To-Test Switch
3. Fire Warning Lamps
4. Fire Extinguisher Discharge Selector Switch
5. Cabin Heater Power Switch
6. External Power Supply Switch
7. Battery Switch
8. Aerial Camera Master Power Switch
9. Cabin Pressure Wing Shutoff Valve Switches
10. Oil Vent Heater Switch
11. Pitot Heater Switches
12. Cabin Temperature Control Valve Indicator Lamp
13. Fire Extinguisher Engine Selector Switches
14. Wing Anti-Icing Temperature Indicator
15. Cabin Heat and Tail Anti-Icing Temperature Indicator
16. Tail Anti-Icing Temperature Indicator
17. Booster Fan Control Switch
18. Cabin Air Supply Temperature Control Switch
19. Wing Anti-Icing Switches
20. Cabin Heating and Anti-Icing Warning Lamps
21. Cabin Heat and Tail Anti-Icing Switches
22. Forward Cabin Altimeter
23. Camera Compartment Altimeter
24. Aft Cabin Altimeter
25. Duct Air Temperature Indicator (Fwd Cabin Pressure)
26. Forward Cabin Pressure Switch
27. Camera Compartment Pressure Switch
28. Aft Cabin Pressure Switch

ENGINEERS' *Table*

1. Engine Analyzer Indicator
2. Exciter Field Flashing Circuit Breaker
3. Carburetor Preheat Switches
4. Air Plug Switches
5. Cylinder Head Temperature Selector Switch
6. Intercooler Shutter Switches
7. Normal Mixture Indicator Lamps
8. Mixture Control Selector Switches
9. Mixture Control Override Switches
10. Spark Advance Switches
11. Circuit Breaker Panel
12. Fan Speed Switches
13. Engine Supercharger Switches
14. Circuit Breaker Panel
15. Turbo Override Fuses
16. Turbo Vernier Switch
17. Turbo Change-Over Switches
18. Turbo Override Switches
19. Turbo Boost Selector Lever
20. Turbo Calibration Potentiometer Knobs
21. Mixture Levers
22. Alternator Breaker Hold-In Switches
23. Turbo Lock Lever
24. Throttle Levers
25. Master Motor Speed Control Lever
26. Propeller Feather Switches
27. Propeller Tel-Lamps
28. Propeller Selector Switches
29. Circuit Breaker Panel
30. Ash Receiver
31. Circuit Breaker Panel
32. Engine Analyzer Attenuating Switch

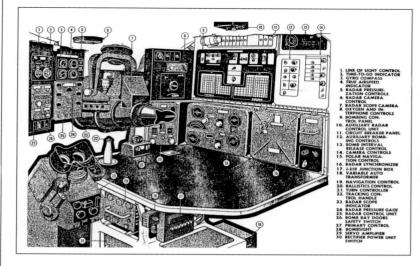

1. LINE OF SIGHT CONTROL
2. TIME-TO-GO INDICATOR
3. GYRO COMPASS
4. TRUE AIRSPEED INDICATOR
5. RADAR PRESSURI-ZATION CONTROLS
6. RADAR CAMERA CONTROL
7. RADAR SCOPE CAMERA
8. OXYGEN AND IN-TERPHONE CONTROLS
9. BOMBING CON-TROL PANEL
10. AUXILIARY RADAR CONTROL UNIT
11. CIRCUIT BREAKER PANEL
12. AUXILIARY BOMB-ING CONTROLS
13. BOMB INTERVAL RELEASE CONTROL
14. CAMERA CONTROLS
15. POLAR NAVIGA-TION CONTROL
16. RADAR SYNCHRONIZER
17. J-218 JUNCTION BOX
18. VARIABLE AUTO TRANSFORMER
19. NAVIGATION CONTROL
20. BALLISTICS CONTROL
21. TURN CONTROLLER
22. TRACKING CON-TROL HANDLE
23. RADAR SCOPE INDICATOR
24. RADAR PRESSURE GAGE
25. RADAR CONTROL UNIT
26. BOMB BAY DOORS SAFETY SWITCH
27. PRIMARY CONTROL
28. BOMBSIGHT
29. SERVO AMPLIFIER
30. RECTIFIER POWER UNIT SWITCH

The radar-bombardier station. Note the radar scope on the extreme left – towards the very end of the B-36's career this was changed from a 5-inch scope to a 10-inch unit. The bombsight (number 28) was the Farrand Y-3 periscopic bombsight that ran vertically through the fuselage and protruded through the lower fuselage, offset slightly to the right side of the aircraft. The box at number 15 (just above the right part of the table) and the box just to the right of it were part of the GEM polar navigation modification. The smaller box has a three-position switch marked NORMAL, POLAR, and POST-POLAR that fed offsets into the navigation system that allowed it to handle crossing over magnetic north. Even given this, it was still largely left to the navigator to take star sightings to ensure the aircraft remained on course at northern latitudes. It was not until the advent of reliable inertial navigation systems that polar flight became routine. (photo: Lockheed Martin; drawing: U.S. Air Force)

The original radio operator's position was very simple. Note the telegraph key on the table – messages were still sent using Morse code as often as they were using voice since the low data rates for Morse translated to longer range for the signal. This station was on the bottom deck in the rear of the forward compartment. Although difficult to read at this resolution, the large radio sitting on the right side of the desk says "SIGNAL CORPS – US ARMY" on its data plate. (Lockheed Martin)

RB-36 radar-navigator station on the left side of the nose compartment. (Lockheed Martin)

RB-36 radar-observer station on the right side of the nose compartment. (Lockheed Martin)

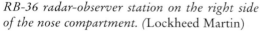

1. LORAN SET
2. OXYGEN PANEL
3. INTERPHONE CONTROL PANEL
4. CIRCUIT BREAKER PANEL
5. RADAR SCOPE
6. C-1 CAMERA
7. EXPOSURE FREQUENCY CONTROL BOX
8. AERIAL CAMERA READY LIGHT
9. DURATION CONTROL
10. DRIFT ANGLE CONTROL
11. BOMBSIGHT
12. CAMERA CONTROL PANEL
13. BOMBING CONTROL PANEL
14. PHOTO-NAVIGATOR'S SIGHTING STATION
15. INSTRUMENT PANEL
16. RADIO COMPASS CONTROL PANEL

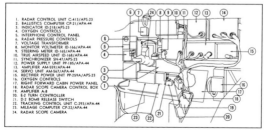

1. RADAR CONTROL UNIT C-413/APS-23
2. BALLISTICS COMPUTER CP-21/APA-44
3. INDICATOR ID-318/APS-23
4. OXYGEN CONTROLS
5. INTERPHONE CONTROL PANEL
6. RADAR PRESSURE CONTROLS
7. VOLTAGE TRANSFORMER
8. MONITOR VOLTMETER ID-166/APA-44
9. STEERING METER ID-165/APA-44
10. TRUE AIRSPEED UNIT ID-168/APA-44
11. SYNCHRONIZER SN-47/APA-23
12. POWER SUPPLY UNIT PP-185/APA-44
13. AMPLIFIER AM-559/APA-44
14. SERVO UNIT AM-567/APA-44
15. RECTIFIER POWER UNIT PP-259A/APS-23
16. OXYGEN CONTROLS
17. RIGHT FORWARD CABIN POWER PANEL
18. RADAR SCOPE CAMERA CONTROL BOX
19. AMPLIFIER A-8
20. E-2 TURN CONTROLLER
21. D-2 BOMB RELEASE SWITCH
22. TRACKING CONTROL UNIT C-293/APA-44
23. MILEAGE COMPUTER CP-22/APA-44
24. RADAR SCOPE CAMERA

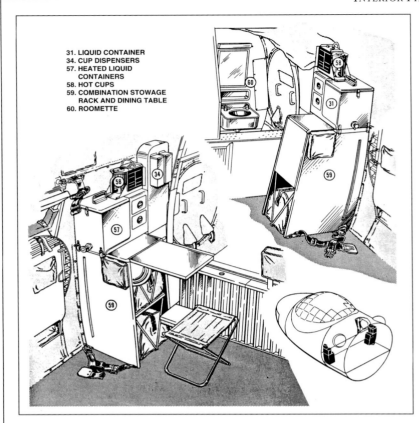

31. LIQUID CONTAINER
34. CUP DISPENSERS
57. HEATED LIQUID CONTAINERS
58. HOT CUPS
59. COMBINATION STOWAGE RACK AND DINING TABLE
60. ROOMETTE

Convair went to great lengths to add crew comfort items such as better bunks and galleys beginning with the B-36H, but all of the equipment was deleted during the Featherweight program. (U.S. Air Force)

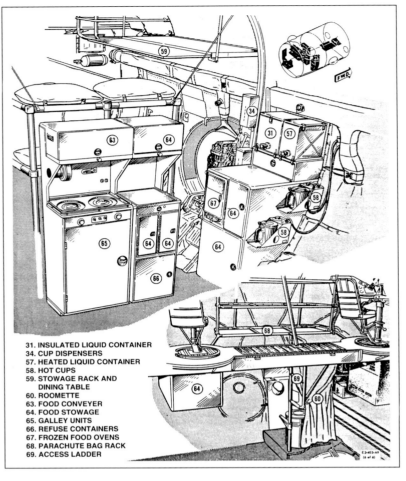

31. INSULATED LIQUID CONTAINER
34. CUP DISPENSERS
57. HEATED LIQUID CONTAINER
58. HOT CUPS
59. STOWAGE RACK AND DINING TABLE
60. ROOMETTE
63. FOOD CONVEYER
64. FOOD STOWAGE
65. GALLEY UNITS
66. REFUSE CONTAINERS
67. FROZEN FOOD OVENS
68. PARACHUTE BAG RACK
69. ACCESS LADDER

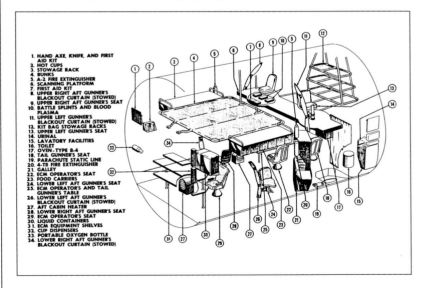

1. HAND AXE, KNIFE, AND FIRST AID KIT
2. HOT CUPS
3. STOWAGE RACK
4. BUNKS
5. A-2 FIRE EXTINGUISHER
6. SCANNING PLATFORM
7. FIRST AID KIT
8. UPPER RIGHT AFT GUNNER'S BLACKOUT CURTAIN (STOWED)
9. UPPER RIGHT AFT GUNNER'S SEAT
10. BATTLE SPLINTS AND BLOOD PLASMA
11. UPPER LEFT GUNNER'S BLACKOUT CURTAIN (STOWED)
12. KIT BAG STOWAGE RACKS
13. UPPER LEFT GUNNER'S SEAT
14. URINAL
15. LAVATORY FACILITIES
16. TOILET
17. OVEN-TYPE B-4
18. TAIL GUNNER'S SEAT
19. PARACHUTE STATIC LINE
20. 4-TB FIRE EXTINGUISHER
21. GALLEY
22. ECM OPERATOR'S SEAT
23. FOOD CARRIERS
24. LOWER LEFT AFT GUNNER'S SEAT
25. ECM OPERATOR'S AND TAIL GUNNER'S TABLE
26. LOWER LEFT AFT GUNNER'S BLACKOUT CURTAIN (STOWED)
27. AFT CABIN HEATER
28. LOWER RIGHT AFT GUNNER'S SEAT
29. ECM OPERATOR'S SEAT
30. LIQUID CONTAINERS
31. ECM EQUIPMENT SHELVES
32. CUP DISPENSERS
33. PORTABLE OXYGEN BOTTLE
34. LOWER RIGHT AFT GUNNER'S BLACKOUT CURTAIN (STOWED)

This is how the rear compartment was configured before the Featherweight program. Note the upper gunner's seats and various crew comfort items. Cramped, perhaps, but comfortable compared to the B-29. (U.S. Air Force)

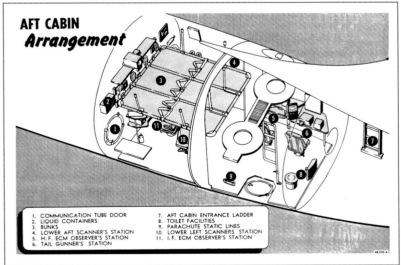

AFT CABIN Arrangement

1. COMMUNICATION TUBE DOOR
2. LIQUID CONTAINERS
3. BUNKS
4. LOWER AFT SCANNER'S STATION
5. H.F. ECM OBSERVER'S STATION
6. TAIL GUNNER'S STATION
7. AFT CABIN ENTRANCE LADDER
8. TOILET FACILITIES
9. PARACHUTE STATIC LINES
10. LOWER LEFT SCANNERS STATION
11. I.F. ECM OBSERVER'S STATION

The Featherweight III B-36H and RB-36H models show that most crew comfort items and the gunner positions have been deleted. The lower gunner chairs and upper platforms remained. (U.S. Air Force)

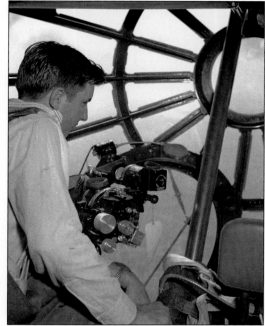

The Farrand Y-1 periscopic bombsight being designed for the B-36 ran into serious development problems, and the early bombers carried an M-9 Norden bombsight that was only a minor evolution of the ones used during World War II. The flat glazed panel had a windshield wiper and was defrosted. (Lockheed Martin)

The B-36H introduced many crew comfort items, such as this galley, that made the long duration flights much easier on the crew. Unfortunately, the reprieve was short-lived – the Featherweight program removed the galleys, tables, mattresses, and other items in order to save weight. (Lockheed Martin)

The photographer did very little operating of most of the cameras – they were usually controlled by the photo-navigator in the nose. Instead, the photographer monitored the operation of the cameras and their associated vacuum and anti-icing systems and loaded film as required. (Lockheed Martin)

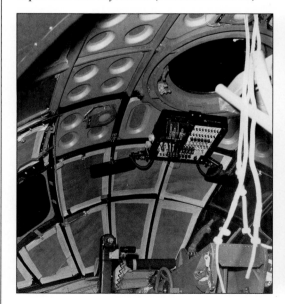

The inside of the cockpit canopy of an RB-36E (44-92019) showing the waffle-pattern tiles, jet controls, and the astrodome hatch. (Convair)

The nose gunsight, this time on a B-36F-1-CF (49-2670) on 14 March 1951. Note the comfortable seat. (Convair)

From the front of the camera compartment looking aft at the empty Trimetrogon camera area. The hatch to the communications tube is visible on the right, and another hatch into bomb bay No. 2 is on the extreme right. This was the RB-36E (44-92019) that was rebuilt as part of Operation PINOCCHIO at Travis AFB. (Convair via the Jay Miller Collection)

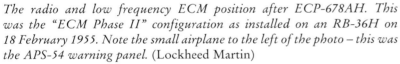

The radio and low frequency ECM position after ECP-678AH. This was the "ECM Phase II" configuration as installed on an RB-36H on 18 February 1955. Note the small airplane to the left of the photo – this was the APS-54 warning panel. (Lockheed Martin)

One of the largest changes made by the Phase II ECM program was the installation of dual APT-16 transmitters at the intermediate and medium frequency position. The electronics were located below the table and are not readily visible in this photo. (Lockheed Martin)

The Phase II ECM high-frequency position (left) and tail gunner station (right) after ECP-678AH. Again, this is an RB-36H on 18 February 1955. The tail gunner was moved to face the right side wall of the aft compartment, with the HF ECM position also facing the right wall immediately forward of the tail gunner. The turret control panel is visible in both photos, showing the relationship of the two stations to each other. (Lockheed Martin)

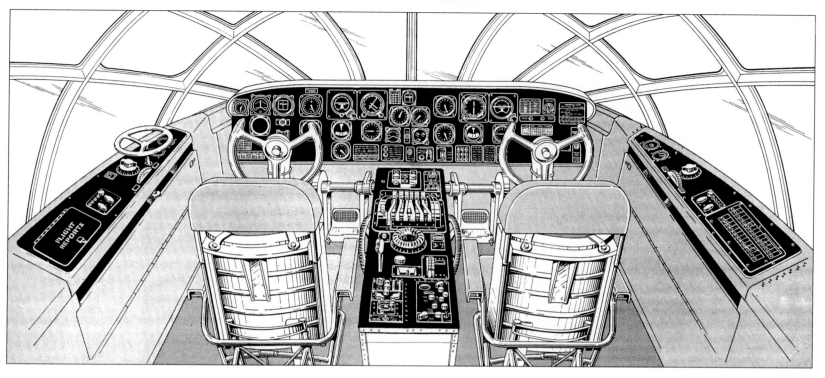

The pilot's position in a B-36B from the 16 November 1948 issue of the flight manual. Compare this to the D-model on page 114. (U.S. Air Force)

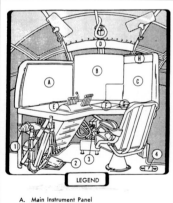

LEGEND

A. Main Instrument Panel
B. Auxiliary Instrument Panel
C. Control Panel
D. Auxiliary Control Panel
E. Engineer's Table
F. Propeller Control Panel
G. Hydraulic Controls
H. Auxiliary Fuel Control Panel
  1. Oxygen Regulator
  2. Microphone Switch
  3. Propeller Synchronizer
  4. Cabin Pressure Dump Valve Control

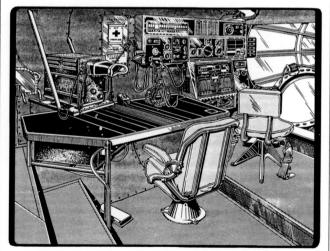

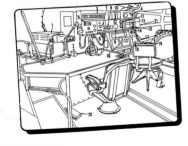

1. Loran Set
2. Table Lamp Rheostat
3. Circuit Breaker Panel
4. Intervolometer Control
5. Interphone Control Panel
6. Oxygen Controls
7. Radio Compass Control Panel
8. Magnetic Compass Indicator
9. Radio Compass Indicator
10. Clock
11. Altimeter
12. Airspeed Indicator
13. Check List
14. Windshield Wiper Switch
15. Servo Heaters Switch
16. Bombing Control Panel
  (See figure 4-11 for detail)
17. Interphone Control Panel
18. Oxygen Controls
19. Bomb Sight
20. Microphone Switch
21. Auxiliary Bomb Rack Control Panel

The B-36B flight engineer station was a great deal different than the later H-model station detailed on page 116. Only a single seat was provided, and the main panel faced the right side of the airplane instead of facing rearward. The bombardier's station (right) was also much simpler, although the Norden bombsight that was found in all of the B-36Bs is mostly hidden by the chair in this illustration. The bombardier in later models would use the Y-3 periscopic bombsight instead of the Norden. (U.S. Air Force).

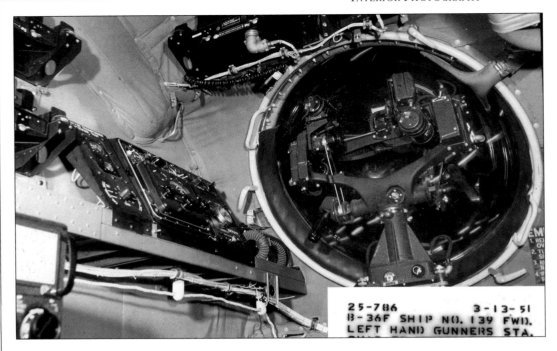

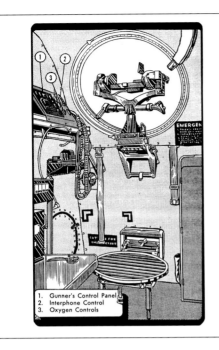

1. Gunner's Control Panel
2. Interphone Control
3. Oxygen Controls

The forward upper sighting station. The photo illustrates the left station in a B-36F (49-2670) taken on 13 March 1951, but is generally applicable to both sides in all models. The drawing is from the B-36B flight manual. Unlike the upper stations in the aft compartment, the forward gunners did not have a chair since they had other jobs when not manning the guns. (photo: Convair via Frank Kleinwechter via Don Pyeatt; drawing: U.S. Air Force)

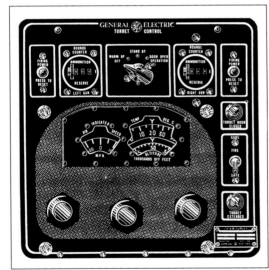

The nose sight in the navigator's compartment of a B-36H (51-1352) on 30 March 1953. Note the "target size" dial below the eyepiece, which the gunner used to set the wingspan of the fighter he was tracking. The computer used this information to determine the distance to the target, and hence the ballistics for the cannon. All of the sights worked in a similar manner. (Lockheed Martin)

A gun control panel was mounted at each sighting blister. Note that the speed indicator is in miles per hour (English units) while the temperature is in degrees Celsius (metric units). Each gun had a rounds-remaining indicator. The nose and tail positions had similar panels that did not have the controls and indicators to retract the turrets and open the doors. (U.S. Air Force)

 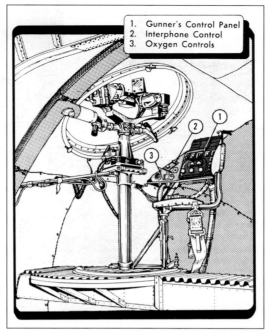 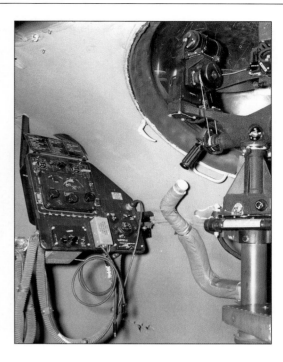

1. Gunner's Control Panel
2. Interphone Control
3. Oxygen Controls

The aft upper sighting stations (left on left; right on right). The photos, taken on 9 August 1954, illustrate an RB-36H (52-1352). The drawing is from the B-36B flight manual. The turret control panel (at right) was identical at all six sighting blisters. (photos: Lockheed Martin; drawing: U.S. Air Force)

 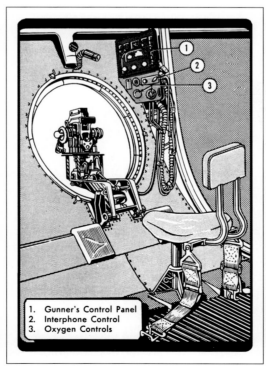 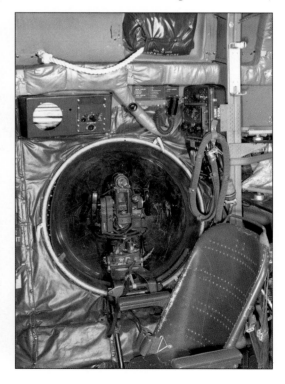

1. Gunner's Control Panel
2. Interphone Control
3. Oxygen Controls

The aft lower sighting stations (left on left; right on right). The photos, taken on 9 August 1954, illustrate an RB-36H (52-1352). The drawing is from the B-36B flight manual. Note the escape rope hanging above the blister in both photos – these allowed rapid egress on the ground after the gunner had opened the blister and swiveled the sight in and down towards the chair. (photos: Lockheed Martin; drawing: U.S. Air Force)

Chapter 6

R-4360-5   9-28-43   C-984

Above: *One of the early hand-built R-4360-5 test engines showing the original cooling fan design. The Wasp Major was probably the ultimate expression of the aircraft piston engine.* (C. Roger Cripliver Collection)

Right: *R-4360 engines engine build-up area at Convair in Fort Worth. After the engines were received from Pratt & Whitney, additional components were installed, then the engines were installed on B-36s being manufactured nearby.* (Lockheed Martin)

THE WASP MAJOR

The first radial aircraft engine was a six-cylinder unit featuring two banks of three cylinders and a double-throw crankshaft built by J. W. Smith in Cicero, Illinois, during 1913. Since the air-cooled engine did not require a heavy cooling system and radiator, it garnered a fair amount of interest quickly. Other companies soon began producing similar designs, but it was Pratt & Whitney that found ultimate success with radial engines. However, it was not obvious from the start that the company would flourish – or even exist.

When Frederick B. Rentschler and a group of engineers left Wright Aeronautical in 1925 to produce the nine-cylinder R-1340 Wasp, they had not formally formed a company or decided upon a name before submitting the design to the U.S. Navy for evaluation.

The Pratt & Whitney Machine Tool Division of Niles-Bement-Pond Corp. (Hartford, Connecticut) had made the castings for the prototype and, as was custom at the time, cast its name in the metal housing. Navy evaluators dutifully transcribed this name into their records, and a company was born, although there was no actual connection with the original tool manufacturer. The original 410-hp Wasp was designed by George Mead and Andy Willgoos, completed on Christmas Eve 1925, and passed its initial Navy tests in March 1926. The Boeing F2B-1 was the first operational aircraft to use the new engine. Ten years later, the 14-cylinder 1,000-hp R-1830 Twin Wasp was available, and by 1941 the 18-cylinder 2,000-hp R-2800 Double Wasp was being produced.

Towards the end of 1940, the Department of War authorized Pratt & Whitney to begin development of what would be known as the Wasp Major. Even prior to starting the formal development program, engineers at P&W had been investigating such diverse subjects as cylinder and crankshaft arrangements for optimum air flow, variable-speed supercharger drive mechanisms, simplified ignition systems, and cooling requirements. At the time the engine was generally called the X-Wasp, and the first engine – X-101 – was run in a ground-test facility on 28 April 1941. This 10-minute test resulted in 18 modifications being made to the engine prior to the second test on 8 May 1941 when the engine ran for over two hours, producing 1,325 horsepower with little effort. The X-101 would continue to be used in the development effort until the end of the 1940s, although by that time very little of the original engine remained.[1]

Officially, the new engine was designated R-4360 – the "R" signifying its radial configuration and the "4360" being its approximate displacement in cubic inches. The Wasp Major featured 28 cylinders arranged in a spiral pattern in four rows of seven each, giving the engine a frontal area no greater than that of the Double Wasp. In fact, the new engine was only one-inch larger in diameter than the original 410-hp Wasp. Despite this, Pratt & Whitney was quick to point out various engineering innovations and improvements:[2]

Deep-finned forged aluminum cylinder heads and duralumin* cylinder muffs; cylinders which are completely interchangeable, even to the extent that they may be used with either tractor or pusher installations; scientifically correct cylinder cooling baffles; the elimination of the conventional ignition harness through the use of seven interchangeable magnetos, one for each bank of four cylinders; a vibration-free crankshaft and improved automatically controlled, hydraulically driven, variable-speed supercharger; and the radial mounting of accessories about the periphery of the accessory drive case, instead of on the rear of the engine, to provide excellent maintenance accessibility.

An early XB-36 engine mount static test rig with the skeletal portion of an R-4360 installed. (Lockheed Martin)

---

* Duralumin™ is an aluminum alloy, developed in 1910, consisting of four percent copper with small amounts of iron, magnesium, manganese, and silicon.

In reality the engine made use of parts and designs from several other projects. The reduction gear had been developed for an earlier P&W liquid-cooled engine that was subsequently cancelled. All 28 cylinders were essentially identical to those used on the first row of the Double Wasp. The crankshaft was drop-forged on modified dies from the Twin Wasp. The cams and valve gears were of the same general design as those of all previous Wasp engines. Most of this reuse was the decision of W.D. Gove, the Wasp Major project engineer from 1941 until 30 June 1946 when he was promoted to development engineer over all P&W piston engines. On 1 July 1946 Ross Begg became project engineer for the R-4360.[3]

One of the most innovative aspects of the new engine was the crankshaft that had been designed to accommodate the spiral layout of the 28 cylinders. In order to save time, Pratt & Whitney decided to use a cast-steel crank in the X-101 prototype engine, instead of the forged-steel crank that would be used in production engines. It was reasoned that the cast part would be rugged enough to survive early development tests to prove the basic design of the four-row engine. An automobile manufacturer (probably Ford) was selected to cast the crank, but security restrictions dictated that nobody know that a four-row engine was being developed. The problem was "solved" by having the manufacturer cast a five-row crank – the superfluous throw was simply cut off once the part had been delivered to P&W. The new crank worked, and the cast part managed to survive 172 hours on the test stand. However, as the power level surpassed the 3,000-hp mark, the crank finally broke – exactly in half. By then, however, there were supplies of the forged-steel part, and the prototype engine was quickly up and running again.[4]

The unique offset cylinder arrangement was an attempt to obtain better cooling characteristics without increasing the frontal area. Many multi-cylinder arrangements were flow tested, and the spiral offset configuration was judged to have the best distribution of cooling air to all cylinders with the minimum amount of drag. As design work progressed, P&W found that many other design features fell in line to produce a happy combination. For instance, the crankshaft

became nearly perfectly balanced, and the intake and exhaust ducting proved to be remarkably efficient due to the spiral layout.

The Wasp Major completed its 150-hour qualification test in December 1944 by which time 23 test engines had accumulated almost 20,000 hours of full-scale testing. In addition, over 40,000 hours of single-cylinder testing had been completed, along with 2,000 hours of single-row testing. During this time the engine had gone through several significant changes from the original X-101. For instance, the side intake and top exhaust valve configuration was replaced by top intake and side exhaust valves. The design of the intake runners was changed, and the cylinder heads were switched from cast to forged. The ignition system underwent several changes. Perhaps the largest change was in the propeller drive gear at the front of the engine, where the original "Jimmie Durante" nose grew progressively shorter. Each change in shape was the result of making the gears stronger to handle increased horsepower and torque. Unfortunately, these changes added several hundred pounds to the weight of the engine, much to the dismay of the aircraft manufacturers scheduled to use it.[5]

On 25 May 1942, a Vultee Model V-85 Vengeance made its first flight with the third R-4360 mounted in its nose. Test pilot H.H. Sargent, Jr. was at the controls for the occasion and the flight was generally successful. As it happened, Sargent, along with Richard G. Smith, was in the same aircraft later in the year when fuel system problems starved the engine, forcing Sargent to make an emergency landing in a tobacco field just north of Hartford. Unfortunately a series of wires that were used to hold canvas tenting to shade the crop fouled the propeller and tipped the Vengeance on its back as it tried to land. Sargent and Smith were trapped in the inverted cockpit, but local farmers soon extricated them relatively unharmed.

The flow of flight test information resumed when engines were installed in a Vultee XA-41 attack bomber, Vought F4U Corsair, and the Republic XP-72. By the end of 1942 progress on the engine was deemed satisfactory for the Army to authorize P&W to construct ten 'semi-production' engines for various prototype aircraft. Some of

The left two photos show the nacelle test stand that was constructed at Fort Worth. This rig supported engine tests, propeller tests, and cooling system tests while it was operating. At right is an early full-scale powered nacelle in the 40x80-foot wind tunnel at the N.A.C.A. Ames Laboratory in California. The rig was supporting 19-foot Curtiss-Electric propeller vibration tests on 24 October 1945. (left and center: Convair via the C. Roger Cripliver Collection; right: N.A.C.A. via the C. Roger Cripliver Collection)

these would find their way into ground test rigs for the XB-36. Ground testing also continued, with a Wasp Major subjected to a test run of 578 hours – 78 hours at rated power (3,000 hp), 138 hours at more than rated power, and the remainder at less than rated power. This test was a great deal more stringent that the proof test conducted on the original Wasp 20 years earlier – only 10 hours at rated power and 40 hours at 90 percent power.

By this time the development of the Wasp Major had cost over $25 million – a substantial sum for the day. Nevertheless this represented somewhat of a bargain since the earlier Double Wasp had consumed over $30 million in development, and total engineering costs on the earlier single- and double-row Wasps had been in excess of $50 million.[6]

TECHNICAL DESCRIPTION

The Pratt & Whitney R-4360 Wasp Major engine was used to power the B-36, B-50, C-97, C-119, and C-124 aircraft. It represents the most technically advanced and complex reciprocating aircraft engine produced in large numbers in the United States. The retirement of the KC-97 from the Air Force inventory in the late 1970s marked the closing of the era of both the large piston engine and the turbosupercharger within the Air Force.

The R-4360 was a 28-cylinder, 4-row radial, air-cooled engine with both gear-driven and exhaust-driven turbosuperchargers. As the name suggests, the engine displaced 4,363 cubic inches (71.5 liters), and each cylinder had a 5.75-inch bore and 6.00-inch stroke (155.8 cubic inches per cylinder). The engine had a compression ratio of 6.7:1 in most applications. The R-4360 was 96.5 inches long, with a diameter of 55.0 inches. At maximum revs, each piston was covering 2,700 feet per minute. The engine weighed 3,670 pounds (the weight and dimensions are for the basic engine only, without the external turbochargers or reduction gears). The engine used 2,500 pounds of 115/145-grade aviation fuel and 25,000 pounds of air per hour at maximum output.[7]

The engine's output was impressive. Rated at 3,500 hp (3,000 in early –25 engines; 3,800 in late –53 units), what is frequently overlooked is the torque provided by these engines. At 1,000 rpm, each engine provided 840 pound-feet of torque – by 3,000 rpm this had increased to a staggering 7,506 pound-feet, measured at the crankshaft. Because of the gearing selected, this was increased to over 20,000 pound-feet at the propeller shaft (which, incidentally, was turning at 1,125 rpm).

The cylinders were generally similar to those used in the front row of the earlier R-2800 series, and were arranged spirally around the crankcase to facilitate cooling of each cylinder. The cylinders used steel barrels, shrunk-on forged aluminum alloy cooling muffs, and forged aluminum alloy heads. Unlike many other radial engines, all of the cylinder jugs were completely interchangeable. The pistons were also generally similar to the R-2800, although they were reinforced slightly for use with the R-4360. The connecting rod assembly for each row of seven cylinders consisted of a master rod with detachable cap, two-piece lead silver bearing, and six I-section articulated or link rods. Each link rod had a bronze bushing at the piston end and rode on a silvered knuckled pin.

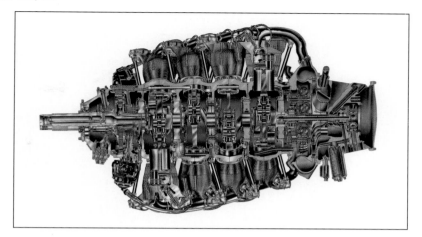

An internal look at the R-4360 Wasp Major. (Pratt & Whitney)

The one-piece forged steel crankshaft had four throws and was supported by five steel-backed lead-silver main bearings. The weight of the reciprocating parts connected to the crankpin were counterbalanced by two fixed and two bifilar counterweights. The power section case was made up of five sections, all except the front and rear sections being substantially similar. The parts for the power section were machined from aluminum forgings and were held together with bolts. All other crankcase sections were magnesium castings. The magneto section was attached to the front of the power section and contained two or four interchangeable magnetos and the torque meter.

Rocker arms with plain bearings were actuated by enclosed pushrods. Double-track self-mounted cams inside the crankcase between the rows of cylinders operated the exhaust valves of the forward row of cylinders and the intake valves of the aft row. The cams were driven by reduction-gears from the crankshaft at one-sixth crankshaft speed. There was a single inlet and a single exhaust valve per cylinder. The inlet valve was a conventional stainless steel unit, while the exhaust valve was made from the rather exotic Inconel-M alloy.

A single Bendix-Stromberg PR-100B3 four-barreled pressure-type carburetor with automatic mixture control was provided on each of the early engines. The carburetor had a throat 20 inches in diameter. There were several different dash numbers of carburetors in use, and frequently a single B-36 might use different versions on each engine. There were minor operating differences between the various dash numbers and the flight engineer had to determine what versions were installed in his aircraft and use them appropriately. The –53 engines used Bendix direct-fuel injection, providing a major increase in reliability and maintainability. In both cases, metered fuel was carried through internal passages and was thrown centrifugally through small holes between the impeller blades to mix with the combustion air. The fuel-air mixture, after passing through the diffuser to the blower rim, was carried to the cylinders through seven intake pipes, one for each bank of four cylinders. Each cylinder had two spark plugs. On –41 and –53 engines, water injection was available for limited times

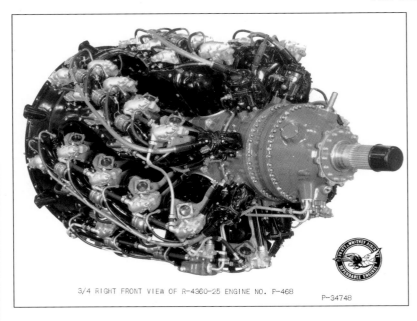

3/4 RIGHT FRONT VIEW OF R-4360-25 ENGINE NO. P-468   P-34748

The B-36A used the R-4360-25, shown here without its two-speed cooling fan. Later engines were basically similar. (Pratt & Whitney)

er was somewhat of a trade-off, for although it provided a doubling of the intake pressure (from 30 inches to over 60 inches), it also added a lot of heat to the intake charge, which is generally undesirable. It was felt that the benefits outweighed the drawbacks. Interestingly, it took 435 hp to drive the supercharger. It was worth it – the supercharger increased the power output by a staggering 1,930 hp.

Each engine was also provided with two General Electric Model B-1 (or BH-1 on later models) exhaust-driven turbosuperchargers[*] arranged in parallel. The primary purpose of the turbos was not to increase the power rating of the engine. Instead, they allowed the sea-level power rating to be maintained up to 35,000 feet, with a gradual degradation at altitudes above that. At sea level, the turbos had the theoretical ability to provide 300 inches of manifold pressure – obviously something that could not be allowed to happen. Automatic controls kept the turbos from overcharging the system at any given altitude. Each turbo had an impeller diameter of 14 inches and was equipped with an intercooler to remove waste heat from the air.[10]

The right-hand turbosupercharger on each engine also provided air for cabin pressurization. The flight engineer had the ability to select dual or single operation of the turbosuperchargers for each engine. When single mode was selected, all exhaust gases were passed through the right-hand turbo – there was no option to select using the left turbo only. A turbo boost selector on the flight engineer's panel was mechanically interconnected to a similar lever on the pilot's pedestal. Each lever had travel graduations from 0 to 10. Position 7 was used for takeoff and there was an indent to stop the lever at that position. However, the lever could be forced through the indent towards position 10 to obtain additional boost when needed.[11]

Heat rejection was a major concern with an engine as powerful as the R-4360. The design of the cylinders and the use of forged aluminum alloy for the heads and barrel muffs permitted the machining of closely-spaced deep fins that provided a 30-percent increase in exposed fin area over that previously available from cast heads. Cooling air was inducted at the leading edge of the wing and was boosted by a large two-speed engine cooling fan before being routed by a series of baffles around the engine. The fan could be set to LOW or HIGH by the flight engineer, and on some aircraft the fan could be set to NEUTRAL where the fan was disengaged from the engine. Control over the amount of cooling air admitted to the nacelle was controlled by positioning a ring-shaped "air plug" located between the trailing edge of the nacelle and the propeller. These air plugs performed the same function as the cowl flaps on tractor installations.[12]

The temperature of the intercooler air – and consequently of the air entering the carburetor – was accomplished by varying the volume of cooling air entering the intercoolers. This was accomplished by opening or closing shutters in front of the intercooler, either automatically via a thermostat, or manually from the flight engineer panel. In low ambient temperatures, the carburetor air could be preheated by recirculating induction air through the turbosuperchargers. A car-

(takeoff and target penetration), adding about 8 percent more power. Each engine included a 9-gallon water tank good for about 5 minutes of operation. In reality, water injection used a mixture of alcohol and distilled water, usually in a 50–50 mix. Once the flight engineer activated water injection, the system operated automatically when the manifold pressure of each engine exceeded 53.5 inches.[8]

There were two magnetos per engine on early engines, and four on the R-4360-53. The flight engineer had a master ignition switch and individual engine ignition switches. Positions on the individual ignition switches were marked OFF, L, R, and BOTH. Interestingly, there was an unmarked position located between L and R that also activated both magnetos. An emergency cutoff switch that stopped all six engines was located on the pilot's instrument panel. The flight engineer also had six two-position switches that selected either 20 or 35 degrees of advance for the ignition spark. The normal setting was 20 degrees. Starting the engines was accomplished by using three three-position switches. Each switch controlled a pair of engines – outboard, middle, and inboard. The middle position on the switch was OFF, with the left engines started when the switch was moved to the L position, and the right engines when the switch was moved to the R position.[9]

At 20,000 feet altitude, without the use of turbosupercharging, the R-4360-41 would have had an output of only 1,000 hp – with its use the power output improved to 3,500 hp. The R-4360 used two different supercharging techniques. An "internal supercharger" was mounted in the airstream immediately behind the carburetor and before the cylinders. This impeller was driven by the crankshaft by a gear train at a fixed ratio. At takeoff the impeller was turning at 17,212 rpm, with a tip speed of nearly 700 mph. The use of this supercharg-

* References are inconsistent about the use of a hyphen here – some use "turbo-supercharger;" others "turbo-supercharger." In modern parlance, these would be called turbochargers.

buretor air temperature gauge for each engine was located on the flight engineer's instrument panel. It should be noted that the intercooler could only remove heat introduced by the exhaust-driven turbochargers – the mechanical supercharger was located internally and downstream from the intercoolers, so there was no practical way to remove the heat introduced by it.[13]

Each engine had its own independent oil system with a separate 190-gallon tank. The oil was required to conform to Specification No. AN-0-8 (later Mil-L-6082). There were oil shut-off valves that could be operated remotely from the flight engineer's control panel, or were manually accessible from the wing crawlway and could be operated manually. Oil temperature was controlled automatically – during ground operations air was drawn through the oil cooler by the engine-driven fan; during flight, ram air independent of the fan was used. The switchover was accomplished when the main landing gear was retracted.[14]

Fuel was contained in eight integral wing tanks (only six on the B-36B; ten on the B-36J) and also in auxiliary fuel tanks that could be loaded into one or more of the bomb bays. Each fuel tank was equipped with an electric booster pump and a tank valve. All of the tanks were interconnected by cross-feed valves, making it possible to supply fuel from any tank to any engine, including the jets on later models. Each of the R-4360 engines was equipped with a mechanically-driven fuel pump and an engine fuel cut-off valve. The normal operating fuel was 115/145 octane Specification No. AN-F-48 (later Mil-F-5572), but Grade 100/130 fuel could be used as an alternative with some restrictions. The integral fuel tanks liked to leak – especially on the early aircraft – and represented one of the more significant problems experienced by the B-36 fleet.[15]

Each aircraft was equipped with six 19-foot diameter Curtiss-Wright constant-speed, full-feathering, reversible propellers. Early aircraft used propellers with rounded tips, but square-tip units were introduced on the B-36H and retrofitted to earlier aircraft. The square tips were an attempt to increase efficiency at high altitude, as well as to solve an earlier propeller fatigue problem and a nagging fuselage buffet. The size of the propellers, and the fast rate-of-pitch change required, eliminated the possibility of using the traditional electric motor to control the variable pitch. Instead the designers developed a system that used part of the power being transmitted via the propeller shaft. Pitch change was accomplished by transmitting power taken from the rotating propeller shaft through a series of gears and four clutch mechanisms. Hydraulic pressure was generated by a self-contained oil pump, and used by either the clutch or the brake on each blade, as directed via electrical control signals from the cockpit. A small electric motor drove the blades in the last of the feathering and the beginning of the unfeathering cycles when the engine was operating below 450 rpm and was unable to furnish sufficient power to operate the pitch change mechanism. Pitch change during normal operations was 2.5 degrees per second, but this increased to 45 degrees per second during feathering and for reversing. Although it was possible to reverse the propellers in flight, this was procedurally prohibited by the flight manual. Engine exhaust was directed via the propeller hub through the hollow blades to prevent ice buildup.[16]

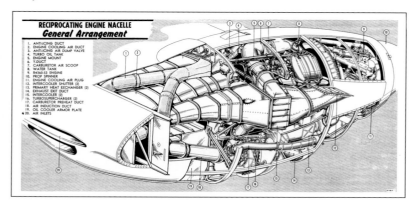

The B-36H used the ultimate version of the Wasp Major – the fuel injected R-4360-53 that developed 3,800 horsepower. (U.S. Air Force)

The propellers could be automatically or manually synchronized in both forward and reverse pitch. Synchronization was accomplished by making the speed of all engines compare with the speed of an electrically-driven master motor. The master motor speed was set by a control lever on the flight engineer's table, or via a mechanically interconnected lever on the pilot's pedestal. A propeller alternator on each engine supplied an electrical indication of engine speed to a contactor assembly on the master motor. If the engine speed did not coincide with that of the master motor, corrective electrical impulses were transmitted to the pitch change mechanism on the propeller until the engine was operating at the same rpm as the master motor. All engines operated at the master motor rpm when their respective selector

An Army instructor uses a cut-away version of an early R-4360-5 as an instructional tool for students learning to become engine mechanics. The cut-away cylinder laying horizontally in the center of the photo gives a good look at the valve configuration. (U.S. Air Force)

Convair developed a concept where a B-36 could transport four spare engines during deployments. Each "pod" was essentially two complete engines and their accessories with their nacelles in place mounted front-to-front. The tapered end at the front and back were covers where the propellers would normally go. A beam running between the pods attached to the normal bomb racks in bomb bay No. 1. This concept only worked with the original sliding bomb bay doors – the later snap-action doors interfered with the attachment mechanism – and was never used operationally. (left: Jay Miller Collection; others: Lockheed Martin)

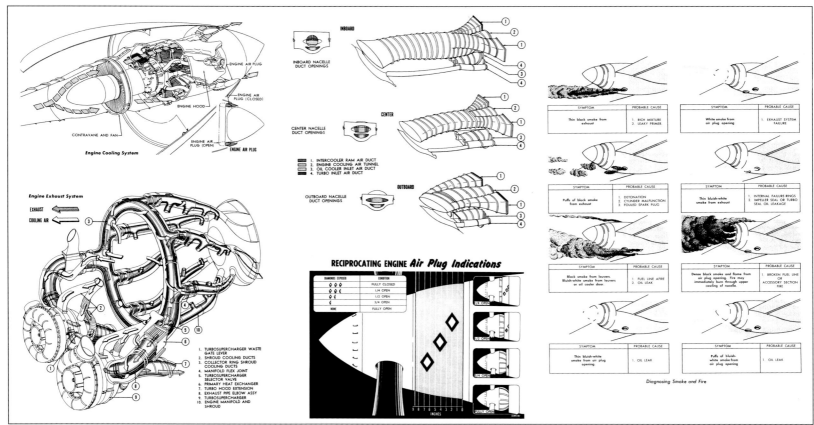

Drawings from B-36 manuals showing various aspects of the R-4360 installation and operation. (U.S. Air Force)

switches were placed in the AUTOMATIC OPERATION position and their throttles were advanced sufficiently for the engine to attain master motor rpm. In the event of a master motor failure, a protective relay caused each propeller to remain at the pitch in effect at the time of the failure. The flight engineer could then adjust each propeller individually using switches on his control panel.[17]

The R-4360 usually was operated for 200–300 hours between major overhauls, but it was not unusual for an engine to last considerably longer with proper maintenance. For instance, during 1952 the No. 3 engine on the XC-99 remained on the aircraft for 814.5 hours before being removed for overhaul. Two of the other engines had logged 524.3 and 630.6 hours. It must be remembered, however, that 500 hours only represented 20 or so flights.[18]

VDT ENGINES

The jet engine was beginning to make progress during the mid-1940s, but early models still suffered from numerous problems, most notably low power and high fuel consumption. This led engine designers to experiment using some jet engine technology coupled with existing concepts. In the end, the most successful of these experiments was the turboprop – essentially a jet engine driving a conventional propeller. But along the way, several manufacturers explored ways of linking existing piston engines with turbines – usually called compounding.

When the original Wasp engine had been developed in 1926, it had an internal mechanically-driven supercharger, and this became standard for all subsequent Wasp engines, including the R-4360. However, there was nothing new in the concept of moving supercharging outside the engine – exhaust-driven superchargers (at the time called turbosuperchargers; more often now simply turbochargers) had been used on the Liberty engines during World War I. During World War II it became fairly common practice for some engines to use the exhaust gases to drive the supercharger. This arrangement provided a "cheap" source of power since the only mechanical power required was that needed to offset the nominal increase in exhaust backpressure created by the turbosupercharger. This meant the pistons had to work a little harder to expel the exhaust gases from the cylinder on each stroke, but this was a small percentage of the power required to drive a mechanical supercharger. With the development of alloys capable of withstanding the high temperatures of the engine exhaust gases and the evolution of satisfactory controls, it was natural for power plant engineers to look for ways for the exhaust gases to do even more of the work.

However, the internal supercharging on the Wasp had demonstrated certain benefits. It helped to equally distribute the fuel-air mixture to each of a growing number of cylinders, and also allowed a more compact and self-contained power plant. This latter advantage was considered so compelling during World War II that when additional supercharging was required for combat at higher altitudes, various Wasp-family engines were developed with a second auxiliary stage of mechanically-driven supercharging. These engines, with their elongated rear sections, were used in various models of F4F Wildcats, F4U Corsairs, and F6F Hellcats.

Nevertheless, even proponents of mechanical superchargers were aware of the drawbacks of the concept. The largest of these was that it took a considerable amount of the engine's power to drive the internal supercharger. The 600-hp Wasp engine required 44 hp to drive its supercharger – the 3,500-hp R-4360 required 435 hp. In theory, for the Wasp Major to produce 4,000 hp at 40,000 feet, it would need to divert over 1,200 hp to the supercharger. The power required went up quickly the higher the altitude. There was another disadvantage to the internal supercharger – engineers could not cool down the intake air prior to using it. On aircraft with external superchargers, it was already common practice to use intercoolers (or aftercoolers) to cool the compressed air before it entered the cylinders. The cooler the air, the less likely it would pre-detonate ("ping" or "knock"), allowing more spark advance and hence greater power.[19]

Compounding appeared to solve both of these problems. By eliminating the internal supercharger, the R-4360-VDT instantly gained 435 hp from the current production engine – unfortunately, it also lost the 1,930 hp that was provided by the supercharger. The engine itself would have to make up the resulting loss of 1,500 horsepower. In retrospect, it is hard to see how the engineers intended to accomplish this. Since compounding compressed the air outside the R-4360, it was possible to run the air through a large aftercooler prior to using it in the cylinders, providing much cooler air. This allowed the engine to run more efficiently, providing a few hundred horsepower boost. The jet thrust from the turbine could add another 300 hp or so, but this still left 1,000 hp unaccounted for.

As envisioned by Pratt & Whitney engineers, compounding had four major design goals: (1) provide more power for takeoff to get heavier loads into the air, (2) give more power for continuous operation at high altitudes, (3) fuel savings, and (4) be less complex.

To accomplish these goals, Pratt & Whitney investigated four "compounding" concepts. The simplest was one where the exhaust gases were passed through a conventional exhaust gas turbine that transmitted power back to the crankshaft through a suitable mechanical drive. This was the approach taken by Wright for the R-3350 Compound. As proposed for the R-4360, this type of compound was confined to low-altitude operation because its maximum-altitude performance was limited by the capacity of its internal-engine supercharger.

Another compounding arrangement was to add conventional exhaust-driven superchargers (turbochargers) to the combination just described. This partially compensated for the altitude restrictions of the first concept, but offered little advantage to the standard R-4360.

The third concept was to duct the hot exhaust gases from the R-4360 directly into the burner cans of a conventional jet engine. A compressor on the front of the jet unit supplied additional air to mix with the engine exhaust and complete the combustion of residual fuel. The resultant hot gas mixture was then passed through the turbine unit to produce power for operating the compressor. Excess power was transmitted back to the R-4360 through suitable shafting and the exhaust was discharged rearward to provide additional thrust.[20]

The fourth concept was the variable discharge turbosupercharger (or turbine, depending on when the description was written). In actuality, the VDT selected for development was the 17th configuration studied by Don Hersey and P.S. Hopper in an attempt to find the ultimate configuration for extracting more power from the R-4360. The Wasp Major VDT was made public on 2 August 1945 at a "semi" open house to celebrate the twentieth anniversary of Pratt & Whitney. At the back of the experimental hangar was a full-scale engineering model of the new R-4360-VDT with a sign that indicated the engine was to develop "Combat, 4,360 horsepower; takeoff, 3,800 horsepower; normal, 2,800 horsepower." This claimed output was sort of the Holy Grail for engine designers – one horsepower per cubic inch.[21]

The development go-ahead for the new engine was received from the War Department in April 1946 with the expected applications being the B-36C, B-50C (later redesignated B-54), and the Republic XR-12 Rainbow reconnaissance aircraft. An R-2800 Double Wasp was used as a proof-of-concept engine and completed a ten-hour endurance test in March 1947. Eight experimental engines were ordered, and by the end of 1948 they had accumulated 1,725 hours of test time. An additional 8,321 hours of testing was also accomplished on various partial test engines. A 150-hour qualification test was completed in August 1948, clearing the way for flight testing to begin. An R-4360-VDT was installed at the No. 2 position (left wing, inside) on a B-50 for the initial flight tests. In this installation, the R-4360 engine sat in its normal position, with the GE turbine below and behind it in the nacelle. This would be remarkably different from the installation planned for the B-36C.[22]

Conceptually, the VDT* engine was fairly simple – all of the piston engine's exhaust gases were discharged through a turbine to provide jet thrust. This could, in the case of the R-4360, add several hundred pounds of thrust to each engine – the equivalent of adding about 300 hp. The R-4360 Wasp Major-VDT engine included three primary components: the Wasp Major, a variable discharge turbosupercharger, and an aftercooler. Engine exhaust gases were used to spin the turbine before being discharged through the variable-area nozzle. On the same axis with the turbine was a two-stage, centrifugal compressor that supercharged all of the intake air for the Wasp Major. The temperature of the intake air was reduced by the large air-to-air aftercooler (conceptually identical to the intercooler used by the non-VDT engines). The cooled air passed through a metering unit into the engine, and fuel was injected into the individual cylinders and ignited.[23]

The VDT installation differed from the normal turbosupercharged R-4360 mainly because there was no wastegate to divert part of the hot exhaust gases overboard at intermediate altitudes. Instead, the VDT passed all of its exhaust gases through the turbine at all times. The R-4360 itself, while appearing little changed externally, deleted the internal supercharger used by other R-4360s.

The General Electric CHM-2 turbine had all of the elements of a contemporary turbojet engine – air compressor, nozzle guide vanes, turbine rotor, tail pipe, and exhaust nozzle – except that the Wasp Major performed the function of the jet burners. As in a jet engine, the air was first compressed. Then, instead of being mixed with fuel and burned in the usual jet engine burners, the air was fed into the 28 cylinders of the R-4360. After fuel was injected and burned inside the

cylinders of the piston engine, the exhaust gases were routed back to the turbine and directed by guide vanes through the turbine rotor and discharged out the tailpipe.

The discharge nozzle of the turbine could be varied in size to maintain the most efficient discharge speed regardless of altitude – a concept not used on most jet engines of the era. This nozzle was also used to control the power output of the Wasp Major since opening or closing the nozzle changed the difference in pressures of the exhaust gas forward and aft of the turbine and determined the amount of exhaust energy extracted by the turbine. The quantity of supercharged air delivered to the Wasp Major dictated its power output. The conventional throttle was used on the VDT only at slow speeds and low altitudes where the turbine was ineffective.

Although the concept was appealing, difficulties in providing proper cooling eventually caused its demise. The problem lay more in the B-36 installation than with the engine itself – a similar R-4360-VDT performed adequately when tested in the B-50C configuration and on the XR-12 Rainbow. The packaging of the B-36 caused the problem. In order to not seriously effect the center-of-gravity of the B-36, and also to reuse as much structure as possible, the R-4360 engine was installed near its normal position in the rear of the wing, with the turbine even further back. This made cooling both units difficult – a problem compounded by the rarified atmosphere at the expected 40,000–45,000-foot cruising altitude. Ground tests indicated that the new engine would actually provide less power than the basic R-4360-41, and the project was finally cancelled. Additional discussion of the problems associated with the B-36C installation may be found in Chapter 3.

J47 JET ENGINES

General Electric (GE) had a long history of developing turbosuperchargers for aircraft engines, including those found on the R-4360 used on the B-36. Because the principles and challenges encountered in turbosuperchargers apply to gas turbines as well, GE was a logical choice to build the first U.S. jet engine. In 1941, the Army Air Corps picked the GE facility in Lynn, Massachusetts, to build a jet engine based on the British design developed by Sir Frank Whittle. Six months later, on 18 April 1942, GE engineers successfully ran the first I-A engine.[24]

With a modest 1,250 lbf, the I-A engine launched America into the jet age. The early jet engines – American, British, or German – all suffered from a variety of problems, most notably poor reliability and miserable fuel consumption. Nevertheless, almost immediately the quest for more power began. Two years later, what would be the first U.S. operational jet fighter, the P-80 Shooting Star, flew powered by a J33 engine rated at 4,000 lbf.[25]

The victory was brief for General Electric. The Army Air Corps, concerned about disrupting supplies of turbosuperchargers, placed production of GE's jet engines with other manufacturers. Finding itself with no jet engines to produce, GE set about designing another.

---

* This originally meant variable discharge turbosupercharger, but later became variable discharge turbine in order to sound more 'modern.'

Two views of the jet pods. At the far right the intake doors are completely closed, although this was a relative term – some air was allowed to enter to keep the compressor turning slowly to prevent it from freezing at altitude. The intake doors are completely open in the photo at near right. The pods themselves were nearly identical to those being manufactured for the Boeing B-47 but did not contain the outrigger landing gear and its supporting structure. (San Diego Aerospace Museum Collection)

The J47 was developed from the earlier J35 and was first flight-tested in May 1948 as a replacement for the J35 used in the North American XF-86 Sabre. During September 1948, a J47 powered an F-86A to a new world's speed record of 670.981 mph. The J47 was a 12-stage axial flow compressor, single-stage axial flow turbine, turbojet engine. The basic engine weighed 2,700 pounds and in the –11 and –19 configurations used by the B-36, produced 5,200 lbf. Each engine cost approximately $50,000.[26]

The J47 put GE back in the business of building jet engines, and dictated that a new manufacturing facility be found to meet the anticipated demand. General Electric subsequently selected a government-owned plant near Cincinnati that had manufactured Wright Aeronautical piston engines during World War II. GE formally opened the plant on 28 February 1949, with the second J47 produc-

tion line. Later, the plant would be known as Evendale and would become GE Aircraft Engines' world headquarters. More than 30,000 engines of the basic J47 type were built before production ended in 1956. The engine was produced in at least 17 different series and was used to power such Air Force aircraft as the F-86, XF-91, B-36, B-45, B-47, XB-51, and C-97. The J47 left service when the last Boeing KC-97J was retired from the Air National Guard in 1978.[27]

With the Korean War boosting demand, the J47 became the world's most produced gas turbine. More than 35,000 J47 engines were delivered by the end of the 1950s. The engine scored two major firsts: it was the first turbojet certified for civil use by the U.S. Civil Aeronautics Administration, and the first to use an electrically-controlled afterburner to boost its thrust, although not in the configurations used by the B-36 or the civil variants.[28]

During manufacture, the engines and jet pods were built-up as a unit then hung on the B-36 wing very late during final assembly. This way the addition of the jets had minimal impact on the already established assembly line. (San Diego Aerospace Museum Collection)

Chapter 7

Above: *One of the ten B-2 "Hydraulic Bomb Lift, Mobile, 50,000 pounds" that were built during World War II to lift the 43,000-pound T-12 bombs. At least two of these would be modified to lift early thermonuclear weapons into B-36 bomb bays. This one is shown with a conventional T-12 bomb at Eglin AFB on 3 January 1950. (Air Force Historical Research Agency)*

Right: *Nose detail of a DB-36H-15-CF (52-5710) on 22 December 1954. Compare the very center of the glazed area with other panels – this aircraft has replaced the small glass area usually there with an antenna for the APS-54 radar warning receiver. Aircraft equipped with the Y-3 periscopic bomb sight had the bombardier's glazed panel covered over. (Lockheed Martin)*

TECHNICAL WONDERS

The 1950s were a time of wonder. Advances in materials and the birth of mechanical and electromechanical computers had opened entirely new avenues of research. The pace of change, when compared to 20 years earlier, was incredible. The thermonuclear bomb was one of the primary signs of the advance, although the widespread use of electricity, radio, and the beginnings of television were more visible to the general populace. For the first time, there appeared to be no limit to what technology could accomplish.

Not surprisingly, the weapons in the early 21st Century are vastly more accurate and reliable than their counterparts from fifty years earlier. However, many of the concepts developed for the B-36 and its contemporaries – drone decoys, guided glide bombs, and electronic countermeasures – have finally found routine and successful use on modern combat aircraft. Ironically, most of the modern weapons are remarkably less complex – at least mechanically – than their predecessors. The digital revolution that began in the 1970s and escalated throughout the 1980s and 1990s allowed designers to replace immensely complicated electromechanical systems with small solid-state components. Modern materials and construction techniques have allowed remarkably lightweight structures, while advances in navigation and aerodynamics have provided precision targeting. The 1950s attempted to develop capabilities with what today would be called brute-force approaches. Remarkably, some of them actually worked.

DEFENSIVE ARMAMENT

The defensive armament installed on the B-36 represented the ultimate expression of the self-defense concept first discussed by Douhet and the Air Corps Tactical School during the 1920s. Although most later bombers (up through the RB-69) would continue to include tail armament, the B-36 was the last that made extensive use of turrets to provide complete hemispheric coverage.

Initial XB-36 designs showed a variety of manned turret configurations. This continued to evolve during the development period until it was decided to use a variation of the remote control turret (RCT) that had found its first extensive use on the B-29 and A-26 during World War II. General Electric continued to develop the concept, and was selected to manufacture an improved system for the B-36.[1]

The basic B-36 defensive armament consisted of eight remotely-controlled turrets, each equipped with two 20-mm cannon. The use of 20-mm cannon was somewhat of a trade-off and always controversial. The 0.50-caliber bullet had better ballistic characteristics, but the 20-mm projectile was more destructive. A proposed 0.60-caliber round would have combined the best attributes of both, but was never developed. Given the increased speed of attacking fighters, designers opted for the bigger punch.

The nose of a B-36 showing the original configuration of the center panel before the installation of the APS-54 antenna. The hemispheric sight for the nose turret is offset slightly to the right side of the aircraft. Note the ARN-58 instrument approach set antenna just ahead of the cockpit. The glazed bombardier window only appeared on early bombers and the reconnaissance models with the Norden bombsight. (Peter M. Bowers)

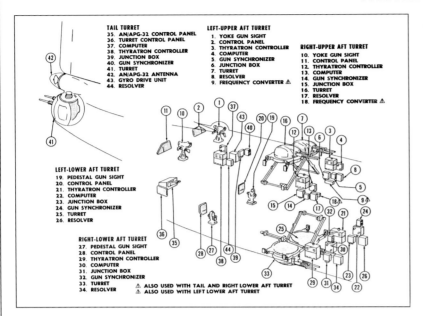

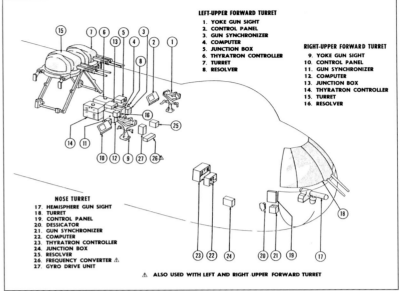

These drawings depict the defensive armament on a B-36F, but are generally applicable to all models that were equipped with guns. The largest difference would be the tail radar installed – an APG-3 or APG-41 could be used instead of the APG-32 depending upon the model. (U.S. Air Force)

The nose and tail turret were nonretractable and provided limited coverage directly ahead and behind the aircraft. Six other turrets were located in pairs on the upper forward fuselage, upper rear fuselage, and lower rear fuselage. Another pair of turrets had been intended for the lower forward fuselage, but were replaced on all production aircraft by the radome for the bomb/nav system. These turrets all retracted into the fuselage and were covered by flush doors when not in use. The turrets were designed to operate at altitudes up to 50,000 feet in temperatures between –50 degF and 122 degF.[2]

Each turret was operated electrically from a gunner's sighting position located apart from the turret it controlled. There were three sighting positions on each side of the fuselage, one forward and two aft to control the retractable turrets. The nose turret was controlled by a sight in the glazed bombardier's compartment, while the tail turret was controlled by a radar operator's position in the aft pressurized compartment.

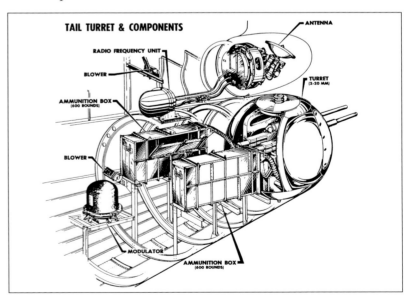

The nose and tail turret details from the B-36F. The other models were substantially similar. (U.S. Air Force)

The electrical units in the RCT system were connected in such a manner that every movement of the sight was immediately followed by a corresponding movement of the cannon and turret. The sighting station controlled the turret movement in elevation and azimuth by means of two separate channels, which allowed the cannon to move in elevation independently of turret rotation in azimuth.

The following is a simplified explanation of the system as it appeared in the *SAC B-36 Gunnery Manual*. The example is for the elevation channel, but the azimuth channel worked the same way.[3]

"When the gunner moves his sight in elevation, the selsyn generator on the sight transmits an AC (alternating current) signal corresponding to the sight's position in elevation to the control transformer on the turret. From this AC signal and the position of the turret, the control transformer generates an output voltage called the error signal (elevation). This error signal is proportional in voltage to the amount of displacement between the sight and the turret. The error signal is sent to the thyratron controller where the AC error signal is amplified and converted to a DC (direct-current) signal with polarity dependent on the phase of the AC input. This DC signal controls the firing of the power thyratron tubes in the controller. The output of the power thyratron tubes goes to the elevation drive motor which elevates the turret into correspondence with the sight."

The basic RCT system was composed of one sight, one turret, one thyratron controller, a signal system, an input resolver, a computer, and various controls to monitor and activate the system. The upper and lower fuselage turrets also had retracting mechanisms. The entire system was very dependent upon a constant and well-regulated electrical supply, and this was one source of early problems. Since all movement of the turrets and cannon was based on the differential voltage between two signals, each signal had to start from a very precise baseline. The voltage regulators in the late 1940s were not truly up to the task, resulting in large errors in movement in early systems.

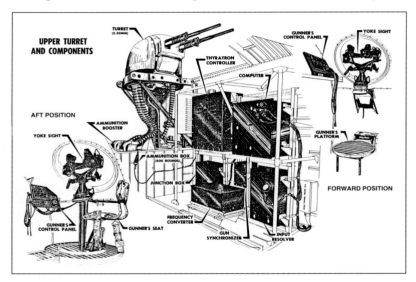
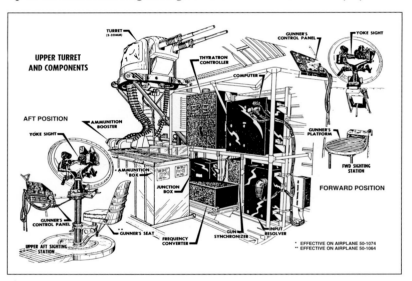

The upper and lower turrets and their associated components changed on the B-36F and later models. The drawing on the left shows the configuration prior to the F-model; on the right is the later configuration. There were also a couple of minor changes within the F-model production run as noted in the drawings. The major differences were the configuration of the ammunition boxes and the seats at each station. (U.S. Air Force)

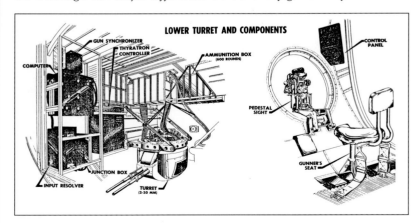
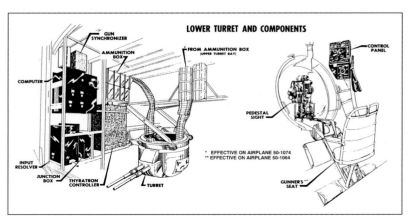

The forward upper turrets of an RB-36 are loaded at Rapid City AFB. (Ed Griemsmann Collection via Frederick A. Johnsen)

Technicians load the nose turret – the sight may be seen offset from the center of the glazed area. (Air Force Historical Research Agency)

A forward upper turret in the fully-deployed position showing the open door that slid along the side of the fuselage. (Peter M. Bowers)

Note the early A/B-model "island" in the turret bay in this photo compared to the one above. Both are looking rearward. (Convair)

Details of the M24A-1 20-mm cannon in the aft upper turrets with the covers removed. (U.S. Air Force)

All six of the turrets were structurally identical, although they differed in some details, mainly ammunition feeds. (Convair)

The purpose of all the B-36 sights (and any aircraft sight, for that matter) was to provide the system with the position, range, and angular velocity of a target in relation to the aircraft. Four different types of sights were used on the B-36: yoke, pedestal, hemisphere, and tail.

The yoke sights were located in the four upper sighting blisters, and were used to control the upper turrets. The retiflector-type optic head mounted on the yoke had an illuminated recticle which indicated the precise direction the sight was pointed. Two restrained gyroscopes were mounted on each sight, one to transmit azimuth lead data and the other to transmit elevation data. The yoke sight could be rotated in elevation from 90 degrees above to 45 degrees below horizontal, and in azimuth from 110 degrees forward to 110 degrees aft of broadside. The gunner tracked the target by manipulating the entire sight.

The pedestal sights were located in the two lower blisters and controlled the lower turrets. As in the yoke sights, each sight was equipped with a retiflector-type optic head and two restrained gyroscopes. The pedestal sight could be rotated in elevation from 45 degrees above to 90 degrees below horizontal, and in azimuth from 105 degrees forward to 105 degrees aft of broadside.

The yoke and pedestal sights had a small clear glass plate through which the gunner looked while aiming. When the sight was powered on, a view through the plate showed a center aiming dot surrounded by a circle of dots. By setting the attacking fighter's wingspan with the target dimension knob and framing the target correctly, the gunner supplied the range of the attacking fighter to the computer. At the same time the gunner was expected to track the fighter accurately and smoothly, providing azimuth, elevation, and relative speed (relative angular velocity) to the computer.

The hemisphere sight controlled the nose turret and was offset to the right side of the nose section, below the turret. The sight was a horizontally-mounted, double-prism periscopic sight designed to give the gunner a full hemisphere of vision. The gunner, without changing his position, could see 90 degrees to the right or left of straight ahead, as well as 90 degrees up or down from the aircraft waterline. The eyepiece of the sight was fixed, and the gunner controlled the turret by manipulating control handles immediately below the sight. Since the sight protruded from the nose of the aircraft into the airstream, a desiccating system was provided to keep the prism free of moisture and a heating unit prevented frost from forming.

The hemisphere sight operated on much the same principle as the yoke and pedestal sights, except the gunner sighted through a single eyepiece with one eye. A dummy eyepiece blocked the unused eye, and could be rotated to accommodate right or left eye-dominant gunners.

The tail sight was a radar set which was controlled by a gunner facing rearward (for no particular reason) in the aft compartment (some RB-36s shifted the gunner facing left on the port side of the aft cabin). The *SAC B-36 Gunnery Manual* boasted that, "The gun-laying radar is highly developed and unbelievably accurate." Three different gun-laying radars were used: the AN/APG-3 in the B-36B was quickly replaced by the AN/APG-32, in the D-model while the AN/APG-41 was used beginning on late H-models (51-5742 and subs). The early sets used a single antenna, while the APG-41 used two antennas above the tail turret, although in some later aircraft these were covered by a single elongated radome.

The thyratron controller was the heart of the RCT system. It was an early electronic device that amplified and converted small AC error signals to DC power for driving the turret drive motors. An individual thyratron controller was provided for each sight-turret combination.

The cannon could move in elevation independently of turret rotation. The turret and guns could move at two different rates, called 1- and 31-speed. The 31-speed was used to quickly move from one position to another, while the 1-speed was used to accurately track targets.

Each of the turrets was equipped with two M24A1 or M24E2 20-mm automatic cannon with a selectable rate of fire between 550 and 820 rounds per minute. Late in their careers the rate of fire was fixed at 700 rounds per minute for the tail guns and 600 for all others. Each gun

weighed 100 pounds, was 77.7 inches long (52.5 inches of this was the barrel), and had a muzzle velocity of 2,730 feet per second.

Convair installed two ammunition boxes for each turret. The nose turret had 800 rounds (400 per box), while all other turrets had 1,200 rounds (600 per box). The boxes were attached to the aircraft structure and were loaded by hand with belts of ammunition prior to each mission. There was an approved modification to replace the ammunition boxes with frames that would support plastic cans, allowing ammunition to be loaded on the aircraft prepacked. This would also have allowed spare ammunition to be more easily carried. It appears that this modification was not installed in any aircraft, although available documentation is not conclusive.

The ammunition was pulled out of an ammunition box by an ammunition booster mounted on the box (except for the lower turrets and some nose turrets) and fed through ammunition chutes to the gun feeders. The lower turrets used gravity to feed the ammunition.

Four different types of 20-mm ammunition were approved for use on the B-36: M96 incendiary, M97 high-explosive incendiary, AP1 armor-piercing incendiary, and AP-T armor-piercing with tracer. An M95 target practice round was also available, as was a nonfunctional "drill" round that could be used to practice loading and handling. Two different fuzes, T196E4 and M75, could be used interchangeably.

The retractable turrets were equipped with fire interrupters to prevent self-inflicted damage to the propellers, wings, or tail. The fire interrupters did not protect the landing gear in the extended position (although why the guns would be firing when the landing gear was extended is unclear). The retractable turrets were also equipped with contour followers to prevent the guns from striking the aircraft, and to prevent the guns from pointing at parts of the aircraft housing personnel. Neither the nose or tail turrets were equipped with fire interrupters or contour followers since it was physically impossible for them to aim at the aircraft. All turrets had electrically operated limit

The tail turret from inside the fuselage looking aft. The dual ammunition boxes were on each side of the fuselage just forward of bulkhead 17.0 (upper left corner) and had a long feed back to the cannon in the tail turret. (U.S. Air Force)

The original APG-3 and mid-life APG-32 were externally identical, but easily distinguishable from the later APG-41 (right). Each of the early systems had only a single antenna above the tail turret. (C. Roger Cripliver Collection)

The dual-antenna APG-41 was introduced during H-model production. Initial plans had been to retrofit the entire Featherweight III fleet, but this never occurred due to financial constraints. (C. Roger Cripliver Collection)

switches to prevent the turret or guns from exceeding their elevation or azimuth limits.

The upper turrets were limited in azimuth travel to 100 degrees either side of broadside. In elevation, fire coverage was limited to approximately 89 degrees upfire. Downfire coverage was dependent on the contour follower; however maximum downfire could be as much as 24 degrees at broadside. Used links and cartridges were collected in spent case containers.

The lower turrets were essentially the same as the upper turrets, but with a few adaptations due to their inverted position. Azimuth rotation was limited to 100 degrees either side of broadside, while elevation was limited to 89 degrees downfire. Upfire was dependent on the contour follower, but could be as much as 24 degrees at broadside. Used links and cartridges were ejected overboard.

The nose turret was located in the upper part of the nose section, and was limited in azimuth rotation to ±30 degrees of straight forward. In elevation it was limited to 26.5 degrees downfire and 26 degrees upfire. No contour follower, fire interrupter, or retraction mechanism was used on the nose turret. Used links and cartridges were collected in a spent case compartment.

The tail turret was, logically enough, located in the tail (this was actually pointed out in the *SAC B-36 Gunnery Manual*). The turret was approximately 40 inches in diameter, and was limited in azimuth rotation to ±45 degrees of straight aft. The turret was limited to 36.8 degrees downfire and 37.5 degrees upfire. No contour follower, fire interrupter, or retraction mechanism was used with the tail turret. Used links and cartridges were ejected overboard.

The control panels next to each sighting station contained switches to extend/retract the turrets (if appropriate), control the various heaters (guns, gyros, feed mechanisms, etc.), arm/safe the guns, and round counters that let the gunner know how much ammunition remained for each gun.

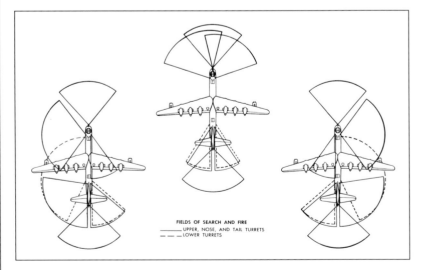

The HOMETOWN defensive tactics were based on a three-ship formation with each aircraft covering a specific quadrant. (U.S. Air Force)

The upper and lower fuselage turrets were electrically retractable in order to reduce drag. Each turret was covered by a flush panel that slid down the outside of the fuselage when opened. Each turret could also be extended or retracted manually by means of a handcrank. The turrets were stowed in unpressurized compartments that could be entered in flight if required, and also served as a means of emergency escape during ground accidents (explaining why many photos show the upper turret doors open during taxi).

Each turret had an early electric (not electronic) computer that provided corrections for parallax (angle), ballistics, lead (target speed), and windage. The computer and sighting system could accurately track targets to 1,499 yards (at exactly 1,500 yards one of the potentiometers in the computer was at its limit, and could cause the guns to hunt). The *SAC B-36 Gunnery Manual* recommended bursts of 2–3 seconds and checking the aiming and computer settings between bursts, but also noted that no cooling cycle was necessary and the guns could be fired continuously if required.

Gun cameras were installed on most sights (early pedestal sights were not camera-equipped), although their primary use was during gunner training and certification. The principal camera used on the B-36 was the Fairchild AN-N6, although the earlier Fairchild N-6 and various Bell and Howell cameras could also be used. The cameras had selectable speeds of 16, 32, and 64 frames per second. The gunners had a surprising amount of control over the cameras, including selecting color filters, aperture settings, etc.

SAC determined that a three-ship "V" formation provided the maximum defensive firepower. In this formation, the aircraft in the lead trained all of its turrets forward (the lower and upper aft turrets swiveled completely forward and provided upward and downward coverage). The aircraft on each side trained all of its turrets to that side. The exception, of course, was the tail turret that always faced aft. This plan left no area covered by less than two turrets (four cannon), and simplified coordination between the gunners. This formation was called HOMETOWN, and was the standard attack formation at altitudes under 35,000 feet.

Above 35,000 feet the importance of beam attacks was lessened since it was thought that very few contemporary fighters could actually keep up with the B-36 at high altitudes. Consequently, the HOMETOWN areas of search and fire were modified to provide more protection to the rear. This formation was called TAIL HEAVY, and primarily involved training the lower aft turrets of all aircraft to the rear (and downward). At these altitudes it was expected that most attacks would come from below and rearward, although there was a chance of a fighter climbing to altitude and waiting for the bombers directly ahead. There were, of course, other formations and tactics available to the bomber crews. Pretty much all of them centered around the same three-ship "V" formation, but modified the search and fire areas for each of the turrets.

The guns were eventually removed from the B-36s that were modified into Featherweight Configuration III aircraft. But there had been other proposals to defend the bomber. In 1947 the MX-802 project began to develop a bomber defense missile called the Dragonfly. This small, solid-fueled rocket had a speed of Mach 2.5 and a range of 3 miles. The missile was a beam-rider directed by small radars aboard the bomber. It was to be fired from a multi-tube launcher that would replace the upper and lower gun turrets.

The MX-802 project was eventually replaced by MX-904, a 75-pound Mach 2.5 rocket with semiactive radar homing. In March 1948 the missile was named Falcon, and for a while was considered a leading candidate for the defensive armament of the B-36 and the proposed B-55. By July 1950 the missile was redirected towards a new generation of interceptors, with a bomber defense version to follow later. In the end, the missile never equipped any bombers, although it went on to a long career on a variety of fighters.

DECOYS

The use of the McDonnell ADM-20B (formerly GAM-72) Quail decoy missile aboard the B-52 during the 1960s was not a new idea. On 16 August 1954 the Air Force issued contract AF33(600)27337 to Convair to develop the GAM-71 Buck Duck decoy missile for the B-36. Convair had been investigating the concept using company funds for several years prior to the official contract, going so far as to manufacture a production-representative prototype. Conceptually this decoy was identical to the later Quail – a small missile that was carried in the bomb bay and launched during the final target penetration. The Buck Duck was designed to accurately simulate the radar return of a B-36, and it was initially expected that one aircraft per formation would carry four bomb bays full (7 decoys) while the other aircraft carried bombs. There was, however, no reason that each bomber could not carry a couple of decoys in one bomb bay and still carry bombs in the others.[4]

Although not terribly challenging from a technical perspective, the Buck Duck program ran into delays due to funding constraints and other priorities at Convair. The first production decoy was completed on 24 November 1954 and an engineering inspection was held on 2–3 December 1954. Three additional decoys were manufactured, although a dozen serial numbers (55-3490 – 55-3501) had been allocated. A couple of months later than expected, the Buck Duck program began captive-carry flights under the wing of a B-29 on 14 February 1955, and the first of at least seven glide flights from the same B-29 were conducted a month later. For reasons that could not be ascertained – but probably relating to the imminent B-36 phase-out – the Buck Duck program was cancelled in January 1956. No record could be found indicating that the missile had ever flown a powered flight, or been carried by a B-36.[5]

Naturally, Buck Duck was a small vehicle, with an overall length of 13 feet and a wing span of 14 feet. The wings folded to produce a package only 5 feet wide. The launch weight was just 1,550 pounds. Most records indicate that a single XLR85 rocket engine produced 900-lbf and could propel the decoy to Mach 0.55 and a range of 230 miles. There are reports, however, that the decoy used a small turbojet engine instead. Radar reflectors were fitted around the Buck Duck in order to approximate the radar return of the big bomber. Two Buck Ducks could be carried in each bomb bay except No. 3, which could only carry a single decoy due to the wing spar.[6]

The GAM-71 Buck Duck decoy was initially developed using Convair funds, but the Air Force subsequently funded the development program. Although Buck Duck was later cancelled, the overall concept was resurrected as the GAM-72 Quail decoy for the B-52. (Lockheed Martin)

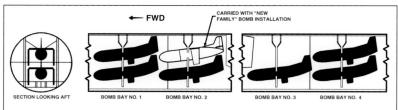

The normal load of Buck Ducks was going to be six missiles, although a special installation would allow a second missile to be carried in bomb bay No. 2 for a total of seven. Alternately – and more likely – each B-36 would carry one bomb bay full of GAM-71s (probably bay No. 2), a fuel tank in bomb bay No. 3, and weapons in Nos. 1 and 4. In any event, the Buck Duck was cancelled before any production models were built. (U.S. Air Force)

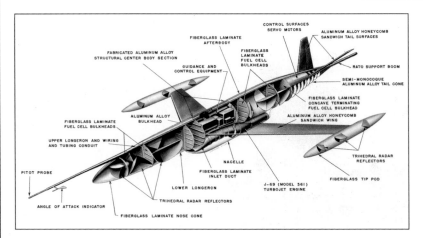

The Convair MX-2223 was an attempt to develop a long-range ground-based decoy that would be launched ahead of the bomber formations to deceive or saturate enemy defenses. (Convair)

A more bizarre concept was embodied in the Long Range Decoy Program. Instead of carrying the decoys on the aircraft, the Air Force decided that it could use a ground-launched, long-range decoy to accompany the bombers. The decoys would be prestaged at locations near the Soviet Union (Alaska and Greenland), and would be launched when a strike order was given to the bomber fleet. The decoys could be launched in support of a strike, or as a diversion as the strike progressed from a different direction. The idea was that the decoys would be put into place, then left unattended for several weeks (or perhaps months) and launched by remote control.

Work on the concept began in December 1952, and on 1 July 1954 the Air Force awarded Convair contract AF33(616)-2642 for a preliminary study into the MX-2223 concept. The study was to determine the "optimum basic design and performance characteristics of a complete long range, surface launched, decoy missile system." Brief data "on such allied factors as: storage, assembly, check-out, repair and launching equipment …" was also to be provided. The study was to examine missiles having ranges between 3,450 and 4,600 miles at speeds of Mach 0.8 to 0.9 at altitudes between 35,000 and 50,000 feet. The decoy was to simulate B-36, B-47, B-52, and B-58 radar returns over a frequency of 65 to 11,000 megacycles.[7]

The final concept described by Convair was basically a small aircraft capable of high subsonic speeds. It used a streamlined circular-section fuselage with a 10:1 fineness ratio, 35-degree swept-wings with tip pods for carrying radar reflectors, and a vee-tail for stability. Most of the fuselage used composite construction, considered very advanced for the time. The nose cone, forebody, and afterbody were of molded fiberglass laminate with the pieces bonded together with a thermo-setting plastic glue. However, the major structural portions of the fuselage – the central cylindrical section that supported the wing and engine, and the tail cone that supported the vee-tail – were of normal semi-monocoque aluminum construction.

Trihedral radar reflectors were located in each fuel cell and the wing-tip pods to simulate the various types of bombers. The reflectors within the fuel cells also acted as baffles during the early part of the mission. The reflectors in the wing tip pods were designed to oscillate as the wing flexed, further enhancing the radar return from the decoy. Provisions were included to add active radar transmitters, chaff, or other electronic equipment as necessary. Although the decoy was probably fast enough to simulate the subsonic bombers, it could not accurately portray a B-58 during supersonic flight.

Convair investigated two different methods to launch the decoys – rail launching using a small booster was rejected in favor of a zero-length system using a larger booster. Acceleration was limited to 5-g to ensure any onboard electronics were not damaged.[8]

The MX-2223 program did not result in a specific development program, but it gave the Air Force the confidence to move forward with a similar program. This time it was the Fairchild B-73 (later redesignated XSM-73) Bull Goose as part of WS-123A. A General Operational Requirement (GOR-16) was released in March 1953, and a development contract was signed with Fairchild in December 1955. Like the MX-2223 concept, the XSM-73 was to be launched from ground sites adjacent to designated SAC bases located in the far north along probable strike routes to the Soviet Union.

The requirements for the XSM-73 were a maximum range of at least 4,600 miles with a speed of at least 0.85 Mach at an altitude of 50,000 feet. A payload of 500 pounds was to be carried, mainly reflectors and electronics to simulate the radar return of a B-47 or B-52 in S-band, L-band, and lower frequencies. By this time the B-36 was being phased out and it was not included in the requirements. The performance of the missile was to simulate both the B-47 and B-52 over the final 1,750 nautical miles of flight. The subsonic speed requirement again meant the B-58 could not be accurately simulated, so the requirement to emulate a Hustler was dropped. The requirements specified that 85 percent of those missiles that arrived at the 4,600-mile range would be within a lateral deviation of plus or minus 110 miles of their designated target under no-wind conditions. The SM-73 weapon system (WS-123A) was to be capable of launching 50 percent of the operational stock of SM-73 missiles within the first hour after an alert and the remaining missiles within the second hour. In theory the missile could be launched from a "ready state" (gyros spun up) in under 2 minutes. The electronic package could be left unattended (no maintenance) for up to 60 days, and the engine could go 28 days between inspections while on alert.[9]

The XSM-73 used an autopilot stabilization system with low-drift, integrating-rate gyro for directional control with provisions for preflight programming of turn in either direction. Aircraft pitch control was provided by elevons operating in phase, roll control was by asymmetrical elevon operation, and yaw damping by a conventional rudder. All of the control surfaces were positioned by hydraulic actuator movement initiated by electrical signal from the flight control system.

The final design for the delta-wing XSM-73 weighed 7,700 pounds at launch, including a 500-pound payload of electronics. The missile was 33.5 feet long with a wing span of 24.4 feet. A single 2,450-lbf J83 turbojet provided a top speed of Mach 0.85 and a projected range of 5,500 miles. A large rocket booster producing 50,000-lbf provided the initial thrust. On 13 May 1958 the name of the program was changed to Goose (no Bull) on orders from the Air Materiel Command.

The Air Force planned to field ten Goose squadrons and purchase 53 development and 2,328 operational missiles. The first squadron was to be operational at the end of FY61, with the final one coming 2 years later. Sled tests began at Holloman AFB, New Mexico, in February 1957, with the first of 20 flights taking place at the Atlantic Missile Range in June 1957. The five flights conducted in 1957 were generally successful, but the remaining 15 (in 1958) were less so, mainly because of problems with the Fairchild-developed YJ83 engine. Problems with funding and the fiberglass-resin bonded wing also delayed the program. Construction of some operational sites in Alaska had begun in August 1958, but on 12 December 1958 the program was cancelled. A total of 28.5 flight hours had been accumulated, and the entire program had cost $70 million.[10]

The Fairchild XSM-73 Bull Goose was a conceptual follow-on to the MX-2223 decoy intended to simulate the B-47 and B-52. (45th SW/HO)

CONVENTIONAL BOMBS

Interestingly, the *SAC B-36 Gunnery Manual* contained a fairly large chapter on bombs and bombing equipment. This was because "as a gunner, you have duties and responsibilities not directly concerned with flexibly gunnery ... you will assist [the bombardier] in the loading, fuzing, and arming of all bombs."

The B-36 was equipped with four large bomb bays. The B-36A and B-36B used electrically-controlled, cable-operated doors that slid in tracks up the side of the lower fuselage. The doors on bomb bays No. 1 and No. 4 were single-piece units that slid up the left side of the fuselage. The two middle bomb bays had doors split down the centerline and slid up both sides of the fuselage – the location of the wing prevented using a single-piece design. Each door was 16.1 feet long. The doors were slow to operate, tended to stick in the extremely cold temperatures at 40,000 feet, and created undesirable drag at a time when speed was of the essence. Beginning with the B-36D, the aircraft were equipped with hydraulically-actuated "snap-action" doors that opened in approximately 2 seconds. There were two sets of 32.375-foot long doors per aircraft, one set covering the combined bomb bays Nos. 1 and 2, and the other set covering Nos. 3 and 4. The B-36A/B models were retrofitted with the new doors as they became RB-36Es and B-36Ds, respectively.

Initially the RB-36 was not configured to carry bombs, only photo flash bombs in bomb bay No. 2 and an auxiliary fuel tank in bomb bay No. 3. Reconnaissance versions installed a pressurized compartment into the space previously used by bomb bay No. 1 that housed up to 14 cameras, a darkroom that allowed film cartridges to be reloaded, and the crew to operate and maintain the equipment. A special pallet that contained various ferret ECM equipment was carried in the area that was bomb bay No. 4 on the bombers, and was easily identified by the three large radomes protruding below the same area. Later this equipment was moved into the aft fuselage and the radomes were placed under the lower aft fuselage, allowing bomb bay No. 4 to be configured to carry a nuclear weapon. The bomb bay doors were also changed to more closely match the bomber models – Nos. 3 and 4 were covered by a single set of new 32.375-foot long doors, while bomb bay No. 2 was covered by a set of 16-foot doors that were modified from the original set of doors. Previously, bomb bays Nos. 2 and 3 had been covered by a single set of doors that were 33.66 feet long.

The B-36 was capable of carrying 67 different types of conventional, incendiary, cluster, and chemical bombs, as well as several types of mines. On aircraft equipped to carry nuclear weapons, any airborne nuclear or thermonuclear weapon in the inventory could be carried – the B-36 was the only aircraft that could do so. Only a single type of bomb could be carried in each bomb bay, although each bay could carry different types if necessary. The end bomb bays (Nos. 1 and 4) could carry a maximum of thirty-eight 500-pound bombs, nineteen 1,000-pound bombs, eight 2,000-pound bombs, or three 4,000-pound bombs. The two middle bomb bays (Nos. 2 and 3) were not as tall as the other two due to the wing carry-through structure, and could carry twenty-eight 500-pound bombs, sixteen 1,000-pound bombs, six 2,000-pound

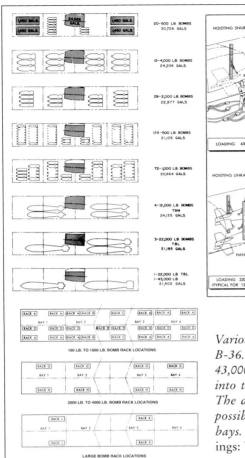

20-500 LB. BOMBS 30,726 GALS
12-4,000 LB. BOMBS 24,204 GALS
28-2,000 LB. BOMBS 22,877 GALS
129-500 LB. BOMBS 21,105 GALS
72-1,000 LB. BOMBS 20,464 GALS
4-12,000 LB. BOMBS TBM 24,135 GALS
3-22,000 LB. BOMBS TBL 21,185 GALS
1-22,000 LB TBL, 1-43,000 LB 21,402 GALS

HOISTING SNUBBER — ADJUSTMENT — HOISTING SNUBBER — LARGE BOMB DOLLY — LARGE BOMB CRADLE (43000 LB. BOMB) — LOADING 43000 LB. BOMB — HAND CRANK FOR ROLLING BOMB — HOISTING LINKAGE — FORE AND AFT POSITIONER HANDLE — HOISTING LINKAGE — DOLLY — DOLLY BRAKE — HAND CRANK — C-8 HOIST UNIT — CRADLE ADAPTER — MANUAL RELEASE BRAKE LEVER — C-8 HOIST UNIT — LOADING 22000 LB. BOMBS. (TYPICAL FOR 12000 LB. BOMBS)

100 LB. TO 1000 LB. BOMB RACK LOCATIONS
2000 LB. TO 4000 LB. BOMB RACK LOCATIONS
LARGE BOMB RACK LOCATIONS

IDENTIFICATION BANDS

Type of bomb	Color of body	Color	Number of bands and location			Color of Marking
			Nose	Center	Tail	
GP and LC (TNT or Amatol loaded), FRAGMENTATION, (TNT or Ednatol, loaded), AP, DEPTH, and SAP.	Olive-drab	Yellow	1*	None	1*	Black
GP and FRAGMENTATION (COMP B loaded).	do	do	2	do	2	do
GP and LC (Tritonal loaded).	do	do	1 narrow between 2 wide bands.	do	1 narrow between 2 wide bands.	do
PHOTOFLASH.	Gray		None	do	None	do
PRACTICE	Blue		do	do	do	White
DRILL	Olive-drab	Black	1	do	1	Black
CHEMICAL:						
Smoke	Gray	Yellow	1	1	1	Yellow
Incendiary	do	Purple	1	1	1	Purple
Persistent gas	do	Green	2	2	2	Green
Nonpersistent gas	do	Green	1	1	1	do
Irritant gas	do	Red	1	1	1	Red

*Small fragmentation bombs (under 90 lb.) are painted on the head and base instead of with an actual color band.

Various aspects of carrying bombs in the B-36. The photo at right shows a 43,000-pound T-12 bomb being loaded into the bomb bay of an early B-36A. The drawings at left show some of the possible configurations of the bomb bays. (photo: Lockheed Martin; drawings: U.S. Air Force)

bombs, or three 4,000-pound bombs. Alternately, two 12,000-pound bombs, or a single 22,000-pound or 43,000-pound bomb could be carried in the combined bay 1/2 and bay 3/4. A portion of the separating bulkhead could be moved to accommodate the larger bombs.[11]

Bombs weighing up to 4,000 pounds were carried on 15 different types of removable bomb racks. The racks were mounted along the sides of the bomb bay in the traditional style. Larger bombs used special slings instead of conventional suspension lugs and shackles.

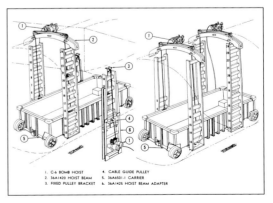

1. C-6 BOMB HOIST
2. 36A1420 HOIST BEAM
3. FIXED PULLEY BRACKET
4. CABLE GUIDE PULLEY
5. 36A6501-1 CARRIER
6. 36A1425 HOIST BEAM ADAPTER

When deploying overseas the B-36 could carry many of its own tools and supplies on these cargo carriers. A total of seven carriers could be carried in the bomb bays (two in each except No. 2). Many of the early demonstration flights flown by the B-36As used the cargo carriers to load zinc bars that were used to simulate the armament and other systems that were not installed on the A-models. (photos: Lockheed Martin; drawing: U.S. Air Force)

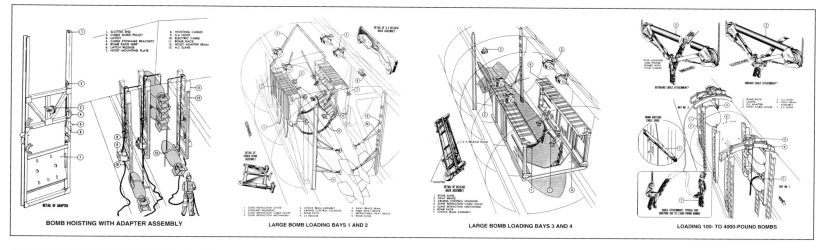

BOMB HOISTING WITH ADAPTER ASSEMBLY   **LARGE BOMB LOADING BAYS 1 AND 2**   **LARGE BOMB LOADING BAYS 3 AND 4**   **LOADING 100- TO 4000-POUND BOMBS**

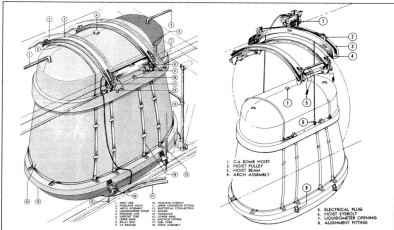

The auxiliary fuel tanks that could be carried in the bomb bays were little more than a shell with a rubber fuel cell inside. The tanks could be jettisoned while the B-36 was in flight, but it required that a crewmember to manually disconnect the fuel and electrical connections first. (U.S. Air Force)

The maximum 86,000-pound bomb load carried by later B-36s is easily the largest bomb load ever carried by an American bomber. Even the "big belly" B-52Ds used during Vietnam could only carry 60,000 pounds (twenty-four 750-pound and eighty-four 500-), and the B-1B carries only 42,000 pounds (eighty-four 500-pound) of bombs (although its theoretical load limit is 75,000 pounds). As a point of reference, one of the most respected interdiction aircraft in the current Air Force inventory is the F-15E Strike Eagle. Fully loaded, with a maximum fuel and weapon load, the F-15E weighs 86,000 pounds – the B-36 could carry that amount of bombs!

Bomb bay No. 3 could carry a 3,000-gallon auxiliary fuel tank in all aircraft, and bomb bay No. 2 could carry one in some aircraft. Other sources report that all four bomb bays in some aircraft could carry these fuel tanks, but this could not be confirmed through official sources. The original auxiliary fuel tank was interesting in that it was basically a metal frame with a fuel-proof "rubberized" canvas bag suspended from it. The bag, made by the Firestone Tire and Rubber Company, contained the fuel. A later version of the fuel cell, manufactured by Goodyear in Akron, Ohio, consisted of a pliocel nylon bladder inside a metal shell. The auxiliary fuel tanks could be dropped during flight if necessary, although the fuel and power connections had to be disconnected manually beforehand.[12]

In a rather unique concept to assist the B-36 in deployments, both the ground power carts and a special cargo carrier were designed to be loaded into the bomb bays. Two cargo carriers were supplied by Convair with each aircraft, complete with wheels and tow bars to facilitate ground handling. Each cargo carrier could carry up to 14,000 pounds of loose items. Bomb bays Nos. 1 and 4 could each carry two of the cargo carriers, while the middle two bomb bays could each carry a single carrier.[13]

A good balancing act, considering the T-12 bomb weighed 43,000 pounds. Each of the ten B-2 "Hydraulic Bomb Lift, Mobile" had a nominal 50,000-pound capacity, although at least two were modified to handle 55,000-pound hydrogen bombs. (Air Force Historical Research Agency)

Most bombs (and other items) under 4,000 pounds each were hoisted into the bomb bays by electric C-6 Hoist Units temporarily installed on top of the fuselage above the bomb bays. Holes in the upper fuselage were provided for the lifting cables. Very large bombs were lifted into the bomb bays with hydraulic lifts.

ATOMIC BOMBS

Interestingly, the B-36 was not designed to carry atomic bombs. But then, at the time no other bomber had been so designed either, and in 1946 only a few specially-modified B-29s were capable of carrying the new atomic devices. By the end of 1947, the Air Force had only 32 B-29s modified under Project SADDLE TREE available to carry atomic weapons. Many of these were described as "quite weary" after their wartime service, and all were assigned to the 509th Bombardment Group. Even more frustrating was a lack of training, mainly due to tight security requirements from the organizations* that controlled the bombs. At the beginning of 1948 only six crews were fully qualified to drop the atomic bomb, although sufficient partially trained personnel existed to assemble another 14 crews if necessary. Other complications included the fact that no air base in the world had all the equipment on hand necessary to assemble and load an atomic bomb, and there were only two qualified bomb assembly teams in the country.[14]

Part of the reason the Northrop flying wings did not garner more support within the Air Force was that the XB-35 had bomb bays too small to accommodate the 5-foot diameter, 10-foot long Mk III "Fat Man" or its Mk 4 replacement. The bombs had to be carried semisubmerged, resulting in a 6-percent loss in top speed and a 10 percent loss in combat range. The B-29 (and the B-50) had bomb bays that could only accommodate weapons shorter than 12 feet long, eliminating carriage of bombs such as the 15-foot long Mk 7.

Part of the problem during the late 1940s was that weapons developers would not tell the Air Force what the physical characteristics of their weapons were until they were in production, and then the data was highly classified. The designers provided "preliminary data" that was often substantially different from the weapon that finally emerged. This had been most evident on the North American B-45 program where the final weapon would not fit in the bomb bay of the light bomber. Modifications to aircraft bomb bays to accommodate atomic weapons was also considered "restricted" under the Atomic Energy Act of 1946. This was reiterated in May 1947 when the AEC stated "...any aircraft modification which would allow a reasonably accurate estimate of size, weight, or shape of the bomb ... must con-

---

* The bombs had been built and were controlled by the Manhattan Engineer District project which became the Armed Forces Special Weapons Project after the war. Eventually the manufacture and control of nuclear weapons passed to the Atomic Energy Commission.

Two shots of empty bomb bays: No. 4 looking aft showing the four aft turrets in their retracted position (left) and No. 3 looking forward showing the wing carry-through structure. At top right Frank Kleinwechter poses with a dummy Mk 17 thermonuclear weapon. Conventional bombs loaded for Eglin firepower demonstration in October 1955 as shown at lower right. (left and center: Lockheed Martin; Frank Kleinwechter via Don Pyeatt)

tinue to be Restricted Data." This meant that you had to be cleared in order to simply look inside an empty bomb bay (many officials tried to enforce this restriction years after it had been officially lifted). The Air Force finally convinced the AEC that an empty bomb bay should be unclassified until the suspension lugs and sway braces were installed, since little information could be gained from the geometric shape of most bomb bays.[15]

The early nuclear weapons were designed without much regard to the aircraft that might carry it. Each bomb had a different center of gravity, sometimes radically different shapes, and required different suspension equipment and sway braces. This greatly complicated the design of aircraft bomb bays. The problem is exemplified by the situation surrounding the Mk 6 weapon. As early as August 1949 the Air Force had requested that Sandia Laboratory supply drawings of the weapon to allow the Air Force to begin planning for its introduction to the inventory. Sandia refused, indicating they would turn over the data after the bomb design had been frozen for production (something that did not occur until mid-1951). The Air Force commented that Sandia "consistently ignored our requirements and had used dimensions which required redesigning of handling, loading, and carrying equipment." The B-36 was impacted less by these problems than most aircraft simply because it was essentially a large tube – a very large tube. In the end it could be modified relatively easily to carry almost any size or shape bomb the designers could dream up. It was the only aircraft ever capable of carrying the monstrous 25-foot long, 42,000 pound Mk 17 thermonuclear weapon.[16]

The components required to enable a bomber to carry early atomic weapons were relatively simple. A special bomb suspension system was installed, along with the appropriate sway braces and suspension lugs. Electronic "T-boxes" controlled, tested, and monitored the bomb during flight, while arming controls and a method to insert the "capsule" that allowed the bomb to go critical were also required.

Concurrently with the weapons programs, Project GEM (global electronics modernization) provided worldwide navigation equipment and some cold weather modifications that allowed bombers to operate over and around the Arctic Circle. Project SADDLE TREE was the first effort to convert B-29s and B-36s to carry the Mk III "Fat Man" type atomic bomb, the weapon being produced immediately after the war. Primarily this involved installing the appropriate suspension equipment and the T-Boxes. Between May 1947 and June 1948 the first 18 B-36Bs were modified to the SADDLE TREE configuration while the last 54 B-models were scheduled to come off the production line with most of the changes already in place. By the end of 1950 SAC had 52 B-36s equipped with the GEM/SADDLE TREE modifications, although at any given time many of these were out of service undergoing maintenance or being modified.[17]

In late December 1950, Project ON TOP began modifying additional aircraft, this time to carry the Mk 4, Mk 5, and Mk 6 devices. At the same time the Air Force began the development of the universal bomb suspension (UBS) system that could be easily reconfigured to accommodate atomic weapons 15–60 inches in diameter up to 128 inches long. The UBS was to be installed in B-29, B-36, B-47, B-50,

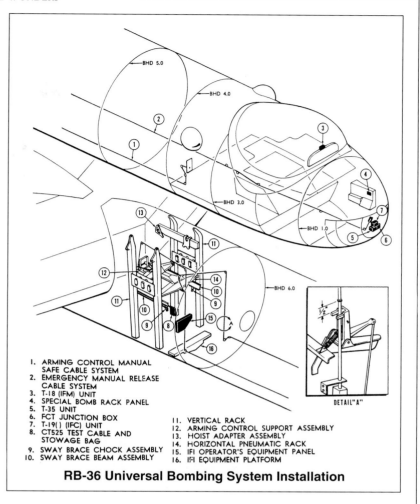

1. ARMING CONTROL MANUAL SAFE CABLE SYSTEM
2. EMERGENCY MANUAL RELEASE CABLE SYSTEM
3. T-18 (IFM) UNIT
4. SPECIAL BOMB RACK PANEL
5. T-35 UNIT
6. FCT JUNCTION BOX
7. T-19( ) (IFC) UNIT
8. CT525 TEST CABLE AND STOWAGE BAG
9. SWAY BRACE CHOCK ASSEMBLY
10. SWAY BRACE BEAM ASSEMBLY
11. VERTICAL RACK
12. ARMING CONTROL SUPPORT ASSEMBLY
13. HOIST ADAPTER ASSEMBLY
14. HORIZONTAL PNEUMATIC RACK
15. IFI OPERATOR'S EQUIPMENT PANEL
16. IFI EQUIPMENT PLATFORM

RB-36 Universal Bombing System Installation

The original UBS installation in RB-36s was in bomb bay No. 2 only. Later modifications added a weapon capability (but not necessarily a UBS) into bomb bay No. 4. (U.S. Air Force)

and B-54 aircraft. When used aboard the B-36, the UBS could support Mk 4, Mk 5, Mk 6, Mk 8, and Mk 18 atomic bombs, and Mk 15, Mk 21, Mk 36, and Mk 39 thermonuclear weapons. The development of the UBS by North American Aviation was afforded the highest national priority available – even higher than the ongoing police action in Korea. All of these modifications resulted in the B-36 being able to carry a single nuclear weapon in bomb bay No. 1 where it was most convenient for crew members to arm the weapon.[18]

It was not until July 1950 that SAC decided that B-36s should be able to carry more than one atomic weapon at a time. No less than three separate configurations evolved from this requirement as part of later phases of ON TOP. At least 30 aircraft (12 B-36Ds and 18 B-36Hs) were modified to carry the UBS in all four bomb bays. Other aircraft were modified to carry the UBS in bomb bay No. 1 and another weapon in bomb bay No. 4. Some aircraft could reportedly

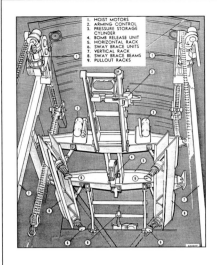

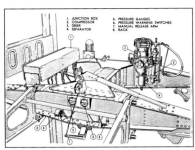

The early model UBS installed on aircraft prior to 52-1360. Later aircraft had slightly simplified systems. (U.S. Air Force)

"medium cargo system" in bomb bay No. 4 capable of carrying anything except the Mk 14, 17, 21, and 36. By this time all RB-36s had a UBS in bomb bay No. 2. T.O. 1B-36(R)-216 installed the large cargo system in bomb bay No. 3 and made provisions for installing the large cargo system in bomb bay No. 4. T.O. 1B-36(R)-506 installed the medium cargo system in bomb bay No. 4. Still pretty confusing.

In 1951 a tentative configuration of the first hydrogen bomb was released to the Air Force – at six feet in diameter, 20 feet long, and weighing 50,000 pounds, only the B-36 was capable of carrying it. Project CAUCASIAN modified four B-36Hs to carry the TX-14 weapon as part of the test series. Unlike the modifications required for the atomic bombs, the H-bombs required structural modifications to the main wing spar to support the heavier loads. A method of lifting the bomb into the aircraft also had to be found, and the Air Force decided to modify two of the ten B-2 bomb lifts that had been built during World War II to load the Grand Slam bombs. Unlike the TX-14, the TX-16 (and EC-16) devices were fueled with cryogenic orthohydrogen, and Project BAR ROOM equipped the CAUCASIAN B-36Hs with the necessary fittings and piping necessary to support them.

The first two modified B-36Hs arrived at Kirtland on 3 November and 3 December 1952 after receiving their special equipment in Fort Worth. The first trial run model (TRM) of the TX-14 arrived at Kirtland in May 1953, and by late June the last two modified B-36Hs had arrived. The modifications included a "cargo platform" in the bomb bay, various sway braces, a U-2 bomb-release and adapter, a pneumatic system, manual bomb release system, suspension slings, sling retractors and snubbing equipment, arming equipment, parachute arming controls (to allow a choice of free-fall or retarded delivery), and various weapon and parachute safety systems.

carry multiple weapons of the same type in a single bomb bay. Beginning in 1952 the RB-36s (all models) were modified to carry nuclear weapons in bomb bay No. 4. The factory began to equip aircraft with the UBS beginning with the B-36F, and by the time the B-36H began to roll off the production line, they could carry the UBS in two bomb bays. It was a confusing time.

By mid-1956 the configurations had stabilized somewhat. All B-36s had UBS installations in bomb bays Nos. 1 and 4 capable of carrying the Mk 6 and Mk 18 atomic weapons. After T.O. 1B-36-783 was incorporated, UBS systems were installed in bomb bay Nos. 2 and 3, again capable of carrying Mk 6 and Mk 18 weapons. On airplanes modified by T.O. 1B-36-852 the "large cargo system" (capable of carrying any weapon) was installed in bomb bay No. 3. T.O. 1B-36-973 installed a

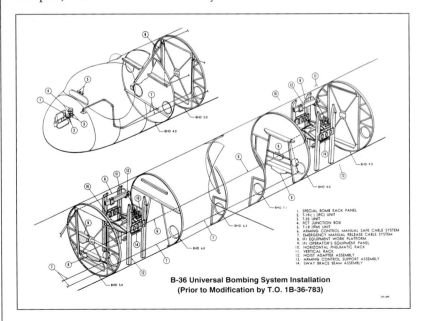

1. SPECIAL BOMB RACK PANEL
2. T-19( ) (IFC) UNIT
3. T-35 UNIT
4. FCT JUNCTION BOX
5. T-18 (IFM) UNIT
6. ARMING CONTROL MANUAL SAFE CABLE SYSTEM
7. EMERGENCY MANUAL RELEASE CABLE SYSTEM
8. IFI EQUIPMENT WORK PLATFORM
9. IFI OPERATOR'S EQUIPMENT PANEL
10. HORIZONTAL PNEUMATIC RACK
11. VERTICAL RACK
12. HOIST ADAPTER ASSEMBLY
13. ARMING CONTROL SUPPORT ASSEMBLY
14. SWAY BRACE BEAM ASSEMBLY

B-36 Universal Bombing System Installation
(Prior to Modification by T.O. 1B-36-783)

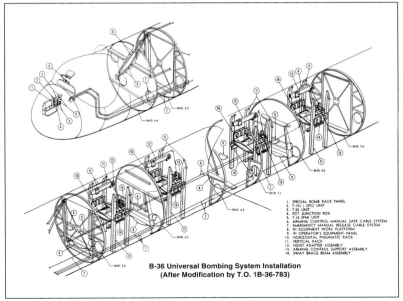

1. SPECIAL BOMB RACK PANEL
2. T-19( ) (IFC) UNIT
3. T-35 UNIT
4. FCT JUNCTION BOX
5. T-18 (IFM) UNIT
6. ARMING CONTROL MANUAL SAFE CABLE SYSTEM
7. EMERGENCY MANUAL RELEASE CABLE SYSTEM
8. IFI EQUIPMENT WORK PLATFORM
9. IFI OPERATOR'S EQUIPMENT PANEL
10. HORIZONTAL PNEUMATIC RACK
11. VERTICAL RACK
12. HOIST ADAPTER ASSEMBLY
13. ARMING CONTROL SUPPORT ASSEMBLY
14. SWAY BRACE BEAM ASSEMBLY

B-36 Universal Bombing System Installation
(After Modification by T.O. 1B-36-783)

Drawings showing the two primary configurations of the B-36 in 1956 – a version that had the UBS in two bomb bays, and one that had the UBS in all four bomb bays. Some aircraft had alternate systems in some bomb bays that allowed a variety of other nuclear weapons to be carried. (U.S. Air

In the first few months after the B-36s arrived at Kirtland, more than 40 dummy TX-14 drops were made. A similar series was also conducted on dummy TX-16 shapes. The TX-14 was 61.4 inches in diameter, 222 inches long, and weighed about 30,000 pounds – the TX-16 was 75 inches longer and weighed an additional 13,000 pounds. No particular problems were noted with either shape. On 7 December 1953 the first full-up drop test of a dummy TX-16 was conducted using the "production" design bomb-release system and including the simulated use of two small hydrogen pumps to top off the cryogenic orthohydrogen (liquid deuterium). By the end of the year, the design of the TX-16 was complete, and the Air Force committed to modifying 220 B-36s to carry the weapon (the B-47 had also been selected, and successfully dropped test shapes; however the range of the medium bomber was deemed insufficient to make an effective carrier and modifications were apparently not widely completed).

As a result of the Operation CASTLE atmospheric tests, the TX-16 was cancelled on 2 April 1954 and the TX-14 and TX-17 were selected for production (called "stockpiled" by the AEC) as the Mk 14 and Mk 17, respectively. With the withdrawal of the TX-16, Project BAR ROOM was renamed CAUTERIZE. A high-priority program was undertaken to modify B-36s to carry production versions of the devices. By the end of 1953 there were 20 B-36s equipped to carry thermonuclear weapons; by the middle of 1955 there were 208 aircraft. CASTLE had demonstrated the devices were capable of yielding the equivalent of 13.5 megatons, and the production Mk 17 yield was estimated at 20 megatons – the most powerful weapon ever deployed by the United States, and only deliverable by the B-36.[*]

BOMBING SYSTEMS

The original plan was to equip the B-36 with the Western Electric AN/APQ-7 Eagle radar bombing system. This system had been designed during World War II and was successfully used on a relatively small number of B-24s and B-29s against Japan late in the war. The system demonstrated an accuracy equal to, or perhaps better than, the best bombardier could achieve using the Norden bombsight in clear weather – and the APQ-7 could accomplish the task at night or during marginally bad weather. However, the APQ-7 only had a range of 30 miles and needed an antenna that was 16-feet long. On the B-29, the antenna had been suspended beneath the fuselage between the bomb bays, looking like a small wing. The B-36 designers hoped to house the antenna in the leading edge of the wing, eliminating the additional drag created by the installation used on the B-29.

After the war ended, the Army Air Forces began the development of a new high-performance bombing system capable of operations at 50,000 feet and up to 500 knots. This was the desired operating environment for the next generation of heavy bombers, and the Norden bombsight would be essentially useless at these altitudes and speeds, as would the APQ-7.

This requirement gave birth to what is now known as a "bomb/nav" system where all of the aircraft bombing and navigation equipment were integrated into a single system. The first of these systems was the AN/APQ-23, essentially an AN/APS-13 search radar

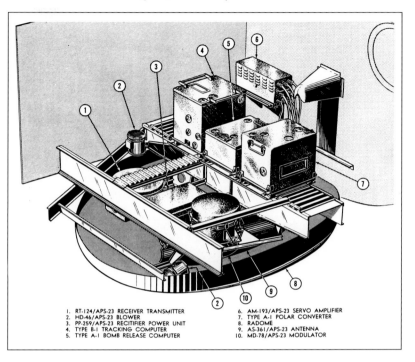

1. RT-124/APS-23 RECEIVER TRANSMITTER
2. HD-46/APS-23 BLOWER
3. PP-259/APS-23 RECITIFIER POWER UNIT
4. TYPE B-1 TRACKING COMPUTER
5. TYPE A-1 BOMB RELEASE COMPUTER
6. AM-193/APS-23 SERVO AMPLIFIER
7. TYPE A-1 POLAR CONVERTER
8. RADOME
9. AS-361/APS-23 ANTENNA
10. MD-78/APS-23 MODULATOR

All B-36 and RB-36 aircraft had an AN/APS-23 search radar located in the lower forward turret compartment instead of guns. The fiberglass radome protruded below the fuselage as shown below. (above: U.S. Air Force; below: Lockheed Martin)

---

[*] The weapon physically would have fit into the early B-52s, but it had been withdrawn from the stockpile prior to the B-52 becoming operational.

BROKEN ARROWS

"I don't know what's scarier – losing nuclear weapons or that it happens so often, there's actually a term for it."[19]

Although it is unlikely that the following code names were in use during the period that the B-36 was active, they are provided here because they have received a great deal of publicity in the last 5 years as a result of being used in various movies and books. Currently, DoD Directive 5230.16 defines a "Nuclear Weapon Accident," as:

An unexpected event involving nuclear weapons or nuclear components that results in any of the following:

- Accidental or unauthorized launching, firing, or use by U.S. forces or U.S. supported Allied forces of a nuclear-capable weapons.
- An accidental, unauthorized or unexplained nuclear detonation.
- Non-nuclear detonation or burning of a nuclear weapon or nuclear component.
- Radioactive contamination.
- Jettisoning of a nuclear weapon or nuclear component.
- Public hazard, actual or perceived."

As a tool for indicating the severity of a nuclear weapon accident, DoD officials are provided the following code words to be used only in internal communications: (listed in order of most to least serious)
Broken Arrow: "A Chairman of the Joint Chiefs of Staff term to identify and report an accident involving a nuclear weapon or warhead."
Bent Spear: "A Chairman of the Joint Chiefs of Staff term used in the Department of Defense to identify and report a nuclear weapon significant incident involving a nuclear weapon or warhead, nuclear components, or vehicle when nuclear loaded."
Empty Quiver: "A reporting term to identify and report the seizure, theft, or loss of a U.S. nuclear weapon."
Faded Giant: "A reporting term to identify an event involving a nuclear reactor or radiological accident."

In April 1981, the Department of Defense and the Department of Energy jointly released a "Narrative Summaries of Accidents Involving U.S. Nuclear Weapons: 1950–1980." This report described 32 accidents involving U.S. nuclear weapons. The report stressed that "There has never been even a partial inadvertent U.S. nuclear detonation despite the very severe stresses imposed upon the weapons involved in these accidents. All 'detonations' reported in the summaries involved conventional high explosives (HE) only."

With most early nuclear weapons, it was standard procedure during most operations to keep a capsule of nuclear material separate from the weapon for safety purposes. While a weapon with the capsule removed did contain a quantity of natural (not enriched) uranium with an extremely low level of radioactivity, accidental detonation of the HE element would not cause a nuclear detonation of contamination.

The following descriptions are straight from the DoD/DoE report. Only the two accidents involving B-36 aircraft are reproduced here. Where known, the serial number of the aircraft has been added.[20]

14 FEBRUARY 1950, PACIFIC OCEAN OFF BRITISH COLUMBIA

"A B-36[B (44-92075)] was enroute from Eielson AFB, Alaska, to Carswell AFB, Texas, on a simulated combat profile mission. The weapon aboard the aircraft had a dummy capsule installed. After six hours of flight the aircraft developed serious mechanical difficulties, making it necessary to shut down three engines. The aircraft was at 12,000 feet altitude. Icing conditions complicated the emergency, and level flight could not be maintained. The aircraft headed out over the Pacific Ocean and dropped the weapon from 8,000 feet. A bright flash occurred on impact, followed by a sound and shock wave. Only the weapon's high explosive material detonated. The aircraft was then flown over Princess Royal Island where the crew bailed out. The aircraft wreckage was later found in British Columbia, although initially the Air Force indicated it had been located on Vancouver Island."

It should be noted that classified correspondence from the period indicates that the weapon probably exploded at an altitude of 3,800 feet since that was where the detonator had been set. Other reports indicate that the 7th BW aircraft was carrying 17 crew members and a Mk 4 "Fat Man" atomic weapon at the time of the accident.[21]

22 MAY 1957, KIRTLAND AFB, NEW MEXICO

"The B-36 was ferrying a weapon from Biggs AFB, Texas, to Kirtland AFB. At 11:50 a.m., MST, while approaching Kirtland at an altitude of 1,700 feet, the weapon dropped from the bomb bay taking the bomb bay doors with it. Weapon parachutes were deployed but apparently did not fully retard the fall because of the low altitude. The impact point was approximately 4.5 miles south of the Kirtland control tower and 0.3 miles west of the Sandia Base reservation. The high explosive material detonated, completely destroying the weapon and making a crater approximately 25 feet in diameter and 12 feet deep. Fragments and debris were scattered as far as 1 mile from the impact point. The release mechanism locking pin was being removed at the time of release. (It was standard procedure at that time that the locking pin be removed during takeoff and landing to allow for emergency jettison of the weapon if necessary.) Recovery and cleanup operations were conducted by Field Command, Armed Forces Special Weapons Project. Radiological survey of the area disclosed no radioactivity beyond the lip of the crater at which point the level was 0.5 milliroetgens. There were no health or safety problems. Both the weapon and capsule were on board the aircraft but the capsule was not inserted for safety reasons. A nuclear detonation was not possible."

Classified correspondence from the time indicated that the crewman who removed the locking pin had inadvertently brushed against the release wire, probably snagged it with his clothing, and caused it to partially release. Normal aircraft vibration and buffeting released the weapon completely shortly thereafter. There were some changes to procedures implemented after the accident to minimize the chances of a repeat accident. Unofficial reports indicate the weapon as a Mk 17.[22]

combined with a CP-16 analog computer. This system used a 60-inch diameter antenna, and found use on B-36A, B-29, and B-50 aircraft. In its final configuration the system was fairly accurate at altitudes of 30,000 feet and speeds up to 400 knots. The APQ-23 supplied range, azimuth, distance, and drift information to both the pilot and bombardier, and could be used for both direct and offset bomb aiming. The radar had a limited tracking range, only 17 miles, and could be linked to the Norden bombsight that was still carried by bombers after the war. Against an ideal target (i.e., good radar definition and a calm day) the APQ-23 could achieve an accuracy of 35 mils (meaning it would be within 350 feet of its target from an altitude of 10,000 feet; by 40,000 feet this had deteriorated to ≈2,000 feet).[23]

The Air Force was not satisfied with this performance, so Western Electric combined the new APA-59 electric analog bombing computer (also called a "ground position indicator") with an APS-23 search radar to form the APQ-24 bomb/nav system. Originally this system was to use a new Farrand Y-1 retractable vertical periscopic optical bombsight, but development problems resulted in the tried-and-true Norden again being used in the B-36B and some B-50s.

The APQ-24 required that the bombardier designate a known landmark that was optically (if using the Norden) or radar significant. The "offset" between this landmark and the actual target was entered into the computer. Using this information the APQ-24 would direct the aircraft to the target even during evasive maneuvers during the bombing run – a tremendous improvement over the straight-and-level bomb runs required during World War II. The system automatically computed ground speed, ground track, wind velocity and direction, and the aircraft's absolute position (longitude and latitude). At 30,000 feet the APQ-24 had a search range of up to 200 miles against large targets (i.e., cities). The design accuracy was 25 mils against an ideal target, and best scores from the SAC bombing competitions – ≈1,000 feet from 40,000-feet altitude – generally indicated that this could be achieved.

The introduction of the APQ-24 necessitated some changes in procedures for the ground and flight crews. The system was extremely maintenance intensive, frequently failing multiple times during a single flight. The crews had to become experts at diagnosing and repairing a very (for the 1950s) complex system. Both the radar and computer had to be calibrated very carefully, and very frequently. But a properly maintained and operated APQ-24 proved remarkably accurate. Approximately 300 sets were manufactured by Western Electric, equipping all B-36Bs and some B-50s.

Still, the Air Force was not completely satisfied. Work continued on the Y-1 retractable vertical periscope bombsight. A new A-1 electromechanical bombing computer was also under development, providing a significant increase in processing speed and accuracy. These two items were combined with the APS-23 search radar to create the K-1 bomb/nav system. In reality this was just an improved APQ-24, and was meant as an interim step on the way to the K-3 system also under development. The K-1 was initially fitted to all B-36Ds, and many APQ-24 systems were brought up to the same standard during maintenance periods. (This system was apparently also designated AN/APQ-31, although it was universally known as K-1.)

Early operations with the APQ-24 and K-1 soon revealed a serious problem – a general lack of reliability. The APQ-24 was operational only 25 percent of the time, with "random and unpredictable" vacuum tube failures being the primary culprit. The K-1 was not much better, averaging only a 40-percent readiness rate. By contrast, the original APQ-23 had been operational over 70 percent of the time. Much of the blame was placed on poorly-trained ground and flight crews. SAC was having a major personnel retention problem at the time, and training frequently took a backseat to exercises and just keeping aircraft in the air. It should be noted that when properly operated and maintained, the K-1 was capable of relatively long periods of operation without failure – during one test in 1950 a K-1 remained operational for 86 hours.

By the end of 1950 the Air Force embarked on Project RELIABLE, a concerted attempt to improve the reliability of the K-systems. One of the first steps was to relocate various components inside the pressurized compartments of the B-36 so that in-flight calibration, adjustment, and maintenance could be performed. In addition, provisions were made for more efficient cooling of the vacuum tubes, and an effort was made to find more reliable tubes. Beginning with the B-36H, most of the system components were located in accessible locations when the aircraft were built.

Beginning in 1950, Sperry redesigned the A-1 bombing computer, adding an improved amplifier, tracking computer, and navigational control. The improved device was designated the A-1A, and Sperry began to subcontract some A-1A production work to the A.C. Spark Plug Division of General Motors. Farrand designed a less-complicated non-retractable version of the Y-1 designated the Y-3, portions of which were subcontracted to Eastman Kodak. Combined with the APS-23 search radar these formed the K-3A bomb/nav system, which became standard equipment on the B-36F and subsequent models. It was also retrofitted to all of the B-36Ds. (The stillborn K-3 would have been similar to the K-3A, but used the Y-1 bombsight.) Most documentation

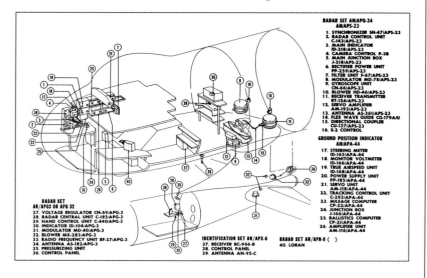

The locations of the equipment for the APQ-24 and APG-32 radar systems on a B-36F. (U.S. Air Force)

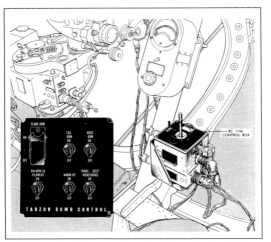

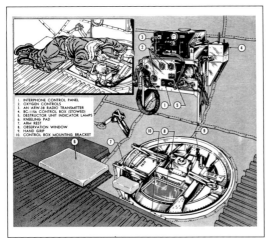

The Bell VB-13 Tarzon was an early attempt at a guided bomb. The first 18 B-36Bs were equipped to carry two Tarzons each, with a special guidance position in the aft compartment (above right) and another guidance position at the normal bombardier's station. (photos: Jay Miller Collection; drawings: U.S. Air Force)

refers to the bomb/nav systems generically as "K( ) systems" or "K-systems" since the versions between various types of aircraft were generally similar (for instance, the K-4A on the B-47 was very similar to the K-3A on the B-36 except using a different bombsight).

The K-3A was effective at altitudes between 4,700 and 50,000 feet and speeds between 137 and 597 knots. The Y-3 bombsight offered magnifications of one, two, or four power with a 76-degree field of view. The system still used the APS-23 radar that could scan continuously 360 degrees, or in 40-degree or 180-degree sector scans to provide faster updates of specific areas. The radar was effective at ranges between 5 and 200 miles, and could vary its pulse duration and pulse repetition frequencies to obtain optimum radar images and defeat jamming. The 60-inch antenna was located in a protruding radome under the forward fuselage and rotated at either 8 or 26 rpm.

It should be noted that, as built, none of the RB-36 models carried a bomb/nav system, mainly because they were not configured to carry

bombs. The aircraft did carry the same search radar and navigation components as their bomber equivalents, but lacked the optical bombsights and computer. When later phases of ON TOP added a nuclear strike capability to the reconnaissance aircraft, the radar bombing system was brought up to the same standard as the B-36s, however the Y-3 optical bombsight was not installed; most aircraft used Norden bombsights instead.

In bomber versions, provisions were initially included to carry a bomb damage assessment camera just forward of the lower aft turret bay. A variety of different camera types (K-17, K-18, K-19B, K-21, K-22, and K-24) could be mounted in this location and were operated from the radar-bombardier station. If the K-19B camera was installed, a photocell was used to trigger the camera when flash bombs were used. The camera was later moved into the aft pressurized compartment, beneath the bunks. This enabled the crew to better monitor the camera and to reload film during flight.

Beginning with the 81st B-36 (a B-36B, 44-92081), most B-36s were equipped with a system code-named CRAWFISH – its more formal designation was Formation Bomb Release, AN/ARW-9 and AN/ARW-10A. The ARW-9 was a transmitter and the ARW-10A was a receiver that allowed the lead aircraft of a formation to release the bombs from other aircraft. The antenna for the system was located on top of the fuselage behind the pilots, and the controls were located at the radar-bombardier's station.

An early attempt at a precision-guided weapon was the Bell VB-13 Tarzon. This was essentially a British 12,000-pound "Tall Boy" bomb fitted with forward and rear shrouds for control surfaces that allowed the bomb to be guided to its target. The 21-foot long, 54-inch diameter, free-falling weapon was tracked visually by means of a colored flare in its tail, and guided to its target via an AN/ARW-38 radio link with the aircraft that dropped it. Development of the bomb had begun during World War II, but had been halted when the war ended.

The program was resurrected briefly in 1950, and 18 B-36Bs (44-92045/92062) were equipped to carry two Tarzons each, although it is unclear how often the weapon was actually dropped from the aircraft. Interestingly, the provisions for carrying and controlling the bombs were retained when the aircraft were converted to B-36Ds. Although the bombs did not see action with the B-36, approximately 30 Tarzons were dropped from B-29s during the Korean conflict, with about eight of them destroying or damaging the bridges they were aimed at. A similar 4,000-pound Razon was also used by the B-29 but proved to be too small to be effective against hardened targets.

The control equipment consisted of the AN/ARW-38 radio transmitter and a separate bomb control panel for each Tarzon. The control equipment for the forward bomb (in combined bomb bays Nos. 1 and 2) was located at the radar-bombardier's station, while a dedicated station was installed in the aft compartment to control the Tarzon carried in the aft bomb bays (Nos. 3 and 4). The aft station consisted of a window and periscope located in the bottom of the fuselage which the operator used while lying prone on a padded surface. A joystick was provided at each location, allowing the operator to control the bomb during its glide to the target.

ELECTRONIC COUNTERMEASURES

One crucial advantage held by the B-36, and later the B-52, was that its size and load-carrying capacity gave it a great deal of room in which to incorporate new equipment. The first operational B-36s were equipped with essentially the same limited ECM equipment as contemporary B-29s. The radio operator served as the additional duty ECM operator, as in the B-29. During 1951, B-36s from the 7th and 11th BWs flew test missions at Eglin AFB to evaluate the effectiveness of the ECM systems. These tests indicated that the B-36s could successfully penetrate existing radar defenses using their ECM. Earlier tests against Royal Air Force night fighters equipped with airborne intercept radars had proven ineffective against B-36Bs equipped with their standard ECM suite. It appeared that the B-36's best defense was a combination of high altitude and ECM.

Late production B-36s were equipped with more ECM systems than any other Air Force aircraft, yet all the jammers dated back to World War II. Only the APR-9 radar receiver and the A-7 chaff dispenser were of modern design. The A-7 had been designed specifically for the B-36 and was capable of dispensing a chaff bundle that was five times larger than the standard bundle – necessary to produce a radar echo similar in size to the B-36.

As new systems were developed and placed into operation the EW engineers had to work hard to keep the equipment close to the antennas – the further the antenna was from the actual jammer the more power was lost in the cabling, especially with the newer microwave jammers. Those radiating in the E-band, for example, lost half of the transmitted power for every 30 feet of cabling, and jammers in the I-band lost half

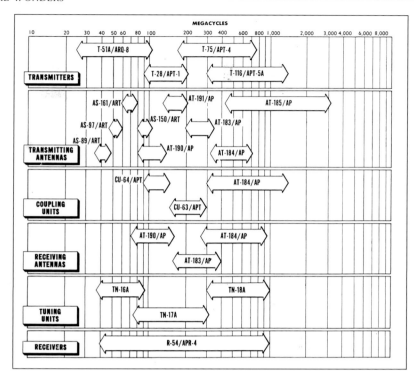

Chart showing the frequencies covered by the early ECM equipment installed in the B-36. This would expand considerably as the aircraft was modified in later years. (U.S. Air Force)

of their power in only 10 feet. Thus one of the major advantages of the bigger airplanes such as the B-36, the size in which to place equipment, could also be a disadvantage because of the distances involved.

As most aircraft were delivered from Convair, they contained racks and antenna-mounting locations for various ECM equipment but not the electronics. The aircraft maintenance manuals stated that "tactical organizations [the Bomb Wings] will supply and install the ECM equipment." Surprisingly, although the ECM equipment was not provided with the aircraft, the numerous antennas were, although they were stowed in plywood boxes in the aft compartment and one of the cargo carriers. The antennas were installed by whatever organization supplied the ECM equipment itself.[24]

Initially, the ECM equipment for the bomber versions consisted of two configurations known as Group I and Group II, depending upon the frequency coverage desired. Group I consisted of two APT-4 transmitters that covered approximately 200–800 MHz (called megacycles at the time). Group II substituted an APT-1 transmitter for one of the APT-4s, extending coverage down to 90 MHz. In both cases a pair of APR-4 receivers were installed, covering approximately 40–1,000 MHz. This equipment would be significantly expanded on later bomber versions as electronic warfare became increasingly important. For instance, the APT-5A transmitter capable of covering 300–1,500 MHz was later added. By late 1954, a Group III had been developed

ELECTRONIC WARFARE EQUIPMENT CARRIED BY MOST RB-36 AIRCRAFT, CIRCA 1953

The following description was written as an introduction to the RB-36 ECM systems for an Air Force training class. It represents the pre-Phase II ECM modifications. It should be noted that this description only talks about the "Ferret ECM (FECM)" positions.*

The RB-36 aircraft contains four ECM positions. The frequency range covered in each position is as follows:

1. Low Frequency Position (38 to 300 mc)
2. Intermediate Frequency Position (300 to 1,000 mc)
3. Medium Frequency Position (1,000 to 4,400 mc)
4. High Frequency Position (4,400 to 11,000 mc)

The Low Frequency position is located in the forward pressurized compartment directly behind the flight engineer's pedestal. This is a combination Radio Operator and ECM Operator position and all the normal radio operator's equipment is also installed in the racks facing the operator. This position contains a single seat and it is probable that the low frequency ECM operator will also be the radio operator. ECM equipment installed in this position is as follows:

1	ARR-5	Communications Search Receiver
2	APR-4	Radar Search Receiver
1	TN-16	Tuning Unit (38 to 95 mc)
1	TN-17	Tuning Unit (74 to 320 mc)
1	ARR-8	Panoramic Receiver
1	APA-74	Pulse Analyzer
1	APA-17	Direction Finder Equipment
1	AS-370	Low Frequency Antenna System
2	ANQ-1	Wire Recorder
1	O-15	Radar camera

The Low Frequency operator may select the audio output of any receiver individually or may select the mixed outputs of any combination by the use of toggle switches.

The AS-222 DF antenna [20 to 250 mc] is mounted in a dome directly under the nose of the aircraft. The non-directional (search) antennas are installed in pairs, one on the right and one on the left side of the aircraft. The inputs of each pair of antennas are fed to a balance and then to the receiver. With this antenna hook up, the LEFT-RIGHT system of determining on which side of the aircraft signals are being received is not possible. The APA-17 DF system is connected to the APR-4/TN-17 combination through a DF switch.

---

* Excerpted from "A Guide to Airborne Electronic Countermeasures," prepared by the Air Force ECM Flying Training School, Barksdale, Louisiana.

All antenna switching for this and all the other ECM positions of the aircraft is done by electrically operated RF switches controlled by toggle switches located on the ECM panel at each position.

The Intermediate Frequency position was located in the rear pressurized compartment. The equipment is located on racks mounted against the rear bulkhead on the right side of the aircraft. The operator sits facing aft. The equipment installed in this position is as follows:

1	APR-4	Radar Search Receiver
1	TN-18	Tuning Unit (300 to 1,000 mc)
3	ARR-8	Panoramic Receiver (three ranges: 300 to 1,000 mc)
1	APA-64	Pulse Analyzer
1	APA-17	Direction Finding Assembly with AS-108 antenna
1	ANQ-1	Wire Recorder
1	O-15	Radar Camera

The Intermediate Frequency operator may select either DF or search antenna operation by means of a toggle switch. The DF antenna is located underneath the aircraft at the rear bomb bay section. The doors have been removed from this bomb bay and replaced by permanently closed stressed skin.

The Medium Frequency position was located in the rear pressurized compartment. The equipment is located on racks mounted against the rear bulkhead on the left side of the aircraft. The operator sits facing aft. The equipment fitted in this position is as follows:

1	APR-9	Radar Search Receiver
1	TN-128	Tuning Unit (1,000 to 2,600 mc)
1	TN-129	Tuning Unit (2,300 to 4,450 mc)
1	APA-17	Direction Finding Assembly with AS-186 antenna
1	APA-74	Pulse Analyzer
1	ANQ-1	Wire Recorder
1	O-15	Radar Camera

The Medium Frequency operator selects either DF or search antennas by means of a toggle switch on the panel at his position. He may also select either the TN-128 or TN-129 tuning unit by means of a toggle switch mounted on the panel in this position. This switch controls a remotely operated switching unit which is located in the rear bomb bay compartment.

The DF antenna is located underneath the aircraft at the rear bomb bay section [the non functional bomb bay No. 4]. Due to the fact that the RF cables between the antenna and the RF units must be kept as short as possible, the RF units are located in the rear bomb bay section.

The High Frequency position is located in the rear pressurized compartment. The equipment is mounted on racks against the left side of the aircraft just forward of the lower left gunner's blister. The operator sits facing the left side of the aircraft. The equipment in this position is as follows:

1	APR-9	Radar Search Receiver
1	TN-130	Tuning Unit (4,150 to 7,350 mc)
1	TN-131	Tuning Unit (7,050 to 10,750 mc)
1	APA-74	Pulse Analyzer
1	APA-17	Direction Finding with AS-247 antenna
1	O-15	Radar Camera

The High Frequency operator may select DF or search operations by means of an RF switch remotely controlled by a toggle switch on the control panel. He may also select either tuning unit, TN-130 or TN-131 by means of a remotely controlled switching unit. The toggle switch controlling this unit is located on the operator's panel.

The TN-130, TN-131, and the switching unit are all located in the rear bomb bay [No. 4] compartment. The DF antenna is located underneath the rear bomb bay compartment.

In the RB-36 each ECM operator performs search and DF operations. The aircraft installation is comfortable for the operating personnel and most of the equipment is well positioned. It is not necessary for the operator to call the engineer to request AC [alternating current] power since the aircraft system is basically AC. The frequency of the AC system is kept within the equipment tolerance so that no extra inverter is needed for selsyn power. All the AC and DC inputs to each set are fused by circuit breakers. This reduces the number of fuses required for the spare parts kit.

All RF tuning units for the APR-9 receivers are located in the unpressurized rear bomb bay section. The extreme cold at altitude and the inability of personnel to perform in-flight maintenance, should one of these units become inoperative, makes this an undesirable feature. [Moving this equipment during ECP-678 did not really improve this situation since the receivers were moved to a different unpressurized area under the aft compartment floor that was also not readily accessible during flight.]

As noted, the above description was for the receiver layout in the RB-36, usually referred to as the Ferret ECM (FECM) equipment. In addition, the aircraft carried much the same defensive ECM (DECM) equipment as the normal B-36 bomber models, including:

1	ARA-3	communications jammer (2 to 18.1 mc)
1	ARQ-8	noise jammers (25 to 105 mc)
1	APT-1	noise jammers (93 to 210 mc)
1	APT-4	noise jammers (160 to 800 mc)
1	APT-5	noise jammers (300 to 1,625 mc)
1	A-6	chaff dispenser
1	A-7	chaff dispenser

Some aircraft carried a second A-7 unit instead of the A-6.

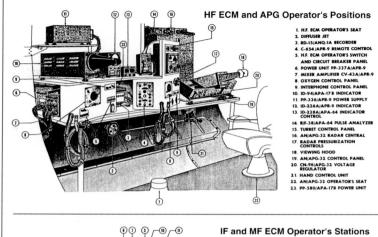
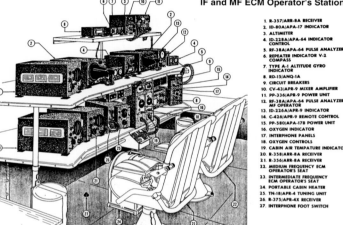
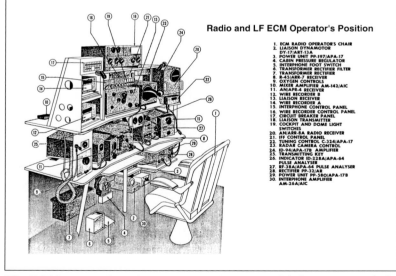

The ECM operator's stations on reconnaissance models beginning with the block-15 RB-36Fs. The Radio and LF ECM operator was in the forward compartment; the other two in the aft. (U.S. Air Force)

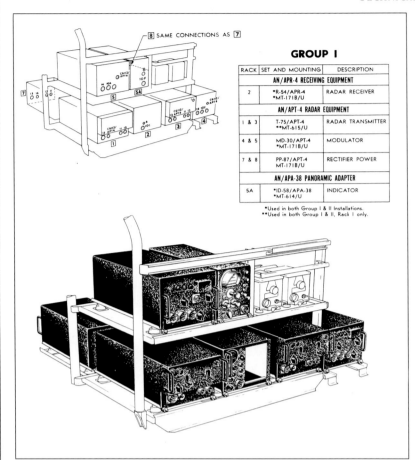

GROUP I

RACK	SET AND MOUNTING	DESCRIPTION
AN/APR-4 RECEIVING EQUIPMENT		
2	*R-54/APR-4 *MT-171B/U	RADAR RECEIVER
AN/APT-4 RADAR EQUIPMENT		
1 & 3	T-75/APT-4 **MT-615/U	RADAR TRANSMITTER
4 & 5	MD-30/APT-4 *MT-171B/U	MODULATOR
7 & 8	PP-87/APT-4 MT-171B/U	RECTIFIER POWER
AN/APA-38 PANORAMIC ADAPTER		
5A	*ID-58/APA-38 *MT-614/U	INDICATOR

*Used in both Group I & II Installations.
**Used in both Group I & II, Rack I only.

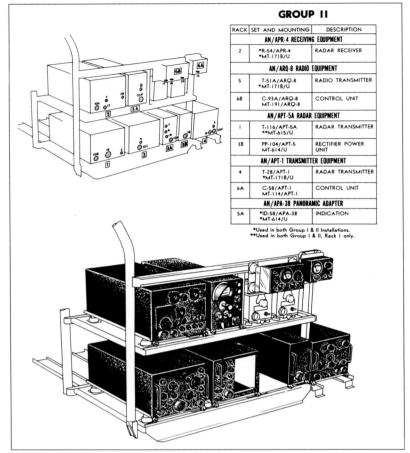

GROUP II

RACK	SET AND MOUNTING	DESCRIPTION
AN/APR-4 RECEIVING EQUIPMENT		
2	*R-54/APR-4 *MT-171B/U	RADAR RECEIVER
AN/ARQ-8 RADIO EQUIPMENT		
5	T-51A/ARQ-8 *MT-171B/U	RADIO TRANSMITTER
6B	C-93A/ARQ-8 MT-191/ARQ-8	CONTROL UNIT
AN/APT-5A RADAR EQUIPMENT		
1	T-116/APT-5A **MT-615/U	RADAR TRANSMITTER
3B	PP-104/APT-5 MT-614/U	RECTIFIER POWER UNIT
AN/APT-1 TRANSMITTER EQUIPMENT		
4	T-28/APT-1 *MT-171B/U	RADAR TRANSMITTER
6A	C-58/APT-1 MT-114/APT-1	CONTROL UNIT
AN/APA-38 PANORAMIC ADAPTER		
5A	*ID-58/APA-38 *MT-614/U	INDICATION

*Used in both Group I & II Installations.
**Used in both Group I & II, Rack I only.

The original Group I and Group II defensive ECM stations in both bombers and reconnaissance versions looked like this. (U.S. Air Force)

that included the APR-4 and APT-4, an IP-69/ALA-2 panoramic receiver, APT-6 transmitter, APR-9 receiver, and APT-9 transmitter.[25]

The reconnaissance versions carried yet more ECM equipment, although most of it was actually "ferret" equipment designed to record and analyze enemy radio and radar transmissions. The defensive ECM systems (DECM) were located in the forward compartment and operated at an ECM station located in the same location as on the bomber versions. An additional station was added directly behind the normal ECM station to operate the low frequency (LF) ferret ECM (FECM) equipment that had its primary antenna behind the large radome under the extreme nose. As built, all RB-36s had three large radomes protruding from what should have been bomb bay No. 4, and a pallet between bulkheads 8.0 and 9.0 contained most of the intermediate (IF), medium (MF), and high frequency (HF) ferret ECM equipment. Control stations for this FECM equipment were installed in the aft compartment, with new IF and MF stations facing forward at bulkhead 10.0 at the front of the compartment. The HF operator shared the tail gunner station, which was relocated to face the right-side fuselage wall instead of towards bulkhead 12.0 at the

rear of the compartment. When SAC directed that the Featherweight RB-36s should have expanded bombing capabilities, the aft FECM equipment was relocated into the aft fuselage between bulkheads 10.0 and 12.0, and the radomes were moved 20 feet aft under the rear fuselage. This freed bomb bay No. 4 to again carry bombs.[26]

Late B-36Hs and all B-36Js added an AN/APS-54 radar warning receiver to notify the crew if the aircraft was being illuminated by a surface or airborne radar. Indicators were positioned at the bombardier (or photo-navigator in RBs), tail gunner, and low frequency ECM positions. The APS-54 was a wide-band crystal video RWR that was effective from 2.6–11 GHz. Antennas were added to the "island" between the elevator and aft fuselage (requiring the normal position lights to be relocated somewhat) and also to the center of the glazed windows in the extreme nose. The system provided limited azimuth data – basically indicating if the threat was ahead-of or behind the B-36. One problem was that the APS-54 could be easily damaged if it was illuminated by the APS-23 search radar of a nearby B-36. This was the first "modern" RWR to enter service with SAC, and quickly became standard equipment on most SAC bombers. The APS-54 was

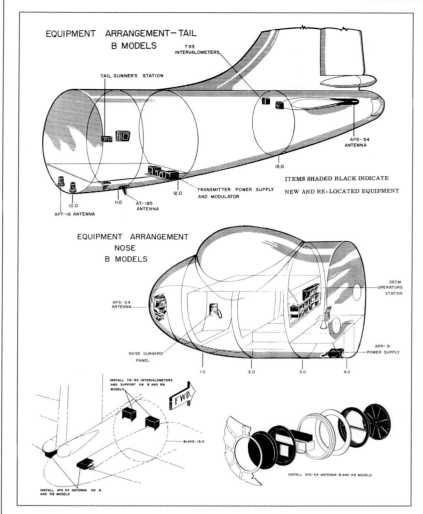

EQUIPMENT ARRANGEMENT—TAIL
B MODELS

EQUIPMENT ARRANGEMENT
NOSE
B MODELS

EQUIPMENT ARRANGEMENT—TAIL
RB MODELS

EQUIPMENT ARRANGEMENT
NOSE
RB MODELS

ITEMS SHADED BLACK INDICATE
NEW AND RE-LOCATED EQUIPMENT

In July 1954 Convair began the ECM Phase II program to update the B-36 fleet. Two related ECPs were issued - 678AG to cover the bomber models, and 678AH to cover the reconnaissance aircraft. This was the modification that moved the RB-36 ferret ECM equipment out of the bomb bay No. 4 area into the aft fuselage, although it was ON TOP Phase X that activated the bomb bay itself. The installation of the APS-54 (shown above) was common to both configurations. (Convair)

retrofitted to other models as they cycled through various ON TOP and ECM Phase II modification programs.[27]

Modernization of the ECM equipment was a large part of the Featherweight program, although the modifications were actually conducted under the Phase II ECM program (ECPs 678AH and 678AG). The $30,000,000 price tag included several significant equipment additions, such as the APS-54 radar warning receiver, two low-frequency radar jammers, and the new APT-16 S-band jammer. The alterations also included the addition of another ECM operator position in RB-36s, so that there were individual crew positions for crew

members operating low, intermediate, medium, and high-frequency radar jammers. The A-6 and A-7 manual chaff dispensers were replaced by the ALE-7 automatic dispenser on most aircraft.

On the GRB-36D FICON aircraft, a single AN/APX-29A IFF/rendezvous set was installed. The antenna was located under a large radome on top of the forward fuselage, and proved to be one of the more recognizable features of the GRB-36D. The APX-29A allowed the RF-84K fighter to easily locate the waiting bomber when returning from a mission. The JRB-36F used for the Tom-Tom and FICON projects also was equipped with an APX-29A set.

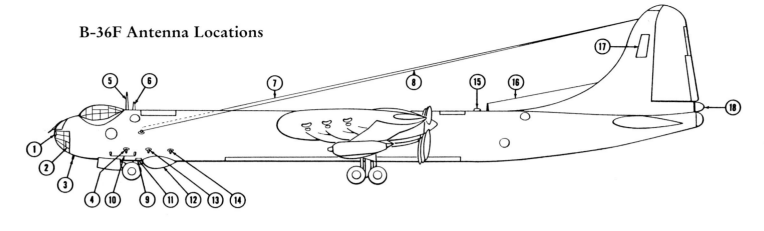

B-36F Antenna Locations

POS.	STA.	ANTENNA	SET	RECEIVER
1	20	MN-92(A)	GLIDE PATH	R-268B/ARN-5B
2	53 L&R	AT219/APR-9	DEFENSIVE E.C.M.	TN-128/APR-9/CV-43( ) TN-129/APR-9/APR-9
3	69	AT-183( )/AP or AT184( )/AP or AS89/ART or AS97/ART or AS161/ART	DEFENSIVE E.C.M.	T-249/APT-6 or T-75/APT-4
4	227 L&R	AT-183( )/AP or AT-184( )/AP	DEFENSIVE E.C.M.	T-75/APT-4
5	230	AS-89/ART or AS-97/ART or AS-150/ART or AS-161/ART	DEFENSIVE E.C.M.	R-375/APR-4X
6	240	AN-104-B	COMMAND	R-77/ARC-3
7	272 R	NO NUMBER	LORAN	R-65/APN-9
8	272 L	NO NUMBER	LIAISON	BC-348-Q
9	272	AT-234/APX-6	IFF	RT-82/APX-6
10	275	NO NUMBER	MARKER BEACON	R-122/ARN-12

POS.	STA.	ANTENNA	SET	RECEIVER
11	276	AT-230/APT-9	DEFENSIVE E.C.M.	T-147/APT-9
12	283	AS-161/APS-23	NAVIGATION RADAR	RT-124/APS-23
13	295 L&R	AT-183( )/AP or AT-184( )/AP or AT-190( )/AP	DEFENSIVE E.C.M.	R-375/APR-4X
14	352 L&R	AT-184( )/AP or AT-185( )/AP or AT-190( )/AP or AT-191( )/AP	DEFENSIVE E.C.M.	T-249/APT-6 T-147/APT-9
15	1308	AS-313A/ARN-6	RADIO COMPASS	R-101/ARN-6
16	1332	SENSE ANTENNA	RADIO COMPASS	R-101/ARN-6
17	1770	NO NUMBER	V.H.F. OMNI RANGE	R-252/ARN-14
18	1950	AS-448/APG-32	GUN DIRECTING RADAR	AN/APG-32

The locations and descriptions of all the antennas on a B-36F in August 1951. This was before the ECM Phase II modifications. (U.S. Air Force)

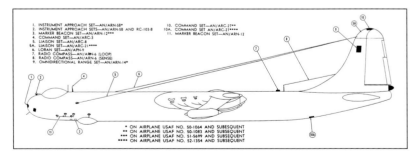

A slightly later (1954) antenna diagram shows a few new antennas. When the B-36 was first introduced, no flush antennas were installed on it. Later, flush antennas appeared on each side of the vertical stabilizer (for the ARN-14 omni), on top of the vertical stabilizer (for the ARC-27 radio), and on the bottom of the fuselage (also for the ARC-27). Due to its relatively slow speed, however, the original wire antennas remained throughout its service career. (U.S. Air Force)

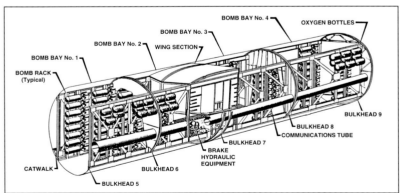

The overall configuration of the bomb bays. A catwalk on the right side of the airplane allowed crewmembers to work in the bays, while the pressurized communications tube on the left allowed relatively comfortable transfer between the forward and aft compartments. (U.S. Air Force)

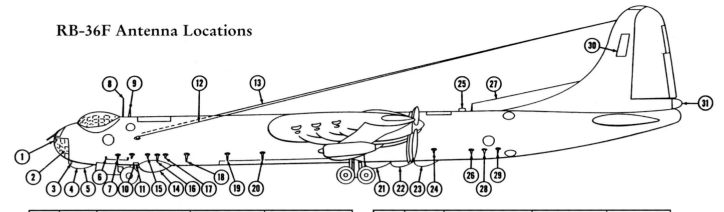

RB-36F Antenna Locations

POS.	STA.	ANTENNA	SET	RECEIVER
1	1	MN-92(A)	GLIDE PATH RECEIVER	R-2688/ARN-5B
2	53 L&R	AT-219/APR-9	DEFENSIVE E.C.M.	TN-128/APR-9/CV43/APR-9
3	69	AT-184( )/AP	DEFENSIVE E.C.M.	T-75/APT-4
4	74	AS-222/APA-178	LOW FREQUENCY FERRET E.C.M.	R-375/APR-4X
5	111	AS-89/ART or AS-97/ART or AS-161/ART	DEFENSIVE E.C.M.	T-24S/APT-6
6	168	NO NUMBER	MARKER BEACON	R-111/ARN-12
7	227 L&R	AT-183( )/AP or AT-184( )/AP or AT-190( )/AP	DEFENSIVE E.C.M.	R-375/APR-4X
8	229	AS-09/ART or AS-161/ART	DEFENSIVE E.C.M.	R-375/APR-4X
9	240	AN-104B	COMMAND RADIO	R-77/ARC-3
10	262	AT-238/APT	IFF	RT-82/APX-6
11	266	AT-238/APT	DEFENSIVE E.C.M.	T-147/APT-9
12	272 L	NO NUMBER	LIAISON RADIO	DC-348
13	272 R	NO NUMBER	LORAN	R-65/APN-9
14	283	AS-361/APS-23	NAVIGATION RADAR	RT-124/APS-23
15	295 L&R	AT-103( )/AP or AT-184( )/AP or AT-185/AP	DEFENSIVE E.C.M.	T-75/APT-4 or R-375/APR-4X
16	350 L&R	AT-184( )/AP or AT-185 ( )/AP AT-190( )/AP or AT-191( )/AP	DEFENSIVE E.C.M.	T-249/APT-6 or T-147/APT-9
17	371 L&R	AT-183( )/AP	LOW FREQUENCY FERRET E.C.M.	R-375/APR-4X

POS.	STA.	ANTENNA	SET	RECEIVER
18	449 L&R	AT-183( )/AP	LOW FREQUENCY FERRET E.C.M.	R-355/APR-8A
19	556 L&R	AT-190( )/AP	LOW FREQUENCY FERRET E.C.M.	R-355/APR-8A
20	665 L&R	AT-190( )/AP	LOW FREQUENCY FERRET E.C.M.	R-375/APR-4X
21	999	AS-214/APR or AS-247/APA-17	HIGH FREQUENCY FERRET E.C.M.	TN-130/APR-9 or TN-131/APR-9
22	1072	AS-125/APR or AS-186/APA-17	MED. FREQUENCY FERRET E.C.M.	TN-128/APR-9 or TN-129/APR-9
23	1162	AS-545/APA-17B	INT. FREQUENCY FERRET E.C.M.	R-375/APR-4X
24	1178 L&R	AS-184( )/AP	INT. FREQUENCY FERRET E.C.M.	R-356/APR-8A
25	1308	AS-313A/ARN-6	RADIO COMPASS	R-181/ARN-6
26	1317 L&R	AS-184( )/AP	INT. FREQUENCY FERRET E.C.M.	R-375/APR-4X
27	1332	SENSE	RADIO COMPASS	R-181/ARN-6
28	1341 L&R	AS-185( )/AP	INT. FREQUENCY FERRET E.C.M.	R-358/APR-8A
29	1404 L&R	AS-185( )/AP	INT. FREQUENCY FERRET E.C.M.	R-357/APR-8A
30	1770 L&R	NO NUMBER	V.H.F OMNI	R-252/ARN-14
31	1950	AS-448/APG-32	GUN DIRECTING	AN/APG-32

The locations and descriptions of all the antennas on an RB-36F in August 1951. This was before the ECM Phase II modifications. (U.S. Air Force)

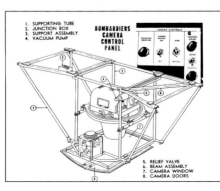

1. SUPPORTING TUBE
2. JUNCTION BOX
3. SUPPORT ASSEMBLY
4. VACUUM PUMP

BOMBARDIERS CAMERA CONTROL PANEL

5. RELIEF VALVE
6. BEAM ASSEMBLY
7. CAMERA WINDOW
8. CAMERA DOORS

Even the bombers carried a camera – a strike camera in the aft fuselage. Originally the camera was located just ahead of the aft lower turret bay, but was later moved into the aft pressurized compartment where the crew could service and reload it easier. (U.S. Air Force)

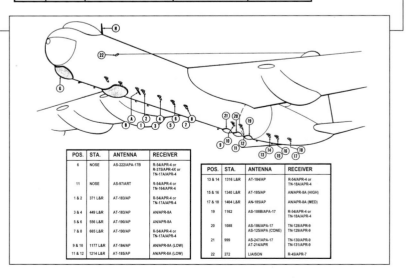

POS.	STA.	ANTENNA	RECEIVER
6	NOSE	AS-222/APA-17B	R-54/APR-4 or R-375/APR-4X or TN-17A/APR-4
11	NOSE	AS-97/ART	R-54/APR-4 or TN-164/APR-4
1 & 2	371 L&R	AT-183/AP	R-54/APR-4 or TN-17A/APR-4
3 & 4	449 L&R	AT-183/AP	AN/APR-8A
5 & 6	556 L&R	AT-190/AP	AN/APR-8A
7 & 8	665 L&R	AT-190/AP	R-54/APR-4 or TN-17A/APR-4
9 & 10	1177 L&R	AT-184/AP	AN/APR-8A (LOW)
11 & 12	1214 L&R	AT-185/AP	AN/APR-8A (LOW)

POS.	STA.	ANTENNA	RECEIVER
13 & 14	1316 L&R	AT-184/AP	R-54/APR-4 or TN-18A/APR-4
15 & 16	1340 L&R	AT-185/AP	AN/APR-8A (HIGH)
17 & 18	1404 L&R	AN-185/AP	AN/APR-8A (MED)
19	1162	AS-108B/APA-17	R-54/APR-4 or TN-18A/APR-4
20	1088	AS-186/APA-17 AS-125/APA (CONE)	TN-128/APR-9 TN-129/APR-9
21	999	AS-247/APA-17 AT-214/APR	TN-130/APR-9 TN-131/APR-9
22	272	LIAISON	R-45/APR-7

MAGNESIUM

One of the B-36's many nicknames was "magnesium overcast," appropriate considering the aircraft represented one of the few truly large-scale aviation uses of the metal. Almost 4 tons of various magnesium alloys accounted for approximately 10 percent of the structural weight of the aircraft. It is estimated that the use of the metal saved 1,900 pounds, extending range by 190 miles.[28]

Magnesium was used as a skin material for about one-half of the fuselage, including the entire area around the bomb bays and bomb bay doors. The leading edges of the wings used 0.025-0.040-inch thick magnesium skin. The trailing edge of the wing and all control surfaces (after metal replaced fabric) were also magnesium. In some of these applications the magnesium skin needed stiffening, and "waffle" was attached to the back of the skin with a metal adhesive (Convair Metlbond or Chrysler Cycleweld). The use of an adhesive instead of more conventional fasteners (rivets, spot welding, etc.) gave a continuous attachment and avoided stress concentrations. Fatigue testing also revealed that the adhesive had a much longer service life. Originally the waffles were made from 0.016-inch aluminum alloy, but production difficulties at Convair eventually forced the subcontracting of the effort to Dow Chemical which produced the waffles from 0.025-inch magnesium alloy, providing approximately the same weight and stiffness.

One of the major external differences on the reconnaissance model was the switch from dull magnesium skin around bomb bay No. 1 to shiny aluminum skin. This was because magnesium does not respond well to pressure cycles, and when this area of the fuselage was turned into a pressurized compartment, the skin (and several bulkheads) were changed to accommodate the new requirements. Both of the other pressurized areas (forward and aft compartments) also used aluminum skin.

All of the control surfaces on the B-36A and B-36B had been covered with doped fabric, a construction technique that was tried and true. However, the increased speeds promised for the B-36D forced Convair to switch to 0.016-inch magnesium alloy to cover the elevators and rudder. Even the magnesium was heavier than fabric, but was necessary since the fabric tended to "balloon" at high speeds. Eventually, all models also had the fabric ailerons replaced by magnesium units.

Magnesium castings were used for the control system drums and bellcranks, and also for numerous fittings throughout the aircraft, Very few castings (of any sort) were used for hinge supports due to worries about hidden flaws. Magnesium was also used for many of the air ducts throughout the aircraft, although the material was difficult to seal. Most gasket materials in use at the time absorbed moisture, which corroded the flange ends on magnesium parts more so than on aluminum ones. Other materials such as silicone rubber, asbestos, or fiberglass were used in places but were not considered ideal.

Initially, there were considerations for using magnesium other than its light weight. For one thing, the material was less "strategic" than aluminum, meaning the United States had more of it available – this had been considered important during the war. The metal was easier to mine and process as an ore, but it was more difficult to fabricate into useable pieces. Magnesium was also more expensive than aluminum. A variety of problems cropped up while using the metal, although it proved to be very successful on the B-36. Convair ended up developing many better techniques for using the material, including new anodizing processes that continue to be used. Ultimately, new supplies of aluminum and improved techniques to mine and process it made the widespread use of magnesium unnecessary, and the B-36 represents the ultimate large-scale use of the material.

Interestingly, during early 1952 the Air Force awarded Convair a $200,000 research contract to investigate changing some parts of the B-36 to a titanium alloy. Convair prototyped several parts of a jet pod in titanium and subjected them to an extensive static test series. The parts included the upper firewall, aft engine support, rear spar terminal fitting, upper front spar web, and the inter-nacelle fairing. Two complete jet pods were then manufactured using the titanium parts and flown on a B-36D (44-92054) for several months before the program ended. Approximately 180 pounds were saved between the two pods and their normal production counterparts.[29]

In late 1952 Convair announced that "Approximately 700 pounds of titanium will be used on each B-36 coming off the assembly line beginning after the first of the year," but provided precious few details about exactly where the titanium would be used. However, the article did state that "… fire walls and other non-structural parts in the B-36 reciprocating engines" would be switched to the new alloy. The article went on to mention the difficulties encountered in working with the metal, as well as its extreme cost ($21.50 per pound, compared to $13 per pound for sterling silver). It is uncertain if the increased use of titanium was ever actually implemented in the B-36 production.

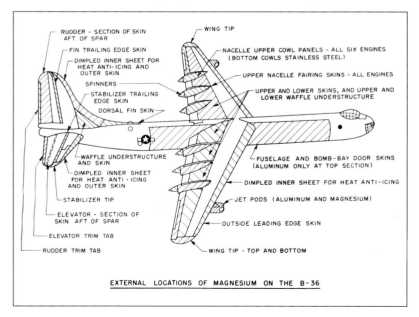

A great deal of the surface skin on the B-36 was magnesium alloy. Reconnaissance versions used slightly less – the pressurized area around the photo compartment used aluminum instead. (Convair)

Believe-it-or-Not

In October 1957, Convair released a short list of believe-it-or-not items about the B-36 (the drawing is for a B-36D).[30]

- The wingspan of the B-36 – 230 feet – is longer than the first flight made by the Wright Brothers' Kitty Hawk Flyer in 1903.
- The B-36 can carry a heavier load of bombs for a greater distance than any other airplane in existence. It has flown more than 10,000 miles while carrying 10,000 pounds of bombs halfway.
- At high speeds, the B-36's ten engines deliver the equivalent of more than 44,000 horsepower, roughly comparable to that of nine locomotives, or about as much horsepower as that generated by 400 average passenger cars.
- The tremendous bomb load of the B-36 is clearly indicated by the fact that a B-36 can haul up to 84,000 pounds of bombs – more than a wartime B-24 bomber weighed when fully loaded.
- The volume of the B-36 bomb bays is 12,300 cubic feet, approximately the capacity of three railroad freight cars.
- The volume of the entire B-36 bomber, nearly 18,000 cubic feet, approximates the volume of three average five-room houses.
- An automobile could easily circle the globe 18 times with the 30,000-plus gallons of high-test gasoline in the wing tanks of a B-36.
- More than 27 miles of electrical wiring are required in the Convair B-36 electrical system, equal to the amount needed to wire 280 five-room houses.
- A 600-room hotel, or 120 five-room houses, could be heated by the anti-icing equipment installed on the B-36 superbomber. In an hour, the giant plane's anti-icing equipment turns out 4,920,000 British thermal units.

- There are 68,000 different shop-made parts and 11,000 different assemblies per B-36 bomber, not counting the thousands upon thousands of parts in government-furnished equipment.
- To construct one 10,000-foot runway, plus a taxiway and small apron, to support B-36 operations, takes 45 four-ton trucks, moving 10 loads per day for 362 days, just to move the required concrete. If the runway was outside the continental U.S., it would take 20 Victory ships or 12,000 C-54 cargo aircraft just to haul the cement (not the sand or gravel).

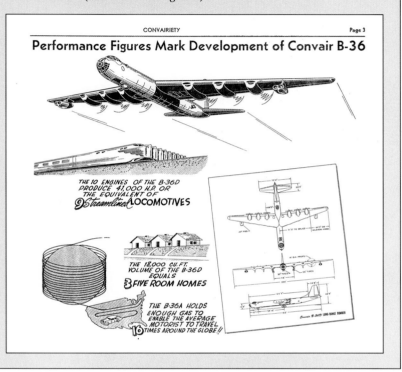

The original configuration on all the reconnaissance models had a single set of doors covering bomb bays Nos. 2 and 3. (Lockheed Martin)

Right: *Some of the 27 miles of wiring in a B-36. (U.S. Air Force)*

Chapter 8

0747-B

Left: *A B-36H-10-CF (51-5703) and B-36D-35-CF (49-2665) were blown into a hangar at Carswell. Both aircraft were returned to Convair for repairs. (U.S. Air Force via C. Roger Cripliver)*

Below: *In the center, with its tail mostly severed, is a B-36D-10-CF (44-92043). The aircraft just behind it, responsible for the tail damage, is a B-36F-1-CF (49-2675), while a B-36H-5-CF (50-1095) is completely missing its aft fuselage and tail at left. (U.S. Air Force via C. Roger Cripliver)*

0756-H-G 2 SEPT 52 CAFB A/C 2046 REST.

TORNADO!

Ironically, the most serious setback to the readiness of the B-36 force came at a high point in the program. On Labor Day, Monday, 1 September 1952, B-36s from the 7th and 11th Bomb Wings sat parked at Carswell AFB. Various maintenance procedures were being carried out and most of the aircraft were parked and not tied down. The weather forecast called for thunderstorms and gusting winds, not unusual for this part of Texas during the summer. At about 18:00 hours, a few people observed heavy clouds moving towards the base, and within a few minutes the anemometer climbed to 91 mph before breaking. At 18:42 a tornado made a direct hit on the base and scattered the huge planes like they were toys. A few fuel tanks were damaged and high-octane aviation gasoline poured onto the ramp. The duty officer from the 7th BW saw that power lines were down near the fuel spills and hurried to get the power turned off, averting a possible catastrophe.[1]

As the storm subsided, approximately two-thirds of the American very heavy bomber fleet lay incapacitated. Not surprisingly, the original news accounts of the damage were less than accurate. For instance, the Convair employee newspaper reported that one B-36 had been destroyed (correct) "… and a number damaged …" (a gross understatement) with total damage estimated at $250,000. The paper did report that nine B-36s at Convair had been damaged, including four that sustained severe damage after they were "… rocked back on their tail sections." The maintenance docks at both Convair and Carswell sustained heavy damage and were the subject of several newspaper articles. Not mentioned was that the docks also were the cause of a great deal of damage to various aircraft.[2]

Starting at dawn the following day the Air Force made a quick estimate of the damage. One aircraft (B-36D 44-92051) had been virtually destroyed and 82 others were damaged – including 10 at the Convair plant across the runway. Twenty-four of these were considered "seriously damaged." Upon receiving the news, General LeMay removed the 19th Air Division from the war plan, and the base went on 84-hour work weeks until repairs were completed. The Air Force called in engineers from Convair to assist with the work and on Wednesday a team of Convair employees headed by Tom Neely arrived at Carswell. Engineering, Quality, and Production emergency response teams were quickly formed at Convair and the plant was put on an intense work schedule to provide assistance to the Air Force.[3]

Twenty-six of the damaged aircraft were turned over to Convair to repair as part of Project FIXIT. By the end of September the Convair newspaper was reporting that the total cost of Project FIXIT was likely to exceed $48,000,000 – a considerable increase from the original report. Interestingly, the paper still did not provide any real indication of just how widespread the damage had been, although it did publish

Convair put together an eight-chart briefing outlining the estimated costs and timeline for fixing the tornado damage – chart No. 7 is reproduced below. It could not be ascertained precisely how accurate these costs turned out to be, but most reports indicated the final expenses were over double this amount. This only covered aircraft repaired by Convair, not the ones repaired by the units based at Carswell or personnel from the San Antonio Air Materiel Area. (C. Roger Cripliver Collection)

CVAC *TENTATIVE FIXIT* COSTS

FIXIT SEQUENCE NUMBER	MODEL	SERIAL NUMBER	APPROXIMATE COST
1	H	50 1096	449 812
2	H	50 1097	349 228
3	H	51 5703	579 624
4	H	50 1088	714 618
5	D	44 92066	559 355
6	F	49 2680	587 650
7	H	50 1099	846 958
8	H	50 1094	448 274
9	H	51 5705	696 044
10	H	51 5715	814 020
11	H	51 5710	635 127
12	D	44 92043	817 034
13	H	51 5718	781 092
14	D	44 92046	1 326 222
15	D	44 92097	1 000 599
16	F	49 2678	647 862
17	H	51 5706	626 102
18	D	44 92040	947 600
19	H	50 1090	1 197 569
20	H	51 5712	1 027 160
21	H	50 1095	1 114 672
22	F	49 2675	792 857
23	D	49 2665	970 947
24	H	50 1094	640 715
25	D	44 92051	2 084 448
TOTAL			20 930 579
IVY	D	49 2653	115 000
			21 045 579 *

POSSIBLE REDUCTION
1. Eliminate Field Operations on 12 Rollbacks
2. Airplane No. 44-92051 - Class 26
3. Reappraisal of Cost on Most Severely Damaged Aircraft

POSSIBLE ADDITIONS
1. Salvage of Airplane No. 44-92051

* Exclusive of Fee

Chart No. 7

a photo of the one aircraft that had been written off. Of the 26 returned to Convair, 8 required the replacement of major portions of the airframes: 2 had from bulkhead 4 forward replaced, 5 had the empennage (bulkhead 12 and aft) replaced, and 1 had from Bulkhead 10 aft replaced.[4]

The aircraft listed as destroyed (44-92051) had been blown completely off the pavement, across a field, and came to rest in a ravine adjacent to the South fence. Its fuselage was broken in half and the left wing and the tail assembly were severed. The aircraft was partially disassembled and a path was graded to the pavement to allow it to be moved back to the ramp. All serviceable equipment, including control surfaces, etc., were stripped off the aircraft and used to fix other damaged airplanes or returned to inventory. The remains of the airframe were later shipped to New Mexico to serve as a ground test vehicle in a nuclear bomb test.

Widespread tail section damage resulted in a heavy demand for replacement parts. The Master Assembly Fixture for the vertical stabilizer was normally limited to producing two assemblies per week and was the focus of an attempt to produce additional assemblies. Under the direction of Joe Carr, Manager of fin production, the production rate was increased to satisfy the demand. Other departments responded to the unusual demand in a similar manner and, by working around the clock, were able to provide all of the parts and assemblies that were needed.

Working jointly, Convair and the Air Force returned one aircraft to service the first week, and nine more in less than 2 weeks. Within 10 days of the storm, the 7th BW was declared operationally ready. In fact, on 2 October, the 7th BW dispatched six aircraft on a night tactics mission that included a simulated bomb run on Tampa, Florida, and actual armament firing on the Eglin test range. Interestingly, by the end of September the two Bomb Wings at Carswell were operating more aircraft than before the storm. Fifty-one more aircraft were back in service by 5 October, and 19 were at Convair awaiting repair. The last of the aircraft deemed repairable was back in the air on 11 May 1953.

The units at Carswell learned a lesson from the tornado. On 9 February 1953 high winds, thunderstorms, and hail again threatened the base. The 7th BW evacuated 22 of its 45 B-36s to Biggs AFB near El Paso, Texas. The aircraft returned to Carswell the following day. On 19 February, the B-36s were again evacuated when high winds threatened the area. This time the aircraft went to Davis-Monthan AFB, Arizona, returning the following day. This scenario would be repeated many times in the future in an effort to make sure the entire B-36 force was not exposed to severe weather at Carswell.[5]

In addition to the single aircraft destroyed in the storm, one additional aircraft (B-36H 51-5712) was not returned to SAC – its damage was considered severe enough to not warrant repair. This aircraft was later converted into the NB-36H. See Chapter 11 for further details on the atomic-powered airplane program.[6]

This B-36D-15-CF (44-92077) and B-36H-5-CF (50-1096) were intertwined in an odd manner. The D-model sustained a fair amount of damage to the right horizontal stabilizer and the leading edge of the vertical stabilizer. (U.S. Air Force via C. Roger Cripliver)

Here a couple of Convair workers examine the damage to the forward upper turret doors on the B-36H-5-CF (50-1096) also shown in the photo at left. Note the markings on the upper fuselage walkway and the BAY NO. 1 marking over the first bomb bay. (Convair via Don Pyeatt)

The only aircraft that was not eventually returned to flying status was this B-36D-10-CF (44-92051) that had been blown into a nearby field and severely damaged. (U.S. Air Force via C. Roger Cripliver)

44-92051 was salvaged by Convair and all serviceable parts were used to restore other aircraft or put into the parts inventory. It was fortunate that this was the only aircraft written-off after the tornado, and that nobody was seriously injured during the event. (Convair via Don Pyeatt)

0754-1-G 2 SEPT 52 CAFB A/C 1076 REST.

754-F-G 2 SEPT 52 CAFB A/C 1076 REST.

Photographed the night of the tornado, B-36H-10-CF (51-5705) and B-36F-15-CF (50-1076) show the damage caused by aircraft being blown into a maintenance dock. (U.S. Air Force via C. Roger Cripliver)

The same two aircraft the next day. The B-36F (50-1076) had been under-going work in its fixed maintenance dock when the B-36H (51-5705) was blown into, and over, it. (U.S. Air Force via C. Roger Cripliver)

0756-K-G 2 SEPT 52 CAFB A/C 2675 REST.

0756-L-G 2 SEPT 52 CAFB A/C 2046 REST.

The first B-36B (by this time a B-36D-1-CF, 44-92026) got together with a B-36F-1-CF (49-2675), resulting in significant tail damage to both air-craft. The empennage was the victim of a great deal of the serious damage caused by the tornado and kept Convair busy for several weeks manufac-turing replacement parts. (U.S. Air Force via C. Roger Cripliver)

What is left of an Air Force maintenance dock rests against the wing of a B-36D-45-CF (44-92046). This particular aircraft had more serious prob-lems since it had been blown backwards into two other parked aircraft (B-36H-5-CF, 50-1095 and B-36F-1-CF, 49-2675), causing considerable damage to both. (U.S. Air Force via C. Roger Cripliver)

This B-36H-5-CF (50-1095) had most of its vertical, both horizontals, and the entire aft fuselage ripped away. Note the 8th Air Force emblem on what is left of the tail. (Convair via Don Pyeatt)

The maintenance docks wrapped around each wing while the aircraft was being worked on. This B-36H-1-CF (50-1089), like many others, was damaged when the dock moved. (U.S. Air Force via C. Roger Cripliver)

Convair workers repair damaged fuselage skin on a B-36H-5-CF (50-1096) the day after the tornado. (Convair via Don Pyeatt)

The horizontal stabilizer of this B-36F-1-CF (49-2675) suffered damage when another B-36 was blown into it. (Convair via Don Pyeatt)

All damage was not confined to the tail area. This B-36H-20-CF (51-5715) suffered extensive nose damage. (U.S. Air Force via C. Roger Cripliver)

Several aircraft were blown into hangars or other buildings on the flight line. Left and center: B-36D-35-CF (49-2665); right: B-36-H-10-CF (51-5703). Note the airmen cleaning up the debris and taking a careful look at the damage caused by the short, intense wind storm. Although not shown here, several buildings on the base also sustained considerable damage. (U.S. Air Force via C. Roger Cripliver)

Another tail ripped off, this time from B-36D-5-CF, 44-92043. (U.S. Air Force via C. Roger Cripliver)

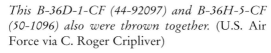

The right J47 pod from B-36H-20-CF 51-5715. The access doors have been removed by workers. (U.S. Air Force via C. Roger Cripliver)

This B-36D-1-CF (44-92097) and B-36H-5-CF (50-1096) also were thrown together. (U.S. Air Force via C. Roger Cripliver)

The wing tip of an unidentified B-36 hit the wing and engine of B-36D-20-CF, 44-92040. (U.S. Air Force via C. Roger Cripliver)

Another maintenance dock that caused considerable damage. This dock was blown under and around a B-36F-5-CF (49-2678), ripping large gashes in the wing skin panels and damaging some structure. Note that most of the cowling access panels are missing. (U.S. Air Force via C. Roger Cripliver)

This B-36H-25-CF (51-5720) had the lower part of the aft fuselage ripped out, causing the tail turret to fall out – here it is held up only by the ammunition feeds. (U.S. Air Force via C. Roger Cripliver)

Although the images presented here focus on the damage to the B-36 fleet at Carswell, other aircraft were also involved. This F-51D Mustang was thrown from the flight line onto a lawn in front of the transient aircraft office. The aircraft was relatively unhurt during the unexpected flight. (U.S. Air Force via C. Roger Cripliver)

Not all of the maintenance docks were demolished by the storm. Here is one that was only slightly damaged, along with the vertical stabilizer stand. The "REST." in some of these photos stood for the "restricted" security classification in effect when the photographs were taken. (U.S. Air Force via C. Roger Cripliver)

Chapter 9

Above: *Early tests of the FICON concept were made with this JRB-36F (49-2707) and the prototype YF-84F (49-2430). All of the RB-36s used as carrier aircraft had the FECM radomes moved under the aft fuselage during the conversion process.* (Convair)

Right: *The X-15 program was initially going to use a B-36 as a carrier aircraft. This would have allowed the pilot to enter the X-15 from the carrier instead of on the ground, providing a slight amount of additional safety. However, the increased performance available from the B-52 ultimately led to that aircraft being used instead.* (Johnny Armstrong Collection via Frederick A. Johnsen)

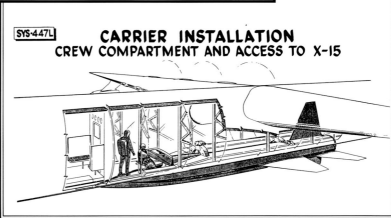

SYS-447L

CARRIER INSTALLATION
CREW COMPARTMENT AND ACCESS TO X-15

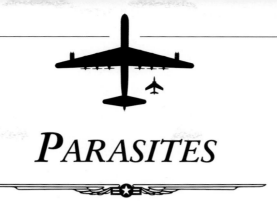

PARASITES

The concept for parasite aircraft was not new by the 1950s. Although several countries had investigated the idea, perhaps the most successful application was the U.S. Navy's Curtiss F9C Sparrowhawk biplanes from the 1930s. First ordered in June 1930, the F9C was less than 20 feet long with a wingspan of only 25.5 feet. A single 420-hp Wright R-975 engine could propel the 2,000-pound fighter to a top speed of 175 mph. When the Navy began building two large airships – *Akron* and *Macon* – it was decided that each airship would be equipped with a small hangar deck that allowed up to five Sparrowhawks to be carried. The original XF9C-1 prototype was modified with a hook device in front of the canopy and tests were conducted using the airship *Los Angeles* beginning on 23 October 1931. Six production F9C-2 Sparrowhawks had been ordered a week earlier.[1]

By all accounts the little fighters were quite successful as parasites. Unfortunately, the *Akron* was lost on 4 April 1933, followed by the *Macon* on 12 February 1935, effectively ending the program. A decade later, the U.S. military would try again.

XP-85 GOBLIN

The first jet fighters introduced near the end of World War II had insufficient range to escort the long-range B-35 and B-36 bombers then on the drawing boards – in fact it was doubtful they could escort B-17s. As one possible solution to this problem, the Army Air Forces revived the parasite fighter idea of the early 1930s and proposed that the long-range bombers carry their protective fighters with them. On 29 January 1944, the Army Air Forces invited the industry to submit conceptual proposals for parasite jet fighters.

The McDonnell Aircraft Corporation was the only company to respond, and proposed a small fighter aircraft to be carried partially inside a parent B-29, B-35, or B-36 heavy bomber. However, the AAF rejected this plan in January 1945, concluding that the fighter would have to be carried entirely inside the B-35 or B-36.

On 19 March 1945, McDonnell submitted a revised proposal for an even smaller aircraft with an egg-shaped fuselage, a triple vertical tail, a tailplane with pronounced dihedral, and vertically-folding swept-back wings. The engine was to be a 3,000-lbf Westinghouse J34-WE-7 (later a –22) axial-flow turbojet with a nose intake and a straight-through exhaust. The aircraft had a pressurized cockpit, an ejection seat, and the eventual armament was to be four 0.50-caliber machine guns in the forward fuselage sides. The top speed was over-optimistically estimated at 648 mph. It would be launched and recovered from a trapeze-like structure that would be extended from its parent aircraft.

The Army Air Forces liked the proposal, and ordered two XP-85 prototypes (46-523 and 46-524) and a static test article from McDonnell on 9 October 1945. At the same time, the Army Air Forces specified that the 24th (the first B-36B) and subsequent B-36s would be capable of carrying one P-85 in addition to a reduced bomb load. It was even planned that some B-36s would be modified so that they could carry three P-85 fighters and no bomb load. Despite later events, it appears that the first few B-36Bs actually had the mounting brackets for the trapeze included in bomb bay No. 1.

Conditional upon the results of flight trials with the XP-85, the Army Air Forces had intended to order an initial batch of 30 production examples. However, before the completion of the first prototype, this plan was shelved in favor of a more cautious approach in

The diminutive McDonnell XP-85 Goblin can best be described as "funny looking." Not surprisingly, performance was disappointing and the aircraft was a handful to fly. (U.S. Air Force via the Tony Landis Collection)

Since the XF-85 never flew with a B-36, there obviously are no photos of the pair together. However, in July 1946 the XF-85 (designated XP-85 at the time) mock-up inspection at the McDonnell plant in St. Louis used a mock-up of a B-36 bomb bay to demonstrate how the XF-85 concept would work. Note that the bomb bay doors bear little resemblance to reality – they are neither the old-style sliding doors nor the newer "snap-action" doors. Based on these photos, either type of production door would likely have worked, so these doors were probably just something the McDonnell craftsmen could easily build and were not representative of any proposed change to the B-36. Unlike the RF-84Ks used in the later FICON program, the XF-85 was designed to fit entirely inside a single bomb bay – meaning that, in theory, a B-36 could carry more than one parasite. The photo at the top right of the opposite page shows the XF-85

with its wings folded vertically nestled completely inside the bomb bay mock-up. The pilot could egress the aircraft while it was secured in the bomb bay (above left) – note the details of the trapeze and its associated hook on the XF-85. The power cables running into the belly of the fighter were used to power the folding wing mechanism and canopy. (The Boeing Company/Military Aircraft & Missiles Systems Group)

Convair also liked to build mock-ups– this is the B-36/F-84 FICON mock-up in Fort Worth during April 1950. Notice that Convair also constructed a very detailed mock-up of the Republic Aviation-manufactured RF-84F. Like the XF-85 mock-up four years earlier, these were used extensively to determine the configuration of the bomb bays to allow FICON operations. Although only a week separates the two interior photos at left, considerable progress was made in determining the location of handholds on the main wing spar and other details. (Jay Miller Collection)

One of the XF-85s in the pit at Edwards being attached to the trapeze extending from the B-29B. Note the additional wingtip stabilizers added during the development program. (Tony Landis Collection)

which only the two experimental aircraft would be acquired. If flight tests were favorable, more could be ordered later.

Since the XP-85 was to be launched and recovered from a retractable trapeze underneath its parent bomber, no conventional landing gear was fitted. Instead, a retractable hook was installed on top of the fuselage in front of the cockpit. During recovery, the XP-85 would approach its parent bomber from underneath and the hook would gently engage the trapeze. Once securely attached, the aircraft would be pulled up into the bomb bay. If an emergency landing were necessary, the prototypes were provided with a retractable steel skid underneath the fuselage, and the wingtips were protected by steel runners. These would have been deleted from any production aircraft.

A mockup of the parasite fighter and the B-36 bomb bay was constructed at the McDonnell facility in St. Louis during June 1946. Since a B-36 could not be spared for the project, a Bell/Atlanta-built B-29B-65-BA (44-84111) was modified with a special launch-and-recovery trapeze for use in the initial testing. With a wry humor, the B-29 was named *Monstro*, after the whale that swallowed Pinocchio. The first flight (using 46-524) was on 23 August 1948, but as the XF-85 attempted to return to the carrier aircraft the trapeze smashed through the canopy and Ed Schoch was forced to make an emergency landing using the belly skid.

A few more test flights were made with the XP-85, but the recovery operation proved to be much more difficult than expected, forcing several emergency landings using the retractable steel skid. Because of the turbulence encountered as the XF-85 approached the trapeze, only three of the seven free flights ended in a successful hookup. The other four flights ended in skid landings on Rogers dry lakebed at Edwards AFB. The second Goblin to fly (46-0523) made its only captive flight on 19 March 1949 and its only free flight, the last flight of the program, on 8 April 1949.

The Air Force reluctantly concluded that since the recovery operation was so difficult a job for even experienced test pilots, it would probably be far beyond the capabilities of the average squadron pilot. In addition, it was projected that the performance of the XF-85 would likely be inferior to that of foreign interceptors that would soon enter service. Furthermore, a budget crunch in the autumn of 1949 led to a severe shortage of funds for developmental projects. Consequently, the Air Force terminated the XF-85 program on 24 October 1949. The first XF-85 survives in the Air Force Museum, while the second may be seen at the Strategic Air Command Museum.

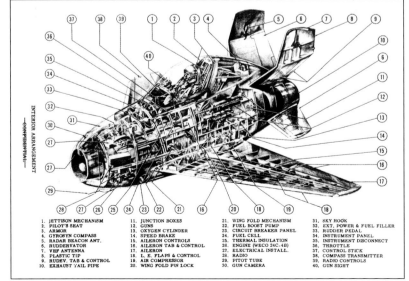

INTERIOR ARRANGEMENT
—CONFIDENTIAL—

1.	JETTISON MECHANISM	11.	JUNCTION BOXES	21.	WING FOLD MECHANISM	31.	SKY HOOK
2.	PILOT'S SEAT	12.	GUNS	22.	FUEL BOOST PUMP	32.	EXT. POWER & FUEL FILLER
3.	ARMOR	13.	OXYGEN CYLINDER	23.	CIRCUIT BREAKER PANEL	33.	RUDDER PEDAL
4.	GYROSYN COMPASS	14.	SPEED BRAKE	24.	FUEL CELL	34.	INSTRUMENT PANEL
5.	RADAR BEACON ANT.	15.	AILERON CONTROLS	25.	THERMAL INSULATION	35.	INSTRUMENT DISCONNECT
6.	RUDDERVATOR	16.	AILERON TAB & CONTROL	26.	ENGINE (WECO 24C-4B)	36.	THROTTLE
7.	VHF ANTENNA	17.	AILERON	27.	ELECTRICAL INSTALL.	37.	CONTROL STICK
8.	PLASTIC TIP	18.	L. E. FLAPS & CONTROL	28.	RADIO	38.	COMPASS TRANSMITTER
9.	RUDEV. TAB & CONTROL	19.	AIR COMPRESSOR	29.	PITOT TUBE	39.	RADIO CONTROLS
10.	EXHAUST TAIL PIPE	20.	WING FOLD PIN LOCK	30.	GUN CAMERA	40.	GUN SIGHT

The interior arrangement diagram from the XF-85 flight manual. Note how far aft the guns (number 12) would have been mounted. It was truly amazing that an entire, functional, jet fighter could be designed into such a small package in the age before computers. (U.S. Air Force)

The YF-84F approaches and docks with the JRB-36F. The B-36 was generally flying just above the stall speed of the F-84, and both aircraft had a positive angle of attack until after the F-84 was hard-attached to the trapeze, after which the B-36 began to level out. Unlike operational FICON carriers, the JRB-36F did not have a complete set of bomb bay plug doors. Note the observer in the lower blister in the photo above center. (Lockheed Martin)

FICON

The FICON (FIghter CONveyor)* project was essentially a follow-on to the earlier XP-85 experiments. It was reasoned that many of the difficulties encountered with the XP-85 were due to that aircraft's unique shape, largely dictated by the requirement that it fit entirely into the bomb bay of a B-35 or B-36. If that requirement was relaxed, a more conventional fighter configuration could be used. A straight-wing Republic F-84E Thunderjet was chosen as the subject of the next round of experiments.

The idea was fairly simple, and much like the Goblin concept. The F-84 had a probe and hook attached to the extreme nose. The B-36 would lower a large trapeze structure so that it was well clear of the bomber. The F-84 would fly up under the B-36 and insert the probe into a funnel at the end of a boom hanging from the trapeze. Once the fighter was locked into place at the nose, the boom would rise until latching pins aft of the cockpit slipped into a saddle on the fighter and locked. This would secure the F-84 at three points, then the entire contraption would be raised mostly into the bomb bays on the B-36.[2]

On 19 January 1951, Convair was authorized to use an RB-36F (49-2707) to carry the F-84E parasite. The bomb bay of the JRB-36F† was extensively modified, and the usual bomb racks were replaced by a retractable H-shaped cradle that was securely fastened to the rear wing spar. Major Clarence E. "Bud" Anderson was selected to fly the F-84. Just before the testing began in early 1952, the Air Force project engineer, Ben Hohmann, decided one more safety feature needed to be added – explosive bolts. Hohmann worried that the redundant locks on the trapeze could fail in such a way that Anderson would not be able to unhook if necessary in an emergency. It took a bit of convincing, but ultimately the new emergency safety system was installed.[3]

A single F-84E (49-2115) from the 31st Fighter Group was used to test the basic concept by engaging its nose in a large basket on the end of the cradle. The first test was simply to push the nose of the F-84 into a funnel attached to the cradle in order to evaluate the turbulence during the rendezvous maneuver. The first attempt proved somewhat difficult, and as the F-84 pushed into the funnel, the fighter began bucking and porpoising. On the next flight it was decided to go ahead and try to fight through the bucking and lock the aircraft in place. Anderson managed to link-up with the boom, but the fighter turned "grossly unstable" and Anderson attempted to release the hook. Nothing happened. The emergency safety system worked – the explosive bolts fired and the airplanes separated cleanly.[4]

The engineers decided that the boom was not rigid enough, so the solution was to redesign the boom and trapeze. The boom was shortened 100 inches, and a snubber and self-centering device were installed to keep the boom from tilting. The hook on the F-84 was moved from the nose to a location on top of the fuselage just ahead of the cockpit. It would mean the fighter would have to fly closer to the bomber, but hopefully the entire structure would be more rigid.

---

* There have been many variations of what people believe this stood for (FIghter reCONnaissance, etc.), but FIghter CONveyer is what is on the official documentation.

† There is some debate over the exact designation of this aircraft – some sources say GRB-36F, others JRB-36F. Since "J" designates special modifications (usually for testing), it seems more appropriate and will be used here. It is also possible it was designated ERB-36F; "E" briefly preceded "J" as a test designation.

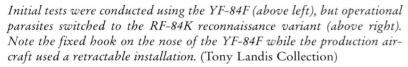

Initial tests were conducted using the YF-84F (above left), but operational parasites switched to the RF-84K reconnaissance variant (above right). Note the fixed hook on the nose of the YF-84F while the production aircraft used a retractable installation. (Tony Landis Collection)

Right: *One of the operational GRB-36Ds (49-2695) in the snow shows the open bomb bay plug doors and the APX-29 radome on top of the fuselage. The reason for the large black panel on the lower forward fuselage is a mystery.* (Frederick A. Johnsen Collection)

The first test of the revised system seemed to be working well. The F-84 successfully engaged the trapeze without any unexpected problems. But as the trapeze operator in the B-36 began to raise the F-84 into the bomb bay Anderson heard a loud bang and the F-84 lurched hard to the right. One of the 2-inch diameter aft locking pins had sheared. Again, Anderson executed an emergency release. The entire incident had taken 3/24ths of a second from the initial bang to the fighter falling away free. Unfortunately, at this point the F-84 was falling at less than its stall speed, and Anderson had shut down the engine after he was solidly connected to the trapeze. Fortunately, even with only 10,000 feet of altitude to play with, Anderson managed to get the engine restarted and made a safe landing at Carswell.

Anderson thought the docking procedure was too difficult and thought the entire program should be cancelled. In response, several other fighter pilots were brought in for further tests – all agreed it was difficult but could be made workable if the mating technique was simplified somehow. Convair responded by devising a better method for making initial contact. After a dozen or so flights with the revised hardware, everybody agreed the concept could be made to work.

By this time there was less emphasis on using the FICON concept for fighter escorts, but a new need had developed. Increasing Soviet air defenses were making it increasingly difficult for large strategic reconnaissance aircraft to penetrate Soviet airspace. The Air Force was not as worried about bomber formations penetrating since by that time the two nations would be at war and fleets of bombers could assist in protecting each other. However, reconnaissance aircraft penetrated one at a time, hopefully without being detected. The FICON concept offered

a way to transport a relatively small reconnaissance aircraft near the Soviet border where it could be released, make its reconnaissance run, and return to the waiting carrier aircraft. Given the 10,000-mile range of a B-36 and the 2,000-mile range of a fighter-reconnaissance aircraft, the system would have an effective range of almost 12,000 miles. The new Republic RF-84F Thunderflash was selected since it could also carry a small atomic weapon if the need ever arose.

In 1953, the first swept-wing YF-84F (49-2430) was modified in much the same manner as the F-84E except that its horizontal stabilizer (which had been relocated in the swept-wing version) was sharply canted downwards in order to clear the bottom of the B-36 during launch and recovery. Early tests revealed an unacceptable amount of flutter around the empennage of the F-84 when it was stowed. Changing the contours of what remained of the B-36 bomb bay doors cured the problem.

The project was revealed to the public in late August 1953, and the aircraft performed at the National Aircraft Show in Dayton, Ohio over the Labor Day weekend. For 3 days the JRB-36F and YF-84F flew a demonstration where the F-84 was launched from the carrier at an altitude of several thousand feet. Ray Fitzgerald was at the controls of the B-36 and Major C. E. Good was at the controls of the F-84. There was no lack of B-36 participation in the air show. In addition to the FICON aircraft, two B-36s landed at the show after a 33-hour nonstop flight from Japan. Two other bombers landed after a flight from England, although the jet stream had forced these to land twice enroute to refuel. In the next several months the FICON concept would also be demonstrated to the public at Eglin and at Carswell.[5]

In January 1954 Convair announced that the Air Force had awarded a contract to modify 10 RB-36Ds and 25 RF-84Fs* (52-7254/7278). The B-36s were scheduled to be modified to the Featherweight III configuration, receive the ECM Phase II modifications, and go through SAM SAC maintenance at the same time. This was far below

Carrier Plug and Clearance Door Operation Sequence

(From Retrieving to Landing)

A ALL DOORS CLOSED
Parasite launched and trapeze retracted to take-off position.

B CLEARANCE DOORS OPEN
Plug doors remain in closed position, although the left forward plug doors and aft plug doors travel with the clearance doors.

C PLUG DOORS OPEN
Trapeze extended for retrieving. Right forward plug door positioned for use as a catwalk.

1. AFT FIXED FAIRING
2. AFT PLUG DOORS
3. LEFT CLEARANCE DOOR
4. LEFT PLUG DOOR
5. TORQUE TUBES
6. FAIRING DOOR
7. FORWARD FIXED FAIRING
8. CATWALK PLUG DOOR
9. RIGHT CLEARANCE DOOR
10. YOKE PLUG DOOR
11. POSITIONING JACK PLUG DOOR

■ SEAL

D CLEARANCE DOORS CLOSED
Parasite retracted to cruise position. Yoke plug doors are open Rubber seals are flush to parasite surfaces.

E CLEARANCE DOORS RETRACTED TO TAKE-OFF POSITION
Catwalk plug door retracted and parasite retracted for landing.

59-354-A4

the number of aircraft SAC originally had in mind – 30 RB-36s and 75 RF-84s. Given the small number of aircraft being modified, Convair did not tool up to make large numbers of parts, and each GRB-36 was essentially modified using hand-built assemblies. The B-36 modifications would be performed concurrently with SAM-SAC maintenance, although the bombers would be out of service a little longer than normal due to the substantial changes required. The modified aircraft were redesignated GRB-36D-III and RF-84K, respectively. The first GRB-36D-III (49-2696) carrier made its initial flight on 28 July 1954 piloted by Ray Fitzgerald, with Fred B. Petty as copilot. At this point the aircraft had been equipped with the trapeze, but had been otherwise unmodified. Initial testing was to be complete by 22 September 1954, but an RF-84K was not available until 17 December, causing considerable delays in the program. Perhaps it was just as well; in the interim the main trapeze jack failed during ground tests and needed to be redesigned. This slipped the beginning of production flight tests until 1 April 1955, which proceeded smoothly. Despite this, the first GRB-36D was delivered to the Air Force in February 1955, 6 months ahead of the first parasite RF-84K.[6]

FICON operations were conceptually, if not practically, simple. Carriers and parasites could fly out of different bases if desired, and the parasite could be picked up in midair enroute to the target area. Alternately, the pair could be mated on the ground prior to takeoff. Convair designed a special set of loading ramps that could elevate the back end of the bomber to allow the parasite to be loaded on the ground. In a more permanent solution, a special loading pit was constructed at Fairchild AFB at a cost of some $55,000 – the fighter was towed into the pit, then the B-36 was positioned over it and the fighter lifted into position.

In a typical mission, the RF-84K was ferried about 2,800 miles and released at an altitude of 25,000 feet. After completion of the mission, the RF-84K would be recovered by the GRB-36D and returned to

---

* Called RBS-84Fs in some documentation. These were carried on the books as GRF-84Fs for quite a while, and most of the flight manuals and other documentation continued to use that designation or simply RF-84F. Very late in the program the RF-84K designation was applied, so that is what will be used here.

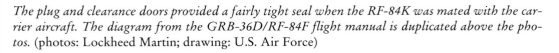

The plug and clearance doors provided a fairly tight seal when the RF-84K was mated with the carrier aircraft. The diagram from the GRB-36D/RF-84F flight manual is duplicated above the photos. (photos: Lockheed Martin; drawing: U.S. Air Force)

It was a tight squeeze, but the F-84 pilot could get out while the aircraft were docked – the YF-84F is shown here. (Lockheed Martin)

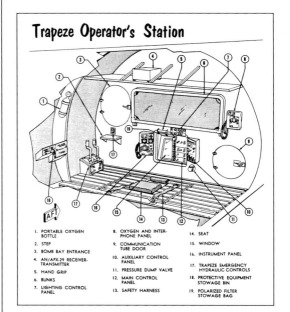

Trapeze Operator's Station

1. PORTABLE OXYGEN BOTTLE
2. STEP
3. BOMB BAY ENTRANCE
4. AN/APX-29 RECEIVER-TRANSMITTER
5. HAND GRIP
6. BUNKS
7. LIGHTING CONTROL PANEL
8. OXYGEN AND INTER-PHONE PANEL
9. COMMUNICATION TUBE DOOR
10. AUXILIARY CONTROL PANEL
11. PRESSURE DUMP VALVE
12. MAIN CONTROL PANEL
13. SAFETY HARNESS
14. SEAT
15. WINDOW
16. INSTRUMENT PANEL
17. TRAPEZE EMERGENCY HYDRAULIC CONTROLS
18. PROTECTIVE EQUIPMENT STOWAGE BIN
19. POLARIZED FILTER STOWAGE BAG

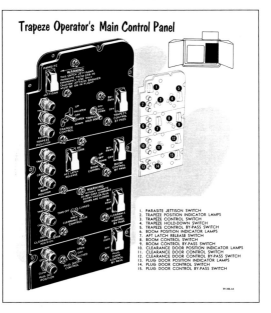

Trapeze Operator's Main Control Panel

1. PARASITE JETTISON SWITCH
2. TRAPEZE POSITION INDICATOR LAMPS
3. TRAPEZE CONTROL SWITCH
4. TRAPEZE HOLD-DOWN SWITCH
5. TRAPEZE CONTROL BY-PASS SWITCH
6. BOOM POSITION INDICATOR LAMPS
7. AFT LATCH RELEASE SWITCH
8. BOOM CONTROL SWITCH
9. BOOM CONTROL BY-PASS SWITCH
10. CLEARANCE DOOR POSITION INDICATOR LAMPS
11. CLEARANCE DOOR CONTROL SWITCH
12. CLEARANCE DOOR CONTROL BY-PASS SWITCH
13. PLUG DOOR POSITION INDICATOR LAMPS
14. PLUG DOOR CONTROL SWITCH
15. PLUG DOOR CONTROL BY-PASS SWITCH

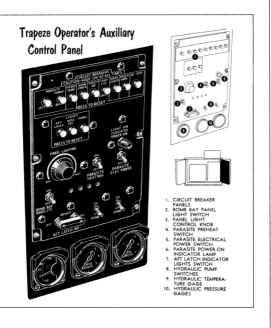

Trapeze Operator's Auxiliary Control Panel

1. CIRCUIT BREAKER PANELS
2. BOMB BAY PANEL LIGHT SWITCH
3. PANEL LIGHT CONTROL KNOB
4. PARASITE PREHEAT SWITCH
5. PARASITE ELECTRICAL POWER SWITCH
6. PARASITE POWER-ON INDICATOR LAMP
7. AFT LATCH INDICATOR LIGHTS SWITCH
8. HYDRAULIC PUMP SWITCHES
9. HYDRAULIC TEMPERA-TURE GAGE
10. HYDRAULIC PRESSURE GAGES

A control station was added at the rear bulkhead of the camera compartment with a large window that opened into the bomb bay. A small indicator panel and an emergency "parasite jettison" switch were added to the pilot's station. (photo: Lockheed Martin; drawings: U.S. Air Force)

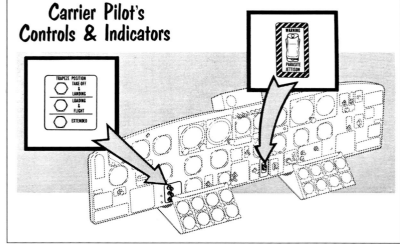

Carrier Pilot's Controls & Indicators

TRAPEZE POSITION
TAKE-OFF & LANDING
LOADING & FLIGHT
EXTENDED

WARNING
PARASITE JETTISON

base. The idea was that the RF-84K would be released about 800–1,000 miles from the target and within a relatively safe area. The pilot of the RF-84K would continue on to the target, obtain high- or low-level photography as desired, then return to the waiting carrier aircraft.[7]

The GRB-36Ds were modified with plug-and-clearance doors instead of bomb bay doors. The clearance doors fit tightly around the parasite during flight, while the plug doors filled the hole that remained when the RF-84K was not being carried. The doors consisted of an aluminum honeycomb core, internal extruded tubing, and aluminum external skins to form a sandwich panel assembly. The

lower cradle assemblies that formed the bottom of bulkheads 7.0 and 8.0 were removed to make way for the RF-84K to be hoisted into the bomb bays. The ECM compartment in what should have been bomb bay No. 4 was removed (the electronics and radomes moved into the aft fuselage the same as other RB-36s), and the lower section of bulkhead 9.0 was strengthened to accommodate the attachment of the aft end of plug-and-clearance doors.[8]

The boom and trapeze consisting of an upper drag strut, lower drag strut, drag strut positioning jack, main jack and yoke, snubber jack, forward and aft latch assemblies, boom assembly, probe receiver

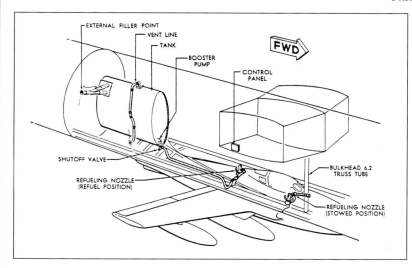

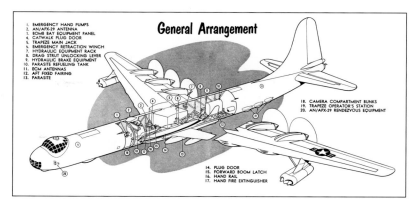

The FICON general arrangement diagram (above) and trapeze operation diagram (below) from the flight manual. (U.S. Air Force)

The RF-84K could be refueled while tucked in the bomb bay of the GRB-36D. Since the B-36 did not normally carry jet fuel (the jet engines ran on avgas), a special jet fuel tank was installed in the back of bomb bay No. 4 offset slightly to the right in order to clear the F-84's tail. (U.S. Air Force)

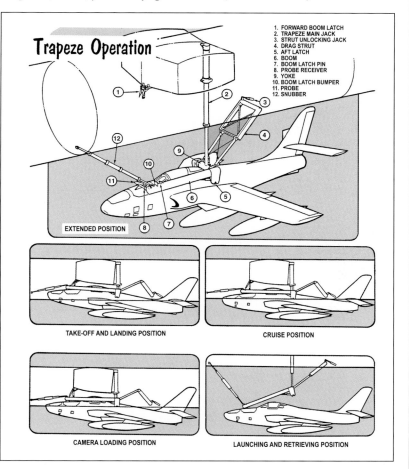

and shaft, and a boom-positioning cylinder were installed to actually catch and release the RF-84K. The hydraulic parts (mainly the jacks and cylinders) were off-the-shelf commercial items and were purchased from outside vendors. The rest of the assemblies were manufactured by Convair in Fort Worth. The boom was considered the most critical piece, and consisted of two extruded aluminum sections welded together. Bulkheads 6.0 and 8.0 were strengthened to support the trapeze assembly, while fittings for the main jack were installed on the rear wing spar. The front wing spar was modified with fittings for the forward latch assembly. Two independent hydraulic systems were installed for trapeze operation and door actuation.[9]

A trapeze operator's station was installed facing aft on bulkhead 6.0 in the camera compartment. This involved the relocation of the lower bunk and safety straps, strengthening bulkhead 6.0 for trapeze snubber jack fittings, relocating the bomb bay light switch, mounting lights for trapeze operation, installing the trapeze operator's window in bulkhead 6.0, and the installation of the control panel and seat. The access door in bulkhead 6.0 was made larger to allow a fully-suited RF-84K pilot to enter the camera compartment.[10]

Special night and rendezvous lighting were installed on the horizontal stabilizers and under the fuselage, and an APX-29A IFF/rendezvous set was installed. The bomb bay was equipped with a catwalk, safety wires, and handholds so that the RF-84K pilot could ingress/egress during flight. Since the B-36 did not normally carry jet fuel (the jet engines were modified to run on aviation gas), a 1,140-gallon fuel tank filled with JP-4 was carried offset to the left side (to clear the RF-84K's tail) in bomb bay No. 4 so that the RF-84K could be refueled while mated. This tank was constructed of a riveted sheet metal structure with welded and riveted skins. Access doors were pro-

vided so that the rubber fuel bladder inside could be inspected. The GRB-36D could also supply electrical power, preheat air, and pressurization air to the parasite during flight.[11]

The operational Air Force crews began training at Convair during late 1955 when 13 pilots from Fairchild AFB arrived. After initial daylight training at Convair, the pilots returned to Fairchild where more

Convair built a set of ramps that allowed the B-36 to be towed into a tail-high attitude. This allowed the F-84 to be towed under the carrier and hoisted into the bomb bay. This is the first GRB-36D (49-2696) to be converted by the production program. Despite appearances, the F-84 shown here (52-8847) is not an RF-84K – it is one of three RF-84Fs bailed to Convair for tests; the other two (848 and 849) were used on the Tom-Tom program. (Lockheed Martin)

extensive training, including night and high-altitude operations continued. The GRB-36D carriers saw limited service with the 99th Strategic Reconnaissance Wing (SRW) based at Fairchild AFB, operating with RF-84Ks from the 91st Strategic Reconnaissance Squadron of the 71st SRW initially based at Great Falls AFB, Montana, then moved to Larson AFB, Washington (now Boeing's Moses Lake facility).[12]

In at least one case, the GRB-36D proved to be an adequate emergency landing field. On 12 December 1955 an RF-84K piloted by Captain F. P. Robbinson was practicing night operations when his hydraulic system began to fail. The pilot suspected he did not have sufficient time to return to base, but radioed a GRB-36D that was nearby and explained the situation. Major Jack R. Packwood, the pilot of the bomber, arranged to rendezvous with the fighter and a hookup was made without incident. The mated pair returned to Fairchild AFB without further incident. The Air Force quoted

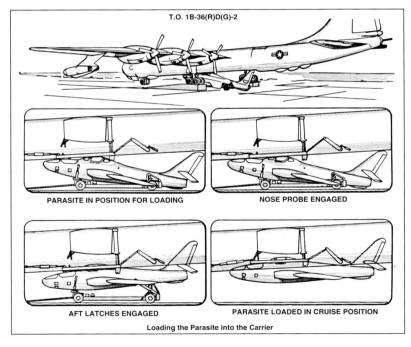

T.O. 1B-36(R)D(G)-2

PARASITE IN POSITION FOR LOADING

NOSE PROBE ENGAGED

AFT LATCHES ENGAGED

PARASITE LOADED IN CRUISE POSITION

Loading the Parasite into the Carrier

Above: *This drawing shows the steps needed to load the parasite on the ground using the ramp system – it did not really differ using the pit at Fairchild.* (U.S. Air Force)

Left: *It was possible to load or unload the parasite on the ground without using either the ramps or pit. However, this required that the tail of the RF-84K be removed and the parasite be laid on the ground as seen in the photo at left taken at Edwards on 2 May 1956.* (AFFTC via Tony Landis)

A special pit was built at Fairchild AFB that allowed the RF-84Ks to be loaded into the carrier aircraft without the ramps that were used at Convair. Although the operation worked, it was generally easier for the two aircraft to fly out separately and then dock in flight. The RF-84Ks almost always carried at least two drop tanks. Note how the parasite's horizontal stabilizer barely cleared the bomb bay despite the anhedral modification. (Frederick A. Johnsen Collection)

There was minimal clearance between the RF-84K drop tanks (or weapons, if carried) and the ground, another reason it was more desirable to mate the aircraft in flight. When operating in this configuration, the B-36 pilot had to make sure not to over-rotate. (below: Tony Landis Collection; above right: Lockheed Martin; others: Robert F. Dorr Collection)

Captain Robbinson: "The GRB-36 was the best emergency alternate I ever heard of. If it hadn't been there, it's a cinch I would have had to bail out." The same bomber crew had made 19 other hookups and drops earlier in the day during routine practice. The bomber belonged to the 348th BS of the 99th BW.[13]

Other stories have circulated about new operations personnel at Larson being confused by RF-84K pilots that filed 48-hour long flight plans with no stopovers listed.

No details have been released concerning the missions flown by the FICONs, but rumors have persisted that the RF-84Ks made several overflights of the north-eastern Soviet Union on reconnaissance missions prior to the U-2 becoming available. No available documentation supports these rumors, but not a great deal has been released about the operations of the 99th SRW during that time period. Once the U-2 had proven its ability, the FICONs were quickly phased out of service.

Project TIP TOW used a pair of EF-84Ds (48-611 and 48-661) and an EB-29A (44-62093) to validate the concept of free-floating panels attached to the wing tips. Tragically, the entire TIP TOW formation would be lost, effectively ending the program. (Peter M. Bowers Collection)

Tom-Tom

The XP-85 and FICON were not the only seemingly bizarre experiments performed during the late 1940s and early 1950s to evaluate enhancing the range of jet fighters by having them carried into the combat zone by bombers or other large aircraft.

Perhaps the most unusual of these range-extension experiments were Projects TIP TOW and Tom-Tom where jet fighters were attached to the wingtips of B-29s and B-36s. The concept had first been put forward by Dr. Richard Vogt, a German scientist who came to America after World War II. Dr. Vogt intended to use the idea to increase the range of an aircraft by attaching two "free floating" panels to carry extra fuel. This could be accomplished without undue structural weight penalties if the extensions were free to articulate and were self-supported by their own aerodynamic lift. In addition, the panels would effectively increase the aspect ratio of the overall wing, providing a significant reduction in wing drag. Therefore, as the theory went, the extra fuel was being carried "for free" by the more efficient wing and the range of the aircraft was increased by the extra fuel. Other potential uses for this concept quickly became apparent. The one that sparked the most interest was for a bomber to carry two escort fighters, one on each wingtip. The Germans had apparently experimented with the concept during late 1944 and early 1945.[14]

During 1949, initial U.S. experiments had successfully used a Douglas C-47A and Culver PQ-14B. These tests involved a very simple coupling device which was a single-joint attachment that permitted 3 degrees of freedom for the PQ-14. A small ring was placed on a short boom attached to the right wingtip of the C-47. Only local structural reinforcement was required since the PQ-14 would be supported by its own lift. A lance was mounted on the left wingtip of the PQ-14, and by facing the lance rearward, no locking mechanism was required since drag would keep the aircraft in place. The PQ-14 would position itself slightly ahead of the C-47 and essentially "back" the lance into the ring. To uncouple, the PQ-14 would simply speed up. The first attempt at coupling was made on 19 August 1949 over Wright Field, Ohio. Problems with wingtip vortex interference were encountered, forcing the engineers to reevaluate the concept. The solution was to move the ring further away from the C-47's wingtip, and on 7 October 1949 a successful coupling was made with Major C.E. "Bud" Anderson at the controls of the PQ-14B.[15]

At the same time as the C-47/PQ-14 experiments, a full-scale program was initiated using a B-29 to tow two straight-wing F-84 fighters. Republic Aviation Corporation was awarded a contract to design, build, and evaluate the combination under Project TIP TOW. Two F-84D-1-REs (48-641 and 48-661) were modified for the initial TIP TOW tests under the designation EF-84D. The wingtips of the EF-84Ds were modified so that they could be attached to flexible mounts fitted to the wingtips of a specially modified EB-29A (44-62093). This idea proved to be highly dangerous, although several successful linkups were made. Tragically, midway through the planned test series, the entire three-plane EF-84D/EB-29A/EF-84D array crashed as a unit on 24 April 1953, killing everybody on all three aircraft. TIP TOW was immediately cancelled. The cause was subsequently traced to one of the EF-84Ds going out of control during the link-up and flipping over onto the wing of the B-29.

Early Tom-Tom flight tests were made with very simplified mock-ups of the attachment hardware. Neither of these installations was capable of actual operation, but they were sufficient to allow pilots to attempt the docking maneuver in order to evaluate wingtip turbulence and other phenomena. The F-84 installation was slightly inboard from the wingtip, which would eventually be modified to have a variety of electrical and fluid connectors on it. (Lockheed Martin)

The actual hardware used for the limited flight test series. The claws on the F-84 grabbed the retractable receiver on the B-36. The B-36 then retracted the receiver until the F-84 wingtip mated with a series of electrical, fluid, and pneumatic connections inside the fairing on the B-36. The F-84 could then shut down its engine and be supplied with pressurization air and power from the B-36. Any production models would have been able to refuel the F-84 while it was attached. Initial trials were conducted on the ground at Fort Worth with the B-84 suspended from a gantry while it was slowly moved into place and the mechanism tested. (Lockheed Martin)

One of the RF-84Fs (51-1849) mated to the right wingtip of the JRB-36F (49-2707) on 8 June 1956. Note that both wingtips on the B-36 are modified to tow F-84s, but all three aircraft were very rarely together. Wingtip vortices from the B-36 made the hookup a very dangerous operation, but once the aircraft were coupled the concept seemed to work as expected. The B-36 has an air data probe protruding from its nose. (Lockheed Martin)

A parallel project was undertaken with a pair of RF-84F-5-REs (51-1848 and 51-1849) attached to wingtip hook-up assemblies on the JRB-36F (49-2707 – the initial FICON testbed). The B-36 was formally assigned to the Tom-Tom project on 8 May 1954. Interestingly, the Tom-Tom moniker was derived from the first names of two men – Major General Tom Gerrity and Convair contract manager Tom Sullivan – which is why it is not written in all caps.

The B-36 system included provisions to launch and retrieve the fighters in flight, and to provide fuel, pressurization, and heating air to the parasites while coupled. The wing structure of the B-36 and F-84s were substantially strengthened to tolerate the expected stress of coupled flight. Interestingly, the actual design of the Tom-Tom mechanisms was accomplished by the Thieblot Engineering Company under subcontract to Convair. A fixed mockup of the coupling mechanism was attached to the wing of the JRB-36F and one RF-84F and 7 hours of proximity flight tests were completed on 30 September 1954. Each of the F-84s was equipped with an articulating jaw that was designed to firmly clamp onto a retractable member on the wingtip of the B-36. Once a firm attachment was made, the B-36 would retract the member into a streamlined fairing where fluid, electrical and air connections would be made to allow the F-84 to shut down its engine.[16]

After the TIP TOW crash, tests continued for a few months with the RF-84F/JRB-36F/RF-84F array. Only a few hookup attempts* were made, and wingtip vortices and turbulence made this operation a very dangerous affair. The first hookup – using only the left-hand fighter – was made on 2 November 1955. In what became the final Tom Tom flight, on 26 September 1956 Beryl Erickson found the F-84 he was piloting oscillating violently up and down while attached to the B-36 wing tip. Fortunately, the part of the attachment broke and the F-84 fell away from the bomber before any serious damage was done. Since experiments with midair refueling techniques seemed to offer greater promise for increased fighter ranges with far less risk to the lives of aircrews, the Tom-Tom experiments were cancelled.

---

* Some reports say as many as 50 hookups were made, but no confirmation of this could be found.

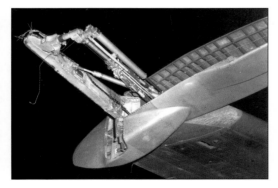

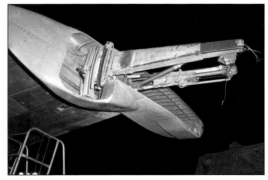

On 26 September 1956 Convair chief test pilot Beryl Erickson found himself piloting an F-84 that was beginning to oscillate wildly while attached to the right wing tip of the B-36. Before Erickson could do anything about the situation, the part of the B-36 mechanism that the F-84 claw clamped onto sheared away, allowing the F-84 to break free. The photos above show the damage – note the gouges in the F-84 claw and the missing piece at the very end of the B-36 mechanism. This ended up being the last flight of the Tom-Tom program. (Lockheed Martin)

More Parasites

Although not directly related to the B-36 program *per se*, there were a couple of other parasite concepts that made use of the basic B-36 airframe. In October 1946 the Air Force began the Generalized Bomber (GEBO) study that would ultimately study some 10,000 different bomber configurations. Convair was heavily involved in these studies and released several reports describing aircraft based, at least partially, on the B-36. In a 1950 GEBO II report, a small aircraft that looked much like an XP-92 sitting atop a B-58 weapons pod was carried partially submerged inside the bomb bay of a B-36. The two-man "return component" had a turbojet engine and sufficient resources to return after attacking the target. The jettisonable pod contained three more engines, a 10,000-pound weapons load, and most of the offensive avionics. The parasite had a launch weight of 100,000 pounds, and a landing weight of 17,500 pounds. It was to be capable of Mach 1.6 at 48,500 feet. The B-36 would carry the parasite for the first 2,000 miles, then return to base after launch. As with many of the GEBO concepts, this one quietly faded into oblivion with no hardware development being initiated.[17]

Another of the GEBO studies expanded on the concept that gave birth to TIP TOW and Tom-Tom. Three B-36s would link up in mid-air, wingtip to wingtip. The increase in wing aspect ratio was supposed to significantly increase the range of the trio, each of which would be equipped with a parasite bomber similar to that described above. There were several other variations on these general themes. For a more complete look into some of these concepts, please see Jay Miller's excellent *Convair B-58* book from Midland Publishing.[18]

The illustration at upper right shows a NASA concept that was a performance follow-on to the X-15 rocket plane and would have reached Mach 10 if it had been built. Plans called for using the same B-36 proposed for use by the X-15 project as a carrier aircraft. The drawings at right and below illustrate various concepts investigated by the GEBO study during the early 1950s. In each instance a small parasite was carried semisubmerged under the B-36. (upper right: NASA; others: Jay Miller Collection)

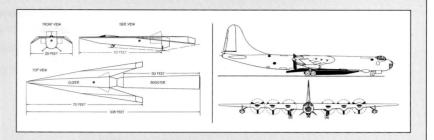

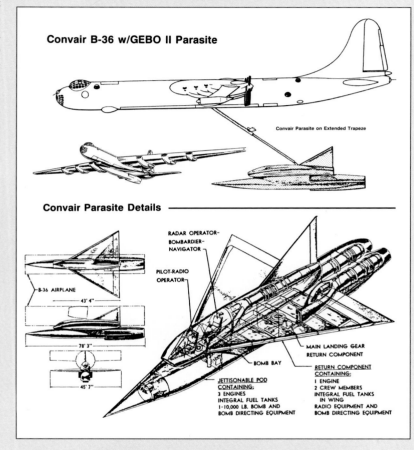

Convair B-36 w/GEBO II Parasite

Convair Parasite on Extended Trapeze

Convair Parasite Details

RADAR OPERATOR-
BOMBARDIER-
NAVIGATOR

PILOT-RADIO
OPERATOR

B-36 AIRPLANE

43' 4"

78' 3"

45' 7"

MAIN LANDING GEAR
RETURN COMPONENT

BOMB BAY

RETURN COMPONENT

RETURN COMPONENT
CONTAINING:
1 ENGINE
2 CREW MEMBERS
INTEGRAL FUEL TANKS
IN WING
RADIO EQUIPMENT AND
BOMB DIRECTING EQUIPMENT

JETTISONABLE POD
CONTAINING:
3 ENGINES
INTEGRAL FUEL TANKS
1-10,000 LB. BOMB AND
BOMB DIRECTING EQUIPMENT

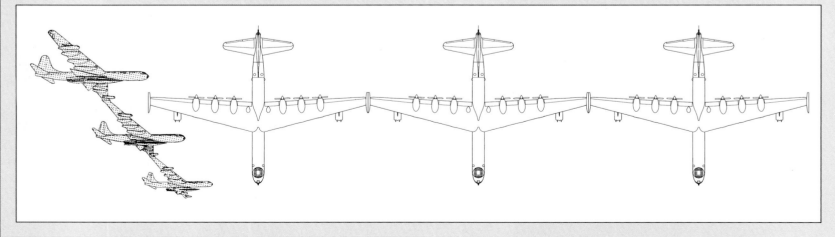

Chapter 10

                                                                                             Magnesium Overcast

The swept wings and empennage transformed the B-36 into a sleek-looking modern aircraft. Unfortunately, the performance provided by the still-thick wing and low-powered engines was not revolutionary. (Tony Landis Collection)

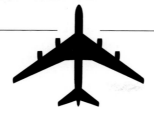

SWEPT WING SLUGGER

It was clear early on that the B-36 replacement was going to be the Boeing B-52, although at the beginning it was not nearly as evident whether the B-52 was going to be a turboprop or a pure-jet aircraft. In January 1946 the Army Air Forces issued a specification for an intercontinental bomber to eventually replace the B-36, although the Convair aircraft had yet to fly. Boeing responded to this specification with the Model 462, which had a 360,000 gross weight and was powered by six Wright XT35-W-1 turboprop engines on a long, straight wing. The military was sufficiently impressed by the concept to award a development contract in June 1946, and followed 2 years later with a contract for two prototype XB-52s. Boeing would call them Stratofortress, continuing their line of "strato" names.[1]

When the prototypes were ordered, the design still used six XT35 engines, but the wing had developed a 20-degree sweep on its leading edge. However, 2 years of study had convinced Boeing engineers that a pure turbojet design would offer higher performance, and testing of the early B-47 medium bombers seemed to be confirming this. By September 1948 Boeing engineers believed that the new Pratt & Whitney XJ57 turbojet engine offered a better chance at the large jump in speeds the Air Force was seeking. Switching to the Model 464-49 with eight J57s suspended in pods below a 35-degree swept wing was accepted by the Air Force on 27 October 1948, and a mock-up was approved in April 1949. Although promising to almost double the cruising speed of early B-36s, the design would likely have very short legs. This prompted the Strategic Air Command to invest heavily in the concept of aerial refueling, including the development of dedicated KC-97 piston-engine and KC-135 jet-powered tankers. Once the equipment and procedures for aerial refueling became commonplace, the scheme worked remarkably well. But it came at considerable expense.

As an alternative, Boeing offered the Model 474 – designated XB-55 – to the Air Force in 1949. This design was powered by four 5,643-hp Allison T40-A-2 turboprop engines slung below a slightly swept wing. Unlike the XB-52, which included only a tail turret for self defense, the XB-55 had a dozen 20-mm cannon arranged in three turrets. Although the development risk was considered to be lower for the XB-55, the resulting 490 mph top speed was substantially less than the 600+ mph envisioned for the XB-52 and the Air Force did not pursue the design.

By January 1951 the first two B-52s were being assembled and the general configuration of the eight-engine jet bomber was well known. The first of these to fly – actually the second aircraft – would make its maiden flight on 15 April 1952.[2]

However, the B-52 was always considered a high-risk program, and the Air Force continued to support the B-36 development and production program until it was obvious that the B-52 would indeed work. Although the Air Force never conducted an actual competition for possible B-52 alternatives, both Convair and Douglas worked on various designs that could fill the role if necessary.

The Douglas design that was considered the most promising was the 1211-J turboprop submitted in January 1951. The design was for a swept-wing aircraft with a gross weight of 322,000 pounds, a speed of 450 knots at 55,000 feet, and a maximum range of 11,000 miles. Originally the 1211-J used six turboprop engines, but by early 1952 this had been changed to four larger turboprops driving counter-rotating propellers. The design looked similar to the Soviet Tu-95 Bear

---

The forward fuselage assembly of aircraft No. 151 carried the name Swept Wing Slugger *for a short time prior to being assembled into the first YB-60 prototype.* (Lockheed Martin)

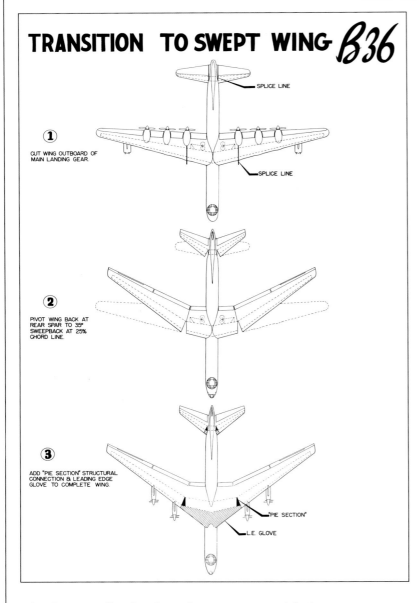

TRANSITION TO SWEPT WING *B36*

① CUT WING OUTBOARD OF MAIN LANDING GEAR.

SPLICE LINE

SPLICE LINE

② PIVOT WING BACK AT REAR SPAR TO 35° SWEEPBACK AT 25% CHORD LINE.

③ ADD "PIE SECTION" STRUCTURAL CONNECTION & LEADING EDGE GLOVE TO COMPLETE WING.

"PIE SECTION"

L.E. GLOVE

This drawing tells a lot about the B-60 program. The basic structure was pure B-36, with the wing spars being cut just outboard of the main landing gear structure and angled back. New "pie sections" and a "leading edge glove" were added, as was an entirely new trailing edge. Note that the final configuration shows four turboprop engines, not the B-52-style jet pods used by the prototypes. (Lockheed Martin)

bomber. The normal combat radius was estimated at 5,000 miles, but this could be increased to 5,750 miles by using wingtip drop tanks that held 50,000 pounds of fuel. Perhaps the design's most unique feature was that it lacked any landing gear, using instead a jettisonable takeoff dolly then landing on skids built into the underside of the fuselage.[3]

Like Boeing, engineers at Convair also wrestled with the question

of pure-jet versus turboprop propulsion. Convair had proposed turboprop-powered variants of the B-36 as early as February 1947, but the Air Force remained unconvinced. At one point the Convair options included a six-turboprop design that had each engine housed in its own pod slung beneath the wings, and a pure-jet version that used 12 General Electric J47 engines in six pods beneath the wings. These evaluations ultimately led Convair engineers to the same conclusion as their Boeing counterparts – the new Pratt & Whitney XJ57 turbojet seemed to be the best solution.[4]

On 25 August 1950, Convair submitted an unsolicited proposal for an all-jet, swept-wing version of the B-36. The design made heavy use of existing B-36 parts, including most of the fuselage and wing structure. Eight P&W J57 engines would be suspended from the wings in pods identical to those being developed for the B-52. The cost of each aircraft was later estimated at $5,000,000, although the first airplane probably cost somewhat less since it was not fully equipped.

The Strategic Air Command was firmly committed to the B-52 as the next heavy bomber. However, the Air Materiel Command was sufficiently interested and on 3 March 1951 authorized Convair to convert two uncompleted B-36Fs (49-2676 and 49-2684) into B-36Gs. This was accomplished as a change order to the existing B-36 production contract (AF-33(038)-2182). The primary motivation was to secure a possible fall-back in case the B-52 ran into significant difficulties, and in any event, the overall cost was expected to be modest. Since the aircraft was so radically different from the existing B-36, the designation was soon changed to YB-60.

The new aircraft would use a wing with a 206.4-foot span that provided 5,239.1 square feet of area. The leading edge had a sweep just less than 38 degrees, with an aspect ratio of 8.02 and a mean aerodynamic chord at 356.6 inches. A NACA 66-015.6A section was used at the root, tapering to a NACA 63-515.1A section at the tip. The fuse-

Below left: This was a speculative drawing published by Aviation Week *in the 26 March 1951 issue. Although most of the major attributes are correct, it is interesting to note that the artist continued the rounded wing and stabilizer tips used on the B-36 instead of the more modern squared-off versions used by the YB-60. (Aviation Week)*

Above right: Convair operated a dedicated J57 test nacelle in support of the YB-60 program, shown here on 1 April 1952. The strut, nacelle, and engines were essentially identical to those used on the Boeing XB-52. (Convair photo via Frank Kleinwechter; scan by Don Pyeatt)

lage was 171.2 feet long and the vertical stabilizer was 50.35 feet* high. The airframe had a projected empty weight of 136,292 pounds, and the all-up weight was the same as the upcoming B-36J model at 410,000 pounds. Also like the B-36J, the B-60 would have 10 wing tanks (instead of eight as in the other B-36 models), although the arrangement was slightly different than that of the B-36J. The tanks held a total of 42,106 gallons of JP-3, and the center and outer tanks

were listed as self-sealing. The aircraft had a design maneuvering limit of +2/-1-g at the design gross weight.[5]

The wing sweep of 37 degrees 56 minutes and 21 seconds was accomplished by cutting each main wing spar outboard of the main landing gear, and inserting a wedge-shaped structure to angle the main spar 35 degrees. A glove was added to the leading edge of the center wing to continue to the sweep line to the fuselage. Entirely new leading and trailing edges were fabricated, including new single-slotted flaps and servo-tab-operated ailerons. The ailerons had a total area of 264.8 square feet, with the servo-tabs accounting for 20.2 of this. The

---

* This is often reported as 60 feet 5 inches, which is incorrect. Even at 50.35 feet the vertical stabilizer protruded into the structure holding the roof of the Hangar Building – another 10 feet would have projected *through* the roof. The AFFTC flight test report concurs with Convair documentation at 50.35 feet high.

The first YB-60 (49-2676) under construction in the Hangar Building at Fort Worth. What is unusual in this seldom-seen photograph is that the aircraft has a production-style nose, not the streamline test nose that it was flown with. The nose shown here was different than the 'tactical' nose fitted to the second prototype, being about 4 feet shorter and not equipped with the AN/APG-32 radar. The shape of the antiglare shield paint makes more sense here than it did after the test nose was fitted just before the aircraft was rolled out. The second aircraft can be seen in the background to the left, confirming that both aircraft were under construction at the same time, not sequentially as is often reported. (Lockheed Martin)

Just before the first YB-60 was completed, a decision was made to fit the aircraft with a more streamline nose carrying a flight test alpha-beta boom. The demarcation line where the removable nose attaches can be seen just forward of the windscreen where the pattern on the anti-glare shield changes. (Lockheed Martin)

The basic tricycle landing gear was identical to the strengthened units used on the B-36J. However, the swept wing had upset the normally excellent center-of-gravity characteristics of the B-36, especially when the two outer wing tanks were full of fuel or the aft bomb bay was loaded. Under these conditions, the aircraft had a tendency to tip backwards while on the ground, necessitating the installation of an auxiliary tail wheel under the aft fuselage. This unit was similar to the normal nose wheel, including the capability to be steered. Many accounts report that the tail wheel was always extended during ground operations, but many photos show otherwise. It was likely highly dependent on how the aircraft was loaded at the time. Since the aircraft could not rotate with the tail wheel extended, it was necessary to retract the tail wheel while still on the ground but after sufficient speed had been gained during the takeoff roll for the elevators to become effective. Once the elevators did become effective, they were used to unload the tail wheel, which was then retracted. Anticipating the higher landing speeds inherent with the swept wing, Convair engineers included provisions for a 67-foot diameter drag chute in the aft fuselage, although it is unclear if it was actually fitted to either prototype. During landing, the tail wheel remained retracted until the main and nose gear were firmly on the ground. While the elevator was still effective, nose-down elevator was applied and the tail wheel was lowered during rollout.[7]

The original B-60 concept had only five crew members, all seated in the heated and pressurized forward compartment – pilot, copilot, navigator, bombardier/radio operator, and radio operator/tail gunner. The K-3A bombing/navigation system and Y-3A bomb sight were retained, with the antenna for the APS-23 search radar in its normal B-36 location under the forward fuselage. ECM equipment consisted of an APR-4 receiver, APR-9 radar receiver, ALA-2 panoramic indicator, and APT-4, –6, and –9 jammers. A full set of radio and navigation aids, including an APN-9A Loran receiver and APX-6 IFF set were included. The first YB-60 was completed more-or-less to this standard, although it lacked any tactical equipment (armament, etc.).

Although the rest of the structure appeared similar to the very latest model B-36, the maximum bomb load was listed as 72,000 pounds, the same as a B-36B. Only a single T-12 43,000-pound bomb could be carried, although the chart listed a possible load of three T-14 22,000-pound "Grand Slam" bombs. The normal B-36 defensive armament was eliminated except for the tail turret, which was remotely directed by an APG-32 radar. The newly-designed streamlined turret would house two M24 20-mm cannon with 400 rounds each.[8]

The initial performance estimates for the new aircraft were good, if not in the same league as the B-52. Maximum speed – limited by structural concerns – was 516 mph at 35,000 feet. Average cruising speed was expected to be 470 mph with a maximum altitude of 52,500 feet. The sea-level rate of climb was a tremendous improvement over the B-36 at 2,820 feet per minute. The estimated combat range was 5,750 miles dropping 10,000 pounds of bombs at the 2,800 mile point. The total mission duration was estimated at 12.25 hours.[9]

In the interest of economy, as many components as possible from the in-production B-36F were used to build the two YB-60s. The

YB-60 was also fitted with swept vertical and horizontal stabilizers, making the aircraft slightly taller than the B-36F. Most of the structure inside the new horizontal and vertical surfaces was common with the B-36, simply angled appropriately, covered with new skin, and fitted with new control surfaces. The horizontal surfaces spanned 64.25 feet, and totaled 985.5 square feet in area. The elevators accounted for 284.7 square feet and could deflect 22 degrees up and 18 degrees down. The vertical stabilizer had 613.9 square feet of area with the rudder taking up 177.8 square feet. Eight Pratt & Whitney YJ57-P-3 turbojets were housed in four pairs suspended below and forward of the wing leading edge. It was hoped that moving the engines ahead of the wing would help compensate for the center-of-gravity shift generated by the swept wing. Each engine was 183.5 inches long, 41 inches in diameter, and weighed 4,348 pounds. The engine's continuous thrust rating was 7,500 lbf, although MIL power of 8,700 lbf could be maintained for up to 30 minutes.[6]

Three views of the first YB-60 just prior to rollout. The lifting frame attached to the nose (at left) and the carts under the main wheels (middle) were the same as those used for normal B-36s. Note the mostly-completed second airplane in the background of the photo at right. (Lockheed Martin)

fuselage, main wing structure, landing gear, most of the tail structure, and ancillary systems such as fuel pumps and electrical distribution were essentially identical to the B-36F. The two airframes (Nos. 151 and 165) progressed through major subassembly along with the other F-models, then were removed from the line and taken to the Hangar Building (not in the main production building) for assembly and conversion. The work progressed quickly with few unexpected problems, and by the end of October 1951 the aircraft was essentially complete except for minor systems and engines. All remaining work – except for the installation of engines – was completed by the end of the year.

During January 1951, the first YB-60 was subjected to a series of vibration tests in order to determine the flutter characteristics of various panels. Electric "shakers" were attached to the aircraft and the vibrations were measured on the 43 areas in question, including the wings, empennage, and engine nacelles. This information was then used to build a scale model of the YB-60 for further tests in the wind tunnel at Convair San Diego.[10]

The B-52 program benefited from a much higher priority than the YB-60 program, and all available flight engines were being delivered to Boeing. Not that there were many to begin with. Full-scale testing of the J57 had only begun in early 1951, and quantities were limited to what amounted to hand-built prototypes. Engines finally began to trickle into Convair during early 1952, although the eighth and last YJ57-P-3 flight engine did not arrive until 4 April. Two days later the first airplane was rolled out of the Hangar Building – tail first with the nose jacked up until the aft fuselage almost scraped the ground. The engines were run for the first time on 9 April, followed by a full-power test on 12 April and taxi tests on 15 April.[11]

The YB-60 made its maiden flight on 18 April 1952, with Convair chief test pilot Beryl A. Erickson and Arthur S. "Doc" Witchell at the controls. Also aboard were J.D. McEachern and William "Bill" P. Easley, who along with Erickson had been on the first flight of the XB-36 six years earlier. The rest of the crew consisted of E.J. Nodolski, L.C. Brandvig, R.P. Scott, and C.T. Jones. The aircraft lifted off at 16:55 hours, landing back at Fort Worth 66 minutes later. As

was procedure at the time, the landing gear was left down for the entire flight. Interestingly, the photographs released by the Air Force after the flight had the landing gear air-brushed out for security reasons that are not understood.[12]

The Boeing YB-52 took to the air for the first time only 3 days later. Although there was never any formal competition between the YB-60 and the YB-52, the B-52 quickly exhibited a clear superiority. The B-52's future would be relatively quickly assured, and the aircraft will have served for 80 years before its planned retirement in 2030.

The cockpit of the first YB-60 shows a fairly radical departure from the B-36. Note that complete engine instrumentation is located in the center of the main panel, and that the old-style control wheels have been replaced by more modern units. (Frederick A. Johnsen Collection)

The YB-60 had a center-of-gravity problem under many conditions. When more than one engine was removed, the c.g. shift was too much for the tail wheel alone to correct. The solution was relatively easy – a large set of weights was attached to the nose wheel. (Lockheed Martin)

MOCK-UP INSPECTION

After the Air Force had accepted the idea of building the YB-60, Convair began receiving input from the Strategic Air Command and other organizations that indicated the original B-60 concept needed to be refined. A total of 11 master change requests (MCR) were generated that significantly altered the interior layout of any future production B-60s. One of these (MCR 5009) moved the APS-23 antenna from the radome under the fuselage into a flush radome under the nose, very similar to the B-52 installation. Another (MCR 5011) added an aft pressurized compartment to the configuration and moved the ECM-radio operator and tail gunner into the aft cabin. Provisions for probe-and-drogue-style, in-flight refueling equipment were added by MCR 5014. Oddly, MCR 5015 added back four of the six retractable turrets that had originally been deleted from the original B-60 configuration. The upper forward and lower aft turrets were to be identical to the standard B-36 units – the upper aft turrets remained deleted.[13]

As late as the mock-up inspection – an odd name considering it was the mostly complete second prototype being examined – that ran from 20 to 22 August 1951, Convair had still been estimating that the first flight would be on 17 October 1951. The lateness of the maiden flight had nothing to do with Convair or the YB-60, but it nevertheless dampened the enthusiasm of all involved.

The future looked somewhat brighter during the inspection. The eight-member mock-up inspection board was chaired by Brigadier General Lewis R. Parker and included 13 technical representatives from the Air Materiel Command, 29 representatives from the Wright Air Development Center, 3 from the Strategic Air Command, and a single representative from Air Force Headquarters.[14]

Convair presented a fair amount of detail on the proposed production B-60 at the inspection. For instance, Convair engineers disclosed that the ECM-radio operator had been moved to the aft cabin and now faced forward. The orientation was considered advantageous since he shared a common reference with the pilots and could offer suggestions on evasive maneuvers as required. The location in the aft cabin was selected since the "area was not congested and there is no cross traffic." All equipment was located in front of the operator, and there were space provisions for adding new ECM equipment as it became available. In addition, the aft cabin location was close to the flush antennas that were mounted in the horizontal and vertical stabilizers for the ECM equipment. This was important since radio signals degrade quickly between the antenna and the electronic equipment. Space was also available on the bottom of the aft fuselage for additional flush antennas. Similarly, the tail gunner faced aft since this orientation was considered optimal for operation of the tail turret.[15]

The second YB-60 and any production aircraft would have carried a crew of nine: pilot, copilot-engineer, bombardier, navigator-gunner, engineer-gunner in the forward compartment; and ECM-radio operator, tail gunner, and two aft gunners in the aft compartment. A dedicated flight engineer was not carried on the YB-60s; instead, the copilot's seat tracks were arranged such that he could move his entire seat to the engineer's panel if necessary during flight. All of the seats were designed to allow "easy mobility while performing combat and normal flight duties and to give maximum comfort ...." Seats rated for 16-g were provided for all crew members (although not necessarily at their normal flight positions) to provide better survivability during crash landings. Convair spent considerable time on human factors during the early 1950s, and for the B-60 "the color scheme used throughout the cabins has been given considerable thought in an effort to create an atmosphere that will add to crew comfort and still give maximum serviceability." Unfortunately, the available documentation does not describe what this color scheme was.

Interestingly, the tunnel that B-36 crewmembers could use to move between the two compartments was deleted because "… the arrangement of equipment and functions of crew members make it unnecessary." The forward and aft cabin were both provided with food lockers and an icebox for storage of perishable foods. Both cabins also had large trash containers, a concession to the increasing use of disposable packaging on food and other comfort items. Each cabin contained bunks with personal storage areas, mattresses, pillows, and blankets. A nylon fabric "which is not easily damaged nor will readily show soil" was used to cover the mattresses and pillows. Lavatory facilities were provided in both cabins, including a toilet, toilet paper, urinal (aft cabin only), relief tube (forward cabin), sink with soap dispenser and hot water, towel hangers, mirror, medicine chest, shaving light, and oxygen equipment. The lavatories were equipped with curtains for privacy.[16]

The fuel system for production aircraft consisted of 10 fuel tanks in the wings with a total of 42,106 gallons. The tanks were connected with a manifold-type fuel system using 3-inch diameter pipes. All of the fuel valves were accessible via the wing crawlway in case they needed to be serviced in flight. The tanks in the outer wing panels had two booster pumps each, while all of the other tanks had a single pump each. A carbon dioxide purging system, similar to that used on early B-36s, was provided. Unlike the B-36, which required each wing tank to be filled separately from on top of the wing, the B-60 would have a single-point refueling system with the connector located on the lower fuselage under the wing, accessible from the ground. A removable refueling probe was to be mounted on the forward fuselage.[17]

Electricity was provided by four alternators powered by constant speed gas turbine motors driven by engine bleed air. Two alternators and two turbines comprised a package unit, and a single package was installed in each wing. Each package was enclosed in a fire-proof stainless steel box and contained fire warning and extinguishing systems. A gas turbine compressor located in the left wing provided bleed air for running the alternators when the main engines were not running. Bleed air from this compressor was also used to provide cool cabin air on the ground. This arrangement proved less than satisfactory during testing.[18]

The tail wheel was added in order to provide sufficient aft stability, particularly for takeoff where the jet thrust (and even greater turboprop thrust planned for later models) increased the tail-down moment due to the aft c.g. location. The tail wheel also ensured that the nose wheel remained adequately loaded to allow steering control. The tail wheel could be retracted in approximately 3 seconds after a sufficient speed had been attained to ensure elevator authority. The tail wheel was lowered after landing rollout but before taxi. Convair included a lengthy explanation of why the tricycle-plus-tail-wheel landing gear was superior to the bicycle (quadracycle) arrangement chosen by Boeing for the B-52, but neglected to add it had really been chosen for maximum commonality with the B-36.

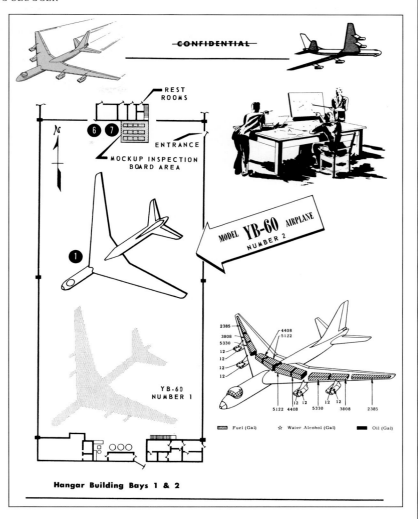

The B-60 mockup inspection was held 20–22 August 1951 and focused on the tactical configuration (i.e., weapons and electronics) installed in the second airplane. At this point it was planned that the first aircraft would fly on 28 February 1952, and that both aircraft would be converted to turboprop engines by June 1953. (Lockheed Martin)

Although a minimal development effort, the B-60 nevertheless introduced a few innovations. As an example, a high-pressure pneumatic system was selected to operate the tail wheel, brakes, and engine-starting system instead of the normal hydraulics. Convair felt this offered significant weight savings while increasing both speed of operation and safety. The system consisted of two 4-cubic-feet-per-minute, 3,000-psi electric compressors that pumped air through both mechanical water separators and chemical dryers into storage tanks. The storage tanks were integral with the main gear and tail wheel structure, resulting in very little added weight.[19]

The main landing gear struts were used for storing air and held almost 10 cubic feet each. This stored air was used to start the turbines.

From almost any angle, the YB-60 was an impressive looking aircraft. Notice the deployed tail wheel in some of the photos. The aircraft was in natural metal finish that highlighted the difference between the dull magnesium and shiny aluminum skin. The fuselage stripe, lettering, and nacelle trim were bright red, and the anti-glare shield was flat black. National insignia and other markings were typical of the B-36 family. (Lockheed Martin)

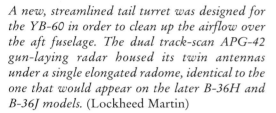

A new, streamlined tail turret was designed for the YB-60 in order to clean up the airflow over the aft fuselage. The dual track-scan APG-42 gun-laying radar housed its twin antennas under a single elongated radome, identical to the one that would appear on the later B-36H and B-36J models. (Lockheed Martin)

The first YB-60 at Edwards AFB in January 1953 with a B-36 (probably an F-model) in the background. Despite sharing the same fuselage, the aircraft looked completely different because of the swept wings and empennage. Note the large ladders positioned to provide access to the top of the wings. (Marty Isham Collection)

Beautifully staged photo of the first airplane with a young cowboy (Billie Whiteside, son of an Air Force Captain). This was taken at the same time as the one in the center during the YB-60's only visit to Edwards AFB. The Swept Wing Slugger *markings had given way to a simple "Convair YB-60." (Tony Landis Collection)*

The main landing gear truss support tubes were used for storing both normal and emergency brake air. The normal brakes were operated by means of dual tension-regulated cables from the brake pedals to the power valves at the rear spar. The non-differential emergency brakes were operated by levers readily accessible to either pilot on each side of the center pedestal, and were also used as a parking brake. An electric anti-skid mechanism modulated the supply of air pressure.[20]

The defensive armament system installed on the second B-60 was an evolution of that used on the B-36. The system included a high-power APG-42 dual search-track radar mounted in the nose to furnish information to the pilot for evasive maneuvering. The APG-42 also provided secondary tracking information for the two upper forward turrets. A similar system was eventually evaluated on the dedicated armament test B-36D aircraft (44-92054) with good results. Two optical yoke-type sighting stations were installed in the forward compartment to control the two upper forward turrets, and two pedestal-type sights were installed in the aft cabin to control the lower aft turrets. The tail defense system consisted of a tail turret controlled by another APG-42.

The nose defense system comprised a removable nose capsule containing the radome, antenna, pressure pump, and power section for the APG-42. The remaining radar equipment was installed in the navigator's compartment. An indicator panel was installed at the pilot's station that provided directional (which nose quadrant) and "time to evade" indications. The APG-42 could also be used to provide formation flying ("station keeping") information in adverse weather. The navigator was provided with a radar scope, while the upper right gunner was provided hand controls for slaving the radar and upper turrets. All of the electronics were inside pressurized areas of the nose to allow in-flight maintenance. On the second YB-60, an earlier APG-32 radar was used

since APG-42 components were in short supply, explaining conflicting reports of which radar would have been carried.[21]

Two upper forward and two lower aft turrets each mounted two 20-mm M24A1 cannon supplied with 350 rounds (although the ammo boxes could hold 600 rounds). The same electric computer, resolver unit, and thyratron controller used in the B-36F were provided for each turret. Nevertheless, a number of improvements were introduced on the B-60 installation. Additional clearance around the gunsight allowed the upper gunners unobstructed body motion through 200 degrees of azimuth. The lower sighting positions were raised higher in the fuselage to improve the gunner's comfort during scanning and tracking operations. This was possible partly because the upper aft turrets and associated sighting positions had been deleted, freeing room in the aft compartment. All of the gunner's control panels were relocated to the opposite side of the sight action switch to permit control operations with one hand while the opposite hand was depressing the action switch.[22]

The tail defensive system consisted of a tail turret with two 20-mm cannon, each with 400 rounds (although, again, the ammo boxes could hold 600 rounds). Otherwise, the APG-42 installation was the same as planned for later B-36s, with a tail gunner located in the aft compartment facing aft. The normal APR-4, APR-9, ALA-2, and APT-9 ECM equipment would have been replaced with APR-14 and APT-16 units.[23]

Space provisions were included for the future installation of the Convair-GE "Package Type Defensive Armament System" then under development. This system repackaged the defensive armament components into "packages" that could be easily installed or removed on aircraft as needed for a particular mission or for maintenance. The turrets were modified to retract flush with the surface of the fuselage, and did not require the doors used on the B-36/YB-60 installation.

The tail wheel was similar to the nose wheel, and could be steered during taxi. The pilots could extend and retract the tail wheel separately from the other landing gear based on gross weight and other considerations. The tail wheel had to be retracted before the aircraft could rotate on takeoff, but after sufficient speed had been gained to allow the elevators to become effective. The assembly retracted forward into the unpressurized area of the aft fuselage. (left and center: Lockheed Martin; right: Richard Freeman Collection via Don Pyeatt)

This allowed them to react more quickly to threats and also lowered drag considerably when the turrets were deployed. Convair proposed installing the system in a B-36F for an engineering evaluation, but this apparently never took place.[24]

Convair engineers spent a considerable amount of time devising a more workable installation for the K-3A bomb/nav system in the B-60. This was a concerted effort to eliminate all of the known deficiencies in the B-36 installation and to improve overall reliability and maintainability. The most interesting feature was that the entire system, including the APS-23 antenna and radome, were installed in a removable nose section. If major maintenance was required, the nose section would be removed and taken to a repair shop while a replacement nose was installed on the aircraft. This also allowed the radar and computer components to be installed in close proximity to each other, keeping interconnecting cabling to a minimum. This lowered cable losses, allowed the system to operate at higher power levels, and also eliminated a great deal of "noise" that hampered accuracy. The use of a flush radome minimized drag, and all equipment was installed in a

Convair employees and their families gather around the first YB-60 during an open house in the photo at left. The aircraft was displayed with its bomb bay doors open and the tail wheel extended. At right, the first YB-60 shows the upper surface details on the swept wing and horizontal stabilizer. It is not completely obvious that the wing was structurally similar to the B-36 unit, but in fact most of it was identical. The single-slotted trailing edge flaps, ailerons, and leading edge were unique to the YB-60, as was the large triangular glove that continued the leading edge into the fuselage The size of the rudder and its trim tab are evident here. On 24 June 1952, during the eighth test flight of the first airplane, a flutter condition resulted in the trim tab disintegrating and the rudder suffering severe torsional wrinkles while flying at 263 mph and 35,000 feet. The rudder was replaced with the unit manufactured for the second airplane, which never did receive a replacement. (Lockheed Martin)

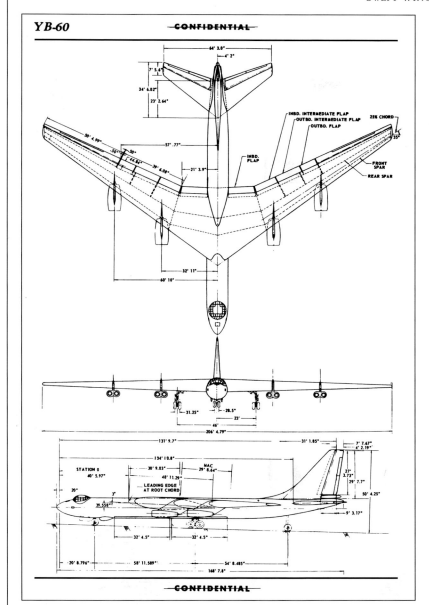
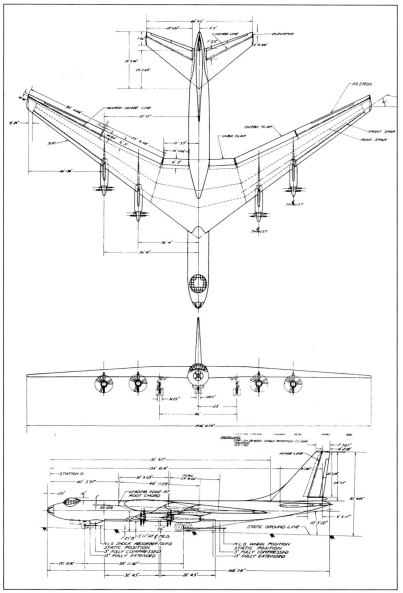

Two drawings of proposed B-60s reveal some interesting details. The all-jet version at left – essentially what was built as the two prototypes – shows J47 engines (instead of J57s) and the APS-23 radar installed in a belly radome, much like the B-36. The turboprop version at right is one of the earliest concepts with a glazed bombardier's nose and single-segment flaps. Production B-60s would have used a similar turboprop installation. (Lockheed Martin)

pressurized and heated area that was accessible for in-flight servicing as needed. In fact, to expedite in-flight maintenance, all of the system information not already available on terminals strips or junction boxes was brought out to new terminal strips where the crew could access it. Three commonly used pieces of test equipment (oscilloscope, multimeter, and a vacuum tube voltmeter) were permanently installed in a convenient location along with a "service table" that also served as an auxiliary table for the bombardier to view maps, etc.[25]

BACK TO TURBOPROPS?

The difficulty in obtaining J57 engines was not lost on Convair, although the problem would become more acute several months in the future. Even during the mockup review, it was noted that the turbojet engines on both prototypes would likely be replaced by turboprop engines in June 1953.

Some officers within the Air Force wanted to procure sufficient turboprop B-60s to equip two Bomb Wings by the middle of 1954, and there was talk about ordering 100 of the aircraft using FY52 funds. Convair indicated that the manufacture of production aircraft, in either jet or turboprop configuration, could begin in March 1953 if authorization was received by 1 January 1952. In many respects, this was contingency planning in case the B-52 ran into development problems – much the same tactic that had resulted in the B-32 being ordered as "insurance" in case the B-29 encountered difficulties. Production B-60s would have presented a very tangible benefit given the budget restrictions of the time; it cost only half as much ($4.1 million versus $8 million) as the B-52. This was largely due to the fact that the cost of the B-36 tooling had been amortized years before, and the B-60 could reuse much of the existing assembly fixtures. However, the Air Force, firmly committed to seeing the B-52 enter production, delayed any decision until both the B-52 and YB-60 entered flight test. It was the beginning of the end.[26]

By July 1952, Convair had revised the proposed production configuration somewhat. The overall length of the proposed production aircraft had grown 4 feet to 175.2 feet, mainly the result of flush-mounting the APS-23 antenna and installing the APG-42 in the nose. This also helped mitigate the center-of-gravity problems experienced by the first aircraft. The wing center section fuel tanks were slightly smaller, reducing overall capacity to 41,462 gallons of JP-4 (instead of the earlier JP-3). The addition of armament and other equipment had caused the empty weight to increase to 153,016 pounds, although the maximum gross weight remained at 410,000 pounds for structural reasons. Unfortunately, performance estimates had been lowered slightly, based mainly on the increase in gross weight. Maximum speed was down 8 mph to 508 mph at 39,250 feet altitude while cruising speed was down 3 mph. Perhaps most surprisingly, the maximum altitude was down almost 8,000 feet to 44,650 feet.[27]

FLIGHT TESTING

Following the first flight on 18 April 1952, Convair conducted 20 flights with the YB-60 totaling 66 hours during the Phase I contractor tests. During these flights there were four major in-flight anomalies. The first occurred during May 1952 on the fourth flight. The intent was to demonstrate high-altitude performance, and the takeoff and initial climb were uneventful. At 26,000 feet a surging condition developed in three of the YJ57 engines, and at 28,000 feet minor explosions were followed by smoke and flame from the engine tail pipes. Pratt & Whitney later determined that the high-pressure compressor on the YJ57 had been to blame and initiated modifications.[28]

During flight number seven on 12 June 1952, all four of the gas turbine motor units refused to operate above 17,000 feet. Convair determined that the turbines were not a dependable source of auxiliary power at high altitudes, and flight testing was postponed until a bank of batteries was installed in one bomb bay and an independent auxiliary power unit was added. In all, 12 of the gas turbine motor units had been procured to support the two YB-60 prototypes, but by July 1952 ten of them had already been expended supporting only the first aircraft.

The first flight after the short grounding, on 24 June 1952, substantiated an early concern regarding the flutter characteristics of the

Judging by the lack of smoke from the J57s, this is likely a landing photograph. The tail wheel had to be retracted prior to the aircraft attempting to rotate, and was not extended until after the aircraft had landed and slowed to a taxi. Considering over 70 percent of the structure of the YB-60 was common to the B-36, the aircraft presented a much more modern appearance. (Terry Panopalis Collection)

The early Pratt & Whitney J57s would not have won any environmental contests, spewing black smoke when advanced to full throttle for takeoff. Anybody familiar with early B-52 takeoffs will instantly feel at home. Photos of the YB-60 taking off never show the tail wheel extended simply because most photos show the aircraft near or after rotation – and the tail wheel had to be retracted prior to this event. (Tony Landis Collection)

Witchell had served as copilot, Erickson and Grubaugh had flown all of the Phase I flights together. The initial plan was to conduct 20 Phase II flights from Fort Worth, but the third flight ended up traveling to Edwards AFB since it was the only location equipped to measure the thrust of such a large aircraft. This single flight was the only time the YB-60 landed someplace other than Fort Worth.[29]

An AFFTC crew conducted four flights totaling 15 hours and 45 minutes between 20 December 1952 and 10 January 1953. During the Phase II tests, the crew consisted of pilot Grubaugh (later killed in a midair between a B-57 and an F-100); Captain Patrick Ferrell (later killed in an F-84F accident), copilot on one flight; Captain Fitzhugh L. Fulton, copilot on the other three flights; Frederick N. Stoliker, USAF Civilian Flight Test Performance Engineer; Donald R. Smith, USAF Civilian Flight Test Flying Qualities Engineer; MSgt. Harvey A. Cook, Flight Engineer; and MSgt. Harold W. "Ridge" Ridge, Flight Engineer (later 1st Lieutenant). Three Convair flight test engineers, Fiske Hanley, Frank P. Jones, and Roger P. Scott also participated in the tests. Only very limited stability, control, and performance data were obtained before the tests were cancelled by the Air Research and Development Command Headquarters on 20 January 1953. The four flights were:[30]

rudder. On this flight, the rudder trim tab disintegrated and the rudder suffered severe torsional wrinkles following the onset of trim-tab flutter at 263 mph and 35,000 feet. The aircraft landed safely, and the rudder from the uncompleted second prototype was subsequently fitted to the first airplane for the remainder of its flight test program. A replacement rudder was never manufactured for the second prototype since it had already been determined that it would never fly.

The final Phase I test flight occurred on 2 December 1952, with Beryl Erickson and Lt. Colonel Boyd L. "Danny" Grubaugh at the controls. With the exception of the first two flights, where Doc

FLT. NO.	DATE	TAKEOFF WEIGHT	FLIGHT TIME	DEPART	ARRIVE
1	20 Dec 52	225,000 lbs.	2 hrs. 40 mins.	Ft. Worth	Ft. Worth
2	31 Dec 52	328,000 lbs.	4 hrs. 10 mins.	Ft. Worth	Ft. Worth
3	01 Jan 53	328,000 lbs.	4 hrs. 55 mins.	Ft. Worth	Edwards
4	10 Jan 53	328,000 lbs.	4 hrs. 00 mins.	Edwards	Ft. Worth

The limited evaluation proved disappointing, and five areas were found where the YB-60 was "… found to be unsatisfactory in that

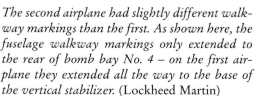

The second airplane had slightly different walkway markings than the first. As shown here, the fuselage walkway markings only extended to the rear of bomb bay No. 4 – on the first airplane they extended all the way to the base of the vertical stabilizer. (Lockheed Martin)

The difference between the prototype nose (center) and the production (or "tactical") nose is clearly evident here. Like the B-52, the production B-60 would have used a flush radome to cover the search and attack radar, contributing to the streamlining necessary to achieve the desired high speeds. The radome on the extreme nose housed an APG-42 radar. The production nose was four feet longer than the prototype nose, and slightly more pointed overall. By the time the photo at right was taken, the second B-60 had been mothballed, never having flown. (Lockheed Martin)

existing handling specifications were not satisfied." This included excessive static control friction, control forces that were too high, a distinct dutch roll characteristic, marginal aileron effectiveness, and imprecise stall warning. However, the report noted that the dutch roll was satisfactorily controlled by the yaw damper. The report also warned that the "characteristics of the stall are sufficiently violent that the airplane should not be intentionally stalled" and that the "lack of [aileron] damping was very irritating to the pilot." Engine operation was also found to be "generally unsatisfactory" but it was acknowledged that the YJ57 was in an early state of development.[31]

On the positive side, the report found that rudder control effectiveness was very good and the static longitudinal stability was very positive at all speeds. The evaluation also found the cockpit arrangement to be generally satisfactory although it made several recommendations for improvements. The major exception was that the evaluation pilots found it difficult to access the pilot and copilot seats while wearing standard flying gear.

The overall conclusions of the evaluation – limited as it was – indicated that, "[M]aximum level flight speed was not materially greater than the B-36 type airplane while the present engine installation prevented the airplane from exceeding the maximum altitude performance of existing B-36 aircraft." In fact, most of the performance demonstrated during both Phase I (Convair) and Phase II (Air Force) testing had been very disappointing. For instance, the rate of climb – at 10,000 feet the measured rate of climb matched Convair's estimate of 1,940 feet per minute, but by 32,000 feet the actual rate was only 730 fpm versus 1,060 fps predicted.[32]

The swept wing required Convair to develop new trailing-edge flaps. Unlike the complex system used by the Boeing B-52, Convair selected a simple multi-segment, single-slotted configuration. Note that the wing still required small bumps to clear the main landing gear, and the lack of doors for the upper rear turrets. (Lockheed Martin)

As assembled, the YB-60 vertical stabilizer extended well into the framework at the top of the Hangar Building. This meant the aircraft could not simply be towed out of the building, so the nose was jacked up to the point the aft fuselage almost scraped the ground. Note that the rudder and elevons have not yet been installed. Both YB-60s were equipped with the elongated tail gun radome. Contrary to many reports, the photo on the right depicts the first airplane, not the second – the serial number is clearly readable. (Convair via the San Diego Aerospace Museum)

Convair put a lot of thought into the arrangement of the radar and bombing systems for the B-60 based on the poor reliability of the B-36 installation. Essentially the entire system was mounted in a removable nose section that could easily be swapped out. The antenna for the APS-23 search and attack radar was behind the flush radome that is the subject of attention in the photo at right. The radome in the extreme nose contained the APG-42 antenna. The K-3A electronics were housed in the larger section in the photo at left, and were accessible to the crew in flight. (Lockheed Martin)

By this time the Air Force had concluded that the B-52 program would succeed in a timely manner, and the YB-60 effort was cancelled. The second prototype was never flown, although it was 93 percent complete, basically only missing its engines. The second prototype (which Convair called a B-60, not a YB-60) was equipped to the expected production standard, including a full offensive and defensive avionics suite, turrets and guns, etc.

Convair vainly attempted to convince the Air Force to produce the B-60, even offering to complete the remaining B-36Fs on the production line as B-60s at the same cost (of course, engines were government-furnished equipment, and they were the expensive part). This proposal was turned down. Convair then tried to convince the Air Force that the YB-60 could be used as an experimental testbed for turboprop engines, but this too was rejected.

The two YB-60s were parked on a corner of the Fort Worth facility where they sat out in the weather for several months. Finally, on 24 June 1954, the aircraft were officially accepted by the Air Force, but no money was allocated for their continued storage (approximately $60 per day was needed). On 1 July 1954 workmen took axes and blow torches to the aircraft, and by the end of July 1954, they had both been scrapped, with some of the components that were common with the B-36F being scavenged for spare parts. It was estimated that $800,000 worth of material was salvaged, including the $29,000 radar computer and two $4,200 landing gear struts from the second airplane, and eight $605 main wheels. The total cost of the YB-60 program was $14,366,022, including the fee paid to Convair.[33]

Convair also considered trying to adapt the YB-60 as a commercial jet airliner, again to no avail. A proposal for a 380,000-pound gross weight commercial version powered by eight P&W J57-P-1 engines would cost $7 million, plus an additional $1 million for engines. The airliner would carry 261 passengers, a flight crew of five, and a cabin crew of four. The aircraft would have a maximum range of 3,450 miles, and could have been available in December 1956. Interestingly, although the aircraft could fly nonstop from New York to London with 261 passengers, it could only carry 22 passengers on the return flight because of the prevailing 100 mph east wind encountered at cruising altitude.[34]

As part of this proposal, Convair surveyed a variety of commercial airports to determine if they could handle an aircraft of this size. None of the three major airports (Los Angles, Chicago Midway, or New York Idlewild) could accommodate the proposed wingspan or gross weight. None of the airport managers were interested in making significant infrastructure improvements beyond those necessary for the upcoming Boeing 707, which was 50,000 pounds lighter and had 100-foot less wing span than the proposed Convair airliner. Convair estimated that operating costs could be covered with an average of 215 passengers per flight. Engineers also noted that the YB-60 derivative only had a projected speed of 432 mph, compared with 600 mph for the Boeing 707 and other competitors. In the end Convair decided to concentrate on the 880-series of jet transports instead.

There were also proposals to use the YB-60 as a test vehicle for the nuclear-powered X-6. See Chapter 11 for more details.

This view (see the inside back cover for another) of the second YB-60 under construction has seldom been seen outside of the Convair photo archives. Note the deployed forward gun turrets on the upper fuselage – graphic confirmation that the "tactical" configuration included retractable turrets and that they were indeed provided to Convair by the government for inclusion on the aircraft. At this stage each turret only has a single cannon installed (or perhaps a dummy cannon for fitting purposes). The vertical stabilizer was a tight fit for the Hangar Building and disappears into the rafters. This would require that the aircraft's nose be jacked up so that the tail would clear both the rafters and the door frame when it was rolled out. Reports that the YB-60 used a vertical over 60 feet high are erroneous since the aircraft would not have fit under the roof of the Hangar Building. An engine container may be seen in the foreground just ahead of the inboard engine pylon, and the removable nose section is in the lower right corner. (Lockheed Martin)

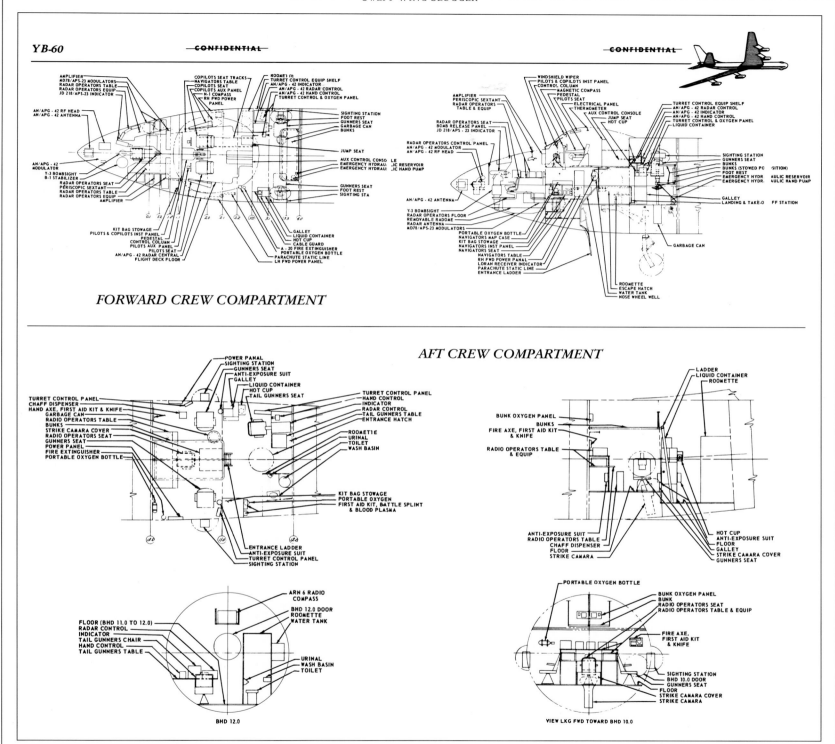

FORWARD CREW COMPARTMENT

AFT CREW COMPARTMENT

Most published sources describe the B-60 as having only a forward pressurized compartment and a five-man crew. This was true of the first prototype, but was not representative of either the second airplane or the planned production model. Here are the production forward and aft crew compartment layouts for the nine-man crew that were presented at the YB-60 Mock-up Review showing the gunner's positions and other tactical and comfort equipment. (Convair via the San Diego Aerospace Museum)

Two at right: *During July 1954, the two YB-60s were broken up using hand axes, blow-torches, and a bulldozer equipped with chains. These photographs ran in the* <u>Fort Worth Star-Telegram</u> *on 1 July 1954, but the effects of aging have taken their toll on them – wrinkling and bubbling of the negative required the photos be retouched to be printable.* (Fort Worth Star-Telegram photo courtesy of the University of Texas at Arlington)

There was a long black stripe under the fuselage leading up to where the tail wheel was located. The tail wheel doors themselves were not painted. No explanation for the stripe has been found. The tail wheel doors were divided into a small forward section and a larger rear section that was attached to the strut. The lack of a protruding APS-24 radome under the forward fuselage lends a sleek appearance. (Tony Landis Collection)

The first YB-60 at Edwards AFB during early January 1953. The aircraft only visited Edwards once, to use the engine thrust measuring equipment installed at the Air Force Flight Test Center. The aircraft returned to Fort Worth after a few days of ground testing. (Tony Landis Collection)

Below left: *The crew that took the first YB-60 on its maiden flight: (left to right) C.T. Jones, J.D. McEachern, R.P. Scott, L.C. Brandvig, E.J. Nodolski, Arthur S. "Doc" Witchell, Beryl A. Erickson, and William "Bill" P. Easly. Six years earlier, Erickson, Easley, and McEachern had been aboard the XB-36's first flight.* (Convair photo via Frank Kleinwechter; scan by Don Pyeatt)

Above right: *Beryl A. Erickson, Convair chief test pilot and manager of flight test waves from the cockpit of the first YB-60 after its maiden flight. Although the aircraft is generally listed as a YB-60-1-CF, the data block on the side of the aircraft has a blank where the block number should be.* (Convair via the San Diego Aerospace Museum)

A.S. "Doc" Witchell (pilot) and J.D. McEachern (flight engineer) show off the new David Clark Company T-1 pressure suits used on the YB-60, as well as the high-altitude B-36s. The green nylon suits came in 12 sizes and a crew member always wore the same suit. Note the pitot tube on the aircraft just below the "Y" in YB-60. (Lockheed Martin)

There are not many photos of the two YB-60s together. Here the two aircraft are shown in storage at the north end of the Fort Worth plant. A slightly different angle taken on the same day gives a good indication of how busy the facility was conducting SAM-SAC and other B-36 modification programs during 1952–1954. (Lockheed Martin)

The government-owned plant at Fort Worth that was run by Convair (and now produces Lockheed Martin F-16 fighters) occupied over 546 acres across the field from Carswell AFB. The buildings occupied 62 acres, with over 4,000,000 square feet of enclosed space and 8,600,000 square feet of paved working areas. Building No. 4 consisted of a 200-foot wide bay that was used for the main production line for the B-36, and a parallel 120-foot bay that was used for parts manufacturing. Both bays stretched over 4,000 feet. The adjacent structure, Building 5, was largely uninvolved in B-36 production. Over 31,000 people produced an average of one B-36 per week for most of the run. The plant produced over 68,000 separate parts, in addition to those made by 57 major subcontractors (excluding Convair's San Diego plant) and 1,553 suppliers located in 36 states and the District of Columbia. A total of 2,500 machine tools and 126,500 production tools were used for B-36 production. The assembly line integrated 8,500 separate subassemblies and 27 miles of wiring. The single B-36 line took up more space in the Fort Worth plant than had been occupied by two B-32 production lines during World War II. (Lockheed Martin)

Chapter 11

Above: *The classic shot of the NB-36H (51-5712) during its seventh flight on 23 December 1955. Note the large cooling scoops where the aft lower sighting blisters used to be.* (Lockheed Martin)

Right: *Various ground equipment was modified for use with the atomic airplanes. The tracked vehicle was designed to quickly (and safely) remove the reactor from the NB-36H and X-6 in the event of a problem.* (Jay Miller Collection)

ATOMIC-POWERED AIRCRAFT

Public interest in atomic energy became almost an obsession following World War II. The scientists who had developed the atomic bomb had also postulated a number of other uses for the atom. Ideas ranged from power generation (commonplace today), to nuclear excavation (Project Plowshare), to nuclear propulsion for vehicles on land, sea, and in the air – there were proposals for atomic-powered ships, submarines, locomotives, automobiles, and aircraft. By today's standards, most were incredibly farfetched, but in the 1950s all were considered worth pursuing – often at considerable expense.[1]

ATOMIC WONDERS

As early as 1942 Enrico Fermi and his associates involved with the Manhattan Engineer District (usually incorrectly described as the Manhattan Project) discussed the use of atomic power to propel aircraft. A study during 1946 by the John Hopkins Applied Physics Laboratory defined the potential benefits and challenges associated with using atomic power for aircraft propulsion. Chief amongst the problems at the time was the lack of data on the effects of radiation on materials which would be used in a design. Other concerns were the possible release of radioactive products during normal operation or due to an accident, shielding the crew and persons on the ground, and the selection of test sites. Although the full effects of radiation were not fully understood, the requirements for an operational nuclear aircraft were to not materially increase the general background radiation levels, and that all harmful radiation would be restricted to within the aircraft or a predesignated exclusion area.[2]

Given the seemingly immense benefits, in May 1946 the Air Force initiated the Nuclear Energy for the Propulsion of Aircraft (NEPA) project to support developing long-range strategic bombers and other high-performance aircraft. The NEPA contract was awarded to the Fairchild Engine & Airframe Co., and the work was conducted at Oak Ridge, Tennessee. By the end of 1948 the Air Force had invested approximately $10 million, and studies continued until 1951.

When the Atomic Energy Commission (AEC) was created in January 1947, the fate of the military-only NEPA effort became uncertain, and the program was continued mainly to allow time for the AEC to devise its own strategy. In May 1951 the NEPA project was effectively replaced by the Aircraft Nuclear Propulsion (ANP) program, a joint effort between the AEC and the Air Force to develop a full-scale aircraft reactor and engine system. Another factor that led to the ANP program was a 1948 MIT study that concluded that "… nuclear aircraft (manned) were likely less difficult than nuclear ramjets, which, in turn, would be less difficult than nuclear rockets to develop." Ironically, this turned out to be the opposite of how events turned out. Although nuclear ramjets (Project Pluto) and nuclear rockets (Project Rover) were successfully tested at the levels needed for operational use, an operational-level atomic aircraft powerplant was never developed. During early 1951 the Joint Chiefs of Staff had endorsed the military necessity of an atomic powered aircraft, clearing the way to continue the program at a higher priority.

TECHNOLOGY

As part of the ANP program, contracts were issued to General Electric to develop the P-1 (later P-3) direct-cycle turbojet and to Pratt & Whitney to develop an indirect cycle turbojet. Work was also begun on the new Connecticut Aircraft Nuclear Engine Laboratory (CANEL) to provide research and test facilities.

In the direct-cycle engine, air from the compressor stage of a turbojet is directed through a reactor core to be heated instead of burning jet fuel like a normal engine. The air, also acting as the reactor coolant, is rapidly heated then directed into the turbine section to be discharged through the tailpipe. The hot air spinning the turbine provides the power to run the compressor, and the cycle continues indefinitely.

An indirect system is very similar, except that the air passes through a heat exchanger instead of passing through the reactor itself. The heat generated by the reactor is carried by a working fluid (either liquid sodium or pressurized water) to the heat exchanger, theoretically allowing more heat energy to be transferred, thereby increasing the efficiency of the system. In both systems, there is no need for a continual flow of chemical fuel (kerosene) to the engines, although almost all designs allowed the engines to burn conventional fuel to spool them up and down as needed.

General Electric ran a series of successful experiments using the direct-cycle concept. The Heat Transfer Reactor Experiment (HTRE) series used three reactors, HTRE-1 through HTRE-3. The water-moderated HTRE-1 successfully ran a single modified J47 engine –

The 1 September 1952 tornado damage to 51-5712 did not look nearly as severe as some of the other aircraft, but the estimated $1 million repair bill made it a good candidate for the NTA. (below right: U.S. Air Force via Don Pyeatt; others: U.S. Air Force via C. Roger Cripliver)

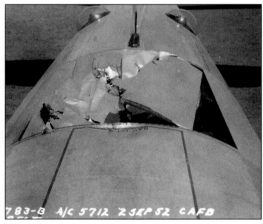

designated X39 by GE – solely under nuclear power. HTRE-1 was principally a proof-of-concept reactor, but achieved a number of full-power runs that demonstrated the feasibility of operating a jet engine on nuclear power. HTRE-2 was simply HTRE-1 modified to test advanced reactor sections in a central hexagonal chamber. The experience gained from HTRE-1 and HTRE-2 was used in the construction of HTRE-3, which was the final test item designed to prove the feasibility of producing an actual aircraft powerplant. HTRE-3 was the closest to a flight article the program came – a solid moderated reactor that powered two X39s at higher power levels. The proposed P-1 powerplant was based on the HTRE-3 configuration and used four modified 17,500-lbf General Electric J53 engines (designated X40) instead of the J47/X39s, but the J53 was a paper engine that never materialized.

The modifications to a standard turbojet engine (J47 or J53) to enable it to be "atomic powered" were relatively straight forward. The entire combustion section was replaced with a ducted compres-

sor outlet and an inlet scroll. Air entered the compressor in the normal fashion and was compressed. But instead of flowing into the combustor, the air was ducted into the reactor core where it was heated as it made its way through the reactor. On the other side it was ducted into the turbine section of the engine, which then turned the compressor section through the normal shaft connecting the two. In many ways, it was not unlike some of the compounding techniques investigated that used an R-4360 as a heat source for a turbine engine.

Most of the proposed X39 and X40 configurations included a chemical combustor just upstream from the turbine. This combustor allowed the turbojets to be started on chemical power (i.e. kerosene) and then be switched over to atomic heat as the reactor was brought up to operating temperatures. The operational system could also utilize the chemical combustor during takeoff and landing, and possibly during target penetration when the relatively slow response time of the reactor could be a disadvantage.

Although all of the HTRE reactors had cores roughly the size needed to fit into an aircraft, none of them were designed to be a prototype of a flight system. The series demonstrated that it appeared "possible and practical with the technology in hand to build a flyable reactor of the same materials as HTRE-3 and similar in physical size." The fact that HTRE-3 didn't produce flight power was mainly because it was not an optimized design; it was intended only as a research reactor to prove the concepts needed for a flight article.

While GE was working on the direct-cycle HTRE series, Pratt & Whitney* was investigating the indirect-cycle design. Progress, however, was much slower and P&W never ran a practical test system. In fact their work was limited mainly to component testing, although significant progress was made in liquid metal† cooling loops, corrosion prevention, and heat exchanger design. In the long run the indirect cycle showed more promise, but it also required a great deal more developmental work. As it happened, the indirect-cycle engine would experience considerable delays and was never seriously in contention for an operational system.

On 19 March 1951, the Air Force signed a letter contract with General Electric to develop the P-1 flight engine, an auxiliary propulsion system in case of a failure in the primary system, an external heat source for testing the engines prior to integrating them with the reactor, servicing equipment, and to support Convair on developing the X-6 airframe. GE was also tasked with investigating advanced propulsion systems for future supersonic atomic-powered aircraft. On 30 April 1951, the AEC contracted with General Electric for the design and construction of the nuclear reactor that would power the J53/X40 turbojets. In June 1951 the AEC and Air Force expected that a ground-based test powerplant would be available in mid-1954, with the first flight-worthy reactor being installed in the X-6 aircraft during 1956. The complete P-1 engine package included an R-1 reactor and four X40 turbojets.

In November 1951, the government contracted with an architectural and engineering firm – Parson-Macco-Liewit – to recommend a remote site for ground tests of the P-1 powerplant. If possible, the site should also be capable of supporting flight tests of the eventual X-6. A month later Parsons had recommended Arco, Idaho, and began work on a facilities master plan. This location became home to the Flight Engine Test Facility, which cost over $8 million. Unfortunately, the facility was never used before the flight program was cancelled.

NB-36H

Despite its problems, the ANP program did spawn plans for two flight vehicles. Both were to be B-36s modified by Convair under contract AF33(038)-2117 as part of the MX-1589 project. The first was an effort to more fully understand the shielding requirements for an airborne reactor. A decision was made to build a small reactor and flight test it aboard a B-36. The reactor would not provide any power to the aircraft, but both the reactor and its associated radiation levels would be carefully monitored during a series of flight tests. This would give designers actual flight data to use in determining the characteristics of the operational shielding, as well as insight into various operational factors. This aircraft was referred to as the Nuclear Test Aircraft (NTA).

The construction of the Nuclear Aircraft Research Facility at Fort Worth to support MX-1589 was carried out under contract AF33(600)-6216. In addition, the AEC awarded Convair a support contract under AT(11-1)-171 on 29 June 1951 to support operations of the flight vehicles. The first public announcement of the MX-1589 program was made by Convair Fort Worth division manager August C. Esenwein on 5 September 1951, and the contracts were signed on 11 November 1951. At the same time, Lockheed was awarded study contracts in case Convair ran into serious trouble. Separately, Boeing, Convair, Douglas, and Lockheed were studying requirements for an operational supersonic atomic-powered aircraft.[3]

The decision to use the B-36 for the initial experiments was based primarily on an analysis that showed that the big bomber could be modified fairly easily to carry the large reactor/engine assembly. Performance would not be outstanding given the speed limitations of the B-36 airframe, but it would serve as an adequate proof-of-concept. There was never any intention of producing more than the single NTA and two experimental X-6 aircraft. No tactical requirements were levied on either design, and they were to be optimized for their test functions with no regard to future operational utility.

The forward fuselage mock-up was used for both the NTA and X-6 programs. Note that the crew access hatch is separate from the nose landing gear well, unlike the B-36. (Lockheed Martin)

At left is the NB-36H in the Hangar Building on 4 March 1953 as restoration begins. In the center is the aircraft on 27 November 1953 – note the FICON mock-up in background and the large cooling scoop protruding from the aft lower blister hole. This scoop provided air for the reactor's air-to-water heat exchanger. At right the aircraft is mostly completed on 27 December 1954. The new nose area was skinned in aluminum even though the area would not suffer pressure cycles. The large opening is where the separate crew module would be installed. (Lockheed Martin)

In preparation for the NTA experiments, Convair installed a small nuclear Ground Test Reactor (GTR) at Fort Worth during 1953. The initial public announcement of the reactor – the first in Texas – came on 20 August 1954. The GTR had gone "critical" on 17 November 1953. The Aircraft Shield Test Reactor (ASTR) – the unit that would be carried aboard the NTA – first went critical on 17 November 1954.[4]

Convair spent a surprising amount of time defining the crew compartment for the NTA. The preliminary design for an appropriate crew compartment – and its associated shielding – exceeded the structural limitations of the B-36 forward fuselage by a rather large margin, and was rejected. A decision on 4 June 1952 to delete some crew comfort items and to move some equipment to other locations on the aircraft resulted in weight estimates within the structural limitations of the aircraft. After evaluating seven alternatives, the final design had side-by-side pilot and copilot stations that were located lower in the fuselage than the standard B-36 (actually, at approximately the same level as the original XB-36). Two nuclear engineers were located immediately aft of the pilots, facing forward. The flight engineer was located in the extreme necked-down aft end of the compartment on the centerline of the airplane, also facing mostly forward.

The XB-36H was rolled out (left) of the Hangar Building on 4 April 1955 much like any other B-36 – with its nose in the air so that the tail cleared the door frame. The shielded crew compartment was installed on 27 April 1955 using a large crane (center and right), then the aerodynamic cover was installed. Note that at this time the cheat line stripe has not been painted on the aircraft, nor has the anti-glare shield or other markings (except a serial number on the tail). (Lockheed Martin)

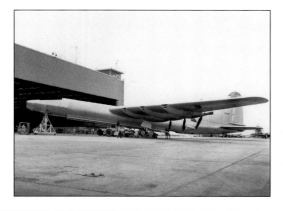

The NB-36H aircraft commander's (left) and pilot's (right) stations as seen from the entrance way on 15 May 1956. (Lockheed Martin)

Construction of a crew compartment mock-up began in July 1952. The new nose section would replace the nose on the B-36 forward of Bulkhead 5. The contours of the nose changed substantially in detail – the cross section of the extreme nose was ogive instead of round, for instance. However, from a distance the only major difference was that the "bubble" cockpit of the B-36 had been replaced by a more conventional-looking "airliner" configuration. Also, the nose landing gear would be moved 6 inches forward to accommodate the entry hatch to the crew compartment. The construction of the flight-rated crew compartment took most of 1953, and the early part of 1954 was spent testing the module. These tests revealed the need for additional shielding materials, some revised instrumentation, and a new windshield. These modifications were completed in early 1955.[5]

Although the B-36 was a large aircraft, and the normal crew compartment provided a fair amount of room for the crew, the NTA would not have this luxury. The amount of shielding required to protect the crew greatly decreased the space available, and the final result was very cramped. The station arrangements were carefully planned to obtain the maximum efficiency from the crew and their equipment within the confined area of the compartment. For example, one problem concerned the placement of the nuclear engineer's oxygen regula-

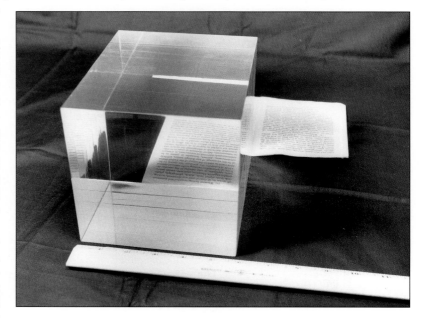

A sample of the 6-inch thick plexiglass windshield for the NB-36H showing its optical clarity on 26 June 1953. (Lockheed Martin)

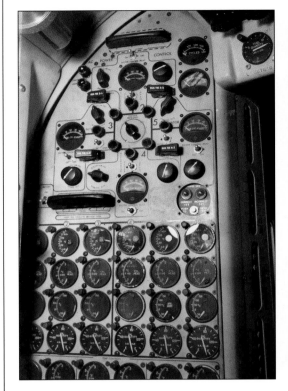

The flight engineer's station was radically different from that of a normal B-36. The flight engineer sat in the very back of the crew module, with panels on either side of him (the left panel is in the two photos at left; the right panel in the center above). Throttles were located below the right panel as seen in the shot of the seat (upper right). A TV system was installed that allowed the flight engineer to monitor aspects of the aircraft (looking forward at the propellers, etc.). The TV monitor was mounted above the doorway to the flight deck between the nuclear engineer and the flight test engineer. (Lockheed Martin)

tors and interphone panels. It was finally decided that the instruments could be mounted on a drop-door hinged to the base of each nuclear engineer's seat. When let down, the door fell between the engineer's legs just above his feet, allowing him to see the instruments. When not in use, the door was pushed upright against the seat, out of the way.

At the pilot's stations, there was only a single set of instruments, located in the middle of the panel since there was not sufficient room behind the panel for all the normal plumbing and electrical wiring. The engine scanning normally performed by crewmembers in the aft compartment was performed instead by using television cameras. A location for the television monitor could not be found, however, until it was decided to locate it in the overhead area between the two

nuclear engineers, where it could be seen relatively easily by the flight engineer. Although the two pilots had movable seats, the other three seats were fixed since there was insufficient room. The area underneath the seats was used for storage.

A drinking water container was provided in the aft portion of the copilot's seat, while the aft side of the pilot's seat contained a relief tube. This location was chosen since it allowed crewmembers to stand at the only location in the compartment that was full-height. A conventional toilet was located outside the crew compartment in the fuselage near the entrance hatch.

The 6-inch thick plexiglass used in the windshield to provide shielding for the crew was very thick, but had excellent optical quali-

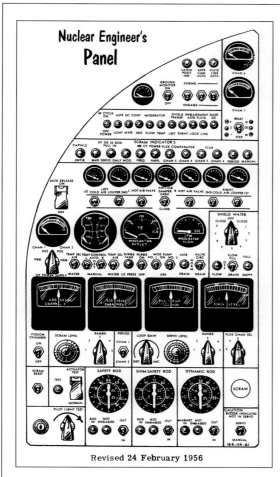

The nuclear engineer's station (left) contained the operating controls for the ASTR reactor. The flight test engineer (center) was responsible for data gathering during the flight. The bottom hatch (right) was the normal way for the crew to embark and disembark from the aircraft. (Lockheed Martin)

ties. The yellow tint of the plexiglass made the conventional gray color normally used in cockpits turn a very undesirable color. After much experimenting, designers found that using a lavender paint in the pilots' area gave the illusion of being gray when illuminated by daylight through the yellow windshield. The pilots' instrument panel was painted black, but all other panels were painted a very pale gray that made the compartment appear roomier. The seats were upholstered in light gray cloth, and the floors were covered in darker gray carpet. A curtain was installed between the pilots and the nuclear engineers to block sunlight.[6]

All portions of the aircraft exterior seen from the pilots' compartment were painted anti-glare black to diffuse direct sunlight. The initial design of a simple antiglare shield produced an unattractive pattern when combined with the black radome. The two areas were subsequently blended together and a small amount of trim extended upward and aft to provide a more appealing look.

Since the crew compartment was designed to be removable during maintenance, a method had to be devised to easily connect and disconnect the flight controls. Instead of the normal cables, a series of push-pull rods projecting from the bottom of the crew compartment were devised that could easily be connected to the cables in the lower fuselage. Push-pull rods were also used for the throttle and mixture

control that connected to the normal cables underneath the crew compartment. The construction of the shielded crew compartment required the perfection of a method to bond rubber and lead to the metal alloys used in aircraft construction. The rubber, in its natural state, was procured from the Goodyear Rubber Company. The rubber was chemically cured and bonded to the alloys using special adhesives. Virgin lead was also bonded to the compartment using a technique that resulted in the entire compartment – alloy, lead, and rubber – being a complete one-piece unit.[7]

The original XB-36 (42-13570) was turned over to the NTA program (called NEBO – Nuclear Engine Bomber – by Convair) in mid-1951 and was used for preliminary ground tests of radiation effects and shielding. The aircraft did not participate in any flights during its NEBO tenure, being strictly a ground-test article.

The NTA began its life as a B-36H-20-CF (51-5712) that had been damaged during the tornado at Carswell AFB on 1 September 1952. The estimated cost to restore the aircraft to an operational configuration was over $1,000,000 – almost 50 percent of the cost of a new aircraft (minus the Government equipment). In particular, the nose of the bomber had been extensively damaged, and since a new shielded crew compartment was part of the plan for the NTA, this airframe was a logical choice. The aircraft was formally assigned to MX-1589

NB-36H FLIGHT LOG

[Flight log data by Steve Andrich, NB-36H Flight Test Engineer, via Lockheed Martin]

Date	Program Flt. No.	ASTR Flt. No.	Flt. Time (hh:mm)	Comments
20 Jul 55	1	–	1:15	Dummy ASTR; vibration survey; empty water system
13 Aug 55	2	–	5:50	Dummy ASTR; vibration survey; full water system
01 Sep 55	3	–	0:30	No ASTR; shakedown flight; empty water system
02 Sep 55	4	0	3:55	ASTR checkout; non-critical; vibration survey
16 Sep 55	5	–	0:15	Upper hatch opened on takeoff
17 Sep 55	6	1	5:50	ASTR checkout; 1st critical; 5 and 10KW
23 Dec 55	7	–	5:05	Shakedown flight; empty water system
07 Jan 56	8	–	2:15	No data
07 Feb 56	9	–	0:25	No data; engine No. 6 fire warning
13 Feb 56	10	2	8:55	First experiment data flight
21 Feb 56	11	–	0.25	
26 Feb 56	12	3	8:15	Data flight
16 Mar 56	13	–	3:40	Dummy ASTR; instrumentation checkout
29 Mar 56	14	4	4:50	Data flight; cut short due to stuck valves
04 Apr 56	15	–	2:05	No data; gasket leak
07 Apr 56	16	–	3:45	No data; electrical control problems
12 Apr 56	17	–	0:20	No data; shakedown flight for #3 and #4 propellers
13 Apr 56	18	5	8:40	Data flight
25 Apr 56	19	–	0:20	No data; landing gear did not retract
27 Apr 56	20	6	10:10	Data flight
10 May 56	21	–	1:15	No data; C-119 chase broke down
12 May 56	22	7	9:30	Data flight
23 May 56	23	8	10:55	Data flight
13 Jun 56	24	9	9:40	Data flight
22 Jun 56	25	10	9:10	Data flight
29 Jun 56	26	11	7:30	Data flight
31 Jul 56	27	–	2:10	No data; autopilot test and shakedown flight
09 Aug 56	28	–	1:40	No data; autopilot problem
17 Aug 56	29	–	2:00	No data
28 Aug 56	30	–	1:20	No data; autopilot problem
30 Aug 56	31	12	5:20	Data flight
07 Sep 56	32	13	8:35	Data flight
13 Sep 56	33	–	1:10	
26 Sep 56	34	14	8:10	Data flight
11 Oct 56	35	15	6:25	Data flight
26 Oct 56	36	16	7:30	Data flight
27 Oct 56	37	17	6:35	Data flight
22 Nov 56	38	–	2:45	
28 Nov 56	39	18	8:40	Data flight
28 Dec 56	40	19	6:15	Data flight
17 Jan 57	41	–	1:45	
27 Feb 57	42	20	9:05	Data flight; low altitude (400 feet) over Gulf of Mexico
08 Mar 57	43	–	0:25	
09 Mar 57	44	–	0:50	
12 Mar 57	45	–	0:55	
14 Mar 57	46	–	0:30	
28 Mar 57	47	–	8:10	Data flight; last flight of program

215:75 hours total NB-36H flight time (47 flights)
167.0 hours nuclear flight test time (17 flights)
89.0 hours ASTR flight operating "critical" time (21 flights)

The NB-36H (above) on 31 July 1956 during a shakedown flight around Fort Worth. The twin APG-41 radomes (below) remained on the tail, but the turret was replaced by a fiberglass cover with a vent in it. (Lockheed Martin)

A view of the top of the ASTR reactor while it was in its special loading pit on the north end of the Convair reservation in Fort Worth. The remarkably compact device did not provide any power to the B-36. (Lockheed Martin)

in early 1953. By the start of 1955 the aircraft had received its new forward fuselage, and the wiring, tubing, instrument capsule, and crew compartment cooling systems had been completed and installed. The aircraft was redesignated XB-36H on 11 March 1955, and was again redesignated as NB-36H on 6 June 1955. The name *Convair Crusader* was painted on each side of the forward fuselage during the early portion of the test series.[8]

The NB-36H was modified to carry the 1,000-kilowatt air-cooled ASTR in the aft bomb bay and to provide shielding for the crew. The NTA incorporated shielding around the reactor itself and there were also water jackets in the fuselage and behind the crew compartment to absorb radiation. A 4-ton lead disc shield was installed in the middle of the aircraft. The ASTR weighed 35,000 pounds and was installed in a container that could be carried in bomb bay No. 4. A number of large air intakes and exhausts were installed in the sides and bottom of the rear fuselage to cool the reactor. The reactor could be removed from the aircraft while on the ground.

Boral, a metal that contained a sandwich of boron carbide and aluminum was used extensively in the ASTR shielding. Because of the hardness and high abrasive nature of Boral, new techniques had to be developed to drill holes, cut, and form the material. Other new materials developed in support of the ANP program included corrosion-proof stainless steel, leaded glass, and various plastics.[9]

The first flight of the NB-36H was on 17 September 1955, with test pilot A.S. Witchell, Jr. at the controls. Flying alongside the NB-36H on every flight was a C-97 carrying a platoon of armed Marines ready to parachute down and surround the test aircraft in case it crashed. An instrumented B-50D (48-058) also accompanied the NTA on most flights to gather data. A total of 47 flights were made up to March of 1957, although the ASTR reactor was only critical on 21 of them. The flight program showed that the "aircraft normally would pose no threat, even if flying low." The principal concerns would be: (a) accidents which cause the release of fission products from the reactors, and (b) the dosage from exposure to leakage of

The NTA next to the reactor loading pit on 13 July 1955. Note that the fuselage clearly says "XB-36H" and that the "Crusader" is not on the cheat line. This was just a week prior to the first flight of the program. (Lockheed Martin)

A model of the ASTR reactor from the NB-36H. From left to right are the top, right, and left views, respectively. (Lockheed Martin)

radioactivity (in the direct-cycle concept). It was subsequently decided that the risks caused by radiation under normal circumstances were no greater than the risks that had been incurred during the development of steam and electric power, the airplane, the automobile, or the rocket. The consequences of an accident, however, could be severe.

In addition to the NB-36H, Convair developed and built a fair amount of support equipment and facilities in Fort Worth. Special transport and emergency vehicles were built to support the NB-36H and X-6 programs. An entire nuclear complex was built on an isolated area at the extreme north end of the Convair plant.

The NB-36H was decommissioned at Fort Worth in late 1957 and was parked in the nuclear area at the Fort Worth plant pending final disposition. As the B-36 phase-out progressed, the Air Materiel Command (which was in charge of scrapping the B-36s) asked the Air Research and Development Command (which owned the NB-36H) when it could be scrapped. No answer was forthcoming. This complicated the AMC's job since the agreement between AMC and ARDC required that AMC maintain sufficient spares on hand to support the NB-36 in case it was needed again. ARDC finally responded that flying activities had been curtailed due to the general FY58 defense funding issues, and that ARDC planned to restart flight tests in FY59. ARDC requested AMC to take over the responsibility for storing the aircraft at Fort Worth, but AMC responded that estimated storage costs of $13,000 had not been budgeted. Air Force Headquarters subsequently directed ARDC to pay the storage costs since the aircraft was scheduled to be tested again the following year when funds were available. As it turned out, FY59 funds for the NB-36H were not forthcoming, and in September 1958 the aircraft was scrapped at Fort Worth.[10]

X-6

The second flight vehicle envisioned by the ANP program would actually use the reactor to provide power for flight. The B-36 was also to provide the basis for the X-6 since it was the only existing airframe large enough to carry the expected engine and shield weight although

This is not how you are supposed to take off; the upper hatch (below left) is supposed to be closed! On the fifth flight – 15 September 1955 – the upper hatch suddenly opened during the takeoff run, resulting in a shaken crew and paperwork scattered everywhere. The aircraft safely landed 15 minutes later with no permanent effects. The shot in the center shows the hatch (on 15 May 1956) from inside the crew module; the photo at right shows it from outside. This gives a good indication of how thick the shielding was around the crew compartment, and at least partially explains why the interior was so cramped. (Lockheed Martin)

  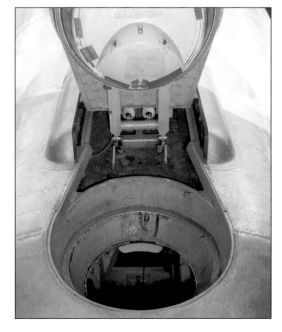

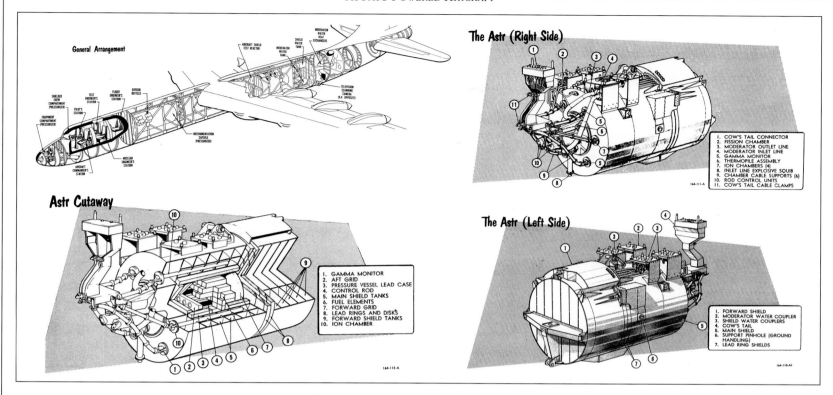

The NB-36H general arrangement is at top, along with three diagrams showing the configuration of the ASTR reactor. (U.S. Air Force)

some consideration was also given to using the two YB-60 airframes.*

At the time, it was expected that the J53 turbojet would form the basis of the X40 direct-cycle atomic-powered engine. The J53 was a high-performance design and it was felt that conversion to nuclear power would present no more difficulty than any other design then in use. The propulsion system would weigh 165,000 pounds, consisting of a 10,000 pound reactor, 60,000 pounds of reactor shielding, 37,000 pounds of crew shielding, and a total engine weight of 18,000 pounds plus an additional 40,000 pounds for ducts and accessories.

The complete X-6 was expected to have a gross takeoff weight of 360,000 pounds. The reactor shield was 60 feet long and 12 feet in diameter, extending basically the entire length of the normal B-36 bomb bays and a 4-inch thick lead gamma shield was installed directly in front of the reactor. Additional side shielding around the reactor was provided by a 2.5-inch thick layer of polyethylene sandwiched between two sheets of aluminum, one of which was the exterior skin.[11]

An additional shield was located on the back of the crew compartment, about 65 feet forward of the reactor. This shield was designed to allow an exposure of 0.25 Roentgen per hour – considerably less than the 1 Roentgen estimated in 1951. The crew compartment itself was identical to the one designed for the NTA with the exception of modified controls and displays to accommodate the new P-1 powerplant.

The four J53/X40 engines were arranged in a horizontal bank under the fuselage slightly forward of the reactor itself. Each engine was positioned so that air from its compressor stage could be ducted straight into the reactor, then be discharged through the engine turbine section. The R-1 reactor was air-cooled and water-moderated, but the water could also serve as additional core coolant if necessary. The core was 5.25 feet in diameter, 3 feet long, contained 143 pounds of enriched Uranium, and weighed a total of 4,000 pounds.

In operations, the X-6 would take off and climb to test altitude using the six R-4360 piston and four J47 turbojet engines (or eight J57s in the case of the YB-60 design). The four X40 engines would be idling using kerosene (JP-4) with the reactor shut down for safety reasons. Once the test altitude was reached, the reactor would be made critical and the four atomic engines would be spooled up using the chemical fuel. Once the X40s were up to speed they would be switched to reactor power and the 10 conventional engines would be shut down or idled (actually, the J47s would probably have been shut down as soon as the desired altitude was reached, as on a normal B-36 flight). When it was time to land, the procedure would be reversed.

As the program progressed, there began to be concerns over the proposed J53 engine. As a result, the Air Force, AEC, and General Electric examined the J47, a proposed GE-X-5-0, the Pratt & Whitney J57-P-5, and the Wright YJ67-W-1. All had drawbacks. The J47 was rejected as not being powerful enough to allow a meaningful

---

* For a much more complete description of the X-6 aircraft, please see Jay Miller, *The X-Planes, X-1 to X-45*, Midland Publishing, April 2001.

Three views of the NB-36H in flight. Note the B-50 (48-058) chase plane in the photo at left, as well as the "Convair Crusader" name on the fuselage of the NB-36H. (Lockheed Martin)

test. The GE-X-5-O was a true paper engine that would require at least 48 months of development. The J57-P-5 was also considered underpowered, but two banks of three engines would probably provide sufficient thrust for the flight-test series. The YJ67 suffered a similar problem, but it was believed that a single bank of five engines would be adequate.

By this time the flight-worthy propulsion package had been designated P-3, but retained the same basic components as the original P-1 installation. The most significant change was that the airflow through the reactor was now back-to-front (compressor air would enter the rear of the reactor), allowing a better center-of-gravity location in the X-6 airframe. The entire R-3 engine package, including the necessary shielding, weighed 140,000 pounds. Assuming the J53/X40

engines could be brought to maturity, a total of 26,000-lbf would propel the X-6 at 300 mph at 15,000 feet.

CANCELLATION

But it was not to be. During early 1953 the Eisenhower Administration determined that a nuclear-powered aircraft had no military value, and Secretary of Defense Charles Wilson did not include the ANP in the FY54 budget. After several weeks of negotiation and compromise, the ANP project avoided complete cancellation, but the X-6 experiment was history. The NB-36H flight tests, however, continued.

Throughout most its life the ANP program was plagued by a lack of direction. Neither the Air Force, the Department of Defense (DoD),

At left is the ASTR reactor being loaded into the NB-36H. The reactor is shown on its stand above center. The unusual shape of the NB-36 nose is shown above left. Below is the B-50D-75-BO instrumentation aircraft (48-058) – note the Holloman A.D.C. badge on the vertical stabilizer. (Lockheed Martin)

nor the AEC maintained a concise set of goals. The Air Force favored the development of an atomic-powered bomber because they wanted to keep manned aircraft an integral part of the deterrent force. Missiles were not showing a great deal of promise and, in fact, the Air Force set the priority for the ANP much higher than that for strategic missiles.[12]

The program was waning when a new motivation rocketed onto the scene, quite literally – the Soviets launched *Sputnik I*. The launch of Sputnik not only started the space race, but also a general techno-logical race. President Eisenhower was urged to speed up the ANP program in order to produce an operational atomic-powered aircraft in answer to the Soviet's space endeavors.

In October 1954, the Strategic Air Command issued a mission requirement for an advanced jet heavy bomber to replace the upcoming B-52 and B-58 beginning in 1965. General LeMay want-ed a bomber that had the range and payload capability of the B-52, combined with the supersonic speed of the B-58. The ARDC responded by issuing Weapon System requirements WS-110A and WS-125A during February 1955. These called for advanced bombers that would have a Mach 0.9 cruise speed to an area some 1,150 miles from their target, then "dash" at Mach 2-plus to the target at high altitude, slowing again to Mach 0.9 for the trip home. The WS-110A was to use conventional jet fuel, while the WS-125A was to be nuclear powered. SAC wanted one, or both, of these advanced bombers to be operational by 1963.

Contracts were awarded to Convair/General Electric and Lockheed/Pratt & Whitney teams in March 1955. The Convair/GE team proposed the NX-2, which used two atomic-powered 55,000-lbf X211 (XJ87) engines along with two conventional turbojets. The com-panies also investigated the possibility of installing chemical (kerosene)-fueled afterburners on the atomic engines, but the exhaust was consid-ered too radioactive for this to work well. The aircraft had a large swept-wing mounted on the aft fuselage and a delta canard mounted far forward. This concept continued for a while in direct competition with the North American XB-70A Valkyrie, but was cancelled in 1956 as technical problems and cost overruns mounted. The concept was revived for a short time as the Continuous Airborne Missile Air Launcher (CAMAL), but this too fell by the wayside during 1958.[13]

Many involved in the ANP program came out in favor of an early flight date to support the WS-125 requirements. Additional impetus came from a spreading rumor that the Soviets had already flown an atomic-powered aircraft. Senator Richard B. Russell from Georgia issued a statement saying: "The report the Russians have test-flown an atomic-powered aircraft is an ominous new threat to world peace, and yet another blow to the prestige and security of our nation and the free world. It follows in tragic sequence the Russian success of last fall in launching the first earth satellite."

On 1 December 1958, *Aviation Week* ran an editorial in which it announced that the Soviets had flown an atomic-powered bomber prototype. This was accompanied by sketches, complete with large red stars, and speculative data. Time has shown this information to be false. There were, however, other rumors. One aircraft, a flying boat, proposed in 1950 would have had a flying weight of 2,000,000 pounds and used four atomic turbo-prop engines. The wing span was more than 420 feet, and the total power of the engines exceeded 500,000 hp. This airplane was supposed to carry 1,000 passengers and 200,000 pounds of cargo at a speed of 450 mph. In fact, the Soviets did modify a Tupolev TU-95 to carry a small reactor for airborne tests much like the NB-36H. A later version was to have been flown using nuclear-powered Kuznetsov turboprop engines, but this never took place.

Ultimately the dwindling federal budget made the Air Force choose between the rather far-fetched WS-125, and the more conven-tional WS-110. The Air Force chose the WS-110, which eventually resulted in the North American XB-70 Valkyrie. In the end the ANP program had simply been around for too long while producing too few results. On 28 March 1961 President Kennedy issued a statement cancelling the ANP program. In it he wrote, "Nearly 15 years and about $1 billion have been devoted to the attempted development of a nuclear-powered aircraft; but the possibility of achieving a militari-ly useful aircraft in the foreseeable future is still very remote."

At the time of cancellation, the total amount spent on atomic air-plane development was $1,040 million, broken down as $839 million for research and development, and $201 million for facilities and equipment. Funding was provided by the Air Force, AEC, and Navy, supplying $518 million, $508 million, and $14 million, respectively.[14]

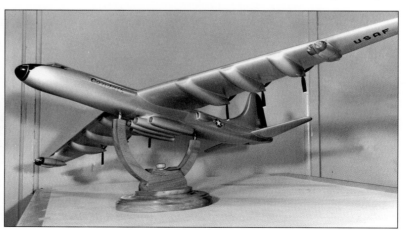

Models of the proposed X-6. The entire reactor/engine assembly could be removed for servicing as shown above. The model at right shows how the engine package would look after it was installed. (Jay Miller Collection)

Chapter 12

Left: *A B-36H-10-CF (51-5704) flies formation with its B-52 replacement.* (Lockheed Martin)

Below: *This Featherweight III B-36H-40-CF (51-5737) was flown to Davis-Monthan in January 1958 and was reclaimed a few months later. The markings on the nose were fairly typical for aircraft of the period, and the white anti-flash paint shows up well here.* (Frank Kleinwechter)

RECLAMATION

The end of the B-36 was much like the beginning – protracted and somewhat confused. It should not have been. By 1953 the Air Force had decided to phase out the B-36 in favor of the new Boeing B-52 Stratofortress. The B-52 promised a quantum leap in performance over the B-36, but it would come at a tremendous cost in time and money, and its development lagged several years. The B-36 was certainly outmoded by mid-1955, but it had served well as SAC's primary strategic bomber and perhaps the major deterrent to Soviet aggression. In February 1956, the B-36 finally began to be replaced by B-52s. However, defense cutbacks in FY57 and FY58 slowed the B-52 procurement process and caused the final phase-out date for the B-36 to be changed from the end of FY57 to the end of FY59.

Nevertheless, the first early model B-36s began arriving at Davis-Monthan AFB, outside Tucson, Arizona, in February 1956. The San Antonio Air Materiel Area (SAAMA) of the Air Materiel Command was responsible for disposing of the retired B-36s, just as it had been responsible for supporting operational B-36s. Over the next 39 months, a two-step process would strip useable parts off the retired aircraft, cut them into manageable pieces, and smelt the metal into ingots. The first step involved the Mar-Pak Corporation and Air Force personnel removing a carefully controlled list of parts from each aircraft that would eventually find use on still-operational B-36s and other aircraft types. The second step used a large guillotine to chop the airframes into small pieces and portable ovens to smelt them into metal ingots.

However, during those 39 months it was not a simple matter of scrapping the aircraft. The delay in B-52 procurement meant that the B-36 would need to serve longer than originally planned. This was complicated by the fact that the procurement of spare parts had been halted in anticipation of the aircraft's retirement, leaving the remaining B-36 squadrons short of some critical components. The need to keep the B-36s operational occurred so abruptly that the contracts with Mar-Pak had to be modified.[1]

Originally, a total of 135 B-36s had been authorized for disposal during FY58 on contract AF33(600)-33903. In August 1957 this number was reduced to 95, at a rate of ten per month. This was a drop in the bucket compared to the quantities of other aircraft being retired – partially due to the defense cutbacks, and partially due to an across-the-board modernization of the Air Force in the post-Korea period. In FY58 alone 3,945 aircraft were scheduled to be disposed of; FY59 showed 1,529 and FY60 had 1,148. All of this presented a problem for the Air Force, particularly the Air Materiel Command, which was responsible for procuring, storing, and transporting spare parts for the operational units. If the economic times had been good, it is likely that retired aircraft would simply have been stripped of major serviceable items (engines, mainly) and cut up for scrap. However, the fiscal crunch forced the Air Force to salvage many more parts from the retired aircraft in order to keep similar operational aircraft flyable. Yet, at the same time, it was not desirable to salvage too many parts, since counting and storing them would have put unacceptable burdens on other parts of the logistics system.[2]

This is reportedly the first B-36 to arrive at Davis-Monthan AFB for reclamation. Note the tail-bumper extended from the aft fuselage, indicating that this was a B-model that had been converted into a B-36D. Interestingly, the aircraft still has the old-style round propeller blade tips. The AASB was not equipped with any of the large maintenance docks, and preparing the aircraft for storage was accomplished using portable work stands and ladders. (Frederick A. Johnsen Collection)

This required a careful juggling act on the part of the Air Force and the personnel on-site at Davis-Monthan. In the case of the B-36, parts could be used not only on other B-36s, but on many other contemporary aircraft. Since they still represented a significant portion of the strategic deterrent, it was essential that the operational portion of the B-36 fleet be maintained until its eventual retirement. Interestingly, most B-36s that arrived at Davis-Monthan did so straight from their last operational sortie.

Various configurations of the basic R-4360 engine used by the B-36 were also used on the B-50, C-97, C-119, and the C-124. As a result of the phase-out of the B-36, 1,218 R-4360-41/41A engines were surplused, the last in December 1959. A further 2,830 R-4360-53 engines became available as later model B-36s were retired, including engines held as spares and war reserves. As the engines became available, personnel from SAAMA began to reclaim crankshafts, cylinders, and other items common to all R-4360 configurations. A total of $22,000 worth of parts were taken off of each R-4360 engine. These parts were then refurbished as needed and utilized by other users, particularly the C-97 and C-124 units. This recycling of parts saved several million dollars during FY58–59.[3]

Left: *All serviceable equipment was removed from the aircraft, along with any "sensitive" equipment such as the Y-3 periscopic bomb sight (shown), gun sights, radar, and other electronics. Since many aircraft were flown to the storage yard directly from their last operational mission, most of this equipment was still installed.* (via Frank Kleinwechter; scan by Don Pyeatt)

Workers from the Mar-Pak Corporation and the AASB remove a R-4360 engine at Davis-Monthan on 4 April 1957. Reclaiming these engines for use on C-124s and other aircraft saved the U.S. Air Force a considerable amount of money. (via Frank Kleinwechter; scan by Don Pyeatt)

After all serviceable and sensitive equipment had been stripped from the aircraft, the carcass was chopped up using a large blade suspended by a crane. The pieces were then loaded into a portable smelter and transformed into ingots on site. (Frederick A. Johnsen Collection)

There were some unexpected requirements for reclaimed B-36 parts. In April 1958 the commander of the 19th Air Division requested SAAMA save 100 crash axes with insulated handles from B-36s being reclaimed. It turned out that the crash axes being procured with the new B-52s were deemed unsatisfactory by the flight crews. Although new axes only cost $7.00 each, there were no funds available to procure them. Salvaging axes from the retired B-36s proved to be the answer, and it is likely that these axes flew with the early model B-52s until they were retired.[4]

In April 1958 Convair was authorized to dispose of all the special tooling required to build and support the B-36 production line at Fort Worth. The value of this tooling was estimated at $500,000, but the Air Force did not want to incur the estimated $20,000 expense to store the tooling until the final B-36 phase out. It was also decided to dispose of 13 all-weather maintenance docks, 7 empennage work stands, and 446 miscellaneous work stands and platforms located in Fort Worth. Past experience had shown that the cost of dismantling such structures by contractor personnel generally exceeded the return generated from selling the scrap – in this case estimated at $38,000 for Convair to perform the work. The Air Force decided instead to solicit bids on a per-pound "as-is/where-is" basis, with all necessary dismantling, loading, and hauling to be at the bidder's risk and expense. A bidder was selected in early June, and by the end of July 1958 all of the material had been removed from the Fort Worth facility. The Air Force realized a profit of $28,051 from the transaction.[5]

Reclamation reached past simply disposing of the aircraft. In 1953 a series of 10 permanent maintenance docks had been installed at Kelly AFB to support the B-36. These docks had originally cost $352,000, and later modifications added another $137,900. By the end of 1958 the docks had been declared excess and SAAMA began a search for any Air Force unit that had potential uses for them. Eventually the San Bernardino Air Materiel Area (SBAMA) inquired if the docks could be modified for use with C-133s. SAAMA engineers determined that they could be used for the new transport aircraft and sent an engineering package to SBAMA for approval. After a long period of silence, SAAMA proceeded with disposing of the docks, partially through donations to local schools and some through sales to contractors (for $700 each). When SBAMA finally did request the docks they were no longer available, although SAAMA found some suitable replacements. All of the docks at Kelly had been disposed of by September 1959.[6]

A total of 385 B-36-type aircraft had been manufactured, including the two original prototypes (XB-36 and YB-36). Of these, 41 had been destroyed or otherwise disposed of during the service life of the type – this included the original XB-36 and the YB-36A. This left 344 aircraft to be reclaimed as the B-36 was phased out of service. SAAMA awarded four separate contracts to Mar-Pak Corporation for the reclamation of these aircraft. The first contract – AF33(600)-33547 – was signed on 30 June 1956 and covered the reclamation of 26 early-model aircraft. The second contract, AF33(600)-33903, was signed on 3 December 1956 and originally covered 135 aircraft. However, the Air Force removed 11 aircraft from this contract and allowed 10 of them to be

The B-36F-1-CF (49-2672) in foreground had not been converted to the Featherweight III configuration – note the deployed top turret. Unlike many aircraft that are held in storage for a prolonged period of time, the B-36s were almost immediately reclaimed – this aircraft arrived in late 1956 and was scrapped during early 1957. (Frederick A. Johnsen)

reclaimed by government personnel to determine if that method was more cost effective. The eleventh aircraft (44-92024) was selected by the Arizona Aircraft Storage Branch (AASB) for extended storage at Davis-Monthan AFB, with the intent of eventually displaying it at the Air Force Museum. After a later B-36J (52-2220) was pulled from the last Mar-Pak contract for display at the Museum, the original aircraft was reclaimed and the carcass transferred to the Davis-Monthan fire department and used as a fire trainer.[7]

The center aircraft is an RB-36H-25-CF (51-13723) with an RB-36F-1-CF (49-2710) behind it in line (to its left in the photo). Both aircraft were among the last group to arrive at Davis-Monthan, and were scrapped during 1959. Note the radomes that covered the DECM and FECM antennas have already been removed. (via Don Pyeatt)

The storage yard at Davis-Monthan showing reclaimed B-36s awaiting the smelter. Note the long row of propellers in the foreground that have been removed from the aircraft. All of the aircraft are missing their R-4360 and J47 engines. (AMARC/Teresa Vanden-Heuvel)

Aerial view of the B-36 area at Davis-Monthan, probably in late 1957 or early 1958. (Jack Kerr via Frank Kleinwechter via Don Pyeatt)

The experiment to determine if it was more economical for personnel from the AASB to reclaim aircraft had some unexpected repercussions. During early 1957 the AASB, eager to increase its usefulness, requested and received permission to reclaim 10 B-36s which were subsequently removed from the second Mar-Pak contract. The reclamation of the 10 aircraft began on 3 June 1957 and was completed on 28 June 1957. The unit cost for reclamation was calculated as $5,193.23 per aircraft. The cost for Mar-Pak to accomplish the same work was $6,000 per aircraft. However, the AASB pointed out that when Mar-Pak did the work, the AASB incurred $1,214 in expenses during the receiving and processing of the aircraft prior to transferring them to Mar-Pak – this made the contractor cost $7,214 – almost 50 percent higher than the AASB cost. If this saving was spread over the remaining 184 B-36s, the total savings to the government was $372,026.12, a considerable amount of money at the time.[8]

After studying the results of the service test and analyzing the cost figures, SAAMA recommended to higher headquarters that AASB be allowed to reclaim the remaining B-36s. Headquarters AMC concurred with the recommendation and on 13 August 1957 advised SAAMA that AASB should conduct further reclamation work at a rate of 10 aircraft per month. However, 18 days later the authorization was rescinded and the AASB was informed that additional contracts should be negotiated with Mar-Pak to accomplish the work. The AASB was restricted to receiving the aircraft and processing them into storage prior to transferring them to Mar-Pak. The mystery behind this sudden reversal was cleared up when it was learned that Congressional pressure had been applied to award the contracts to Mar-Pak.[9]

In support of the Mar-Pak request for reinstatement, cost figures had been compiled by the contractor alleging to prove that the work could be accomplished more economically by Mar-Pak. These figures were in direct contradiction to the figures previously compiled by the AASB – which set of figures was correct was never cleared up. Informal reports indicate that Mar-Pak used long-range cameras that showed up to 50 people working on (or standing near) one B-36 aircraft during the AASB reclamation. This photo was used to allege poor work methods and excessive personnel used by the AASB for the task. If the photos in fact existed the AASB explained they were probably taken during a shift change when people were simply transiting the area and were not directly involved in the ongoing work. It really did not matter – the Ohio congressional delegation had made sure that all future work would go to Mar-Pak. To ensure the AASB could not again try to wrest the work away from Mar-Pak, Headquarters AMC immediately cut the AASB staff by 130 people.[10]

In fairness to Mar-Pak Corporation, it should be noted that the experience gained during the learning-curve on the earlier contract did allow the company to increase the efficiency of the operation and lower costs. It might well be that it was in the best interests of the U.S. Government for the reclamation program to be continued by contract. In any case, it was a moot point.[11]

The signing of the third contract, AF33(600)-35907, had been delayed while the Air Force determined the relative merits of contractor versus Air Force reclamation. When it was finally signed on 16 October 1957, the contract covered the reclamation of 95 aircraft. Subsequently, two supplemental agreements added eight additional aircraft. As it turned out, one of the 103 aircraft on this contract was given to the New Mexico Institute of Mining and Technology at Socorro, New Mexico. The aircraft (51-5720) was slowly dismantled and portions of it used in live weapons effects testing conducted under Navy auspices. As late as 1990 significant portions of the center wing structure remained in the aircraft scrapyard at New Mexico Tech (as the school was subsequently renamed). Members of the restoration team restoring the B-36J at Fort Worth have removed portions of skin from the remains in Socorro for use on their aircraft.[12]

The fourth and final Mar-Pak contract – AF33(600)-37911 – was signed on 31 July 1958 and originally covered 81 aircraft, mostly late-model B/RB-36Hs and B-36Js. Four of the aircraft (51-13730, 52-2217, 52-2220, and 52-2827) were later withdrawn from the contract and given to various museums around the country. The last B-36 was flown to Davis-Monthan on 11 February 1959 from Biggs AFB, and on 24 April 1959 Mar-Pak completed the last reclamation contract. All that remained now was the final smelting of the skeletonized airframes by another contractor.[13]

Mar-Pak (and the AASB in some instances) had been responsible for reclaiming all useful and hazardous equipment from the B-36 airframes. Among the hazardous materials to be removed were 20 separate assemblies that contained minor amounts of radioactive material. It was common practice at the time to use elements such as Radium-226 as a light source for instruments, and to include Thorium-232 in some optical glass. Other Thorium isotopes were also used to impart strength to the magnesium alloys on the B-36, but this was such a trace amount as to be considered inconsequential (it is still used for the same purpose).[14]

ITEM	ISOTOPE	LOCATION
8-Day Clock	Ra-226	Flight Engineer Station
Bomb Bay Setting Gage	Ra-226	Bombardier Station
Bombsight Azimuth	Ra-226	Bombardier Station
Bombsight Housing	Ra-226	Bombardier Station
Bombsight Lens	Th-232	Bombardier Station
Bombsight Sighting Angle	Ra-226	Bombardier Station
Circuit Breaker	Ra-226	Copilot Station
Circuit Breaker (2)	Ra-226	Flight Engineer Station
Long Range Switch	Ra-226	Tail Gunner Station
Oxygen Mask	Ra-226	Navigator Position (left side)
Oxygen Pressure Gage	Ra-226	Radio Operator Compartment
Oxygen Regulator	Ra-226	Throughout Aircraft
Range Switch	Ra-226	Aft Left Gunner Station
Range Switch	Ra-226	Aft Right Gunner Station
Switch	Ra-226	Pilot Overhead (right side)
Switch	Ra-226	Pilot Console
Tachometer	Ra-226	Pilot Panel (left side)
Target Switch	Ra-226	Tail Gunner Station
Tune For Max	Ra-226	Navigator Station

The carcasses then needed to be smelted into ingot form in order to recycle the metals. The smelting was accomplished on-site at Davis-Monthan by various contractors. For instance, a total of 95 carcasses were sold to Page Airways for $8,751 each. However, Page could only sell the residual metal for $4,000 per aircraft, and the contractor submitted a claim to recover the $452,675 loss they incurred on the contract. Page subsequently was awarded other contracts covering the smelting of the remaining carcasses, but in this instance Page was reimbursed only for the labor involved and all metals and other residue remained the property of the Government.[15]

As of 1 July 1957, the value of all assets that had been reclaimed from B-36s totaled $53,541,682.22; $36.5 million of this represented material that had direct application to other aircraft in the Air Force inventory. Expenses incurred by the Air Force and Mar-Pak totaled $1,125,927.34, as well as an additional $209,271.50 in transportation costs.

A year later the total value of reclaimed assets had climbed to $108,243,731.28, and another year later amounted to $159,030,324.17, exclusive of reclamation and transportation costs. An additional savings of $39,580,155.75 was realized by not procuring items (i.e., using reclaimed parts) for various aircraft types. The total cost to reclaim the B-36 assets were placed at $2,812,434.87, with $4,125,347.01 being spent to repair the parts and put them into a serviceable condition. Transportation added $450,645.96 to this total. This represented an actual return to the Government of $151,641,896.33 – almost 10 percent of the roughly $1,532 million cost of the B-36 procurement.

The remains of 51-5720 at New Mexico Tech (formerly the Institute of Mining and Technology) at Socorro, New Mexico. This shows part of one wing, upside down, with the internal ducting from the leading edge (at left) to the engine. (Wendell Montague)

An overall view of one of the junk yards at New Mexico Tech showing various parts of B-29s and external fuel tanks, as well as the remains of 51-5720 (circled). The aircraft were used in ballistic survivability studies conducted under Navy auspices. (Wendell Montague)

The forward fuselage of B-36H-25-CF (51-5720) was rescued from Socorro and displayed at the Ontario Air Museum (now the Planes of Fame). Here, a young aviation historian Frederick A. Johnsen is seen posing in front of it during September 1969. Unfortunately, over the years the section was heavily vandalized in the loosely-guarded museum. The remains were sold to David Tallichet in 1975 for possible use at a new museum, but this never happened and the section was scrapped sometime during the late 1970s. (Kenneth G. Johnsen)

Seen during reclamation at Davis-Monthan during early 1959, this Featherweight III RB-36H-15-CF (51-5748) had been modified to photograph high-altitude atomic airburst tests. Note the row of camera ports on the upper forward fuselage, and the enlarged forward blister opening. No photo could be located of this aircraft during operations and little is known of what it did, but it is known that it photographed one airburst 86,000 feet over the Pacific test range. A second RB-36H (51-5750) was similarly modified. (via Frank Kleinwechter; scanned by Don Pyeatt)

The YB-36 (42-13571) – rebuilt as an RB-36E – was the original aircraft selected for display at the old Air Force Museum at Wright-Patterson AFB. For unexplained reasons, several sections of skin are missing off the forward fuselage and wing leading edge in two of the photos below. Also note the FICON YF-84F and XF-85 in the photos below. When the Museum received the B-36J that is currently on display, the RB-36E was "demilitarized" using a bulldozer, and in 1971 the remains sold to Ralph Huffman for $760. The parts were then sold to Walter Soplata who moved them to his farm in nearby Newbury, Ohio. What is left of the aircraft still exists on Soplata's farm, although the bulldozer and 30 years of weather have taken their toll. (left: William J. Balogh, Sr. via Dave Menard; below left: Frederick A. Johnsen Collection; center via Richard Marmo; right: via Don Pyeatt)

Appendices

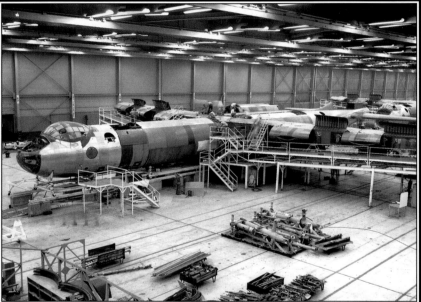

Left: *The jet demonstrator (44-92057) takes shape on the assembly line as a B-36B-10-CF. Note the sliding door covering bomb bay No. 1 – the doors were not changed until the aircraft went through the B-to-D conversion in early 1951.* (Lockheed Martin)

Right: *A bunch of B-36A forward fuselages await being remanufactured into RB-36Es. The area around bomb bay No. 1 would be completely removed and a new camera compartment would be added in its place. Note that some aircraft have astrodomes on top of the cockpit while others do not.* (Lockheed Martin)

SERIAL NUMBERS

Cum No.	CVAC No.	Serial Number	Lot No.	As-Built Configuration	Contract Number	Accepted by Air Force	Final Configuration	Featherweight Configuration	Final Disposition (Contract No. if scrapped)	Notes
1	–	42-13570	1	XB-36-CF	W535-ac-22352	Jun 48		—	Used as fire trainer at Carswell	
2	"YB"	42-13571	1	YB-36-CF	W535-ac-22352	May 49	RB-36E-5-CF	III	Scrapped in 1971 at the Air Force Museum	First aircraft through SAM-SAC; retired to Air Force Museum; remains saved by Walter Soplata in Ohio
–	–	43-52436	–	XC-99-1-CO	W535-ac-34454	May 49		—	Donated to Disabled American Veterans	In storage at former Kelly AFB
3	1	44-92004	1	B-36A-1-CF	AF33-038-AC7	Aug 47	YB-36A-1-CF	—	Tested to Destruction at W-P AFB	First production four-wheel main gear
4	2	44-92005	1	B-36A-1-CF	AF33-038-AC7	May 48	RB-36E-10-CF	III	Scrapped by Mar-Pak, FY57 [AF33(600)33903]	
5	3	44-92006	1	B-36A-1-CF	AF33-038-AC7	Jun 48	RB-36E-5-CF	III	Scrapped by Mar-Pak, FY57 [AF33(600)33903]	
6	4	44-92007	2	B-36A-5-CF	AF33-038-AC7	Jun 48	RB-36E-5-CF	III	Scrapped by Mar-Pak, FY57 [AF33(600)33903]	According to some Convair documentation, the first 13 airplanes on contract AC7 were originally designated YB-36.
7	5	44-92008	2	B-36A-5-CF	AF33-038-AC7	Jun 48	RB-36E-1-CF	III	Scrapped by Mar-Pak, FY57 [AF33(600)33903]	
8	6	44-92009	2	B-36A-5-CF	AF33-038-AC7	Jun 48	RB-36E-5-CF	III	Scrapped by Mar-Pak, FY57 [AF33(600)33903]	
9	7	44-92010	2	B-36A-5-CF	AF33-038-AC7	Jun 48	RB-36E-1-CF	III	Scrapped by Mar-Pak, FY57 [AF33(600)33903]	
10	8	44-92011	2	B-36A-5-CF	AF33-038-AC7	Jul 48	RB-36E-5-CF	III	Scrapped by Mar-Pak, FY57 [AF33(600)33903]	
11	9	44-92012	3	B-36A-10-CF	AF33-038-AC7	Jul 48	RB-36E-5-CF	III	Scrapped by Mar-Pak, FY57 [AF33(600)33903]	
12	10	44-92013	3	B-36A-10-CF	AF33-038-AC7	Jul 48	RB-36E-5-CF	II	Scrapped by Mar-Pak, FY57 [AF33(600)33903]	
13	11	44-92014	3	B-36A-10-CF	AF33-038-AC7	Jul 48	RB-36E-5-CF	II	Scrapped by Mar-Pak, FY57 [AF33(600)33903]	
14	12	44-92015	3	B-36A-10-CF	AF33-038-AC7	Jul 48	RB-36E-5-CF	II	Scrapped by Mar-Pak, FY57 [AF33(600)33903]	First to SAC; Original *City of Fort Worth*
15	13	44-92016	3	B-36A-10-CF	AF33-038-AC7	Aug 48	RB-36E-5-CF	II	Scrapped by Mar-Pak, FY57 [AF33(600)33903]	
16	14	44-92017	3	B-36A-10-CF	AF33-038-AC7	Aug 48	RB-36E-10-CF	II	Scrapped by Mar-Pak, FY57 [AF33(600)33903]	Second to SAC
17	15	44-92018	4	B-36A-15-CF	AF33-038-AC7	Aug 48	RB-36E-10-CF	II	Scrapped by Mar-Pak, FY57 [AF33(600)33903]	
18	16	44-92019	4	B-36A-15-CF	AF33-038-AC7	Aug 48	RB-36E-10-CF	II	Scrapped by Mar-Pak, FY57 [AF33(600)33903]	Operation Pinocchio
19	17	44-92020	4	B-36A-15-CF	AF33-038-AC7	Sep 48	RB-36E-10-CF	II	Scrapped by Mar-Pak, FY57 [AF33(600)33903]	
20	18	44-92021	4	B-36A-15-CF	AF33-038-AC7	Sep 48	RB-36E-10-CF	III	Scrapped by Mar-Pak, FY57 [AF33(600)33903]	
21	19	44-92022	4	B-36A-15-CF	AF33-038-AC7	Sep 48	RB-36E-10-CF	II	Scrapped by Mar-Pak, FY57 [AF33(600)33903]	
22	20	44-92023	4	B-36A-15-CF	AF33-038-AC7	Sep 48	RB-36E-10-CF	II	Scrapped by Mar-Pak, FY57 [AF33(600)33903]	
23	21	44-92024	4	B-36A-15-CF	AF33-038-AC7	Sep 48	RB-36E-1-CF	—	Used as fire trainer at Davis-Monthan	
24	22	44-92025	4	B-36A-15-CF	AF33-038-AC7	Feb 49	RB-36E-10-CF	II	Scrapped by Mar-Pak, FY57 [AF33(600)33903]	
25	23	44-92026	5	B-36B-1-CF	AF33-038-AC7	?	B-36D-10-CF	III	Scrapped by Mar-Pak, FY56 [AF33(600)33547]	Propeller vibration tests; converted at Ft. Worth
26	24	44-92027	5	B-36B-1-CF	AF33-038-AC7	?	B-36D-20-CF	III	Scrapped by Mar-Pak, FY56 [AF33(600)33547]	
27	25	44-92028	5	B-36B-1-CF	AF33-038-AC7	?	B-36D-30-CF	III	Scrapped by Mar-Pak, FY56 [AF33(600)33547]	
28	26	44-92029	5	B-36B-1-CF	AF33-038-AC7	?	B-36D-30-CF	III	Written Off 08 Feb 55	
29	27	44-92030	5	B-36B-1-CF	AF33-038-AC7	?	B-36D-20-CF	II	Written Off 06 Mar 55	
30	28	44-92031	5	B-36B-1-CF	AF33-038-AC7	?	B-36D-30-CF	II	Scrapped by Mar-Pak, FY56 [AF33(600)33547]	
31	29	44-92032	5	B-36B-1-CF	AF33-038-AC7	?	B-36D-15-CF	II	Written Off 29 Mar 54	Converted at Ft. Worth
32	30	44-92033	5	B-36B-1-CF	AF33-038-AC7	?	B-36D-50-CF	II	Scrapped by Mar-Pak, FY57 [AF33(600)33903]	
33	31	44-92034	5	B-36B-1-CF	AF33-038-AC7	?	B-36D-10-CF	II	Scrapped by Mar-Pak, FY57 [AF33(600)33903]	
34	32	44-92035	5	B-36B-1-CF	AF33-038-AC7	?		—	Written Off 22 Nov 50	
35	33	44-92036	5	B-36B-1-CF	AF33-038-AC7	?	B-36D-30-CF	III	Scrapped by Mar-Pak, FY57 [AF33(600)33903]	
36	34	44-92037	5	B-36B-1-CF	AF33-038-AC7	Dec 48	B-36D-40-CF	II	Scrapped by Mar-Pak, FY56 [AF33(600)33547]	
37	35	44-92038	6	B-36B-5-CF	AF33-038-AC7	Dec 48	B-36D-10-CF	—	Written Off 12 Jun 52	
38	36	44-92039	6	B-36B-5-CF	AF33-038-AC7	Dec 48	B-36D-20-CF	III	Scrapped by Mar-Pak, FY57 [AF33(600)33903]	
39	37	44-92040	6	B-36B-5-CF	AF33-038-AC7	Dec 48	B-36D-20-CF	III	Scrapped by Mar-Pak, FY57 [AF33(600)33903]	
40	38	44-92041	6	B-36B-5-CF	AF33-038-AC7	Dec 48	B-36D-30-CF	III	Written Off 10 Jan 56	
41	39	44-92042	6	B-36B-5-CF	AF33-038-AC7	Dec 48	B-36D-40-CF	III	Scrapped by Mar-Pak, FY56 [AF33(600)33547]	
42	40	44-92043	6	B-36B-5-CF	AF33-038-AC7	Dec 48	B-36D-10-CF	II	Scrapped by Mar-Pak, FY56 [AF33(600)33547]	First B-to-D conversion at San Diego
43	41	44-92044	6	B-36B-5-CF	AF33-038-AC7	Dec 48	B-36D-30-CF	III	Scrapped by Mar-Pak, FY57 [AF33(600)33903]	
44	42	44-92045	6	B-36B-5-CF	AF33-038-AC7	Feb 49	B-36D-30-CF	III	Scrapped by Mar-Pak, FY57 [AF33(600)33903]	
45	43	44-92046	6	B-36B-5-CF	AF33-038-AC7	Jan 51	B-36D-45-CF	III	Scrapped by Mar-Pak, FY56 [AF33(600)33547]	High-altitude tests with J47 engines
46	44	44-92047	6	B-36B-5-CF	AF33-038-AC7	Feb 49	B-36D-40-CF	II	Scrapped by Mar-Pak, FY56 [AF33(600)33547]	
47	45	44-92048	6	B-36B-5-CF	AF33-038-AC7	Feb 49	B-36D-10-CF	II	Scrapped by Mar-Pak, FY57 [AF33(600)33903]	
48	46	44-92049	6	B-36B-5-CF	AF33-038-AC7	Jan 49	B-36D-10-CF	III	Scrapped by Mar-Pak, FY56 [AF33(600)33547]	
49	47	44-92050	7	B-36B-10-CF	AF33-038-AC7	Mar 49	B-36D-40-CF	—	Written Off 15 Apr 52	
50	48	44-92051	7	B-36B-10-CF	AF33-038-AC7	Mar 49	B-36D-10-CF	—	Written Off 01 Sep 52	Unrepairable tornado damage at Carswell AFB

Cum No.	CVAC No.	Serial Number	Lot No.	As-Built Configuration	Contract Number	Accepted by Air Force	Final Configuration	Featherweight Configuration	Final Disposition (Contract No. if scrapped)	Notes
51	49	44-92052	7	B-36B-10-CF	AF33-038-AC7	Mar 49	B-36D-30-CF	III	Scrapped by Mar-Pak, FY57 [AF33(600)33903]	
52	50	44-92053	7	B-36B-10-CF	AF33-038-AC7	Apr 49	B-36D-10-CF	III	Scrapped by Mar-Pak, FY57 [AF33(600)33903]	Converted at Ft. Worth
53	51	44-92054	7	B-36B-10-CF	AF33-038-AC7	Apr 49	B-36D-10-CF	—	Scrapped by Mar-Pak, FY58 [AF33(600)35907]	Dedicated armament test aircraft; -53 engine testbed; converted at Ft. Worth
54	52	44-92055	7	B-36B-10-CF	AF33-038-AC7	Jun 49	B-36D-40-CF	III	Scrapped by Mar-Pak, FY57 [AF33(600)33903]	
55	53	44-92056	7	B-36B-10-CF	AF33-038-AC7	Jun 49	B-36D-40-CF	II	Scrapped by Mar-Pak, FY57 [AF33(600)33903]	
56	54	44-92057	7	B-36B-10-CF	AF33-038-AC7	Jan 51	B-36D-40-CF	II	Scrapped by Mar-Pak, FY57 [AF33(600)33903]	Flight test J35 and J47 engine survey; 4-blade propeller vibration test; -53 engine tests
57	55	44-92058	7	B-36B-10-CF	AF33-038-AC7	Jun 50	B-36D-20-CF	II	Scrapped by Mar-Pak, FY57 [AF33(600)33903]	Defensive armament tests
58	56	44-92059	7	B-36B-10-CF	AF33-038-AC7	Jan 49	B-36D-40-CF	II	Scrapped by Mar-Pak, FY57 [AF33(600)33903]	
59	57	44-92060	7	B-36B-10-CF	AF33-038-AC7	Aug 49	B-36D-40-CF	II	Scrapped by Mar-Pak, FY57 [AF33(600)33903]	
60	58	44-92061	7	B-36B-10-CF	AF33-038-AC7	Jul 49	B-36D-40-CF	III	Scrapped by Mar-Pak, FY56 [AF33(600)33547]	
61	59	44-92062	7	B-36B-10-CF	AF33-038-AC7	Jul 49	B-36D-45-CF	III	Scrapped by Mar-Pak, FY56 [AF33(600)33547]	
62	60	44-92063	7	B-36B-10-CF	AF33-038-AC7	Jul 49	B-36D-40-CF	III	Scrapped by Mar-Pak, FY56 [AF33(600)33547]	
63	61	44-92064	7	B-36B-10-CF	AF33-038-AC7	Jul 49	B-36D-30-CF	II	Scrapped by Mar-Pak, FY57 [AF33(600)33903]	
64	62	44-92065	8	B-36B-15-CF	AF33-038-AC7	Aug 49	B-36D-45-CF	II	Scrapped by Mar-Pak, FY57 [AF33(600)33903]	
65	63	44-92066	8	B-36B-15-CF	AF33-038-AC7	Aug 49	B-36D-45-CF	III	Scrapped by Mar-Pak, FY56 [AF33(600)33547]	
66	64	44-92067	8	B-36B-15-CF	AF33-038-AC7	Aug 49	B-36D-45-CF	II	Scrapped by Mar-Pak, FY57 [AF33(600)33903]	
67	65	44-92068	8	B-36B-15-CF	AF33-038-AC7	Sep 49	B-36D-45-CF	II	Scrapped by Mar-Pak, FY57 [AF33(600)33903]	
68	66	44-92069	8	B-36B-15-CF	AF33-038-AC7	Oct 49	B-36D-45-CF	—	Written Off 27 Feb 54	
69	67	44-92070	8	B-36B-15-CF	AF33-038-AC7	Oct 49	B-36D-45-CF	II	Scrapped by Mar-Pak, FY57 [AF33(600)33903]	
70	68	44-92071	8	B-36B-15-CF	AF33-038-AC7	Dec 49	B-36D-45-CF	—	Written Off 11 Dec 53	
71	69	44-92072	8	B-36B-15-CF	AF33-038-AC7	Jun 49	B-36D-30-CF	II	Scrapped by Mar-Pak, FY56 [AF33(600)33547]	Defensive armament tests; K-System tests
72	70	44-92073	8	B-36B-15-CF	AF33-038-AC7	Jul 49	B-36D-50-CF	III	Scrapped by Mar-Pak, FY57 [AF33(600)33903]	
73	71	44-92074	8	B-36B-15-CF	AF33-038-AC7	Jul 49	B-36D-45-CF	II	Scrapped by Mar-Pak, FY57 [AF33(600)33903]	
74	72	44-92075	8	B-36B-15-CF	AF33-038-AC7	Aug 49		—	Written Off 14 Feb 50	
75	73	44-92076	8	B-36B-15-CF	AF33-038-AC7	Jul 49	B-36D-50-CF	III	Scrapped by Mar-Pak, FY57 [AF33(600)33903]	
76	74	44-92077	8	B-36B-15-CF	AF33-038-AC7	Aug 49	B-36D-50-CF	II	Scrapped by Mar-Pak, FY57 [AF33(600)33903]	
77	75	44-92078	8	B-36B-15-CF	AF33-038-AC7	Aug 49	B-36D-50-CF	II	Scrapped by Mar-Pak, FY57 [AF33(600)33903]	
78	76	44-92079	8	B-36B-15-CF	AF33-038-AC7	Aug 49		—	Written Off 15 Sep 49	First B-36 to be lost
79	77	44-92080	8	B-36B-20-CF	AF33-038-AC7	Aug 49	B-36D-45-CF	—	Written Off 29 Jan 52	
80	78	44-92081	9	B-36B-20-CF	AF33-038-AC7	Aug 49	B-36D-50-CF	II	Scrapped by Mar-Pak, FY57 [AF33(600)33903]	Last B-to-D conversion in San Diego
81	79	44-92082	9	B-36B-20-CF	AF33-038-AC7	Sep 49	B-36D-50-CF	III	Scrapped by Mar-Pak, FY57 [AF33(600)33903]	
82	80	44-92083	9	B-36B-20-CF	AF33-038-AC7	Sep 49	B-36D-50-CF	II	Scrapped by Mar-Pak, FY57 [AF33(600)33903]	
83	81	44-92084	9	B-36B-20-CF	AF33-038-AC7	Oct 49	B-36D-50-CF	II	Scrapped by Mar-Pak, FY57 [AF33(600)33903]	
84	82	44-92085	9	B-36B-20-CF	AF33-038-AC7	Jan 50	B-36D-45-CF	III	Scrapped by Mar-Pak, FY57 [AF33(600)33903]	
85	83	44-92086	9	B-36B-20-CF	AF33-038-AC7	Feb 49	B-36D-50-CF	II	Scrapped by Mar-Pak, FY57 [AF33(600)33903]	
86	84	44-92087	9	B-36B-20-CF	AF33-038-AC7	Apr 51	B-36D-45-CF	II	Scrapped by Mar-Pak, FY57 [AF33(600)33903]	Defensive armament tests; wing structure integrity evaluations
87	85	44-92088	9	RB-36D-1-CF	AF33-038-AC7	Dec 49	ERB-36D-1-CF	—	Scrapped at Kelly AFB, FY55	Ordered as B-36B; modified to carry the "Boston Camera"
88	86	44-92089	9	RB-36D-1-CF	AF33-038-AC7	Dec 49		III	Scrapped by Mar-Pak, FY57 [AF33(600)33903]	Ordered as B-36B
89	87	44-92090	9	RB-36D-1-CF	AF33-038-AC7	Jan 50	GRB-36D-1-CF	III	Scrapped by Mar-Pak, FY57 [AF33(600)33903]	Ordered as B-36B; accelerated service tests
90	88	44-92091	9	RB-36D-1-CF	AF33-038-AC7	Feb 50		II	Scrapped by Mar-Pak, FY57 [AF33(600)33903]	Ordered as B-36B
91	89	44-92092	9	RB-36D-1-CF	AF33-038-AC7	Jun 50	GRB-36D-1-CF	III	Scrapped by Mar-Pak, FY57 [AF33(600)33903]	Ordered as B-36B
92	90	44-92093	9	RB-36D-1-CF	AF33-038-AC7	Jun 50		II	Scrapped by Mar-Pak, FY57 [AF33(600)33903]	Ordered as B-36B
93	91	44-92094	9	RB-36D-1-CF	AF33-038-AC7	Jul 50	GRB-36D-1-CF	III	Scrapped by Mar-Pak, FY57 [AF33(600)33903]	Ordered as B-36B
94	92	44-92095	9	B-36D-1-CF	AF33-038-AC7	Apr 50		III	Scrapped by Mar-Pak, FY56 [AF33(600)33547]	Ordered as B-36B; E-5 autopilot tests
95	93	44-92096	9	B-36D-1-CF	AF33-038-AC7	Jul 50		III	Scrapped by Mar-Pak, FY56 [AF33(600)33547]	Ordered as B-36B; propeller vibration tests
96	94	44-92097	9	B-36D-1-CF	AF33-038-AC7	Jul 50		—	Written Off 28 Aug 54	Ordered as B-36B
97	95	44-92098	9	B-36D-1-CF	AF33-038-AC7	Aug 50		II	Scrapped by Mar-Pak, FY57 [AF33(600)33903]	Ordered as B-36B
98	96	49-2647	10	B-36D-5-CF	AF33-038-2182	Aug 50		III	Scrapped by Mar-Pak, FY56 [AF33(600)33547]	
99	97	49-2648	10	B-36D-5-CF	AF33-038-2182	Jul 50		III	Scrapped by Mar-Pak, FY56 [AF33(600)33547]	E-6 autopilot tests; prop vibration tests
100	98	49-2649	10	B-36D-5-CF	AF33-038-2182	Aug 50		II	Scrapped by Mar-Pak, FY56 [AF33(600)33547]	
101	99	49-2650	10	B-36D-5-CF	AF33-038-2182	Sep 50		III	Scrapped by Mar-Pak, FY56 [AF33(600)33547]	
102	101	49-2651	10	B-36D-5-CF	AF33-038-2182	Sep 50		III	Scrapped by Mar-Pak, FY57 [AF33(600)33903]	
103	102	49-2652	10	B-36D-5-CF	AF33-038-2182	Aug 50		III	Scrapped by Mar-Pak, FY57 [AF33(600)33903]	Named *Pretty Girl*
104	103	49-2653	10	B-36D-5-CF	AF33-038-2182	Aug 50		III	Written Off 28 Jun 55	Nuclear "effects" aircraft for Operations IVY, UPSHOT-KNOTHOLE, and CASTLE; named *Ruptured Duck!*
105	104	49-2654	10	B-36D-5-CF	AF33-038-2182	Aug 50		III	Scrapped by Mar-Pak, FY57 [AF33(600)33903]	
106	135	49-2655	12	B-36D-35-CF	AF33-038-2182	Apr 51		III	Scrapped by Mar-Pak, FY57 [AF33(600)33903]	Crew comfort prototype prior to delivery
107	110	49-2656	11	B-36D-15-CF	AF33-038-2182	Nov 50		III	Scrapped by Mar-Pak, FY57 [AF33(600)33903]	
108	111	49-2657	11	B-36D-15-CF	AF33-038-2182	Nov 50		II	Scrapped by Mar-Pak, FY56 [AF33(600)33547]	
109	115	49-2658	12	B-36D-25-CF	AF33-038-2182	Aug 50		—	Written Off 27 Apr 51	
110	116	49-2659	12	B-36D-25-CF	AF33-038-2182	Jan 51		II	Scrapped by Mar-Pak, FY56 [AF33(600)33547]	
111	117	49-2660	12	B-36D-25-CF	AF33-038-2182	Sep 50		—	Written Off 06 May 51	
112	121	49-2661	12	B-36D-25-CF	AF33-038-2182	Jan 51		—	Written Off 05 Aug 52	
113	122	49-2662	12	B-36D-25-CF	AF33-038-2182	Jan 51		II	Scrapped by Mar-Pak, FY57 [AF33(600)33903]	

44-92099 through 44-92103 (5 airplanes) on contract AF33-038-AC7 were cancelled to pay for the stillborn B-36C project.

Cum No.	CVAC No.	Serial Number	Lot No.	As-Built Configuration	Contract Number	Accepted by Air Force	Final Configuration	Featherweight Configuration	Final Disposition (Contract No. if scrapped)	Notes
114	123	49-2663	12	B-36D-25-CF	AF33-038-2182	Mar 51		III	Scrapped by Mar-Pak, FY56 [AF33(600)33547]	
115	127	49-2664	12	B-36D-35-CF	AF33-038-2182	Mar 51		III	Scrapped by Mar-Pak, FY56 [AF33(600)33547]	
116	128	49-2665	12	B-36D-35-CF	AF33-038-2182	Mar 51		III	Scrapped by Mar-Pak, FY57 [AF33(600)33903]	
117	129	49-2666	12	B-36D-35-CF	AF33-038-2182	Mar 51		II	Scrapped by Mar-Pak, FY57 [AF33(600)33903]	
118	133	49-2667	12	B-36D-35-CF	AF33-038-2182	Mar 51		III	Scrapped by Mar-Pak, FY57 [AF33(600)33903]	
119	134	49-2668	12	B-36D-35-CF	AF33-038-2182	Apr 51		II	Scrapped by Mar-Pak, FY56 [AF33(600)33547]	
120	109	49-2669	11	B-36F-1-CF	AF33-038-2182	Apr 51		III	Scrapped by Mar-Pak, FY58 [AF33(600)35907]	−53 engine tests; F-model prototype
121	139	49-2670	13	B-36F-1-CF	AF33-038-2182	Aug 51		II	Scrapped by Mar-Pak, FY57 [AF33(600)33903]	
122	140	49-2671	13	B-36F-1-CF	AF33-038-2182	Aug 51		II	Scrapped by Mar-Pak, FY57 [AF33(600)33903]	First F-model delivered to the Air Force
123	141	49-2672	13	B-36F-1-CF	AF33-038-2182	Aug 51		II	Scrapped by AASB FY57 [Project A-7-5014-SB]	
124	145	49-2673	13	B-36F-1-CF	AF33-038-2182	Aug 51		II	Scrapped by Mar-Pak, FY57 [AF33(600)33903]	
125	146	49-2674	13	B-36F-1-CF	AF33-038-2182	Sep 51		II	Scrapped by AASB FY57 [Project A-7-5014-SB]	
126	147	49-2675	13	B-36F-1-CF	AF33-038-2182	Jul 51		II	Scrapped by AASB FY57 [Project A-7-5014-SB]	
127	151	49-2676	13	YB-60-1-CF	AF33-038-2182	Jul 54		—	Scrapped at Carswell AFB, July 1954	Ordered as B-36F; redesignated B-36G, then YB-60
128	152	49-2677	13	B-36F-1-CF	AF33-038-2182	Aug 51		II	Scrapped by Mar-Pak, FY58 [AF33(600)35907]	Carried B-58 static test article
129	153	49-2678	14	B-36F-5-CF	AF33-038-2182	Aug 51		II	Scrapped by Mar-Pak, FY57 [AF33(600)33903]	
130	157	49-2679	14	B-36F-5-CF	AF33-038-2182	Sep 51		II	Written Off 04 Aug 52	
131	158	49-2680	14	B-36F-5-CF	AF33-038-2182	Sep 51		II	Scrapped by Mar-Pak, FY57 [AF33(600)33903]	
132	159	49-2681	14	B-36F-5-CF	AF33-038-2182	Sep 51		II	Scrapped by AASB FY57 [Project A-7-5014-SB]	
133	163	49-2682	14	B-36F-5-CF	AF33-038-2182	Jan 52		II	Scrapped by Mar-Pak, FY57 [AF33(600)33903]	ECP983AQ prototype
134	164	49-2683	14	B-36F-5-CF	AF33-038-2182	Aug 51		II	Scrapped by AASB FY57 [Project A-7-5014-SB]	
135	165	49-2684	14	YB-60-2-CF	AF33-038-2182	Jul 54		—	Scrapped at Carswell AFB, July 1954	Ordered as B-36F; redesignated B-36G, then YB-60; never flew
136	170	49-2685	14	B-36F-5-CF	AF33-038-2182	Oct 52		II	Scrapped by Mar-Pak, FY57 [AF33(600)33903]	
137	100	49-2686	10	RB-36D-5-CF	AF33-038-2182	Sep 50		II	Scrapped by Mar-Pak, FY57 [AF33(600)33903]	
138	105	49-2687	11	RB-36D-10-CF	AF33-038-2182	Dec 50	GRB-36D-10-CF	III	Scrapped by Mar-Pak, FY57 [AF33(600)33903]	
139	106	49-2688	11	RB-36D-10-CF	AF33-038-2182	Sep 50		II	Scrapped by Mar-Pak, FY57 [AF33(600)33903]	
140	107	49-2689	11	RB-36D-10-CF	AF33-038-2182	Jan 51		II	Scrapped by Mar-Pak, FY57 [AF33(600)33903]	
141	108	49-2690	11	RB-36D-10-CF	AF33-038-2182	Oct 50		II	Scrapped by Mar-Pak, FY57 [AF33(600)33903]	
142	112	49-2691	11	RB-36D-10-CF	AF33-038-2182	Nov 50		II	Scrapped by Mar-Pak, FY57 [AF33(600)33903]	
143	113	49-2692	11	RB-36D-10-CF	AF33-038-2182	Nov 50	GRB-36D-10-CF	III	Scrapped by Mar-Pak, FY57 [AF33(600)33903]	
144	114	49-2693	11	RB-36D-10-CF	AF33-038-2182	Nov 50		II	Scrapped by Mar-Pak, FY57 [AF33(600)33903]	
145	118	49-2694	12	RB-36D-15-CF	AF33-038-2182	Jan 51	GRB-36D-15-CF	III	Scrapped by Mar-Pak, FY57 [AF33(600)33903]	
146	119	49-2695	12	RB-36D-15-CF	AF33-038-2182	Dec 50	GRB-36D-15-CF	III	Scrapped by Mar-Pak, FY57 [AF33(600)33903]	
147	120	49-2696	12	RB-36D-15-CF	AF33-038-2182	Mar 51	GRB-36D-15-CF	III	Scrapped by Mar-Pak, FY57 [AF33(600)33903]	First production FICON carrier
148	124	49-2697	12	RB-36D-15-CF	AF33-038-2182	Mar 51		II	Scrapped by Mar-Pak, FY57 [AF33(600)33903]	
149	125	49-2698	12	RB-36D-20-CF	AF33-038-2182	Mar 51		II	Scrapped by Mar-Pak, FY57 [AF33(600)33903]	
150	126	49-2699	12	RB-36D-20-CF	AF33-038-2182	Apr 51		II	Scrapped by Mar-Pak, FY57 [AF33(600)33903]	
151	130	49-2700	12	RB-36D-20-CF	AF33-038-2182	Apr 51		II	Scrapped by Mar-Pak, FY57 [AF33(600)33903]	
152	131	49-2701	12	RB-36D-20-CF	AF33-038-2182	Apr 51	GRB-36D-20-CF	III	Scrapped by Mar-Pak, FY57 [AF33(600)33903]	
153	132	49-2702	12	RB-36D-20-CF	AF33-038-2182	Apr 51	GRB-36D-20-CF	III	Scrapped by Mar-Pak, FY57 [AF33(600)33903]	
154	136	49-2703	13	RB-36F-1-CF	AF33-038-2182	Jul 51		II	Scrapped by Mar-Pak, FY59 [AF33(600)37911]	Introduced C-1 fire control system
155	137	49-2704	13	RB-36F-1-CF	AF33-038-2182	Jul 51		II	Scrapped by Mar-Pak, FY59 [AF33(600)37911]	
156	138	49-2705	13	RB-36F-1-CF	AF33-038-2182	Aug 51		II	Scrapped by Mar-Pak, FY59 [AF33(600)37911]	
157	142	49-2706	13	RB-36F-1-CF	AF33-038-2182	Sep 51		II	Scrapped by Mar-Pak, FY59 [AF33(600)37911]	
158	143	49-2707	13	RB-36F-1-CF	AF33-038-2182	May 51	JRB-36F-1-CF	—	Scrapped by Mar-Pak, FY57 [AF33(600)33903]	FICON and Tom-Tom test aircraft
159	144	49-2708	13	RB-36F-1-CF	AF33-038-2182	Sep 51		II	Scrapped by Mar-Pak, FY59 [AF33(600)37911]	
160	148	49-2709	13	RB-36F-1-CF	AF33-038-2182	Aug 51		II	Scrapped by Mar-Pak, FY58 [AF33(600)35907]	
161	149	49-2710	13	RB-36F-1-CF	AF33-038-2182	Aug 51		II	Scrapped by Mar-Pak, FY59 [AF33(600)37911]	
162	150	49-2711	13	RB-36F-1-CF	AF33-038-2182	Aug 51		II	Scrapped by Mar-Pak, FY59 [AF33(600)37911]	
163	154	49-2712	14	RB-36F-5-CF	AF33-038-2182	Aug 51		II	Scrapped by Mar-Pak, FY59 [AF33(600)37911]	
164	155	49-2713	14	RB-36F-5-CF	AF33-038-2182	Sep 51		II	Scrapped by Mar-Pak, FY59 [AF33(600)37911]	
165	156	49-2714	14	RB-36F-5-CF	AF33-038-2182	Sep 51		II	Scrapped by Mar-Pak, FY59 [AF33(600)37911]	
166	160	49-2715	14	RB-36F-5-CF	AF33-038-2182	Sep 51		II	Scrapped by Mar-Pak, FY59 [AF33(600)37911]	
167	161	49-2716	14	RB-36F-5-CF	AF33-038-2182	Sep 51		II	Scrapped by Mar-Pak, FY58 [AF33(600)35907]	
168	162	49-2717	14	RB-36F-5-CF	AF33-038-2182	Sep 51		II	Scrapped by Mar-Pak, FY59 [AF33(600)37911]	
169	166	49-2718	14	RB-36F-5-CF	AF33-038-2182	Sep 52		II	Scrapped by Mar-Pak, FY59 [AF33(600)37911]	
170	167	49-2719	14	RB-36F-5-CF	AF33-038-2182	Oct 52		II	Scrapped by Mar-Pak, FY59 [AF33(600)37911]	
171	168	49-2720	14	RB-36F-5-CF	AF33-038-2182	Oct 52		II	Scrapped by Mar-Pak, FY59 [AF33(600)37911]	
172	169	49-2721	14	RB-36F-5-CF	AF33-038-2182	Oct 52		II	Scrapped by Mar-Pak, FY59 [AF33(600)37911]	
173	171	50-1064	15	B-36F-10-CF	AF33-038-2182	Sep 52		III	Scrapped by Mar-Pak, FY58 [AF33(600)35907]	Introduced C-2 fire control system
174	172	50-1065	15	B-36F-10-CF	AF33-038-2182	Oct 52		III	Scrapped by Mar-Pak, FY58 [AF33(600)35907]	
175	173	50-1066	15	B-36F-10-CF	AF33-038-2182	Oct 52		—	Written Off 28 May 52	
176	175	50-1067	15	B-36F-10-CF	AF33-038-2182	Oct 52		—	Written Off 06 Mar 52	
177	176	50-1068	15	B-36F-10-CF	AF33-038-2182	Nov 52		II	Scrapped by Mar-Pak, FY58 [AF33(600)35907]	
178	177	50-1069	15	B-36F-10-CF	AF33-038-2182	Oct 52		II	Scrapped by AASB FY57 [Project A-7-5014-SB]	
179	178	50-1070	15	B-36F-10-CF	AF33-038-2182	Oct 52		II	Scrapped by Mar-Pak, FY57 [AF33(600)33903]	
180	180	50-1071	15	B-36F-10-CF	AF33-038-2182	Dec 52		II	Scrapped by Mar-Pak, FY58 [AF33(600)35907]	

Cum No.	CVAC No.	Serial Number	Lot No.	As-Built Configuration	Contract Number	Accepted by Air Force	Final Configuration	Featherweight Configuration	Final Disposition (Contract No. if scrapped)	Notes
181	181	50-1072	15	B-36F-10-CF	AF33-038-2182	Nov 52		II	Scrapped by Mar-Pak, FY58 [AF33(600)35907]	
182	182	50-1073	15	B-36F-10-CF	AF33-038-2182	Nov 52		II	Scrapped by Mar-Pak, FY58 [AF33(600)35907]	
183	183	50-1074	15	B-36F-15-CF	AF33-038-2182	Nov 52		II	Scrapped by Mar-Pak, FY58 [AF33(600)35907]	
184	185	50-1075	15	B-36F-15-CF	AF33-038-2182	Nov 52		II	Scrapped by Mar-Pak, FY57 [AF33(600)33903]	
185	186	50-1076	15	B-36F-15-CF	AF33-038-2182	Nov 52		II	Scrapped by AASB FY57 [Project A-7-5014-SB]	
186	187	50-1077	15	B-36F-15-CF	AF33-038-2182	Nov 52		II	Scrapped by Mar-Pak, FY58 [AF33(600)35907]	
187	188	50-1078	15	B-36F-15-CF	AF33-038-2182	Dec 52		II	Scrapped by Mar-Pak, FY58 [AF33(600)35907]	
188	190	50-1079	15	B-36F-15-CF	AF33-038-2182	Dec 52		II	Scrapped by Mar-Pak, FY58 [AF33(600)35907]	
189	191	50-1080	15	B-36F-15-CF	AF33-038-2182	Jan 53		II	Scrapped by Mar-Pak, FY58 [AF33(600)35907]	
190	192	50-1081	15	B-36F-15-CF	AF33-038-2182	Dec 52		III	Scrapped by Mar-Pak, FY58 [AF33(600)35907]	
191	193	50-1082	15	B-36F-15-CF	AF33-038-2182	Dec 52		II	Scrapped by Mar-Pak, FY58 [AF33(600)35907]	
192	195	50-1083	16	B-36H-1-CF	AF33-038-2182	May 52		III	Scrapped at Carswell AFB (?)	4925th Test Group (Atomic) aircraft
193	196	50-1084	16	B-36H-1-CF	AF33-038-2182	May 52		III	Scrapped by Mar-Pak, FY58 [AF33(600)35907]	
194	197	50-1085	16	B-36H-1-CF	AF33-038-2182	May 52	EDB-36H-1-CF	II	Scrapped by Mar-Pak, FY57 [AF33(600)33903]	Operation IVY; third Rascal carrier–never used; listed as scrapped in Dec 56
195	198	50-1086	16	B-36H-1-CF	AF33-038-2182	May 52		III	Scrapped by Mar-Pak, FY58 [AF33(600)35907]	*Miss Featherweight*; 4925th Test Group (Atomic)
196	200	50-1087	16	B-36H-1-CF	AF33-038-2182	May 52		II	Scrapped by Mar-Pak, FY58 [AF33(600)35907]	
197	201	50-1088	16	B-36H-1-CF	AF33-038-2182	May 52		II	Scrapped by Mar-Pak, FY58 [AF33(600)35907]	
198	202	50-1089	16	B-36H-1-CF	AF33-038-2182	May 52		II	Scrapped by Mar-Pak, FY58 [AF33(600)35907]	
199	204	50-1090	16	B-36H-1-CF	AF33-038-2182	Jun 52		II	Scrapped by Mar-Pak, FY58 [AF33(600)35907]	
200	205	50-1091	16	B-36H-1-CF	AF33-038-2182	Jun 52		III	Scrapped by Mar-Pak, FY58 [AF33(600)35907]	
201	207	50-1092	16	B-36H-5-CF	AF33-038-2182	Jun 52		II	Scrapped by Mar-Pak, FY58 [AF33(600)35907]	Introduced C-3 fire control system
202	208	50-1093	16	B-36H-5-CF	AF33-038-2182	Jun 52		III	Scrapped by Mar-Pak, FY58 [AF33(600)35907]	
203	210	50-1094	16	B-36H-5-CF	AF33-038-2182	Jun 52		III	Scrapped by Mar-Pak, FY58 [AF33(600)35907]	
204	211	50-1095	16	B-36H-5-CF	AF33-038-2182	Jun 52		II	Scrapped by Mar-Pak, FY58 [AF33(600)35907]	
205	213	50-1096	16	B-36H-5-CF	AF33-038-2182	Jan 52		II	Scrapped by Mar-Pak, FY57 [AF33(600)33903]	
206	214	50-1097	16	B-36H-5-CF	AF33-038-2182	Jan 52		II	Scrapped by Mar-Pak, FY58 [AF33(600)35907]	
207	174	50-1098	15	RB-36F-10-CF	AF33-038-2182	Oct 52		II	Scrapped by Mar-Pak, FY59 [AF33(600)37911]	
208	179	50-1099	15	RB-36F-10-CF	AF33-038-2182	Oct 52		II	Scrapped by Mar-Pak, FY59 [AF33(600)37911]	
209	184	50-1100	15	RB-36F-15-CF	AF33-038-2182	Nov 52		II	Scrapped by Mar-Pak, FY59 [AF33(600)37911]	
210	189	50-1101	15	RB-36F-15-CF	AF33-038-2182	Nov 52		III	Scrapped by Mar-Pak, FY59 [AF33(600)37911]	
211	194	50-1102	15	RB-36F-15-CF	AF33-038-2182	Dec 52		II	Scrapped by Mar-Pak, FY59 [AF33(600)37911]	
212	199	50-1103	16	RB-36H-1-CF	AF33-038-2182	Feb 52		III	Scrapped by Mar-Pak, FY59 [AF33(600)37911]	
213	203	50-1104	16	RB-36H-1-CF	AF33-038-2182	Jan 52		III	Scrapped by Mar-Pak, FY58 [AF33(600)35907]	
214	206	50-1105	16	RB-36H-1-CF	AF33-038-2182	Jan 52		III	Scrapped by Mar-Pak, FY58 [AF33(600)35907]	
215	209	50-1106	16	RB-36H-5-CF	AF33-038-2182	Jan 52		III	Scrapped by Mar-Pak, FY58 [AF33(600)35907]	
216	212	50-1107	16	RB-36H-5-CF	AF33-038-2182	Feb 52		III	Scrapped by Mar-Pak, FY58 [AF33(600)35907]	
217	215	50-1108	16	RB-36H-5-CF	AF33-038-2182	Feb 52		III	Scrapped by Mar-Pak, FY59 [AF33(600)37911]	
218	216	50-1109	16	RB-36H-5-CF	AF33-038-2182	Feb 52		III	Scrapped by Mar-Pak, FY59 [AF33(600)37911]	
219	217	50-1110	16	RB-36H-5-CF	AF33-038-2182	Feb 52		III	Scrapped by Mar-Pak, FY59 [AF33(600)37911]	
220	249	51-13717	18	RB-36H-20-CF	AF33-038-2182	Jun 52		II	Scrapped by Mar-Pak, FY59 [AF33(600)37911]	
221	251	51-13718	18	RB-36H-20-CF	AF33-038-2182	Jul 52		II	Scrapped by Mar-Pak, FY57 [AF33(600)33903]	
222	253	51-13719	18	RB-36H-20-CF	AF33-038-2182	Jul 52		—	Written Off 18 Feb 53	
223	255	51-13720	18	RB-36H-25-CF	AF33-038-2182	Jul 52		II	Written Off 15 Nov 56	
224	257	51-13721	18	RB-36H-25-CF	AF33-038-2182	Jul 52		—	Written Off 18 Mar 53	
225	259	51-13722	18	RB-36H-25-CF	AF33-038-2182	Aug 52		—	Written Off 27 Aug 54	
226	261	51-13723	18	RB-36H-25-CF	AF33-038-2182	Aug 52		III	Scrapped by Mar-Pak, FY59 [AF33(600)37911]	
227	263	51-13724	18	RB-36H-25-CF	AF33-038-2182	Aug 52		II	Scrapped by Mar-Pak, FY57 [AF33(600)33903]	
228	265	51-13725	18	RB-36H-25-CF	AF33-038-2182	Sep 52		II	Scrapped by Mar-Pak, FY57 [AF33(600)33903]	
229	267	51-13726	19	RB-36H-30-CF	AF33-038-2182	Aug 52		II	Scrapped by Mar-Pak, FY57 [AF33(600)33903]	
230	269	51-13727	19	RB-36H-30-CF	AF33-038-2182	Sep 52		II	Scrapped by Mar-Pak, FY59 [AF33(600)37911]	
231	271	51-13728	19	RB-36H-30-CF	AF33-038-2182	Sep 52		II	Scrapped by Mar-Pak, FY57 [AF33(600)33903]	
232	273	51-13729	19	RB-36H-30-CF	AF33-038-2182	Sep 52		II	Scrapped by Mar-Pak, FY57 [AF33(600)33903]	
233	275	51-13730	19	RB-36H-30-CF	AF33-038-2182	Sep 52		II	Donated to Chanute AFB, Illinois Museum	Now at Castle AFB Museum
234	277	51-13731	19	RB-36H-30-CF	AF33-038-2182	Oct 52		II	Scrapped by Mar-Pak, FY57 [AF33(600)33903]	
235	279	51-13732	19	RB-36H-35-CF	AF33-038-2182	Oct 52		II	Scrapped by Mar-Pak, FY57 [AF33(600)33903]	
236	281	51-13733	19	RB-36H-35-CF	AF33-038-2182	Oct 52		II	Scrapped by Mar-Pak, FY57 [AF33(600)33903]	Named *Mathew B. Brady*
237	283	51-13734	19	RB-36H-35-CF	AF33-038-2182	Oct 52		III	Scrapped by Mar-Pak, FY57 [AF33(600)33903]	
238	285	51-13735	19	RB-36H-35-CF	AF33-038-2182	Nov 52		III	Scrapped by Mar-Pak, FY58 [AF33(600)35907]	
239	287	51-13736	19	RB-36H-35-CF	AF33-038-2182	Nov 52		II	Scrapped by Mar-Pak, FY58 [AF33(600)35907]	
240	289	51-13737	19	RB-36H-35-CF	AF33-038-2182	Nov 52		II	Scrapped by Mar-Pak, FY57 [AF33(600)33903]	
241	291	51-13738	20	RB-36H-40-CF	AF33-038-2182	Nov 52		III	Scrapped by Mar-Pak, FY58 [AF33(600)35907]	
242	293	51-13739	20	RB-36H-40-CF	AF33-038-2182	Dec 52		III	Scrapped at Carswell FY58 [AF33(600)35907]	
243	295	51-13740	20	RB-36H-40-CF	AF33-038-2182	Dec 52		II	Scrapped by Mar-Pak, FY58 [AF33(600)35907]	
244	297	51-13741	20	RB-36H-40-CF	AF33-038-2182	Dec 52		II	Scrapped by Mar-Pak, FY58 [AF33(600)35907]	
245	218	51-5699	17	B-36H-10-CF	AF33-038-2182	Jun 52		III	Scrapped by AASB FY57 [Project A-7-5014-SB]	
246	219	51-5700	17	B-36H-10-CF	AF33-038-2182	Jul 52		III	Scrapped by Mar-Pak, FY58 [AF33(600)35907]	
247	220	51-5701	17	B-36H-10-CF	AF33-038-2182	Jul 52		III	Scrapped by Mar-Pak, FY58 [AF33(600)35907]	
248	222	51-5702	17	B-36H-10-CF	AF33-038-2182	Jul 52		III	Scrapped by Mar-Pak, FY58 [AF33(600)35907]	

Cum No.	CVAC No.	Serial Number	Lot No.	As-Built Configuration	Contract Number	Accepted by Air Force	Final Configuration	Featherweight Configuration	Final Disposition (Contract No. if scrapped)	Notes
249	224	51-5703	17	B-36H-10-CF	AF33-038-2182	Jul 52		III	Scrapped by Mar-Pak, FY58 [AF33(600)35907]	
250	226	51-5704	17	B-36H-10-CF	AF33-038-2182	Oct 52		III	Scrapped by Mar-Pak, FY58 [AF33(600)35907]	
251	228	51-5705	17	B-36H-10-CF	AF33-038-2182	Jul 52		II	Scrapped by Mar-Pak, FY58 [AF33(600)35907]	
252	230	51-5706	17	B-36H-15-CF	AF33-038-2182	Jul 52	JDB-36H-15-CF	II	Scrapped by Mar-Pak, FY58 [AF33(600)35907]	TANBO XIV experiments; EDB-36H Rascal
253	232	51-5707	17	B-36H-15-CF	AF33-038-2182	Aug 52		II	Scrapped by AASB FY57 [Project A-7-5014-SB]	
254	234	51-5708	17	B-36H-15-CF	AF33-038-2182	Aug 52		III	Scrapped by Mar-Pak, FY58 [AF33(600)35907]	
255	236	51-5709	17	B-36H-15-CF	AF33-038-2182	Aug 52		II	Scrapped by AASB FY57 [Project A-7-5014-SB]	
256	238	51-5710	17	B-36H-15-CF	AF33-038-2182	Aug 52	JDB-36H-15-CF	II	Scrapped by Mar-Pak, FY57 [AF33(600)33903]	YDB-36H/EDB-36H Rascal carrier (prototype); listed as scrapped in Aug 57
257	240	51-5711	17	B-36H-15-CF	AF33-038-2182	Aug 52		III	Scrapped by Mar-Pak, FY58 [AF33(600)35907]	
258	242	51-5712	18	B-36H-20-CF	AF33-038-2182	Jun 52	NB-36H-20-CF	—	Scrapped by Convair at Carswell, FY58	Designated XB-36H from 11 Mar 55 to 6 Jun 56
259	244	51-5713	18	B-36H-20-CF	AF33-038-2182	Jun 52		III	Scrapped by Mar-Pak, FY58 [AF33(600)35907]	
260	246	51-5714	18	B-36H-20-CF	AF33-038-2182	Jun 52		III	Scrapped by Mar-Pak, FY58 [AF33(600)35907]	
261	248	51-5715	18	B-36H-20-CF	AF33-038-2182	Jun 52		III	Scrapped by Mar-Pak, FY58 [AF33(600)35907]	
262	250	51-5716	18	B-36H-20-CF	AF33-038-2182	Jul 52		III	Scrapped by Mar-Pak, FY58 [AF33(600)35907]	
263	252	51-5717	18	B-36H-20-CF	AF33-038-2182	Jul 52		III	Scrapped by Mar-Pak, FY58 [AF33(600)35907]	
264	254	51-5718	18	B-36H-25-CF	AF33-038-2182	Jul 52		III	Scrapped by Mar-Pak, FY58 [AF33(600)35907]	
265	256	51-5719	18	B-36H-25-CF	AF33-038-2182	Jul 52		—	Written Off 07 Feb 53	
266	258	51-5720	18	B-36H-25-CF	AF33-038-2182	Aug 52		III	To New Mexico Institute, FY58	
267	260	51-5721	18	B-36H-25-CF	AF33-038-2182	Aug 52		III	Scrapped by Mar-Pak, FY58 [AF33(600)35907]	
268	262	51-5722	18	B-36H-25-CF	AF33-038-2182	Aug 52		III	Scrapped by Mar-Pak, FY58 [AF33(600)35907]	
269	264	51-5723	18	B-36H-25-CF	AF33-038-2182	Aug 52		III	Scrapped by Mar-Pak, FY58 [AF33(600)35907]	
270	266	51-5724	19	B-36H-30-CF	AF33-038-2182	Sep 52		III	Scrapped by Mar-Pak, FY58 [AF33(600)35907]	
271	268	51-5725	19	B-36H-30-CF	AF33-038-2182	Sep 52		III	Scrapped by Mar-Pak, FY58 [AF33(600)35907]	
272	270	51-5726	19	B-36H-30-CF	AF33-038-2182	Sep 52	JB-36H-30-CF	III	Scrapped by Mar-Pak, FY57 [AF33(600)33903]	EB-36H until 1955; red, white, and blue paint
273	272	51-5727	19	B-36H-30-CF	AF33-038-2182	Sep 52		III	Scrapped by Mar-Pak, FY58 [AF33(600)35907]	
274	274	51-5728	19	B-36H-30-CF	AF33-038-2182	Sep 52		III	Scrapped by Mar-Pak, FY58 [AF33(600)35907]	
275	276	51-5729	19	B-36H-30-CF	AF33-038-2182	Sep 52		—	Written Off 12 Feb 53	
276	278	51-5730	19	B-36H-35-CF	AF33-038-2182	Oct 52		III	Scrapped by Mar-Pak, FY58 [AF33(600)35907]	
277	280	51-5731	19	B-36H-35-CF	AF33-038-2182	Oct 52	JB-36H-35-CF	III	Scrapped by Mar-Pak, FY57 [AF33(600)33903]	EB-36H until 1955
278	282	51-5732	19	B-36H-35-CF	AF33-038-2182	Oct 52		III	Scrapped by Mar-Pak, FY58 [AF33(600)35907]	
279	284	51-5733	19	B-36H-35-CF	AF33-038-2182	Oct 52		III	Scrapped by Mar-Pak, FY58 [AF33(600)35907]	
280	286	51-5734	19	B-36H-35-CF	AF33-038-2182	Nov 52		III	Scrapped by Mar-Pak, FY58 [AF33(600)35907]	Star of *Strategic Air Command* movie
281	288	51-5735	19	B-36H-35-CF	AF33-038-2182	Nov 52		III	Scrapped by Mar-Pak, FY58 [AF33(600)35907]	
282	290	51-5736	20	B-36H-40-CF	AF33-038-2182	Nov 52		III	Scrapped by Mar-Pak, FY58 [AF33(600)35907]	
283	292	51-5737	20	B-36H-40-CF	AF33-038-2182	Nov 52		III	Scrapped by Mar-Pak, FY58 [AF33(600)35907]	
284	294	51-5738	20	B-36H-40-CF	AF33-038-2182	Dec 52		III	Scrapped by Mar-Pak, FY58 [AF33(600)35907]	
285	296	51-5739	20	B-36H-40-CF	AF33-038-2182	Dec 52		III	Scrapped by Mar-Pak, FY58 [AF33(600)35907]	
286	298	51-5740	20	B-36H-40-CF	AF33-038-2182	Jan 53		III	Scrapped by Mar-Pak, FY58 [AF33(600)35907]	
287	299	51-5741	20	B-36H-40-CF	AF33-038-2182	Jan 53		III	Written Off 07 Jan 57	
288	300	51-5742	20	B-36H-40-CF	AF33-038-2182	Dec 52		III	Scrapped by Mar-Pak, FY58 [AF33(600)35907]	
289	221	51-5743	17	RB-36H-10-CF	AF33-038-2182	Mar 52		III	Scrapped by Mar-Pak, FY59 [AF33(600)37911]	
290	223	51-5744	17	RB-36H-10-CF	AF33-038-2182	Mar 52		III	Scrapped by Mar-Pak, FY59 [AF33(600)37911]	
291	225	51-5745	17	RB-36H-10-CF	AF33-038-2182	Mar 52		III	Written Off 09 Nov 57	
292	227	51-5746	17	RB-36H-10-CF	AF33-038-2182	Apr 52		III	Scrapped by Mar-Pak, FY59 [AF33(600)37911]	
293	229	51-5747	17	RB-36H-10-CF	AF33-038-2182	Apr 52		III	Scrapped by Mar-Pak, FY59 [AF33(600)37911]	
294	231	51-5748	17	RB-36H-15-CF	AF33-038-2182	Apr 52	JRB-36H-15-CF	III	Scrapped by Mar-Pak, FY59 [AF33(600)37911]	Modified to observe high-altitude atomic tests
295	233	51-5749	17	RB-36H-15-CF	AF33-038-2182	May 52		II	Scrapped by Mar-Pak, FY57 [AF33(600)33903]	
296	235	51-5750	17	RB-36H-15-CF	AF33-038-2182	Apr 52	JRB-36H-15-CF	II	Scrapped by Mar-Pak, FY59 [AF33(600)37911]	Modified to observe high-altitude atomic tests
297	237	51-5751	17	RB-36H-15-CF	AF33-038-2182	Apr 52		II	Scrapped by Mar-Pak, FY57 [AF33(600)33903]	
298	239	51-5752	17	RB-36H-15-CF	AF33-038-2182	May 52		II	Scrapped by Mar-Pak, FY57 [AF33(600)33903]	
299	241	51-5753	17	RB-36H-15-CF	AF33-038-2182	Jun 52		II	Scrapped by Mar-Pak, FY59 [AF33(600)37911]	
300	243	51-5754	18	RB-36H-20-CF	AF33-038-2182	May 52		II	Scrapped by Mar-Pak, FY59 [AF33(600)37911]	
301	245	51-5755	18	RB-36H-20-CF	AF33-038-2182	May 52		II	Scrapped by Mar-Pak, FY59 [AF33(600)37911]	
302	247	51-5756	18	RB-36H-20-CF	AF33-038-2182	Jun 52		II	Scrapped by Mar-Pak, FY59 [AF33(600)37911]	
303	304	52-1343	20	B-36H-45-CF	AF33-038-5793	Jan 53		III	Scrapped by Mar-Pak, FY58 [AF33(600)35907]	
304	306	52-1344	20	B-36H-45-CF	AF33-038-5793	Mar 53		III	Scrapped by Mar-Pak, FY58 [AF33(600)35907]	
305	308	52-1345	20	B-36H-45-CF	AF33-038-5793	Feb 53		III	Scrapped by Mar-Pak, FY58 [AF33(600)35907]	
306	310	52-1346	20	B-36H-45-CF	AF33-038-5793	Feb 53		III	Scrapped by Mar-Pak, FY58 [AF33(600)35907]	
307	312	52-1347	20	B-36H-45-CF	AF33-038-5793	Mar 53		III	Scrapped by Mar-Pak, FY58 [AF33(600)35907]	
308	314	52-1348	21	B-36H-50-CF	AF33-038-5793	Mar 53		III	Scrapped by Mar-Pak, FY58 [AF33(600)35907]	
309	316	52-1349	21	B-36H-50-CF	AF33-038-5793	Mar 53		III	Scrapped by Mar-Pak, FY58 [AF33(600)35907]	
310	318	52-1350	21	B-36H-50-CF	AF33-038-5793	Apr 53		III	Scrapped by Mar-Pak, FY58 [AF33(600)35907]	
311	320	52-1351	21	B-36H-50-CF	AF33-038-5793	Apr 53		III	Scrapped by Mar-Pak, FY58 [AF33(600)35907]	
312	322	52-1352	21	B-36H-50-CF	AF33-038-5793	Apr 53		III	Scrapped by Mar-Pak, FY58 [AF33(600)35907]	
313	324	52-1353	21	B-36H-50-CF	AF33-038-5793	Jun 53		III	Scrapped by Mar-Pak, FY58 [AF33(600)35907]	
314	326	52-1354	21	B-36H-55-CF	AF33-038-5793	May 53		III	Scrapped by Mar-Pak, FY58 [AF33(600)35907]	
315	328	52-1355	21	B-36H-55-CF	AF33-038-5793	May 53		III	Scrapped by Mar-Pak, FY58 [AF33(600)35907]	
316	330	52-1356	21	B-36H-55-CF	AF33-038-5793	Jun 53		III	Scrapped by Mar-Pak, FY58 [AF33(600)35907]	

Cum No.	CVAC No.	Serial Number	Lot No.	As-Built Configuration	Contract Number	Accepted by Air Force	Final Configuration	Featherweight Configuration	Final Disposition (Contract No. if scrapped)	Notes
317	331	52-1357	21	B-36H-55-CF	AF33-038-5793	May 53	JB-35H-55-CF	—	Scrapped by Mar-Pak, FY58 [AF33(600)35907]	EB-36H until 1955
318	334	52-1358	21	B-36H-55-CF	AF33-038-5793	Jun 53	JB-36H-55-CF	—	Scrapped by Mar-Pak, FY57 [AF33(600)33903]	EB-36H until 1955; red, white, and blue paint
319	336	52-1359	21	B-36H-55-CF	AF33-038-5793	Jul 53		III	Scrapped by Mar-Pak, FY58 [AF33(600)35907]	
320	338	52-1360	22	B-36H-60-CF	AF33-038-5793	Jul 53		III	Scrapped by Mar-Pak, FY58 [AF33(600)35907]	
321	340	52-1361	22	B-36H-60-CF	AF33-038-5793	Jul 53		III	Scrapped by Mar-Pak, FY58 [AF33(600)35907]	
322	342	52-1362	22	B-36H-60-CF	AF33-038-5793	Aug 53		III	Scrapped by Mar-Pak, FY58 [AF33(600)35907]	
323	344	52-1363	22	B-36H-60-CF	AF33-038-5793	Aug 53		III	Scrapped by Mar-Pak, FY58 [AF33(600)35907]	
324	346	52-1364	22	B-36H-60-CF	AF33-038-5793	Aug 53		III	Scrapped by Mar-Pak, FY58 [AF33(600)35907]	
325	348	52-1365	22	B-36H-60-CF	AF33-038-5793	Sep 53		III	Scrapped by Mar-Pak, FY58 [AF33(600)35907]	
326	350	52-1366	22	B-36H-60-CF	AF33-038-5793	Sep 53		III	Scrapped by Mar-Pak, FY58 [AF33(600)35907]	
327	301	52-1367	20	RB-36H-45-CF	AF33-038-5793	Jan 53		II	Scrapped by Mar-Pak, FY58 [AF33(600)35907]	
328	302	52-1368	20	RB-36H-45-CF	AF33-038-5793	Jan 53		II	Scrapped by Mar-Pak, FY58 [AF33(600)35907]	
329	303	52-1369	20	RB-36H-45-CF	AF33-038-5793	Jan 53		II	Written Off 05 Aug 53	
330	305	52-1370	20	RB-36H-45-CF	AF33-038-5793	Feb 53		II	Scrapped by Mar-Pak, FY59 [AF33(600)37911]	
331	307	52-1371	20	RB-36H-45-CF	AF33-038-5793	Mar 53		II	Scrapped by Mar-Pak, FY59 [AF33(600)37911]	
332	309	52-1372	20	RB-36H-45-CF	AF33-038-5793	Feb 53		II	Scrapped by Mar-Pak, FY59 [AF33(600)37911]	
333	311	52-1373	20	RB-36H-45-CF	AF33-038-5793	Feb 53		II	Scrapped by Mar-Pak, FY57 [AF33(600)33903]	
334	313	52-1374	21	RB-36H-50-CF	AF33-038-5793	Mar 53		II	Scrapped by Mar-Pak, FY59 [AF33(600)37911]	
335	315	52-1375	21	RB-36H-50-CF	AF33-038-5793	Mar 53		II	Scrapped by Mar-Pak, FY57 [AF33(600)33903]	
336	317	52-1376	21	RB-36H-50-CF	AF33-038-5793	Apr 53		II	Scrapped by Mar-Pak, FY59 [AF33(600)37911]	
337	319	52-1377	21	RB-36H-50-CF	AF33-038-5793	Apr 53		II	Scrapped by Mar-Pak, FY57 [AF33(600)33903]	
338	321	52-1378	21	RB-36H-50-CF	AF33-038-5793	Apr 53		II	Scrapped by Mar-Pak, FY59 [AF33(600)37911]	
339	323	52-1379	21	RB-36H-50-CF	AF33-038-5793	May 53		II	Scrapped by Mar-Pak, FY57 [AF33(600)33903]	
340	325	52-1380	21	RB-36H-50-CF	AF33-038-5793	May 53		II	Scrapped by Mar-Pak, FY59 [AF33(600)37911]	
341	327	52-1381	21	RB-36H-55-CF	AF33-038-5793	May 53		II	Scrapped by Mar-Pak, FY59 [AF33(600)37911]	
342	329	52-1382	21	RB-36H-55-CF	AF33-038-5793	Jun 53		II	Scrapped by Mar-Pak, FY58 [AF33(600)35907]	
343	331	52-1383	21	RB-36H-55-CF	AF33-038-5793	Jun 53		II	Scrapped by Mar-Pak, FY58 [AF33(600)35907]	
344	333	52-1384	21	RB-36H-55-CF	AF33-038-5793	Jun 53		II	Scrapped by Mar-Pak, FY58 [AF33(600)35907]	
345	335	52-1385	21	RB-36H-55-CF	AF33-038-5793	Jul 53		II	Scrapped by Mar-Pak, FY58 [AF33(600)35907]	
346	337	52-1386	21	RB-36H-55-CF	AF33-038-5793	Jul 53		III	Scrapped by Mar-Pak, FY57 [AF33(600)33903]	4925th Test Group (Atomic) aircraft
347	339	52-1387	22	RB-36H-60-CF	AF33-038-5793	Jul 53		III	Written Off 04 Jan 56	
348	341	52-1388	22	RB-36H-60-CF	AF33-038-5793	Aug 53		II	Scrapped by Mar-Pak, FY58 [AF33(600)35907]	
349	343	52-1389	22	RB-36H-60-CF	AF33-038-5793	Aug 53		III	Scrapped by Mar-Pak, FY57 [AF33(600)33903]	
350	345	52-1390	22	RB-36H-60-CF	AF33-038-5793	Aug 53		II	Scrapped by Mar-Pak, FY59 [AF33(600)37911]	
351	347	52-1391	22	RB-36H-60-CF	AF33-038-5793	Sep 53		II	Scrapped by Mar-Pak, FY59 [AF33(600)37911]	
352	349	52-1392	22	RB-36H-60-CF	AF33-038-5793	Sep 53		II	Scrapped by Mar-Pak, FY57 [AF33(600)33903]	
353	351	52-2210	23	B-36J-1-CF	AF33-038-5793	Sep 53		III	Scrapped by Mar-Pak, FY59 [AF33(600)37911]	
354	352	52-2211	23	B-36J-1-CF	AF33-038-5793	Sep 53		III	Scrapped by Mar-Pak, FY59 [AF33(600)37911]	
355	353	52-2212	23	B-36J-1-CF	AF33-038-5793	Oct 53		III	Scrapped by Mar-Pak, FY59 [AF33(600)37911]	
356	354	52-2213	23	B-36J-1-CF	AF33-038-5793	Oct 53		III	Scrapped by Mar-Pak, FY59 [AF33(600)37911]	
357	355	52-2214	23	B-36J-1-CF	AF33-038-5793	Nov 53		III	Scrapped by Mar-Pak, FY59 [AF33(600)37911]	
358	356	52-2215	23	B-36J-1-CF	AF33-038-5793	Nov 53		III	Scrapped by Mar-Pak, FY59 [AF33(600)37911]	
359	357	52-2216	23	B-36J-1-CF	AF33-038-5793	Nov 53		III	Scrapped by Mar-Pak, FY59 [AF33(600)37911]	Last aircraft through SAM-SAC
360	358	52-2217	23	B-36J-1-CF	AF33-038-5793	Dec 53		III	Donated to Offutt AFB Museum	
361	359	52-2218	23	B-36J-1-CF	AF33-038-5793	Dec 53		III	Scrapped by Mar-Pak, FY59 [AF33(600)37911]	
362	360	52-2219	23	B-36J-1-CF	AF33-038-5793	Dec 53		III	Scrapped by Mar-Pak, FY59 [AF33(600)37911]	
363	361	52-2220	23	B-36J-1-CF	AF33-038-5793	Jan 54		III	Donated to the Air Force Museum	
364	362	52-2221	23	B-36J-1-CF	AF33-038-5793	Jan 54		III	Scrapped by Mar-Pak, FY59 [AF33(600)37911]	
365	363	52-2222	24	B-36J-5-CF	AF33-038-5793	Jan 54		III	Scrapped by Mar-Pak, FY59 [AF33(600)37911]	
366	364	52-2223	24	B-36J-5-CF	AF33-038-5793	Feb 54		III	Scrapped by Mar-Pak, FY59 [AF33(600)37911]	
367	365	52-2224	24	B-36J-5-CF	AF33-038-5793	Feb 54		III	Scrapped by Mar-Pak, FY59 [AF33(600)37911]	
368	366	52-2225	24	B-36J-5-CF	AF33-038-5793	Feb 54		III	Scrapped by Mar-Pak, FY59 [AF33(600)37911]	
369	367	52-2226	24	B-36J-5-CF	AF33-038-5793	Mar 54		III	Scrapped by Mar-Pak, FY59 [AF33(600)37911]	
370	368	52-2812	24	B-36J-5-CF	AF33-038-5793	Mar 54		III	Scrapped by Mar-Pak, FY59 [AF33(600)37911]	
371	369	52-2813	24	B-36J-5-CF	AF33-038-5793	Mar 54		III	Scrapped by Mar-Pak, FY59 [AF33(600)37911]	
372	370	52-2814	24	B-36J-5-CF (III)	AF33-038-5793	May 54		III	Scrapped by Mar-Pak, FY59 [AF33(600)37911]	
373	371	52-2815	24	B-36J-5-CF (III)	AF33-038-5793	May 54		III	Scrapped by Mar-Pak, FY59 [AF33(600)37911]	
374	372	52-2816	24	B-36J-5-CF (III)	AF33-038-5793	May 54		III	Scrapped by Mar-Pak, FY59 [AF33(600)37911]	
375	373	52-2817	24	B-36J-5-CF (III)	AF33-038-5793	May 54		III	Scrapped by Mar-Pak, FY59 [AF33(600)37911]	
376	374	52-2818	24	B-36J-5-CF (III)	AF33-038-5793	Jun 54		III	Written Off 25 May 55	
377	375	52-2819	25	B-36J-10-CF (III)	AF33-038-5793	Jun 54		III	Scrapped by Mar-Pak, FY59 [AF33(600)37911]	
378	376	52-2820	25	B-36J-10-CF (III)	AF33-038-5793	Jun 54		III	Scrapped by Mar-Pak, FY59 [AF33(600)37911]	
379	377	52-2821	25	B-36J-10-CF (III)	AF33-038-5793	Jun 54		III	Scrapped by Mar-Pak, FY59 [AF33(600)37911]	
380	378	52-2822	25	B-36J-10-CF (III)	AF33-038-5793	Jun 54		III	Scrapped by Mar-Pak, FY59 [AF33(600)37911]	
381	379	52-2823	25	B-36J-10-CF (III)	AF33-038-5793	Jul 54		III	Scrapped by Mar-Pak, FY59 [AF33(600)37911]	
382	380	52-2824	25	B-36J-10-CF (III)	AF33-038-5793	Jul 54		III	Scrapped by Mar-Pak, FY59 [AF33(600)37911]	
383	381	52-2825	25	B-36J-10-CF (III)	AF33-038-5793	Jul 54		III	Scrapped by Mar-Pak, FY59 [AF33(600)37911]	
384	382	52-2826	25	B-36J-10-CF (III)	AF33-038-5793	Jul 54		III	Scrapped by Mar-Pak, FY59 [AF33(600)37911]	
385	383	52-2827	25	B-36J-10-CF (III)	AF33-038-5793	Aug 54		III	Donated to the City of Fort Worth	Second *City of Ft. Worth* ("Ft."not "Fort")

Some Air Force and Convair documentation continued the H-model block numbers into the B-36J production run. Under this scheme, the J-1 airplanes were J-65s, the J-5s were J-70s, and the J-10s were J-75s. However, all Air Force technical orders used the –1, –5, and –10 block numbers, so that is what is shown here.

The jet demonstrator (44-92057) during March 1949. Note that the bomb bay doors are still the early sliding type, not the later "snap action" units. At this point the aircraft was essentially a B-36B equipped with J47 engines. (Convair via the San Diego Aerospace Museum Collection)

The third RB-36D (49-2688) gives a good contrast to the bomber variant at the top of the page. Note the use of shiny aluminum skin around the camera compartment, while the bomber uses dull magnesium skin around the same area (which is bomb bay No. 1). (Convair)

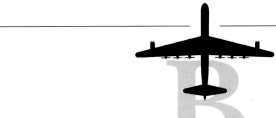

THE FIRST 95 AIRPLANES

The B-36 in general, but the first 95 airplanes in particular, spent an abnormally high percentage of their careers being modified or converted from one configuration to another, or undergoing major maintenance. The following chart shows the time each airplane spent in various modification or maintenance programs. The "1, 2, 3" shown at the start of each line (plus at the end of the A-to-E remanufacturing) equates to "major mate, final assembly, and field operations," respectively. "A–E" indicates the airplane was undergoing remanufacture from a B-36A to an RB-36E. "B–D" shows aircraft being converted from B-models into B-36Ds. "Tank" indicates resealing the fuel tanks. "Worth" is short for Project WORTHMORE. An "L" was when latent defects were being taken care of. The exact nature of Project 983 could not be ascertained. ① indicates defensive armament flight tests. ② indicates propeller vibration flight tests and maximum-range demonstrations with –25 engines. ③ indicates offensive armament flight tests. ④ indicates bomb dropping demonstrations. ⑤ indicates high-altitude cruise control flight tests. ⑥ indicates landing gear flight tests. ⑦ indicates 40,000-foot altitude range flight tests. ⑧ indicates maximum-range and duration flight tests. A black square indicates the aircraft was written-off during that month (see Appendix C for more complete loss data).

The original chart supplied by Roger Cripliver had been drawn by hand and was several feet wide by 8 feet long. Unfortunately, the chart only documented through the end of 1953 – but this covered the more interesting period of modifications. When the chart was recreated electronically in order to make it more readable, all events were rounded to the nearest whole month. The bars were lengthened or shortened as seemed appropriate based on the original. Although this has skewed some events, the overall presentation is still noteworthy and fairly accurate.

Serial Number	CVAC No.	1946	1947	1948	1949	1950	1951	1952	1953
42-13570	–		FLIGHT TESTS; PROPELLER SURVEY; -25 ENGINES		NOSE REPAIR / TRACK GEAR			IN STORAGE; ASSIGNED TO NEBO PROJECT	
42-13571	"YB"	1	2 — FLIGHT TESTS; TEST BED FOR -41 ENGINES		A–E	1 2 3		TANK SEAL	SAM-SAC
44-92004	1	1	2 — 3 — A.M.C. STATIC TESTS						
44-92005	2		1 — 2 — FLIGHT TESTS		A–E		1 2 3	SAN-SAN	SAM-SAC
44-92006	3		1 — 2 — 3	A–E	1 2 3			SAN-SAN	
44-92007	4		1 — 2 — 3	A–E	1 2 3		SAN-SAN		SAM-SAC
44-92008	5		1 — 2 — 3	① 3	A–E; M.M. & F.A. IN YARD 3			SAN-SAN	
44-92009	6		1 — 2 — 3		A–E	1 2 3		SAN-SAN	SAM-SAC
44-92010	7		1 — 2 — 3		A–E	1 2 3		TANK SEAL	SAM-SAC
44-92011	8		1 — 2 — 3		A–E	1 2 3		SAN-SAN	SAM-SAC
44-92012	9		1 — 2 — 3		A–E	1 2 3	TANK	SAN-SAN	
44-92013	10		1 — 2 — 3	②	A–E	1 2 3		SAN-SAN	
44-92014	11		1 — 2 — 3		A–E	1 2 3		SAN-SAN / SAM-SAC	
44-92015	12		1 — 2 — 3		A–E	1 2 3		SAN-SAN	
44-92016	13		1 — 2 — 3		A–E	1 2 3		SAN-SAN	SAM-SAC
44-92017	14		1 — 2 — 3		A–E	1 2 3			
44-92018	15		1 — 2 — 3		A–E	1 2 3		SAN-SAN	SAM-SAC
44-92019	16		1 — 2 — 3		A–E	1 2 3		PINOCCHIO / WORTHMORE	
44-92020	17		1 — 2 — 3		A–E	1 2 3		SAN-SAN	
44-92021	18		1 — 2 — 3		A–E	1 2 3		SAN-SAN	
44-92022	19		1 — 2 — 3		A–E	1 2 3		SAN-SAN	
44-92023	20		1 — 2 — 3		A–E	1 2 3		SAN-SAN	SAM-SAC
44-92024	21		1 — 2 — 3		A–E	1 2 3			
44-92025	22		1 — 2 — 3		A–E	1 2 3		SAN-SAN	
44-92026	23		1 — 2 — 3 FLIGHT TESTS; PROP VIBRATION		B–D; @ FT. WORTH			SAN-SAN	WORTH
44-92027	24		1 — 2 — 3	L	B–D	3		SAN-SAN / 983	WORTH
44-92028	25		1 — 2 — 3		B–D	3		SAN-SAN	SAM-SAC
44-92029	26		1 — 2 — 3	③ L	B–D	3		SAN-SAN	
44-92030	27		1 — 2 — 3		B–D	3		SAN-SAN	

Serial Number	CVAC No.	1946	1947	1948	1949	1950	1951	1952	1953
44-92031	28			1 2 3 ④	L	B–D 3		SAN-SAN 983	
44-92032	29			1 2 3	L		B–D 3		WORTH
44-92033	30			1 2 3	L / TANK		B–D 3		WORTH
44-92034	31			1 2 3 ⑤		B–D; @ FT. WORTH	SAN-SAN	WORTH	SAM-SAC
44-92035	32			1 2 3	L	TANK ■			
44-92036	33			1 2 3	L	B–D 3		SAN-SAN	SAM-SAC
44-92037	34			1 2 3	TANK SEAL @ OKC	B–D 3		SAN-SAN	
44-92038	35			1 2 3	L TANK	B–D 3		SAN-SAN ■	
44-92039	36			1 2 3		B–D 3	SAN-SAN		WORTH
44-92040	37			1 2 3	L	B–D 3	SAN-SAN	WORTH	
44-92041	38			1 2 3	L	B–D 3		SAN-SAN	SAM-SAC
44-92042	39			1 2 3	L		B–D 3	SAN-SAN	SAM-SAC
44-92043	40			1 2 3	L	B–D 3	SAN-SAN	WORTH	
44-92044	41			1 2 3	L	B–D 3	SAN-SAN 983		WORTH
44-92045	42			1 2 3		B–D 3	SAN-SAN		SAM-SAC
44-92046	43			1 2 / J47 HIGH-ALTITUDE TESTS		B–D 3		WORTH	
44-92047	44			1 2 3		B–D 3		WORTH	
44-92048	45			1 2 3	L	B–D 3	SAN-SAN	WORTH	
44-92049	46			1 2 ⑥ 3	L	B–D 3	SAN-SAN 983	WORTH	
44-92050	47			1 2 3	TANK SEAL @ OKC	B–D 3	■		
44-92051	48			1 2 3	TANK B–D 3		SAN-SAN ■		
44-92052	49			1 2 3		B–D 3		SAN-SAN	SAM-SAC
44-92053	50			1 2 3	B–D; @ FT. WORTH		SAN-SAN 983	WORTH	
44-92054	51			1 2 3	L B–D; @ FT. WORTH / DEFENSIVE ARMAMENT FLIGHT TESTS; C-1, C-2, C-3 FIRE CONTROL; NOSE RADAR				
44-92055	52			1 2 3		B–D 3	SAN-SAN		SAM-SAC
44-92056	53			1 2 3		B–D 3	SAN-SAN		SAM-SAC
44-92057	54			1 2 / J35 AND J47 ENGINE SURVEY; 4-BLADE PROP VIB.; -53 ENGINE		B–D 3		WORTH	
44-92058	55			1 2 / DEFENSIVE ARMAMENT; B-1, B-2		B–D 3	SAN-SAN		SAM-SAC
44-92059	56			1 2 3		B–D 3		WORTH	SAM-SAC
44-92060	57			1 2 3 ⑦		B–D 3		WORTH	
44-92061	58			1 2 3		B–D 3		WORTH	
44-92062	59				1 2 3 / TANK	B–D 3		WORTH	
44-92063	60				1 2 3	B–D 3		WORTH	
44-92064	61				1 2 3	B–D 3	SAN-SAN		SAM-SAC
44-92065	62				1 2 3	B–D 3		WORTH	SAM-SAC
44-92066	63				1 2 3	B–D 3		F WORTH	
44-92067	64				1 2 3	B–D 3		WORTH	
44-92068	65				1 2 3 / TANK	B–D 3		WORTH	
44-92069	66				1 2 3 / TANK	B–D 3		WORTH	
44-92070	67				1 2 3 / TANK	B–D 3		WORTH	
44-92071	68				1 2 3 L	B–D 3		WORTH	
44-92072	69				1 2 3 / FLIGHT TESTS	B–D 3	SAN-SAN		
44-92073	70				1 2 3	B–D 3		WORTH	
44-92074	71				1 2 3	B–D 3		WORTH	
44-92075	72				1 2 3 ■				
44-92076	73				1 2 3 ⑧ / RESIDUAL FUEL TESTS	B–D 3		WORTH	
44-92077	74				1 2 3	B–D 3		WORTH	
44-92078	75				1 2 3		B–D 3	WORTH	
44-92079	76				1 2 3 ■				
44-92080	77				1 2 3	B–D 3	■		
44-92081	78				1 2 3		B–D 3	WORTH	
44-92082	79				1 2 3 / TANK	B–D 3		WORTH	
44-92083	80				1 2 3	B–D 3		WORTH	
44-92084	81				1 2 3	B–D 3		WORTH	
44-92085	82				1 2 3	B–D 3		WORTH	
44-92086	83				1 2 3	B–D 3		WORTH	
44-92087	84				1 2 3 / DEFENSIVE ARMAMENT TESTS	B–D 3		WORTH	
44-92088	85				1 2 3 / CAMERA TESTS	"BOSTON"			
44-92089	86				1 2 3 / FLIGHT TESTS	TANK SEAL	SAN-SAN		
44-92090	87				1 2 3 / SERVICE TESTS	ENGINE SURVEY			
44-92091	88				1 2 3 / FLUX GATE COMPASS TESTS	SAN-SAN			
44-92092	89				1 2 3	SAN-SAN			
44-92093	90				1 2 3	TANK SEAL	SAN-SAN		SAM-SAC
44-92094	91				1 2 3	SAN-SAN			
44-92095	92				1 2 3 / FLIGHT TESTS	MCR 1474		WORTH	
44-92096	93				1 2 3 / PROPELLER VIBRATION TESTS	MCR 983AQ		WORTH	
44-92097	94				1 2 3 / RADIO NOISE TESTS	SAN-SAN		WORTH	
44-92098	95				1 2 3			WORTH	SAM-SAC

WRITE-OFFS

	Date	Model	Serial No.	Unit	Location	Remarks
1	15 Sep 49	B-36B-15-CF	44-92079	7th BW/9th BS	Carswell AFB	Crashed into Lake Worth on take off. Five of 13 crewmembers killed.
2	14 Feb 50	B-36B-15-CF	44-92075	7th BW/436th BS	British Columbia	Returning from Alaska. Severe icing and engine fire. Abandoned by crew in-flight. Five of 17 crewmembers killed. Broken Arrow.
3	22 Nov 50	B-36B-1-CF	44-92035	11th BW/26th BS	Cleburne, Texas	Three engines – two on one side – failed. Crashed 20 miles south of runway. Two of 17 crewmembers killed.
4	27 Apr 51	B-36D-25-CF	49-2658	7th BW/436th BS	Oklahoma	55 miles northeast of Oklahoma City. Mid-air collision with F-51 fighter. F-51 pilot killed; 13 of 17 B-36 crewmembers killed.
5	06 May 51	B-36D-25-CF	49-2660	7th BW	Kirtland AFB	Landing during high winds. Twenty-three of 25 crewmembers killed.
6	29 Jan 52	B-36D-45-CF	44-92080	92nd BW	Fairchild AFB	Landed short. All crewmembers survived.
7	06 Mar 52	B-36F-10-CF	50-1067	7th BW/436th BS	Carswell AFB	Landing gear collapsed on touchdown. Burned at ramp. Only minor injuries.
8	15 Apr 52	B-36D-40-CF	44-92050	92nd BW	Fairchild AFB	Crashed on take off. Fifteen crewmembers killed.
9	28 May 52	B-36F-10-CF	50-1066	11th BW	Carswell AFB	Landed short. Seven crewmembers killed.
10	12 Jun 52	B-36D-10-CF	44-92038	Convair	San Diego	Fuel fire on the ground during SAN-SAN. No one aboard.
11	04 Aug 52	B-36F-5-CF	49-2679	7th BW/436th BS	Carswell AFB	Fuel fire on the ground. Only minor injuries to three crewmembers.
12	05 Aug 52	B-36D-25-CF	49-2661	Convair	Pacific near San Diego	Wing fire in flight. Two crewmembers killed.
13	01 Sep 52	B-36D-10-CF	44-92051	11th BW	Carswell AFB	Tornado damage not repaired. No one aboard.
14	07 Feb 53	B-36H-25-CF	51-5719	7th BW/492nd BS	RAF Fairford, England	Adverse weather caused the aircraft to run out of fuel. All crewmembers survived.
15	12 Feb 53	B-36H-30-CF	51-5729	7th BW/9th BS	Goose Bay	Misguided by GCA – flew into hill. Two of 17 crewmembers killed.
16	18 Feb 53	RB-36H-20-CF	51-13719	28th SRW	Walker AFB	Landing gear collapsed. Burned on ground. All survived.
17	18 Mar 53	RB-36H-25-CF	51-13721	28th SRW	Newfoundland	Controlled flight into terrain. Twenty-three crewmembers killed.
18	05 Aug 53	RB-36H-45-CF	52-1369	5th SRW	Atlantic off Scotland	Loss of power. Nineteen crewmembers killed, four survivors.
19	11 Dec 53	B-36D-45-CF	44-92071	7th BW/492nd BS	El Paso	Controlled flight into terrain during approach. The entire crew of nine was killed.
20	27 Feb 54	B-36D-45-CF	44-92069	92nd BW	Fairchild AFB	Landing gear collapsed. Burned on ground. All crewmembers survived.
21	29 Mar 54	B-36D-15-CF	44-92032	92nd BW	Fairchild AFB	Takeoff practice abort. Seven crewmembers killed.
22	27 Aug 54	RB-36H-25-CF	51-13722	28th SRW	Ellsworth AFB	Controlled flight into terrain. Twenty-six crewmembers killed, one survivor.
23	28 Aug 54	B-36D-1-CF	44-92097	95th BW	Biggs AFB	Loss of power on landing. One crewmember killed.
24	08 Feb 55	B-36D-30-CF	44-92029	95th BW	Carswell AFB	Pilot landed short after misjudged approach. Two crewmembers killed.
25	06 Mar 55	B-36D-20-CF	44-92030	42nd BW	Loring AFB	Wingtip hit snowbank during landing. All crewmembers survived.
26	25 May 55	B-36J-5-CF	52-2818	6th BW	Sterling City, Texas	In-flight breakup during overflight of thunderstorm. Fifteen crewmembers killed.
27	27 Jun 55	B-36D-5-CF	49-2653	11th BW	Carswell AFB	Delayed salvage. Aircraft damaged during Operation CASTLE atomic tests.
28	04 Jan 56	RB-36H-60-CF	52-1387	28th SRW	Ellsworth AFB	Landing accident. Burned on ground. All crewmembers survived.
29	10 Jan 56	B-36D-10-CF	44-92041	95th BW	Biggs AFB	Hard landing. Four longerons at Bulkhead 10.0 failed (i.e., tail broke off). All survived.
30	15 Nov 56	RB-36H-25-CF	51-13720	28th SRW	Denver	Loss of power after takeoff; crash landed. Fire on ground. All crewmembers survived.
31	07 Jun 57	B-36H-40-CF	51-5741	7th BW	Carswell AFB	Aircraft heavily damaged on 25 April 1957 during a storm fly-through. No injuries. Delayed salvage on 7 June 1957.
32	09 Nov 57	RB-36H-10-CF	51-5745	72nd SRW	Ramey AFB	Explosion and ground fire. All crewmembers survived.

The first major accident involved a B-36B (44-92079) crashing in Lake Worth on 15 September 1949 while attempting a takeoff from Carswell AFB during a nighttime "maximum effort" mission. The cause was attributed to two propellers unexpectedly going into reverse pitch. Five of the 13 crewmembers aboard were killed. Contrary to many reports, the remains of the B-36 were salvaged from the lake and subsequently scrapped. (via Don Pyeatt)

On 28 May 1952 this B-36F (50-1066) from the 11th BW had just taken off from Carswell on a training mission. An engine cowling panel came loose and they returned to attempt a high weight landing. The landing gear broke and the aircraft skidded down the runway and burned on the ground. Seven crewmembers died in the accident. (above: via Ed Calvert via Don Pyeatt; below and right: via the San Diego Aerospace Museum Collection)

A B-36B (44-92075) crashed in British Columbia on 14 February 1950. This was the only B-36 crash where the aircraft was known to be carrying a nuclear weapon. The photo at left shows the Mark 4 detonator case that was discovered in the wreckage. A pair of 20-mm cannon are visible in the center photo. The photo at right shows the left wing, still with USAF markings. The wreckage was rediscovered in August 1997 with Scott Deaver visiting it on the 10th and Doug Craig and Doug Davidge on the 11th. The site has been visited several times since. (Doug Davidge)

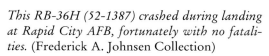

This RB-36H (52-1387) crashed during landing at Rapid City AFB, fortunately with no fatalities. (Frederick A. Johnsen Collection)

Returning from a deployment on 12 February 1953, this B-36H (51-5729) crashed at Goose Bay when the GCA controller issued incorrect instructions during landing. Another B-36H (51-5719) had crashed in England a week earlier during the same deployment. (via Don Pyeatt)

SURVIVORS

Of the 386 aircraft that were produced by Convair, only five remain intact – the single XC-99, one RB-36H, and three B-36Js. The future of three of the aircraft is certain – they are in government-funded museums and will most probably be on display for many years. The future of the XC-99 is more in doubt, despite Air Force assurances that it will be preserved. The B-36J at Fort Worth also faces an uncertain future, although it is unlikely anything untoward will happen to the aircraft anytime soon.

43-52436

The XC-99-1-CF was permanently grounded in August 1957 after logging 7,430 hours of flight time while carrying over 60,000,000 pounds of cargo. On 6 November 1957, title for the aircraft was transferred to the Disabled American Veterans, which put the aircraft on public display in a field next to Kelly AFB for the next 30 years. Regrettably, the aircraft fell into disrepair, and in 1993 the Kelly Field Heritage Foundation purchased it for $65,000 and the aircraft was towed back to the west side of the Kelly ramp near the Texas Air National Guard flight line. Plans to establish a museum at Kelly to house the aircraft proved fruitless, and the aircraft was subsequently donated to the Air Force Museum. Officials have stated that the aircraft will be preserved, but its exact future remains uncertain, especially given the closing of Kelly AFB in June 2001.[1]

51-13730

This Featherweight II RB-36H-30-CF was originally displayed at the Chanute AFB museum. It is the only surviving RB-36. When Chanute was closed, volunteers from Castle disassembled the aircraft and loaded the parts on 11 railroad cars supplied by the Santa Fe Rail Road. The volunteers then reassembled the aircraft. At the time of its retirement, the aircraft was operated by the 28th BW(H) at Ellsworth AFB, and is currently displayed in those markings.[2]

52-2217

This Featherweight III B-36J-1-CF was flown from Biggs AFB to Offutt AFB, Nebraska, for display at the Strategic Air Command Museum. The donation of this aircraft touched off an unusual problem: SAAMA had assumed that the aircraft would be donated without engines, classified items, or weapons. However, SAC refused to

The XC-99 as it appeared in May 1999 at Kelly AFB. Given the lack of care the aircraft has received for the past 30 years, it is remarkably intact. Most of the leading edge panels and hatches that are missing in these photos are inside the aircraft. The fabric-rudder looks the worse for wear. (Tony Landis)

The RB-36H at Chanute during October 1981. For some reason the aircraft was fictitiously painted as a B-36D (44-92065) in the markings of the 92nd BW. Note the FECM radomes are missing. (via Terry Panopalis)

As it sits at the Castle AFB Museum, the RB-36H is still not correct, but at least it is displayed in 28th SRW markings. Note the FECM radomes under the aft fuselage are still missing, and that the aircraft is configured with the original-style bomb bay doors that covered bomb bays No. 2 and No. 3 instead of the later ON TOP doors that more closely resembled the bombers. The nose radome is still in place. (Dennis R. Jenkins)

accept the aircraft unless the engines remained. Since this was a J-model with R-4360-53 engines, which were in short supply, SAAMA offered to swap the engines for earlier –41 models that were less critical. SAC refused, wanting a completely authentic aircraft for display. It was a battle SAAMA could not win, and the aircraft, as well as the ones at Fort Worth and the Air Force Museum were eventually displayed complete with their –53 engines.[3]

The aircraft is now part of the collection of the Strategic Aerospace Museum at Offutt. An XF-85 is also on display nearby. During its career the B-36 had served with the 7th, 28th, 42nd, and 95th BWs.

52-2220

The Air Force Museum has actually had three B-36s assigned to it for display. The first was the original YB-36 (42-13571), which had been converted into an RB-36E. The aircraft was delivered to the museum on 18 February 1957 after a 12-hour and 10-minute flight from Ramey AFB, Puerto Rico, where it had served with the 72nd BW. The pilot on the flight was Captain Blaine E. Thomas. This aircraft remained at the museum until 1971 when it was sold for scrap and the remains fell into the collection of Walter Soplata. What little remains of the aircraft is still on Soplata's farm in Ohio. The second aircraft selected for display was another RB-36E (44-92024) that was pulled from the second Mar-Pak contract. This aircraft remained in storage at Davis-Monthan until a B-36J (52-2220) was selected for display from the final batch of aircraft to be retired. The RB-36E was reclaimed and the carcass transferred to the Davis-Monthan fire department for use as a fire trainer during late 1958.[4]

The Museum's B-36J was flown to Wright Field from Davis-Monthan on 30 April 1959 from its assignment with the 95th BW(H) at Biggs AFB. This was the only unit the aircraft had served with during its relatively short career. This was the last flight ever made by a B-36. The aircraft presented some unique challenges for the designers of the new Museum building that was to house it. Because of the large wingspan it was finally decided to roll the aircraft into the building before the last wall was constructed. Also on display near the B-36 are an XF-85 parasite and the YF-84F prototype.

The B-36J at the Air Force Museum is the only B-36 inside a building, ensuring that it will remain in top condition. Despite being restored to a high standard, the aircraft is not completely accurate – for instance, the white paint has a masked demarcation, unlike operational aircraft that were sprayed without masking, leading to a fuzzy line. The museum also has one of the XF-85 prototypes and the FICON YF-84F displayed near the B-36. (Terry Panopalis)

52-2827

By December 1958, only 22 B-36Js remained in the operational inventory. A symbol of global airpower during the early days of the United States Air Force, the B-36 was now at the end of its career. On 12 February 1959, the last B-36J (52-2827) left Biggs AFB, Texas, where it had been on duty with the 95th BW, and was flown to Amon Carter Field in Fort Worth as part of Operation SAYONARA* The aircraft had originally been delivered to the 92nd BW(H) at Fairchild AFB. The Amon G. Carter Foundation supplied a $5,000 grant to build a concrete apron in front of the Carter Air Terminal to display the aircraft, and the Convair Management Club assumed the responsibility to maintain the aircraft. The retirement of the last B-36 marked the beginning of a new era – SAC became an all-jet bomber force on that day. Within 2 years, all but the four B-36s that had been saved for museum display had been scrapped.[5]

The aircraft was rolled across a grassy field on heavy steel matting and placed on display on the main approach to the airport terminal building in a memorial park that was constructed and donated by the Amon G. Carter family through the Amon G. Carter Foundation. Nearly 4,000 people were present for the park dedication ceremony on 17 May 1959. After hosting thousands of visitors for the next 10 years, the plane was evicted from its park due to closing of what was now the Greater-Southwest International Airport. Of the different plans suggested for its rescue, the most ambitious was made by Sam Ball, a Convair aeronautical engineer. He proposed the plane be restored sufficiently to allow it to fly to nearby Meacham Field where it would be further restored and maintained as a flying museum. The Peacemaker Foundation was established and received permission from the City of Fort Worth to restore and fly the plane. All six piston engines were started before the project was halted. One engine was allowed to run for 15 minutes and operated flawlessly after sitting idle for nearly 12 years. Alarmed by the possibility of the plane becoming airworthy, the Air Force decreed that work cease on the flyout effort. During the next 2 years, work on the aircraft scaled down while negotiations continued – unsuccessfully – with the Air Force.

The years of moving between several display sites and vandalism had taken their toll on the B-36J at Fort Worth. Over the past few years the aircraft has undergone a loving restoration by many of the people that originally built her, along with many others that are drawn to the history surrounding the largest piston-engine bomber in the world. (Bob Adams via 7th Bomb Wing B-36 Association)

Eventually the aircraft was turned over to a new group that put it on display near the General Dynamics (former Convair) facility that had built it. Here the aircraft was displayed with several other aircraft for many years, but it slowly deteriorated due to lack of maintenance and funds. In 1993 a new group formed to save the B-36J. With full support from the City of Fort Worth, it was moved into a hangar at the plant, now operated by Lockheed Martin. The aircraft has been beautifully restored, but the immediate plans for its future are in a state of flux. The most likely scenario is that a new museum will be built at the Dallas-Fort Worth airport with the B-36 as its cornerstone. But as always when discussing new museums, funding is an unknown issue, and it is probable that the B-36 will sit – mostly disassembled – at the Lockheed Martin facility for some time to come.

---

* Sayonara means goodbye in Japanese.

B-36: Saving The Last Peacemaker
An epic story of saving the last B-36

By Ed Calvert, Don Pyeatt, Richard Marmo
Foreword by Walter J. Boyne

A pictorial documentary of the rescue, restoration and preservation of the last Convair B-36 intercontinental bomber. Historical references, 408 photographs and two sound recordings provide the reader an accurate record of the preservation of a national treasure.

Revised 2002 by G.D. Pyeatt
Edited by Dennis R. Jenkins

HTML version. Requires an Internet browser. Internet connection not required.

The Fort Worth B-36 has become a lifetime cause for many former Convair and SAC personnel who built and flew the Peacemakers. One person in particular, Mr. C.E. (Ed) Calvert deserves special mention for devoting his life to the preservation of this aircraft. Mr. Calvert has volunteered as a caretaker of 52-2827 since the aircraft was retired from SAC in 1959 and continues to do so as this book goes to print. After learning of Mr. Calvert's dedication to his cause, ProWeb Fort Worth, a Fort Worth based web publisher, published an E-book on Compact Disk that details the post-service history of this aircraft and the many obstacles it has met while waiting to be placed on permanent public display. *B-36: Saving the Last Peacemaker* (ISBN 0-9677593-1-5), co-authored by Ed Calvert, Don Pyeatt, and Richard Marmo, describes the plight of the aircraft and those who undertook the monumental task of saving it from total destruction. The book is available online from Amazon.com and from the publisher's website http://www.prowebfortworth.com.

ATOMIC BOMB TEST PARTICIPATION

The following atomic tests were supported by B-36 aircraft in some manner. The B-36 probably participated in other tests, but no conclusive documentation was uncovered. In many of these instances, the B-36 actually dropped the weapon being tested – but there were other detonations where the aircraft that dropped the device could not be ascertained. Various other B-36s were used as "sampler" aircraft to measure the radiation released from the tests, and "effects" aircraft to measure overpressures. It was a dangerous job.

There were at least five B-36s dedicated for long periods of time to the atomic test mission. A single Featherweight III B-36D-5-CF (49-2653) was used as an "effects" aircraft for almost all of the early major tests. Four B-36Hs (50-1083, 50-1086, 51-5726, and 52-1386) were used extensively by the 4925th Test Group (Atomic) at Kirtland AFB, New Mexico, in support of atomic testing. In addition, two RB-36H-15-CFs (51-5748 and 51-5750) were modified with a series of upward-looking cameras to photograph the mushroom clouds at high altitudes (see page 223 for a photo).

The B-36 was chosen for use in the atomic tests for a couple of reasons. First, they were still the mainstay of the strategic deterrence armada, although it was obvious they were on their way out as the B-47 and B-52 came online. Second, they were large enough to carry meaningful equipment over long distances and were among the only aircraft that could fly high enough to obtain some of the data the Los Alamos scientists needed. Surprisingly, the Air Force was concerned about the effects of atomic detonations on fabric control surfaces, and the B-29 and B-50 still used fabric – most B-36s had been converted to metal surfaces during various mod programs, and the few that still had fabric rudders were quickly modified.

EFFECTS AIRCRAFT

When high-yield nuclear weapons (both fission and fusion) began to be developed, both the Atomic Energy Commission and the Air Force began to be concerned over their potential effects on the delivery aircraft. Largely to determine the maximum yield weapon that could be delivered by an aircraft (and have it survive to return home), the Air Force agreed to fly instrumented B-36, B-47, and B-50 aircraft near various atomic tests. These would be known as "effects" airplanes to determine what effects the heat, blast, and overpressure of a nuclear detonation had on an aircraft. The best estimates using strict-

ly theoretical data indicated that the B-36 should be able to deliver weapons in the megaton range, while the B-47 would probably be limited to about half of that. Operational considerations meant that the B-50 would likely never be called upon to deliver high-yield weapons, and the type was removed from testing after Operation IVY.

A single Featherweight III B-36D-5-CF (49-2653) was modified at Wright-Patterson AFB between 9 May and 15 June 1952, including the addition of a metal rudder (an approved modification for the B-36 fleet, but one that had not been universally implemented). The aircraft was heavily instrumented with thermocouples to measure heat, accelerometers to measure movement, strain gages, recording meters, and oscilloscopes. All of the data was recorded aboard the aircraft using either photographs of the oscilloscopes, or on wire recorders. This was before telemetry was a widely-used concept, and the electromagnetic pulse of the detonation would likely have rendered any

The Ruptured Duck *was a B-36D-5-CF (49-2653) that was used as an "effects" aircraft during many atmospheric nuclear tests. Note how high on the fuselage the white paint has been applied – this was well before the "high altitude camouflage" used on the operational B-36 fleet.* (George Savage)

telemetry unusable in any event. Calibration of the sensors was completed on 15 August and the aircraft was flown to Carswell AFB for maintenance. On 21 September 1952 the aircraft arrived at Kwajalein Island in the Pacific, followed by a B-47B on 2 October 1952 that would be used for similar tests.

OPERATION TEXAN

This was a full-scale rehearsal for Operation IVY that was conducted from Bergstrom AFB, near Austin, Texas, on 13 August 1952. A target ship was positioned in the Gulf of Mexico at the same distance (425 miles) from Bergstrom that the Eniwetok test site at Runit Island was from the Kwajalein airfield. A total of 39 aircraft participated in simulated bomb drops, sampling missions, drone control, and cloud-tracking tasks. Of these, three were B-36s – the dedicated B-36D effects aircraft, and two B-36H drop aircraft. One of the H-models would actually drop a live device during IVY, while the other would serve as a sampler control aircraft with scientists from Los Alamos aboard to direct the efforts of the sampler fleet. The device dropped during TEXAN was a modified T-59 training shape (really a Mk 4 bomb shape) that simulated the Mk 18 that would be dropped at Eniwetok. The device was 60 inches in diameter, 128 inches long, and weighed 8,600 pounds.

OPERATION IVY

In mid-October 1952 the Wright Air Development Center (WADC) published a report that attempted to specify the minimum safe altitudes to be used by a B-36D for surface-burst and air-burst weapons. In all cases the B-36 was assumed to be traveling at high speed in level flight when the weapon was dropped, with some scenarios including an immediate sharp breakaway turn. None of the weapons were parachute retarded. Surprisingly, the altitudes were not terribly high.[1]

	ALTITUDE IN FEET FOR		
SCENARIO	20 KT	45 KT	100 KT
Level flight sea-level burst	10,800	13,800	19,100
Level flight 3,000-foot air burst	12,600	16,700	21,800
Breakaway sea-level burst	4,460	6,880	9,830
Breakaway 3,000-foot air burst	7,390	9,520	11,410

The first tests of devices with yields greater than a megaton were undertaken during Operation IVY in the fall of 1952. Two devices were tested – a liquid-fueled thermonuclear device during Shot Mike, and a Mk 18 fission device during Shot King.

For Shot Mike the effects B-36D was flown from the airfield at Kwajalein, and was 15 miles away at an altitude of 40,000 feet at the time of detonation on 1 November 1952. The Mike device was too heavy to be airdropped, and was detonated on the ground. The 10.4 megaton detonation created a crater 164 feet deep and 6,240 feet in diameter, and a fireball 3.5 miles in diameter, and When the shock wave

arrived at the B-36D, the aircraft was at 38,500 feet at a slant range of 25 miles from the detonation. The aircraft had a true airspeed of 278 knots, and a true ground speed of 254 knots, away from the blast. The B-36D experienced a temperature of 93 degF on the wingtip nearest the explosion and a peak overpressure of 0.33 psi (only 62 percent of the design limit). This data was of a considerably lesser magnitude than expected and yielded little useful information.[2]

One of the conclusions from Shot Mike was that the B-36 was not fast enough to escape the potentially disastrous effects of a thermonuclear device unless the bomb was equipped with a retarding parachute that gave the bomber extra time to escape. Unfortunately, at the time, the Strategic Air Command strongly opposed the use of parachutes on nuclear weapons. Eventually, SAC relented and allowed the use of retarding parachutes on almost all nuclear weapons.[3]

The Shot King device was a prototype of the Mk 18 super oralloy bomb (SOB). The device consisted mostly of standard stockpiled components – it was based on the stockpiled Mk 6D bomb, but used the 92 point implosion system developed for the Mk 13. The normal uranium-plutonium composite core was replaced by a new design made up of approximately 132 pounds of highly enriched uranium (oralloy) in a natural uranium tamper. The complete bomb weighed 8,600 pounds.

A dry run for Shot King was held on 8 November 1952 with a modified T-59 training shape being loaded into the B-36H drop aircraft. The next morning the shape was dropped into the ocean near the Shot King surface target, northeast of Runit Island in Eniwetok Atoll. Most of the other aircraft and ships scheduled to support the actual test were involved in this dry run. All went well.

The actual Mk 18 prototype had arrived on Kwajalein via C-124 on 7 November. Following the successful dry run, on 12 November the device and all of its components were checked out and loaded in the B-36H. The next day the aircraft took off, but the drop was cancelled because of a solid overcast over the test area. The weapon was unloaded from the B-36H, underwent minor maintenance, and was reloaded on 16 November. Following a 06:30 departure, the B-36H conducted practice bombing runs over the target for 3 hours. In this case the "target" consisted of a series of brightly-painted oil drums mounted on pilings that provided a good optical target from 25 miles. Radar reflectors had also been installed, providing a radar target that was visible at a range of 60 miles. The bombardier used the optical sight, and dropped the device from 40,000 feet. He missed the target by a remarkably small 215 feet, and 56 seconds after release the device exploded at an altitude of 1,480 feet with a yield of 500 kilotons.

The effects B-36D was about 28,000 feet out of position during Shot King, and provided little useful data. The B-36H drop aircraft, however, sustained minor damage from the blast. Unfortunately, the H-model was not instrumented, but engineers later calculated that the empennage had been exposed to approximately 80 percent of its design limit. One of the results of this test was the development of a "thermal protection device" for the inside of the glazed panels on aircraft. The original curtains were made from an aluminized asbestos, but these could only be used once due to a severe blackening of their exposed surfaces. An improved material was subsequently selected –

a white duck fabric similar to canvas – that could be used multiple times. The B-36s participating in Shot Mike were equipped with the aluminized asbestos curtains, and these would remain through the end of Operation CASTLE when they were finally replaced by the updated material. Another change that resulted from the IVY tests was the decision to develop a highly reflective white paint to help protect the delivery aircraft. Eventually, almost all SAC nuclear bombers would have their bottom surfaces coated with a special heat-resistant white paint. However, for the remainder of the Pacific test series, the local units experimented with various white paints and the areas covered differed considerably from the later operational schemes.

Operation UPSHOT-KNOTHOLE

This operation was conducted at the Nevada Test Site and consisted of 11 atmospheric tests conducted between 17 March and 4 June 1953 – three airdrops, seven tower tests, and one airburst. The purpose of the tests included validating new theories using both fission and fusion devices. Approximately 21,000 Department of Defense military and civilian personnel participated in Operation UPSHOT-KNOTHOLE as part of the Desert Rock V exercise. Unfortunately, Operation Upshot-Knothole, particularly Shot Harry, drew a great deal of criticism as resultant fallout levels produced increased offsite radiation exposures. The tests comprising the 1953 Operation UPSHOT-KNOTHOLE included:[4]

Shot	Date	Launch	Type	Yield
Annie	17 Mar	tower	weapons related	16 kilotons
Nancy	24 Mar	tower	weapons related	24 kilotons
Ruth	31 Mar	tower	weapons related	200 tons
Dixie	06 Apr	air drop	weapons related	11 kilotons
Ray	11 Apr	tower	weapons related	200 tons
Badger	18 Apr	tower	weapons related	23 kilotons
Simon	25 Apr	tower	weapons related	43 kilotons
Encore	08 May	air drop	weapons effects	27 kilotons
Harry	19 May	tower	weapons related	32 kilotons
Grable	25 May	cannon	weapons related	15 kilotons
Climax	04 Jun	air drop	weapons related	61 kilotons

The B-36 did not participate in all of these tests. However, 12 B-36s were part of a 53-aircraft armada that participated in Shot Nancy on 24 March 1953. The lead B-36 was commanded by Brigadier General Joe W. Kelly, commander of the 19th Air Division from Carswell. The predawn detonation was used to provide firsthand knowledge of what an atomic explosion looked and felt like. The B-36s were from a variety of squadrons, but all landed at Carswell AFB following the explosion.[5]

The blast induced loads obtained during the two IVY shots had been too low to provide adequate verification of the blast load theory at levels approaching the maximum capabilities of the aircraft. In addition, the response data from IVY showed that the aft fuselage and

The fleet at Kirtland AFB included at least two EB-36Hs, an EB-50, and several F-84s. All were used to deliver nuclear weapons during various atmospheric test series. (National Archives via Stan Piet)

empennage of the B-36 were more vulnerable than had previously been predicted. As part of the tests, the effects B-36D (49-2653) received additional instrumentation after it had returned to Wright-Patterson AFB on 21 November 1952, but the instrumentation could not be completely calibrated prior to departing for Kirtland AFB. Nevertheless, the aircraft was exposed to Shot Encore as part of Project 5.3 over the Nevada Proving Grounds. The aircraft crew included aircraft commander Lieutenant Colonel Jerry Hunt, radar operator Lieutenant Colonel Harold Upton, and flight engineer Major Samuel Baker. In order to more accurately simulate an operational aircraft, this time the B-36D was loaded with 25,000 pounds of dummy bombs in bomb bay No. 1. The effects aircraft had to fly a widely separated formation with the drop aircraft to ensure it was in the proper position when the device was dropped. The shot was detonated on 8 May 1953, but again the data was not truly satisfactory, partially because the instrumentation had not been adequately calibrated. After this test the aircraft was sent to Fort Worth where Convair performed a complete instrument calibration with assistance from the Cook Research Laboratories.[6]

On 4 June 1953, an unidentified B-36H dropped a high-yield Mk 7 atomic device over Area 7 of the Nevada Proving Ground for Shot Climax. This was the 11th and final test of Operation UPSHOT-KNOTHOLE. Interestingly, since the B-36 was not normally equipped to handle the tactical Mk 7, a bomb rack from an F-84 fighter was temporarily installed on the B-36 for the test. The 1,334-foot altitude detonation was 172 feet west and 232 feet north of the designated ground zero. The predicted yield of this device was 50–70 kilotons, and the actual 61 kiloton yield was the highest of any U.S. continental test up to that time. This test was meant to test the "Cobra" core that was subsequently used as a primary in the TX-14, TX-17, and TX-21 thermonuclear devices fired during Operation CASTLE.

In addition to airborne support, the B-36 also participated in UPSHOT-KNOTHOLE on the ground, at least sort of. The Air Force wanted to expose various portions of an aircraft structure to higher blast effects than could be safely obtained by a manned aircraft in flight. Therefore, various assemblies – box beams, tension ties, stabilizer and elevator assemblies, outer wing panels, and parts of bonded metal structures – were manufactured and placed on the ground near the detonation. In each case, three identical parts were manufactured. One was shielded from the blast effects, one from thermal radiation, and the other was unshielded and exposed to the full force of the detonation. The stabilizer, elevator, and outer wing panels were placed under load to simulate flight conditions. These components were exposed to both Shot 9 and Shot 10 of UPSHOT-KNOTHOLE as part of Project 8.1a. The data collected was considered satisfactory.[7]

The tests resulted in a wide range of damage. For temperatures of approximately 350 degF, the tests showed that waffle panels were less vulnerable to skin buckling than hat panels. Honeycomb core panels were the most vulnerable due to bond release, with failures occurring as low as 300 degF. The overpressure required to produce panel buckling on the B-36 stabilizer and elevator assembly was found to be between 1.2 and 3.2 psi (at 13,000 feet from the detonation). An overpressure of 5.7 psi caused the wing panel, positioned 4,774 feet from ground zero, to fail.

Operation CASTLE

This nuclear test series was conducted between February and May 1954 at Eniwetok, in the Pacific Marshall Islands.

SHOT	DATE	EXPECTED YIELD (MT)	ACTUAL YIELD (MT)	ALTITUDE	SLANT RANGE
Bravo	01 Mar	4–8	15	33,000	60,580
Romeo	27 Mar	1.5–7	11	37,000	63,580
Koon	07 Apr	0.33–2.5	0.11	40,000	56,570
Union	26 Apr	1–6	6.9	37,000	62,700
Yankee	05 May	6–10	13.5	40,000	56,990
Nectar	14 May	1–2.5	1.69	33,000	126,380

As part of the tests, the effects B-36D (49-2653) was flown on all six tests as part of Project 6.2a with the call sign of "Elaine l." The aircraft was manned by crew S-36 from the 42nd Bomb Squadron, 11th Bomb Wing at Carswell AFB with Lieutenant Colonel George J. Savage the aircraft commander for each flight. For the first five shots, the aircraft was positioned in such a manner as to simulate that it had just dropped the weapon being detonated (i.e., flying away from the blast). On the last shot, the aircraft flew towards the blast in order to acquire data for

Without doubt, the most colorful B-36s were the two EB-36Hs (52-1358 and 51-5726, inset) from Kirtland AFB in this red, white, and blue scheme (see page 112 for a color photograph). Contrary to some reports, this scheme was not used during the atomic bomb tests, but was applied when the aircraft were used as high-altitude photo targets for ground-based cameras on the Atlantic Missile Range at Cape Canaveral. (Jay Miller Collection)

this orientation. On five of the shots, the yields of the detonations were such that good data were obtained – the unexpectedly low yield of Shot Koon provided no useful information. Shot Yankee provided the highest thermal and gust loading, 64 percent and 76 percent, respectively, of the theoretical aircraft limit. In fact, a 322 degF thermal pulse buckled the elevator skin in four places and blistered a large portion of the paint off the lower surface of the horizontal stabilizer – despite newly added painted gloss white with a clear overcoat. Shot Bravo resulted in overpressures in excess of 100 percent of the theoretical limits, and resulted in significant damage to various parts of the aircraft skin, although no primary structure was damaged (see below).[8]

In addition, two B-36Hs (50-1083 and 50-1086) were used as sampling aircraft during the tests, and a single RB-36H was used as a sampler controller, directing the sampling aircraft into the correct areas of the cloud. The sampling B-36s reached 55,000 feet, although it often took them over two hours of climbing to do so. The crew wore partial pressure suits, but even so each aircraft was limited to approximately 90–100 minutes above 50,000 feet before encountering either crew or equipment problems.[9]

[Excerpt from Operation CASTLE final report]

The "effects" B-36 flew during the six CASTLE shots to collect definitive blast and thermal response data near the aircraft's design limits so that the B-36 weapons delivery handbook could be completed.

The yield of the first CASTLE shot, Bravo, was approximately 150% greater than the positioning yield used for the effects studies of aircraft in flight. The weapons effects program B-36D – the same plane used during Operation IVY [and UPSHOT-KNOTHOLE] – was exposed to overpressure load, which caused mechanical damage that required replacement of the bomb bay doors, all four lower plexiglass scanners' blisters, and the radar antenna radome.

The undersides of all six engine nacelles and the landing gear and lower aft gun turret bay doors were also damaged. The radome was 'dished in' about seven inches, both bomb bay doors were buckled, the skin on the nose wheel doors was cracked, the main landing gear 'canoe' doors were dented, and several access doors were either blown off or unlatched by the blast.

Considerable thermal damage ensued. The heat pulse from the explosion buckled several small, unpainted inspection panel doors, scorched the left wing root fabric filler, blistered and scorched the paint at the wing roots, peeled and blistered paint on the middle of each horizontal stabilizer, blistered the paint and buckled metal on the elevator trim and servo tabs, burned and charred black rubber padding inside the two lower aft scanner's blisters [the upper blisters were covered over], and damaged many other components, including retracted gun turrets, propeller spinners, and even the bomb bay communications tunnel between the forward and rear crew compartments.

The crew reported seeing an intense bright red glow through the thermal curtains that had been pulled shut just before the blast [on all shots, the crew saw two distinct light pulses near the beginning of the thermal pulse]. The thermal pulse lasted about 15 seconds.

Shortly after the Bravo burst, the aft crew compartment was filled with smoke from blister padding, miscellaneous lubricating fluids, and charred components outside the crew cabin. Fire warning lights on four of the reciprocating engines lit up for about four seconds as thermal radiation impinged on sensors located in the engines and all jet engine exhaust temperature gauges pegged but engines returned to normal operation.

Thermal effects on this airplane during the 13.5MT CASTLE Yankee shot were also considerable: a 322 degree F. thermal pulse buckled the elevator skin in four places and blistered and peeled a large portion of the paint on the lower surfaces of the horizontal stabilizer and elevators, despite the plane's underside having been painted with a protective coat of clear lacquer over white enamel to improve the reflecting properties of the skin. The thermal pulse was accompanied by a 20 second duration radiation pulse.

The damage from the first CASTLE flight had required 818 man hours to repair. Somewhat laconically, the final project report for CASTLE noted that these phenomena also had a deleterious effect on the mental attitude of the crew.

The report concluded that "… for the relatively slow-speed, propeller-driven aircraft such as the B-36, the effects of the blast wave resulting from the detonation of a nuclear weapon may very well limit the operational capabilities during a strategic mission …"[10]

Information gathered during the CASTLE tests resulted in a B-36 delivery handbook being developed. The preferred delivery flight began at 345 knots at 40,000 feet (about the maximum speed possible), followed by a violent turn away from the target immediately after the weapon was dropped. It was estimated that the aircraft could survive a surface burst from a 10.8 megaton free-fall or 100 megaton parachute-retarded bomb (no 100 megaton bombs were actually developed). If the bomb was set to explode at 6,000 feet, these figures dropped to 1.5 and 35 megatons, respectively.[11]

OPERATION TEAPOT

Several operational B-36 crews participated as observers during Operation TEAPOT as part of Project 40.4. Shot Turk on 7 March and Shot MET of 15 April were both observed by crews from the 7th BW at Carswell as part of Project 40.0. These were considered operational training missions to verify "nuclear bomb delivery and escape procedures … from the SAC [weapons] delivery handbook for the B-36" The B-36s both used the call sign "Powder Burn." For the 45-kiloton Shot Turk, the aircraft was 1 mile east of ground zero, tail-on, flying eastbound at 250 mph and 23,000 feet. For the 24-kiloton Shot MET, the aircraft was directly overhead at 26,000 feet and 250 mph. After experiencing the effects of the detonation, the aircraft returned to Carswell. When the data was analyzed, it was determined that the radiation exposure was essentially nil – each crew member received less than 3 mrem of neutron exposure and 27 mrem of gamma exposure. In each case, this was less than what would trigger the "film badges" worn by the crew during the missions, and the recorded crew dose was zero.[12]

As part of Shot Wasp on 18 February, an unidentified B-36 dropped a Mk 12 (TX 12) case being used to test a 1.2-kiloton air defense weapon using the venerable Ranger Able uranium core in a new compact, lightweight implosion system. The test was at Area 7 of the Nevada Proving Grounds. The detonation had been scheduled for 07:30 hours, but was postponed until 12:00 noon when the B-36 take off was delayed, and again by clouds over the test location. Approximately 35 major experiments were conducted during the detonation, all for either weapons development or civil effects (Plowshare) purposes. The implosion system was a sphere 22 inches in diameter but only weighed 120 pounds. The total device weight was 1,500 pounds. The unretarded (free-fall) device detonated at 762 feet altitude. Although the bomb was much heavier, the implosion system was the lightest nuclear explosive system fired up until this time (broken the following year during Operation REDWING).[13]

On 25 March 1955, largely to test procedures of the nuclear test 4 days later, a B-36 dropped a non-nuclear high-explosive device from an altitude of 30,000 feet over Yucca Flat, Nevada. The device detonated against a background of intricate smoke trails and puffs positioned just before the burst by six F-86s and another B-36. The smoke provided photo reference points.[14]

The Wasp test was largely repeated as part of Shot Wasp Prime on 29 March 1955. The unretarded Mk 12 case was dropped from 15,000 feet and exploded at approximately 740 feet. About 40 Air Force aircraft participated in the test, mostly performing cloud sampling missions. Within 5 minutes of the detonation, the cloud had topped 30,000 feet altitude, and had largely vanished within 20 minutes. This device used a slightly higher yield core for weapons development purposes. The yield was about the same as predicted. As a minor footnote – this shot was fired 5 hours and 5 minutes after Apple-1, the first time in U.S. history that two nuclear explosions were set off in one day.[15]

Shot HA (high altitude) was on 6 April 1955 over Yucca Flat. This B-36H airdrop was a test of a 3.2-kiloton air-to-air missile warhead similar to the Wasp Prime device (17-inch spherical system weighing 125 pounds) in a 1,085 pounds Mk 5 ballistic case. The device was dropped from 42,000 feet and the device was parachute retarded to permit the B-36 to escape to a safe distance, marking the first parachute weapon drop conducted at the Nevada Proving Ground. The device was still at 32,650 feet when it detonated. The B-36H had dropped a series of radiosondes to record air pressure just prior to dropping the HA device. In addition, thermal and radiation sensors were installed in the aft fuselage. Two RB-36s were used during Shot HA to collect radioisotope samples from the cloud, but one bomber could not climb high enough to obtain useful samples.[16]

Operation REDWING

This test series was conducted between April and July 1956 at Eniwetok, in the Pacific Marshall Islands and included the first air drop of a U.S. thermonuclear weapon. Originally, a B-36 was going to be used to drop the TX-51-X1 from an altitude of 40,000 feet. However, further analysis determined that the B-36 was too slow to escape the expected thermal effects of the device, and a B-52B (52-013) was ultimately selected for the Shot Cherokee drop aircraft. A B-36 was, however, used to drop diagnostic canisters in support of Cherokee.

A B-36 was used to drop the low-yield TX-28 device used in Shot Osage on 17 June 1956. The device detonated at an altitude of 670 feet within 180 feet of the desired target and yielded 70 kilotons. This was a proof test of the W-25, a lightweight, low yield, plutonium warhead intended for air defense and other tactical applications. This spherical implosion device had a diameter of 17.4 inches, was 25.7 inches long and weighed 174.6 pounds. It was dropped in an instrumented Mk 7 drop case, which had a total weight of 3,150 pounds. This was the last nuclear test in which a B-36 participated.[17]

Operation MIAMI MOON

This was an operation to gather radioisotope samples from British nuclear weapons tests conducted during Operation GRAPPLE on Malden Island (south of Hawaii) in May and June 1957. Four specially-equipped RB-36s from the 5th BW were modified with four large external sampling pods (two per side) on the sides of the fuselage just ahead of the wing. The pods held removable fine-mesh paper filters to trap the radioactive particles which were later

Right: *Decontaminating the B-36s that participated in the nuclear tests was a manpower-intensive job. Primarily workers scrubbed the aircraft with a mixture of gunk and kerosene, followed by a lot of water. Note the lack of full-protection suits.* (via C. Roger Cripliver)

Left: *Decontamination at Convair sometimes involved disassembling major parts of the aircraft to ensure all surfaces could be cleaned.* (Lockheed Martin)

analyzed on the ground – no in-flight analysis was conducted. Originally four sampling flights were to be conducted during each of the four planned British tests, but ultimately the British only tested three devices, and the Air Force could only afford to fly two sampling missions per test. A 17-hour calibration mission was flown on 11 May 1957, and two missions were flown on 15 May, two on 31 May, and two on 19 June, all from Hickam AFB, Hawaii. Each sampling mission lasted 19 hours, with approximately 2.5 hours spent inside the mushroom cloud at an altitude of 40,000 feet.[18]

OPERATION OLD GOLD

A similar program was flown to gather data from Soviet nuclear tests, although the aircraft would necessarily not be able to fly as near to the cloud. During late 1957 and early 1958 two RB-36s from the 5th BW deployed to Eielson AFB, Alaska. This time each aircraft only carried two sampling pods, mounted on the side of the fuselage at the side-oblique camera position. A door in each pod opened at particular times during flight, exposing small tubes inside the pod that collected slipstream air and ducted it to containers located inside the camera compartment. The pods had originally been mounted parallel to the aircraft waterline, but were later angled slightly to correspond to the wing angle-of-attack. This was done to solve a problem where the pods were subjected to excessive aerodynamic forces because the B-36 tended to fly slightly nose high – in fact, one pod had been ripped off an aircraft as it departed Fairfield-Suisun AFB. The flights were flown along the edges of Soviet airspace for several days following each of the Soviet tests.

COSMIC RAYS

Although not actually a part of the atomic test series, one of the EB-36Hs (51-5726) from the 4925th Test Group (Atomic) at Kirtland AFB was used by the University of California Radiation Laboratory at Berkley during an investigation into the number and energy of cosmic ray neutrons in the upper atmosphere. The project began in November 1956 and continued through 1 February 1957 when the aircraft was scheduled for periodic maintenance. The tests were considered very successful, and were later continued using a B-52.[19]

DECONTAMINATION

As a result of supporting these nuclear tests, at least four B-36s (49-2653, 50-1083, 50-1086, and 52-1386) were heavily contaminated with radioactive material. Initially, the Air Force attempted to use normal maintenance personnel to decontaminate the aircraft. They were not totally successful. "From the experience gained following shot BRAVO in decontamination of B-36 aircraft it was apparent that the techniques and utilization of personnel and equipment must be revised. Entirely too much time was used to decontaminate the aircraft and excessive radiation exposures were being accumulated by B-36 maintenance personnel who participated in the decontami-

nation. … Decontamination is not 100% effective due to the nature of radioactivity and the inherent problem of completely cleaning all aircraft surfaces and engines."[20]

The initial attempt after CASTLE Shot Bravo was indeed manpower intensive. After the completion of a mission the two B-36Hs were parked in an isolated area and allowed to "cool" for 20 hours. Work stands were positioned and engine cowlings removed. Then a 1:5 ratio mixture of gunk and kerosene was applied over the exterior surfaces of the aircraft and engines. These surfaces were thoroughly scrubbed using brooms while the mixture was applied. A warm water and detergent mixture was applied to remove the emulsion formed by the gunk, followed by a fresh water rinse to remove all residue. The aircraft was then allowed to drain for 30 minutes before radiation measurements were taken. The procedure was repeated three times. The entire procedure required 17 personnel, took 4–5 days, and used 5,200 gallons of water, 220 gallons of gunk, and 1,010 gallons of kerosene for each aircraft.

After CASTLE Shot Romeo the Air Force decided to allow the aircraft to cool for 44 hours. Additional personnel (for a total of 26) were assigned to wash each aircraft, this time using 2,350 gallons of water, 83 gallons of gunk, and 321 gallons of kerosene. The warm water was heated and a couple of small drain holes were drilled in each engine cowling to prevent trapping contaminated water. Overall, this was considered a much better way to decontaminate aircraft in the field, and these procedures were used for the duration of the CASTLE tests.

On 30 September 1954 the Air Force awarded Convair a contract to figure out how to decontaminate the aircraft. The contract had two purposes: "(1) reduce the radioactive contamination of three B-36 airplanes to a level the Air Force considers safe for operating personnel and, (2) modernize each airplane to conform with the current SAM-SAC Cycle I configuration."[21]

The decontamination task had never been attempted before and forced Convair to overcome several unique problems. Special facilities had to be constructed at Fort Worth to handle the disposal of contaminated wash water and certain liquid and solid waste materials. It was necessary to indoctrinate each worker in the proper methods of handling radioactive parts and materials to ensure personal safety. This included the need to wear protective clothing, showering each day before going to lunch or before going home, and observing special precautions during smoke breaks and trips to the rest room. These precautions effectively limited each 8-hour shift to 6 hours of productive work.

Each aircraft was largely disassembled and thoroughly washed. A few badly contaminated skin sections were replaced, as were many rubber and plastic components. The aircraft were redelivered to the Air Force on 1 April, 17 June, and 19 August 1955, respectively.[22]

The four RB-36s used during Operation MIAMI MOON were decontaminated at Hickam Field, Hawaii, following that test series. Each aircraft was parked in a remote section of the field and allowed to cool for 3 days. The decontamination process was generally similar to that performed after CASTLE, using gunk and kerosene.[23]

PAINT AND MARKINGS

The XB-36 was delivered in an overall dull aluminum paint, although under some lighting conditions it appeared to have a natural metal finish. The XC-99 was delivered in all natural metal but used aluminum skin exclusively, leading to an overall shiny finish. The YB-36 and all B-36A aircraft were delivered in natural metal finish, revealing the two different materials (shiny aluminum and dull magnesium) used for their skins. The doped fabric control surfaces were painted an aluminum color that closely matched the dull finish of the natural magnesium. National insignia were located on both sides of the aft fuselage and the upper left and lower right wing surfaces. Large "buzz" numbers were painted on the forward fuselage ("BM" was the B-36 code, plus the last three digits of the serial number). Some aircraft also had the buzz number painted on the lower left wing.

The B-36B introduced having "USAF" painted on the lower left and upper right wing surfaces, displacing the lower buzz number. The USAF and national insignia were much further inboard (almost adjacent to the outboard R-4360 nacelle) than on later aircraft, when the markings were moved outboard of the jet nacelles. As part of Project GEM, most B-36Bs (and a few B-36As) had the top and bottom surfaces of the outer wing panels and both horizontal and vertical stabilizers painted a bright red to aid visibility in the white-out conditions experienced during arctic operations. The first B-36Bs left the factory without the red paint and it was added in the field. Later B-36Bs were painted on the assembly line. The area around the serial numbers, "USAF," and national insignia were left unpainted. Beginning sometime in 1950, most of the standard markings were applied in decal form instead of being painted on.

Sometime during B-36B production the buzz numbers disappeared from the forward fuselage and were replaced with "UNITED STATES AIR FORCE" in 9-inch letters on the forward fuselage just aft of the forward turret compartment. The marking appeared insignificant given the size of the fuselage. Some aircraft included both the small UNITED STATES AIR FORCE and the buzz numbers.

As the red markings disappeared, the round "numbered Air Force" insignia and geometric tail code (triangle, circle, etc.) began to appear on both sides of the vertical stabilizer. At least a couple of "red tails" had triangle markings along with the 8th Air Force insignia on the vertical stabilizers. Later, a letter representing the specific bomb wing would appear inside the geometric marking (triangle J representing the 7th BW, for instance).

If aircraft were assigned to a specific squadron within a wing, the squadron color was often applied to the tip of the vertical stabilizer, the nose gear doors, and infrequently to the front of the jet pods and the propeller spinners. When two Bomb Wings were assigned to the same Group (such as the 7th and 11th at Carswell) one of the wings used striped colors while the other used solid colors. Buzz numbers began to return late during B-36D production, but now omitted the "BM" and just used the last three or four digits of the serial number.

In 1954 the Strategic Air Command began painting the familiar "star spangled band" down each side of the nose, with the SAC shield on the left side. The right side was usually unadorned except for the band, but some aircraft displayed the wing insignia over the band.

During late 1955, the small "UNITED STATES AIR FORCE" on the forward fuselage was replaced with 36-inch-high "U.S. AIR FORCE" markings. This did not leave room for the buzz numbers, and they were usually deleted, although a few aircraft simply moved them forward of the new markings.

The "high altitude camouflage" white undersides also began appearing about this time. In reality, this was anti-thermal white paint meant to provide a small amount of additional protection against the thermal pulse of a nuclear detonation. The paint added almost 200 pounds to each B-36. At the same time the aircraft were given a coat of acrylic paint to inhibit corrosion, particularly on the magnesium skin. The fuselage generally used a clear coat, but the wings were often painted with an aluminum color that obscured the natural metal finish. The "USAF" marking on the lower left wing was usually deleted at this time. Since most of the units changed to a consolidated maintenance squadron, the individual color markings also began to disappear. The large buzz numbers continued on some aircraft however, usually written in front of the U.S. AIR FORCE in the same size. Other aircraft had the last four digits of their serial numbers written in 12-inch letters on the forward fuselage just above the white demarcation line under the crew hatch.

The Convair production number was frequently left painted in 9-inch numbers on both the extreme forward fuselage and the aft fuselage. Even if the units removed these, Convair simply repainted them the next time the aircraft went through maintenance or modification. Oddly, many photographs have these numbers scratched out by the censors, although the serial numbers were left intact.

There were, of course, many variations to these markings.

Wing	Tail Code	Location	Begin	End
5th Bomb Wing (Heavy)* [23rd, 31st, and 72nd BS]	Circle X	Travis AFB, CA	14 Nov 50	01 Jun 58
6th Bomb Wing (Heavy) [24th, 39th, and 40th BS]	Triangle R	Walker AFB, NM	16 Jun 52	01 Jun 57
7th Bomb Wing (Heavy) [9th, 436th, 492nd BS]	Triangle J	Carswell AFB, TX	01 Aug 48	01 Feb 58
9th Strategic Reconnaissance Wing [1st, 5th, 99th SRS] [1]	Circle X	Travis AFB, CA	01 May 49	01 May 50
11th Bomb Wing (Heavy) [26th, 42nd, 98th BS]	Triangle U	Carswell AFB, TX	18 Nov 48	01 Oct 57
28th Bomb Wing (Heavy)* [77th, 717th, and 718th BS]	Triangle S	Ellsworth AFB, SD	16 May 49	01 Feb 57
42nd Bomb Wing (Heavy) [69th, 70th, and 75th BS]	none +	Loring AFB, MN	25 Feb 53	01 Dec 55
72nd Bomb Wing (Heavy)* [60th, 73rd, and 301st BS]	Square F	Ramey AFB, PR	16 Jun 52	01 Jan 59
92nd Bomb Wing (Heavy) [325th, 326th, and 327th BS]	Circle W	Fairchild AFB, WA	16 Jun 51	15 Nov 56
95th Bomb Wing (Heavy) [334th, 335th, and 336th BS]	none +	Biggs AFB, TX	08 Nov 52	01 Jan 59
99th Strategic Reconnaissance Wing [346th, 347th, and 348th BS]	Circle I	Fairchild AFB, WA	01 Jan 53	04 Sep 56

* = redesignated from Strategic Reconnaissance Wing (SRW).

+ = the geometric tail codes were phased out before these Wings were activated.

Square was the 2nd Air Force; Triangle was the 8th Air Force; Circle was the 15th Air Force.

The "High Altitude Camouflage" was added to all operational B-36s by Time Compliance Technical Order 1B-36-895 dated 4 February 1955. The 20 gallons of Gloss White Enamel paint conformed to MIL-E-7729, Type I (it did not have an FS number). The paint was "feathered" onto the aircraft instead of having areas masked off, so the edge was not crisp. The feathering could extend up to 3 inches beyond the dimensional limits in the drawings. A 50-inch diameter National insignia was carried on the fuselage and upper left wing surface. (Convair via C. Roger Cripliver)

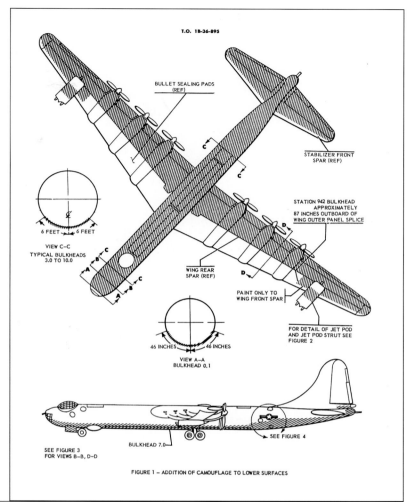

FIGURE 1 – ADDITION OF CAMOUFLAGE TO LOWER SURFACES

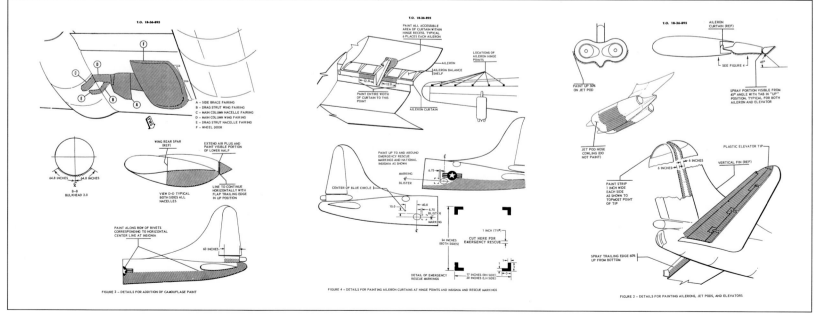

FIGURE 3 – DETAILS FOR ADDITION OF CAMOUFLAGE PAINT

FIGURE 4 – DETAILS FOR PAINTING AILERON CURTAINS AT HINGE POINTS AND INSIGNIA AND RESCUE MARKINGS

FIGURE 2 – DETAILS FOR PAINTING AILERONS, JET PODS, AND ELEVATORS

NOTES AND CITATIONS

Chapter 1 Citations

1. H.G. Wells, *The War in the Air*, originally published in 1908, republished by Quiet Vision in March 2001.
2. See, for example: Raymond R. Flugel, "United States Air Power Doctrine: A Study of the Influence of William Mitchell and Giulio Douhet at the Air Corps Tactical School, 1921-1935," (PhD dissertation, University of Oklahoma, 1965) pp. 183-234; and John F. Shriner, *Foulois and the U.S. Army Air Corps, 1931-1935*, (Washington DC: Office of Air Force History, 1983), pp. 44-46. Both are in the files of the Air Force Historical Research Agency (AFHRA), Maxwell AFB. The quote is from: Giulio Douhet, *The Command of the Air*, translated by Dino Ferrari, (New York: Coward-McCann, 1942), p. 34.
3. *Employment of Combined Air Force*, (Langley Field, VA: Air Corps Tactical School, 1926), passim; Thomas A. Fabyanic, "A Critique of United States Air War Planning, 1941-1944," (PhD dissertation, St. Louis University, 1973), p. 2.
4. *Employment of Combined Air Force*, passim.
5. Jeffery G. Barlow, *Revolt of the Admirals: The Fight for Naval Aviation, 1945-1950*, (Washington DC: Naval Historical Center, 1994), p. 13.
6. The Arnold quote is from *A Brief History of Strategic Bombardment, 1911–1971*, (March AFB, California, 15th Air Force, 1971), p. 17.
7. Barlow, *Revolt of the Admirals:*, pp. 14-15.
8. *The Effects of Strategic Bombing on the German War Economy*, (Washington DC: USSBS, 1945), p. 146; *Over-All Report (European War)*, (Washington DC: USSBS, 1945), pp. 42-45.
9. *Over-All Report (European War)*, (Washington DC: USSBS, 1945), p. 72.
10. *Very Heavy Bombardment in the War Against Japan*, (Washington DC: USSBS, 1946), passim; Robert F. Futrell, *Ideas, Concepts, Doctrine: A History of Basic Thinking in the United States Air Force, 1907-1964*, Volume 1, (Maxwell AFB: Air University, 1971), pp. 147-148.
11. *Very Heavy Bombardment in the War Against Japan*, p. 11.
12. Ibid, pp. 13-14.
13. Marcelle Size Knack, *Post-World War II Bombers*, (Washington DC: Office of Air Force History, 1988), p. 3.
14. Ray Wagner, *American Combat Planes*, 3rd Edition, (New York: Doubleday, 1982), pp. 210-211, 214-215, and 400-401.
15. Knack, *Post-World War II Bombers*,, pp. 5-6.
16. Ibid p. 7.
17. Convairiety, 18 January 1950, pp. 3-4.
18. Convairiety, 18 January 1950, pp. 3-4.
19. Meyers K. Jacobsen, "Design Development of the XB-36," AAHS Journal, Winter 1970, p. 227.
20. Knack, *Post-World War II Bombers*, p. 8; The map in Convairiety, 1 September 1948, p. 5 provides the distance between San Diego and Fort Worth.
21. Convairiety, 8 April 1953, p. 1; Knack, *Post-World War II Bombers*, p. 5.
22. Knack, *Post-World War II Bombers*, pp. 10-11.
23. Ibid, pp. 10-11.
24. Letter, General B.E. Meyers, Air Materiel Command, to Harry Woodhead, no subject, dated 7 July 1944, in the archives at the San Diego Aerospace Museum.
25. Knack, *Post-World War II Bombers*, p. 11.
26. "Investigation of Workmanship on the XB-36 Airplane," report from the AAF Air Technical Services Command, Engineering Division, 3 August 1945; Walton S, Moody, *Building a Strategic Air Force*, (Washington DC: Air Force History and Museums Program, 1996), p. 100.
27. The quote is from Hearings before the Subcommittee on Appropriations, House of Representatives, *Military Establishment Appropriations, 1947*, 79th Congress, 2nd Session, 8 May 1946, p. 23.
28. Frank Perkins, "The Crash That Saved the B-36," Fort Worth Star-Telegram, 13 March 1997.
29. Memorandum, subject: Track Landing Gear, to the USAF Chief of Staff from the Engineering Division, AMC, 1948; Convairiety, 29 March 1950, p. 8.
30. "7th BMW B-36 Chronology," TSgt Gregory S. Byard, 7th BW Historian, undated, p. 16, in the files at the Air Force Historical Research Center.
31. Move under power data from Convairiety, 30 January 1952, p. 1; Convairiety, 29 May 1957, pp. 1-2.
32. Robert Hotz, "Why B-36 Was Made USAF Top Bomber," *Aviation Week*, 15 August 1949, p. 14.
33. Convairiety, 13 October 1948, p. 1 and p. 8; Convairiety, 5 January 1949, p. 5.
34. Wagner, *American Combat Planes*.
35. Convair report ZP-XM-001, "Flying Wing Design, Six Engine, Long Range, Heavy Bombardment Airplane," 9 May 1942, in the archives at the San Diego Aerospace Museum.
36. Letter from Mr. H.A. Sutton to Mr. I. M. Laddon, Subject: Flying Wing Study, 9 May 1942, in the archives at the San Diego Aerospace Museum.
37. See, for instance, Convair report ZP-014, "Comparison Tailless vs. Conventional Four Engine Army Bombardment Design," 16 October 1943; Convair report ZP-020, "Two-Engine Bombardment Airplane, Tailless Type," 3 December 1943; Unsigned letter, "Status of Tailless Design," 11 March 1944. All in the archives of the San Diego Aerospace Museum.

Chapter 2 Citations

1. Convair report ZP-36-001, "Commercial Land Plane 6 Engines (Turbosupercharged) Model 36," 20 May 1942, in the archives at the San Diego Aerospace Museum.
2. Hoover was identified in Convairiety, 2 March 1949, p. 5 (and yes, his first name was Roberts).
3. *Aviation Week*, 2 June 1952, p. 12; "Convair XC-99 Press Book," undated, p. 18.
4. "Flight Operating Instructions for the XC-99 Airplane," 31 March 1949.
5. Marcelle Size Knack, *Post-World War II Bombers*, (Washington DC: Office of Air Force History, 1988), p. 8; "Convair XC-99 Press Book," p. 1.
6. "Convair XC-99 Press Book," p. 30.
7. "Convair XC-99 Press Book," p. 26; Convairiety, 15 February 1950, p. 1.
8. "Convair XC-99 Press Book," p. 11.
9. Ibid, p. 20.
10. Ibid, p. 28.
11. "Flight Operating Instructions for the XC-99 Airplane"; Convair Field Service Letter No. 56, 11 June 1951; Convairiety, 5 January 1949, p. 5; Convairiety, 2 February 1949, p. 1.
12. Convairiety, 5 January 1949, p. 5; Convairiety, 16 February 1949, p. 1; Convairiety, 13 April 1949, p. 1; Convairiety, 27 April 1949, p. 1; Convairiety, 2 August 1950, p. 1.
13. Convairiety, 11 May 1949, p. 1.
14. "7th BMW B-36 Chronology," TSgt Gregory S. Byard, 7th BW Historian, undated, pp. 11-12, in the files at the Air Force Historical Research Center.
15. Convairiety, 21 June 1950, p. 1; Convairiety, 19 July 1950, p.1 and p. 8.
16. Convair Field Service Letter No. 56, "New Developments: the XC-99 Airplane," 11 June 1951; a great deal more narrative on the Operation ELEPHANT flight may be found in Meyers K. Jacobsen, et. al., *Convair B-36: A Comprehensive History of America's "Big Stick,"* (Atglen, PA: Schiffer Military/Aviation History), pp. 327-330.
17. Convair Field Service Letter No. 56, 11 June 1951.
18. Ibid.
19. Ibid.
20. Convairiety, 22 November 1950, pp. 1-2.
21. Convairiety, 20 June 1951, p. 1.
22. Convairiety, 26 September 1951, p. 1; Convairiety, 16 January 1952, p. 8; *Aviation Week*, 2 June 1952, p. 12; Convairiety, 16 July 1952, p. 1 and p. 8.
23. Convairiety, 1 July 1953, p. 2; Convairiety, 26 August 1953, p. 1.
24. Convairiety, 26 August 1953, p. 1.
25. Convairiety, 7 August 1957, p. 2.
26. *Aviation Week*, 5 December 1949, p. 14, Convairiety, 23 November 1949, p. 1 and p. 8.
27. A great deal more narrative on the Post Office proposal may be found in Jacobsen, *Convair B-36*, pp. 331-332.
28. Convair report ZD-37-004, "CVAC Model 37 for Pan American Airways," 15 February 1945.
29. Convair report ZH-026, "A Comparison of Performance Between the Model 37 and a Flying Boat Version of the Same Airplane," 17 August 1945.
30. Ibid.

Chapter 3 Citations

1. "Development of Airborne Armament: 1910-1961," Volume II, Historical Division, Aeronautical Systems Division, October 1961, pp. 192-193.
2. Ibid, pp. 193-194.
3. Ibid, pp. 195-197.
4. Marcelle Size Knack, *Post-World War II Bombers*, (Washington DC: Office of Air Force History, 1988), p. 19.
5. "Development of Airborne Armament: 1910-1961," pp. 197-198.
6. Convairiety, 5 January 1949, p. 5.
7. Wayne Wachsmuth, *Detail & Scale Volume 47, B-36 Peacemaker*, (Fort Worth, TX: Detail & Scale, 1997), p. 16.
8. Convair report FZA-36-061, "Preliminary Proposal for Global Flight of the B-36 Airplane," 6 January 1947.
9. AN-01-5EUB-1, *Flight Operating Instructions, USAF Series B-36B Aircraft*, 16 November 1948, p. 22.
10. Delivery data in Convairiety, 15 June 1955, p. 1.
11. Knack, *Post-World War II Bombers*, p. 18.
12. AN-01-5EUB-1, *Handbook, Flight Operating Instructions, USAF Series B-36B Aircraft*, 16 November 1948, p. 22.
13. Test conducted during 1951 found that even on a 103 degF Texas day, the airframe could experience temperatures as low as −103 degF at 40,000 feet. The test rig used 240 transducers and 17,000 feet of wiring.
14. AN-01-5EUB-1, p. 95.
15. Ibid, p. 96.
16. "Development of Airborne Armament: 1910-1961," pp. 196-197.
17. "7th BMW B-36 Chronology," TSgt Gregory S. Byard, 7th BW Historian, undated, pp. 4-5, in the files at the Air Force Historical Research Center.

18. Convair report FZA-36-091, "Summary Report of B-36A Airplane Long Range Simulated Tactical Mission Flight Two," 4 June 1948; Convairiety, 5 January 1949, p. 5; "7th BMW B-36 Chronology," pp. 5-6.
19. Convair report FZA-36-100, "Summary Report of B-36A Long Range Simulated Tactical Mission Flight Three," 9 August 1948.
20. "7th BMW B-36 Chronology," pp. 7-8.
21. Knack, Post-World War II Bombers, p. 23; Convairiety, 5 January 1949, p.5; Aviation Week, 18 October 1948, p. 12; "7th BMW B-36 Chronology," pp. 5-6.
22. Convairiety, 27 October 1948, p. 1 and p. 8.
23. Knack, Post-World War II Bombers, pp. 21.
24. Aviation Week, 18 October 1948, p. 12; Walton S. Moody, Building a Strategic Air Force, (Washington DC: Air Force History and Museums Program, 1996), p. 238.
25. "Development of Airborne Armament: 1910-1961," pp. 47-48.
26. "Convair Statement of Work for a Modified B-36 Airplane Powered with Four Wright T-35-1 Gas Turbines with Extension Shafts," 14 February 1947.
27. Ibid.
28. "Development of Airborne Armament: 1910-1961," pp. 198-199.
29. Convairiety, 8 December 1948, p. 1 and p. 8.
30. "7th BMW B-36 Chronology," p. 10.
31. Knack, Post-World War II Bombers, p. 25; Convairiety, 5 January 1949, p. 5; Convairiety, 1 March 1950, p. 6: For a better description of the growing pains being experienced by the Air Force, see Moody, Building a Strategic Air Force, pp. 266-268, and 271.
32. Convairiety, 21 December 1949, p. 5.
33. Convairiety, 21 December 1949, p. 5; Convairiety, 25 October 1950, p. 8.
34. Convairiety, 21 December 1949, p. 5.
35. Convairiety, 8 December p. 1. As an aside, on the same page was a small article about a written request for a subscription to the Consolidated-Vultee News (the previous name of Convairiety) – the address was "Biblioteka, Frunze 19, Moscow, USSR." Convair declined.
36. Convairiety, 22 December 1948, p. 1 and p. 8.
37. Convairiety, 16 March 1949, p. 1.
38. Convairiety, 16 March 1949, p. 1.
39. Convairiety, 16 March 1949, p. 1 and p. 8.
40. Convairiety, 30 March 1949, p. 1.
41. Convairiety, 13 April 1949, p. 1.
42. Convairiety, 27 April 1949, p. 1 and p. 8; Convairiety, 3 August 1949, p. 1.
43. Convairiety, 21 June 1950, p. 5; Convairiety, 30 July 1952, p. 1; Convairiety, 10 September 1952, p. 1; "7th BMW B-36 Chronology," TSgt Gregory S. Byard, 7th BW Historian, undated, p. 40, in the files at the Air Force Historical Research Center.
44. "7th BMW B-36 Chronology," p. 9.
45. "Development of Airborne Armament: 1910-1961," pp. 51-52.
46. The Ladd field information is from Convairiety, 2 March 1949, p. 5; Convairiety, 12 October 1949, p. 1; Convairiety, 4 January 1950, p. 5; Convairiety, 1 March 1950, p. 1; Convairiety, 12 April 1950, p. 1.
47. Convairiety, 16 February 1949, p.1 and p. 8.
48. Convairiety, 13 April 1949, p.1; Convairiety, 12 October 1949, p.3.
49. Convairiety, 13 April 1949, p.1 and p. 8; Aviation Week, 15 August 1949, p. 14.
50. Moody, Building a Strategic Air Force, p. 267.
51. "7th BMW B-36 Chronology," p. 13.
52. "7th BMW B-36 Chronology," p. 13; Moody, Building a Strategic Air Force, p. 332.
53. "7th BMW B-36 Chronology," p. 13; Convairiety, 4 January 1950, p. 5; Convairiety, 1 March 1950, p. 1; Convairiety, 12 April 1950, p. 1; Convairiety, 5 December 1951, p. 5.
54. Convairiety, 6 June 1951, p. 1.
55. Fort Worth data from Convairiety, 1 March 1950, p. 1; San Diego data from Convairiety, 21 June 1950, p. 8.
56. Convairiety, 21 June 1950, p. 5; Convairiety, 30 July 1952, p. 1; Convairiety, 10 September 1952, p. 1.
57. Meyers K. Jacobsen, "B-36 Production, Part 2," in the AAHS Journal, Fall 1973, p. 168.
58. Knack, Post-World War II Bombers, pp. 15-16.
59. Telegram from R. G. Mayer, Plant Manager, Convair Fort Worth, to the Commanding General, Air Materiel Command, 4 September 1947.
60. Letter, Major General Lawrence C. Craigie, Chief of the Research and Engineering Division, Wright Field, to the Commanding General, Air Materiel Command, 10 September 1947; Letter, Lieutenant General Nathan F. Twining, Commanding General, AMC, Wright Field, to the Chief of Staff of the Air Force, 30 September 1947.
61. During this debate the independent Air Force finally became a reality and General Joseph T. McNarney replaced Lieutenant General Nathan F. Twining as the Commander of the Air Materiel Command. Letter, General Joseph T. McNarney, Commanding General, AMC, Wright Field, to the Air Force Chief of Staff, 16 October 1947; Moody Building a Strategic Air Force, pp. 180-181.
62. Letter from General Joseph T. McNarney, Commanding General, AMC, Wright Field, to the Air Force Chief of Staff, 21 April 1948.
63. Robert Hotz, "Why B-36 Was Made USAF Top Bomber," Aviation Week, 15 August 1949, p. 13.
64. Knack, Post-World War II Bombers, pp. 16-17; Jacobsen, "B-36 Production, Part 2," in the p. 168.
65. Letter from Frank A. Learman, Sales Manager, Convair Fort Worth, to the Commanding General, AMC, Wright Field, 4 May 1947; Knack, Post-World War II Bombers, pp. 16-17.
66. Letter from Frank Watson, Contract Manager, Convair, Fort Worth, to Commanding General, AMC, 10 December 1947.
67. Letter from Brigadier General, H. A. Shepard, Acting Director of Procurement, AMC, to Convair, Fort Worth, 30 December 1947.
68. Knack, Post-World War II Bombers, p. 20.
69. Letter, General Joseph T. McNarney, Commanding General, AMC, Wright Field, to the Air Force Chief of Staff, 21 April 1948.
70. Aviation Week, 15 August 1949, p. 14; AF-WP-O-APR 61 250, Index of AF Serial Numbers Assigned to Aircraft 1958 and Prior, Part 1: Numerical Listing; Prepared by the Procurement Division, Programmed Procurement Branch, Reports Section, MCPPSR, p. 125, in the files at the Jay Miller Collection.

Chapter 4 Citations

1. The fact that Bell manufactured the pods, instead of Boeing, came from Convairiety, 15 February 1950, p. 4; Convairiety, 23 May 1951, p. 8.

2. "Development of Airborne Armament: 1910-1961," Volume I, Historical Division, Aeronautical Systems Division, October 1961, pp. 50-51.
3. Convairiety, 11 October 1950, p. 8.
4. A reproducible photo of the first flight could not be found, but see Convairiety, 13 April 1949, p. 1.
5. Aviation Week, 12 September 1949, p. 37.
6. Convairiety, 7 June 1950, p. 1; Convairiety, 22 November 1950, p. 1 and p. 8.
7. Marcelle Size Knack, Post-World War II Bombers, (Washington DC: Office of Air Force History, 1988), p. 34; Convairiety, 13 April 1949, p. 1; Convairiety, 12 October 1949, p. 3; conversations with C. Roger Cripliver (retired Convair engineer); "7th BMW B-36 Chronology," TSgt Gregory S. Byard, 7th BW Historian, undated, p. 18, in the files at the Air Force Historical Research Center.
8. Cannon data from Convairiety, 6 December 1950, p.1 and p. 8; Convairiety, 10 January 1951, p. 5; Building 3 data from Convairiety, 9 May 1951, p. 8.
9. Convairiety, 20 June 1951, p. 5.
10. Convairiety, 20 June 1951, p. 5.
11. Convairiety, 31 January 1951, p. 1; Convairiety, 19 December 1951, p. 1.
12. Proseal data from Convairiety, 31 January 1951, p. 2.
13. "Development of Airborne Armament: 1910-1961," pp. 196-197.
14. "7th BMW B-36 Chronology," p. 14.
15. Convairiety, 18 September 1957, p. 2.
16. Order/quantity data comes from Convairiety, 4 January 1950, p. 3.
17. "Development of Airborne Armament: 1910-1961," pp. 198-201.
18. Convairiety, 28 March 1951, p. 1.
19. Convair Field Service Letter No. 56, 11 June 1951.
20. "7th BMW B-36 Chronology," pp. 22-23.
21. Knack, Post-World War II Bombers, p. 41.
22. "7th BMW B-36 Chronology," pp. 26-28.
23. Convairiety, 25 April 1951, pp. 1-2.
24. Mock-up inspection from Convairiety, 30 August 1950, p. 1; "Drag Evaluation of the YDB-36H," AFFTC report 53-31, October 1953, originally classified SECRET, declassified on 31 December 1972, Appendix I, p. 3.
25. "Development of Airborne Armament: 1910-1961," pp. 199-203.
26. Ibid.
27. Mock-up inspection from Convairiety, 30 August 1950, p. 1.
28. "High-altitude propeller" comment from Mike Moore in conversation with the author, 11 May 2001.
29. Knack, Post-World War II Bombers, p. 45.
30. Convairiety, 23 March 1955, p. 8.
31. "7th BMW B-36 Chronology," p. 31.
32. Ibid, p. 36.
33. "Convair Development Department Annual Report 1953," 27 May 1954, p. 23.
34. "Drag Evaluation of the YDB-36H," Appendix I, p. 3; "B-36 Rascal Mock-up Inspection," a brochure released on 18 November 1952 in support of the mockup inspection, originally classified SECRET.
35. Standard Aircraft Characteristics, Consolidated-Vultee DB-36H, 20 April 1954; Standard Aircraft Characteristics, Consolidated-Vultee DB-36H-II, 3 October 1955.
36. Aircraft History Cards supplied by Mike Moore, Lockheed Martin, Fort Worth; "Drag Evaluation of the YDB-36H," Appendix I, p. 3; "B-36 Rascal Mock-up Inspection," p. 25.
37. "B-36 Rascal Mock-up Inspection," p. 9.
38. Ibid.
39. "B-36 Rascal Mock-up Inspection"; "Semi-Annual Progress Report," Holloman Air Development Center, 8 July 1955.
40. "Convair Development Department Fourth Annual Report," 8 September 1955, p. 9, in the files at the AEC, Little Rock; "Drag Evaluation of the YDB-36H," Appendix I, p. 4.
41. "Drag Evaluation of the YDB-36H," p. 1.
42. "Convair Development Department Fourth Annual Report," p. 9.
43. "Semi-Annual Progress Report," Holloman Air Development Center, 8 July 1955; "Weekly Test Report Status," Holloman Air Development Center, 19 June 1955. Both were originally classified SECRET and are in the files of the Air Force Historical Research Agency.
44. "Convair Development Department Annual Report 1953," 27 May 1954, p. 27; "Convair Development Department Fourth Annual Report," p. 25.
45. Ray Wagner, American Combat Planes, third edition, (New York: Doubleday and Company, 1982), p 428. Some sources indicate Rascal was cancelled on 29 November instead of 9 September.
46. "7th BMW B-36 Chronology," p. 34.
47. "Convair Development Department Annual Report 1953," 27 May 1954, p. 25.
48. Knack, Post-World War II Bombers, p. 51; Convairiety, 25 August 1954, p. 1.
49. Knack, Post-World War II Bombers, p. 51; Convairiety, 30 June 1954, p. 1.
50. SAC Programming Plan 10-54, "Featherweight Modification for the B-36 Fleet," (TOP SECRET), 28 January 1954; History of the Fifteenth Air Force, 1 January 1954 to 30 June 1954, Top Secret Supplement, Project Featherweight, 3 December 1954, p. 1, in the files of the AFHRA as K670.01-15.
51. History of the Fifteenth Air Force, p. 2.
52. History of the Fifteenth Air Force, p. 2.
53. History of the Fifteenth Air Force, p. 3; "Featherweight Project Manufacturing Plan," Convair Fort Worth, 1954, passim.
54. "Featherweight Project Manufacturing Plan," p. 9.
55. "Featherweight Project Manufacturing Plan," p. 9-10.
56. History of the Fifteenth Air Force, pp. 3-4.
57. "Featherweight Project Manufacturing Plan," p. 7.
58. History of the Fifteenth Air Force, pp. 4-6.
59. "Featherweight Project Manufacturing Plan," passim; "Phase II ECM Manufacturing Plan," Convair Fort Worth ECP-678AH and ECP-678AG, 14 July 1954, passim; "Phase II ECM and Phase X ON TOP Manufacturing Plan," Convair Fort Worth, 22 October 1954, (no page numbers).
60. History of the Fifteenth Air Force, pp. 7-8=.
61. "ECP 2308 Phase 10 ON TOP Manufacturing Plan," 13 September 1954, p. 2-3.
62. Notes and documentation supplied by C. Roger Cripliver, who was responsible for writing many of the TCTOs used in these programs.
63. Ibid.

64. Untitled report dated 10 August 1967, supplied by C. Roger Cripliver.
65. Convairiety, 17 June 1953, p. 1 and p. 8.
66. "Operation SAM-SAC," prepared by Convair Tool Project Engineering, undated, pp. 28-29.
67. Conclusion of B-36 Aircraft Phase-Out, Historical Monograph Nr. 1, Headquarters, San Antonio Air Materiel Area, Kelly AFB, Texas, March 1960; "Operation SAM-SAC," prepared by Convair Tool Project Engineering, undated, pp. 16-18.
68. Convairiety, 22 February 1956, p. 1 and p. 3.
69. Convairiety, 17 June 1953, p. 8; Convairiety, 15 July 1953, p. 2; Convairiety, 27 July 1955, p. 1.
70. Convairiety, 17 June 1953, p. 8; Convairiety, 15 July 1953, p. 2; Convairiety, 27 July 1955, p. 1.
71. Convairiety, 1 June 1955, p. 1; "Operation SAM-SAC," p. 14.
72. Convairiety, 22 February 1956, p. 1 and p. 3.
73. Convairiety, 17 April 1957, p. 2; Notes and documentation supplied by C. Roger Cripliver, who was responsible for writing many of the TCTOs used in these programs.

Chapter 5 Citations

1. Convairiety, 23 November 1949, p. 1; quote is from Convairiety, 4 January 1950, p. 1.
2. 1B-36(R)H(III)-1, Flight Handbook, USAF Series RB-36H-III Aircraft, Featherweight – Configuration III, 21 October 1955, pp. 218-282.
3. Report from Colonel A. A. Fickel, USAF, Assistant to the Commanding General, ARDC to General Schlatter and General Cook (HQ, ARDC, Wright-Patterson AFB), 19 March, 1951.
4. Convairiety, 15 February 1950, p. 3.
5. "Phase II ECM Manufacturing Plan," Convair Fort Worth ECP-678AH and ECP-678AG, 14 July 1954, pp. 28-29; "ECP 2308 Phase 10 ON TOP Manufacturing Plan," Convair, 13 September 1954, passim.
6. RB-36 Aircraft Weather Reconnaissance Manufacturing Plan," Convair, 12 August 1954, passim; "Phase II ECM and Phase X ON TOP Manufacturing Plan," Convair Fort Worth, 22 October 1954, (no page numbers).
7. Convairiety, 4 January 1950, p. 1; Flight logs belonging to Berton L. Woods, who flew on almost every B-36 at Fort Worth – his entry on 14 December 1949 for 44-92088 indicates it was a "10-engine" reconnaissance model (other entires around it indicate B-models as "6-engine").
8. Convairiety, 15 February 1950, p. 3.
9. Convairiety, 10 May 1950, p. 3.
10. Wayne Wachsmuth, Detail & Scale Volume 47, B-36 Peacemaker, (Fort Worth, TX: Detail & Scale, 1997), p. 20.
11. Rapid City data from Convairiety, 14 March 1951.
12. Convairiety, 15 June 1955, pp. 1-2.
13. Convairiety, 2 August 1950, p. 1; Convairiety, 1 August 1951, p. 5.
14. Convairiety, 1 August 1951, p. 5.
15. Order/quantity data comes from Convairiety, 4 January 1950, p. 3; Convairiety, 12 September 1951, p. 1.
16. Conversation between the author and Cargill Hall, Historian at the National Reconnaissance Office (NRO), 12 January 2001.
17. History of the Fifteenth Air Force, 1 January 1954 to 30 June 1954, Top Secret Supplement, Project Featherweight, 3 December 1954, pp. 12-13, in the files of the AFHRA as K670.01-15.

Chapter 6 Citations

1. Pratt & Whitney Bee-Hive (employee newsletter), January 1946 (pp. 8-9), Spring 1947 (pp. 10-14), and January 1949 (pp. 7-11). These were thoughtfully provided to me by Tom A. Heppenheimer. The X-101 engine was continually updated to reflect the current engineering configuration. By 1947 it resembled an "old farmer's ax which had seven new handles and five new heads, but was still the same old ax."
2. Pratt & Whitney Bee-Hive, January 1946, pp. 8-9.
3. Pratt & Whitney Bee-Hive, Spring 1947, pp. 10-14.
4. Pratt & Whitney Bee-Hive, Spring 1947, pp. 10-14.
5. Pratt & Whitney Bee-Hive, Spring 1947, p. 12.
6. Pratt & Whitney Bee-Hive, Spring 1947, p. 14. It is somewhat unclear as to if these figures had been adjusted for inflation since the development efforts took place over a span of 15 years or so. Regardless, it gives a relative indication of the costs associated with the development of the R-4360.
7. SAC Manual 50-35, Aircraft Performance Engineer's Manual for B-36 Aircraft Engine Operation, 1953.
8. AN-01-5EUB-1, Handbook, Flight Operating Instructions, USAF Series B-36B Aircraft, 16 November 1948, p. 7; 1B-36H(III)-1, Flight Handbook, USAF Series B-36H-III Aircraft, 26 November 1954, p. 1-4; 1B-36(R)H(III)-1, Flight Handbook, USAF Series RB-36H-III Aircraft, Featherweight – Configuration III, 21 October 1955, p. 80.
9. AN-01-5EUB-1, p. 7; 1B-36H(III)-1, p. 2.
10. AN 01-5EUC-2 (1B-36D-2), Erection and Maintenance Instructions, USAF Series B-36D Aircraft, 3 June 1954; "Drag Evaluation of the YDB-36H," AFFTC report 53-31, October 1953, originally classified SECRET, declassified on 31 December 1972, p. 1, Appendix II, p. 7.
11. AN-01-5EUB-1, p. 8.
12. SAC Manual 50-35, passim; 1B-36H(III)-1, p. 1-13; AN-01-5EUB-1, p. 4.
13. AN-01-5EUB-1, p. 6.
14. Ibid, p. 13.
15. Ibid.
16. AN-01-5EUB-1, pp. 8-9; 1B-36H(III)-1, p. 1-16.
17. 1B-36H(III)-1, p. 1-17.
18. Convairiety, 5 November 1952, p. 3.
19. Pratt & Whitney Bee-Hive, January 1949, pp. 8-9.
20. Pratt & Whitney Bee-Hive, January 1949, pp. 10-11.
21. Pratt & Whitney Bee-Hive, January 1949, p. 10.
22. Pratt & Whitney Bee-Hive, January 1949, p. 11.
23. Pratt & Whitney Bee-Hive, January 1949, p. 7.
24. http://www.geae.com/aboutgea/history.html, accessed on 21 March 2001.
25. http://www.geae.com/aboutgea/history.html, accessed on 21 March 2001.
26. http://www.wpafb.af.mil/museum/engines/eng49.htm, accessed on 21 March 2001.
27. http://www.geae.com/aboutgea/history.html, accessed on 21 March 2001; http://www.wpafb.af.mil/museum/engines/eng49.htm, accessed on 21 March 2001.
28. http://www.geae.com/aboutgea/history.html, accessed on 21 March 2001.

Chapter 7 Citations

1. A very detailed history of the defensive systems may be found in Meyers K. Jacobsen, et. al., Convair B-36: A Comprehensive History of America's "Big Stick," (Atglen, PA: Schiffer Military/Aviation History), pp. 246-287; see also "Development of Airborne Armament: 1910-1961," Volume II, Historical Division, Aeronautical Systems Division, October 1961, pp. 169-206.
2. SAC Manual 50-30, B-36 Gunnery, November 1954, passim.
3. Ibid.
4. "Convair Development Department Annual Report 1953," 27 May 1954, p. 7; "Convair Development Department Fourth Annual Report," 8 September 1955, p. 23; both in the files at the AEC, Little Rock.
5. Kenneth P. Werrell, The Evolution of the Cruise Missile, Air University Press, Maxwell AFB, AL, September 1985, pp. 123-124; AF-WP-O-APR 61-250, Index of AF Serial Numbers Assigned to Aircraft 1958 and Prior, Part 1: Numerical Listing; Prepared by the Procurement Division, Programmed Procurement Branch, Reports Section, MCPPSR, p. 125, in the files at the Jay Miller Collection.
6. Werrell, The Evolution of the Cruise Missile, p. 236; Ferrest E. Armstrong, "From New Technology Development to Operational usefulness – B-36, B-58, F-111/FB-111," a paper written for an AIAA conference, but unfortunately, I do not know when or why.
7. Convair report ZN-175/1, undated but probably late 1954, passim, originally classified SECRET, declassified on 15 January 1968, in the files of the San Diego Aerospace Museum.
8. Ibid.
9. http://www.wpafb.af.mil/cgi-bin/quiz.pl/research/bombers/b5/b5-70.htm, accessed on 7 May 2001.
10. Werrell, The Evolution of the Cruise Missile, p. 124; Information in various flat files in the 45th SW History Office, Patrick AFB, Florida.
11. AN-01-5EUB-1, Handbook, Flight Operating Instructions, USAF B-36B Aircraft, 16 November 1948, p. 94.
12. AN-01-5EUB-1, p. 13 and 94; AN 01-5EUC-2 (1B-36D-2), Erection and Maintenance Instructions, USAF Series B-36D Aircraft, 3 June 1954, p. 637; Convairiety, 14 March 1951, p. 5; Aviation Week, 12 September 1949, p. 37.
13. Aviation Week, 18 October 1948, p. 94.
14. Walton S. Moody, Building a Strategic Air Force, (Washington DC: Air Force History and Museums Program, 1996), pp. 167-170.
15. Ibid, passim.
16. "History of Project Saddletree," Air Material Command, Wright-Patterson AFB, May 1963.
17. Moody, Building a Strategic Air Force, pp. 244-245.
18. A more in-depth, but somewhat confusing, look at the various early bomb modifications to the B-36 may be found in Jacobsen, et. al., Convair B-36, pp. 235-240. Other data from AN01-5EUE-2 (undated), T.O. 1B-36D-2-1 dated 23 March 1956, and T.O. 1B-36D-4 dated 16 November 1956.
19. From the movie "Broken Arrow," ©1995 Twentieth Century Fox Film Corporation
20. "Narrative Summaries of Accidents Involving U.S. Nuclear Weapons: 1950–1980," Department of Defense report 322434, April 1981. Provided by the DoE Nevada Test Site archives.
21. Letter, Major General Thomas D. White, USAF, to William L. Borden, Chairman, Joint Committee on Atomic Energy, 17 March 1950. Originally classified TOP SECRET, declassified on 26 April 1968. Provided by the DoE Nevada Test Site archives; Frank Perkins, "Nightmare at Midnight," Fort Worth Star-Telegram, 16 February 1997.
22. Letter, Herbert B. Loper, Assistant to the Secretary of Defense (Atomic Energy), to the Honorable Carl. T. Durham, Chairman of the Joint Committee on Atomic Energy, 15 July 1957. Originally classified SECRET, declassified on 2 May 1992. Provided by the DoE Nevada Test Site archives.
23. The K-system history is condensed from "Development of Airborne Armament: 1910-1961," Volume I, Historical Division, Aeronautical Systems Division, October 1961, pp. 1-63.
24. AN 01-5EUC-2 (1B-36D-2), p. 519.
25. 1B-36H(III)-1, p. 229.
26. "Phase II ECM Manufacturing Plan," ECP-678AH and ECP-678AG, 14 July 1954, passim.
27. Ibid, pp. 28-29.
28. Aviation Week, 12 July 1948, p. 21.
29. Convairiety, 12 March 1952, pp. 1-2; Convairiety, 19 November 1952, pp. 1-2; Convairiety, 10 March 1954, pp. 1-2
30. From a release by Convair dated 15 October 1957. Supplied courtesy of C. Roger Cripliver; "Track landing gear for the B-36 Strategic Bomber," prepared for the Air Command and Staff School of the Air University, May 1949, in the files of the Air Force Historical Research Agency.

Chapter 8 Citations

1. Walton S. Moody, Building a Strategic Air Force, (Washington DC: Air Force History and Museums Program, 1996), pp. 412-414.
2. Convairiety, 10 September 1952, pp. 1-2.
3. Convairiety, 24 September 1952, p. 1.
4. "7th BMW B-36 Chronology," TSgt Gregory S. Byard, 7th BW Historian, undated, pp. 30-31, in the files at the Air Force Historical Research Center.
5. "7th BMW B-36 Chronology," p. 29; Moody, Building a Strategic Air Force, pp. 412-414.

Chapter 9 Citations

1. Ray Wagner, American Combat Planes, third edition, (New York: Doubleday and Company, 1982), pp. 141-142.
2. Clarence E. "Bud" Anderson, To Fly and To Fight, (New York: St. Martin's Press, 1990), pp. 199-200.
3. Ibid, pp. 201-202.
4. Ibid.
5. Convairiety, 9 September 1953, p. 1; Convairiety, 23 September 1953, pp. 1-2; Convairiety, 5 May 1954, p. 1.
6. Convairiety, 13 January 1954, p. 1; "FICON Manufacturing Plan," 11 May 1954, p. 6, originally classified SECRET, declassified on 3 August 1961; "Convair Development Department Fourth Annual Report," 8 September 1955, p. 26, in the files at the AEC, Little Rock.
7. Convairiety, 28 December 1955, p. 1.
8. "FICON Manufacturing Plan," passim.
9. Ibid.
10. Ibid, pp. 20-64.
11. 1B-36(R)D(G)-1, FICON Flight Manual, 17 June 1955; "FICON Manufacturing Plan," p. 10.
12. Training data from Convairiety, 16 November 1955.

13. <u>Convairiety</u>, 28 December 1955, p. 1 and p. 8.
14. C.E. "Bud" Anderson, "Aircraft Wingtip Coupling Experiments," a paper prepared for the Society of Experimental Test Pilots, passim.
15. Ibid.
16. "Convair Development Department Fourth Annual Report," 8 September 1955, p. 22.
17. Jay Miller, *Convair B-58*, Aerograph #4, Aerofax, Inc. 1985, pp. 17-21.
18. For a more complete accounting of the GEBO designs, see Jay Miller, *Convair B-58*, Aerograph #4, Aerofax, Inc. 1985, pp. 17-21 (now available from Midland Counties Publishing, Hinckley, UK).

Chapter 10 Citations

1. Ray Wagner, *American Combat Planes*, third edition, (New York: Doubleday and Company, 1982), p 432.
2. Ibid.
3. *Aviation Week*, 29 January 1951, p. 13.
4. *Ibid.*
5. "YB-60 Standard Aircraft Characteristics," 21 September 1951, classified SECRET, declassified 16 December 1966. In the files at the Air Force Museum; "Phase II Flight Test of the YB-60 Airplane," AFFTC report 53-10, April 1953, originally classified SECRET; declassified on 29 March 1977, Appendix II, p. 4.
6. "YB-60 Standard Aircraft Characteristics;" "Transition to Swept Wing B-36," a small paper published by Convair and classified Secret at the time (undated). Copies are in the files at the San Diego Aerospace Museum, Air Force Historical Research Agency, and the National Archives; "Phase II Flight Test of the YB-60 Airplane," p. 1.
7. "YB-60 Standard Aircraft Characteristics;" "Transition to Swept Wing B-36;" "Phase II Flight Test of the YB-60 Airplane," Appendix I, p. 4.
8. "YB-60 Standard Aircraft Characteristics."
9. Ibid.
10. <u>Convairiety</u>, 16 January 1952, p. 1 and p. 8.
11. <u>Convairiety</u>, 7 May 1952, p. 8.
12. <u>Convairiety</u>, 23 April 1952, p. 1.
13. "Mockup Inspection of the Model YB-60 Airplane," Convair, Contract AF-33(038)-2182, 20 August 1951, p. 11.
14. Ibid, p. 3.
15. Ibid, p. 16.
16. Ibid, pp. 16-17.
17. Ibid, p. 17.
18. Ibid, p. 18; "Phase II Flight Test of the YB-60 Airplane," p. 2.
19. "Mockup Inspection of the Model YB-60 Airplane," pp. 18-20.
20. Ibid, p. 20.
21. Ibid, pp. 20-21.
22. Ibid, p. 21.
23. Ibid, p. 11. This represented the inclusion of MCRs 5009-5012, 5014-5016, and 5020-5022.
24. Ibid, pp. 21-22.
25. Ibid, p. 22.
26. Ibid, p. 3; "Experimental All-Jet Versions of B-36 Are Given the Ax at Carswell," <u>Fort Worth Star-Telegram</u>, 1 July 1954.
27. "YB-60 Standard Aircraft Characteristics."
28. YB-60 flight history source data were the accident files at the Directorate of Flight Safety Research OTIG, Norton AFB, California, and at the Federal Records Center, Alexandria, Virginia.
29. <u>Convairiety</u>, 17 December 1952, p. 1; <u>Convairiety</u>, 14 January 1953, p. 1.
30. "Phase II Flight Test of the YB-60 Airplane," p. 1 and Appendix III, p. 1; <u>Convairiety</u>, 31 December 1952, p. 2; <u>Convairiety</u>, 14 January 1953, p. 1; conversations and email between Fred Stoliker and the author, various dates in March 2001.
31. "Phase II Flight Test of the YB-60 Airplane," p. 2.
32. "Phase II Flight Test of the YB-60 Airplane," p. 3.
33. <u>Fort Worth Star-Telegram</u>, various dates in July 1954; Meyers K. Jacobsen, et. al., *Convair B-36: A Comprehensive History of America's "Big Stick*," (Atglen, PA: Schiffer Military/Aviation History), p. 339.
34. "YB-60 Commercial Transport," Convair report FZP-36-1001, 4 April 1953.

Chapter 11 Citations

1. The majority of this chapter, unless otherwise cited, is from Jay Miller, *The X-Planes, X-1 to X-45*, (Hinckley, England: Midland Publishing, April 2001), pp. 98-111; other data is from Convair report ZP-276, "Nuclear Aircraft Systems Background," undated but probably late 1959 or early 1960.
2. R.W. Bussard and R.D. DeLauer, *Fundamentals of Nuclear Flight*, (New York, NY: McGraw Hill, 1965), p. 1; J.A. Conner, Jr., "Aerospace Nuclear Power Safety Considerations, *Aerospace Engineering*, May 1960, p. 26-58.
3. Convair report XM-566, "Short History of the Design and Development of the Nose Section and Crew Compartment Mock-Up for the XB-36H," 20 March 1956; <u>Convairiety</u>, 12 September 1951, p. 1; Convair Development Department Fourth Annual Report," 8 September 1955, p. 19, in the files at the AEC, Little Rock.
4. <u>Convairiety</u>, 25 August 1954, p. 1; Convair Development Department Fourth Annual Report," p. 19.
5. Convair Development Department Fourth Annual Report," p. 19.
6. "Short History of the Design and Development of the Nose Section and Crew Compartment Mock-Up for the XB-36H," Convair report XM-566, 20 March 1956.
7. "Convair Development Department Fourth Annual Report," p. 20.
8. Ibid.
9. Ibid.
10. *Conclusion of B-36 Aircraft Phase-Out*, Historical Monograph Nr. 1, Headquarters, San Antonio Air Materiel Area, Kelly AFB, Texas, March 1960.
11. Miller, *The X-Planes, X-1 to X-45*, pp. 106-111.
12. "Review of the Manned Aircraft Nuclear Propulsion Program," published jointly by the Atomic Energy Commission and the Department of Defense, 1963, pp. 31-58.
13. Miller, *The X-Planes, X-1 to X-45*, pp. 106-111; John Wegg, *General Dynamic Aircraft and their Predecessors*, Putnam Publishing, p. 211.
14. "Review of the Manned Aircraft Nuclear Propulsion Program," passim.

Chapter 12 Citations

1. *Conclusion of B-36 Aircraft Phase-Out*, Historical Monograph Nr. 1, Headquarters, San Antonio Air Materiel Area, Kelly AFB, Texas, March 1960, passim.
2. Ibid.
3. Ibid.
4. Ibid..
5. Ibid.
6. Ibid.
7. Ibid.
8. Ibid.
9. Ibid.
10. Ibid.
11. Ibid.
12. Ibid; email between the author and Dave Collis at NM Tech; conversation between the author and Mike Moore at LMTAS/Fort Worth.
13. *Conclusion of B-36 Aircraft Phase-Out*, passim.
14. "Radioactive Items List," at http://www.abwem.wpafb.af.mil/em_coldfusion/emb/aircraft/itemlist.cfm?, accessed 1 March 2001; http://pearl1.lanl.gov/periodic/
15. *Conclusion of B-36 Aircraft Phase-Out*, passim.

Appendix D Citations

1. <u>Convairiety</u>, 7 August 1957, p. 2; Conversations between the author and officials at the Air Force Museum during June and July 2001.
2. "Welcome to the Castle Air Museum," a brochure at the museum, 1997.
3. *Conclusion of B-36 Aircraft Phase-Out*, Historical Monograph Nr. 1, Headquarters, San Antonio Air Materiel Area, Kelly AFB, Texas, March 1960.
4. <u>Convairiety</u>, 20 March 1957, p. 4; *Conclusion of B-36 Aircraft Phase-Out*, passim.
5. *Conclusion of B-36 Aircraft Phase-Out*, passim.

Appendix E Citations

1. Julius King, "Special Weapons Effects on Aircraft," Historical Branch, Wright Air Development Center, July 1957, pp. 41-51.
2. Chuck Hansen, *U.S. Nuclear Weapons: The Secret Story*, Aerofax, Inc. 1988, pp. 56-59; "Operation UPSHOT-KNOTHOLE, Nevada Proving Grounds, Blast Effects on B-36 Type Aircraft in Flight," report WT-750, March 1955. Originally classified SECRET, declassified 10 July 1985. Copy provided by the Department of Energy Nevada Test Site. (This report also covered Operation IVY, although the title does not indicate this.)
3. King, "Special Weapons Effects on Aircraft," pp. 51-52.
4. http://www.osti.gov/historicalfilms/opentext/data/0800015.html, accessed on 21 June 2001.
5. <u>Convairiety</u>, 8 April 1953, pp. 1-2.
6. "Operation UPSHOT-KNOTHOLE, Nevada Proving Grounds, Blast Effects on B-36 Aircraft in Flight."
7. Ibid.
8. "Operation CASTLE, Project 6.2a, Blast and Thermal Effects on B-36 Aircraft in Flight," report WT-925, Aircraft Laboratory, Wright Air Development Center, Dayton, Ohio, 29 June 1959. Originally classified SECRET, declassified and provided by the DoE Nevada Test Site archives.
9. "Operation CASTLE, Project 6.2a, Blast and Thermal Effects on B-36 Aircraft in Flight;" Letter (with attachments), Colonel Herschel D. Mahon, Chief of Staff to Commander, SAC, Subject: Aircraft decontamination, 2 June 1954. Originally classified SECRET, declassified on 5 August 1986. Provided by the DoE Nevada Test Site.
10. "Operation CASTLE, Summary Report to the Commander, Task Unit 13, Military Effects, Programs 1-9, Pacific Proving Ground, March-May 1954," 30 January 1959, pp. 1-10, 76.
11. King, "Special Weapons Effects on Aircraft," pp. 80-92.
12. Memorandum, from J. Goetz and R. Weitz at SAI to AFNTPR, subject: Estimate of Radiation Dose to B-36 Flight Crews, Shots Turk and MET, Operation TEAPOT, 13 July 1982. Obtained from the Department of Energy, Nevada Test Site.
13. Press Release, AEC-DoD, 23 February 1955; Press Release AEC #JOTI-55-26, 18 February 1955.
14. Press Release AEC #JOTI-55-74, 25 March 1955.
15. <u>Convairiety</u>, 6 April 1955, p. 5; Press Release, AEC #JOTI-55-83, 29 March 1955.
16. Press Release #JOTI-55-88, 6 April 1955; Hansen, *U.S. Nuclear Weapons*, pp. 176-177.
17. Hansen, *U.S. Nuclear Weapons*, pp. 72-74.
18. "History of the 15th Air Force, January-June 1957," pp. 264-269; "Operation MIAMI MOON," Colonel Tom Doyle, USAF (Ret.), Klaxon, Volume 2, Issue 4, Fall 1994, pp. 8-10.
19. Letter, Wilmot H. Hess, University of California, to Commander, Air Force Special Weapons Center, Kirtland AFB, 14 January 1957.
20. Letter (with attachments), Colonel Herschel D. Mahon, Chief of Staff to Commander, SAC, Subject: Aircraft decontamination, 2 June 1954. Originally classified SECRET, declassified on 5 August 1986. Provided by the DoE Nevada Test Site archives.
21. "Convair Development Department Fourth Annual Report," 8 September 1955, p. 21.
22. "Convair Development Department Fourth Annual Report," p. 21.
23. "History of the 15th Air Force, January-June 1957," pp. 264-269; "Operation MIAMI MOON," pp. 8-10.

Appendix F Citations

1. The 9th SRW is not generally credited with operating B-36s. However, C. Roger Cripliver from Convair remembered the 1st SRS of the 9th operating "a few RB-36s" and further investigation with both Dave Menard (formerly of the Air Force Museum) and Coy Cross III (the Historian at the current 9th RW at Beale AFB, California) during June 2001 confirm that the wing did indeed operate a few B-36s between May 1949 and May 1950. Although the records indicate these were RB-36s, this is unlikely since there were only three RB-36s delivered by 1 May 1950, and none before December 1949. It is more probable that a few B-36As and/or early B-36Bs were operated in a training role, and most likely only by the 1st SRS. The Circle X tail code was later reassigned to the 5th BW(H).

INDEX

Addendum

The B-36F-1-CF (49-2677) carrying the B-58 static test article arrives at Wright-Patterson AFB on 12 March 1957. Note the external bracing between the B-36 main landing gear well and the top of the B-58 wing. (Bill Shiner via James Baldwin)

The Boeing Model 462 was powered by six Wright T35 turboprops and was the beginning of the B-52. This design nominally competed with the YB-60. (Boeing Historical Archives)

This is the original J35 installation used on the B-36B jet demonstrator. Note that the bottom of the pod is not sculptured and there is no sway brace between the pylon and the wing. (Convair)

This B-36J-5-CF (52-2222) exhibits the typical markings for the type at the end of their service career. Note the peeling on the white fuselage paint. (Ben Whitaker via Don Pyeatt)

The permanent maintenance docks made life a lot easier, providing platforms and shade for the mechanics. (Ben Whitaker via Don Pyeatt)

This B-36A-5-CF (44-92010) was part of a display at Andrews AFB during February 1949. Another photo is on page 43. (Jay Miller Collection)

Chipping ice off the wing of a B-36 There was a lot of surface area to chip, and it was a long drop if you fell. (Frank Kleinwechter via Don Pyeatt)

A view of the Convair plant in Fort Worth showing the number of B-36s surrounding the facility. (Jack Kerr via Frank Kleinwechter via Don Pyeatt)

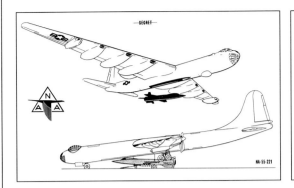
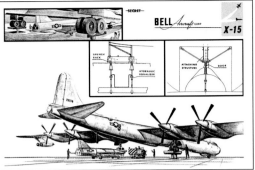
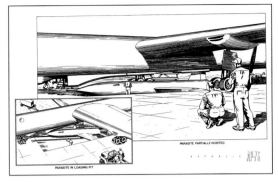

In 1955, three of the four designs for the Project 1226 (X-15) competition used a B-36 as a carrier aircraft. From left above: North American ESO-7487, Bell D-171, and Republic AP-76. The fourth competitor, Douglas, used a Boeing B-50. In all three cases with the B-36, the research airplane would have been carried partially submerged in the bomb bays (using all four in the case of Republic; only three in the other two instances). NASA and the Air Force worried that the big bomber would become unsupportable after it was phased out of SAC service, and the X-15 program obtained two Boeing B-52s for use as carrier aircraft just before modifications began on the B-36. See page 170 for another drawing. (Dennis R. Jenkins Collection)

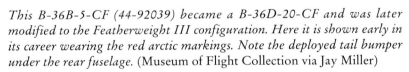

Without an RF-84K, this GRB-36D-15-CF (49-2694) poses at an airshow with the aft plug and clearance doors open. Note the APX-29 radome on top of the fuselage, something unique to the FICON carriers. (Museum of Flight Collection via Jay Miller)

This B-36B-5-CF (44-92039) became a B-36D-20-CF and was later modified to the Featherweight III configuration. Here it is shown early in its career wearing the red arctic markings. Note the deployed tail bumper under the rear fuselage. (Museum of Flight Collection via Jay Miller)

One of life's little mysteries. The Convair log for these two photographs indicates that they are the forward fuselage from 51-5712 after it was removed when the aircraft was converted to the NB-36H. However, it appears that the tornado damage to the forward fuselage and canopy greenhouse has been repaired, although there is no record of this being accomplished. See page 208 for more photos. (Convair via James Baldwin)

This B-36H-25-CF (51-5718) shows the striped markings on the jet pods that adorned most of the fleet for a short time. Note the unit badge on the nose. (Museum of Flight Collection via Jay Miller)

An early XB-36 model using a Davis wing with six tractor X-Wasp engines instead of the pusher configuration ultimately chosen. There is no discernable date on the photo, but the twin vertical stabilizers indicate that it was a fairly early concept. (Convair via Don Pyeatt)

An in-flight view of the armament systems test airplane (B-36D-10-CF, 44-92054) that spent its entire career testing defensive weapons and systems for the B-36 and B-58. Note that all six retractable gun turrets are deployed, and the protruding radome for an experimental nose-defense radar. The tail radar is also not the APG-3 or APG-32 normally carried on the D-model, but appears to be similar to the APG-41 carried on late H-models. Another photo of this aircraft is on page 67. (Convair via the C. Roger Cripliver Collection via Don Pyeatt)

This RB-36H-50-CF (52-1375) was accepted by the Air Force in March 1953, converted to a Configuration II Featherweight, then scrapped in FY57; a short career. (Museum of Flight Collection via Jay Miller)

The XC-99-1-CO (43-52436) is shown with both of its sliding cargo doors open, providing a good indication of their relative position on the fuselage. The aircraft in the background under the tail are a bunch of North American B-25s. (Museum of Flight Collection via Jay Miller)

A shot of the "Boston Camera" airplane (ERB-36D-1-CF, 44-92088) showing the large opening in the side of the camera compartment for the lens of the 240-inch focal-length camera (under the "United States Air Force" marking on the forward fuselage). The other two round openings near the cockpit are the normal crew access hatch and the upper sighting blister. Note the protrusion below the camera opening that was necessary to house part of the camera. Additional related photos may be found on pages 68 and 92. (Museum of Flight Collection via Jay Miller)

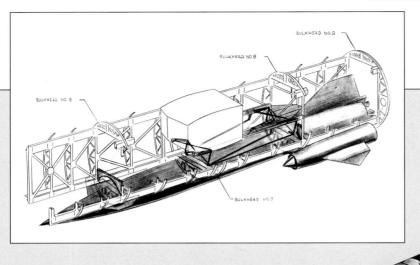

This early NA-704 Navaho intercontinental cruise missile design would have used a B-36 as a carrier aircraft. A single rocket engine in the fuselage provided initial boost, and the two wing-mounted ramjets provided near-Mach-3 cruise power. (U.S. Air Force)

The two photos at right show an early NA-704 design in the "cruise" (top) and "ready-to-drop" (bottom) positions in the B-36. Note that even in the cruise position the nose of the missile is below the B-36 due to the position of the canard surfaces. The drawing below depicts a much later Navaho design being launched from a B-36. This is very similar – except for the air intakes – to the Navaho that was actually built. (all courtesy of the U.S. Air Force)

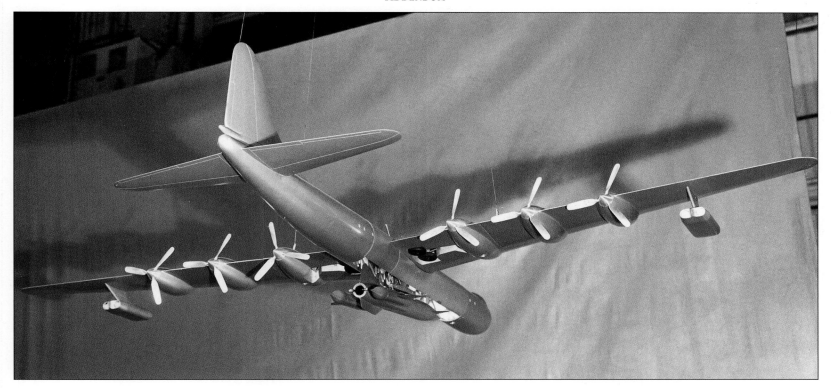

This early NA-704 concept for the North American Aviation B-64 (later SM-64) Navaho cruise missile took up all four bomb bays on the B-36. During the late 1940s and early 1950s the Air Force was certain that it wanted to develop long-range missiles, but was unsure if the resulting design would be a ballistic missile or a high-speed cruise missile. The Navaho was one of the latter. In the end the Atlas and Titan intercontinental ballistic missiles (ICBM) were chosen for further development. Nevertheless, later versions of the Navaho were the first large aircraft to fly at Mach 2 and provided an interesting technology base for high-speed winged flight. Note the tight clearance between the missile and the B-36 landing gear in the bottom view at lower right. The final Navaho concept abandoned the use of a B-36 as a carrier and opted for a large rocket booster instead. Although linked directly to the Navaho program, this booster led directly to the creation of the Rocketdyne Division of the North American that supplied rocket engines for many launch vehicles and ICBMs. (U.S. Air Force)

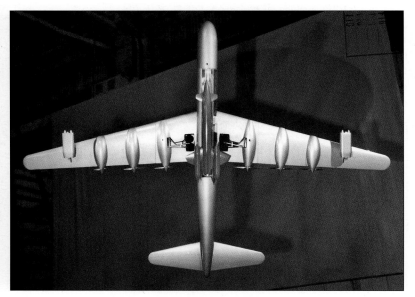

The end. (Lockheed Martin)

A simple plaque at Arlington National Cemetery remembers the B-36 aircrews and ground personnel. (Ann Ascol-Roberts)

It is likely that this photo has never been seen outside Convair before. This is the second YB-60 prototype during final assembly. Contrary to most published reports, the production B-60s would have been equipped with defensive turrets, and this aircraft shows the forward upper turrets in the deployed position. Also note the people standing in the nose of the aircraft – missing here is the extreme forward section that housed the attack radar and equipment. (Lockheed Martin Tactical Aircraft Systems)